H andbook of Basel III Capital opens up a
peerless perspective on how different
elements affect a bank's regulatory
capital. The large number of real-life case
studies provide a strategic approach to
capital that practitioners may find useful
to improve a bank's capital and risk-return
profiles. While Basel III is global in scope,
its practice varies by nation. This treatment
thoroughly examines the European Union's
Capital Requirements Directive IV (CRD IV
and CRR), but the versatile framework is
completely useful across all jurisdictions.

Going far beyond general regulatory explanations found in other books, this advanced
guide digs deep into the vulnerable Common Equity Tier 1 capital, the core capital of
a bank according to Basel III, and proposes
a strategic approach to identifying opportunities to enhance regulatory capital levels.
Regulatory capital professionals, investment
bankers, auditors and consultants can put
their capital enhancement strategies way
ahead of the curve by:

- Seeing how other banks increased
  Common Equity Tier 1 capital, decreased
  risk weighted assets or did both
  simultaneously

- Understanding the latest information and
  strategies surrounding the filters from
  Common Equity Tier 1 and the Additional
  Tier 1 instruments

Handbook of Basel III Capital equips you
with the true, comprehensive grasp of the
regulatory mechanisms so you can make
them work for you.

JUAN RAMIREZ is a senior professional at Deloitte in London, assessing the regulatory capital impact, accounting treatment, and risk management of complex transactions. He has a strong expertise in providing advice on the design of specific complex financial instruments and transactions to enhance regulatory capital. During his career mostly in London, he has worked for BNP Paribas, JP Morgan, Lehman Brothers, Barclays Capital, and Banco Santander. He has devoted more than twenty years to marketing structured derivatives solutions, including commodity, credit, equity, fixed income, and FX. He is the author of *Accounting for Derivatives* and *Handbook of Corporate Derivatives and Equity Capital Markets*, both published by Wiley. Juan holds a BSc in Electrical Engineering from ICAI in Spain and an MBA from University of Chicago.

Handbook of Basel III Capital

Handbook of Basel III Capital

Enhancing Bank Capital in Practice

JUAN RAMIREZ

WILEY

Library of Congress Cataloging-in-Publication Data is available

ISBN 9781119330820 (hardcover) ISBN 9781119330806 (ePDF)
ISBN 9781119330899 (ePub)

Cover Design: Wiley
Cover Image: © Vasiliy Yakobchuk/iStockphoto

Set in 9/11pt and Sabon LT Std by SPi-Global, Chennai, India
Printed in the UK

To my wife Marta and our children Borja, Martuca and David

Contents

Preface

Often banks feel Basel III regulations are excessively conservative and act as a deterrent to investors looking for attractive returns. However, Basel III is an opportunity for banks to improve their asset quality and risk-return profiles. It encourages a strategic approach to decisions about businesses and assets, allocating precious capital toward opportunities that fit the bank's actual risk and return profiles, and exerting pressure to shed unattractive positions.

This book tries to fill a gap in the financial literature on regulatory bank capital. I found a substantial number of excellent books often written by developers of quantitative models on the estimation of credit risk parameters (i.e., exposures, probabilities of default and so on). There also several good books providing a general overview of Basel III, which are useful to grasp an introductory knowledge of the regulation, but that might be too elementary for regulatory capital professionals.

This book has two objectives: (i) to provide readers with a deep **understanding** of the principles underpinning the capital dimension of Basel III (i.e., the numerator of the capital ratio calculation) and (ii) to be exposed to real-life cases of initiatives to **enhance capital**. The first objective is a notably challenging one due to the large number of complex rules and because it requires a thorough understanding of the accounting treatment of the items affecting regulatory capital. To meet the second objective, a large number of real case studies have been included.

This book is aimed primarily at capital practitioners at banks, bank equity analysts, institutional investors and banking supervisors. I believe that it is also a useful resource for structurers at investment banks developing capital-efficient transactions and for professionals at auditing, consulting and law firms helping client banks to enhance their capital positions.

Whilst the Basel III rules are intended to provide a common framework for financial institutions, its implementation may vary across the globe, as national supervisors have discretion about the domestic implementation of the Basel III rules. This book is based on the European Union version of Basel III, which is referred to as CRD IV. Whilst some particular changes to the general Basel III framework are introduced by the CRD, most of its contents are likely to be common to the regulation of other jurisdictions.

The interpretations described in this book are those of the author alone and do not reflect the positions of the entities which the author is or has been related to.

About the Author

Juan Ramirez currently works for Deloitte in London, assessing the accounting treatment, risk management and regulatory capital impact of complex transactions.

Prior to joining Deloitte, Juan worked for 20 years in investment banking in sales and trading at JP Morgan, Lehman Brothers, Barclays Capital, Santander and BNP Paribas. He has been involved with interest rate, equity, FX and credit derivatives. Juan holds an MBA from University of Chicago and a BSc in electrical engineering from ICAI.

Juan is the author of the books *Accounting for Derivatives* and *Handbook of Corporate Equity Derivatives and Equity Capital Markets*, both published by Wiley.

CHAPTER 1

Overview of Basel III

Bank executives are in a difficult position. On the one hand their shareholders require an attractive return on their investment. On the other hand, banking supervisors require these entities to hold a substantial amount of expensive capital. As a result, banks need capital-efficient business models to prosper.

Banking regulators and supervisors are in a difficult position as well. Excessively conservative capital requirements may lessen banks' appetite for lending, endangering economic growth. Excessively light capital requirements may weaken the resilience of the banking sector and cause deep economic crises.

1.1 INTRODUCTION TO BASEL III

Basel III's main set of recommendations were issued by the Basel Committee on Banking Supervision (BCBS) in December 2010 (revised June 2011) and titled *Basel III: A Global Regulatory Framework for More Resilient Banks and Banking Systems*.

It is important to note that the BCBS does not establish laws, regulations or rules for any financial institution directly. It merely acts in an advisory capacity. It is up to each country's specific lawmakers and regulators to enact whatever portions of the recommendations they deem appropriate that would apply to financial institutions being supervised by the country's regulator.

1.1.1 Basel III, CRR, CRD IV

With a view to implementing the agreements of Basel III and harmonising banking solvency regulations across the European Union as a whole, in June 2013 the European Parliament and the Council of the European Union adopted the following legislation:

- Capital Requirements Directive 2013/36/EU of the European Parliament and of the Council of 26 June 2013 (hereinafter the "**CRD IV**"), on access to the activity of credit institutions and the prudential supervision of credit institutions and investment firms, amending Directive 2002/87/EC and repealing Directives 2006/48/EC and 2006/49/EC. CRD IV entered into force in the EU on 1 January 2014; and
- Regulation (EU) No 575/2013 of the European Parliament and of the Council of 26 June 2013 on prudential requirements for credit institutions and investment firms and amending Regulation (EU) No 648/2012 (hereinafter the "**CRR**").

National banking regulators then give effect to the CRD by including the requirements of the CRD in their own rulebooks. The national regulators of the bank supervises it on a consolidated basis and therefore receives information on the capital adequacy of, and sets capital requirements for, the bank as a whole. Individual banking subsidiaries are directly regulated by their local banking regulators, who set and monitor their capital adequacy requirements.

- In Germany, the banking regulator is the Bundesanstalt für Finanzdienstleistungsaufsicht ("BaFin").
- In Switzerland, the banking regulator is the Swiss National Bank ("SNB").
- In the United Kingdom, the banking regulator is the Prudential Regulation Authority ("PRA").
- In the United States, bank holding companies are regulated by the Board of Governors of the Federal Reserve System (the "Federal Reserve Board" or "FSB").

1.1.2 A Brief History of the Basel Accords

Global standards for bank capital are a relatively recent innovation, with an evolution along three phases (see Figure 1.1).

During the financial crises of the 1970s and 1980s the large banks depleted their capital levels. In 1988 the Basel Supervisors Committee intended, through the Basel Accord, to establish capital requirements aimed at protecting depositors from undue bank and systemic risk. The Accord, Basel I, provided uniform definitions for capital as well as minimum capital adequacy levels based on the riskiness of assets (a minimum of 4% for Tier 1 capital, which was mainly equity less goodwill, and 8% for the sum of Tier 1 capital and Tier 2 capital). Basel I was relatively simple; risk measurements related almost entirely to credit risk, perceived to be the main risk incurred by banks. Capital regulations under Basel I came into effect in December 1992, after development and consultations since 1988. Basel I was amended in 1996 to introduce capital requirements to addressing market risk in banks' trading books.

In 2004, banking regulators worked on a new version of the Basel accord, as Basel I was not sufficiently sensitive in measuring risk exposures. In July 2006, the Basel Committee on Banking Supervision published *International Convergence of Capital Measurement and Capital Standards*, known as Basel II, which replaced Basel I. The supervisory objectives for Basel II were to (i) promote safety and soundness in the financial system and maintain a certain overall level of capital in the system, (ii) enhance competitive equality, (iii) constitute a more comprehensive approach to measuring risk exposures and (iv) focus on internationally active banks.

The unprecedented nature of the 2007–08 financial crisis obliged the Basel Committee on Banking Supervision (BCBS) to propose an amendment to Basel II, commonly called Basel III. Basel III

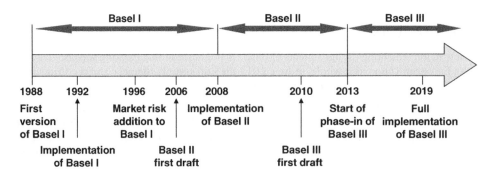

FIGURE 1.1 Bank regulatory capital accords

introduced significant changes in the prudential regulatory regime applicable to banks, including increased minimum capital ratios, changes to the definition of capital and the calculation of risk-weighted assets, and the introduction of new measures relating to leverage, liquidity and funding.

1.1.3 Accounting vs. Regulatory Objectives

It is important to make clear that the accounting and regulatory objectives are not fully aligned. The aim of accounting financial statements is the provision of information about the financial position, performance, cash flow and changes in the financial position of an entity that is useful for making economic decisions to a range of users, including existing and potential investors, lenders, employees and the general public.

The main objective of prudential regulation is to promote a resilient banking sector or, in other words, to improve the banking sector's ability to absorb shocks arising from financial and economic stress, whatever the source, thus reducing the risk of spillover from the financial sector to the real economy.

1.2 EXPECTED AND UNEXPECTED CREDIT LOSSES AND BANK CAPITAL

Let us assume that a bank provided a loan to a client. The worst case one could imagine would be that the client defaults and that, as a consequence, the bank losses the entire loaned amount. This event is rather unlikely and requiring the bank to hold capital for the entire loan would be excessively conservative and the bank is likely to pass the cost of the capital requirement to the client, making the loan too costly for the client. Requiring the bank to hold no capital for the loan would compromise the bank's viability if the borrower defaults. Thus, the bank regulator has to require banks to hold capital levels that assure their viability with a high probability, while maintaining their appetite to extend loans to borrowers at reasonable levels.

Credit losses, within a certain confidence interval, on debt instruments may be divided into expected and unexpected losses.

1.2.1 Expected Losses

The **expected loss** on a debt instrument is the level of credit loss that the bank is reasonably expected to experience on that instrument. The interest priced on the debt instrument at its inception incorporates the expected loss during the life of the instrument.

Banks are expected in general to cover their expected credit losses on an ongoing basis (e.g. by revenues, provisions and write-offs), as shown in Figure 1.2, because they represent another cost component of the lending business. Bank supervisors need to make sure that banks do indeed build enough provisions against expected losses.

1.2.2 Unexpected Losses

The **unexpected loss** on a debt instrument is the level of credit loss in excess of the expected loss that the bank may be exposed to with a certain probability of occurrence. Thus, the size of the unexpected loss depends on the confidence interval chosen. Unexpected losses relate to potentially large losses that occur rather seldomly. In other words, the bank cannot know in advance their timing and severity.

Banks are required to hold regulatory capital to absorb unexpected losses, as shown in Figure 1.2. Thus, risk-weighted assets relate to the unexpected losses only. Bank regulatory capital is needed to cover the risks in such unexpected losses and, thus, it has a loss absorbing function.

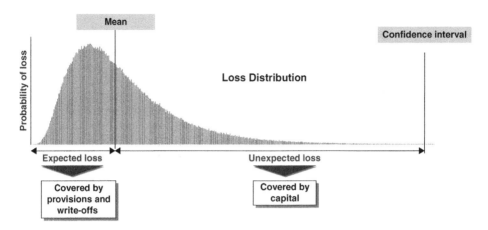

FIGURE 1.2   Expected and unexpected credit losses

1.3 THE THREE-PILLAR APPROACH TO BANK CAPITAL

The capital adequacy framework consists of three pillars (see Figure 1.3), each of which focuses on a different aspect of capital adequacy:

- **Pillar 1**, called "**Minimum Capital Requirements**", establishes the minimum amount of capital that a bank should have against its credit, market and operational risks. It provides the guidelines for calculating the risk exposures in the assets of a bank's balance sheet (the "risk-weighted assets") and the capital components, and sets the minimum capital requirements.
- **Pillar 2**, called "**Supervisory Review and Evaluation Process**", involves both banks and regulators taking a view on whether a firm should hold additional capital against risks not covered in Pillar 1. Part of the Pillar 2 process is the "**Internal Capital Adequacy Assessment Process**" ("**ICAAP**"), which is a bank's self-assessment of risks not captured by Pillar 1.
- **Pillar 3**, called "**Market Discipline**", aims to encourage market discipline by requiring banks to disclosure specific, prescribed details of their risks, capital and risk management.

    This book focuses on Pillar 1.

1.3.1 Pillar 1 – Minimum Capital Requirements

Pillar 1 covers the calculation of capital, liquidity and leverage levels (see Figure 1.4). Pillar 1 covers as well the calculation of risk-weighted assets for credit risk, market risk and operational risk. Distinct regulatory capital approaches are followed for each of these risks.

Leverage Ratio   One of the causes of the 2007–08 financial crisis was the build-up of excessive balance sheet leverage in the banking system, despite meeting their capital requirements. It was only when the banks were forced by market conditions to reduce their leverage that the financial system increased the downward pressure in asset prices. This exacerbated the decline in bank capital. To prevent the excessive deleveraging from happening again, Basel III introduced a leverage ratio. This ratio was designed to put a cap on the build-up of leverage in the banking system as well as to introduce

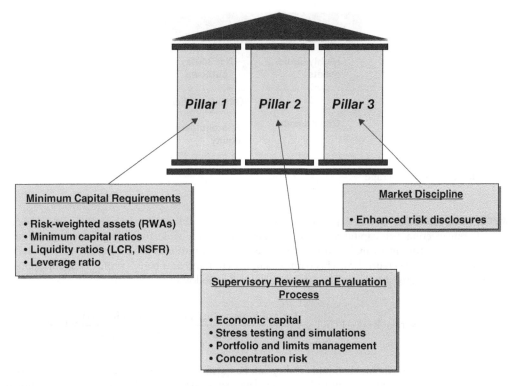

FIGURE 1.3   The three pillars around Basel III

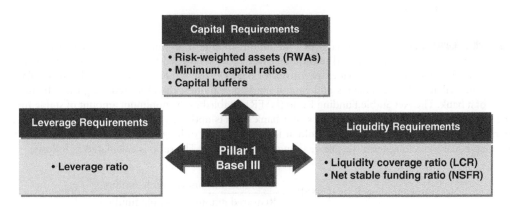

FIGURE 1.4   Pillar 1 of Basel III

additional safeguards against model risk and measurement errors. The leverage ratio is a simple, transparent, non-risk-weighted measure, calculated as an average over the quarter:

$$\text{Tier 1 leverage ratio} = \frac{\text{Tier 1 capital}}{\text{Average total restated balance sheet assets}}$$

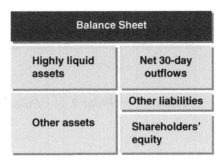

FIGURE 1.5   Liquidity coverage

Liquidity Coverage Ratio   Banks experienced severe liquidity problems during the 2007–08 financial crisis, despite meeting their capital requirements. Basel III requires banks to hold a pool of highly liquid assets which is sufficient to maintain the forecasted net cash outflows over a 30-day period, under stress assumptions (see Figure 1.5). This requirement tries to improve a bank's resilience against potential short-term liquidity shortages. The ratio is calculated as follows:

$$\text{Liquidity Coverage Ratio}\left(\text{LCR}\right) = \frac{\text{Stock of high-quality liquid assets}\left(\text{HQLAs}\right)}{\text{Net cash outflows over a 30-day time period}} \geq 100\%$$

Assets are considered "highly liquid" if they can be quickly converted into cash at almost no loss.
All assets in the liquidity pool must be managed as part of that pool and are subject to operational requirements. The assets must be available for the treasurer of the bank, unencumbered and freely available to group entities.

Net Stable Funding Ratio   Basel III requires a minimum amount of funding that is expected to be stable over a one-year time horizon based on liquidity risk factors assigned to assets and off-balance sheet exposures. This requirement provides incentives for banks to use stable sources to fund banks' balance sheets, off-balance sheet exposures and capital markets activities, therefore reducing the refinancing risks of a bank. The Net Stable Funding Ratio (NSFR) establishes the minimum amount of stable funding based on the liquidity characteristics of a bank's assets and activities over a more than one-year horizon. In other words, a bank must hold at least an amount of long-term (i.e., more than one year) funding equal to its long-term (i.e., more than one year) assets. The ratio is calculated as follows:

$$\text{Net Stable Funding Ratio}\left(\text{NSFR}\right) = \frac{\text{Available amount of stable funding}}{\text{Required amount of stable funding}} \geq 100\%$$

The numerator is calculated by summing a bank's liabilities, weighted by their degree of permanence. The denominator is calculated by summing a bank's assets, weighted by their degree of permanence.

1.3.2 Pillar 2 – Supervisory Review and Evaluation Process

Pillar 2 is an additional discipline to evaluate the adequacy of the regulatory capital requirement under Pillar 1 and other non-Pillar 1 risks. Pillar 2 refers to the possibility for national supervisors to impose a wide range of measures – including additional capital requirements – on individual institutions or groups of institutions in order to address higher-than-normal risk.

Pillar 2 has two aspects. The first requires banks to regularly assess their overall risk profile and to calculate any further capital that should be held against this additional risk. This assessment is called ICAAP. Pillar 1 captures exposures to credit risk, market risk and operational risk. Exposures to risks not captured by Pillar 1 are assessed in Pillar 2. These include credit concentration risk, liquidity risk, reputation and model risk. Consequently, Pillar 2 could add requirements to the amount of capital held by banks (and offset the lower credit-risk capital requirement).

The second aspect of Pillar 2 is its inclusion of a "supervisory review process". In the case of the European Union, the supervisory authorities assess how banking institutions are complying with EU banking law, the risks they face and the risks they pose to the stability of the financial system. This allows supervisors to evaluate each bank's overall risk profile and, if needed, to mandate a higher prudential capital ratio where this is judged to be prudent.

ICAAP – Internal Capital Adequacy Assessment Process   Banks should have a process for assessing their overall capital adequacy in relation to their risk profile and a strategy for maintaining their capital levels. This assessment is called ICAAP – Internal Capital Adequacy Assessment Process. ICAAP assesses the amounts, types and distribution of capital that it considers adequate to cover the level and nature of the risks to which it is or might be exposed. This assessment should cover the major sources of risks to the firm's ability to meet its liabilities as they fall due and incorporate stress testing and scenario analysis.

ICAAP is documented and updated annually by the firm or more frequently if changes in the business, strategy, nature or scale of its activities or operational environment suggest that the current level of financial resources is no longer adequate.

1.3.3 Pillar 3 – Market Discipline

Pillar 3 requires disclosure of information regarding all material risks and the calculation of bank capital positions. Pillar 3 also requires the disclosure of exposures and associated risk-weighted assets for each risk type and approach to calculating capital requirements for Pillar 1.

Its objective is to help investors and other stakeholders to assess the scope of application by a bank of the Basel framework and the rules in their jurisdiction, their capital condition, risk exposures and risk assessment processes, and hence their capital adequacy.

This dimension of Basel III is designed to complement Pillars 1 and 2 by providing additional discipline on bank risk-taking behaviour. The idea is that banks which the market judges to have increased their risk profiles without adequate capital may witness their securities sold down in debt and equity markets. The additional costs that this will impose on financing bank operations will provide an incentive for management to modify either the bank's risk profile or its capital base.

1.3.4 Significant Subsidiaries Disclosure Requirements

[CRR 13(1)] ("Application of disclosure requirements on a consolidated basis") requires that significant subsidiaries of EU parent institutions, and those subsidiaries which are of material significance for their local market, disclose information specified in the following articles on an individual or sub-consolidated basis:

- Own funds [CRR 437];
- Capital requirements [CRR 438];
- Capital buffers [CRR 440];
- Credit risk adjustments [CRR 442];
- Remuneration Policy [CRR 450];
- Leverage [CRR 451]; and
- Credit risk mitigation techniques [CRR 453].

[CRR 13(1)] does not provide explicit criteria for the determination of significant subsidiaries or those subsidiaries which are of material significance for their local market. Commonly, a banking group defines certain quantitative and qualitative criteria to determine which subsidiaries are subject to the requirements set forth in [CRR 13(1)]. These criteria take into account the subsidiary's significance to the group as well as the subsidiary's importance to its local market using quantitative measures such as total assets and RWAs in relationship of the group's consolidated assets and RWAs, as well as certain qualitative aspects of the subsidiary's standalone systemic importance to their local markets using designations and measures as defined by local regulators.

1.4 RISK-WEIGHTED ASSETS (RWAs)

When assessing how much capital a bank needs to hold, regulators weigh a bank's assets according to their risk. Safe assets (e.g., cash) are disregarded; other assets (e.g., loans to other institutions) are considered more risky and get a higher weight. The more risky assets a bank holds, the higher the likelihood of a reduction to earnings or capital, and as a result, the more capital it has to have. In addition to risk weighting on-balance sheet assets, banks must also risk weight off-balance sheet exposures such as loan and credit card commitments.

The risk-weighted assets ("**RWAs**") are a bank's assets and off-balance sheet items that carry credit, market, operational and/or non-counterparty risk (see Figure 1.6):

- **Credit risk:** RWAs reflect the likelihood of a loss being incurred as the result of a borrower or counterparty failing to meet its financial obligations or as a result of deterioration in the credit quality of the borrower or counterparty.
- **Market risk:** RWAs reflect the risk due to volatility of in the fair values of financial instruments held in the trading book in response to market movements – including foreign exchange, commodity prices, interest rates, credit spread and equity prices – inherent in both the balance sheet and the off-balance sheet items.
- **Operational risk:** RWAs reflect the risk of loss resulting from inadequate or failed internal processes, people and systems or from external events.
- **Other risks:** RWAs primarily reflect the capital requirements for equity positions outside the trading book, settlement risk, and premises and equipment.

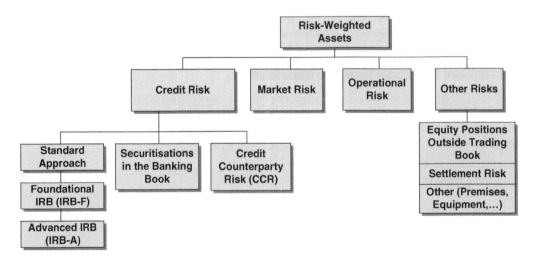

FIGURE 1.6   Main components of RWAs

1.4.1 Calculation of Credit Risk RWAs

Basel III applies two approaches of increasing sophistication to the calculation credit risk RWAs:

- **The standardised approach** is the most basic approach to credit risk. It requires banks to use external credit ratings to determine the RWAs applied to rated counterparties, based on a detailed classification of asset and counterparty types. Other counterparties are grouped into broad categories and standardised risk weightings are applied to these categories using standard industry-wide risk weightings.
- **The internal ratings-based approach** (IRB). The credit RWAs calculation under this approach is based on an estimate of the exposure at default (EAD), probabilities of default (PD) and loss given default (LGD) concepts, using bank-specific data and internal models that are approved by the regulator. The IRB approach is further sub-divided into two applications:
  - **Advanced IRB (AIRB):** where internal calculations of PD, LGD and credit conversion factors are used to model risk exposures;
  - **Foundation IRB (FIRB):** where internal calculations of probability of default (PD), but standardised parameters for LGD and credit conversion factors are used.

1.4.2 Calculation of Counterparty Credit Risk (CCR) RWAs

Counterparty credit risk (CCR) arises where a counterparty default may lead to losses of an uncertain nature as they are market-driven. This uncertainty is factored into the valuation of a bank's credit exposure to such transactions. The bank uses two methods under the regulatory framework to calculate CCR credit exposure:

- The **mark to market method** (MTM, also known as current exposure method), which is the sum of the current market value of the instrument plus an add-on (potential future exposure or PFE) that accounts for the potential change in the value of the contract until a hypothetical default of the counterparty.
- The **internal model method** (IMM), subject to regulatory approval, allows the use of internal models to calculate an effective expected positive exposure (EPE), multiplied by a factor stipulated by the regulator.

1.4.3 Calculation of Market Risk RWAs

RWA calculations for market risk assess the losses from extreme movements in the prices of financial assets. Under the regulatory framework there are two methods to calculate market risk:

- **Standardised approach:** A calculation is prescribed that depends on the type of contract, the net position at portfolio level and other inputs that are relevant to the position. For instance, for equity positions a specific market risk component is calculated that depends on features of the specific security (for instance, country of issuance) and a general market risk component captures changes in the market.
- **Model-based approach:** With their regulator's permission, firms can use proprietary Value-at-Risk (VaR) models to calculate capital requirements. Under Basel III, Stressed VaR, Incremental Risk Charge and All Price Risk models must also be used to ensure that sufficient levels of capital are applied.

1.4.4 Calculation of Securitisation Exposures RWAs

Securitisation exposures that fulfil certain criteria are treated under a separate framework to other market or credit risk exposures. For trading book securitisations, specific risk of securitisation transactions is calculated following standardised market risk rules; general market risk of securitisations is captured in market risk models. For securitisations associated with non-traded banking books, the following approaches are available to calculate risk-weighted assets:

- **Standardised approach:** Where external ratings are available for a transaction, look-up tables provide a risk weight to apply to the exposure amount. For unrated securitisations, depending on the type of exposure and characteristics, standard weights of up to 1250% are applied.
- **Advanced approaches** include:

  - **The ratings-based approach**, where external ratings are available, allows for a more granular assessment than the equivalent standardised approach.
  - For unrated transactions, the **"look through" approach** can be used, which considers the risk of the underlying assets.
  - The **internal assessment approach** can be used on unrated asset-backed commercial paper programmes; it makes use of internal models that follow similar methodologies to rating agency models.

1.4.5 Calculation of Operational Risk RWAs

Capital set aside for operational risk is deemed to cover the losses or costs resulting from human factors, inadequate or failed internal processes and systems or external events. To assess capital requirements for operational risk, the following methods apply:

- **Basic indicator approach (BIA):** Sets the capital requirement as 15% of the net interest and non-interest income, averaged over the last three years. If the income in any year is negative or zero, that year is not considered in the average.
- **Standardised approach:** Under this approach net interest and non-interest income is classified into eight business lines as defined by the regulation. The capital requirement is calculated as a percentage of the income, ranging between 12% and 18% depending on the business line, averaged over the last three years. If the capital requirement in respect of any year of income is negative, it is set to zero in the average calculation.
- **Advanced management approach (AMA):** Under the AMA the firm calculates the capital requirement using its own models, after review and approval of the model and wider risk management framework by the regulator.

1.4.6 Link between RWAs and Capital Charges

The link between capital charges and RWAs is the following:

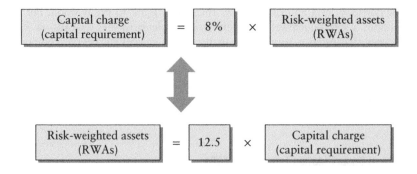

CHAPTER 2

Minimum Capital Requirements

Any financial institution subject to Basel III regulations is required to hold certain types and amounts of capital to help it meet its obligations as they fall due. This chapter addresses the minimum capital requirements for banks. It is important to note that minimum capital requirements are not uniform across all banks: they depend on several factors including the jurisdiction where the bank operates and its presence in the domestic and global financial marketplace.

2.1 COMPONENTS AND MINIMUM REQUIREMENTS OF BANK CAPITAL

Both Pillar 1 and Pillar 2 result in capital requirements for the bank. Pillar 1 sets out the capital needed to absorb unexpected losses or asset impairments stemming from credit risk, counterparty credit risk, market risk and operational risk. Pillar 2 covers the consideration of whether additional capital is required over and above the Pillar 1 capital requirements.

2.1.1 Pillar 1 Capital Requirements

According to Basel III, a bank's regulatory capital is divided into several categories or tiers of capital, which try to group constituents of capital depending on their degree of permanence and loss absorbency, as shown in Figure 2.1.

Tier 1 capital is so called because it is the best-quality capital from the regulator's perspective. The objective of Tier 1 capital is to absorb losses and help banks to remain **"going concerns"** (i.e., to remain solvent, or in other words, to prevent failures). There are two layers of Tier 1 capital:

- **Common Equity Tier 1** capital ("CET1"), which includes permanent shareholders' equity; and
- **Additional Tier 1** capital ("AT1"), which includes some instruments with ability to absorb losses.

Tier 2 capital, a supplementary capital with less loss absorption capabilities, is aimed at providing loss absorption on a **"gone concern"** basis (i.e., in case of insolvency of the bank) to protect depositors. It consists mainly of subordinated notes less prudential deductions.

The sum of Tier 1 and Tier 2 capital is called **"total capital"** or **"own funds"**. Both Tier 1 capital and Tier 2 capital items are subject to deductions that are specific to each type of capital.

2.1.2 Pillar 2 Capital Requirements

Competent authorities are empowered to require banks to hold additional own funds requirements. These are called the "Pillar 2 capital requirements".

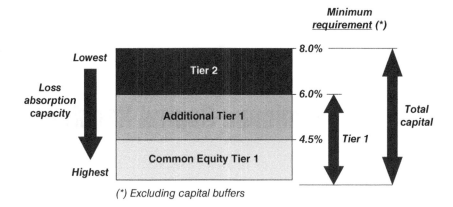

FIGURE 2.1   Components of a bank's regulatory total capital

In accordance with [CRD IV 104(1)(a)] competent authorities in Europe shall be empowered to require banks to hold additional regulatory capital requirements (**"Pillar 2 capital requirements"**). In addition to having this general power to impose Pillar 2 capital requirements, [CRD IV 104(2)] specifies a number of circumstances in which competent authorities must impose them:

- A bank does *not* meet the requirement set out in [CRR 73 and 74] or does *not* have the capacity to identify and manage large exposures as set out in [CRR 393];
- Risks or elements of risks are not covered by the Pillar 1 capital requirements (i.e., the 4.5% minimum CET1 capital, 6% minimum Tier 1 capital and the 8% total capital requirements) or by the CBR;
- The sole application of other administrative measures is unlikely to improve the arrangements, processes, mechanisms and strategies sufficiently within an appropriate timeframe;
- The review referred to in [CRD IV 98(4) or 101(4)] reveals that the non-compliance with the requirements for the application of the respective approach will likely lead to inadequate own funds requirements;
- The risks are likely to be underestimated despite compliance with the applicable requirements of CRD IV and of CRR; or
- A bank reports to the competent authority that the stress test results referred to in [CRR 377(5)] materially exceed its own funds requirement for the correlation trading portfolio.

According to the EBA in its document "Opinion of the European Banking Authority on the Interaction of Pillar 1, Pillar 2 and Combined Buffer Requirements and Restrictions on Distributions" (EBA/Op/2015/24) of 16 December 2015, competent authorities should determine additional regulatory capital requirements, covering:

- The risk of unexpected losses, and of expected losses insufficiently covered by provisions, over a 12-month period (except where otherwise specified in the CRR) ("unexpected losses");
- The risk of underestimation of risk due to model deficiencies as assessed in the context of [CRD IV 101]; and
- The risk arising from deficiencies in internal governance, including internal control, arrangements and other deficiencies.

2.2 COMPONENTS AND MINIMUM REQUIREMENTS OF CAPITAL BUFFERS

In addition to the minimum capital requirements there are three further categories of capital, called regulatory buffers. The objective of these buffers is the introduction of instruments that will move in a countercyclical fashion to the capital levels of banks. In other words, buffers are intended to increase

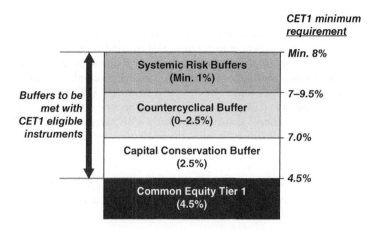

FIGURE 2.2   Minimum CET1 requirements including capital buffers

during economic upturns and to decrease in downturns. Therefore, the regulatory buffers provide a greater sensitivity of regulatory capital requirements to risk profiles of institutions at a given point of time. There are currently three buffers:

- The capital conservation buffer;
- The countercyclical buffer; and
- The systemic risk buffers.

Because the buffer requirements are met with CET1 eligible instruments, the minimum CET1 requirement is in reality much higher than the 4.5% stand-alone minimum, at least 8%, as shown in Figure 2.2.

2.3 CAPITAL CONSERVATION BUFFER

The capital conservation buffer is designed to provide banks with an extra cushion of capital to draw on during times of financial and/or economic stress (when losses are typically incurred), avoiding breaching minimum capital requirements. The minimum capital conservation requirement on an individual and consolidated basis is fixed at 2.5%, to be met only with CET1 eligible instruments.

Under CRD IV the capital conservation buffer is phased in from January 2016, with full implementation by January 2019, as follows:

Year (1-January)	2016	2017	2018	2019
Capital conservation buffer	0.625%	1.25%	1.875%	2.50%

Banks are expected to build up the capital conservation buffer in good times. This ensures that the banking sector builds up capital buffers when it has the earnings capacity to do so and uses those buffers in periods of stress. Requiring capital buffers to rise during periods of strong earnings helps dampen excessive banking sector credit extension and leverage.

> Remember that the minimum CET1 that a bank is required to hold is 4.5% of RWAs, so why did Basel III not impose a 7% CET1 minimum instead?
>
> When a bank's minimum 4.5% CET1 capital level is breached, the entity's solvency is in danger and most probably the bank regulatory supervisor would oblige the bank to raise CET1 capital.

(continued)

In contrast and after 1 January 2019, when a bank's capital conservation buffer level falls below the 2.5% range as it experiences losses, it is able to conduct business as normal, as the constraints imposed relate only to capital distributions (i.e., dividend payments, share buybacks, bonuses, etc.), and not to the operation of the bank. A bank with a combined buffer requirement (which includes the capital conservation buffer) that is below the CBR target faces constraints on capital distributions until the CBR target is reached (see Section 6.4.1). The Basel Committee did not want to impose operational constraints when a CBR target was breached in order to avoid having capital buffers as pure additions to the minimum capital requirements.

Supervisory authorities may exempt Small- or medium-sized investment firms from the requirement to maintain a capital conservation buffer where the exemption does not threaten the stability of the financial system of the supervised jurisdiction.

2.4 COUNTERCYCLICAL BUFFER

During times of strong economic growth banks typically ease the supply of credit and risks are assessed to be low. Later, in a downturn, the riskiness of loans increase, banks reduce the supply of credit, credit losses are recognised and banks are forced to raise capital in notably expensive capital markets.

The **countercyclical buffer** is a pre-emptive measure designed to protect banks against future losses stemming from assets originated during periods of unsustainable levels of leverage, debt or credit growth, and to support bank lending in the economic downturn. According to the Basel Committee of Banking Supervision (BCBS), the countercyclical buffer has three main objectives:

- To protect the banking sector from losses resulting from periods of excessive credit growth followed by periods of stress;
- To help ensure credit remains available during periods of stress; and
- To lean against the build-up of excesses, when credit is being granted at a rapid pace, by reducing the attractiveness of bank lending due to an increase in the cost of credit.

A bank's countercyclical buffer complements its capital conservation buffer (see Figure 2.3). Reducing the cyclicality of credit in the economy means that in periods of rapid growth the countercyclical buffer would be built up, and in periods of stress the requirement would be eased in order to facilitate the availability of credit.

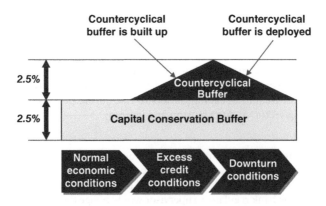

FIGURE 2.3   Interaction of the countercyclical buffer with the capital conservation buffer

The countercyclical buffer is a bank-specific buffer, and ranges from **0% to 2.5%** of RWAs, calibrated in steps of 0.25% and comprised of CET1 capital. National supervisory authorities have to assess and set the appropriate countercyclical buffer rate for its jurisdiction on a quarterly basis. Where a bank is required to hold a larger countercyclical buffer it has 12 months to meet the higher capital levels (unless an earlier date is justified on the basis of exceptional circumstances), while decisions to a lower countercyclical buffer take effect immediately. Both the pre-announced and the actual countercyclical buffer have to be publicly published.

The Basel Committee formulated five principles to guide the authorities in setting the countercyclical buffer:

- It should aim at building the resilience of the banking sector;
- The credit-to-GDP gap is a useful common reference point in taking the buffer decisions;
- In addition to the credit-to-GDP gap, other indicators should be used to arrive at buffer decisions;
- It should be released promptly in times of stress; and
- Its use should be complemented with other macroprudential instruments.

Similarly to the capital conservation buffer, when a bank's countercyclical buffer level falls below the level required by the national supervisory authority as it experiences losses, it is able to conduct business as normal as the constraints imposed relate only to capital distributions (i.e., dividend payments, share buybacks) and not to the operation of the bank. A bank with a combined buffer requirement (which includes the capital conservation buffer) that is below the CBR target face constraints on capital distributions until the CBR target is reached (see Section 6.4.1).

Under CRD IV the maximum countercyclical buffer will be phased in from 1 January 2016, with full implementation by 1 January 2019, as follows:

Year (1-Jan.)	2016	2017	2018	2019
Countercyclical buffer	0.625%	1.25%	1.875%	2.50%

The countercyclical buffer rate for a bank in a jurisdiction is set by the national supervisory authority (ranging from 0% to 2.5%) and must meet *all* the following requirements:

1. The rate must reflect, in a meaningful way, the credit cycle and the risks due to excess credit growth in the jurisdiction;
2. The rate must duly take into account the specificities of the national economy;
3. The buffer guide must be based on the deviation of the ratio of credit to gross domestic product from its long term trend, taking into account:

   a. An indicator of the growth of levels of credit within the jurisdiction and, in particular, an indicator reflecting the changes in the ratio of credit granted in the jurisdiction to gross domestic product; and
   b. In the case of a jurisdiction member of the European Union, any recommendation issued by the European Systemic Risk Board ("ESRB") on setting buffer rates for the countercyclical capital buffer.

Countercyclical Buffer and Pillar 2

While the countercyclical capital buffer requirements are part of Pillar 1, they may interact with Pillar 2 objectives. Pillar 2 tries to capture a bank's exposure to risks not assessed under Pillar 1, like concentration, liquidity, reputational, model risks and so on. Under Pillar 2 a national supervisory authority performs its own risk assessment of the banks operating in its jurisdiction and may require a bank to hold a capital add-on in addition to the capital level required under Pillar 1. As a result, authorities should ensure that a bank's countercyclical capital buffer do not overlap with capital add-ons included in Pillar 2.

2.4.1 The Countercyclical Buffer Ratio and the Credit-to-GDP Gap

The countercyclical buffer aims at reflecting in a meaningful way the credit cycle and the risks due to excess credit growth in the jurisdiction setting the buffer. Basel III specifies that the deviation of the credit-to-GDP ratio from its long-term trend (the "**credit-to-GDP gap**") should serve as "a common starting point for decisions on buffer rates by the relevant national authorities", but it is not an automatic buffer framework. National supervisory authorities have discretion over setting a bank's countercyclical buffer requirement, taking also taking into account "other variables relevant to the risks to financial stability". In this respect the credit-to-GDP gap is intended to be a source of discipline in the application of judgment by national authorities.

According to the Basel Committee, the credit-to-GDP gap is converted into an "indicative" countercyclical buffer level following the following three steps:

First, the credit-to-GDP ratio at time t between the aggregate credit to the non-financial private sector ($Credit_t$), using the broadest credit aggregate available, and nominal GDP (GDP_t) are calculated:

$$Credit\text{-}to\text{-}GDP\ Ratio_t = \frac{Credit_t}{GDP_t}$$

Second, the trend of this ratio is estimated using a one-sided Hodrick–Prescott filter. This filter is a statistical tool that allows for the separation of the cyclical and trend components of a time series. Additionally, the upper (H) and lower (L) boundaries for the trend are determined, and the gap (Gap_t) between the credit-to-GDP ratio and such trend is calculated:

$$Gap_t = Credit\text{-}to\text{-}GDP\ Ratio_t\text{-}Trend_t$$

Third, the countercyclical buffer size (CCB_t) is determined (see Figure 2.4). If the gap is below the lower boundary, the buffer is zero and if the gap is above the upper boundary the CCB is set at its maximum of 2.5%. Between both boundaries, the buffer increases linearly as the level of the credit-to-GDP gap approaches the upper boundary, calibrated in steps of 0.25% points:

$$CCB_t = \begin{cases} Zero & \text{If} & Gap_t < L \\ 2.5\% \times \dfrac{Gap_t - L}{H - L} & \text{If} & L \le Gap_t \le H \\ 2.5\% & \text{If} & Gap_t > H \end{cases}$$

Therefore, the lower and upper boundaries are key factors when setting a countercyclical buffer. A study by the Basel Committee found that L = 2 and H = 10 provided a robust estimate based on historical banking crises.

Many analyses have been performed to test the reliability of the credit-to-GDP gap as an indicator of excess credit growth. These analyses conclude that the credit-to-GDP gap indicator may have certain drawbacks and may thus not transmit the right signals in all circumstances concerning the build-up and release of the buffer. That is why Basel III gives national supervisory authorities discretion over setting a bank's countercyclical buffer requirement, leaving the door open to taking into account other variables besides the credit-to-GDP gap.

2.4.2 The Reciprocity Principle

A cornerstone element of the countercyclical buffer is its reciprocity principle between different jurisdictions. If the supervisory authority in a given country determines the activation of the countercyclical

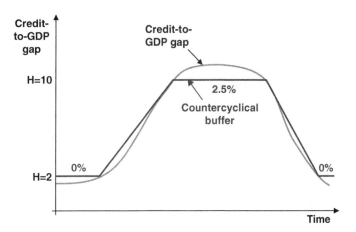

FIGURE 2.4 Interaction of the countercyclical buffer with the credit-to-GDP gap

buffer, all banks with exposures in that country are required to build up that buffer, regardless of their country of origin. The reciprocity principle is particularly important in banking systems characterised by a large share of foreign banks. It makes sure that foreign and domestic banks can compete on equal terms in the country that activated the countercyclical buffer. It also protects international banks from systemic risks arising outside their home country and avoids incentives to circumvent the requirements by host authorities by transferring operations to other countries, which could lead to excessive credit growth not being effectively tackled.

In order to reflect the geographic composition of its credit portfolio, a group's consolidated countercyclical buffer consists of the weighted average of the countercyclical buffers that apply in the jurisdictions where relevant credit exposures of the bank are located. Imagine a banking group active in three jurisdictions (see Figure 2.5): each national supervisory authority will set a countercyclical buffer requirement based on the domestic and foreign exposures relevant to the jurisdiction. The group's countercyclical buffer requirement will be calculated as the weighted-average of the three individual countercyclical buffer requirements:

$$Group\,countercyclical\,buffer = \frac{\begin{array}{c}Countercyclical\,buffer\,1 \times Exposures\,1 + Countercyclical\,buffer\,2 \\ \times Exposures\,2 + Countercyclical\,buffer\,3 \times Exposures\,3\end{array}}{Exposures\,1 + Exposures\,2 + Exposures\,3}$$

Limits on Reciprocal Obligations A banking group's countercyclical buffer depends on the judgement of the national supervisory authorities in each individual jurisdiction in which the group operates. It was

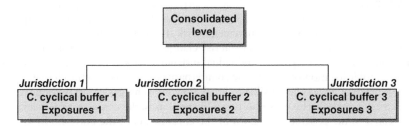

FIGURE 2.5 Countercyclical buffer situation

Example: Reciprocity

To illustrate how reciprocity works, assume that Country 1 and Country 2 had set the countercyclical on domestic exposures of their banks at 2.5% and 1%, respectively. Let us assume further that in these two jurisdictions, four banks were operating: Bank A and Bank B with domestic exposures only to Country 1 and Country 2 respectively, and Bank C and D with exposures to both countries. The following table details each bank's exposures to each country and their **consolidated** countercyclical buffer:

	RWAs in Country 1	RWAs in Country 2	Weighted-average CCB
Bank A	100	0	2.5%
Bank B	0	100	1.0%
Bank C	60	40	1.9%
Bank D	40	60	1.6%

The countercyclical buffer of Bank C was calculated as (60 × 2.5% + 40 × 1%)/(60 + 40) = 1.9%. According to the reciprocity principle, any loan to Country 1 borrowers, irrespective of the location of the bank making the loan, attracted a countercyclical buffer requirement of 2.5%. While Bank A and Bank B, with domestic credit exposures only, were subject to the full amount of the buffer determined by their supervisor, the buffer of internationally active banks reflected the structure of their domestic and foreign exposure.

mentioned previously that if deemed appropriate, national supervisory authorities may require a domestic countercyclical buffer in excess of 2.5% for banks in their jurisdictions, depending on the extent of the build-up of system-wide risk in a given jurisdiction.

In the European Union (like in most jurisdictions) international reciprocity obligations concerning the buffer settings depend on the level of the buffer rate set by the national designated authority:

- If the buffer rate is set up to 2.5%, the mutual reciprocity is mandatory;
- If the buffer rate is set above 2.5%, the mutual reciprocity for the part exceeding 2.5% is voluntary.

This creates a potential scope for regulatory arbitrage among jurisdictions. When a national authority sets a buffer rate above 2.5% (e.g., 3%) while reciprocity by other countries is mandatory only up to 2.5%, the level playing field in these countries is affected. Domestic banks would be required to apply a 3% buffer while foreign banks may be required to apply a 2.5% buffer on the RWAs of such jurisdiction. Therefore domestic banks would operate at a cost-of-capital disadvantage in relation to branches of foreign banks. Such an outcome might dissuade national authorities from setting a buffer above 2.5% in the first place, constraining the flexibility of national authorities to take necessary actions to prevent excessive credit growth.

Calculating Exposures   Credit exposures include all private sector credit exposures (including non-financial sector exposures) that attract a credit risk capital charge or the risk-weighted equivalent trading book capital charges for specific risk, incremental risk (IRC) and securitisation.

For the VaR for specific risk, the incremental risk charge and the comprehensive risk measurement charge, banks translate these charges into individual instrument risk weights that would then be allocated to the geographic location of the specific counterparties that make up the charge.

However, it may not always be possible to break down the charges in this way due to the charges being calculated on a portfolio by portfolio basis. In such cases, the charge for the relevant portfolio should be allocated to the geographic regions of the constituents of the portfolio by calculating the proportion of the portfolio's total exposure at default (EAD) that is due to the EAD resulting from counterparties in each geographic region.

2.5 SYSTEMIC RISK BUFFERS

A "too-big-to-fail" problem arises when the threatened failure of a large financial institution leaves public authorities with no option but to bail it out using public funds to avoid financial instability and economic damage. The Basel Committee once argued that the moral hazard associated with implicit guarantees derived from the perceived expectation of government support can encourage large financial institutions to take excessive risks, reduces market discipline and creates competitive distortions, further increasing the probability of distress in the future. As a result, the direct cost of support associated with moral hazard is borne by taxpayers, representing a large and unacceptable implicit public subsidy of private enterprise.

In addition to the capital conservation buffer and the countercyclical capital buffer, banks need to comply with the **systemic risk buffer** requirements in order to compensate for the risk that such banks represent for the financial system and the potential impact of their failure on taxpayers. There are three systemic risk buffers (see Figure 2.6):

- The systemic risk buffer;
- The global systemically important institution (G-SII) buffer; and
- The other systemically important institution (O-SII) buffer.

The G-SII and O-SII apply only to systemically important institutions. The FSB defines a Systematically Important Financial Institution (SIFI) as a "financial institution whose distress or disorderly failure, because of its size, complexity and systemic interconnectedness, would cause significant disruption to the wider financial system and economic activity".

2.5.1 Systemic Risk Buffer

Basel III sets out a systemic risk buffer to be deployed as necessary by each country with a view to mitigating long-term, non-cyclical systemic or macroprudential risk at a national level. The systemic risk buffer is not set on an individual firm basis, but is to be applied to the whole financial sector or one or more subsets of it. The use of this buffer is predicated on the risk in question potentially having serious negative consequences for the national financial system and the real economy and not already having been adequately mitigated or prevented by other measures included in Basel III.

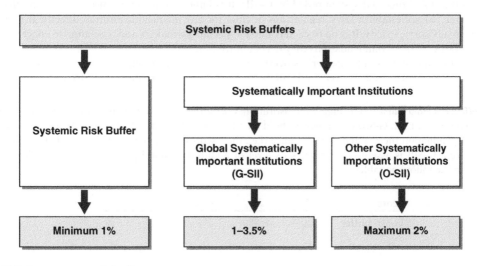

FIGURE 2.6 Systemic risk buffers

Banks may be required to maintain a Systemic Risk Buffer on an individual as well as on a consolidated level. The systemic risk buffer is set at a minimum of **1%** of the exposures to which it applies (individual, sub-consolidated or consolidated basis, as applicable). The Systemic Risk Buffer may apply to exposures located in third countries. Much like the countercyclical capital buffer, the systemic risk buffer also gives national authorities the option of recognising buffer rates set in other countries.

In the European Union the European Systemic Risk Board (ESRB) is the entity responsible for developing the principles and monitoring macroprudential risks across the Union (see Glossary). Each member state competent or designated authority can set a systemic risk buffer:

- A buffer rate between 0–3% does not require prior approval from the European Commission where imposed on exposures in a member state other than the authority's home member state. However, there is an obligation to notify the European Commission, European Banking Authority (EBA) and European Systemic Risk Board (ESRB).
- For a buffer rate between 3–5%, notification as above is required but the Commission will provide an opinion on the measure decided and if this opinion is negative, the Member States will have to "comply or explain".
- Above 5%, the setting member state shall be authorised by the European Commission through a Commission Implementing Act before setting the buffer.

2.5.2 Global Systemically Important Bank (G-SIB) Buffer

The **Global Systemically Important Institution** ("**G-SII**") buffer is designed to mitigate structural macroprudential risk and it is applied only by "**Global Systemically Important Institutions (G-SIIs)**" [CRD IV.131(4)]. SIIs are financial institutions of such size, market importance and interconnectedness that their distress or failure would cause significant dislocation in the financial system and adverse economic consequences. When the SII is a bank, the term "SIB" is often used instead. Therefore a **G-SIB** is a bank that is determined to be a globally systemically important institution. In November 2011, the BCBS published a framework *Global Systemically Important Banks: Updated Assessment Methodology and the Higher Loss Absorbency Requirement* (BCBS 255), complemented with the publication in November 2014 of *The G-SIB assessment methodology – score calculation* (BCBS 296), for dealing with G-SIBs.

G-SIBs are required under Basel III to maintain, on a **consolidated** basis, a buffer of CET1 capital (the **G-SIB Buffer**). This is in order to compensate for the higher risk that such global institutions represent for the financial system and the potential impact of their failure on taxpayers.

The **Financial Stability Board** ("**FSB**") coordinates all of the measures to reduce moral hazard and risks to the global financial system posed by G-SIIs. It is important to note that the FSB, as the Basel Committee, do not establish laws, regulations or rules for any financial institution directly. It merely acts in an advisory capacity. It is up to each country's specific lawmakers and regulators to enact whatever portions of the recommendations they deem appropriate.

The G-SIB designation framework is overly prescriptive and its application is largely mechanical. The case study in Section 2.7 covers in detail the methodology for determining G-SIB buffers.

The Size of the G-SIB Buffer   The bigger an institution, the more effect a potential failure may have on the financial system. Each G-SIB is required to hold an additional buffer of CET1 capital between **1%** and **3.5%** depending on their systemic importance (i.e., their scores under the identification methodology). The score a G-SIB is assigned determines its level of additional capital relative to its total RWAs, as shown in the following table:

Score	1	2	3	4	5
G-SIB buffer	1.0%	1.5%	2.0%	2.5%	3.5%

At the time of writing, no banks are expected to be required a 3.5% rate and, as a result, equity analysts refer to a 1–2.5% rate range for the G-SIB buffer. Where a G-SIB moves to a higher score level, it has 12 months to meet the higher capital levels, while moves to a lower score level decrease capital requirements immediately.

Under CRD IV the systemic risk buffer will be phased in from January 2016, with full implementation by January 2019, as follows:

Year (1-Jan.)	2016	2017	2018	2019
Percentage of systemic risk buffer	25%	50%	75%	100%

2.5.3 Other Systemically Important Institution (O-SII)

The "too-big-to-fail" problem may exist not only at the global level but also at a national level. As the Basel Committee noted, there are many banks that are not significant at the global level but could, if they were to come under stress, have an important impact on their domestic financial system and economy.

An **Other Systemically Important Institution** ("O-SII") or **Domestically Important Institution** ("D-SII") is a financial institution whose distress or disorderly failure could have a serious detrimental impact on either the financial system or the real economy within the country in which the institution operates (i.e., the reference system for the impact of failure of a O-SII should be the domestic economy) [CRD IV.131(5)].

In this respect, national supervisory authorities must undertake regular assessments of the systemic importance of the banks in their jurisdictions to ensure that their assessment reflects the current state of the relevant financial systems.

Whilst the G-SII designation framework is overly prescriptive and its application is largely mechanical, the O-SII framework is more principle-based and its application by national supervisory authorities allows a substantial degree of discretion, especially as to the appropriate relative weights they place, depending on national circumstances, on the following criteria:

- Size;
- Interconnectedness of the institution or group with the financial system;
- Importance for the economy of the country (including substitutability and financial system infrastructure); and
- Complexity within the domestic economy (including additional complexities caused by cross-border activities).

National supervisory authorities need to publicly disclose information that provides an outline of the methodology employed to assess the systemic importance of banks in their domestic economy.

It is up to the national supervisory authorities to designate which entities authorised within their jurisdiction are O-SIIs. The designation may be on an individual, sub-consolidated or consolidated level. As a result of their O-SII assessments, national supervisory authorities may require the maintenance, at that level, of a buffer of up to **2%** of their total RWAs, which must also consist of CET1 instruments.

2.5.4 Interaction between the Systemic Risk Buffers

In theory the O-SII framework is supposed to complement the G-SII regime by focusing on the impact that the distress or failure of banks may have on the domestic economy. Broadly speaking a group and

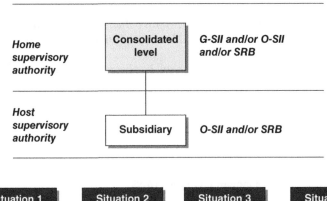

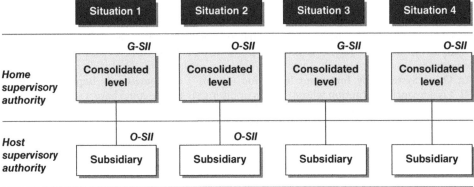

FIGURE 2.7   Group/subsidiary – G-SII/O–SII/SRB combinations

its subsidiaries/branches, designated as G-SII and/or O-SII, fall within one of the following situations (see Figure 2.7):

- At the consolidated group level a bank may be required to hold a G-SII buffer and/or an O-SII buffer and/or a systemic risk buffer by the home supervisory authority. Interestingly, an O-SII buffer may exceed a G-SII buffer.
- At a subsidiary level a bank may be required to hold an O-SII buffer and/or a systemic risk buffer by the host supervisory authority.

Especially at the consolidated level, a double counting may occur when macroprudential risks taken into account by one buffer are also considered by another buffer. Several rules apply regarding the interaction of the G-SII, O-SII and systemic risk buffers, as follows:

- Pursuant to [CRD IV.131(8)]: where an O-SII is a subsidiary of either a G-SII or an O-SII parent institution and subject to an O-SII buffer on a consolidated basis, the buffer that applies at individual or sub-consolidated level for the O-SII shall not exceed the higher of:
  - 1% of the total RWAs; and
  - The G-SII or O-SII buffer rate applicable to the group at consolidated level.
- Pursuant to [CRD IV.131(14)]: where a group, on a consolidated basis, is subject to the following, the higher buffer shall apply in each case:
  - A G-SII buffer and an O-SII buffer;
  - A G-SII buffer, an O-SII buffer and a systemic risk buffer.

- Pursuant to [CRD IV.131(15)] and [CRD IV.133(5)]: notwithstanding [CRD IV.131(14)], where the systemic risk buffer applies to all exposures located in the jurisdiction that sets that buffer to address the macroprudential risk of that jurisdiction, but does *not* apply to exposures outside the jurisdiction, that systemic risk buffer is cumulative with the O-SII or G-SII buffer.
- Pursuant to [CRD IV.131(14)] and [CRD IV.133(4)]: where an institution, on an individual or sub-consolidated basis is subject to an O-SII buffer and a systemic risk buffer, the higher of the two shall apply.
- Pursuant to [CRD IV.131(16)]: where [CRD IV.131(14)] applies and an institution is part of a group or a sub-group to which a G-SII or an O-SII belongs, this shall never imply that that institution is, on an individual basis, subject to a combined buffer requirement that is lower than the sum of the capital conservation buffer, the countercyclical capital buffer and the higher of the O-SII buffer and systemic risk buffer applicable to it on an individual basis.
- Pursuant to [CRD IV.131(17)]: where [CRD IV.131(15)] applies and an institution is part of a group or a sub-group to which a G-SII or an O-SII belongs, this shall never imply that that institution is, on an individual basis, subject to a combined buffer requirement that is lower than the sum of the capital conservation buffer, the countercyclical capital buffer and the sum of the O-SII buffer and systemic risk buffer applicable to it on an individual basis.
- Pursuant to [CRD IV.133(4)]: where a group which has been identified as a SII which is subject to a G-SII buffer or an O-SII buffer on a consolidated basis is also subject to a systemic risk buffer on a consolidated basis, the higher of the buffers shall apply.
- Pursuant to [CRD IV.133(6)]: where [CRD IV.133(6)] applies and an institution is part of a group or a sub-group to which a G-SII or an O-SII belongs, this shall never imply that that institution is, on an individual basis, subject to a combined buffer requirement that is lower than the sum of the capital conservation buffer, the countercyclical capital buffer and the higher of the O-SII buffer and systemic risk buffer applicable to it on an individual basis.
- Pursuant to [CRD IV.133(7)]: where [CRD IV.133(5)] applies and an institution is part of a group or a sub-group to which a G-SII or an O-SII belongs, this shall never imply that that institution is, on an individual basis, subject to a combined buffer requirement that is lower than the sum of the capital conservation buffer, the countercyclical capital buffer and the sum of the O-SII buffer and systemic risk buffer applicable to it on an individual basis.

2.6 GOING CONCERN vs. GONE CONCERN CAPITAL

There are two general types of regulatory capital (Figure 2.8):

- Capital that absorbs losses on a **going concern** basis, allowing a bank to continue its activities and helping to prevent insolvency; and
- Capital that absorbs losses on a **gone concern** basis, helping to ensure that depositors and senior creditors can be repaid in the event the bank is wound up.

Chapter 6 covers in detail the concepts mentioned in this section. In order to explore these concepts in an informal way and how capital levels are supposed to help banks, let us assume a bank that is operating in an economy that worsens over time.

2.6.1 Going Concern

In a normal functioning of the economy and the financial system, the bank periodically increases its capital levels by generating profits. Despite dividends being distributed, capital buffers are being built up.

As the economy deteriorates, the bank reports its first losses and starts eroding its countercyclical buffer, followed by its capital conservation and systemic risk buffers. As the combined buffer

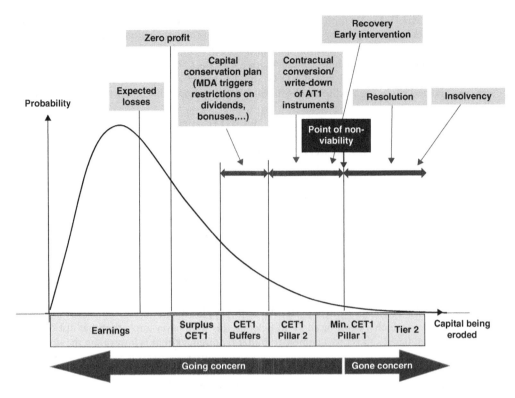

FIGURE 2.8 Going concern vs. gone concern regulatory capital

requirement (i.e., the bank-specific aggregate of the buffers required by the supervisory authority) is not met, a capital conservation plan is executed and a Maximum Distribution Amount (MDA) is set. The bank is prevented from incurring in cash outflows exceeding the MDA related to distributions to CET1 and AT1 instrument holders, and payments of variable remuneration or discretionary pension benefits.

As the economy deteriorates further, the CET1 capital levels of the bank continue to decline. At some point CET1 high triggers on AT1 instruments (e.g., 7.5%) are breached. Equity convertible AT1 instruments are automatically converted into shares of the bank, raising the bank's CET1 levels. Principal write-down AT1 instruments experience their principal amounts automatically being written down, and as the principal is reduced, a gain is recognised, increasing the bank's CET1 levels. At this point is likely that the supervisory authority will ask the bank to raise its CET1 levels further by issuing new ordinary shares in the equity markets.

When a CET1 capital level of 5.125% is reached, the **point of non-viability** is assessed by the supervisory authority. Low triggers (5.125%) of AT1 instruments are breached and, as a consequence, convertible AT1 instruments are converted into ordinary shares and principal on write-down AT1 instruments is reduced. If the conversion is deemed to be insufficient to solve the bank situation, the supervisory authority (and/or the resolution authority) will implement early intervention measures, which are likely to oblige the bank to adopt measures such as issuing new ordinary shares and AT1 instruments in the equity markets, and other capital enhancement initiatives such as disposals of assets.

2.6.2 Gone Concern

If the supervisory authority deems the situation to have reached the point of non-viability, the authority controls the management of the bank and the bank's resolution plan is executed. The bank is restructured and the terms of the financial instruments may be changed to preserve capital. Tier 2 instruments are written down, or converted into other instruments, to try to protect the depositors of the bank. If the write down of Tier 2 instruments are insufficient, other more senior instruments will be written down or converted into other instruments.

2.7 CASE STUDY: UBS vs. JP MORGAN CHASE G-SIB STRATEGIES

This case compares the G-SIB status of UBS and JP Morgan Chase and their contrasting strategies: while UBS decisively shrank its corporate and investment banking activities, achieving a reduction in its G-SIB capital surcharge, JP Morgan Chase preferred to maintain its business model and to implement initiatives that preserved internal synergies but had no substantial impact on its G-SIB status. JP Morgan Chase stressed that the value of its business model – through revenue and cost synergies, scale, risk management and diversified earnings – more than outweighed the capital savings to be obtained by splitting its retail and wholesale businesses.

The case has two main objectives: firstly, to describe in detail the key features and drivers of the Basel III methodology in respect of the G-SIB buffer; and secondly, to provide insights regarding potential strategies to reduce the size of the G-SIB requirement. Whilst reducing the size of a global bank translates into a regulatory capital benefit through a lower G-SIB buffer requirement, the simplification of its business is likely to erode the bank's return on equity as, for example, less synergies are achieved. Therefore the challenge for a global bank is how to determine a size and complexity that maximises return on equity.

2.7.1 G-SIB Methodology

The G-SII designation framework is overly prescriptive and its application is largely mechanical. As mentioned in Section 2.5.2, only a group of notably large banks with a strong presence in multiple jurisdictions are required to hold a G-SIB buffer. The first G-SIBs list was issued by the FSB in November 2011 and has been updated each November since then, based on data from the previous fiscal year-end supplied by banks and validated by national authorities.

Identification of a G-SIB is prescribed by the FSB, following a score-based system dependent upon several indicators. Based on their score, G-SIBs are subsequently assigned to a bucket. Each bucket determines the minimum G-SIB buffer that each bank in the bucket needs to comply with. The scoring system means that the larger the G-SIB, the higher the bucket it is assigned to in the list and hence the more capital it is required to hold as a percentage of risk-weighted assets. Each G-SIB is required to hold a G-SIB buffer of CET1 capital between **1%** and **3.5%**, depending on their bucket (the bucket thresholds were set such that bucket 5 was empty), as shown in the following table:

Bucket	1	2	3	4	5
G-SIB buffer	1.0%	1.5%	2.0%	2.5%	3.5%

The methodology to calculate each score was established by the BCBS in November 2014 in its document *The G-SIB Assessment Methodology – Score Calculation*. There are 12 indicators, grouped into five categories (see Figure 2.9):

- **Size:** The total on and off-balance sheet exposures of the bank, calculated on the basis of the leverage ratio.
- **Interconnectedness:** Capturing transactions with other financial institutions, including loans, debt, equity securities, secured financing transactions (SFTs) and derivative activity. Three are the indicators in this category:
  - Intra-financial system assets;
  - Intra-financial system liabilities; and
  - Securities outstanding.

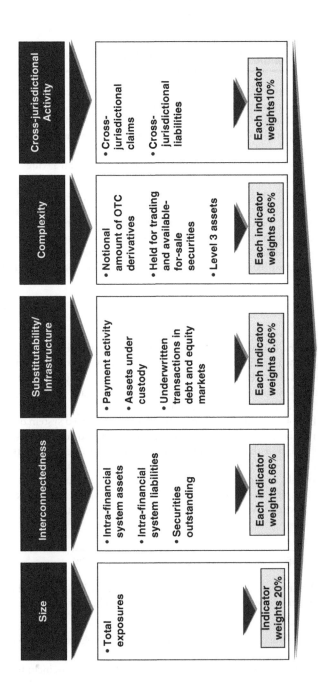

FIGURE 2.8   G-SIIs – Individual indicators of designation criteria

- **Substitutability/financial institution infrastructure:** The extent to which the banks services could be substituted by other institutions. Includes payments data (covering gross wholesale payments during the year excluding internal payments using large-value payment systems such as SWIFT, CHAPs etc.), assets under custody (covering the value of all assets that the bank holds as custodian on behalf of customers, excluding assets under management and assets under administration) and debt and equity underwriting. This category is subject to a cap. There are three indicators in this category:
  - Payment activity;
  - Assets under custody; and
  - Underwritten transactions in debt and equity markets.
- **Complexity:** The degree and number of complex transaction a bank is party to, including OTC derivative notionals, trading and available-for-sale (or at fair value through OCI securities) securities and Level 3 fair value assets. There are three indicators in this category:
  - Notional amount of over-the-counter (OTC) derivatives;
  - Trading and available-for-sale securities; and
  - Level 3 assets.
- **Cross-jurisdictional activity:** Foreign claims on an ultimate risk basis and foreign liabilities. There are two indicators in this category:
  - Cross-jurisdictional claims; and
  - Cross-jurisdictional liabilities.

Each category bears an equal weighting (20%). The indicators in each category are equally weighted, to sum 20%.

Interestingly, when calculating a bank's indicators, the data must be converted from the reporting currency to euros (EUR) – the G-SIB assessment methodology reporting currency – using the exchange rates published on the BCBS website. The average exchange rates over the bank's fiscal year is used to convert the individual payments data into the bank's reporting currency. The 31 December spot rate is used to convert each of the 12 indicator values (including total payments activity) to EUR. These rates should not be rounded in performing the conversions, as this may lead to inaccurate results.

Therefore, banks using a presentation currency other than the EUR are exposed, from a G-SIB perspective, to the exchange rate of their presentation currency relative to the EUR. For example, in the case of USD-based banks a strengthening of the USD relative to the EUR may result in a higher G-SIB buffer requirement.

In the case of UBS, its G-SIB indicators as of 31 December 2013 were translated into EUR using the 1.2276 average CHF/EUR spot rate during the year 2013, as published by the BCBS, in Table 2.1.

It can be seen that the figures related to payment activity and notional amount of OTC derivatives are notably larger than the rest. The G-SIB methodology is not concerned about how these absolute values compare among themselves. Rather, the methodology measures how each individual indicator compares with the EUR-denominated size of that indicator in the financial system (the "sample total"). In other words, indicator values are normalised using sample totals for the purposes of calculating a bank's score. To calculate the score for a given indicator, a bank's EUR-translated reported value for that indicator is divided by the corresponding sample total, and the resulting value is then expressed in basis

TABLE 2.1 UBS's G-SIB Indicators and their Amounts

Category	Indicator	Amount (CHF Million)	Amount (EUR Million)
Size	Total exposures	1,138,759	927,630
Interconnectedness	Intra-financial system assets	148,586	121,038
	Intra-financial system liabilities	139,816	113,894
	Securities outstanding	191,025	155,609
Substitutability/ infrastructure	Payment activity	25,768,760	20,991,170
	Assets under custody	2,919,065	2,377,863
	Debt and equity underwritten transactions	102,763	83,710
Complexity	Notional amount of OTC derivatives	30,199,172	24,600,173
	Held for trading and AFS securities	87,673	71,418
	Level 3	15,035	12,247
Cross-jurisdictional activity	Cross-jurisdictional claims	529,100	431,004
	Cross-jurisdictional liabilities	455,145	370,760

points (bps) (Table 2.2). For example, the score for UBS's Level 3 assets indicator is calculated by dividing UBS's Level 3 assets amount by the aggregate of the total amount of Level 3 assets held by all banks in the sample.

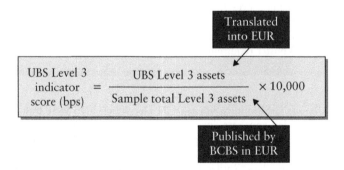

The sample itself consists of the largest 75 banks as determined by the Basel III leverage ratio exposure measure, along with any banks that were designated as a G-SIB in the previous year but are not otherwise part of the top 75 (an unlikely event other than as a result of bank mergers).

The impact on its G-SIB status of a bank's effort to reduce a specific indicator therefore depends on the overall reduction efforts undertaken by the 75 banks in the sample.

TABLE 2.2 UBS's Score of G-SIB Indicators

Category	UBS Amount (EUR Million)	Sample Total (EUR Million)	Score (bps)
Total exposures	927,630	66,313,252	140
Intra-financial system assets	121,038	7,717,966	157
Intra-financial system liabilities	113,894	7,830,852	145
Securities outstanding	155,609	10,836,237	144
Payment activity	20,991,170	1,850,754,574	113
Assets under custody	2,377,863	100,011,716	238
Debt and equity underwritten transactions	83,710	4,487,481	187
Notional amount of OTC derivatives	24,600,173	639,987,527	384
Held for trading and AFS securities	71,418	3,310,507	216
Level 3	12,247	595,405	206
Cross-jurisdictional claims	431,004	15,800,934	273
Cross-jurisdictional liabilities	370,760	14,093,661	263

TABLE 2.3 UBS's Calculation of Final G-SIB Score

Indicator	Average Score	Category Cap	Final Score
Size	140		140
Interconnectedness	(157 + 145 + 144) / 3 = 149		149
Substitutability/infrastructure	(113 + 238 + 187) / 3 = 179	500	179
Complexity	(384 + 216 + 206) / 3 = 269		269
Cross-jurisdictional activity	(273 + 263) / 2 = 268		268
Average final score (rounded)			216

To calculate the scores for each of the five categories, the scores for the indicators that fall within each category are averaged (Table 2.3). For example, the complexity category score is the average of the three complexity indicator scores: OTC derivatives, trading and AFS securities, and Level 3 assets. Since the size category consists of only one indicator, the category score is simply the score for the total exposures indicator. If binding, the substitutability cap must then be applied.

The **substitutability/infrastructure** category score is subject to a **500 bps cap**. It means that a bank holding a "market share" larger than 5% is not penalised for any excess above the 5% cap. For example, a bank with a substitutability/infrastructure category score of 900 bps (i.e., 9%) has little incentive, from a G-SIB perspective, to reduce it to, for instance, 600 bps. Such an effort would have no impact in its substitutability/infrastructure category score.

The final score is produced by averaging the five category scores and then rounding to the nearest whole basis point (fractional values between 0 and 0.5 are rounded down, while values from 0.5 to 1 are rounded up). Nonetheless, a bank's score may be adjusted based on supervisory judgment. In these exceptional cases, the published bucket will not align with the calculated score. The decision to exercise supervisory judgment will generally reflect a variety of quantitative or qualitative factors not captured in the 12 indicators. In the end, the FSB and the relevant supervisory authorities, in consultation with the BCBS, make final decisions regarding the use of supervisory judgment.

Once a bank score is calculated, the score ranges in the following table determines in which bucket the bank falls into and, consequently, the G-SIB buffer requirement (also called the "HLA" – Higher Loss Absorbency – requirement). For example, a bank with a score of 277 would fall into the second bucket, which corresponds to a 1.5% buffer requirement, to be met with CET1 capital.

Bucket	1	2	3	4	5
Score	130–229	230–329	330–429	430–529	530–629
G-SIB buffer	1.0%	1.5%	2.0%	2.5%	3.5%

Interestingly, a bank's ranking for the purpose of allocation of a capital charge on the scale 0% to 3.5% is therefore be driven by its relative complexity, substitutability, etc. compared with the entire reference group of banks, materially influenced by those of the largest banks in the group.

Thus, if a bank were significantly to shrink its size, simplify operations and reduce complexity, but others were to take even greater steps in this regard, then that bank might nevertheless rise in the overall ranking and potentially incur an increased G-SIB buffer.

The 216 final score placed UBS in the first bucket, corresponding to a G-SIB buffer requirement of 1% CET1. This score was very close to the 230 minimum score within the second bucket. Thus, UBS was likely to keep reducing its score in order to maintain its status within the first score.

Finally, note that G-SIB surcharges are applied two years after the data date. For example, UBS's 2014 figures determined the 2016 surcharge.

2.7.2 UBS's G-SIB Strategy

It was shown above that, based on the closing of 2013 G-SIB figures, UBS was positioned within the first bucket, implying a G-SIB capital requirement of 1%. However, based on the closing of 2012 amounts, UBS was placed in the G-SIB second bucket, implying a G-SIB capital requirement of 1.5%. Therefore, UBS's initiatives during 2013 (and the previous years) resulted in a 50 basis points G-SIB capital saving.

UBS's reduction in G-SIB status was the consequence of a strategy of simplifying and derisking its business and thus, in theory, it was able to operate with a lower capital requirement than previously. On the assumption that this freed up capital which could potentially be used to achieve a higher return for shareholders, there was a clear benefit to the strategy.

Prior to 2009 UBS had built up an investment banking franchise that had market leading positions in FX, interest rates, credit and equities. However, the business was a major driver of the G-SIB impact given the size of the OTC derivatives notional, level 3 assets, trading assets and securities financing. The interest rate business had been underperforming for several years due to low volumes on volatility and higher capital requirements.

From 2009, UBS refocused around its robust global wealth management franchise and restructured its investment banking activities to make them more client-focused. The bank aimed at reducing RWAs associated to its investment bank by building on less capital-intensive, flow franchises (e.g. cash equities, FX, money market, and corporate finance) and reducing interest rate and credit businesses. Solely in 2009, the investment bank reduced its balance sheet and RWAs by 41% and 37% respectively.

As at the end of 2014 the re-aligned investment bank consumed CHF 70 billion of RWAs (31% of group total, as shown in Figure 2.10) – achieving its long-term target – and CHF 290 billion of leverage exposure (less than 30% of total group).

2.7.3 JP Morgan Chase's G-SIB Strategy

In contrast to UBS, JP Morgan Chase's position in the G-SIB ladder remained unchanged in 2014 from 2013, according to international G-SIB standards, which are notably different to U.S. G-SIB standards. In 2014 and 2015 American G-SIBs, notably Citigroup and JP Morgan Chase, were under substantial pressure from regulators to reduce the size and complexity of their business models. In the case of JP Morgan, divestments have been peripheral, limited to small subsidiaries in markets where the bank held low market share, driven by a simple desire to improve return on equity.

In November 2014, the U.S. Federal Reserve Board established the guidelines for U.S. G-SIB capital charges, which was built upon the BCBS methodology. The U.S. rules on G-SIB surcharges were more stringent than BCBS rules: it eliminated the "substitutability/infrastructure" category and added a "short-term wholesale funding" category (see Figure 2.11). In order to calculate their score, the "size", "interconnectedness", "complexity" and "cross-jurisdictional activity" categories were calibrated against their "sample total", which comprised the aggregate for each indicator of the 75 largest banks. Therefore, the U.S. version did not represent any changes in the calculation of the score of each indicator score pertaining to these four categories. However, the U.S. version doubled their weights when determining the G-SIB surcharge.

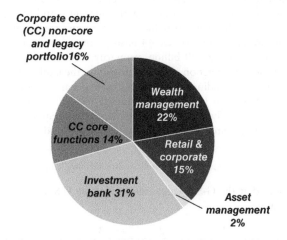

FIGURE 2.10 RWAs divisional breakdown, as at the end of 2014

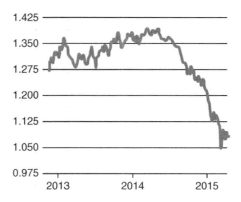

FIGURE 2.11   EUR/USD spot rate (Jan-13 to Apr-15)

Regarding the new category – short-term wholesale funding – it was in line with the U.S. version of the liquidity cover ratio definition. This new category was calibrated against the average RWA rather than against the aggregate of the 75 largest banks as the BCBS did not provide sample total amounts for this category.

> The short-term wholesale funding indicator was expected to increase capital requirements for firms heavily reliant on wholesale financing to reduce systemic risk from fire sales.
>
> In practice, it heavily penalised non-operating deposits. Under the LCR rules, these non-operating deposits were effectively placed as cash at the Federal Reserve, therefore presenting no fire sale risk to either the bank or the financial system.
>
> In the case of JP Morgan Chase, it had at year-end 2014 USD 390 billion of deposits from financial institutions, of which USD 200 billion were non-operating. Providing its balance sheet to financial clients was in part an accommodation. However, these deposits impacted not only the bank's short-term wholesale funding indicator score, but also the score of its size, cross-jurisdictional and interconnectedness indicators. The bank estimated that its was gaining 10 to 15 basis points net on these deposits – an unattractive margin – and they provided no benefit from a U.S. LCR perspective. In order to reduce its large score stemming from its short-term wholesale funding indicator, expected to save 44 basis points in this score by reducing in 2015 its non-operating deposits by USD 100 billion, primarily from international financial institutions. In order to minimise the impact on client relationships, the bank worked with these clients to find potential alternatives, including offering them money market funds.
>
> Whilst the treatment of repo funding was relatively lenient in the short-term wholesale funding indicator, repos are heavily penalised in other regulatory requirements. For example, the leverage ratio does not take into account the collateral received in a repo, as covered in Chapter 17.

It is important to note that the G-SIB surcharges under the U.S. regime are notably larger than those under the BCBS regime:

Bucket	1	2	3	4	5
Score	630–729	730–829	830–929	930–1,029	1,030–1,129
G-SIB buffer	3.5%	4.0%	4.5%	5.0%	5.5%

In the case of JP Morgan, using closing of 2014 figures, the G-SIB score of the bank using the EUR/USD spot rate as of 31 December 2013 was:

Indicator	Size	Interconnectedness	Complexity	Cross-Jurisdictional Activity	Short-Term Wholesale Funding
Score	79	85	139	58	58
Adjustment	×2	2	×2	×2	×2
Adjust. score	158	170	278	116	116
Total score	838				

The total score of 838 implied that the bank was placed within bucket 3, implying a G-SIB buffer of 4.5%. However, due primarily to the substantial appreciation of the USD relative to the EUR in 2014 (see Figure 2.11), JP Morgan expected to be placed within bucket 4, implying a G-SIB buffer of 5%.

Whilst there was a tangible benefit for such a large and complex bank to reduce its size and complexity of its business models in the form of a lower G-SIB charge, JP Morgan Chase assessed whether that such strategy would be beneficial to its shareholders. The bank analysed the implications of a separation between its retail activities – Chase – and the corporate and investment bank – JP Morgan – as seen in Table 2.4.

TABLE 2.4 Implications of a separation between JP Morgan's retail activities and its corporate and investment bank

	Comments	Impact
Revenue and expense	■ While most revenue synergies should remain – modest portion would be lost ■ The ability to invest through-the-cycle and leadership positions could erode ■ Each company would remain at scale, but would need to invest to rebuild ancillary businesses – critical infrastructure – and duplicate Corporate functions, which would impact margins	■ Small negative ■ Negative – not quantified ■ Meaningfully negative
Capital	■ Amount of excess capital available to shareholders would be more modest than implied by G-SIB scores alone – given CCAR would be the binding constraint for Consumer	■ Approx. USD 15 bn
Valuation	■ Valuation range more modest than equity research analysts were implying ■ Upside driven by multiple expansion	■ Value of synergies lost would be greater than capital freed up
Execution risk	■ Managing transition to standalone organisations – separating and rebuilding systems, technology, controls and risk management processes ■ Retaining management and top talent ■ Protecting client franchise and market leadership position	■ Increased uncertainty

JP Morgan Chase quantified the synergies achieved by the organisation were it to remain as one group. The bank estimated USD 15 billion of revenue synergies:

■ The scale and platform enabled a portfolio approach for clients (i.e., profitability was attained through a broad product set and cross-border capabilities). For example, the bank's premier investment banking platform and international footprint was leveraged by commercial banking and asset management businesses and resulted in a robust cross-sell of treasury services and investor services products;

■ The extensive branch network played a critical role as a key sales channel utilised by the commercial banking and asset management businesses; and

■ Its fortress balance sheet provided strategic leverage (e.g., lending growth).

In addition, the bank estimated USD 3 billion of cost synergies, mainly stemming from shared corporate infrastructure (e.g., common finance and risk functions, shared technology and operations, cybersecurity) and scale benefits enabling the bank to service its clients more efficiently. Those synergies were estimated to result in a USD 6 to 7 billion annual benefit in its net income:

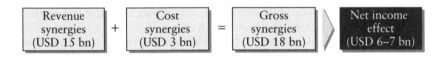

JP Morgan Chase's universal banking model brought in other benefits beyond synergies, like for example:

■ The diversification of businesses allowed for significant investments through-the-cycle;

■ It increased the depth of its product expertise, industry knowledge and access to integrated coverage teams; and

■ It helped the bank to attract and develop top talent.

Based on these figures, JP Morgan Chase concluded that the regulatory capital savings of separating both activities would be lower than the benefits of remaining one entity. Therefore, rather than reducing its size and complexity by splitting its retail and investment banks, JP Morgan Chase decided to focus on implementing initiatives to enhance its G-SIB score.

> In practice it is difficult for a bank to fully control the surcharge calculation because there are factors outside management's control. The proportionality of the calculation means that the impact of any one bank's actions on its surcharge also depends on the collective actions of the other 74 G-SIBs. Furthermore, since the aggregate market indicators are denominated in EUR, U.S. banks are disadvantaged when the USD strengthens as their USD-denominated balance sheet translates into a larger relative proportion of the other 74 G-SIBs. A hedge of the EUR/USD rate has to be carefully designed to not increase volatility in the income statement.

The bank first introduced a G-SIB assessment framework that measured the return of activities on their marginal G-SIB's contribution, and then used this framework to identify actions to reduce the score. There were three dimensions addressed when optimising the bank's G-SIB score, as shown in Figure 2.12:

■ Initiatives to address **absolute values** (i.e., the numerators of the score of each indicator). As the amounts reported by the bank corresponding to each of the four indicators that was benchmarked

FIGURE 2.12   Three-dimensional assessment of G-SIB enhancement initiatives

to the other 74 G-SIBs, was translated into EUR, JP Morgan Chase had to assess whether it made sense to put in place EUR/USD hedges.

- Initiatives to address **market effects**, or in other words, the market size. The denominators in the score calculation for each indicator in the four categories were influenced by sample totals (i.e., the size of each indicator across the largest 75 banks). These initiatives analysed the impact on JP Morgan Chase' score stemming from the collective actions of the other 74 G-SIBs and implemented actions to offset excessively negative impacts.
- Initiatives to take into account **time effects**. The G-SIB surcharge was not fully effective until 1 January 2019, being subject to a three year phase-in period staring on 1 January 2016. This gradual application allowed the bank to not to overreact to market events.

In particular, JP Morgan Chase implemented a number of initiatives to address **absolute values** at its corporate and investment banking (CIB) division activities, the business of the bank more likely to affect the G-SIB scores. The bank first determined the share of the overall score of each CIB business and compared with their share of revenues, as shown in Figure 2.13. The idea was to allocate capital charges through activities based upon their marginal G-SIB contribution. This analysis was complemented with an estimate if the G-SIB indicator distribution within the CIB division (see Figure 2.14).

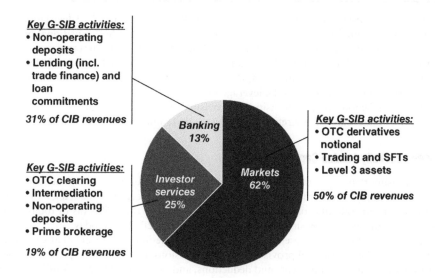

FIGURE 2.13   G-SIB surcharge share of each Corporate and Investment Banking division business (2014)

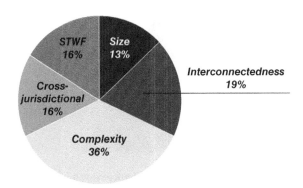

FIGURE 2.14   G-SIB indicator distribution within the Corporate and Investment Banking division (2014)

Initiatives had to be carefully assessed through three lenses – product, business and client – so as not to fundamentally damage the strengths of the business: its profitability, completeness and its global scale. These initiatives included:

- Establishing caps to balance sheet size;
- Establishing a governance process of escalation and approvals for new G-SIB intensive products;
- Repricing existing G-SIB intensive products;
- Intensifying efforts for OTC derivatives compression;
- Intensifying efforts for Level 3 assets rationalisation;
- Intensifying efforts for trading book inventory reduction; and
- Reviewing loans and loan commitments inventory.

G-SIB intensive products, such as non-operating deposits, had to be repriced to incorporate the return expected from their capital consumption.

2.8 TRANSITIONAL PROVISIONS

Basel III introduced substantial requirements relative to Basel II. The Basel III legislation set out a minimum pace of introduction of these enhanced capital requirements (the "**transitional provisions**"). The transitional provisions are designed to implement Basel III requirements in stages over a prescribed period. Basel III permitted a transitional period from 1 January 2014 to 1 January 2018 for a good number of regulations, primarily regarding capital requirements, deductions from capital, capital buffers and certain other measures, such as the leverage ratio.

In the European Union (EU), the transitional provisions were set out in Part Ten of the CRR. Each of the EU Member States has the discretion to accelerate that minimum pace of transition.

2.8.1 Phase-in vs. Fully Loaded Capital

A calculated measure that is presented as being on a "**fully loaded basis**" means that such measure is calculated without applying the transitional provisions. For example, a fully loaded CET1 ratio calculated as of today means the ratio of CET1 capital (as of today) to the RWAs (as of today), assuming that there are no transitional provisions (i.e., it is as if 1 January 2024 was today).

A calculated measure that is presented as being on a "**phase-in basis**" means that such measure is calculated following the transitional provisions. These provisions are (i) phase-in provisions for applying the necessary regulatory adjustments and deductions, and (ii) phase-out provisions for instruments no longer qualifying under Basel III. Phase-in and phase-out transitional provisions are allowed to ease the transition for banks to the "fully loaded" capital rules.

2.8.2 Grandfathering of Non-compliant AT1 and Tier 2 Instruments

Basel III non-compliant AT1 and Tier 2 instruments which were included in an institution capital base before 1 January 2013 (collectively referred to as "extant capital instruments") benefit from a grand-fathering period. Extant capital instruments may be phased out during the 10-year period beginning from 1 January 2013. This progressively reduces the eligible amount by 10% annually, following an initial 20% on 1 January 2014, until they are fully phased out by 1 January 2022. Table 2.5 summa-rises the percentage of base amount of transitional instruments that may be included in AT1 and Tier 2 capital under the phase-out arrangement (base is fixed at the nominal amount of such instruments outstanding on 1 January 2013).

For example, a bank that issued a Tier 1 extant capital instrument in August 2010 was able to count 70% of the notional outstanding amount of the instrument as of 1 January 2015 during calendar year 2015, 60% during calendar year 2016, and so on. As of 1 January 2022, no Tier 1 extant capital instruments will be recognised in Tier 1 capital.

To the extent that an instrument is redeemed, or its recognition in capital is amortised, dur-ing the phase-in period, the nominal amount serving as the base is not reduced. In addition, instruments may only be included under a particular cap to the extent that they are recognised in that tier of capital. That is to say, any amount of instruments issued in excess of the limits allowed for recognition prior to 1 January 2013 (e.g., supplementary capital limited to the institution's core capital; and term debt capital limited to 50% core capital) are eligible for the gradual phasing-out treatment (i.e., any such excess amount is excluded from the calculation of the base amount). Nevertheless, such instruments are allowed to be fully recognised (i.e. without limita-tion) on and after 1 January 2013 if they meet all the qualifying criteria for inclusion in AT1 capital or in Tier 2 capital.

Where an instrument's recognition in capital is subject to amortisation on or before 1 January 2013, only the amortised amount recognised in capital on 1 January 2013 is taken into account in the amount fixed for transitioning rather than the full nominal amount. The instrument continues to amor-tise on a straight-line basis at a rate of 20% per annum during the transition period, while the aggre-gate cap is reduced at a rate of 10% per year.

TABLE 2.5   Phase-in Eligibility AT1 and Tier 2 Instruments

Commencement Date	Percentage of Base Amount
1-Jan-2016	60%
1-Jan-2017	50%
1-Jan-2018	40%
1-Jan-2019	30%
1-Jan-2020	20%
1-Jan-2021	10%
1-Jan-2022	0%

TABLE 2.6   Transitional Provisions Regarding Capital Conservation and G-SIB Buffers

Commencement Date	Capital Requirement
1-Jan-2016	25% × [2.5% capital conservation buffer + G-SIB buffer based on 2014 list]
1-Jan-2017	50% × [2.5% capital conservation buffer + G-SIB buffer based on 2015 list]
1-Jan-2018	75% × [2.5% capital conservation buffer + G-SIB buffer based on 2016 list]
1-Jan-2019	100% × [2.5% capital conservation buffer + G-SIB buffer based on 2017 list]

Share premium may be included in the base provided that it relates to an instrument that is eligible to be included in the base for the transitional arrangements.

Non-qualifying instruments that are denominated in a foreign currency are included in the base using their value in the reporting currency of the institution as at 1 January 2013. The base is fixed in the reporting currency of the institution throughout the transition period. During the transition period, instruments denominated in a foreign currency are valued as they are reported on the balance sheet of the institution at the relevant reporting date (adjusting for any amortisation in the case of Tier 2 instruments).

2.8.3 Transitional Provisions Regarding Capital Conservation and G-SIB Buffers

Table 2.6 summarises the transitional provisions regarding the capital conservation and G-SIB buffers (the countercyclical capital buffer may also be required in addition to these capital requirements). These buffer requirements are subject to a three-year phase-in period, starting 1 January 2016, and increasing each year by one quarter of the total buffer. The total buffer will be completely phased in starting from 1 January 2019.

CHAPTER 3

Common Equity 1 (CET1) Capital

The Common Equity component of Tier 1 capital (commonly referred to as "**Common Equity Tier 1**" capital or "**CET1**"), is the key capital measure as it is considered the element of capital that is the highest quality and the most effective in absorbing losses and enabling an institution to remain as a going concern.

CET1 is calculated in accordance with Chapter 2 (Common Equity Tier 1 capital) of Title I (Elements of own funds) of Part Two (Own Funds) of the CRR.

3.1 CET1 MINIMUM REQUIREMENTS

CET1 ratio means the ratio of a bank's CET1 capital to its risk-weighted assets (RWAs). The minimum requirement for CET1 ratio is 4.5% of RWAs after the application of adjustments. However, when combined with the capital buffers, the resulting CET1 requirement is notably higher (see Figure 2.2). The difference between both requirements is that a bank not meeting the minimum 4.5% CET1 requirement would require supervisor intervention, while not meeting the capital buffer requirements would only restrict distributions (e.g., dividends).

$$\text{Common Equity Tier 1 Capital Ratio} = \frac{\text{Common Equity Tier 1 capital}}{\text{Risk-weighted assets}} \geq 4.5\%$$

3.2 ELIGIBILITY REQUIREMENTS OF CET1 INSTRUMENTS

CET1 is the highest-quality component of a bank's capital. CET1 consists mainly of ordinary shares (i.e., common stock) plus reserves less some deductions. Other instruments can be included which are deemed fully equivalent to ordinary shares in terms of their capital quality as regards loss absorption and do not possess features which could cause the condition of the bank to be weakened as a going concern during periods of market stress. For example, in the rare cases where a bank issued non-voting ordinary shares, to be included in CET1, they must be identical to voting common shares of the issuing bank in all respects except the absence of voting rights.

3.2.1 Criteria Governing Instruments Inclusion in CET1

For an instrument to be included in CET1, the predominant form of Tier 1 capital, it must meet all of the following criteria:

1. It represents the most subordinated claim in liquidation of the bank.
2. It is entitled to a claim of the residual assets that is proportional to its share of issued capital, after all senior claims have been repaid in liquidation (i.e., it has an unlimited and variable claim, not a fixed or capped claim).
3. Principal is perpetual and never repaid outside of liquidation (setting aside discretionary repurchases or other means of effectively reducing capital in a discretionary manner that is allowable under national law).
4. The bank does nothing to create an expectation at issuance that the instrument will be bought back, redeemed or cancelled, nor do the statutory or contractual terms provide any feature which might give rise to such an expectation. This criterion does not oppose banks being market makers in their own shares.
5. Distributions (i.e., dividends and coupons) are paid out of distributable items (retained earnings included). The level of distributions are not in any way tied or linked to the amount paid in at issuance and are not subject to a cap (except to the extent that a bank is unable to pay distributions that exceed the level of distributable items).
6. There are no circumstances under which the distributions are obligatory. Non-payment is therefore not an event of default.
7. Distributions are paid only after all legal and contractual obligations have been met and payments on more senior capital instruments have been made. This means that there are no preferential distributions, including in respect of other elements classified as the highest-quality issued capital.
8. It is the issued capital that takes the first and proportionately greatest share of any losses as they occur. Within the highest-quality capital, each instrument absorbs losses on a going concern basis proportionately and pari passu with all the others.
9. The paid-in amount is recognised as equity capital (i.e., not recognised as a liability) for determining balance sheet insolvency.
10. The paid-in amount is classified as equity under the relevant accounting standards.
11. It is directly issued and paid-up, and the bank cannot directly or indirectly have funded the purchase of the instrument.
12. The paid-in amount is neither secured nor covered by a guarantee of the issuer or related entity or subject to any other arrangement that legally or economically enhances the seniority of the claim. Related entities are the issuer's subsidiaries, the parent undertaking of the issuer or its subsidiaries, the parent financial holding company or its subsidiaries, the mixed activity holding company or its subsidiaries, the mixed financial holding company and its subsidiaries, or any undertaking that has close links with the previous entities.
13. It is only issued with the approval of the owners of the issuing bank, either given directly by the owners or, if permitted by applicable law, by the Board of Directors or by other persons duly authorised by the owners.
14. It is clearly and separately disclosed on the bank's balance sheet.

3.2.2 Major Components of CET1

CET1 consists of the following items (see Figure 3.1):

- Capital instruments and related share premium accounts [CRR 26(1), 27, 28, 29];
- Retained earnings, prior to the inclusion of any interim net profit or losses [CRR 26(1)(c)];
- Independently reviewed interim profits, net of any foreseeable charge or dividend [CRR 26(2)];
- Accumulated other comprehensive income [CRR 26(1)(c)];

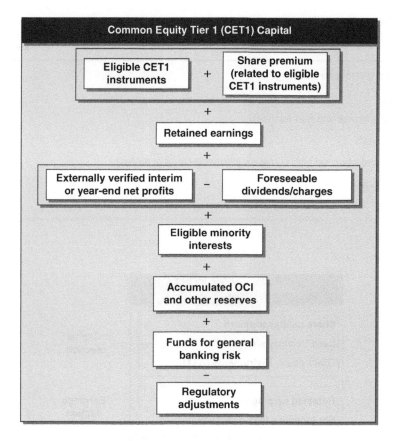

FIGURE 3.1   Components in the calculation of CET1

- Other reserves [CRR 26];
- Funds for general banking risk [CRR 26(1)(f)];
- CET1 eligible minority interests [CRR 84];
- Less regulatory adjustments.

Example: HSBC's CET1 Capital

On 31 December 2015, the British bank HSBC disclosed the CET1 items in Table 3.1.

3.2.3 Accounting Overview of Shareholders' Equity

The shareholders' equity of a bank balance sheet is comprised of different elements, which represent capital invested in the bank by third-party investors and capital generated and not returned to these investors since its constitution. These elements can be grouped into the categories shown in Figure 3.2 (this is my own split, not an official accounting split).

Capital Section   The capital section groups transactions with owners acting in their capacity as owners, comprising:

TABLE 3.1   HSBC's Fully-loaded CET1 Capital as of 31 December 2015

Item	Amount USD mn
Ordinary shares and related share premium	20,858
Retained earnings	143,976
Other comprehensive income (and other reserves)	<453>
Eligible minority interests	3,519
Independently reviewed interim net profits net of any foreseeable charge or dividend	<3,717>
Regulatory adjustments	<33,320>
Total CET1 capital	130,863

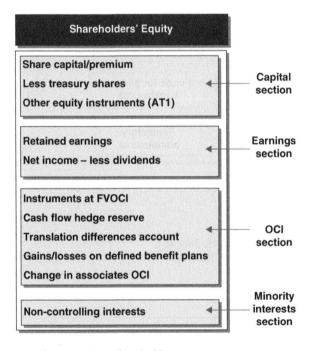

FIGURE 3.2   Main elements of (accounting) shareholders' equity

- **Ordinary shares** (or common stock) represent the basic ownership interest in the reporting entity. It is the residual corporate interest that bears the ultimate risk of loss, as it is subordinate to all other instruments issued by the bank. A reporting entity may have more than one class of ordinary shares;
- **Share premium** (or additional paid-in capital or APIC) is the excess amount paid by an investor over the par value of a stock issue. In addition, non-stock-related contributions from an investor, such as cash or property, are normally reflected in share premium;

- **Treasury shares** (or own shares or treasury stock) are created when a reporting entity reacquires its own ordinary shares. If the treasury shares are not constructively or actually retired upon its reacquisition, the bank presents it on the shareholders' equity of the balance sheet as a reduction from capital; and
- **Other equity instruments** are instruments other than ordinary shares that from an accounting perspective are classified as equity instruments as opposed to liabilities. In a bank, AT1 instruments are included in this section of shareholders' equity.

Earnings Section   The earnings section groups the following items:

- **Retained earnings** represents the earned capital of the bank. Earned capital is the capital that develops and builds up over time from profitable operations. It consists of all undistributed income that remains invested in the bank;
- **Profit or loss** (or net income) represents the bank's net earnings generated during the reporting period. This statement mainly comprises net interest income after provisions for credit losses, net non-interest income and taxes; and
- **Dividends** are distributions to shareholders and owners of other equity instruments (such as equity-classified AT1 instruments). Cash dividends declared are generally reported as a deduction from retained earnings until the retained earnings account is exhausted. In the absence of retained earnings, cash dividends should generally be charged to share premium. Stock dividends declared are generally shown as a deduction from retained earnings and added to common stock and share premium.

Reserves Section – Other Comprehensive Income (OCI)   Other comprehensive income (OCI) mainly represents items that are temporarily recorded in the bank's balance sheet. Whilst a large proportion of the items in OCI will be subsequently reclassified to profit or loss, some items (e.g., remeasurement of gains/losses related to defined benefit pension plans) are reclassified to other sections of shareholders' equity. OCI is further explained in Section 3.5.

Non-controlling Interests Section   Issuances of a subsidiary's ordinary shares and other equity instruments (e.g., AT1 instruments) to third parties are treated as non-controlling interests (i.e., minority interests). Non-controlling interests are shown in the consolidated balance sheet as a separate component of equity, which is distinct from the group's shareholders' equity.

3.2.4 Capital Instruments and Share Premium

The main component of CET1 capital is the capital raised through ordinary shares and other similar instruments. CET1 eligible capital instruments and related share premium accounts are dealt with by [CRR 26(1)(a) (b), 27, 28, 29].

There are some financial institutions, such as mutual, cooperative or saving banks, that do not issue common shares. Taking into account their specific constitution and legal structure, the national supervisors apply the criteria preserving the quality of the instruments to be included in CET1 by requiring that the eligible instruments are deemed fully equivalent to common shares in terms of their capital quality as regards loss absorption and do not possess features which could cause the condition of the bank to be weakened as a going concern during periods of market stress. The EBA periodically publishes a list of capital instruments in EU member states qualifying as CET1 instruments.

Share Premium   Share premium (i.e., stock surplus or additional paid-in capital) is only permitted to be included in CET1 if the shares giving rise to the share premium are also permitted to be included in CET1. This requirement ensures that banks are not given credit in CET1 when they issue shares outside of the CET1 (e.g., AT1 instruments) which may have a low nominal value and high share premium. In this sense the CRR ensures that there is no loophole for including instruments other than common shares in CET1.

Scrip Dividends   New shares issued in lieu of dividends (i.e., scrip dividends) help a bank to enhance its CET1 by keeping shareholders' equity intact. A scrip dividend programme provides shareholders with an opportunity, if they wish, to receive new shares instead of a cash dividend in respect of a dividend, without incurring in transaction costs (e.g. brokerage fees).

The number of new shares that a participant receives for each scrip dividend depends on the number of ordinary shares held at the dividend record date, the amount of the cash dividend to which the investor is entitled, any residual cash balance brought forward from the last scrip dividend, and the scrip reference share price. The formula used for calculating the number of new shares to be received is as follows:

$$\text{Number of new shares} = \frac{\text{Cash available}}{\text{Scrip reference share price}}$$

Where:

- Cash available is the number of ordinary shares held at the relevant dividend record date multiplied by the cash dividend per ordinary share plus any residual cash balance brought forward. The residual cash balance represents the aggregate cash amount not been distributed as of the previous scrip dividend to each shareholder because it resulted in a fraction of a share; and
- Scrip reference share price is the average of the bank's share price over a pre-specified number of consecutive trading days (e.g., five) commonly commencing on (and including) the date on which the ordinary shares are first quoted ex-dividend.

For example, let us assume a bank had 2 billion ordinary shares held, that the dividend was EUR 1.00 per ordinary share and that the residual cash balance from a previous scrip dividend was EUR 0.3 million and that the scrip reference share price was EUR 20.50.

- The cash available (i.e., the cash dividend payable plus the residual cash balance) was EUR 2,000.3 million (= 2 bn × 1.00 + 0.3 mn).
- The number of new shares to be issued (i.e., the cash available divided by the scrip reference share price) was 97.7 million (= 2,000.3 mn/20.50).

Retail investors are commonly interested in receiving new shares, for tax reasons. Individual shareholders are likely to make an election to receive new shares instead of a cash dividend if such new shares are treated as a new asset acquired on the date the new shares are issued while cash dividends are taxed as ordinary income. The "cash equivalent" of the new shares is treated as being the base cost of the new shares. The shareholder will be subject to tax only after disposal of the new shares.

From a bank perspective a scrip dividend retains CET1 and cash, as shown in Figure 3.3. Let us assume that a bank declares a EUR 500 million scrip dividend and that 40% of its shareholding elects distribution in shares. Therefore, EUR 300 million (= 500 mn × 60%) is paid in cash while the bank is able to keep EUR 200 million CET1.

In contrast, a full EUR 500 million cash dividend erodes CET1 and cash balances by that amount, as shown in Figure 3.4.

Employee Share Plans   Similarly to scrip dividends, new shares issued under employee share plans also keep CET1. Imagine a share plan with a 3-year vesting period worth EUR 90 million and a

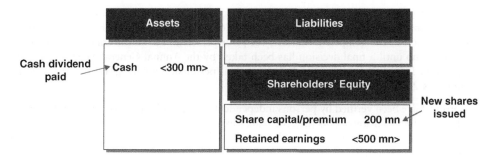

FIGURE 3.3 Balance sheet effects of the scrip dividend

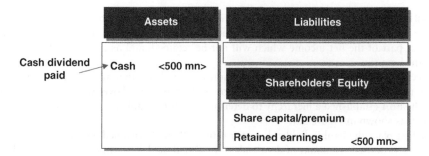

FIGURE 3.4 Balance sheet effects of the cash dividend

corporate tax rate of 30%. Each year during the vesting period, the bank recognised a compensation expense of EUR 30 million (= 90 mn/3). When the shares were issued following the end of the vesting period, the bank had already recognised a EUR 63 million [= 90 mn × (1 − 30%)] expense. By issuing new shares, rather than paying a cash compensation, the bank was able to retain such EUR 63 million CET1.

3.2.5 Retained Earnings and Interim Net Income less Expected Dividends

Items other than capital instruments and share premium are eligible only where they are available to the bank for unrestricted and immediate use to cover risks or losses as soon as these occur.

Retained Earnings   Retained earnings comprise the aggregate of a bank's profit or loss amounts (since it its constitution) which have not been distributed to shareholders. According to [CRR 26(1)], retained earnings is an eligible CET1 item.

Gains and Losses for the Current Financial Year   The profit or loss statement is referred to by various names, such as the net income statement, statement of earnings, or others. Whatever name is used, its purpose is the same: to provide users of the financial statements with a measurement of a reporting entity's results of operations over a period of time (commonly a quarter or a year). This allows users to make important investing, lending and other decisions by understanding trends of key measures such as interest income and net interest margin.

According to [CRR 26(2)], a bank may include interim or year-end **profits** in CET1 capital before it has taken a formal decision confirming the final profit or loss of the institution for the year only with the prior permission of the competent authority. A prior permission from the competent authority is thus compulsory up until a final decision has been taken by the Annual General Meeting confirming the final profit or loss of the institution for the year. This permission will be granted if the conditions detailed in [CRR 26(2)(a), (b)] are met:

- The profits have been verified by persons independent of the bank, who are responsible for auditing the bank financial statements (i.e., the bank's external auditors).
- Any foreseeable charge or dividend has been deducted from the amount of those profits and the basis of this calculation.

Losses for the current financial year as provided in [CRR 36(1)(a)] are deducted for the purpose of calculating CET1. There is no requirement to have such losses verified by an external auditor.

Foreseeable Dividends   Foreseeable charges or dividends have to be deducted from interim or year-end profits. The aim of the determination of the deduction of the foreseeable charges and dividends is to estimate that part of the net income which will not be retained, and as result, not function as stable capital in the long run.

Foreseeable charges or dividends are any charges or dividends that are reasonably expected to be paid out of the interim or year-end profit in relation to the time period over which the profits are being assessed. The EBA established a hierarchy to determine the foreseeable charges or dividends amount to be deducted, as shown in Figure 3.5.

In the first place the bank's dividend payout ratio shall be determined on the basis of the **formally approved – or proposed – amount of dividends** to be distributed. The approval or proposal has to be

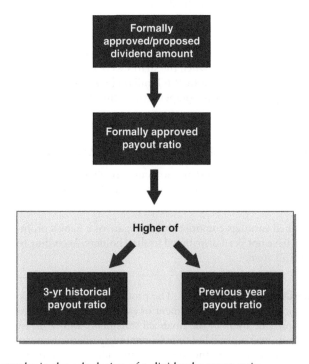

FIGURE 3.5   EBA's hierarchy in the calculation of a dividend payout ratio

made by the management body to the relevant body. The approved or proposed amount shall be deducted from the interim or year-end profits under consideration:

$$\text{Amount to be deducted} = \text{Approved dividend amount}$$

Secondly, in the absence of an approved or proposed dividend amount, the amount of deduction from the interim or year-end profits equals the amount of interim or year-end profits multiplied by the **dividend payout ratio**:

$$\text{Amount to be deducted} = \text{Interim (or year-end) profits} \times \text{Dividend payout ratio}$$

Where a dividend payout ratio has been approved by the management body (or other relevant body) for the relevant body, such ratio should be used. Where a payout range instead of a fixed value has been approved, the upper end of the range is to be used.

In the absence of an approved dividend policy, the dividend payout ratio shall be based on the highest of the following:

- The average of the dividend payout ratios of the three years prior to the year under consideration; and
- The dividend payout ratio of the year preceding that of the year under consideration.

The amount of foreseeable dividends to be paid in a form that does not reduce the amount of CET1 capital shall not be deducted from interim or year-end profits to be included in CET1 capital. Therefore, if the bank has approved a scrip dividend, it does not need to deduct the expected amount of the dividend to be distributed in shares.

The competent authority may authorise the bank to adjust the calculation of the dividend payout ratio to exclude **exceptional dividends** paid during the historical period.

The impact of future regulatory requirements, or actions taken by competent authorities, that may restrict the amount of dividends available for distribution should be factored into the calculation of foreseeable dividends. For example, a deficit in the "combined buffer requirement" may lead to restrictions on the dividend payout policy on a legal entity basis or on a consolidated basis, as governed by the Maximum Distributable Amount – MDA – (see Section 6.4.1). In addition, statutory national laws may restrict the amount of dividends an entity may distribute.

It is important to remember that the competent authority needs to be satisfied that all necessary deductions to the interim or year-end profits and related to foreseeable charges have been made, before consenting that the bank includes interim or year-end profits in CET1 capital.

Using historical payout ratios without adjusting for current market conditions has the advantage of using an objective measure. However, when market conditions in the year under consideration are materially worse or better than in the earlier years of the period on which the calculation was based, the payout ratio is likely to be either over- or understated. For example, a year of strong earnings following several years of economic downturn in which poor earnings were retained resulting in a low payout ratio would result in an excessively low estimation of the dividend payout.

Another element to be taken into account is the expectation among investors that an estimated payout ratio for CET1 capital calculations may create in their investment decisions. This is a delicate subject, and may lead to a capital regulatory authorities being in possession of privileged information not available to the market.

ECB's Recommendation on Dividends   On top of the MDA limitations, other official entities may place particular restrictions on the distribution of dividends. As an example, the European Central Bank (ECB) on 28 January 2015 issued a recommendation on dividend distribution policies (ECB/2015/2) in 2015 for the financial year 2014. The ECB established three categories of banks and issued dividend recommendations for each category, as follows:

- **Category 1:** Banks which satisfied the phase-in capital ratios requirements and which had already reached their fully loaded ratios as at 31 December 2014 should only distribute their net profits in dividends in a conservative manner to enable them to continue to fulfil all requirements even in the case of deteriorated economic and financial conditions;
- **Category 2:** Banks which satisfied the phase-in capital ratio requirements but which had not reached their fully loaded ratios as at 31 December 2014 should only distribute their net profits in dividends in a conservative manner to enable them to continue to fulfil all requirements, even in the case of deteriorated economic and financial conditions. In addition, they should in principle only pay out dividends to the extent that, at a minimum, a linear path towards the required fully loaded capital ratios was secured. In practice, this meant that over a period of four years (i.e., the remaining phase-in period), banks should in principle retain at least 25% per year of the gap towards their fully loaded CET1 capital ratio, their Tier 1 capital ratio and their total capital ratio;
- **Category 3:** Credit institutions which under the 2014 comprehensive assessment had a capital shortfall that would not be covered by capital measures by 31 December 2014, or banks in breach of the phased-in requirements, should in principle not distribute any dividend.

Foreseeable Charges   The amount of foreseeable charges to be taken into account shall comprise taxes, and the amount of any obligations or circumstances arising during the related reporting period which are likely to reduce the profits of the bank and for which the competent authority is not satisfied that all necessary value adjustments, such as additional valuation adjustments according to [CRR 31], or provisions have been made.

3.3 CASE STUDY: UBS DIVIDEND POLICY AND ITS IMPACT ON CET1

This case study highlights the significant variability of dividend policies in banking through changing economic cycles. It also covers the accounting and regulatory capital impact of stock dividends through the distribution of treasury shares and newly issued shares.

3.3.1 UBS Historical Dividend and Buyback Policies

The shareholder remuneration policy of the Swiss bank UBS from 2000 follows three main periods:

- From 2000 to 2007, a period of substantial dividends and buybacks of own shares;
- From 2008 to 2014, a period of no dividends; and
- From 2015 onwards, a period of gradually reinstating dividends.

From 2000 until the 2007 credit crisis, UBS was a high cash flow bank which used to have one of the largest programmes of cash return to shareholders in the European market. Between 2000 and 2007, it distributed just under CHF 46 billion of cash flow in dividends and buybacks (see Figure 3.6). In the fourth quarter of 2007, the markets for US residential sub-prime mortgages and related securities, and the US residential housing market in general started to sharply deteriorate. In December, it became increasingly evident that substantial write-downs would be required. UBS therefore decided to take immediate actions to strengthen its capital position: firstly, UBS's Board of Directors approved the rededication of 36.4 million shares that had previously been bought back and earmarked for cancellation. Secondly, it replaced the cash dividend for 2007 with a stock dividend (a ratio of one free new share for a minimum of every 20 shares already owned).

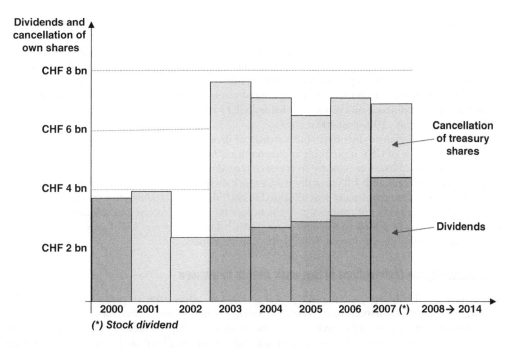

FIGURE 3.6   UBS dividends and buybacks 2000–2014

In 2008, in the context of a severe deterioration in the financial markets which caused heavy write-offs in its CDO and other illiquid portfolios, UBS reported a loss of CHF 19.7 billion. The bank's capital position sharply deteriorated and official assistance had to be obtained. The official aid was implemented through three main measures: firstly, UBS obtained a capital injection by the Swiss government; secondly it was agreed a transfer up to USD 60 billion of illiquid and other positions to a fund owned and controlled by the Swiss National Bank (SNB); and thirdly, UBS placed CHF 6 billion of mandatory convertible notes with the Swiss Confederation. Obviously, the cash return programme to shareholders was cancelled in 2008 and no distributions would take place until 2015.

After seven years of reductions in risk positions, risk-weighted assets, total assets and operating costs, UBS achieved in 2013 a capital level well above the SNB's requirements (see Figure 3.7). In 2014

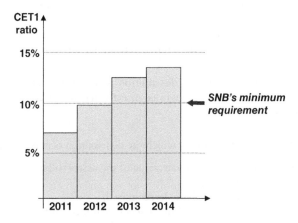

FIGURE 3.7   UBS's 2011–2014 CET1 capital ratio

UBS reached a fully-loaded CET1 capital ratio of 13%, prompting the bank to request permission from the SNB to reinstate paying dividends to its shareholders.

Following SNB's permission, in 2015 UBS announced an ordinary dividend of CHF 0.50 for 2014, an increase of 100% on the prior year and a payout ratio of 53% of the bank's reported net profit. It disclosed an intended dividend payout policy that, besides being associated to its earnings, was linked to its CET1 ratio in order to protect its strong capital position. UBS targeted to pay out at least 50% of its net profits, conditional on both a fully-loaded CET1 ratio of minimum 13% and a fully-loaded CET1 ratio of minimum 10% post-stress.

Although banks plan to distribute stable strings of dividends, in reality dividends can be difficult to forecast. In the case of UBS, it probably forecasted for 2007 a cash dividend in excess of the already substantial 2006 one. However, in order to preserve capital in 2008 (when the dividend corresponding to 2007 would be distributed) UBS actually paid a stock dividend, comprising a combination of newly and existing shares. One entitlement was allocated to each share outstanding after the close of business on the record date. Twenty entitlements gave the holder the right to receive one additional UBS share for free. Before we take a look to the impact on UBS's balance sheet and CET1 capital of that stock dividend, let us review the accounting for distributions to owners.

3.3.2 Accounting for Distributions of Non-cash Assets to Owners

A dividend, or a distribution, is a non-reciprocal transfer of assets from an entity to its owners. The IASB issued IFRIC 17 *Distributions of Non-cash Assets to Owners* on 27 November 2008. It clarified when a dividend payable should be recognised, how the dividend payable should be measured and how to account for the difference between the carrying amount of the distributed asset and the carrying amount of the dividend payable upon its settlement. IFRIC 17 also covered distributions in which the owner is given the choice of receiving either non-cash assets or a cash alternative.

Initial Measurement   A liability is recognised when the distribution is authorised and is no longer at the discretion of the bank. In listed banks, it occurs when the dividend is approved by its shareholders. A corresponding amount is recognised directly in equity.

The liability (i.e., the dividend payable) is initially measured at the fair value of the assets to be distributed. Subsequently, the liability is remeasured at each reporting date and at settlement, with changes recognised directly in equity. Where shareholders can elect between receiving cash and non-cash assets, the measurement of the liability takes into account the fair value of each alternative and their weighted probabilities.

Unless required by other IFRSs, the assets to be distributed are not remeasured to fair value when the liability is recognised. This may create a mismatch, as the liability is recognised at the fair value of the assets from the date of initial recognition while the assets themselves are not remeasured to fair value until settlement.

When the assets are distributed, the payable is settled and the difference between the dividend paid and the carrying amount of the net assets distributed is recognised in profit or loss.

Subsequent Recognition   The liability for the distribution is remeasured at the end of each reporting date and on settlement date, with changes recognised directly in equity. Remeasurement is based on the fair value of the assets to be distributed.

Recognition on Settlement Date   At the date on which the distribution occurs, the following takes place:

- The liability is remeasured based on the fair value of the assets to be distributed and any changes are recognised directly in equity;
- The liability and the assets distributed are derecognised;
- Any difference between the fair value of the assets distributed and their carrying amount in the financial statements is recognised in profit or loss; and

■ Any amounts recognised in other comprehensive income in relation to the assets distributed (e.g., revaluation reserves) are reclassified to profit or loss or transferred directly to retained earnings if required in accordance with other IFRSs, on the same basis that would be required if the non-cash assets had been disposed of.

Example: Accounting for a Non-cash Distribution

As an example, let us assume that a bank wished to distribute to its shareholders shares of a third company, ABC. The shares were classified at fair value through profit or loss. Upon approval of the dividend at a shareholders' AGM, the bank recognised a liability for EUR 1 billion (the fair value of the stake on that date) and debited equity with the same amount, as follows:

Retained earnings (Equity)	1,000,000,000	
Dividend payable (Liability)		1,000,000,000

Let us assume that at the subsequent reporting date, the distribution had not yet occurred. The fair value of the ABC shares to be distributed was EUR 1.2 billion. Therefore, the liability remained outstanding and the fair value of the non-cash asset had changed. The liability was remeasured through equity (i.e., the bank debited to retained earnings) as an adjustment to the amount of the distribution. In addition, the shares were fair valued as if they were unrelated to the upcoming dividend.

Retained earnings (Equity)	200,000,000	
Dividend payable (Liability)		200,000,000
ABC shares (Asset)	200,000,000	
Trading gains (Profit or loss)		200,000,000

Let us assume that on the date of settlement the fair value of the ABC shares had declined by 100 million to EUR 1.1 billion. The net effect of the remeasurement was to credit to retained earnings an additional EUR 100 million and to debit the liability with the same amount. The shares were fair valued as well through profit or loss.

Next, both the liability and the shares are derecognised. Because the shares' carrying amount was identical to its fair value as a result of the shares being fair valued at each reporting date, no additional entries were required.

Dividend payable (Liability)	100,000,000	
Retained earnings (Equity)		100,000,000
Trading losses (Profit or loss)	100,000,000	
ABC shares (Asset)		100,000,000
Dividend payable (Liability)	1,100,000,000	
ABC shares (Asset)		1,100,000,000

3.3.3 Distribution of Treasury Shares as Dividend

The stock dividend related to 2007 included the distribution of 36.4 million shares that UBS had repurchased in previous years. Prior to the distribution, the treasury shares were recognised in UBS's balance sheet at their cost, reducing shareholders' equity under IFRS. Assuming that they were repurchased at an average price of CHF 60.50, the carrying amount of the 36.4 million treasury shares was CHF 2.2 billion (see Figure 3.8). Under Basel III, those own shares reduced UBS's CET1 by an amount equal to its accounting value, thus a CHF 2.2 billion reduction.

Upon declaration of the stock dividend, the treasury shares to be distributed were derecognised and retained earnings was charged (i.e., debited).

From a regulatory perspective, CET1 capital was unchanged as two offsetting impacts had a neutral effect upon dividend declaration (see Figure 3.9):

- Because treasury shares are deducted from CET1 capital, the CHF 2.2 billion own shares derecognition caused a corresponding increase in UBS's CET1 capital;
- Because retained earnings are part of CET1 capital, the CHF 2.2 billion reduction in retained earnings caused a corresponding reduction in UBS's CET1 capital.

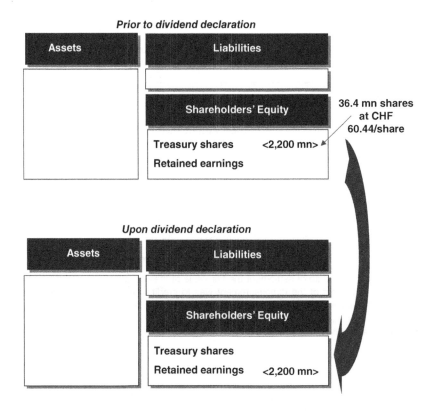

FIGURE 3.8   Accounting impact of UBS's stock dividend paid using treasury shares

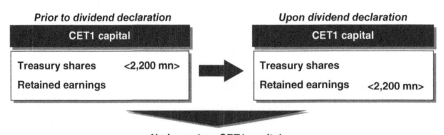

FIGURE 3.9   Impact on CET1 of UBS's stock dividend paid using treasury shares

3.3.4 Distribution of Newly Issued Shares as Dividend

In addition to the delivery of treasury shares, the stock dividend related to 2007 included the distribution of 98.7 million newly issued shares. Let us assume that UBS estimated the fair value of those shares to be CHF 2,961 million. Each share had a par value of CHF 0.10.

The stock dividend covered with newly issued shares was recorded by transferring the fair value of the shares issued from retained earnings to the related share accounts. Retained earnings was charged (debited) for the fair value of the shares (i.e., CHF 2,961 million), and share capital (for the par value of the shares – CHF 9.9 million) and share premium were credited (see Figure 3.10).

Albeit all the accounts impacted – retained earnings, share capital and share premium – upon the dividend declaration were constituents of CET1 capital, there was no overall impact on CET1. The increase in share capital and share premium was fully offset by the reduction in retained earnings (see Figure 3.11).

Comparison with a Cash Dividend   The whole purpose of the stock dividend was to remunerate UBS shareholders while preserving its CET1 capital. Compared with an equivalent cash dividend, a stock dividend was more beneficial for UBS's CET1 capital base.

Imagine that, instead of distributing the new shares just described above, UBS had paid a CHF 2,961 million cash dividend. From an accounting perspective, the cash dividend would have reduced the bank's retained earnings and cash levels by CHF 2,961 million as shown in Figure 3.12.

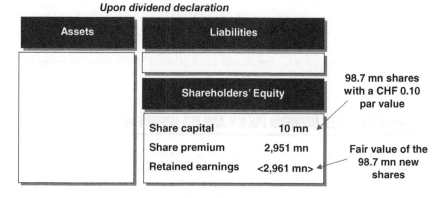

FIGURE 3.10   Accounting impact of UBS's stock dividend paid with newly issued shares

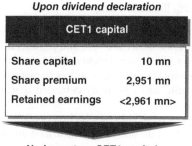

FIGURE 3.11   Impact on CET1 of UBS's stock dividend paid with newly issued shares

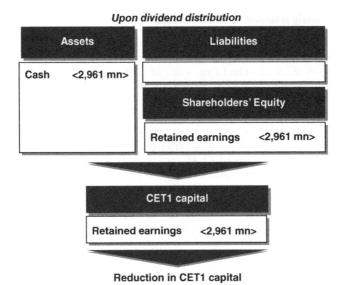

FIGURE 3.12   Impact on UBS's balance sheet and CET1 capital of a CHF 2,961 mn cash dividend

From a regulatory capital perspective, CET1 capital would have be reduced by CHF 2,961 million as a result of the decrease in retained earnings. In contrast, by issuing new shares in lieu of a dividend cash payment, the level of UBS's CET1 capital base was maintained.

Additionally, a cash dividend payment would have affected UBS's liquidity position, at a time when funding costs skyrocketed.

3.4 CASE STUDY: SANTANDER DIVIDEND POLICY AND ITS IMPACT IN CET1

This case describes the implications of Banco Santander's traditional scrip dividend policy and the rationale behind the change in its dividend policy in 2015. Whilst scrip dividends may help a bank keep CET1 capital and offer payout ratios greater than 100% (i.e., in excess of earnings) the continuous creation of new shares may result in unforeseen challenges, such as dilution effects to investors that elect a cash alternative in dividend distributions.

3.4.1 Santander's Traditional Scrip Dividend Policy

The Spanish bank Banco Santander ("Santander") had proudly kept a per-share payout of EUR 0.60 for several years even as earnings came under pressure and payouts in several years exceeded 100% of earnings. This payout represented a 9% dividend yield in 2014, at a time when interest rates were close to zero due to the exceptional quantitative easing measures implemented by the ECB. The charismatic chairman of the bank, Emilio Botín, had repeatedly defended that maintaining the bank's dividend policy was a priority.

From a regulatory capital perspective, the bank had successfully passed the stress tests performed by the ECB in 2014. Whilst its CET1 ratio was one of the lowest among its European peers, Santander defended its capital levels as adequate.

Since 2009 and in order to preserve CET1 capital, Santander adopted a scrip dividend policy. For example, in its 2014 AGM, Santander shareholders approved to apply a scrip dividend scheme whereby they were offered four quarterly scrip dividends of EUR 0.15 per share each, totalling EUR 0.60 per share. The scheme implied that in each of the four distributions, the bank shareholders had the option of receiving an amount equivalent to EUR 0.15 per share, in shares or cash. As part of the scrip dividend scheme, each shareholder received one "right" for every share held. Shareholders could elect among three options (see Figure 3.13):

- Option 1: Shareholders could receive, in exchange for their rights and otherwise free of charge, a certain number of newly issued Santander shares to which they were entitled. This was the default option. The number of shares received depended on the number of rights held and the Santander share price on or around the record date for the scrip dividend. For retail investors, this option had no Spanish withholding tax liability; or
- Option 2: Shareholders could sell their rights on the market (through the Spanish Stock Exchanges) at any time during their trading period and receive cash. The value of the rights would fluctuate depending on market prices and, accordingly, there could be no guarantee of the price received. For retail investors, this option had no Spanish withholding tax liability but shareholders would incur a brokerage fee of 0.3%; or
- Option 3: Shareholders could sell their rights off market to Santander at a fixed price and in exchange receive EUR 0.15 per share cash like a normal cash dividend. For retail investors, this option had the same Spanish withholding tax treatment as a normal dividend paid in cash (i.e., tax withheld at 20%).

On the announcement date, the number of shares to be issued was unknown. The number of rights needed to receive a new Santander share on conversion of the rights – the conversion ratio – was calculated as follows:

$$\text{Conversion ratio} = \frac{A \times B}{C}$$

Where:

- "A" was the number of Santander shares in issue on the date the Board of Directors or the Executive Committee agreed to execute the capital increase (the "Calculation Day");
- "B" was the average price of a Santander share on the Spanish Stock Exchanges in the five business days prior to the Calculation Day, rounded up or down to the nearest EUR thousandth; and
- "C" was the amount of cash available for distribution.

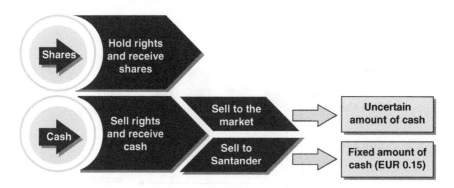

FIGURE 3.13 Santander scrip dividend – alternatives to shareholders

3.4.2 Santander's New Dividend Policy

In 2014 Santander had an 8.5% fully loaded CET1 ratio, one of the lowest among its largest European peers, a main market concern. Another concern from the market was the potentially lower future organic generation of capital due to the slowdown in the Latin American economies, from which Santander derived 34% of its earnings, mostly in Brazil, as a result of the declines in commodity prices.

Following the death of Emilio Botín in 2014, his daughter Ana Patricia Botín became executive chairwoman of Banco Santander. She appointed a new CEO – José Antonio Alvarez – who had previously held the bank's CFO position. The new team announced a fundamental change in the bank's capital and dividend policies.

Capital Increase   To address concerns around low capital levels, in January 2015 Santander announced a EUR 7.5 billion capital increase, representing 9.6% of the share capital of the bank prior to the increase. The capital increase was executed through an accelerated book building without pre-emptive rights led by Goldman Sachs and UBS. The placement was carried out at EUR 6.18, a 10% discount relative to the previous day closing price. The pricing and allocation took place on the 9 January 2015, and the new shares were to start trading on 13 January. The new shares were eligible for the scrip dividends planned for February and May 2015.

Reduction in Dividend   Simultaneously, Santander announced a cut in the annual dividend from four EUR 0.15 scrip dividends (totalling EUR 0.60 per share) to three cash dividends of EUR 0.05 and a scrip dividend of EUR 0.05 (totalling EUR 0.20 per share). Therefore, Santander reduced its dividend by 66.7%.

Advantages of the Capital Increase and New Dividend Policy   The main advantages of the capital increase and new dividend policy were the following:

1. The main objective of the capital increase was to **enhance the bank's CET1 capital levels**. The implementation through an accelerated book building process allowed Santander to quickly place the new CET1 capital in the market. The capital increase addressed market and regulators' concerns about Santander's capital levels. The capital increase took Santander to a 9.7% fully loaded CET1 capital ratio from 8.3%, an increase of 140 basis points, putting Santander in line with its European peers.
2. The main objective of the new dividend policy was to reduce the **enormous progression of Santander's number of shares** caused by the combination of the notably high dividend yield and the scrip. Since 2009, investors were electing shares rather than cash in a notably increasing proportion, as shown in Figure 3.14 (in 2014 the new shares take-up was close to 85%). This was

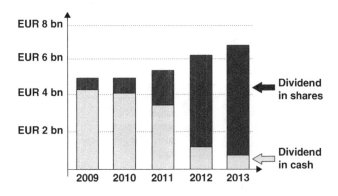

FIGURE 3.14   Santander scrip dividend: cash vs. shares election by shareholders

primarily due to Santander's broad retail investor base (53% retail share ownership at the closing of 2014 according to the bank) and the tax advantages of choosing shares for these investors. As a result, the number of shares outstanding had substantially increase since the bank adopted its scrip dividend policy – in part due to the conversion of mandatory convertible bonds, the share exchange at Santander Brazil and the acquisition of Bancorp as well, as shown in Figure 3.15. Imagine the sharp acceleration in the number of shares outstanding if during several years the bank kept an annual EUR 0.60 dividend and the shareholders kept unchanged their proportion of take-up in shares. The following table compares the number of shares outstanding maintaining the previous dividend policy (and without a capital increase) with those resulting from the new dividend policy (and with the capital increase), depicting how from 2017 the growth in outstanding number of shares under the new strategy would be substantially lower and how the new shares stemming from the capital increase would be offset by the reduction in shares resulting from the scrip dividend in Table 3.2.

3. Another advantage of the new dividend policy was its **enhanced sustainability**. The 2015 dividend represented a 3% dividend yield and approximately a 35% dividend payout, more aligned with dividend payouts at other comparable banks.
4. The lower number of shares resulting from the reduced scrip dividend had the ability to **partially offset the higher number of shares** stemming from the capital increase. If other banks were to raise capital, it would likely be more negative than was the case for Santander.
5. The higher capital levels allowed the bank pursued **organic growth opportunities**.
6. Whilst the bank indicated that the capital raise was for organic growth, the higher capital levels allowed Santander to be **better positioned to pursue acquisitions** of other banking businesses. In recent years, given Santander's relatively low capital levels, the bank had arguably missed out

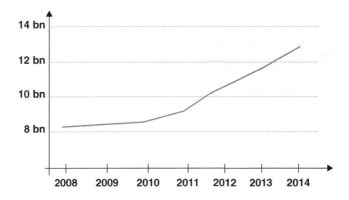

FIGURE 3.15 Santander's outstanding number of ordinary shares

TABLE 3.2 Santander's Outstanding Number of Ordinary Shares under the Previous and New Dividend Policies (in millions)

	2014	2015	2016	2017
Previous dividend policy (no capital increase)	12,584	13,450	14,376	15,365
New dividend policy (with capital increase)	12,584	14,320	14,405	14,491
Difference		+6.4%	+0.2%	−5.7%

acquisition opportunities in the deleveraging process in Europe, especially in Spain. New opportunities could be considered on the basis of maintaining or enhancing the new capital levels.

7. The enhanced capital levels allowed Santander to **gradually abandon its scrip dividends** and restore full cash dividends.

Disadvantages of the Capital Increase and New Dividend Policy   The main disadvantages of the capital increase and new dividend policy were the following:

1. Whilst the new dividend policy was more sustainable, it risked triggering the disposal of Santander's shares by income-oriented investors attracted by the bank's former 9% yield. These investors were a significant driver of the banking sector's outperformance in 2013 and 2014.
2. The capital increase was performed by placing the new shares in the market at a 10% discount to the previous day's closing price.
3. The three cash dividends reduced the CET1 capital.
4. Changes in dividend policies generate uncertainty in equity investors, probably creating a perception that they are taking on more regulatory risk to their Santander dividends than they had anticipated.

3.5 ACCUMULATED OTHER COMPREHENSIVE INCOME

Accumulated other comprehensive income (OCI) is a group of items in shareholders' equity. OCI includes several items which reflect remeasurements as a result of movements in valuations (see Figure 3.16). These items are temporarily recognised in OCI and at a subsequent date would be

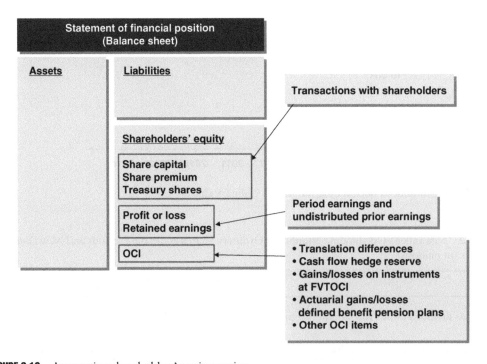

FIGURE 3.16   Accounting shareholders' equity section

reclassified ("recycled") to other parts of shareholders' equity (e.g., profit or loss). The main items in OCI are:

- Translation differences account;
- Cash flow hedge reserve;
- Gains/losses on instruments recognised at fair value through OCI (or recognised as "available for sale" under the previous IAS 39); and
- Actuarial gains and losses on defined benefit pension obligations.

From a disclosure perspective, items in OCI are grouped into:

- Items that may be **reclassified to profit or loss** (recycled) in subsequent periods. These include gains and losses on cash flow hedges, foreign currency translation adjustments, and gains and losses on debt instruments at fair value through OCI; and
- Items that will **not be reclassified to profit or loss** in subsequent periods. These include actuarial gains and losses on defined benefit pension obligations, and gains and losses on equity instruments at fair value through OCI.

3.5.1 Translation Differences

For internationally active banks, the translation differences account may be a notably large component of OCI. Upon consolidation, assets and liabilities of foreign operations are translated into the group's presentation currency (e.g., EUR for banks domiciled in the Eurozone). A foreign operation includes subsidiaries, joint ventures and associates.

Assets, liabilities and equity of foreign operations are translated at the period end closing rate while items of income and expense are commonly translated into the presentation currency at the average exchange rate during the reporting period.

The resulting foreign exchange differences are recognised in the translation (or exchange) differences account within OCI. For foreign operations that are subsidiaries, the amount of exchange differences attributable to any non-controlling interests is recognised in non-controlling interests.

Upon disposal of a foreign subsidiary, joint venture or associate (which results in loss of control or significant influence over that operation), the total cumulative translation differences recognised in OCI are reclassified to profit or loss as part of the gain or loss on disposal.

When a bank disposes of a portion of its interest in a subsidiary that includes a foreign operation but retains control, the related portion of the translation differences is reclassified to non-controlling interests.

When a bank disposes of a portion of its investment in an associate or joint venture that includes a foreign operation while retaining significant influence or joint control, the related portion of the cumulative currency translation balance is reclassified to profit or loss.

Translation differences amounts may include the effects of hedging net investments in foreign operations. The effective portion of gains and losses of these hedging instruments is transferred directly to OCI to offset translation gains and losses on the net investments in foreign branches and subsidiaries. The ineffective portion of gains and losses of these hedging instruments is recognised in profit or loss.

Elements of the Net Assets of a Foreign Subsidiary An investment in net assets of a foreign operation is a collection of the foreign operation's assets and liabilities. More precisely, the net assets are the difference between the foreign operation's assets and liabilities, and the goodwill related to the investment in the foreign operation, which change during the reporting period (see Figure 3.17). The change can be analysed by looking at the variation of goodwill and the shareholders' equity of the foreign subsidiary during the accounting period (see Figure 3.18):

- Profit or loss is generated in the foreign operation during the reporting period;
- Dividends are distributed to the foreign operation's shareholders;

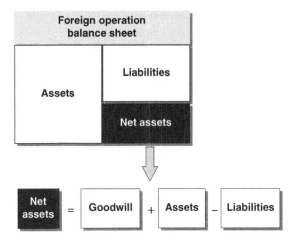

FIGURE 3.17 Net assets of a foreign operation

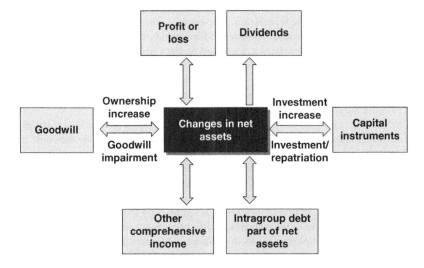

FIGURE 3.18 Elements of the net assets of a foreign subsidiary

- Capital investment is increased by the acquisition of the foreign operation's new or existing capital instruments;
- Capital investment is reduced by the sale or cancellation of the foreign operation's existing capital instruments;
- Additional other comprehensive income is generated or reduced in the foreign operation's financial position during the reporting period;
- Existing or new intragroup loans become part of the group's net investment as a result of it being considered that settlement is neither planned nor likely to occur in the foreseeable future; and
- Existing goodwill is impaired or new goodwill is recognised as a result of an increase in ownership.

Goodwill and statement of financial position items are measured to fair value when a stake is acquired in a foreign operation (so it is consolidated by the group either as a subsidiary, joint operation or associate). The revalued assets and liabilities are translated at the closing exchange rate.

Working Example   Next I cover in a simple example the mechanics of the translation process and how amounts in the exchange differences account of OCI are generated. Let us assume that on 1 January 20X0 ParentCo (the parent bank of a group with a EUR presentation currency) acquired 80% of SubCo (whose functional currency was the USD) for USD 1.43 billion consideration (see Figure 3.19). The fair value of SubCo's identifiable net assets was USD 1.5 billion (USD 3.5 billion of assets and USD 2 billion of liabilities). The closing EUR USD spot rate on 1 January 20X0 was 1.3000.

Translation Process on Acquisition Date   On 1 January 20X0, ParentCo acquired SubCo. Because SubCo's functional currency – USD – was not the currency of a hyperinflationary economy, SubCo's financial position was translated from its functional currency into the consolidated group's presentation currency – EUR – using the closing spot rate at the acquisition date – EUR USD 1.3000 (Table 3.3).

Each component of SubCo's shareholders' equity was also translated using the 1.3000 EUR USD closing spot rate (Table 3.4).

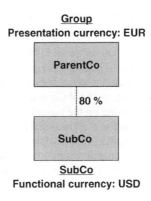

FIGURE 3.19   Group's structure post-acquisition

TABLE 3.3   Translation of Subco's Assets, Liabilities and Shareholders' Equity on Acquisition Date

SubCo's item	Fair Value	EUR USD Rate	Translated EUR Amount
Assets	USD 3,500 mn	1.3000	EUR 2,692 mn
Liabilities	USD 2,000 mn	1.3000	EUR 1,538 mn
Shareholders' equity	USD 1,500 mn	1.3000	EUR 1,154 mn

TABLE 3.4   Translation of Subco's Shareholders' Equity on Acquisition Date

SubCo's Equity Item	Fair Value	EUR USD Rate	Translated EUR Amount
Share capital	USD 500 mn	1.3000	EUR 385 mn
Retained earnings	USD 800 mn	1.3000	EUR 615 mn
Other comprehensive income	USD 200 mn	1.3000	EUR 154 mn
Shareholders' equity	**USD 1,500 mn**	1.3000	**EUR 1,154 mn**

Goodwill   The group's consolidated statements included a goodwill item arising on the acquisition of SubCo. Goodwill was calculated as the difference between the consideration paid and the sum of the fair values of the underlying net assets. Goodwill was treated as a "hidden asset" of SubCo, and therefore expressed in SubCo's functional currency, USD. The initial USD value of the goodwill was calculated as follows:

$$\text{Goodwill} = \text{USD } 1,430 \text{ mn} - 80\% \times 1,500 \text{ mn} = \text{USD } 230 \text{ million}$$

The EUR value of the goodwill on acquisition date was EUR 177 million (= USD 230 mn/1.3000).

Non-controlling interest (NCI)   The 20% of SubCo not owned by ParentCo was recognised as a non-controlling interest (i.e., minority interest). The non-controlling interest (NCI) was measured initially as a proportionate share of SubCo's net identifiable assets, as follows:

$$\text{NCI} = 20\% \times \text{USD } 1,500 \text{ mn} = \text{USD } 300 \text{ mn}$$

The EUR value of the NCI on acquisition date was EUR 231 mn (= USD 300 mn/1.3000).

On consolidation, the EUR 1.1 billion (= USD 1,430 mn/1.3000) carrying amount of the parent's investment in the subsidiary was replaced with the subsidiary's assets and liabilities and the non-controlling interest. Any goodwill arising on the acquisition of SubCo and any fair value adjustments to the carrying amounts of SubCo's assets and liabilities arising on the acquisition were treated as assets and liabilities of the foreign operation, and therefore expressed in the functional currency of the foreign operation.

Table 3.5 represents ParentCo's and SubCo's stand-alone balance sheets, and the consolidated balance sheet as of 1 January 20X0 – the acquisition date – (rounded to the nearest EUR million), for simplicity assuming no intragroup transactions and no other entities in the group.

Translation Process on First Reporting Date   Let us cover the translation process performed at the first reporting date following acquisition. To simplify our analysis, let us assume that the Group reported its financial statements on an annual basis at year end. Thus, the first reporting date following acquisition was 31 December 20X0. Table 3.6 summarises SubCo's stand-alone balance sheet on that date.

The process to calculate the exchange differences can be split into the following steps (see Figure 3.20):

- First, take SubCo's statement of financial position (i.e., balance sheet) and translate each item, excluding goodwill;
- Second, calculate the exchange differences (excluding goodwill) such that the translated assets equal the sum of (1) the translated liabilities and (2) the translated shareholders' equity;
- Third, allocate the exchange differences (excluding goodwill) between the group and the non-controlling interests, based on their share of the net assets; and
- Fourth, add the exchange differences due to the retranslation of goodwill to the group's exchange differences.

Step 1: Translation of the Subsidiary's Statement of Financial Position   The first step on 31 December 20X0 was to translate the subsidiary's balance sheet (excluding goodwill). Because SubCo's functional currency – USD – was not the currency of a hyperinflationary economy, SubCo's results and financial position were translated from its functional currency – USD – into the group's presentation currency – EUR – using the following procedures:

1. SubCo's assets and liabilities were translated at the EUR USD closing rate on the reporting date (assumed to be 1.2000).

TABLE 3.5 ParentCo's, SubCo's and the Group's Balance Sheets as of 1 January 20X0

ParentCo's Stand-alone Balance Sheet

Assets		Liabilities	
Investment in SubCo (USD 1,430 mn)	EUR 1,100 mn	ParentCo's liabilities	
ParentCo's other assets		**Equity**	
		ParentCo's equity	

SubCo's Stand-alone Balance Sheet

Assets		Liabilities	
Assets	USD 3,500 mn	Liabilities	USD 2,000 mn
		Equity	
		Share capital	USD 500 mn
		Retained earnings	USD 800 mn
		Other comprehensive income	USD 200 mn

Group's Consolidated Balance Sheet

Assets		Liabilities	
Goodwill (USD 230 mn)	EUR 177 mn	ParentCo's liabilities	
ParentCo's other assets		SubCo's liabilities (USD 2,000 mn)	EUR 1,538 mn
SubCo's assets (USD 3,500 mn)	EUR 2,692 mn	**Equity**	
		ParentCo's equity	
		Non-controlling int. (USD 300 mn)	EUR 231 mn

2. Subco's profit or loss statement was translated using the average EUR USD FX rate since the last reporting period (assumed to be 1.1500). Alternatively, IAS 21 permits the translation of income and expenses at the FX rates at the dates of the transactions, but this alternative is rarely used as it is operationally more complex.
3. SubCo's distributed dividends were translated at the EUR USD spot rate prevailing on the date that SubCo's shareholders meeting approved the payment of such dividend (assumed to be 1.2500).
4. SubCo's remaining items were translated at their historical EUR USD FX rates. IAS 21 does not state how these items should be translated, but in reality most entities use historical FX rates.
5. All resulting exchange rate differences were recognised in other comprehensive income.

Remember that the EUR USD closing spot rate on 31 December 20X0 and the 20X0 average EUR USD rate were 1.2000 and 1.1500 respectively. Also, that the EUR USD closing spot rate on the day the dividend was approved by SubCo's shareholders was 1.2500. Table 3.7 summarises the translation of SubCo's statement of financial position on 31 December 20X0.

TABLE 3.6 SubCo's Stand-alone Balance Sheet as of 31 December 20X0

SubCo (Stand-alone Balance Sheet) as of 31-Dec-X0

Assets		Liabilities	
Assets	USD 3,800 mn	Liabilities	USD 2,100 mn
		Equity	
		Share capital	USD 500 mn
		Open retained earnings	USD 800 mn
		Profit or loss	USD 100 mn
		Dividends paid	<USD 40 mn>
		Other comprehensive income	USD 340 mn

FIGURE 3.20 Process to calculate exchange differences

TABLE 3.7 Translation of SubCo's Statement of Financial Position on 31 December 20X0

SubCo's Balance Sheet Item	Fair Value	EUR USD Rate	Translated EUR Amount
Assets (A)	USD 3,800 mn	1.2000 (closing)	EUR 3,167 mn
Liabilities (B)	USD 2,100 mn	1.2000 (closing)	EUR 1,750 mn
Share capital (C)	USD 500 mn	1.3000 (historical)	EUR 385 mn
Opening retained earnings (D)	USD 800 mn	1.3000 (historical)	EUR 615 mn
Profit or loss (E)	USD 100 mn	1.1500 (average)	EUR 87 mn
Dividends (F)	USD 40 mn	1.2500 (approval date)	EUR 32 mn
Opening OCI (G)	USD 200 mn	1.3000 (historical)	EUR 154 mn
Change OCI during period (H)	USD 140 mn	1.2000 (closing)	EUR 117 mn
Exchange rate differences (A) – (B) – (C) – (D) – (E) + (F) – (G) – (H)			**EUR 91 mn**

The change in OCI was translated using the closing EUR USD spot rate: 1.2000. This translation assumes that all the change in OCI took place on the closing date. An alternative, probably more realistic, estimate would be to use the average EUR USD rate during the accounting period (i.e., 1.1500), similar to the conversion treatment of the profit or loss statement, assuming that the change in OCI took place gradually during that period.

Step 2: Exchange Differences Calculation Under a second step, exchange differences, excluding goodwill, were calculated such that the translated assets equalled the sum of (1) the translated liabilities and (2) the translated shareholders' equity. Table 3.8 shows the translated balance sheet of SubCo and the carrying value of the exchange differences.

Step 3: Exchange Differences Allocation Under a third step, the EUR 91 mn exchange differences (excluding goodwill retranslation) were allocated to the group and to the non-controlling interests, based on their proportionate share of SubCo's net assets. In our case, ParentCo's share of SubCo's net assets was 80%. Therefore:

- Exchange differences attributable to the group, excluding goodwill retranslation, were EUR 73 mn (= EUR 91 mn × 80%).
- Exchange differences attributable to the non-controlling interests were EUR 18 mn (= EUR 91 mn × 20%).

Step 4: Exchange Differences due to Goodwill Next, the exchange differences related to the goodwill were calculated, as follows:
- Exchange differences attributable to the group, due to goodwill retranslation, were EUR 15 mn (= USD 230 mn/1.2000 – USD 230 mn/1.3000).

Finally, the exchange differences were calculated, as follows:

- Exchange differences attributable to the group EUR 88 mn (= EUR 73 mn + EUR 15 mn).
- Exchange differences attributable to the non-controlling interests were EUR 18 mn.

> The EUR 88 million exchange differences were recognised in OCI. In our case there was an appreciation of the USD vs. the EUR, thus having a positive impact in OCI. As OCI (excluding the cash flow hedge reserve) is part of CET1 capital, the positive impact on the exchange differences account strengthens the group's CET1 capital levels.

TABLE 3.8 Exchange Differences Stemming from the Translation of SubCo's Balance Sheet

SubCo's Translated Balance Sheet as of 31-Dec-X0

Assets		Liabilities	
Assets (USD 3,800 mn)	EUR 3,167 mn	Liabilities (USD 2,100 mn)	EUR 1,750 mn
		Equity	
		Share capital (USD 500 mn)	EUR 385 mn
		Opening ret. earnings (USD 800 mn)	EUR 615 mn
		Profit or loss (USD 100 mn)	EUR 87 mn
		Dividends paid (USD 40 mn)	<EUR 32 mn>
		Opening OCI (USD 200 mn)	EUR 154 mn
		New OCI (USD 140 mn)	EUR 117 mn
		Exchange differences (excl. goodwill)	EUR 91 mn

3.5.2 Cash Flow Hedge Reserve

The amounts in this reserve represent the portion of gains and losses on hedging instruments that are effective cash flow hedges (see Section 3.14 for a more detailed explanation of this item).

3.5.3 Gains and Losses on Instruments at FVTOCI

IFRS 9 *Financial Instruments* considers three categories of financial assets (see Figure 3.21):

- At **amortised cost**. This consists of debt investments that meet both the business model test (i.e., the investment is managed to hold it in order to collect contractual cash flows) and the contractual cash flow test (the contractual terms give rise on specified dates to cash flows that are solely payments of principal and interest on the principal amount outstanding), and for which the fair value option is not applied.
- At fair value through OCI (**FVOCI**). This consists of debt investments that meet both the business model test and the contractual cash flow test, but that are managed to sell them as well. It also consists of equity investments not held for trading, for which the entity chooses not to classify them at FVTPL.
- At fair value through profit or loss (**FVTPL**). This consists of financial assets that are measured neither at amortised cost nor at FVOCI.

Debt Instruments Recognised at FVTOCI   A debt instrument classified at FVOCI is presented in the asset side of the statement of financial position at fair value. The bank also keeps an amortised cost calculation (i.e., using the instrument's effective interest rate) to recognise interest income in profit or loss.

Interest income and impairment are recognised in profit or loss, using the same methodology as for amortised cost (i.e., using the effective interest rate method). Impairment charges can be reversed through profit or loss. Likewise, foreign exchange gains and losses are recognised in profit or loss as if the instrument was carried at amortised cost. The difference between amortised cost (in the currency of denomination) and fair value (also in the currency of denomination) is recognised in OCI and reclassified to profit or loss when the debt instrument is sold.

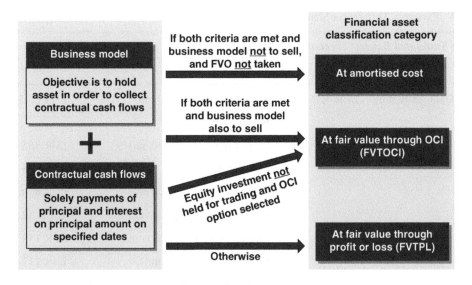

FIGURE 3.21   IFRS 9 financial assets classification categories – summary flowchart

Next I cover the effects on CET1 of investments in debt instruments at FVTOCI through a simple example. Let us assume that a European bank bought, at a small discount, a fixed-rate bond with the terms in Table 3.9.

Let us assume that the bank (whose presentation currency was the EUR) recognised the bond at FVTOCI, that no impairments were recognised and – to keep it simple – that the bank reported financially on an annual basis. The effective interest rate (EIR) was calculated as the rate that exactly discounted estimated future cash flows through the expected life of the bond, as follows:

$$98 \; mn = \frac{5 \; mn}{1 + EIR} + \frac{5 \; mn}{(1 + EIR)^2} + \frac{105 \; mn}{(1 + EIR)^3}$$

Solving the previous equation, EIR was 5.7447%. The EIR governed the interest income recognised at each reporting date (Table 3.10).

Let us assume further that the "clean" fair value (i.e., the fair value excluding accrued interest) of the bond on 31 December 20X0 and 31 December 20X1 was 97 million and 101 million respectively. The change in the bond's clean fair value at each reporting date is shown in Table 3.11.

In order to account for the bond, the bank had to keep track of both the bond's amortised cost and its fair value. Any difference between the bond's clean fair value and its amortised cost was recognised in the FVOCI reserve of OCI (Table 3.12).

The presentation of the investment in the bond on the bank's financial statements at the closing of the second year was as follows (see Figure 3.22):

- On the asset side, the bond was presented at its clean fair value: EUR 101 million.
- In OCI (within shareholders' equity), the difference between the bond's fair value and its amortised cost was presented: EUR 1,704,000.
- In profit or loss, the interest income using the EIR was recognised: EUR 5,666,000.

TABLE 3.9   Fixed-rate Bond Main Terms

Bond Terms	
Purchase price	EUR 98 million
Purchase date	1-Jan-X0
Notional	EUR 100 million
Maturity	Three years (31-Dec-X2)
Coupon	5% annual 30/360 basis

TABLE 3.10   Calculation of Interest Income and Amortised Cost Amounts

Year	Amortised Cost Beginning Year (a)	Interest Income (b) = (a) × EIR	Cash Flow (c)	Amortised Cost End of Year (d) = (a) + (b) − (c)
1	98,000,000	5,630,000	5,000,000	98,630,000
2	98,630,000	5,666,000	5,000,000	99,296,000
3	99,296,000	5,704,000	5,000,000	100,000,000

TABLE 3.11   Period Change in Bond's Clean Fair Value

Year	Clean Fair Value (a)	Previous Clean Fair Value (b)	Change (c) = (a) – (b)
1	97,000,000	98,000,000	<1,000,000>
2	101,000,000	97,000,000	4,000,000
3	100,000,000	101,000,000	<1,000,000>

TABLE 3.12   Amounts recognised in the FVOCI Reserve

Year	Clean Fair Value (a)	Amortised Cost End of Year (b)	FVOCI Reserve (c) = (a) – (b)	Previous FVOCI Reserve (d)	New FVOCI Entry (c) – (d)
1	97,000,000	98,630,000	<1,630,000>	-0-	<1,630,000>
2	101,000,000	99,296,000	1,704,000	<1,630,000>	3,334,000
3	100,000,000	100,000,000	-0-	1,704,000	<1,704,000>

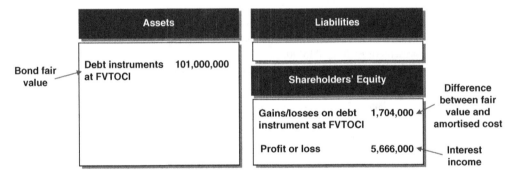

FIGURE 3.22   Second-year impact on the bank's balance sheet of the debt investment at FVTOCI

The bond investment impacted CET1 through two items. Firstly, the EUR 1,704,000 amount in OCI was included in CET1 capital. As a result, the bank's CET1 capital was exposed to the changes in the market value of the bond. Secondly, the after-tax amount of the EUR 5,666,000 interest income helped the bank strengthen its CET1 capital.

The bond in our example was tested for impairment at each reporting date. Any impairments would be recognised in profit or loss, reducing CET1 capital on an after-tax basis.

Commonly, banks hold large amounts of government bonds which are recognised at FVTOCI. These bond portfolios are not held for trading purposes, but they are part of structural hedges in which rate-insensitive funding (demand deposits and equity) is invested in fixed-rate government bonds to lock in a certain net interest margin. Therefore, unrealised gains and unrealised losses on these portfolios (e.g., as a result of a weakening of a government's credit risk) may have a substantial impact in a bank's CET1, contributing to CET1 capital volatility. However, unrealised gains and unrealised losses are treated symmetrically.

Strategic Investments in Equity Instruments   Under IFRS 9 *Financial Instruments*, at initial recognition an entity may make an irrevocable election to present in OCI subsequent changes in the fair value of an investment in an equity instrument that is within the scope of IFRS 9, and that is not held for trading. Amounts presented in OCI are never reclassified to profit or loss. If an equity investment is designated at FVTOCI, dividend income would be recognised in profit or loss. No impairment is recognised.

3.5.4 Actuarial Gains/Losses on Defined Benefit Pension Plans

Remeasurement gains and losses arising on defined benefit pension plans are recognised in OCI and therefore impact **CET1 capital**. The accounting for defined benefit pension plans is covered in Section 3.18.

3.5.5 Other Items in OCI

There are a good number of other items that are recorded in OCI, including:

- Own credit risk reserve. For those financial liabilities designated at fair value through profit or loss, changes in fair value attributable to changes in the liability's credit risk are recognised in OCI (unless an account mismatch occurs by such recognition). These amounts presented in OCI are never recycled to profit or loss.
- Revaluations of property, plant and equipment;
- Options time value hedge reserve. This reserve temporarily includes the changes in time value of options designated as hedging instruments in hedge accounting relationships;
- Forward component of forward instruments reserve. This reserve temporarily includes the changes in the forward components of derivative forwards designated as hedging instruments in hedge accounting relationships;
- Basis spread component reserve. This reserve temporarily includes the changes in the basis spread of cross-currency swaps designated as hedging instruments in hedge accounting relationships.

Tax effects   Items of OCI may be presented either:

- Net of related tax effects; or
- Before related tax effects, with one amount shown for the aggregate amount of income tax relating to those items.

Interim OCI   The guidelines to calculate interim profit or loss apply in the same manner to gains and losses included in accumulated other comprehensive income (see Subsection 3.2.5).

3.6 CASE STUDY: BANCO BPI'S PARTIAL DISPOSAL OF PORTFOLIO OF PORTUGUESE AND ITALIAN GOVERNMENT BONDS

This case study describes the change in approach taken by the Portuguese bank Banco BPI (BPI) on its sovereign investment strategy. This change was driven by the entry into force in January 2014 of European Directive CRD IV, which transposed the Basel III regulatory standards into EU law.

As of 31 December 2013, BPI held EUR 1.7 billion and EUR 975 million of Portuguese and Italian government bonds respectively, maturing in 2019. The bonds were recognised from an accounting perspective as "available for sale" ("AFS"), a category under IAS 39 (the standard for financial instruments preceding IFRS 9) which was similar to the current "at fair value through OCI" asset category under IFRS 9. The bonds were swapped into floating through pay-fixed/receive-floating interest rate swaps (IRSs). An IRS is an agreement between two parties to exchange fixed and floating interest payments, based upon interest rates defined in the contract, without the exchange of the underlying principal amounts. As illustrated in Figure 3.23, the combination of the bonds and the swaps resulted in

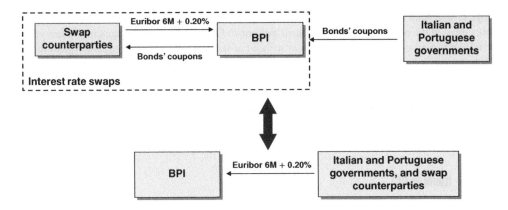

FIGURE 3.23 BPI's asset swap of Italian and Portuguese bond portfolio

BPI receiving an overall interest of Euribor 6-month plus 0.20% by paying the bonds' fixed coupons to the counterparties to the swaps and receiving such interest on a semiannual basis until 2019.

3.6.1 Accounting Treatment of the Combination of the Bonds and Swaps

Let us take a look at the impact of the Italian and Portuguese bond portfolio on BPI's financial statements, assuming that the bonds were acquired at par, and that the swaps had a nil fair value and were entered into simultaneously to the purchase of the bonds. The derivatives were interest swaps that converted the bonds interest from fixed to floating, thus hedging the bonds' interest rate risk. Consequently, BPI was exposed to the bonds' non-interest rate risks, such as credit – Italian and Portuguese sovereign – and liquidity risks.

Fair Value Hedge Accounting BPI applied fair value hedge accounting to the hedging relationship that comprised the bonds (the hedged item) and the derivatives (the hedging instrument). Pursuant to IFRS 9 (and IAS 39), a fair value hedge was accounted for as follows:

- The **hedging instrument** (i.e., each swap) was recorded on the balance sheet at its (clean) fair value (i.e., excluding settlement amounts accruals).
  - Changes during each quarter in the fair value were recognised in profit or loss; and
  - Accrual of the settlement amounts was recognised in profit or loss as well.

- The **hedged item** (i.e., each bond) was recorded on the balance sheet at its (clean) fair value (i.e., excluding coupon accruals).

  - Changes during each quarter in the fair value of the hedged item *for the risk being hedged* (interest rate risk in our case) were recognised in profit or loss;
  - Interest income was recognised in profit or loss each quarter. Interest was calculated using the amortised cost method. Therefore, BPI had to keep track not only of its fair value but of its amortised cost as well; and
  - The difference between the bond fair value (excluding the cumulative change in fair value due to changes in interest rates) and its amortised cost was recognised in OCI in the reserve for instruments at FVTOCI (in the available-for sale reserve under IAS 39).

Figure 3.24 describes the effects of the combination of the bonds and the swaps in the financial statements of BPI, as a result of applying fair value hedge:

- On the **asset** side the bonds were recognised at (clean) fair value;

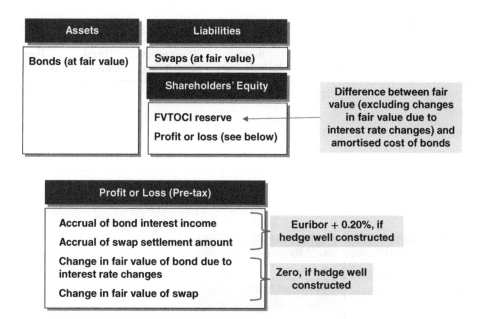

FIGURE 3.24   Balance sheet recognition of BPI's asset swap of Italian and Portuguese bond portfolio

- On the **liability** side the swaps were recognised at (clean) fair value when the swaps had a negative replacement cost (i.e., if unwound, BPI would have to pay the swap counterparties). Were the swaps to have a positive replacement value, they would be recognised on the asset side of the balance sheet;
- In the **FVTPL reserve of OCI** (or AFS reserve) the difference between the bonds' fair value (excluding the cumulative change in fair value due to changes in interest rates) and their amortised cost was recognised;
- In **profit or loss** the accruals of the bonds' interest income and the swaps' settlement amounts were recognised. If the hedge was well constructed, the sum of these two items should have resulted in the accrual of the Euribor 6-month plus 0.20% interest on the notional of the bonds; and
- Also in **profit or loss** were recognised the period variation in fair value of the bonds due to changes in interest rates and the period variation in the fair value of the swap. If the hedge was well constructed, the sum of these two items should have resulted in an amount close to zero (excluding the effect of CVA/DVA on the swap). In other words, the change in the fair value of the bond (stemming from changes in interest rates) would be fully offset by the changes in fair value of the swap. This is why this sort of hedge is called "fair value hedge" under IFRS 9 (and IAS 39).

3.6.2 Regulatory Capital Impact of the Combination of the Bonds and Swaps

As of 31 December 2013, BPI experienced unrealised mark-to-market losses in both the bonds and the derivatives (EUR 77 million and EUR 341 million losses respectively), as shown in Table 3.13.

In order to understand the impact of the asset swaps in BPI's regulatory capital, it is necessary to comprehend the presentation of the investment strategy in the bank's balance sheet (see Figure 3.25):

1. The bonds were recognised at their fair value, which was EUR 2,598 million (= 2,675 mn – 77 mn) on the asset side of the balance sheet. The exposures to the Portuguese and Italian sovereigns were risk-weighted;
2. A negative EUR 418 million was recognised in the FVTOCI reserve, representing the unrealised losses related to changes in the fair value of the bonds due to factors other than interest rate

TABLE 3.13 BPI's Bond Portfolio and Related Hedges Unrealised Losses as of 31 December 2013

	Nominal Value	Bonds Gains/Losses	Derivatives Gains/Losses	Total Before Tax	Total After Tax
OTs 4.75% 2019 (Portugal)	1,700	<130>	<210>	<340>	<240>
BTPs 2019 (Italy)	975	53	<131>	<78>	<55>
	2,675	<77>	<341>	<418>	<295>

*amounts in EUR million

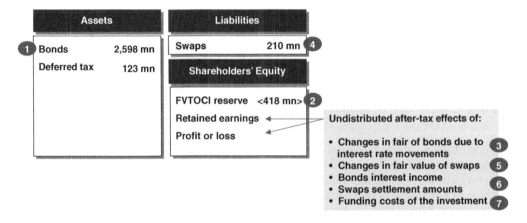

FIGURE 3.25 Balance sheet recognition of BPI's asset swap of Italian and Portuguese bond portfolio

changes. This reserve was part of OCI and thus an ingredient of CET1 capital. Therefore, BPI's CET1 capital was reduced by EUR 418 million;

3. The fair value of the bonds experienced a EUR 341 million increase stemming from changes in interest rates. As BPI applied fair value hedge accounting, these changes were recognised in profit or loss, and as a result impacted CET1 capital. These changes were offset with the changes in (5) below;

4. The swaps were recognised at their fair value (a EUR 210 million negative mark to market) on the liability side as their fair value was negative. From a capital perspective the swaps were risk-weighted as follows:

   ■ As their replacement value (i.e., their accounting fair value) was negative, no capital was required. BPI could net these negative replacement values with other derivatives with positive replacement values, if the derivatives were under the same master agreement;

   ■ The swaps were subject to capital charges related to their counterparty credit risk;

5. The changes in fair value of the swaps were recognised in profit or loss, and as a result affected CET1 capital. These changes were offset with the changes in (3) above;

6. The accruals of the bonds' interest income and the accruals of the swaps' settlement amounts were recognised in profit or loss. The aggregate of these two accrual amounts resulted in BPI recognising an income equivalent to Euribor 6-month plus 0.20% on the bond notionals. The after-tax effect of such interest was part of CET1; and

7. The funding of the bonds and swaps positions were also recognised as an expense on BPI's profit or loss and, therefore, their after-tax amounts were part of CET1.

BPI's CET1 ratio was exposed to the following risks (see Figure 3.26):

- **Interest rate risk:** An increase in interest rates would reduce the fair value of the bonds and increase the fair value of the swaps. These two exposures offset each other in profit or loss. However, an increase in interest rates would mean that the overall interest income would increase, stemming from the increase in Euribor 6-month rates, but this increase would be offset by the corresponding increase in funding costs. Therefore, the effect on BPI's CET1 of changes in interest rates was somewhat neutral;
- **Credit risk to Portugal and Italian sovereigns:** A decrease in the creditworthiness of these sovereigns would reduce the fair value of the bonds, reducing BPI's CET1 capital levels through the corresponding decline in the FVTOCI reserve. Additionally, the risk-weighted assets related to the bonds would increase, reducing BPI's CET1 ratio;
- **Credit risk to the swap counterparties:** A decrease in the creditworthiness of the swap counterparties would increase the risk-weighted assets related to the swaps reducing BPI's CET1 ratio;
- **Liquidity risk:** An increase in the liquidity premium of the bonds would reduce the fair value of the bonds and, in turn, reduce BPI's CET1 capital levels through the corresponding decline in the FVTOCI reserve.

3.6.3 Regulatory Rationale of BPI's Partial Disposal of the Bonds and Swaps Portfolio

During the first quarter of 2014, prices of Portuguese and Italian public debt experienced a substantial recovery. BPI's position in Portuguese and Italian government bonds maturing in 2019 and their related swaps are shown in Table 3.14.

It can be observed that during the period, the bond portfolio had a substantial mark-to-market gain while the derivatives hedging the portfolio deteriorated. Overall, the pre-tax unrealised losses of the portfolio declined by 37%, from EUR 418 million to EUR 262 million during the first quarter of 2014.

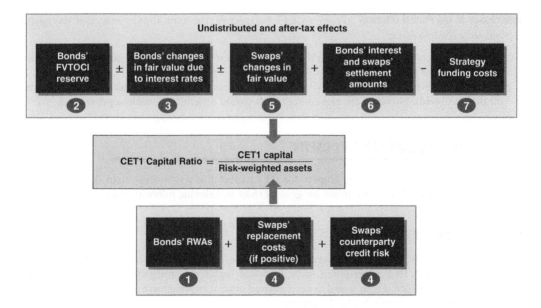

FIGURE 3.26 Impact of BPI's bond investment strategy on CET1 ratio as of 31 December 2013

TABLE 3.14   BPI's Bond Portfolio and related Hedges Unrealised Losses as of 31 March 2014

	Nominal Value	Bonds Gains/Losses	Derivatives Gains/Losses	Total Before Tax	Total After Tax
OTs 4.75% 2019 (Portugal)	1,700	38	<244>	<206>	<159>
BTPs 2019 (Italy)	975	92	<148>	<56>	<43>
	2,675	130	<392>	<262>	<202>

To take advantage of the substantial recovery in sovereign bond prices, BPI sold 50% of its portfolio, recognising a EUR 131 million (= 262 mn / 2) pre-tax loss, or a EUR 101 million (= 202 mn / 2) after-tax loss.

Advantages of the Partial Disposal   From a CET1 perspective, the main advantages of the partial disposal were the following:

- BPI reduced the volatility of its CET1 capital ratio.
- Whilst the FVTOCI reserve in OCI still showed a negative EUR 262 million carrying amount, it has notably recovered from the previous quarter amount, implying a EUR 156 million (= 418 mn – 262 mn) improvement in CET1 capital ignoring taxes. The partial disposal allowed BPI to lock-in half of such improvement.
- The strategic decision permitted the bank to reduce its balance sheet exposure to sovereign risk. BPI followed the recommendations from supervisory and community authorities, which have been advising a reduction of the link between the sovereign risk and the banking sector risk.
- BPI reduced the risk-weighted assets related to the sold bonds and swaps.

Weaknesses of the Partial Disposal   From a CET1 perspective, the main disadvantages of the partial disposal were the following:

- BPI could not benefit thereafter from the positive interest carry (0.20%), assuming funding costs equal to Euribor 6-month.
- BPI could not benefit subsequently from a further recovery in sovereign prices due to credit risk on the sold bonds. However, the remaining bonds would benefit from such improvement.

3.7 OTHER ITEMS ELIGIBLE FOR CET1 CAPITAL

There are three other items that are eligible for CET1 capital: reserves other than the ones already included in the CET1 calculations, funds for general risks and eligible minority interests.

3.7.1 Other Reserves

According to [CRR 4(117)] "other reserves" means reserves within the meaning of the applicable accounting framework that are required to be disclosed under the applicable accounting standard, excluding any amounts already included in accumulated other comprehensive income or retained earnings. These reserves are eligible for CET1 capital.

3.7.2 Funds for General Banking Risks

Banks' stand-alone financial statements are reported using national accounting standards, while on a consolidated basis banks outside the United States apply IFRS. Whilst not permitted under IFRS, national accounting rules may require a bank to set up a fund for general banking risks.

The total value of the fund for general banking risks is presented a separate item on the liability side and its change is shown in profit or loss. Basel III recognises the fund for general banking risks (without any foreseeable charge) as disclosed reserves, and qualifies it as CET1 capital.

3.7.3 Eligible Minority Interests

Under Basel III, a minority interest is included in consolidated CET1 only if it is issued by a genuine subsidiary bank and meets all the criteria for CET1 instruments. Surplus CET1 of the subsidiary attributable to minority interests is excluded from consolidated CET1, dealt with in detail in Chapter 9.

3.8 CET1 PRUDENTIAL FILTERS

CET1 is the key capital measure as it is considered the element of regulatory capital that is the highest quality and the most effective in absorbing losses at all times. Basel III requires the deduction from CET1 capital of items that may not fulfil its loss-absorbing function. These are the so-called "**prudential filters**".

3.8.1 Phase-in Provisions

In order to help banks meet the higher capital standards through reasonable earnings retention and capital raising while still supporting lending to the economy, under CRD IV prudential filters are phased in from January 2014, with full implementation by January 2018, as follows:

Year (1-Jan.)	2016	2017	2018	2019
Phase-in deductions from CET1	40%	80%	100%	100%

During the transition period, the part which is not deducted from CET1 attracts existing treatment. For example, in 2016:

- Regarding the deferred tax assets subject to full deduction in 2018, 40% of their amounts are deducted from CET1 and 60% are not deducted but risk-weighted in 2016;
- If an item is required to be deducted under the existing framework (suppose from Tier 2) and Basel III rules prescribe deduction from CET1, 40% of the amount is deducted from CET1 and the rest is deducted from current tier of deduction (i.e., tier 2) in 2016; and
- In case of minority interest, if such capital is not eligible for inclusion in CET1 but is included under the existing guidelines in Tier 1, then 40% of the amount is deducted from the relevant component of capital (Tier 1) in 2016.

3.8.2 Deductions from CET1

A substantial number of items are deducted from CET1 capital. The CET1 prudential filters are the following:

- Additional valuation adjustments;
- Intangible assets (net of related tax liability);

- Deferred tax assets that rely on future profitability excluding those arising from temporary differences (net of related tax liability);
- Fair value reserves related to gains or losses on cash flow hedges;
- Negative amounts resulting from the calculation of expected loss amounts;
- Any increase in equity that results from securitised assets;
- Gains or losses on liabilities valued at fair value resulting from changes in own credit standing;
- Defined-benefit pension fund assets;
- Direct and indirect holdings by the bank of own CET1 instruments;
- Direct, indirect and synthetic holdings of the CET1 instruments of financial sector entities where those entities have reciprocal cross-holdings with the bank designed to inflate artificially the own funds of the bank;
- Direct, indirect and synthetic holdings by the bank of the CET1 instruments of financial sector entities where the bank does not have a significant investment in those entities (amount above 10% threshold and net of eligible short positions);
- Direct, indirect and synthetic holdings by the bank of the CET1 instruments of financial sector entities where the bank has a significant investment in those entities (amount above 10% threshold and net of eligible short positions);
- Exposure amount of the following items which qualify for a risk weight of 1,250%, where the bank opts for the deduction alternative;
- Deferred tax assets arising from temporary differences, exceeding the relevant threshold;
- Amounts exceeding the 15% threshold;
- Losses for the current financial year;
- Foreseeable tax charges relating to CET1 items;
- Qualifying AT1 deductions that exceed the AT1 capital of the bank; and
- Temporary filter on unrealised gains and losses on available-for-sale instruments.

3.9 ADDITIONAL VALUATION ADJUSTMENTS

[CRR 34] requires banks to apply prudent valuation standards to all positions that are measured at fair value when calculating the amount of their own funds. Any **additional valuation adjustments (AVAs)** necessary to reduce (or increase) the fair value of those asset (or liability) positions as calculated in accordance with the relevant accounting standards, to the relevant prudent value are deducted from CET1 capital. AVAs are covered in Chapter 7.

3.10 INTANGIBLE ASSETS (INCLUDING GOODWILL)

According to [CRR 36(1)(b), 37], intangible assets (net of their related **deferred tax liabilities** that would be extinguished if the intangible assets became impaired or were derecognised under IFRS) are deducted from CET1. This deduction is based on, according to Basel III, the high level of uncertainty regarding the ability of the banking organisation to realise value from these assets, especially under adverse financial conditions. The amount to be deducted includes the **goodwill** part of the valuation of a bank's significant investments. From a regulatory capital perspective, goodwill and intangible assets have the same meaning as under IFRS. Therefore, it is important to understand how IFRS treats these assets.

Because goodwill and any other intangible assets are deducted from CET1, they are excluded from the calculation of credit risk exposure values.

Considering that all intangibles other than goodwill have "high degree of uncertainty" is arguably unfair in situations where the intangible has a real, realisable value that would be taken into account in any transaction transferring a business.

For example, software routines to price complex derivative products in an investment bank could be sold to other banks or software companies if deemed to be necessary. In any case, software is commonly depreciated over a relatively short period of time, reducing the significance of a specific software deduction from CET1 over time.

In another example, mortgage servicing rights (MSRs) represent another intangible asset whose value is relatively apparent and for which a CET1 deduction is arguably excessively conservative. MSRs have identifiable income streams attached to them, which may be reliably measured when prepayment risks fully hedged. Alternatively, MSRs could be sold by a bank as a going concern, or transferred in resolution. As a result of the full deduction of MSRs from CET1, banks are likely to add the cost of capital when pricing these mortgage services, to the detriment of both mortgagors and mortgage investors.

As mentioned in Chapter 8 certain subsidiaries (i.e., consolidated from an accounting perspective) are excluded for regulatory purposes from the calculation of regulatory capital. These primarily include insurance, real estate and SPVs.

Goodwill related to significant investments in the capital of banking, financial and insurance entities that are outside the scope of regulatory consolidation is still deducted from CET1.

3.10.1 Goodwill from an IFRS Accounting Perspective

Goodwill is covered in detail in Chapters 8 and 9 through several case studies. In this Section I cover goodwill in a more general way to provide the reader with an understanding of the concept.

Goodwill is an asset representing the future economic benefits arising from other assets acquired in a business combination that are not individually identified and separately recognised. The amount of goodwill may include:

- The fair value of expected synergies from the combination;
- Assets and liabilities that are not measured at fair value, such as deferred tax and employee benefits;
- Assets that cannot be recognised from an accounting perspective (e.g., non-contractual customer relationships).

Whilst goodwill is not amortised from an accounting point of view, it may be amortised for tax purposes in some jurisdictions.

Initial Recognition of Goodwill   Goodwill arises on the acquisition of subsidiaries, joint ventures and associates. The accounting for business combinations (i.e., acquisition of other entities) is dealt with by **IFRS 3** *Business Combinations*. In the case of the acquisition of a subsidiary, goodwill is a residual amount which represents the excess of the aggregate of the cost of an acquisition and any non-controlling interests in the acquiree over the fair value of the identifiable net assets (i.e., assets, liabilities and contingent liabilities) acquired at the date of the acquisition:

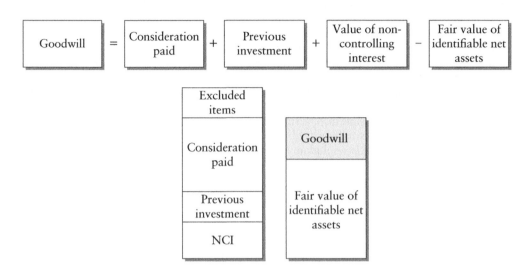

For the purpose of calculating goodwill resulting from a business combination, the following steps are followed:

Firstly, the **excluded items** must be identified. These are consideration items which are not considered to be part of the exchange for the acquiree, and therefore should not be taken into account when calculating the amount of goodwill. For example, the acquirer and the acquiree may have a pre-existing relationship. In another example, the executives of the acquiree may have been granted in the past a stock options plan representing compensation for past services, that would need to be replaced at the date of the transaction.

Secondly, the **"consideration" paid** (i.e., the cost of the acquisition or "consideration" transferred) must be determined at fair value. Consideration paid is the sum of the acquisition date fair values of the assets transferred, the liabilities incurred by the acquirer to the former owners of the acquiree, and the equity interests issued by the acquirer to the former owners of the acquiree (except for the measurement of share-based payment awards). Examples of consideration paid include cash and issuance of the acquirer's ordinary shares.

The consideration paid also incorporates the fair value of **contingent consideration** (also called "earn-out") at the date of the transaction, regardless of the probability of it being disbursed. If the contingent consideration is classified as an asset or liability, it is subsequently fair valued at each reporting date, with fair value changes recognised in the profit or loss statement, therefore *not* adjusting goodwill. If the contingent consideration is classified as an equity instrument, it is not remeasured following initial recognition.

Thirdly, in a business combination achieved in stages, the acquisition-date fair value of the acquirer's **previously held equity interest** in the acquiree needs be determined as well.

Fourthly, the value of the **non-controlling interest** ("NCI") is estimated. The NCI is the portion of equity (i.e., net assets) in a subsidiary not attributable, directly or indirectly, to a parent.

Finally, the net of the acquisition-date amounts of the **identifiable assets acquired and the liabilities assumed** are determined by reference to market values or by discounting expected future cash flows to present value. This discounting is either performed using market rates or by using risk-free rates and risk-adjusted expected future cash flows.

Where the fair value of the bank's share of the identifiable net assets of the acquired entity is greater than the cost of acquisition (i.e., negative goodwill or badwill), the excess is recognised immediately in the profit or loss statement.

Goodwill Related to Investments in Associates and Joint Ventures   Goodwill arises on the acquisition of interests in joint ventures and associates when the cost of investment exceeds the bank's share of the net fair value of the identifiable assets and liabilities of associates or joint ventures. Goodwill arising on acquisitions of associates and joint ventures is included in the bank's "investment in joint ventures and associates" (i.e., goodwill is not disclosed separately from the carrying amount of the investment) and is *not* tested separately for impairment.

At the date of disposal of a subsidiary, the carrying value of attributable goodwill is included in the calculation of the profit or loss on disposal, except where it has been written off directly to reserves in the past.

Example: Goodwill and Non-controlling Interests

This example illustrates how goodwill is determined when a non-controlling interest ("NCI") is present in an acquisition. Assume Bank A acquires 75% of Bank B for EUR 1.3 billion. The fair value of the remaining 25% of entity B is determined to be EUR 350 million. The fair value of the identifiable net assets and liabilities is determined to be EUR 1.2 billion.

Goodwill resulting from a business combination is calculated by comparing the consideration paid plus the value of the NCI to the fair value of identifiable net assets:

$$\boxed{\text{Goodwill}} = \boxed{\substack{\text{Consideration} \\ \text{paid}}} + \boxed{\substack{\text{Value of non-} \\ \text{controlling} \\ \text{interest}}} - \boxed{\substack{\text{Fair value of} \\ \text{identifiable net} \\ \text{assets}}}$$

When determining the value attributed to the NCI in an acquiree, IFRS 3 provides the acquirer with a choice: to measure it either at the non-controlling interests' proportionate share of the acquiree's identifiable net assets ("partial goodwill" or "proportionate share method") or at fair value ("full goodwill" or "fair value method"). This election is made on a transaction-by-transaction basis. The elected choice in turn affects the value attributed to goodwill, a residual amount (see Figure 3.27).

The acquirer – Bank A – can choose to measure the NCI based on the fair value of the identifiable net assets acquired (partial goodwill), or EUR 300 mn (= 1.2 bn × 25%). In our case, this would result in goodwill of EUR 400 million (= 1.3 bn + 300 mn – 1.2 bn) being recognised.

Alternatively, Bank A can measure and recognise the NCI at fair value (full goodwill), that is, EUR 350 million. This method recognises goodwill on the NCI. This would result in goodwill of EUR 450 mn (= 1.3 bn + 350 mn – 1.2 bn) being recognised. The fair value measurement of the NCI may require the use of complex valuation techniques, an important drawback.

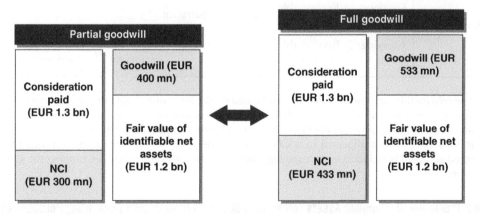

FIGURE 3.27   Goodwill amounts using the partial and full goodwill methods

Accounting perspective   From an accounting perspective and relative to the partial goodwill method, the full goodwill method results in a larger shareholders' equity at the acquisition date, implying a lower level of leverage. However, any subsequent goodwill impairment charge would be higher than under the partial goodwill method, with a negative impact on reported profit or loss.

Additionally, in jurisdictions where goodwill is tax-deductible, electing the full goodwill method results in a larger deductibility, an interesting advantage.

Finally, the full goodwill method would reduce any potential decrease in bank A's shareholders' equity resulting from a subsequent buyout of the NCI.

Regulatory capital perspective   From a regulatory capital perspective, the application of the partial goodwill method makes more sense. The regulatory recognition of the NCI is subject to a cap, as shown in Chapter 9, and the goodwill is deducted from CET1. If the size of the NCI does not exceed the regulatory cap, both methods have the same impact on CET1 capital. In contrast, when the NCI is such that regulatory cap is exceeded, Bank A does not get capital recognition for a part of its NCI while it is required to fully deduct the goodwill.

Subsequent Measurement of Goodwill – Impairment Testing   Goodwill acquired on a business combination is reviewed (i.e., tested) for impairment annually, or more frequently if there are indications that impairment may have occurred.

Because goodwill does not generate independent cash inflows, for the purposes of impairment testing goodwill is allocated to one or more **cash-generating units** ("CGUs"), commonly to several CGUs. The group of CGUs to which goodwill is allocated shall represent the lowest level at which the goodwill will be monitored for internal management purposes. CGUs are the smallest identifiable groups of assets that generate cash inflows largely independent of the cash inflows from other assets or groups of assets and that are expected to benefit from the synergies of the combination. In identifying a CGU various factors are considered, including how management monitors the entity's operations or makes decisions about continuing or disposing of the entity's assets and operations.

For impairment testing purposes, the allocated goodwill forms part of the CGU's (or group of CGUs') carrying amount. Potential impairment of the respective CGU is measured by comparing its **carrying amount**, including any allocated goodwill, to its **recoverable amount**. An impairment charge is recognised if the carrying amount exceeds the recoverable amount, giving rise to a loss in the profit or loss statement. Impairment charges are not subsequently reversed.

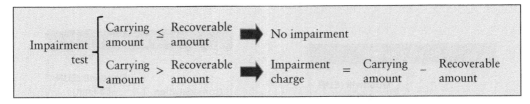

The recoverable amount of a CGU is determined on the basis of its value-in-use, commonly using a discounted cash flow model. This model incorporates assumptions regarding estimated earnings, discount rates and long-term growth rates impacting the recoverable amount of the CGU.

If goodwill has been allocated to a CGU and an operation within that unit is disposed of, the attributed goodwill is included in the carrying amount of the operation when determining the gain or loss on its disposal.

3.10.2 Treatment of Intangible Assets (other than Goodwill) from an IFRS Accounting Perspective

Intangible assets are key value drivers of a business as they provide rights and privileges to owners. Intangible assets can be internally developed or purchased, have an indefinite life or a finite life.

From an IFRS accounting perspective, intangible assets are dealt with by **IAS 38** *Intangible Assets*. In IAS 38, intangible assets are defined as identifiable, non-monetary assets that lack physical substance. An intangible asset is deemed to be **"identifiable"** when it meets either of the following criteria:

- It is separable from the entity (i.e., it can be sold, transferred, licensed, rented or exchanged) either individually or together with a related contract (asset or liability) – the **"separability"** criterion. If the entity faces a restriction on the transfer or sale of the intangible asset, the separability criterion is considered to be *not* met for that asset; or
- It arises from contractual or other legal rights (whether or not those rights are transferable or separable from the entity or from other rights and obligations) – the **"contractual-legal"** criterion.

Initial Accounting Recognition   According to IAS 38, the criteria for recognition in the financial statements of an intangible asset are:

- It meets the definition of an intangible asset;
- It is probable that future economic benefits (e.g., revenues, cost savings, …) attributable to the intangible asset will flow to the bank – the **"probability"** criterion; and
- Its cost can be reliably measured – the **"reliability of measurement"** criterion.

If these criteria are not met, costs must be expensed.

The initial recognition of an intangible asset is dependent on how it has been obtained:

- Acquired through a business combination;
- Acquired separately in exchange for monetary assets;
- Acquired separately in exchange for a consideration that included non-monetary assets or a combination of non-monetary and monetary assets;
- Obtained by way of a government grant; or
- Generated internally.

Regarding intangible assets **acquired in a business combination,** cost is deemed to be their fair value (as part of the purchase price allocation process) at the date of acquisition. The probability criterion and the reliability of measurement criteria are always assumed to be met for intangible assets obtained in this way. All intangible assets that can be reliably measured are recognised, regardless of whether they have been previously recognised in the acquiree's financial statements. If an intangible asset acquired in a business combination has a finite useful life, there is a rebuttable presumption that its fair value can be measured reliably. Fair value will reflect market participants' expectations at the acquisition date about the probability that the expected future economic benefits embodies in the asset will flow to the entity.

Regarding **separately acquired** intangible assets in **exchange for other monetary assets** (e.g., cash), the probability criterion is always assumed to be met. These intangibles are initially measured at cost. Cost comprises the purchase price, including import duties and non-refundable purchase taxes, after deducting trade discounts and rebates, and any directly attributable costs of preparing the asset for its intended use. Their cost can usually be measured reliably, as it is in the form of cash or other monetary assets.

Regarding **separately acquired** intangible assets in **exchange for other non-monetary assets** or for a combination of monetary and non-monetary assets, the probability criterion is always assumed to be met. Assuming that their exchange transactions have commercial substance, these intangible assets are initially measured at fair value of the consideration given unless the fair value of neither the asset given up nor the asset received can be reliably measured. If the intangible asset is not measured at fair value, it is measured at the carrying amount of the asset given up.

Regarding intangible assets **obtained by way of a government grant,** entities have the choice between recognising them either at fair value or nominal value. These intangible assets are sometimes acquired free of charge (i.e., a nil nominal amount) or for a nominal amount. They are relatively uncommon within the banking sector.

Regarding **internally generated** intangible assets, none of the intangibles recognition criteria is automatically assumed to be met, so a bank would need to ascertain that such criteria are satisfied. The initial recognition of internally generated intangibles is somewhat complex, and is covered next.

Recognition of Internally Generated Intangible Assets   The process of internal generation of an intangible asset is divided into a **research phase** and a **development phase**. Research is original and planned investigation undertaken with the prospect of gaining new scientific or technical knowledge and understanding. Development is the application of research findings or other knowledge to a plan or design for the production of new or substantially improved materials, devices, products, processes, systems or services before the commencement of commercial production or use. Development is more closely related to the earnings process than research.

IAS 38 assumes that during the **research phase** an entity is unable to demonstrate that there will be future economic benefits (i.e., the probability criterion is *not* met). As a result, *no* intangible assets arising from the research phase may be recognised and any costs should be expensed as incurred. Interestingly, research projects that are acquired as part of a business combination are treated differently.

During the development phase, only the costs that are directly attributable to generating the intangible asset, and not the general costs of the operation, may be capitalised. An intangible asset arising from the development phase is recognised (i.e., incurred costs are capitalised as an intangible asset) if the recognition criteria are met and when the bank can demonstrate:

- Its technical feasibility of completing the intangible asset so that it will be available for use or sale;
- Its intention to complete the intangible asset and use or sell it;
- Its ability to use or sell the intangible asset;
- How the intangible asset will generate probable future economic benefits. For example, the existence of a market for the output of the intangible asset or for the intangible asset itself, or, if it is to be used internally, the usefulness of the intangible asset;
- The availability of adequate technical, financial and other resources to complete the development and to use or sell the intangible asset; and
- Its ability to measure the attributable expenditure reliably during its development.

Any expenditure expensed during the research or development phase cannot subsequently be capitalised if the project meets the criteria for recognition at a later date.

> In reality, the costs relating to many internally generated intangible items cannot be capitalised (i.e., not recognised as intangible assets) and are expensed as incurred. This includes advertising costs, expenditure on internally generated brands and customer lists.

Subsequent Accounting Recognition   Subsequent to initial recognition, an entity may choose to adopt either the **cost model** or the **revaluation model** as its accounting policy. The revaluation model can only be elected if the intangible asset is traded in an active market, a rather unusual situation.

- Under the **cost model** the intangible asset is, following initial recognition, carried at cost less any accumulated amortisation and impairment losses.
- Under the **revaluation model** the intangible asset is carried at the asset's fair value (the active market price) at the date of valuation less subsequent accumulated amortisation.

Subsequent Accounting Recognition: Amortisation – Finite and Indefinite Useful Life Intangibles   Certain intangible assets are determined to have a **finite useful life**. Commonly these include patents, purchased credit card relationships, internally and externally generated software enhancements, non-compete agreements and client relationships.

Useful life is defined in IAS 38 as either (i) the period over which the asset is expected to be available for use by an entity, or (ii) the number of production or similar units expected to be produced from the asset by an entity.

Intangible assets which have been determined to have a finite useful life are **amortised** on over their estimated useful life, as soon as they are available for use. The depreciable amount is defined as the intangible asset's cost, or other amount substituted for cost, less its residual value. The residual value of an intangible asset with a finite useful life should be assumed to be zero, unless there is either a commitment by a third party to purchase the asset at the end of its useful life or there is an active and continuing market for the intangible asset and the residual value of the asset can be determined by reference to that market. The method of amortisation that is used should reflect the pattern in which the asset's future economic benefits are expected to be consumed by the entity. If that pattern cannot be determined reliably, the straight-line method of amortisation must be used. Amortisation charges are recognised as an expense in the profit or loss statement (unless they are permitted or required by IAS 38 or another standard to be included in the carrying amount of another asset). Amortisation applies to finite useful life intangible assets, whether held at cost or at fair value. The useful life, residual value and amortisation method for an intangible asset with a finite life should be reviewed at least at each financial year end.

Certain intangible assets are determined to have an **indefinite useful life**. Indefinite is not the same as an infinite useful life: it just indicates that there is no foreseeable limit to the period over which the asset is expected to generate net cash inflows for the bank. Commonly these include established or leading brands. Indefinite useful life intangible assets are *not* amortised.

> The British bank HSBC disclosed in its annual report for the year ending 2013 that intangible assets with finite useful lives were amortised, generally on a straight-line basis, over their useful lives as follows:
> - Trade names: 10 years;
> - Mortgage servicing rights: between 5 and 12 years;
> - Internally generated software: between 3 and 5 years;
> - Purchased software: between 3 and 5 years;
> - Customer/merchant relationships: between 3 and 10 years; and
> - Other: generally 10 years.

Subsequent Accounting Recognition: Impairment   Impairment of intangible assets is dealt with by IAS 36 *Impairment of Assets*. Intangible assets are reviewed at each reporting date to assess whether there is any indication that they are impaired. If any such indication exists, the recoverable amount of the asset is determined and in the event that the asset's carrying amount is greater than its recoverable amount, it is written down immediately by the difference between these two amounts.

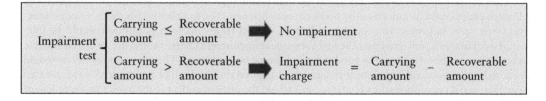

Whilst indefinite useful life intangible assets are not amortised, they are reassessed at least annually to reconfirm that an indefinite useful life remains appropriate. In the event that an indefinite life is inappropriate, a finite life is determined and an impairment review is performed on the intangible asset. This change in the useful life is furthermore an indication that an asset may be impaired. Where impairment is identified, the asset should be written down to its recoverable amount.

Subsequent Expenditure   The nature of many intangible assets is that there are often no additions to the asset or replacements to parts of it. As a result, subsequent expenditure will only rarely meet the criteria for being recognised in the carrying amount of an asset. For example, subsequent expenditure on brands, customer lists and similar items will always be recognised in profit or loss as incurred.

Derecognition   Where an intangible asset is (i) disposed of or (ii) where no future economic benefits are expected from its use or disposal, it should be derecognised. Gains and losses arising on derecognition should be recognised in the profit or loss statement and calculated as the difference between the asset's net disposal proceeds and its carrying amount.

3.11 CASE STUDY: DANSKE BANK'S GOODWILL IMPAIRMENT

In December 2014, the Danish bank Danske Bank announced that it expected to make goodwill impairments of about DKK 9 billion in its 2014 annual report. The goodwill impairments related to Danske Bank's activities in Finland, Northern Ireland and Estonia. Danske Bank's CFO claimed: "The goodwill impairments are of a purely technical nature and do not affect our strategy or business. The impairments also will not affect our regulatory capital or liquidity."

In financial accounting, goodwill is an asset representing the future economic benefits arising from other assets acquired in a business acquisition that are not separately recognised. At 30 September 2014 the bank had total goodwill of DKK 18.6 billion, therefore the DKK 9 billion goodwill impairment charge implied a 48% reduction in the bank's total goodwill. This goodwill impairment charge was the result of Danske Bank's ordinary goodwill impairment testing, changed macroeconomic conditions and its dialogue with the Danish Financial Supervisory Authority regarding the measurement of the bank's goodwill. In particular, more conservative model assumptions were incorporated for future income stream related especially to deposit margins, interest rates and impairment levels.

3.11.1 Accounting and Tax Impact of the Impairment

From an accounting perspective the DKK 9 billion impairment was recognised in consolidated profit or loss as a charge, reducing the bank's pre-tax net income by the same amount. The after-tax effect of the impairment charge depended on three factors:

1. Whether the goodwill was being amortised prior to the charge;
2. Whether the impairment charge was tax-deductible; and if so
3. Whether the charge would help the bank to reduce its tax bill.

I am not an expert in Danish taxes, but my understanding is that at that time goodwill acquired by a Danish entity could be amortised by up to one-seventh annually. In other words, from a tax perspective, seven years following an acquisition all the goodwill related to such acquisition would be fully amortised. Following full amortisation, any subsequent impairment charge would not be tax-deductible (otherwise more than 100% of the goodwill may become tax deducted). Therefore, no tax effects would be caused by the goodwill impairment charge, assuming that the goodwill being impaired was generated more than seven years prior to such charge. As a result, the after-tax effect in the bank's profit or loss of the DKK 9 billion impairment charge was a DKK 9 billion reduction as well.

> Although goodwill was amortised from a tax perspective, its accounting carrying amount was not influenced by such amortisation. As a result, prior to the impairment charge Danske Bank recognised a DKK 18.6 billion goodwill in its balance sheet. Thus, prior to the goodwill impairment and from a regulatory capital perspective, the Danish bank deducted DKK 18.6 billion from its CET1 capital, regardless of the tax amortisation.
>
> Because it generated sufficient taxable profit, the amortisation benefited Danske Bank as it paid less taxes. In other words, the Danish bank profit or loss benefited from a lower tax expense. As profit or loss is a component of CET1 capital, the tax amortisation helped the bank to generate CET1 capital more rapidly.

Similarly, and due to the effect in profit or loss, the impact in Danske Bank's shareholders' equity was a DKK 9 billion reduction to DKK 149.7 billion from DKK 158.7 billion at September 2014 (i.e., a 6% reduction).

3.11.2 Regulatory Capital Impact of the Impairment

The effect of the goodwill impairment charge on Danske Bank's CET1 capital was neutral, as the two main impacts of such charge offset each other:

- Firstly, prior to the impairment Danske Bank had to deduct the DKK 9 billion goodwill from its CET1 capital. The impairment meant that the bank had no longer such goodwill, and therefore such a deduction had to be made, enhancing its CET1 capital by DKK 9 billion.
- Secondly, an element of CET1 capital was its externally verified profit or loss. The DKK 9 billion reduction in the bank's profit or loss implied an identical reduction in its CET1 capital.

3.11.3 Other Impacts

As previously noted, the impact of the goodwill impairment charge on Danske Bank's profit or loss was a DKK 9 billion reduction. The bank had an approved policy of distributing dividends representing 40% of the yearly net income. The impairment charge notably reduced the amount of dividends that could be distributed according to such payout policy. To avoid such constraint on dividend distributions, Danske Bank exceptionally adopted a new payout policy in which, for 2014, dividends would be based on net profit for the year before goodwill impairments.

3.12 CASE STUDY: BARCLAYS BADWILL RESULTING FROM ITS ACQUISITION OF LEHMAN BROTHERS N.A.

Concurrent to Lehman Brothers' bankruptcy filing, on 22 September 2008, Barclays completed the acquisition of Lehman Brothers North America. The total consideration transferred was GBP 874 million (GBP 834 million in cash and GBP 40 million in costs incurred). The acquired business included Lehman Brothers North American fixed income and equities sales, trading and research and investment banking businesses, Lehman Brothers New York head office and two data centres in New Jersey. The transaction resulted in "**badwill**" (i.e., negative goodwill) being recognised.

A transaction in which badwill arises is called a "**bargain purchase**". More precisely, a bargain purchase occurs if the acquisition date amounts of the identifiable net assets acquired, excluding goodwill, exceed the sum of (i) the value of consideration paid, (ii) the value of any non-controlling interest in the acquiree and (iii) the fair value of any previously held equity interest in the acquiree. IFRS 3 considers that a bargain purchase represents an economic gain, which should be immediately recognised by the acquirer in profit or loss.

The transaction badwill amounted to GBP 2,262 million, which was recognised in Barclays' profit or loss statement as a gain on the acquisition. Several points are worth noting (see Figure 3.28):

- Firstly, under IFRS the GBP 2,262 million gain on acquisition was calculated net of deferred tax liabilities included in the acquisition balance sheet and were thus not subject to further tax in calculating the tax charge for the year. Furthermore, Barclays had tax losses previously unrecognised as a deferred tax asset but capable of sheltering part of this deferred tax liability. This gave rise to a tax benefit of GBP 492 million, which, in accordance with IAS 12, was included as a credit within the tax charge for the year.
- Secondly, GBP 888 million of intangible assets were recognised, of which GBP 636 mn related to customer lists.
- Thirdly, under the terms of the acquisition, Barclays assumed an obligation to make payments to employees of the acquired business in respect of their preacquisition service provided to Lehman Brothers. This amount – GBP 163 million – represented the equity-settled portion of that obligation and was recognised as a component of shareholders' equity. That amount was excluded from the calculation of the badwill, since it represented compensation for past services.
- Fourthly, the initial accounting for the acquisition was determined only provisionally. Any revisions to fair values that result from the conclusion of the acquisition process with respect to assets not yet received by Barclays were subsequently recognised as an adjustment to the initial accounting. According to IFRS 3, any such revisions had to be effected within 12 months of the acquisition date and, if any, would have resulted in a restatement of Barclays' 2008 profit or loss statement and balance sheet. In this case, there were no subsequent revisions to the initial accounting disclosed in the 2008 financial statements.
- Finally, Lehman Brothers filed for bankruptcy when the transaction took place. Certain assets were received subsequent to the acquisition date, since it was first necessary to agree their status as assets of Barclays with the relevant regulators, custodians, trustees, exchanges and bankruptcy courts. Such assets were initially classified within loans and advances. Once they were received, the related receivable was derecognised and the resulting asset recognised within the appropriate balance sheet category.

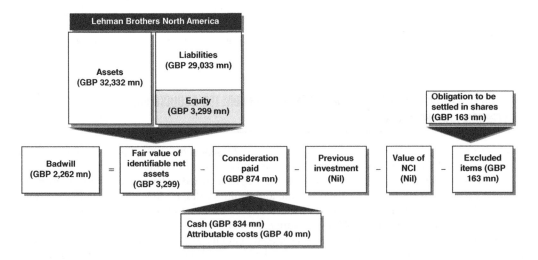

FIGURE 3.28　Badwill resulting from Barclays' acquisition of Lehman Brothers NA

From a regulatory capital perspective, the acquisition of Lehman Brothers increased CET1 capital by GBP 1,374 million (= 2,262 million profit minus 888 million intangibles, ignoring other adjustments). However, assets with a book value of GBP 31,444 million (= 32,332 mn − 888 mn) had to be risk-weighted.

Tax effects (e.g., the potential recognition of deferred tax liabilities) have been ignored to keep the case study simple. Deferred taxes are covered in detail in Chapter 13.

3.13 DEFERRED TAX ASSETS

Deferred tax assets that rely on future profitability are excluded from CET1. Chapter 13 provides a detailed explanation on how these assets are generated, their accounting treatment and their impact in regulatory capital.

3.14 FAIR VALUE RESERVES RELATED TO GAINS OR LOSSES ON CASH FLOW HEDGES

Cash flow hedge reserves are an element of OCI. Pursuant to [CRR 33(1)(a)], fair value reserves related to gains or losses on cash flow hedges of financial instruments that are not valued at fair value, including projected cash flows, are not included in CET1 capital. Therefore, any positive amounts in the cash flow hedge reserve related to such hedges are deducted from CET1 capital. Conversely, any negative amounts related to such hedges are added back to CET1 capital.

The cash flow hedge reserve recognises the gains or losses in the hedges of future cash flows. If the cash flow hedge reserve shows a positive amount this is because the cash flow hedging derivatives are experiencing a gain (i.e., their fair value has increased since the derivatives became part of the cash flow hedging relationships), which offsets an unfavourable movement in the expected cash flows being hedged. Therefore, the cash flow hedge reserve only reflects one half of the picture, the fair value of the derivative but not the changes in fair value of the hedged future cash flows.

Since the values of the cash flow hedge reserve were already taken into account, with the other reserves in OCI, when calculating CET1 capital prior to any deductions, this adjustment basically unwinds such incorporation. In other words, the adjustment ascertains that the amounts in the cash flow hedge do not have any effect in CET1 capital.

The adjustment is only related to cash flow hedges of financial instruments. Typically banks apply cash flow hedging to the hedges of the future coupons of floating rate debt, a financial instrument, when the debt instrument is recognised at amortised cost. Let us assume that a floating rate debt was hedged with an interest rate swap. The changes in the fair value of the swap recognised in the cash flow hedge reserve would be deducted from (in the case of a fair value gain) or added to (in the case of a fair value loss) CET1 capital.

Were a bank to apply cash flow hedges to non-financial instruments, the filter does not apply. Imagine the future acquisition of a mainframe computer denominated in a foreign currency hedged with a FX forward. If the element being hedged is the foreign currency cash flow related to the purchase, the gain or loss on the FX forward recognised in the cash flow hedge reserve of OCI is part of CET1 capital, and no adjustments would be necessary.

What about (in this last example) if the risk being hedged is the payable resulting from the mainframe purchase? The accounts payable is a financial instrument, but it is fair valued at each reporting date. Therefore, no adjustment to CET1 capital would be required related to the gain/loss of the FX forward recognised in the cash flow hedge reserve.

The basis for such deduction is based on the accounting amounts in the cash flow hedge reserve recognised under IFRS. Therefore, it is important to understand how these gains and losses are generated from an accounting perspective.

3.14.1 Cash Flow Hedges – Accounting Mechanics

IFRS prescribes the use of cash flow hedge accounting to avoid a distorted impact on earnings for derivatives which serve to hedge the risk of a change in future cash flows. Cash flow hedges are dealt with by **IFRS 9** *Financial Instruments*. According to IFRS 9, a cash flow hedge is a hedge of the exposure to variability in cash flows that:

- Is attributable to a particular risk associated with all, or a component of, a recognised asset or liability (such as all or some future interest payments on variable rate debt), or a highly probable forecast transaction; and
- Could affect reported profit or loss.

Derivatives used in cash flow hedges are recognised at fair value on the balance sheet. At each reporting date, the period change in fair value of the derivative (the "**hedging instrument**") is calculated and split between an effective and ineffective parts. The recognition of the change in fair value of the hedging instrument is shown in Figures 3.29 and 3.30.

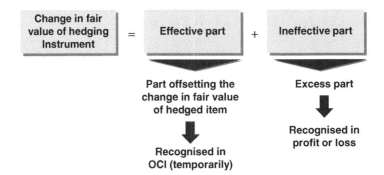

FIGURE 3.29   Recognition of the change in fair value of a hedging instrument

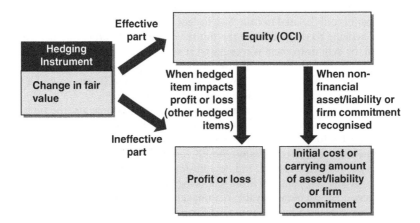

FIGURE 3.30   Accounting for a cash flow hedge

- The **effective** part of the change in the fair value of the derivative is recognised in the cash flow hedge reserve of **other comprehensive income** (OCI). The effective part represents the portion of the change in the fair value of the derivative that is offsetting the change in fair value of the cash flows being hedged (the "hedged item").
- The **ineffective** part is recognised immediately in the **profit or loss** statement.

A bank's cash flow hedges consist principally of interest rate swaps, futures and cross-currency swaps that are used to protect against exposures to variability in future interest cash flows on non-trading floating rate assets and liabilities or which are expected to be re-funded or rein-vested in the future.

Commonly, the amounts and timing of future cash flows, representing both principal and interest flows, are projected for each portfolio of financial assets and liabilities on the basis of their contractual terms and other relevant factors, including estimates of prepayments and defaults. The aggregate principal balances and interest cash flows across all portfolios over time form the basis for identifying gains and losses on the effective portions of derivatives designated as cash flow hedges of forecast transactions.

The accumulated gains and losses recognised in OCI are **reclassified** to the profit or loss statement in the periods in which the hedged cash flows will affect profit or loss (see Figure 3.30). For example, if the hedged item is a variable rate borrowing, the reclassification to profit or loss is recognised in profit or loss within "interest expense", therefore offsetting the borrowing's interest cost. However, when the forecast transaction that is hedged results in the recognition of a non-financial asset or a non-financial liability (e.g., inventory), the gains and losses previously recognised in OCI are removed from equity and included in the initial measurement of the cost of the asset or liability.

Discontinuance of Hedge Accounting When either (i) the hedging instrument expires or is sold, (ii) the future cash flows are no longer expected to occur or (iii) the hedge no longer meets the criteria for hedge accounting, the application of cash flow hedge accounting is discontinued. When an entity discontinues hedge accounting for a cash flow hedge it shall account for the amounts that have been accumulated (related to such hedge) in the cash flow hedge reserve of OCI as follows:

- If the hedged future cash flows are still expected to occur, the amounts remain in the cash flow hedge reserve until the future cash flows occur.
- If the hedged future cash flows are no longer expected to occur, the amounts are immediately reclassified from the cash flow hedge reserve to profit or loss as a reclassification adjustment.

3.14.2 Case Study: Hedging a Floating Rate Liability with an Interest Rate Swap

In order to explain the accounting features of cash flow hedges I cover next an example, a simplified version of a case study taken from my book *Accounting for Derivatives*. It covers the hedge with an interest rate swap of the variability (due to changes in interest rates) in interest payments pertaining to a floating rate debt issued by a bank.

Background Information   Assume that on 31 December 20X0, Bank ABC issued at par a floating rate bond with the characteristics in Table 3.15.

As the bond coupon was linked to the Euribor 12-month rate, the bank was exposed to rising Euribor rates. Bank ABC decided to mitigate that exposure by, simultaneously with the issuance of the bond, entering into an IRS. Bank ABC entered into an IRS with the terms shown in Table 3.16.

The combination of the bond and the IRS allowed Bank ABC to pay a fixed 5.36% (= 3.86% + 1.50%) overall interest at the end of each annual period, as shown in Figure 3.31. Thus, Bank ABC was not exposed to rising Euribor rates.

Accounting Mechanics in Absence of Hedge Accounting Application   The bond was recognised at amortised cost, using the effective interest rate method. In our case, assuming that it reported on an annual basis, Bank ABC recognised each year an interest expense equal to the bond's floating coupon payment. No fair valuation of the bond was required.

TABLE 3.15   Main Terms of Bank ABC's Floating-rate Bond

Bond Terms	
Issue date	31 December 20X0
Issuer	Bank ABC
Maturity	5 years (31 December 20X5)
Notional	EUR 100 million
Issue price	100%
Coupon	Euribor 12-month + 1.50%, annually (Act/360 basis)
Euribor fixing	Euribor is fixed at the beginning of each annual interest period

TABLE 3.16   Main Terms of Bank ABC's Interest Rate Swap

Interest Rate Swap Terms	
Trade date	31 December 20X0
Counterparties	Bank ABC and XYZ Bank
Notional	EUR 100 million
Maturity	5 years (31 December 20X5)
Bank ABC pays	3.86% annually, Actual/360 basis
Bank ABC receives	Euribor 12-month, annually, Actual/360 basis
Euribor fixing	Euribor is fixed at the beginning of the annual interest period
Initial fair value	Nil

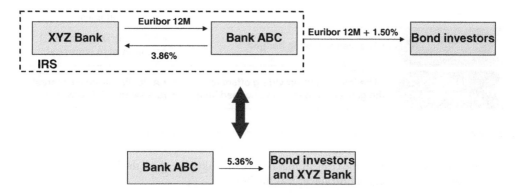

FIGURE 3.31 Overall annual interest expense

In the absence of hedge accounting, the IRS would have a double impact in profit or loss:

- The IRS would be fair valued at each reporting date and the changes in fair value during the accounting period would be recognised in profit or loss; and
- The IRS settlement amounts. The combination of the bond's interest expense and the IRS settlement amounts would result in an interest expense equivalent to a 5.36% interest paid on the bond coupon.

An accounting mismatch would then occur in the profit or loss statement due to the IRS fair valuation, adding volatility to that statement, as shown in Figure 3.32.

Hedged Item and Hedging Instrument The main objective of hedge accounting is to align the risk management and the accounting recognition of the hedging activities of entities. In a hedge accounting relationship there are two elements: the hedged item and the hedging instrument (see Figure 3.33).

- The **hedged item** is the item that exposes the entity to a market risk(s). It is the element that is designated as being hedged. In our case, the hedged item was the string the coupon payments on the bond, excluding the 150 basis points credit spread (i.e., just the Euribor 12-month component was part of the hedge accounting relationship).

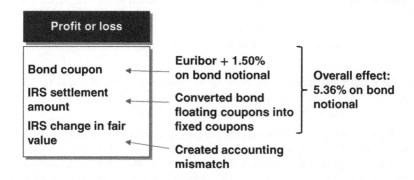

FIGURE 3.32 Effects in profit or loss in absence of hedge accounting application

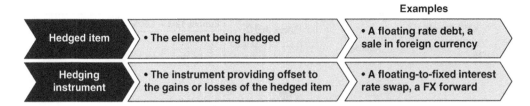

FIGURE 3.33   Hedge accounting terminology: hedged item and hedging instrument

- The **hedging instrument** is the element that hedges the risk(s) to which the hedged item is exposed to. In our case, the hedging instrument was the IRS.

Whilst the application of hedge accounting is voluntary, in order to be applied a hedge needs to meet a number of requirements. A hedging relationship qualifies for hedge accounting only if all the following criteria are met:

1. The hedging relationship consists only of eligible hedge items and hedging instruments. The hedge item was eligible as it was a group of highly expected forecast cash flows that exposed Bank ABC to fair value risk, affected profit or loss and was reliably measurable. The hedging instrument was eligible as it was a derivative that did not result in a net written option;
2. At hedge inception there is a formal designation and documentation of the hedging relationship and the entity's risk management objective and strategy for undertaking the hedge; and
3. The hedging relationship is considered effective. There are three further requirements to meet this effectiveness criterion:

    - There is an economic relationship between the hedged item and the hedging instrument;
    - The effect of credit risk does not dominate the value changes that result from that economic relationship; and
    - The hedge ratio of the hedging relationship is the same as that resulting from the quantity of hedged item that the entity actually hedges and the quantity of the hedging instrument that the entity actually uses to hedge that quantity of hedged item. The hedge ratio should not be intentionally weighted to create ineffectiveness.

I assume that all those requirements were met and, therefore, Bank ABC was able to apply cash flow hedge accounting.

Recognition of the Hedged Item   In a cash flow hedge the recognition of the hedged item is not affected by the application of hedge accounting. Therefore, the bond was recognised at amortised cost and, as a result, the bond's interest expense was recorded in profit or loss. The carrying amount of the bond on the bank's liability side was its EUR 100 million notional amount.

Recognition of the Hedging Instrument   The hedging instrument (i.e., the IRS) was fair valued at each reporting date. The IRS's settlement amounts were recognised in profit or loss, adjusting interest expense. Changes in the fair value of the IRS were recognised as follows:

- The **effective part** of the gain or loss on the hedging instrument was recognised in the cash flow hedge reserve of other comprehensive income (OCI) in equity. The effective part denoted the extent to which the gain or loss on the hedging instrument offset that on the hedged item.
- The **ineffective part** of the gain or loss on the hedging instrument was recognised immediately in profit or loss. The ineffective part represented the excess of the gain or loss on the hedging instrument over the effective part. Therefore, a well designed hedging strategy results in small, ineffective parts relative to the effective parts.

TABLE 3.17   Bond Interest and Swap Settlement Amounts

Date	Period Euribor 12M	Bond Interest [1]	Swap Settlement Amount [2]
31-Dec-20X1	3.21%	<4,775,000>	<659.000>
31-Dec-20X2	4.21%	<5,789,000>	354.000
31-Dec-20X3	3.71%	<5,282,000>	<152.000>
31-Dec-20X4	3.80%	<5,374,000>	<61.000>
31-Dec-20X5	3.95%	<5,526,000>	91.000

Notes:
[1] *< 100 mn > × (Euribor 12M + 1.50%) × 365/360, assuming 365 calendar days in the interest period*
[2] *100 mn × (Euribor 12M) × 365/360 – 100 mn × 3.86% × 365/360, assuming 365 calendar days in the interest period*

TABLE 3.18   Swap Effective and Ineffective Amounts

Date	IRS Fair Value	Period Change	Effective Part	Ineffective Part
31-Dec-20X1	3,243,000	3,243,000	3,237,000	6,000
31-Dec-20X2	850,000	<2,393,000>	<2,393,000>	Nil
31-Dec-20X3	276,000	<574,000>	<574,000>	Nil
31-Dec-20X4	<87,000>	<363,000>	<348,000>	<15,000>
31-Dec-20X5	Nil	87,000	78,000	9,000

Bond Coupon Payments and Swap Settlement Amounts   Let us assume that the bond coupon payments and swap settlement amounts at each relevant date were the values in Table 3.17.

Fair Valuations of Hedging Instrument   Let us assume that the fair value of the hedging instrument (excluding accrued settlement amounts) and the effective/ineffective parts of its fair value change at each relevant date were the numbers in Table 3.18.

Accounting Entries   The required journal entries were the following:

1. Entries on 31 December 20X0
   To record the issuance of the bond:

Cash (Asset)	100,000,000
Financial debt (Liability)	100,000,000

No journal entries were required to record the swap since its fair value was zero at inception.

2. Entries on 31 December 20X1
   The bond paid a EUR 4,775,000 coupon.

Interest expense (Profit or loss)	4,775,000
Cash (Asset)	4,775,000

The change in fair value of the swap since the last valuation was a EUR 3,243,000 gain, of which EUR 3,237,000 was deemed to be effective and recorded in the cash flow hedge reserve of equity, while EUR 6,000 was deemed to be ineffective and recorded in profit or loss.

Derivative contract (Asset)	3,243,000
Cash flow hedge reserve (Equity)	3,237,000
Financial gains (Profit or loss)	6,000

Under the swap the entity paid a EUR 659,000 settlement amount.

Interest expense (Profit or loss)	659,000
Cash (Asset)	659,000

3. Entries on 31 December 20X2
   The bond paid a EUR 5,789,000 coupon.
   The change in fair value of the swap since the last valuation was a EUR 2,393,000 loss, fully effective and recorded in the cash flow hedge reserve of equity.
   Under the swap the entity received a EUR 354,000 settlement amount.

Interest expense (Profit or loss)	5,789,000
Cash (Asset)	5,789,000
Cash flow hedge reserve (Equity)	2,393,000
Derivative contract (Asset)	2,393,000
Cash (Asset)	354,000
Interest income (Profit or loss)	354,000

4. Entries on 31 December 20X3
   The bond paid a EUR 5,282,000 coupon.
   The change in fair value of the swap since the last valuation was a EUR 574,000 loss, fully effective and recorded in the cash flow hedge reserve of equity.

Under the swap the entity paid a EUR 152,000 settlement amount.

Interest expense (Profit or loss)	5,282,000
Cash (Asset)	5,282,000
Cash flow hedge reserve (Equity)	574,000
Derivative contract (Asset)	574,000
Interest expense (Profit or loss)	152,000
Cash (Asset)	152,000

5. Entries on 31 December 20X4
   The bond paid a EUR 5,374,000 coupon.
   The change in fair value of the swap since the last valuation was a EUR 363,000 loss, of which EUR 348,000 was deemed to be effective and recorded in the cash flow hedge reserve of equity, while EUR 15,000 was deemed to be ineffective and recorded in profit or loss.
   Under the swap the entity paid a EUR 61,000 settlement amount.

Interest expense (Profit or loss)	5,374,000
Cash (Asset)	5,374,000
Cash flow hedge reserve (Equity)	348,000
Financial losses (Profit or loss)	15,000
Derivative contract (Asset)	363,000
Interest expense (Profit or loss)	61,000
Cash (Asset)	61,000

6. Entries on 31 December 20X5
   The bond paid a EUR 5,526,000 coupon and repaid the EUR 100 million principal.
   The change in fair value of the swap since the last valuation was a EUR 87,000 gain, of which EUR 78,000 was deemed to be effective and recorded in the cash flow hedge reserve of equity, while EUR 9,000 was deemed to be ineffective and recorded in profit or loss.
   Under the swap the entity received a EUR 91,000 settlement amount.

Interest expense (Profit or loss)	5,526,000
Financial debt (Liability)	100,000,000
Cash (Asset)	105,526,000
Derivative contract (Asset)	87,000
Cash flow hedge reserve (Equity)	78,000
Financial gains (Profit or loss)	9,000
Cash (Asset)	91,000
Interest income (Profit or loss)	91,000

Role of the Cash Flow Hedge Reserve   Let us have a look at the financial statements of Bank ABC on 31-Dec-20X1, the first reporting date following the taking out of the hedge (see Figure 3.34):

- On the asset side, the IRS was recognised at its fair value (excluding accrued settlement amounts), or EUR 3,243,000.
- On the liability side, the bond was carried at its amortised cost value, or EUR 100 million.
- In the bank's profit or loss statement, the bond coupon (EUR <4,775,000>) and the IRS settlement amount (EUR <659,000>) were recognised as interest expense. The IRS's ineffective part (EUR 6,000) was recognised in profit or loss as well, as a financial gain.
- On the shareholders' equity side, the cash flow hedge reserve of OCI showed a EUR 3,237,000 carrying amount, which represented the effective part of the change in fair value of the IRS.

Ignoring ineffective parts, the role of the cash flow hedge reserve was to temporarily keep a record of the change in fair value of the IRS so that the bank's profit or loss statement showed an interest expense approximately equal to the 5.36% target. Hedge accounting aligned the objective of the hedge – to result in a 5.36% interest expense – with its accounting recognition.

Final Remarks   The total interest expense/income recognised during the interest period ending 31 December 20X1 was EUR 5,434,000 (= 4,775,000 + 659,000). The objective of entering into the hedge was to fix the overall interest rate to 5.36%, which represented a EUR 5,434,000 (= 100 mn × (3.86% + 1.50%) × 365/360) interest expense. Therefore, the objective was fully met during that interest period. This was true during all interest periods in which the swap fair value change was fully effective. In periods during which ineffectiveness was present, the difference between the actual and the target interest expenses was notably small.

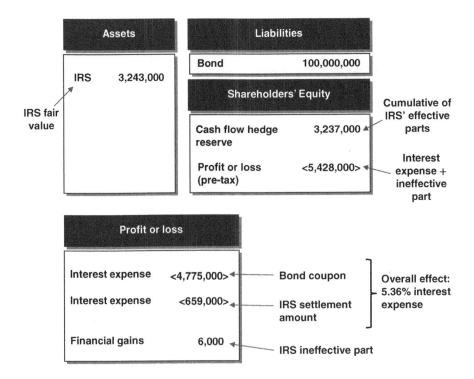

FIGURE 3.34   Effects of the hedge on Bank ABC's financial statements on 31-Dec-20X1

Deferred tax relating to fair value remeasurements of cash flow hedging instruments which are charged or credited directly to OCI, is also charged or credited to OCI and is subsequently recognised in the profit or loss statement when the deferred fair value gain or loss is recognised in the profit or loss statement.

Let us take a look to the impact on CET1 capital of the EUR 3,237,000 cash flow hedge reserve carrying amount on 31-Dec-20X1. From a regulatory perspective, the amounts in the cash flow hedge reserve impacted CET1 capital in a two-step process:

- Firstly, they were added to CET1 capital in conjunction with all other amounts in OCI. In our example, CET1 capital was increased by EUR 3,237,000.
- Secondly, any amounts in the cash flow hedge reserve related to the hedge of financial instruments not measured at fair value were deducted from CET1 capital. In our example, CET1 capital was reduced by EUR 3,237,000.

Therefore, the objective of that second step was to neutralise any effect of the cash flow hedge reserve in CET1 capital. The logic behind it is that amounts in the cash flow hedge reserve represent temporary gains/losses that would be compensating future cash flows (in our case, so that an interest expense rate of 5.36% expense rate would be met). Whilst the IRS's fair value gain meant that Bank ABC was expected to receive future settlement amounts under the IRS, these amounts would be reducing a similar increase in the bond's future coupons.

3.15 NEGATIVE AMOUNTS RESULTING FROM THE CALCULATION OF EXPECTED LOSS AMOUNTS

At the time of writing, the EU has not yet adapted the CRR to incorporate IFRS 9's provisioning rules. The filter described in this Section is based on the rules set out in [CRR 36(1)(d), 40, 159], which as a result of IFRS 9 being implemented may be subject to changes.

3.15.1 Shortfall of Provisions

For banks calculating RWAs using the Internal Ratings-Based (IRB) Approach, negative amounts resulting from the calculation of expected loss amounts are deducted from CET1, as shown in Figure 3.35.

Expected loss in excess of eligible provisions	=	Regulatory expected loss	−	Eligible provisions for regulatory purposes

The objective of this deduction is to eliminate any incentives for under-provisioning. The full shortfall amount is deducted without being reduced by a rise in the level of deferred tax assets that rely on future profitability, or other additional tax effects, that could be expected to occur if provisions were to rise to the level of expected losses.

3.15.2 Excess of Provisions

Unlike a shortfall of provisions, which as pointed out previously is deducted from CET1 for banks using the IRB approach, an excess of provisions is *not* added to CET1, but to Tier 2 capital (see Figure 3.36). This addition is subject to a cap of 0.6% of *credit* RWAs calculated under the IRB approach [CRR Chapter 3 of Title II of Part Three].

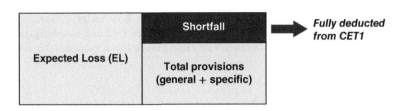

FIGURE 3.35 Treatment of the shortfall in provisions from expected losses calculated under the IRB approach

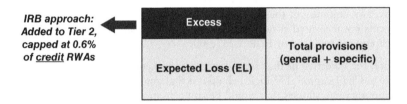

FIGURE 3.36 Treatment of the excess in provisions from expected losses calculated under the IRB approach

Banks are fully penalised for any shortfall, while they are partially compensated in the case of an excess. As a result, banks have no incentives for under-provisioning but at the same time have limited incentives for over-provisioning.

As accounting provisions under IFRS 9 are substantially higher than those under IAS 39, the 0.6% cap (if maintained) will be more likely to be reached, further reducing encouragements for over-provisioning.

In general, except during times of economic downturn, banks generally have substantial provisions in excess of expected losses. Banking supervisors need to carefully assess whether the risks addressed by this filter are already being tackled by the countercyclical buffer. An overlap is likely to unnecessarily impose an additional burden on banks during times of economic weakness, slowing economic recovery.

3.16 EQUITY INCREASES RESULTING FROM SECURITISED ASSETS

Pursuant to [CRR 32(1)] any increase in accounting shareholders' equity that results from securitised assets is excluded from CET1 capital, including the following:

- Gains on sale for the bank associated with future margin income that results in an increase in accounting shareholders' equity;
- Where the bank is the originator of a securitisation, net gains that arise from the capitalisation of future income from the securitised assets that provide credit enhancement to positions in the securitisation.

3.17 GAINS OR LOSSES ON LIABILITIES VALUED AT FAIR VALUE RESULTING FROM CHANGES IN OWN CREDIT STANDING

A deterioration in a bank's own creditworthiness can lead to an increase in the bank's CET1 as a result of a reduction in the value of its liabilities. The Basel III rules seek to prevent this, by requiring banks to derecognise in the calculation of CET1 all unrealised gains and losses that have resulted from changes in the fair value of liabilities that are due to changes in the bank's own credit risk. This filter applies to debt issued by banks and also has implications for the treatment of fair valued derivatives. In order to understand the spirit behind this filter and how to apply it, let us review first the accounting recognition of financial liabilities under IFRS 9.

3.17.1 Financial Liability Categories

A financial is any liability that is a contractual obligation to deliver cash or another financial asset to another entity or to exchange financial instruments with another entity under conditions that are potentially unfavourable.

Under IFRS 9 there are only two categories of financial liabilities (see Figure 3.37) at amortised cost and at fair value through profit and loss (FVTPL). The following table summarises the accounting treatment of each category of financial liabilities:

Liability Category	Measurement	Fair Value Changes
At amortised cost	Amortised cost. Any premium or discount is amortised to profit or loss	Not relevant by virtue of not being fair valued
At fair value through profit or loss (FVTPL)	Fair value	Changes in fair value attributable to changes in credit risk presented in OCI (unless it creates or increases accounting mismatch) Remaining changes in fair value recorded in profit or loss

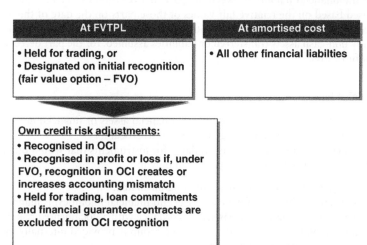

FIGURE 3.37   IFRS 9 financial liabilities classification categories

The category of financial liabilities at FVTPL has two sub-categories: liabilities held for trading and those designated to this category at their inception using the fair value option. Financial liabilities classified as held for trading include:

- Financial liabilities acquired or incurred principally for the purpose of generating a short-term profit (i.e., held for trading);
- A derivative not designated in a cash flow or net investment hedging relationship, or the ineffective part if designated;
- Obligations to deliver securities or other financial assets borrowed by a short seller; and
- Financial liabilities that are part of a portfolio of identified financial instruments that are managed together and for which there is evidence of a recent actual pattern of short-term profit taking.

Debt instruments issued by a bank would be recognised within the "amortised cost" category. Because these debt instruments are not fair valued, the CET1 filter related to own credit risk does not apply to these instruments.

However, debt instruments are fair valued at each reporting date when recognised within the "at FVTPL" category. This is the case when the debt instrument is held for trading or when the bank applies the "fair value option" (to be covered below). Because own credit risk is incorporated in the fair valuation, therefore, the CET1 filter related to own credit risk applies to these debt instruments.

Because all derivatives are fair valued at each reporting date, own credit risk is incorporated in the fair valuation and, therefore, the CET1 filter related to own credit risk applies to derivative instruments.

3.17.2 Partial Repurchases of Financial Liabilities

When a bank repurchases own financial liabilities, the repurchased part is derecognised. According to IFRS 9, "if an entity repurchases a part of a financial liability, the entity shall allocate the previous carrying amount of the financial liability between the part that continues to be recognised and the part that is derecognised based on the relative fair values of those parts on the date of the repurchase. The difference between (a) the carrying amount allocated to the part derecognised and (b) the consideration paid, including any non-cash assets transferred or liabilities assumed, for the part derecognised shall be recognised in profit or loss."

3.17.3 The Fair Value Option

The **fair value option** (FVO) is an option to designate financial assets or financial liabilities at FVTPL. The election is available only on initial recognition and is irrevocable.

In the case of **financial liabilities**, FVO is available for instruments that would otherwise be mandatorily recognised at amortised cost, being permitted only if:

- It eliminates or significantly reduces an **accounting mismatch**; or
- A group of financial liabilities (or financial assets and financial liabilities) is managed and its performance is evaluated on a fair value basis, in accordance with a documented risk management or investment strategy, and the information about the group is provided internally on that basis to the entity's key management personnel; or
- A contract contains one or more embedded derivatives and the host is not a financial asset, then an entity may designate the entire hybrid contract at FVTPL unless the embedded derivative is insignificant or it is obvious that separation of the embedded derivative would be prohibited.

The FVO is only available on initial recognition of the financial asset or liability. This requirement may create a problem if the entity enters into offsetting contracts on different dates. A first financial instrument may be acquired in the anticipation that it will provide a natural offset to another instrument that has yet to be acquired. If the natural hedge is not in place at the outset, IFRS 9 would not allow to record the first financial instrument at FVTPL, as it would not eliminate or significantly reduce a measurement or recognition inconsistency. Additionally, to impose discipline, an entity is precluded from reclassifying financial instruments in or out of the fair value category, unless (in the case of financial assets) the business model for those assets changes.

Accounting Mismatch   Sometimes, a particular market risk that affects a financial asset or a financial liability is hedged with another financial instrument that behaves in an opposite way to movements in such market risk (i.e., an increase in the market variable would increase the fair value of one of the two items while decreasing that of the other item). In this case, the entity would be interested in measuring the financial asset or financial liability at fair value through profit or loss (FVTPL) to benefit from their natural offsetting. The entity could apply the FVO because it will eliminate or significantly reduce the measurement or recognition inconsistency that would otherwise arise from measuring these assets or liabilities, or recognising the gains and losses on them, on different bases.

3.17.4 Changes in Credit Risk in Financial Liabilities at FVTPL – Debt Instruments

The amount of change in the fair value of a debt instrument issued by the bank and designated at FVTPL under the fair value option that is attributable to changes in credit risk must be presented in other comprehensive income (OCI), unless:

- Presentation of the fair value change in respect of the liability's credit risk in OCI would create or enlarge an accounting mismatch in profit or loss. In this case, the fair value change attributable to changes in credit risk must be recognised in profit or loss. This determination is made at initial recognition of the individual liability and will not be reassessed.

The remainder of the change in fair value is presented in profit or loss.

To determine whether the treatment would create or enlarge an accounting mismatch, the entity must assess whether it expects the effect of the change in the liability's credit risk to be offset in profit or loss by a change in fair value of another financial instrument. In reality, such instances are expected to be rare, unless an entity for example holds an asset whose fair value is linked to the fair value of the liability.

The changes in credit risk recognised in OCI are *not* recycled to profit or loss on settlement of the liability.

The following instruments, when recognised at FVTPL, are not required to isolate the change in fair value attributable to credit risk (i.e., all gains and losses are presented in profit or loss):

- Financial guarantee contracts; and
- Loan commitments.

Measurement of a Debt Liability's Credit Risk   IFRS 9 largely carries forward guidance from IFRS 7 on how to determine the effect of changes in credit risk. An entity determines the amount of the fair value change that is attributable to changes in its credit risk either:

- As the amount of change in its fair value that is not attributable to changes in market conditions that give rise to market risk (e.g., a benchmark interest rate, the price of another entity's financial instrument, a commodity price, a foreign exchange rate or an index of prices or rates); or
- Using an alternative method, if it provides a more faithful representation of the changes in the fair value of the liability attributable to the changes in its credit risk.

IFRS 9 clarifies that this would include any liquidity premium associated with the liability.

If the only significant relevant changes in market conditions for a liability are changes in an observed (benchmark) interest rate, under IFRS 9 the amount of fair value changes that are attributable to changes in credit risk may be estimated using the so-called **"default method"**, as follows:

1. The entity first calculates the liability's internal rate of return at the start of the period using the liability's fair value and contractual cash flows at that date. It then deducts from this internal rate of return the observed (benchmark) interest rate at the start of the period so as to arrive at an "instrument-specific component" of the internal rate of return.
2. Next, the entity computes a present value of the cash flows of the liability at the end of the period using the liability's contractual cash flows at that date and a discount rate equal to the sum of (i) the observed (benchmark) interest rate at that date and (ii) the instrument-specific component of the internal rate of return determined in (1).
3. The entity then deducts the present value calculated in (2) from the fair value of the liability at the end of the period. The resulting difference is the change in fair value that is not attributable to changes in the observed (benchmark) interest rate and which is assumed to be attributable to changes in credit risk.

This default method is appropriate only if the only significant relevant changes in market conditions for a liability are changes in an observed (benchmark) interest rate and that, when other factors are significant, an alternative measure that more faithfully measures the effects of changes in the liability's credit risk should be used. For example, if the liability contains an embedded derivative, the change in fair value of the derivative would be excluded in calculating the fair value change amount attributable to changes in credit risk.

3.17.5 Application of Own Credit Gains and Losses to Derivatives – DVA

In December 2011, the BCBS published a consultative document titled *Application of Own Credit Risk Adjustments to Derivatives*. The application of the own credit risk gains and losses filter to fair valued derivatives is not straightforward since their valuations depend on a range of factors other than the bank's own creditworthiness.

In Section 7.1.1 the reader may find a more detailed explanation on the different adjustments to be included in the fair valuation of derivatives. In the case of a Level 2 liability derivative, the adjustment to its credit risk-free mid-market fair valuation would commonly include the following elements:

- An adjustment to reflect that there is a bid-ask in the market, and that if the bank were to unwind the derivative other market participants would require it to trade at the offer price. This adjustment increases the value of the liability.
- An adjustment to incorporate the risk that the bank will default before the maturity of the derivative when the derivative has a negative fair value (i.e., when the counterparty is owed under the derivative by the bank). This adjustment is termed **"Debit Valuation Adjustment"** (DVA), which reduces the absolute value of the liability.
- An adjustment, in the case of uncollateralised derivatives, to take into account the funding costs or benefits of having to hedge the position with other collateralised derivatives. This adjustment is termed **"Funding Valuation Adjustment"** (FVA), which increases the value of the liability.

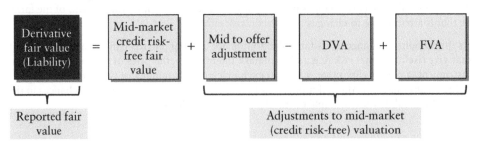

In the case of a Level 3 liability derivative, other adjustments may be needed. For example, an adjustment to incorporate model risk.

> CVA ("credit valuation adjustment") is the opposite of DVA, thus, being applied to derivative assets (i.e., derivatives with a positive fair value) to incorporate the possibility that the counterparty to the instrument may default and the positive fair value may not be realised in full.
>
> Therefore, the fair valuation of a derivative asset follows similar adjustments (mid-to-bid, CVA, FVA). All these adjustments reduce the fair value calculated using the mid-market valuation.

3.17.6 CVA/DVA Calculation from Netting Sets

The estimation of CVA/DVAs requires complex modelling methodologies that estimate the evolution of exposures over time and rely on assumptions and parameters. The process of calculating CVA/DVA can be divided into five steps (see Figure 3.38).

First Step: Collecting Netting Set Data   Commonly, before entering into derivatives trades with a counterparty, the bank and the counterparty have already signed a master agreement (e.g., an ISDA derivatives master agreement). All the derivatives formalised under a master agreement would be subject to the clauses stated in such agreement. If either the counterparty or the bank default, the settlement figure would be a single net amount representing the aggregate fair value, calculated at the time of default, of all the outstanding derivatives and related collateral entered into under such master agreement. All the derivatives under the same master agreement are grouped into a "**netting set**" for purposes of calculating CVA/DVA. A netting set is a group of derivatives, and their related collateral, with a single counterparty to which the entity is credit exposed on a net basis from a legal perspective.

The computation of CVA/DVA must take into account the netting set because the expected exposure becomes a portfolio measure rather than a single-derivative measure.

In a first step, the relevant data relating to a "**netting set**" is collected (see Figure 3.39) and all the market variables (commonly referred to as "**market factors**") that affect the fair valuation of the derivatives in the netting set are identified. Imagine, for example, that a EUR-based bank has an interest rate

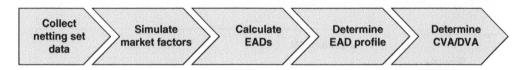

FIGURE 3.38   CVA/DVA calculation steps

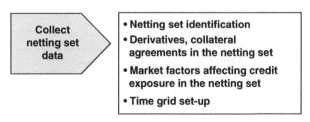

FIGURE 3.39   CVA/DVA calculation first step

swap with a counterparty and that the swap was linked to the Euribor 6-month. In the netting set the Euribor 6-month rate would be a market factor. Imagine further that another swap in the netting set was linked to USD Libor 3-month. That second swap would bring two additional market factors: the USD Libor 3-month rate and the EUR USD FX rate.

Finally, the period from the valuation date until the maturity of the longest derivative in the netting set is divided into time buckets (commonly referred to as the "**time grid**"). It is relatively common to divide the time period into quarterly time buckets.

Second Step: Simulating Market Factors   In a second step, the market factors identified in the previous step are simulated: a large number of paths of future behaviour of the market factors are generated along the time grid. The simulation is often generated using a Monte Carlo simulation method, which can simulate forward in time thousands of potential paths of movements of a market factor, based on a suitably chosen stochastic process for that market factor. This is the most complex part of the simulation process, especially when several market factors affect the netting set. The parameters of this process are calibrated based on historical market data (several years of history). The latest daily close of market values form the starting point of the simulation, and their volatilities and assumed correlations are added as inputs as well.

Imagine a single market factor: the Euribor 6-month rate. The bank would have also incorporated the term structure of volatilities of this interest rate using market cap and floor volatility information. The starting point of the Euribor 6-month rate would be its market level on valuation date (2% in our case). The result would be a large number of paths of future movement of the Euribor 6-month rate, as illustrated in Figure 3.40.

Third Step: Calculating Exposure at Default Profile   In a third step, the netting set's exposure at default profile is determined. In a first task within the third step, the credit risk-free fair value (or mark-to-market, "MtM") of each derivative in the netting set is calculated for each time bucket across each path of market factors. Each MtM represents the claim owed to the bank by the counterparty (a positive MtM) or by the bank to the counterparty (a negative MtM), were one of the two parties to the derivative to default. The MtM calculation takes into account credit mitigants such as collateral and break clauses. In our case, each path of Euribor 6-month rates generated a path of MtMs of the swap, each MtM path starting at EUR 390,000 and ending at a nil (see Figure 3.41).

The next task within the third step is to divide the paths of MtMs into two groups: a first group of positive MtMs and a second group of negative MtMs (see Figure 3.42). A positive MtM means that

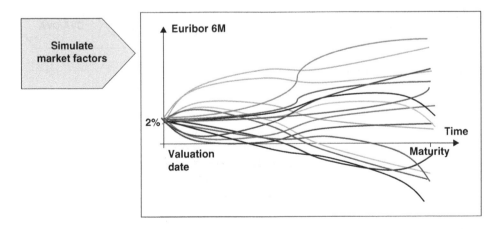

FIGURE 3.40   CVA/DVA calculation second step

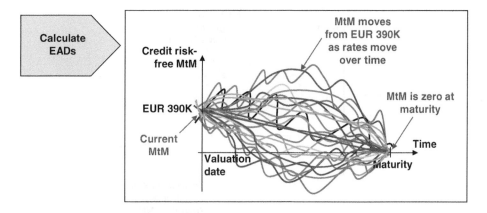

FIGURE 3.41   CVA/DVA calculation third step – first task

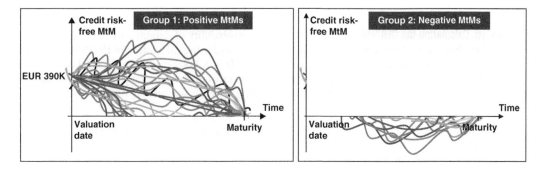

FIGURE 3.42   CVA/DVA calculation third step – second task

the bank is exposed to the counterparty's credit risk. Conversely, a negative MtM means that the counterparty is exposed to the bank's credit risk.

The third task within the third step is, for each group, to determine the EAD at each time bucket. A time bucket's EAD is calculated as the arithmetic average of the group's MtMs at such time bucket, as illustrated in Figure 3.43 for the group encompassing positive MtMs.

The end outcome of the third step is the EAD profile for each group, as illustrated in Figure 3.44.

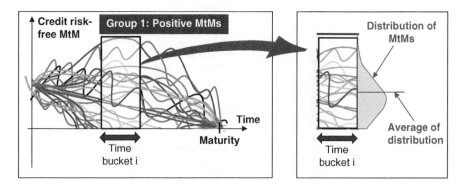

FIGURE 3.43   CVA/DVA calculation third step – third task

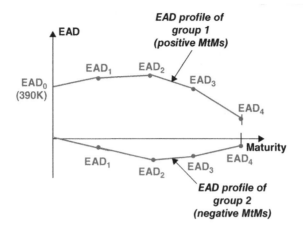

FIGURE 3.44   CVA/DVA calculation third step – final task

Fourth Step: Calculating the CVA/DVA   In a fourth step, the probability of default – PD – of the counterparty and the bank at each time bucket is calculated. The basis for the calculation of the PD is the CDS of the bank (or the counterparty's CDS as the case may be). If no CDS is trading in the market, PDs are calculated from other alternative sources. Figure 3.45 illustrates my own pecking order regarding the use of alternative sources when calculating the entity's PDs (or the counterparty's PDs):

- Yields may be available for publicly traded bonds issued by the entity;
- CDSs may be available for competitors with a financial situation (i.e., rating) similar to that of the entity;
- CDSs may be available for an index of companies in the entity's industry, region and rating;

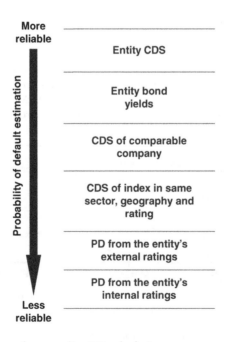

FIGURE 3.45   My own pecking order regarding PD calculation sources

- PDs may be available for the entity's external ratings from the reports published by the rating agencies (e.g., Moody's); or
- The entity's banks may have rated the entity using an internal rating system for which an equivalent external rating may be inferred.

Additionally, a Loss Given Default – LGD – is estimated for each time bucket for both the bank and the counterparty. Normally a constant LGD is assumed across all time buckets.

Next, the CVA/DVA is calculated as the sum of CVA and DVA. Because both amounts have opposite signs, there is a partial (or total) offset between them:

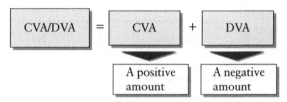

The CVA would be calculated as the sum of the expected loss at each time bucket of Group 1. The expected loss corresponding to a time bucket would be determined by multiplying the bucket's (i) the present value of the EAD, (ii) the counterparty's PD and (iii) counterparty's LGD:

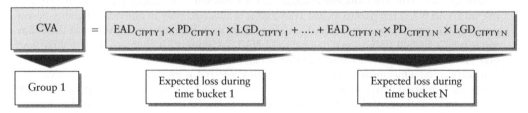

The DVA results in a negative amount, reducing the effect of the CVA. Similarly to the CVA calculation, the DVA would be calculated taking into account the present value of the EAD, and the entity's PDs and LGDs:

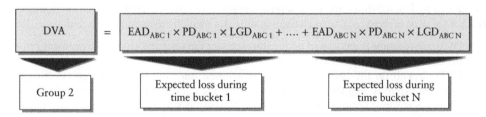

The overall CVA/DVA has been calculated for the portfolio of derivatives being part of the netting set. The final step in this process is to allocate the resulting CVA/DVA to the derivatives being part of the netting set.

When the derivatives and instruments are presented in a single line in the statement of financial position (e.g. because they are all assets or all liabilities or both but presented net) and they are not designated separately in a hedging relationship, disaggregating the single adjustment may not be necessary. However, in all other cases it will be necessary to allocate the net portfolio adjustment to the individual derivatives in the netting set. Whilst neither IFRS 13 nor IFRS 9 provides guidance on how to perform the allocation, IFRS 13 requires this allocation to be done on a reasonable and consistent basis. Two approaches are commonly used:

- A relative fair value approach (Figure 3.46): the overall CVA/DVA is allocated to either the individual asset derivatives or the individual liability derivatives. When the CVA amount exceeds the

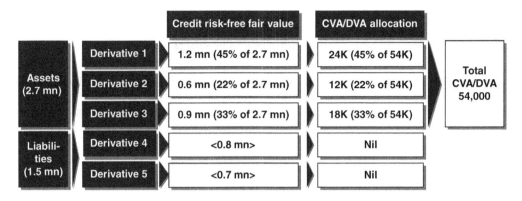

FIGURE 3.46   Example of CVA/DVA allocation using a relative fair value approach

DVA amount resulting in a positive amount, the overall CVA/DVA is referred to as just CVA and it is allocated only to individual asset derivatives based on the relative credit risk-free fair value of each asset derivative. Thus, in that case, liability derivatives would not be allocated any CVA. Conversely, when the DVA amount exceeds the CVA amount, resulting in a negative amount, the overall CVA/DVA is referred to as just DVA and it is allocated only to individual liability derivatives based on the relative credit risk-free fair value of each liability derivative. Figure 3.46 illustrates how a 54,000 CVA (a positive overall CVA/DVA amount) is allocated among three asset derivatives in a netting set according to their credit risk-free valuation;

- A relative credit adjustment approach: the overall CVA/DVA is allocated to each derivative (both assets and liabilities) based on their contribution to the CVA/DVA amount. This approach requires keeping track of the contribution of each derivative to the EAD profile. This method is theoretically sounder than the previous one, but in my opinion adds an operational complexity that is arguably difficult to justify.

Compared to debt liabilities, there are several complications associated with isolating changes in the fair value of derivatives due to changes in a bank's own creditworthiness, including:

- DVAs are commonly calculated taking into account the resulting credit risk exposures to all the derivatives in a netting set;
- DVAs depend on the bank's own creditworthiness and the market factors affecting the expected exposure that the derivative creates for the bank and the counterparty. Therefore, DVAs are sensitive not only to changes in creditworthiness (i.e., probabilities of default) but also to changes in all market factors that affect the expected exposures;
- DVAs exist irrespective of whether the current fair value of a derivative – or a netting set of derivatives – is positive (representing a net asset), zero or negative (representing a net liability).

3.17.7 Basel III Treatment of Own Credit Gains and Losses

Pursuant to [CRR 33(1)(b)], all unrealised gains or losses on liabilities of the bank valued at fair value resulting from changes in its own credit standing are deducted from CET1 capital. The adjustment to CET1 could either be positive or negative. It shall be a positive adjustment if there is a loss due to changes in own credit risk (i.e., if it reduces accounting equity) and vice versa.

CRR provides for an exception by allowing such gains and losses to be offset by a change in the fair value of another financial instrument resulting from changes in the bank's own credit standing.

Debt Instruments

Imagine a bank that issues a bond with an initial fair value of 100 and a claim on insolvency of 100, and that this bond is fair valued on the balance sheet.

When a bank issues a bond at par value, the bank is actually valuing the bond using a discount rate that reflects its own credit risk at the moment of issuance and investors will receive coupon payments that factor in that level of credit risk. There will be *no* own credit risk adjustment to CET1 at inception in respect of this bond.

If, subsequent to the bond issuance, the own credit risk of the bank deteriorates, the bond liability decreases. Let us assume that it decreases from 100 to 95. This (ignoring tax effects) creates 5 of CET1 through a 5 gain in OCI (or in profit or loss). However, it would not be appropriate to rely on this additional 5 of CET1 because if the bank fails, the claim of the bondholder is still 100, not 95. This means that the 5 of CET1 that was generated disappears in insolvency. In other words, the 5 of CET1 is not loss-absorbent.

The own credit risk filter ensures that a bank's capital is not increased when its own creditworthiness deteriorates and as a result there is a reduction in the value of its fair valued liabilities. Thus, this filter appears well advised in principle.

Derivatives

Imagine that a bank takes out a swap with a counterparty of equal credit standing, that the swap has zero fair value on inception and that the swap is the only derivative between the bank and the counterparty. The swap will have no CVA/DVA adjustment at inception, as the CVA would equal the DVA. At the moment of entering into the swap there will be *no* own credit risk adjustment to CET1 at inception in respect of this swap.

Alternatively, imagine that the bank takes out a swap with a counterparty of better credit standing, that the swap has zero value on inception and that the swap is the only derivative between the bank and the counterparty. The fair valuation of the swap would include a DVA adjustment (i.e., the DVA component would exceed the CVA component). Because the fair value of the swap at inception is zero, it would not be recognised on the balance sheet (in other words, it is neither an asset nor a liability). Although the own credit risk filter applies only to financial liabilities, Basel III would *require* the bank to apply own credit risk adjustment to CET1 at inception in respect of this swap. As a result the DVA adjustment at inception would be deducted from CET1 capital.

Then assume that the credit standing of the bank deteriorates. This deterioration leads to an increase of DVA. Let us assume that in this case a DVA increase of 5 is generated. The creation of this additional DVA on the balance sheet leads in turn to the creation of 5 in profit or loss (or in OCI). However, if the bank fails, the claim of the counterparty will likely be zero. In other words, the 5 of CET1 that was created by the DVA asset is not loss-absorbent. Consequently, in order to offset the CET1 creation stemming from the 5 units recognised in profit or loss (or in OCI), the bank would be required to deduct 5 from its CET1 capital.

However, in practice, the CVA/DVA related to this swap will be calculated in conjunction with all the derivatives agreed with the same counterparty under the same derivatives agreement.

3.18 DEFINED-BENEFIT PENSION PLANS

Broadly speaking, there are two types of pension plans: defined contribution pension plans and defined benefit pension plans (DBPPs). DBPPs affect regulatory capital through a specific filter from CET1. Because the starting point in calculating the impact of these plans in regulatory capital is their accounting amounts in the balance sheet, it is crucial for a bank to understand their accounting framework prior to embarking on initiatives on pension plans to enhance CET1 capital.

3.18.1 Defined Contribution vs. Defined Benefit Pension Plans

Defined contribution pension plans are pension plans where the level of benefits depends on the value of contributions paid in respect of each member and the investment performance achieved on those contributions. Therefore, a bank's liability is limited to the fixed contributions it has agreed to pay – it has no legal or constructive obligation to pay further contributions if the fund does not hold sufficient assets to pay the employee benefits. In other words, it is the employee who takes the risk of performance of the plan. The performance of the pension plan has no bearing on the bank's accounting.

Defined benefit pension plans are pension plans in which the bank has a legal obligation to provide agreed benefits to current and past employees. Benefits may be in the form of cash payments or in kind, such as medical, dental or pension benefits, which are usually dependent on one or more factors such as age, years of service and compensation. Defined benefit plans effectively place actuarial and investment risk on the bank as it has an obligation to make good any shortfall in benefits levels as set out in the plans legal agreement. Each agreement specifies the benefits to be paid, and the bank has an obligation to finance them accordingly. The majority of these plans define benefits in relation to an employee's final salary (typically the pension will be based on a percentage of final salary for each year of pensionable service). Another form of defined benefit plan is the average salary plan, where the pension is calculated by reference to average pay over an extended period.

3.18.2 Accounting Treatment of Defined Benefit Pension Plans

From an accounting perspective DBPPs are covered in IAS 19 *Employee Benefits*. IAS 19 assumes that a pension plan is classified as a DBPP unless it meets the criteria of a defined contribution plan. A defined contribution plan is defined as "the company's legal or constructive obligation is limited to the amount that it agrees to contribute to the plan".

In the case of DBPPs, DBPP assets and obligations are not recognised separately. Banks are required to recognise a **net defined benefit liability or asset** in their statement of financial position (i.e., balance sheet). This item represents the difference between (see Figure 3.47):

- DBPP obligations (or **defined benefit obligations**): the present value of the defined benefit obligations (i.e., the expected future payments required to settle the liabilities resulting from employees' past and current services) at the reporting date; and
- DBPP assets: the fair value, as of the reporting date, of any assets out of which the DBPP obligations are to be settled directly. In order to be included in the DBPP surplus/deficit calculations, assets shall meet a set of requirements.

Commonly, the net balance implies a deficit, and as a result, a **net defined benefit liability** is recognised in the balance sheet. This reflects that the bank has not contributed as much as into the plan as its obligations.

In the less frequent situation that the net balance amount is an asset (i.e., a surplus), a **net defined benefit asset** is recognised in the balance sheet. IAS 19 restricts the amount of the surplus that can be recognised. The asset to be recognised is limited the lower of (a) the surplus in the defined benefit plan;

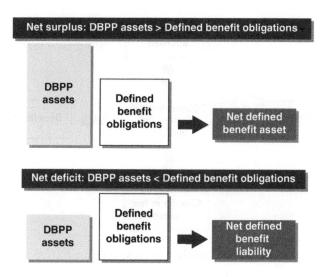

FIGURE 3.47 Defined benefit pension plans balance sheet recognition

and (b) the "**asset ceiling**". The asset ceiling is determined as the present value of any economic benefit available to the bank either in the form of a refund from the plan to which the bank has an unconditional right or a reduction in future contributions to the plan.

Measurement and Recognition of Defined Benefit Pension Plan Assets DBPP assets are measured at their fair value at the end of each reporting period. Where no market price is available, the fair value of plan assets is estimated, for example by discounting expected future cash flows using a discount rate that reflects both the risk associated with the plan assets and the maturity of those assets.

DBPP assets are tightly defined, and only assets that meet the following criteria may be included in the calculations:

- The assets are not held directly by the bank, but by a legally separated entity (commonly a fund or in the form of qualifying insurance policies);
- The assets exist solely for the purpose of meeting the DBPP obligations; and
- The assets cannot be returned to the bank unless all the DBPP obligations have been met.

Plan assets include any insurance policies issued by insurers that are not a related party ("qualifying insurance policies") used only to pay or fund employee benefits under the defined benefit plans and that are not available to the bank's own creditors (even in bankruptcy).

Unpaid contributions due from the bank, non-transferable financial instruments issued by the bank and held by the fund, and non-qualifying insurance policies are excluded from plan assets.

DBPP assets change during the reporting period. Three are the movements in a DBPP's assets (see Figure 3.48):

- **Contributions** represent payments from the bank into the DBPP and thus increase a DBPP's assets. The typical journal entries would be:

> DBPP assets XXX
>   Cash XXX

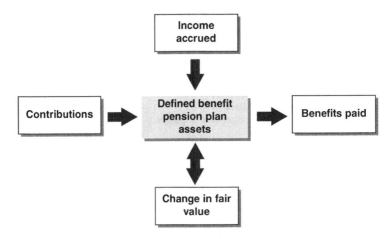

FIGURE 3.48   Changes in the assets of a defined benefit pension plan

- **Settlements** (i.e., benefits paid) are transactions that eliminate all further legal or constructive obligations for part or all of the benefits provided under a defined benefit plan. They represent payments to the DBPP's beneficiaries and therefore reduce liabilities. The typical journal entries would be:

> Defined benefit obligations   XXX
> > DBPP assets   XXX

- **Accrued income** (interest, dividends, and other income) from the DBPP assets. This income increases the amount of assets. The typical journal entries would be:

> DBPP assets   XXX
> > Financial income   XXX

- **Change in the fair value** of the DBPP assets. The typical journal entries would be:

> DBPP assets   XXX
> > DBPP reserve (OCI) income   XXX

Measurement and Recognition of Defined Benefit Obligations   According to IAS 19, a DBPP obligation represents "the expected future payments required to settle the obligation resulting from employee service in the current and prior periods". In other words, it reflects the present value of the expected future outflows that, without deducting any plan assets, will arise in respect of the benefits earned by employees under the bank's DBPPs. These benefits have accrued to employees through services rendered to date. Estimating defined benefit obligations is a complex task, requiring the aid of independent qualified actuaries.

A DBPP obligation (and related service costs) is determined using the "projected unit credit method", which sees each period of service as giving rise to an additional unit of benefit entitlement and measures each unit separately in building up the final obligation. Benefit is attributed to periods of service using the plan's benefit formula, unless an employee's service in later years will lead to a materially higher benefit than in earlier years, in which case a straight-line basis is used. This requires the bank to attribute benefit to the current period (to determine current service cost) and the current and prior periods (to determine the present value of defined benefit obligations).

The use of the projected unit credit method involves a number of actuarial assumptions. Actuarial assumptions are a bank's best estimate of the variables that determine the ultimate cost of providing post-employment benefits. The actuarial assumptions used must be unbiased and mutually compatible, and represent the best estimate of the variables determining the ultimate post-employment benefit cost. These assumptions can be grouped into demographic and financial assumptions:

Demographic assumptions, which are mainly based on past experience, commonly include:

- Mortality assumptions, determined by reference to the best estimate of the mortality of plan members during and after employment;
- Rate of employee turnover, disability and early retirement.

Financial assumptions, which must be based on market expectations at the end of the reporting period, typically include:

- Discount rate and expected rate of return on assets;
- Future expected salaries, medical costs and benefit levels. The assumption for salary increases reflects the long-term expectations for salary growth and takes into account inflation, seniority, promotion and other relevant factors such as supply and demand in the labour market;
- Contributions from employees or third parties.

The **discount rate** used is determined by reference to market yields at the end of the reporting period on high-quality corporate bonds, or where there is no deep market in such bonds, by reference to market yields on government bonds. Currencies and terms of bond yields used must be consistent with the currency and estimated term of the obligation being discounted. Commonly, high credit quality is assumed for AA- or better-rated issuers.

Recognition of Changes in a DBPP Assets and DBPP Obligations IAS 19 requires the recognition of all changes in the value of a net defined benefit liability (or asset) in the accounting period in which they occur. Changes are split into the following components (see Figure 3.49):

- **Current and past service costs** (i.e., the present value of the benefits earned by active employees), attributable to the current and past periods, are recognised in **profit or loss**;
- **Net interest** on the net defined benefit liability or asset, determined using the discount rate at the beginning of the period, is recognised in **profit or loss.** Net interest expense (income) represents the change in the DBPP as a result of the passage of time; and

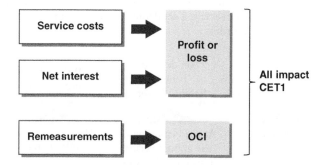

FIGURE 3.49 Items of a defined benefit pension plan recognised in profit or loss, or OCI

- **Remeasurements** of the net defined benefit liability or asset, including actuarial gains and losses, are recognised in **OCI**. Remeasurement gains and losses comprise actuarial gains and losses, return on plan assets (excluding amounts included in net interest on the net defined benefit asset or liability) and any change in the effect of the asset ceiling (excluding amounts included in net interest on the net defined benefit liability or asset). There is *no* subsequent reclassification of these amounts from OCI into profit or loss.

Past Service Costs   Past service costs arise when a bank amends a DBPP to provide lower or additional benefits for services in prior periods. It may be either positive or negative (i.e., it either increases or decreases the present value of the defined benefit obligation). IAS 19 requires all past service costs to be recognised immediately in profit or loss, regardless of vesting requirements. Past service costs arise as a result of either:

- **An amendment to the plan terms**: a change in the terms of a defined benefit plan so that a significant element of future service by current employees will no longer qualify for benefits or will qualify only for reduced benefits, or introduces new benefits to past service. An example would be to set a cap on the amount of benefits that an employee may receive upon retirement. A plan amendment that reduces the obligation to employees will be a negative past service cost; or
- **A curtailment**: a reduction in the number of employees participating in a DBPP. This reduction significantly diminishes the expected years of future service of present employees. A demonstrable commitment to making a significant reduction in the number of employees covered by a DBPP is considered to be a curtailment. An example would be a planned reduction in a bank's global markets group due to greatly diminished client derivatives activity.

Current Service Costs   IAS 19 defines current service costs as "the increase in the present value of the defined benefit obligation resulting from employee service in the current period". It represents the actuarially calculated present value of the pension benefits earned by the active employees in each period and is supposed to reflect the economic cost for each period based on current conditions. This cost is determined independently of the funding of the plan. In principle, therefore, for a given set of employees and benefit formula, the current service cost should be the same, irrespective of whether the plan is in surplus, in deficit or unfunded.

Net Interest   Commonly, there is interest on both a DBPP assets and DBPP obligations. IAS 19 requires interest on a DBPP to be recognised **net** in profit or loss. It represents the unwinding of the discount on the defined benefit obligations and a theoretical return on the DBPP assets. Net interest is calculated as the product of (i) the net benefit liability (or asset) and (ii) the discount rate used to calculate the DBPP obligation at the beginning of the annual period. The net benefit liability (asset) is determined at the beginning of the annual period and is adjusted to take into account any changes during the year as a result of contribution and benefits payments. When the DBPP results in a net defined liability, net interest is recognised as an expense and, conversely, a net defined benefit asset position results in net interest being recognised as income in profit or loss.

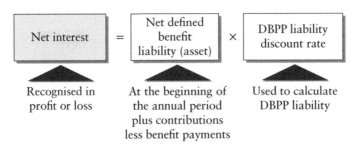

Example: Net Interest

The following simplified example depicts the calculation of net interest:

Net interest calculation	
Fair value of DBPP assets (expected return 4%)	1,200 mn
Present value of DBPP liabilities (discount rate 5%)	1,700 mn
Net defined benefit liability	<500 mn>
Net interest (<500 mn> × 5%)	<25 mn>

Because the rate to calculate net interest is the discount rate used to calculate the DBPP liability, net interest does not take into account the yield on the assets, even if the DBPP results in a net defined benefit asset. Recall that the discount rate is derived from market yields on high-quality corporate bonds and, therefore, it does not reflect the credit quality of the bank.

The riskiness of the DBPP assets is reflected in the fair value of the plan assets and the volatility of such fair valuation. A highly volatile asset portfolio may cause high volatility in OCI through the calculation of the net defined benefit liability (asset).

Settlement Gains/Losses   A settlement arises when the bank, or a third party, makes a payment to the employees covered by the DBPP that eliminates all further liability under the plan. A settlement gain or loss is defined as the difference between (a) the present value on the settlement date of the DBPP obligation being settled, and (b) the settlement price, including any DBPP assets transferred and any payments made directly by the bank. Settlements are recognised in profit or loss when they occur.

Remeasurements   Remeasurements comprise:

- **Actuarial gains and losses**: changes in the present value of the DBPP obligation that result from experience adjustments and changes in the actuarial assumptions;
- The **return on plan assets**, excluding amounts included in net interest on the net defined benefit liability (or asset); and
- Any change in the effect of the **asset ceiling**, excluding amounts included in net interest on the net defined benefit liability (or asset).

Remeasurements are recognised in the bank's balance sheet immediately, with a charge or credit to other comprehensive income (OCI) in the periods in which they occur. Amounts recognised in OCI are *not* reclassified through profit or loss, but through other items of shareholders' equity (e.g., retained earnings).

3.18.3 Regulatory Treatment of Defined Benefit Pension Plans

It was explained previously that on the balance sheet a DBPP is recognised as either a net defined benefit liability or asset. The regulatory treatment of DBPPs is asymmetric, as a regulatory capital filter is applied to net defined benefit assets while no filter exists for net defined benefit liabilities:

- A **net defined benefit liability**, as reported on the balance sheet, is fully recognised in the calculation of CET1 capital; while
- A **net defined benefit asset** is deducted from CET1 capital, subject to some adjustments (to be covered next).

The asymmetric treatment of net defined benefit assets and liabilities provides little encouragement to banks to make contributions in excess to their DBPP obligations.

Net Defined Benefit Asset Deduction from CET1   Pursuant to [CRR 36(1)(e) and 41] any recognised net defined benefit asset, net of any associated deferred tax liability, is deducted from CET1 capital rather than being risk-weighted.

This treatment addresses the concern that assets arising from pension funds may not be capable of being withdrawn and used for the protection of depositors and other creditors of a bank. The concern assumes that their only value stems from a reduction in future payments into the fund.

The amount to be deducted is calculated as follows:

- The amount of defined benefit pension fund assets on the balance sheet of the bank (i.e., the net defined benefit asset); less
- The amount of any associated deferred tax liability which could be extinguished if the assets became impaired or were derecognised under the applicable accounting framework; less
- Subject to prior permission of the competent authority, the amount of assets in the defined benefit pension fund which the bank has an unrestricted ability to use. These assets are risk-weighted instead, as if they were owned directly by the bank.

$$\boxed{\text{Deduction from CET1}} = \boxed{\text{Net defined benefit assets}} - \boxed{\text{Associated deferred tax liabilities}} - \boxed{\text{Defined benefit plans unrestricted assets}}$$

The third component involves DBPP assets over which the bank has unrestricted ability to use them. This entails immediate and unfettered access to the assets such as when the use of the assets is not barred by a restriction of any kind and there are no claims of any kind from third parties on these assets. Unfettered access to the assets is likely to exist when the bank is not required to request and receive specific approval from the manager of the pension funds or the pension beneficiaries each time it accesses excess funds in the DBPP.

3.18.4 Initiatives to Enhance CET1 Impact of Defined Benefit Pension Plans

DBPPs impact CET1 capital through three different elements:

- Through the filter (i.e., a direct deduction) from CET1;
- Through profit or loss; and
- Through OCI.

Enhancements through the Filter   It was explained in the previous sections that, from an accounting perspective, a net defined benefit asset is recognised on the balance sheet when the DBPP assets exceed the DBPP obligations. It was also mentioned above that a net defined benefit asset is deducted from CET1 capital. Therefore, banks with substantial net defined benefit asset values would be inclined to stop making contributions to DBPPs in order to gain a more balanced relation between DBPP assets and DBPP liabilities.

Another CET1 enhancement initiative would be to change the terms of a DBPP to allow the bank have unrestricted access to the amount of assets exceeding the amount of DBPP obligations. Remember that the amount to be deducted from CET1 capital is adjusted for the amount of DBPP assets which the bank has an unrestricted ability to use. This is often a challenging initiative due to legal constraints and the potential emergence of conflicts of interest between the bank and the DBPP beneficiaries.

Enhancements through Profit or Loss　Service costs attributable to the current and past periods, and net interest are recognised in profit or loss, and consequently, affect CET1 capital. Therefore:

- Past service costs (i.e., amendments to the terms of a DBPP or curtailments) which imply lower future benefits strengthen CET1 capital. The opposite also holds true.
- A reduction in the discount rate (i.e., a decrease in market yields on high-quality corporate bonds) in a DBPP which is recognised on the balance sheet as a net defined benefit liability (i.e., the DBPP liabilities exceed the DBPP assets) reduces net interest expense and, as a result, has a positive impact on CET1 capital. The opposite also holds true. This effect partially off-sets the impact on the remeasurement of DBPP liabilities stemming from changes in the discount rate.
- An increase in the discount rate in a DBPP which is recognised as a net defined benefit asset (i.e., the DBPP assets exceed the DBPP liabilities) on the balance sheet increases net interest income and, as a result, has a positive impact on CET1 capital. The opposite also holds true.

Enhancements through OCI　Remeasurement gains and losses arising on DBPPs are recognised in OCI and, therefore, impact **CET1 capital**. CET1 may decline when the fair value of DBPP assets decline, their investment returns decrease or the estimated value of defined benefit obligations increase. The opposite also holds true. Therefore, changes in salaries, turnover, mortality, early retirement and return on assets may affect a bank's level of CET1 capital.

It was observed previously that a DBPP surplus can only be recognised on the balance sheet to the extent that it does not exceed the estimated future economic benefit (i.e., a surplus is subject to the so-called "asset ceiling"). Where the amount of surplus recognised has been capped, any reduction in the asset ceiling will reduce CET1. Changes in the surplus, due to changes in the defined benefit obligations or fair value of DBPP assets, will not affect CET1 until the surplus falls below the cap.

The enhancements through OCI usually target reductions in CET1 volatility and procyclicality rather than addressing CET1 levels directly.

Under IAS 19, remeasurements of DBPP assets and defined benefit obligations at each balance sheet date may be highly volatile, being sensitive to point-in-time fair values of DBPP assets and point-in-time estimations of defined benefit obligations. Reducing volatility in CET1 caused by volatility of DBPP remeasurements requires careful analysis of the variables influencing values of DBPP assets and obligations. For example, a DBPP net position could be adversely affected by any increase in long term inflation assumptions.

Additionally, when reducing the volatility of estimations of defined benefit obligations, banks should take into account the periodicity of such undertakings. Some variables affecting these assessments are estimated every year while other variables are estimated, for instance, every three years.

It is relevant to note that IAS 19's use of yields on high-quality corporate bonds (typically yields on bonds of AA-rated corporate issuers) to discount defined benefit obligations is arguably a rather arbitrary one. Yields on high-quality corporate bonds may bear little relation to the actual funding levels of the bank, especially when DBPP obligations are long term. Banks entering into hedges of these yields to reduce volatility in OCI (and as a result to reduce CET1 volatility) may encounter undesirable effects when these yields bear little relation to the underlying economics of the bank's defined benefit obligations.

Additionally, when hedging CET1 volatility banks should carefully assess the correlation between other variables and yields on high-quality corporate bonds. For example, there may exist a natural offset between inflation and these yields.

It is important to point out that IAS 19's accounting treatment of DBPPs has a procyclical nature which is not corrected by regulatory capital.

During the onset of a financial crisis, fair values of equity instruments and corporate bonds tend to fall as investors fly to higher quality bonds or sell assets to obtain needed liquidity, reducing the value of DBPP assets.

Simultaneously, credit spreads of bonds tend rise while interest rates fall. The effect on defined benefit obligations depends on the net effect of these two variables. Usually, the fall in interest rates exceed the widening in credit spreads on high-quality corporate bonds, increasing the present value of the defined benefit obligations.

Therefore, during times of economic downturn a decrease in CET1 capital levels would be expected, due to the negative remeasurement effects of declining fair values of DBPP assets and rising values of defined benefit obligations. Alternatively, when economic conditions improve, the effect would be the opposite, strengthening CET1 capital levels.

These procyclicality effects are in theory addressed through the countercyclical buffer. However, the requirements on this buffer do not depend on the size of the DBPPs of a bank. Banks with large DBPPs willing to hedge these procyclical effects would need to put in place specific hedges to reduce such effects.

3.18.5 Additional Considerations

My final comments are quite philosophical. The whole purpose of CET1 capital is to absorb losses and help banks remain "going concerns" (i.e., to remain solvent). When a bank has a large net defined liability on its balance sheet, it means that the bank is expected to make substantial contributions in the future to meet the DBPP future payments to its beneficiaries. Thus, in principle it makes sense to require the bank to hold CET1 capital to meet such obligations. However, the remeasurement of DBPP assets at each reporting date while DBPP obligations are long term in nature may contribute to excessively volatile CET1 levels, which is an undesirable outcome.

Another interesting discussion arises on the effect of DBPPs in a "gone concern" (i.e., insolvency) situation, which depends on the bankruptcy laws pertaining to the jurisdiction in which the DBPP is based. Ideally, it would have been better bank capital rules that consider whether a bank is liable for the shortfall of a pension fund when being in a gone concern situation.

3.19 CASE STUDY: LLOYDS' DE-RISKING OF ITS DEFINED BENEFIT PENSION PLANS

As at 31 December 2013, the British bank Lloyds Banking Group ("Lloyds") operated six defined benefit pension schemes (DBPPs) with total assets of GBP 32.6 billion. The amount of pension benefit that a beneficiary employee would receive on retirement was dependent on several factors, such as age, years of service and salary. Around one third of the bank's workforce (around 35,000) were earning pension benefits in these schemes which had been closed to new entrants for a number of years. The remaining two thirds of its workforce were members of a defined contribution scheme called "Your Tomorrow".

Full actuarial valuations of Lloyds' main DBPPs were carried out every three years. with interim reviews in the intervening years; these valuations were updated to 31 December each year by qualified independent actuaries. For the purposes of these annual updates, DBPP assets were included at their fair value and DBPP liabilities were measured on an actuarial basis using the so-called projected unit credit method. The DBPP liabilities were discounted using rates equivalent to the market yields at the balance sheet date on high-quality corporate bonds that were denominated in the currency in which the benefits would be paid, and that had terms to maturity approximating to the terms of the related pension liability.

During 2012 and 2013, Lloyds took several initiatives related to its DBPPs (see Figure 3.50), which are described next.

3.19.1 Changes during 2012

During 2012, following a review of policy in relation to the bank's DBPPs, increases in certain schemes were subsequently linked to the UK Consumer Price Index rather than the UK Retail Price Index. The impact of this change was a reduction in Lloyds' DBPP obligation of GBP 258 million. This change was deemed to be an amendment to the plans' terms, affecting past service costs, and thus recognised as a gain in the bank's 2012 profit or loss statement. The effect on CET1 was a GBP 258 million improvement, assuming that no taxes were levied on such gain (Lloyds had plenty of deferred tax assets in 2012).

3.19.2 Changes during 2013

During 2013, Lloyds assessed the sensitivity of its DBPPs to market and other risks through stress tests. The bank concluded that its DBPPs were exposed to a number of significant risks, including:

- **Inflation rate risk:** the majority of the DBPP obligations were linked to inflation both in deferment and in payment. Higher inflation would lead to higher liabilities, although this would be partially offset by holdings of inflation-linked gilts and, in most cases, caps on the level of inflationary increases were in place to protect against extreme inflation.

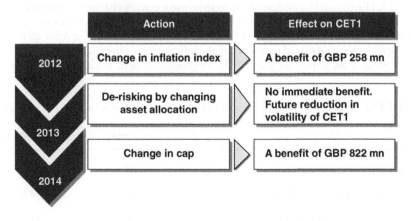

FIGURE 3.50   Initiatives taken by Lloyds on its defined benefit pension plans

■ **Credit risk:** DBPP assets comprised direct investments in bonds and therefore exposed DBPP assets to a widening of credit spreads. However, credit spread risk also arose from the DBPP liabilities discount rate, which partially offset the credit risk from the credit portfolio. DBPP liabilities were determined using a discount rate derived from yields on AA-rated corporate bonds. A decrease in corporate bond yields would increase DBPP liabilities, although this would be partially offset by an increase in the value of bond holdings.

■ **Interest rate risk:** Bond holdings were also exposed to interest rate risk. An increase in interest rates would reduce the value of these bonds. Rising interest rates would reduce DBPP liabilities.

■ **Equity risk:** DBPP assets comprised direct investments in equity instruments and, as a result, were exposed to falling equity prices.

■ **Longevity risk:** The majority of the DBPPs were to provide benefits for the life of the members so increases in life expectancy would result in an increase in the DBPP liabilities. Assumptions were made regarding the expected lifetime of DBPP members based upon recent experience and extrapolated the improving trend. However, given the rate of advance in medical science and increasing levels of obesity, it was uncertain whether they will ultimately reflect actual experience.

■ **Investment risk:** DBPP assets were invested in a diversified portfolio of debt securities, equities and other return-seeking assets. If the assets underperformed the discount rate used to calculate DBPP liabilities, it would reduce the surplus or increase the deficit.

■ **Volatility in asset values and the discount rate** would lead to volatility in the net defined benefit obligation on the bank's balance sheet and in OCI. To a lesser extent this would also lead to volatility in the pension expense in the bank's profit or loss statement.

Next Lloyds ranked the different market risk exposures, as shown in the following table (inflation risk was part of the interest rate bucket):

Market risk exposure				
Interest rate	FX	Credit	Equity	Inflation
Medium	Low	High	Medium	High

In order to reduce the volatility of the net defined benefit liability, a rates and inflation hedging programme was implemented. Additionally, high-quality credit assets and alternative assets were purchased by the pension plans while equities were sold. These changes were expected to reduce OCI volatility, which would translate in a lower CET1 volatility as shown in Table 3.19.

3.19.3 Changes during 2014

In March 2014, Lloyds reached an agreement to implement certain changes to its DBPPs. After consultation with trustees and recognised unions, Lloyds decided to revise the cap on the increases in pensionable pay used in calculating the pension benefit, from 2% to 0% with effect April 2014 (i.e., prior to this change benefits were increased each year by the inflation rate plus 2%). Lloyds believed that while the DBPPs remained an important part of the employees' benefit package, the announced change

TABLE 3.19 Initiatives taken by Lloyds to reduce its OCI Volatility due to its DBPPs

		Dec-2012	Dec-2013
% of assets held in equities	⬇	32%	18%
% of rates exposure hedged	⬆	45%	54%
% of inflation exposure hedged	⬆	54%	71%

represented the right balance between providing fairer pension benefits to all its employees and managing the bank's regulatory capital and risk position.

The effect of this change was to reduce Lloyd's net defined benefit liability recognised on its balance sheet by GBP 822 million, with a corresponding curtailment gain recognised in the profit or loss statement. That gain had a 24 basis points (i.e., 0.24%) positive effect on Lloyds' fully loaded CET1 capital ratio.

The net defined benefit liability recognised in Lloyds' balance sheet at 31 December 2013 in respect of its defined benefit obligations was GBP 998 million, comprising DBPP assets of GBP 98 million and DBPP liabilities of GBP 1,096 million. Six months later, Lloyds reported a net defined benefit liability totalling GBP 659 million, a substantial reduction largely aided by the curtailment:

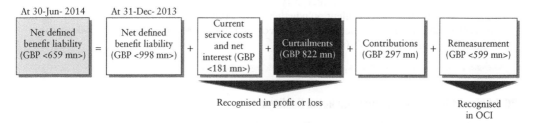

The effect of the curtailment in CET1 capital was the after-tax amount resulting from the GBP 822 million pre-tax gain.

3.20 HOLDINGS BY A BANK OF OWN CET1 INSTRUMENTS

Pursuant to [CRR 36(1)(f), 42] and to avoid double-counting of own capital, a bank is required under Basel III to fully deduct from CET1 capital holdings of own CET1 instruments, whether held directly, indirectly or synthetically (such as through holdings of index securities). The filter applies irrespective of the location of the exposure in the banking book or the trading book. In addition, any such instruments which the bank could be contractually obliged to purchase should also be deducted.

> **Indirect holdings** are defined in [CRR 4(114)] as "any exposure to an intermediate entity that has an exposure to capital instruments issued by a financial sector entity where, in the event the capital instruments issued by the financial sector entity were permanently written off, the loss that the institution would incur as a result would not be materially different from the loss the institution would incur from a direct holding of those capital instruments issued by the financial sector entity".
> By restricting the definition to holdings of capital instruments, the CRR does not capture exposures to financial sector entities gained through other forms of investments in the unconsolidated intermediate entity.
> **Synthetic holdings** are defined in [CRR 4(126)] as "an investment by an institution in a financial instrument the value of which is directly linked to the value of the capital instruments issued by a financial sector entity".

Gross long positions may be deducted net of short positions (i.e., only the net long position is deducted) only if both the following conditions are met:

- The long and short positions are in the same underlying exposure and the short positions involve no counterparty risk; and
- Either both the long and the short positions are held in the trading book or both are held in the banking book.

The requirement that gross long positions may be deducted net of short positions only if the short positions involve "no" counterparty risk is arguably too restrictive and probably difficult to attain on a practical basis.

From a theoretical perspective, a short position may bear no counterparty credit risk only where all the market value of the CET1 instruments being short is posted upfront and in cash by the counterparty, a notably uncommon situation.

The CRR does not state whether a short position in own CET1 instruments settled against a QCCP is considered to be "counterparty risk-free", although from a theoretical perspective the bank would have some degree of counterparty risk to the QCCP.

Similarly, the CRR remains silent on whether a short position a short position taken through a fully collateralised OTC transaction (which involves a low degree of counterparty risk) is considered to be "counterparty risk-free".

3.20.1 Indirect Holdings Arising from Index Holdings

Regarding direct, indirect and synthetic holdings of index securities, banks are required to calculate the underlying exposure to own CET1 instruments included in those indices, and to deduct such exposures from CET1 capital.

An indirect holding arising from an index holding comprises the proportion of the index invested in the CET1 instruments (or AT1 and Tier 2 instruments where the bank calculates its own AT1 or Tier 2 capital) of financial sector entities included in the index. An index includes, but is not limited to, index funds, equity or bond indices or any other scheme where the underlying instrument is a capital instrument issued by the bank.

Banks may net gross long positions in own CET1 instruments, resulting from holdings of index securities against short positions in own CET1 instruments resulting from short positions in the underlying indices, including where those short positions involve counterparty risk, provided that both the following conditions are met:

- The long and short positions are in the same underlying indices; and
- Either both the long and the short positions are held in the trading book or both are held in the banking book.

The requirement to look through index securities is operationally complex, especially when structured options are involved. In my view this requirement is unnecessary as it is quite unlikely that a bank would enter into an index to synthetically buyback its own CET1 instruments. Imagine a bank part of the Eurostoxx 50 index. A synthetic long position in its own shares would require the bank being long the index and short the other 49 constituents of the index, a notably costly position.

Banks active in the equity derivatives market typically have substantial positions in equity indices (e.g., the Eurostoxx50 index, the S&P 500 index, etc.) as part of their market-making and client activities. Fortunately for them, the possibility of netting long and short positions have a strong effect on those banks as they commonly have balanced long and short positions, which facilitates market liquidity. Otherwise, it would lead to an unnecessary imbalance.

Netting of Long and Short Index Positions   [CRR 76] states that banks may reduce the amount of a long position in a capital instrument by the portion of an index that is made up of the same underlying exposure that is being hedged, provided the following conditions are met:

1. Either both the long position being hedged and the short position in an index used to hedge that long position are held in the trading book or both are held in the non-trading book;
2. The positions referred to in the previous paragraph are held at fair value on the balance sheet of the bank; and
3. The short position referred to in point (1) qualifies as an effective hedge under the internal control processes of the bank. The competent authorities shall assess the adequacy of those control processes on at least an annual basis and are satisfied with their continuing appropriateness.

Use of a Conservative Estimate as an Alternative – Operationally Burdensome   Subject to obtaining prior permission from the competent authority, a bank may use a **conservative estimate** of the underlying exposure of the bank to capital instruments included in indices as an alternative to a bank calculating its exposure to the items referred to in either or both:

- Own CET1 (or AT1 and Tier 2 instruments where the bank calculates its own AT1 or Tier 2 capital) included in indices; and
- CET1 (or AT1 and Tier 2 instruments where the bank calculates its own AT1 or Tier 2 capital) instruments of financial sector entities, included in indices.

To use the conservative estimate approach the bank has to demonstrate to the satisfaction of the competent authorities that it would be operationally burdensome for the bank to monitor its underlying exposure to the indices. The conservative estimate of the exposures uses a structure-based approach which, according to the EBA, involves either:

- The use of a **percentage** as an estimate for the value of the holdings that shall be deducted from own funds. This approach can be used when the capital instrument of a financial sector entity which is part of the index cannot exceed a maximum percentage of the index, in accordance with its investment mandate. This maximum percentage is the one applied for the estimate; or
- In the event that the bank is unable to determine the maximum percentage as referred to in the previous paragraph and the index, in particular in accordance with its investment mandate, the bank shall take into account the full amount of the index holdings for the deduction from own funds.

The deduction shall be operated on a corresponding deduction approach (i.e., from CET1, AT1 or Tier 2 capital, as appropriate). In situations where the bank cannot determine the precise nature of the holding, the value of the holding is deducted from CET1 capital.

According to the EBA, operationally burdensome is a situation under which look-through approaches to capital holdings in financial sector entities on an ongoing basis are unjustified, as assessed by the competent authorities. In their assessment of the nature of operationally burdensome situations, competent authorities shall take into account the **low materiality** and **short holding period** of such positions. A holding period of short duration shall require the strong liquidity of the index to be evidenced.

According to the EBA, a position is deemed to be of **low materiality** where all of the following conditions are met:

- The **individual** net exposure arising from index holdings measured before any look-through is performed does not exceed 2% of CET1 items as defined in [CRR 46(1)(a)] (i.e., the CET1 capital used to set the 10% threshold used to calculate the deduction of holdings of CET1 instruments where an institution does not have a significant investment in a financial sector entity);
- The **aggregated** net exposure arising from index holdings measured before any look-through is performed does not exceed 5% of CET1 items as defined in [CRR 46(1)(a)];

■ The sum of the aggregated net exposure arising from index holdings measured before any look-through is performed and any other holdings that shall be deducted pursuant to [CRR 36(1)(h)] (i.e., the applicable amount of direct, indirect and synthetic holdings by the bank of CET1 instruments of financial sector entities where the bank does not have a significant investment in those entities) does not exceed 10% of CET1 items as defined in [CRR 46(1)(a)].

3.20.2 Requirements for the Repurchase of Own CET1 Instruments

Pursuant to [CRR 78] banks need supervisory permission to repurchase or redeem own CET1 instruments, unless the repurchase is carried out for market making or employee remuneration purposes (subject to conditions). The requirements are covered in Section 4.2.6.

3.21 CASE STUDY: DANSKE BANK'S SHARE BUYBACK PROGRAMME

In 2014, the Danish bank Danske Bank ("Danske") decided to initiate a share buyback programme of DKK 5 billion. Using the price prevailing at the time of disclosure, 29 million shares were expected to be bought back, and the programme would run in the period from 30 March 2015 to 31 December 2015.

At 31 December 2014, the CET1 capital ratio and the total capital ratio were 15.1% and 19.3%, respectively, well above the minimum requirements. Such a high capital ratios limited the return on equity of the Danish bank. The purpose of the share buyback programme was to adjust the share capital to better reflect Danske's capital targets.

3.21.1 Legal Background

The share buyback programme would be initiated pursuant to the authorisation granted to the Board of Directors by the general meeting on 18 March 2015. The total number of shares that could be acquired under the programme may not exceed 10% of the total share capital (the legal maximum in the EU). Danske's board of directors intended to propose to the general meeting in 2016 that the shares be cancelled. Danske was entitled to suspend or stop the programme at any time subject to announcement to Nasdaq Copenhagen.

The programme was to be executed under the European Commission's Regulation No. 2273/2003 of 22 December 2003 (the EU's safe harbour regulation). The share buyback would be handled by Danske. Pursuant to this regulation:

■ No shares could be bought back at a price exceeding the higher of (i) the share price of the latest independent trade and (ii) the highest current independent offer price on Nasdaq Copenhagen. In other words, Danske could only take already existing offers, being forbid to make a new price; and
■ The total number of shares that could be purchased on a single trading day could not exceed 25% of the average daily trading volume over the preceding 20 trading days on Nasdaq Copenhagen. In other words, in a given day Danske could not execute a number of shares such as to have a substantial effect on that day's the trading volume.

3.21.2 Accounting Impact

Let us assume that on 31 December 2015 Danske completed its share buyback programme spending DKK 5 billion.

Under IFRS 32, where the bank or any entity of the group purchases the bank's share capital, the consideration paid is deducted from shareholders' equity as treasury shares until they are cancelled.

When such shares are subsequently sold, reissued or otherwise disposed of, any consideration received is included in shareholders' equity, net of any directly attributable incremental transaction costs and related income tax effects. Therefore, the repurchased own shares reduced Danske's shareholders' equity by DKK 5 billion, as shown in Figure 3.51. As the shares were purchased in cash, the carrying amount of its "cash and cash equivalents" item was reduced by DKK 5 billion.

3.21.3 CET1 Capital Impact

Let us assume that Danske's fully loaded CET1 ratio without the buyback comprised DKK 131.1 billion and DKK 865.8 billion of CET1 capital and RWAs respectively (I have taken figures from the end of 2014), resulting in a 15.1% CET1 ratio.

The DKK 5 billion reduction in Danske's shareholders' equity stemming from the share buyback would have an equal impact on its CET1 capital. Consequently, Danske's CET1 capital would be DKK 126.1 billion (= 131.1 bn − 5 bn) and its CET1 capital ratio would be 14.6% (= 126.1 bn/865.8 bn), a 50 basis points reduction but still a substantially high ratio:

The impact on CET1 capital was expected to be partially offset with the organic generation of CET1 stemming from the bank's positive net income.

It is important to note that from a regulatory perspective, the buyback programme had additional impacts:

- The reduction in Tier 1 capital would have a negative impact on Danske's leverage ratio; and
- The outflow of cash would have a negative impact on Danske's liquidity metrics, especially in its liquidity coverage ratio.

3.22 CASE STUDY: DEUTSCHE BANK'S TREASURY SHARES STRATEGY

This case study illustrates the impact on CET1 capital of transactions on own shares, in particular analysing Deutsche Bank's strategy on own shares during 2014. Once again I cover in detail the accounting impact of such transactions before addressing the regulatory capital issues.

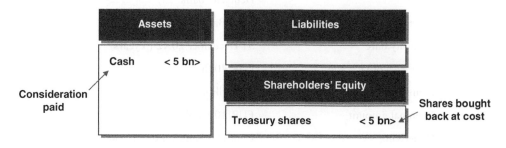

FIGURE 3.51 Impact of its buyback programme on Danske Bank's statement of financial position

3.22.1 Governance Related to Deutsche Bank's Acquisition of Own Shares

Deutsche Bank's shareholders in the 2014 AGM granted the management board the authorisation to buy back up to 10% of the share capital (i.e., 101.9 million shares) before the end of April 2019. A maximum of 51 million shares (5% of the share capital at the time of the resolution by the AGM on this authorisation) could be purchased by using derivatives (put and call options or forward purchase contracts). The bank could accordingly sell to third parties put options based on physical delivery and buy call options from third parties, provided that these options were fulfilled only with shares, which themselves were acquired subject to compliance with the principle of equal treatment. The term of the options had to be selected such that the share purchase upon exercising the option was carried out at the latest on 30 April 2019.

The purchase price to be paid for the shares upon exercise of the **put options** or upon the maturity of the **forward purchase** could not exceed more than 10% or fall below 10% of the average of the share prices (closing auction prices of the Deutsche Bank share in Xetra trading and/or in a comparable successor system on the Frankfurt Stock Exchange) on the last three stock exchange trading days before conclusion of the respective transaction in each case, excluding ancillary purchase costs but taking into account the option premium received.

Call options could only be exercised if the purchase price to be paid did not exceed by more than 10% or fall below 10% of the average of the share prices (closing auction prices of the Deutsche Bank share in Xetra trading and/or in a comparable successor system on the Frankfurt Stock Exchange) on the last three stock exchange trading days before the acquisition of the shares.

In addition to the shareholders' authorisations, Deutsche Bank received approval from the German banking regulator – BaFin – for the execution of these authorisations as required under the CRR rules.

3.22.2 Accounting and Regulatory Impact of Forwards on Own Shares

A physically settled forward on own shares is an obligation to purchase a number of own shares at a pre-specified future date. Let us assume that on 1 January 20X0 Deutsche Bank entered into a forward purchase on its own shares with XYZ Bank that allowed for physical settlement only with the terms in Table 3.20:

TABLE 3.20 Main Terms of Deutsche Bank's Forward on its own Shares

Physically-settled Forward Terms	
Start date	1 January 20X0
Counterparties	Deutsche Bank and XYZ Bank
Buyer	Deutsche Bank
Seller	XYZ Bank
Maturity date	31 December 20X2 (3 years)
Reference price	EUR 40.00
Number of shares	2.5 million
Nominal amount	EUR 100 million
Underlying	Deutsche Bank's ordinary shares
Settlement	Physical delivery only

At maturity (i.e., 31 December 20X2) Deutsche Bank was obliged to acquire 2.5 million own shares and to pay EUR 100 million. Because in all scenarios the instrument implied the exchange of a fixed number of shares for a fixed amount of cash (i.e., it met the so-called "fixed-for-fixed" requirement), it was classified from an accounting viewpoint as an equity instrument, as opposed to a derivative.

Initial Recognition The forward was initially recognised as a deduction of equity and a liability, as shown in Figure 3.52. The initial carrying amount of the liability represented the present value of the settlement amount of the forward, discounted using the yield of debt issued by Deutsche Bank with the same term. The liability represented the future payment obligation under the forward. A corresponding charge was made to shareholders' equity and recorded as "forward on own shares".

Let us assume that 3-year straight bonds issued by Deutsche Bank were trading at a 5% yield on 1 January 20X0. At inception, the present value of the final consideration was EUR 86,384,000 [$= 100 \text{ mn}/(1 + 5\%)^3$]. The accounting entries were the following:

On 1 January 20X0 (trade inception):	
Forward on own shares (Equity)	86,384,000
Forward obligation (Liability)	86,384,000

From a CET1 perspective, the reduction in accounting shareholders' equity, in turn, generated a corresponding reduction in the bank's CET1 capital (see Figure 3.52). As a result, at inception Deutsche Bank's CET1 declined by EUR 86,384,000, the present value of the forward settlement amount.

Subsequent Recognition The liability component was recognised at amortised cost using the effective interest rate method. During the life of the forward the carrying value of the liability would be increasing to reach the final EUR 100 million consideration, as shown in Table 3.21.

On each reporting date, Deutsche Bank recognised the interest expense related to the accrual of the liability. For example, the interest expense recognised during the first year was EUR 4,319,000, or EUR 2,591,000 on an after-tax basis (assuming a 40% tax rate). Supposing that the bank's net profit was externally verified, the impact on CET1 of the interest expense was a reduction of EUR 2,591,000, as shown in Figure 3.53.

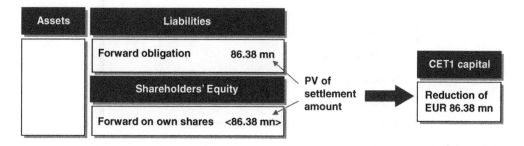

FIGURE 3.52 Initial recognition of Deutsche Bank's forward on own shares

TABLE 3.21   Calculation of Interest Expense and Carrying Amount of the Liability

Date	Interest Expense	Liability Carrying Value
1-Jan-X0		86,384,000
31-Dec-X0	4,319,000[1]	90,703,000
31-Dec-X1	4,535,000[2]	95,238,000[3]
31-Dec-X2	4,762,000	100,000,000

Notes:
[1] $4,319,000 = 86,384,000 \times 5\%$
[2] $4,535,000 = 90,703,000 \times 5\%$
[3] $95,238,000 = 90,703,000 + 4,535,000$

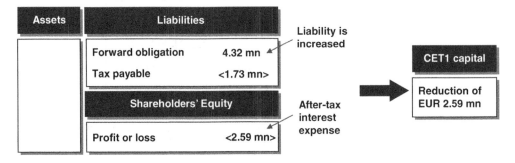

FIGURE 3.53   Recognition of Deutsche Bank's forward on own shares during the first year

The accounting entries, assuming yearly accounting periods for simplicity, were the following:

On 31 December 20X0:		
Interest expense (Profit or loss)	4,319,000	
Forward obligation (Liability)		4,319,000
On 31 December 20X1:		
Interest expense (Profit or loss)	4,535,000	
Forward obligation (Liability)		4,535,000
On 31 December 20X2:		
Interest expense (Profit or loss)	4,762,000	
Forward obligation (Liability)		4,762,000

Recognition at Maturity   Additionally, on 31 December 20X2 the forward was physically settled. Deutsche Bank received 2.5 million own shares and paid to XYZ Bank EUR 100 million. Upon settlement of the forward purchase, the liability was extinguished and the charge to equity was reclassified to common shares in treasury. The related accounting entries were the following:

Forward obligation (Liability)	100,000,000
Cash (Asset)	100,000,000
Treasury shares (Equity)	86,384,000
Forward on own shares (Equity)	86,384,000

Impact on CET1 Capital The impact on CET1 of the forward strategy was the following:

- On trade date – 1 January 20X0 – CET1 was reduced by EUR 86,384,000, as shown in Figure 3.52;
- On each reporting date CET1 was further reduced by the after-tax impact on profit or loss of the interest expense. For example, on the first reporting date – 31 December 20X0 – CET1 was reduced by EUR 2,591,000, as shown in Figure 3.53. Thus, during the life of the forward CET1 capital was reduced by EUR 8,170,000 [= (4,319,000 + 4,535,000 + 4,762,000) × 60%, assuming a 40% tax rate] as a result of the recognition of the after-tax interest expense.
- At maturity – 31 December 20X2 – the settlement of the forward had no additional impact on CET1.

The overall impact of the forward, following its settlement, was a reduction in CET1 capital of EUR 94,554,000, comprising (i) the EUR 86,384,000 reduction stemming from the newly recognised treasury shares and (ii) the EUR 8,170,000 reduction stemming from the after-tax interest expense recognised in profit or loss, as shown in Figure 3.54.

3.22.3 Accounting and Regulatory Impact of Sold Put Options on Own Shares

A physically settled put option on own shares gives the buyer the right, but not the obligation, to sell to the seller (Deutsche Bank in our case) a fixed number of own shares at a pre-specified price at a future date. Let us assume that on 1 January 20X0 Deutsche Bank sold a two-year put option on 2.78 million of its own shares to XYZ Bank that allowed for physical settlement only, with the terms in Table 3.22.

Option Mechanics At inception, Deutsche Bank received a EUR 9 million premium in cash in exchange for selling the put option.

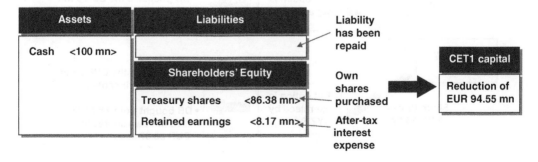

FIGURE 3.54 Impact on CET1 of Deutsche Bank's forward on own shares, following its settlement

TABLE 3.22   Main Terms of Deutsche Bank's Put Option on Own Shares

Physically-settled Put Option Terms

Start date	1 January 20X0
Buyer	XYZ Bank
Seller	Deutsche Bank
Maturity date	31 December 20X1 (2 years)
Strike price	EUR 35.97 (90% of the spot price on trade date)
Number of shares	2.78 million
Strike amount	EUR 100 million (= 35.97 × 2.78 mn)
Underlying	Deutsche Bank's ordinary shares
Premium	EUR 9 million
Settlement	Physical delivery only

At maturity, XYZ Bank would have the right to sell 2.78 million ordinary shares of Deutsche Bank to the German bank. At maturity, XYZ Bank would be assessing whether to exercise the option, as follows (see Figure 3.55):

- If Deutsche Bank's share price is greater than, or equal to, EUR 35.97 (the strike price), XYZ Bank would *not* exercise the put. The option would expire worthless; or
- If Deutsche Bank's share price is lower than EUR 35.97 (the strike price), XYZ Bank would exercise the put and the German bank would buy 2.78 million of its own shares from XYZ Bank for a EUR 100 million cash consideration (i.e., EUR 35.97 per share).

Initial Recognition   The put option sale was classified as an equity instrument as the number of shares was fixed, the strike was fixed and physical settlement was required (i.e., it met the "fixed-for-fixed"

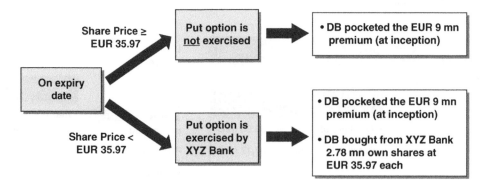

FIGURE 3.55   Scenarios at maturity of Deutsche Bank's sale of put option on own shares

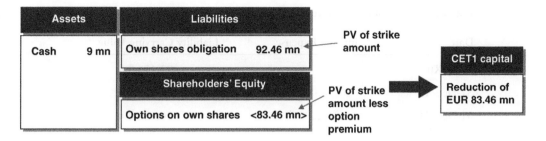

FIGURE 3.56   Initial recognition of Deutsche Bank's sale of put on own shares

condition). Were the fixed-for-fixed condition not met, the option would have been classified as a derivative and, as a result, measured at fair value through profit or loss.

At inception, the put option was initially recognised as deduction of equity and a liability, as shown in Figure 3.56. A liability was recognised because it embodied the bank's potential contractual obligation to repurchase its own equity instruments, which could require a transfer of assets (cash in our case). It was a liability albeit the repurchase feature was conditional on the level of Deutsche Bank's share price. The initial carrying amount of the liability was the present value of the strike amount.

Let us assume that 2-year straight bonds issued by Deutsche Bank were trading at a 4% yield on 1 January 20X0. Therefore, the present value at inception of the strike amount was EUR 92,456,000 [$= 100 \text{ mn}/(1 + 4\%)^2$].

A charge to shareholders' equity was made and reported as "options on own shares". The amount recognised was the difference between the present value of the strike amount and the premium received (EUR 9 million). The accounting entries at inception were the following:

On 1 January 20X0 (trade inception):	
Options on own shares (Equity)	83,456,000
Cash (Asset)	9,000,000
Own shares obligation (Liability)	92,456,000

From a CET1 perspective, the reduction in accounting shareholders' equity, in turn, generated a corresponding reduction in the bank's CET1 capital (see Figure 3.56). As a result, at inception Deutsche Bank's CET1 declined by EUR 83,456,000, the difference between the present value of the strike amount and the premium received. Therefore, both IFRS and Basel III assumed that the put would be exercised, a notably conservative supposition.

Subsequent Recognition   The liability component was recognised at amortised cost using the effective interest rate method. During the life of the forward the carrying value of the liability would be increasing to reach the EUR 100 million strike amount, as shown in Table 3.23.

Interest expense was recognised in profit or loss at each reporting date. For example, the interest expense recognised during the first year was EUR 3,698,000, or EUR 2,219,000 on an after-tax basis (assuming a 40% tax rate). Supposing that the bank's net profit was externally verified, the impact on CET1 of the interest expense was a reduction of EUR 2,219,000, as shown in Figure 3.57.

TABLE 3.23 Calculation of Interest Expense and the Liability Carrying Amount

Date	Interest Expense	Liability Carrying Value
1-Jan-X0		92,456,000
31-Dec-X0	3,698,000 [1]	96,154,000 [2]
31-Dec-X1	4,846,000 [3]	100,000,000

Notes:
[1] $3,698,000 = 92,456,000 \times 4\%$
[2] $96,154,000 = 92,456,000 + 3,698,000$
[3] $4,846,000 = 96,154,000 \times 4\%$

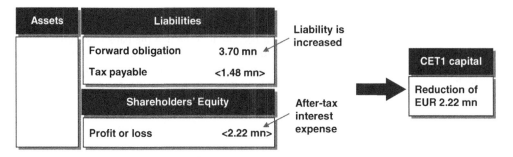

FIGURE 3.57 Recognition of Deutsche Bank's sale of put on own shares on 31 December 20X0

The accounting entries, assuming for simplicity yearly accounting periods, were the following:

On 31 December 20X0:	
Interest expense (Profit or loss)	3,698,000
Own shares obligation (Liability)	3,698,000
On 31 December 20X1:	
Interest expense (Profit or loss)	4,846,000
Own shares obligation (Liability)	4,846,000

Recognition at Maturity – Put Option was Exercised At expiry – 31 December 20X1 – XYZ Bank had the right, but not the obligation, to exercise the put option. Let us assume that at expiry, the price of Deutsche Bank shares were trading below the EUR 35.97 strike price and that, as a result, XYZ Bank exercised the put option. Deutsche Bank acquired 2.78 million own shares and paid the EUR 100 million strike amount.

From an accounting perspective, the liability was extinguished and the charge to equity was reclassified to common shares in treasury, as follows:

On 31 December 20X1 (exercise date):

Own shares obligation (Liability)	100,000,000
Cash (Asset)	100,000,000
Treasury shares (Equity)	83,456,000
Options on own shares (Equity)	83,456,000

The impact on CET1 of the put option strategy was the following:

- On trade date – 1 January 20X0 – CET1 was reduced by EUR 83,456,000, as shown in Figure 3.56;
- On each reporting date CET1 was further reduced by the after-tax impact on profit or loss of the interest expense. For example, on the first reporting date – 31 December 20X0 – CET1 was reduced by EUR 2,219,000, as shown in Figure 3.57. Thus, during the life of the forward, CET1 capital was reduced by EUR 5,126,000 [= (3,698,000 + 4,846,000) × 60%, assuming a 40% tax rate] as a result of the recognition of the after-tax interest expense.
- At expiry – 31 December 20X1 – the exercise of the put option had no additional impact on CET1.

The overall impact of the put option, following its exercise, was a reduction in CET1 capital of EUR 88,582,000, comprising (i) the EUR 83,456,000 reduction stemming from the newly recognised treasury shares and (ii) the EUR 5,126,000 reduction stemming from the after-tax interest expense recognised in profit or loss, as shown in Figure 3.58.

Recognition at Maturity – Put Option was *not* Exercised Let us assume that at expiry, the price of Deutsche Bank shares were trading above (or at) the EUR 35.97 strike price and that, as a result, XYZ Bank did *not* exercise the put option.

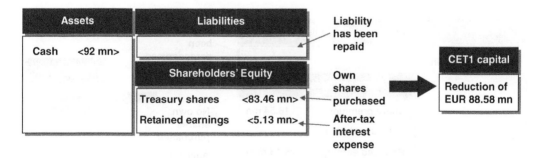

FIGURE 3.58 Overall impact of Deutsche Bank's sale of put on own shares – option exercised

From an accounting perspective, the liability and the "options on own shares" in equity were extinguished and the difference recognised as "share premium" in equity, as follows:

> **On 31 December 20X1 (trade maturity):**
>
> | | |
> |---|---:|
> | Own shares obligation (Liability) | 100,000,000 |
> | Options on own shares (Equity) | 83,456,000 |
> | Share premium (Equity) | 16,544,000 |

The impact on CET1 of the put option strategy was the following:

- On trade date – 1 January 20X0 – CET1 was reduced by EUR 83,456,000, as shown in Figure 3.56;
- On each reporting date CET1 was further reduced by the after-tax impact on profit or loss of the interest expense. For example, on the first reporting date – 31 December 20X0 – CET1 was reduced by EUR 2,219,000, as shown in Figure 3.57. Thus, during the life of the forward CET1 capital was reduced by EUR 5,126,000 [= $(3,698,000 + 4,846,000) \times 60\%$, assuming a 40% tax rate] as a result of the recognition of the after-tax interest expense.
- At expiry – 31 December 20X1 – the initial EUR 83,456,000 impact on CET1 was unwound and the EUR 16,544,000 difference between the strike amount (EUR 100,000,000) and the initial amount recognised in equity (EUR 83,456,000) increased Deutsche Bank's CET1.

The overall impact of the put option, following its worthless expiry, was an increase in CET1 capital of EUR 11,418,000 (= 16,544,000 − 5,126,000), comprising (i) the EUR 5,126,000 CET1 reduction stemming from the after-tax interest expense recognised in profit or loss and (ii) the EUR 16,544,000 CET1 increase stemming from the difference between the strike amount and the initial amount recognised in equity, as shown in Figure 3.59.

3.22.4 Accounting and Regulatory Impact of Bought Call Options on Own Shares

A physically settled call option on own shares gives the buyer (Deutsche Bank in our case) the right, but not the obligation, to buy from the seller a fixed number of own shares at a pre-specified price at a future date. Let us assume that on 1 January 20X0 Deutsche Bank bought a two-year call option on 2.78 million own shares to XYZ Bank that allowed for physical settlement only, with the terms in Table 3.24.

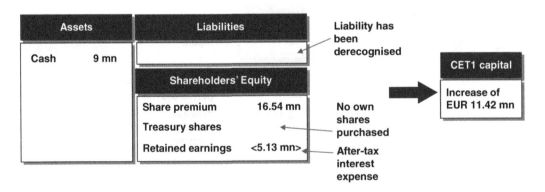

FIGURE 3.59   Overall impact of Deutsche Bank's sale of put on own shares – option *not* exercised

TABLE 3.24   Main Terms of Deutsche Bank's Call Option on Own Shares

Physically-settled Call Option Terms

Start date	1 January 20X0
Buyer	Deutsche Bank
Seller	XYZ Bank
Maturity date	31 December 20X1 (2 years)
Strike price	EUR 44.05 (110% of the spot price on trade date)
Number of shares	2.27 million
Strike amount	EUR 100 million (= 44.05 × 2.27 mn)
Underlying	Deutsche Bank's ordinary shares
Premium	EUR 8 million, to be paid upfront by the buyer
Settlement	Physical settlement only

Option Mechanics   At inception, Deutsche Bank paid a EUR 8 million premium in cash in exchange for buying the call option.

At maturity, XYZ Bank would have the right to buy 2.27 million ordinary shares of Deutsche Bank from XYZ Bank. At maturity, Deutsche Bank would be assessing whether to exercise the option, as follows (see Figure 3.60):

- If Deutsche Bank's share price is lower than, or equal to, EUR 44.05 (the strike price), the German bank would *not* exercise the call. The option would expire worthless; or
- If Deutsche Bank's share price is greater than EUR 44.05 (the strike price), the German bank would exercise the call, buying 2.27 million of its own shares from XYZ Bank for a EUR 100 million cash consideration (i.e., EUR 44.05 per share).

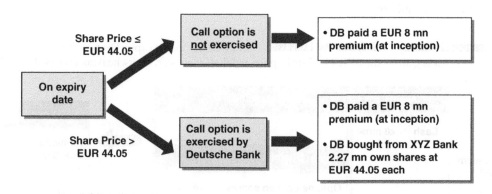

FIGURE 3.60   Scenarios at maturity of Deutsche Bank's purchase of call option on own shares

Initial Recognition   The call option purchase was classified as an equity instrument as the number of shares was fixed, the strike was fixed and physical settlement was required (i.e., it met the "fixed-for-fixed" condition). Were the fixed-for-fixed condition not met, the option would have been classified as a derivative and, as a result, measured at fair value through profit or loss.

At inception, the call option was initially recognised as a deduction of equity. The amount recognised was the fair value of the option, which was the EUR 8 million premium paid. Because Deutsche Bank paid the EUR 8 million premium in cash, the carrying amount of the "cash and cash equivalents" account declined by such amount. The accounting entries at inception were the following:

> **On 1 January 20X0 (trade inception):**
>
> Options on own shares (Equity)   8,000,000
>
>   Cash (Asset)   8,000,000

In contrast with the sale of a put option on own shares, the purchase of a call option on own shares did not require a liability to be recognised at inception. This was because no third party could oblige Deutsche Bank to pay the EUR 100 million strike amount. In other words, it was up to the German bank to exercise the option and incur in such payment.

On the option trade date, the impact on CET1 capital was a reduction of EUR 8 million stemming from the reduction in accounting shareholders' equity, as shown in Figure 3.61.

On trade date, a purchase call option strategy is likely to result in a notably lower CET1 reduction than a forward purchase or sale of put strategies. The reason is the negative impact on shareholders' equity of the present value of the future settlement/strike amount to be paid under the forward or the put option.

Subsequent Recognition   There was no requirement to fair value the call option as it was an equity instrument. No accounting entries were performed until expiry. Therefore, there was no further impact on CET1 capital until expiry.

Recognition at Maturity – Call Option *was* Exercised   Let us assume that at expiry Deutsche Bank's ordinary shares were trading above the EUR 44.05 strike price and that, as a result, Deutsche Bank exercised the call

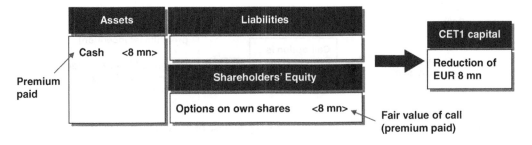

FIGURE 3.61   Initial recognition of Deutsche Bank's purchase of call on own shares

option. Deutsche Bank paid EUR 100 million in exchange for 2.27 million own shares. The overall cost of the repurchased treasury shares was EUR 108 million, the sum of the strike amount and the upfront premium. The accounting entries to recognise the repurchase of its own shares were the following:

On 31 December 20X1 (expiry date):	
Treasury shares (Equity)	100,000,000
Cash (Asset)	100,000,000
Treasury shares (Equity)	8,000,000
Options on own shares (Equity)	8,000,000

The impact on CET1 of the call option strategy was the following:

- On trade date – 1 January 20X0 – CET1 was reduced by the EUR 8 million option premium, as shown in Figure 3.61;
- On each reporting date, the call option had no further impact on CET1;
- At expiry – 31 December 20X1 – CET1 was further reduced by the EUR 100 million strike amount paid.

The overall impact on CET1 of the call option, following its exercise, was a decline of EUR 108 million (see Figure 3.62), comprising (i) the EUR 8 million CET1 reduction stemming from the premium paid and (ii) the EUR 100 million paid for the shares acquired through the exercise of the call.

Recognition at Maturity – Call Option was *not* Exercised   Let us assume that at expiry, Deutsche Bank's ordinary shares were trading below (or at) the EUR 44.05 strike price. The option expired worthless and, as a result, XYZ Bank did *not* exercise the call option. The amount in equity was reclassified to "share premium" within equity, as the option ceased to exist. The accounting entries were the following:

On 31 December 20X1 (option expiry):	
Share premium (Equity)	8,000,000
Options on own shares (Equity)	8,000,000

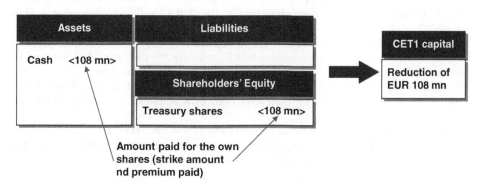

FIGURE 3.62 Overall impact of Deutsche Bank's purchase of call on own shares – option exercised

The impact on CET1 of the call option strategy was the following:

- On trade date – 1 January 20X0 – CET1 was reduced by the EUR 8 million option premium, as shown in Figure 3.61;
- On each reporting date, the call option had no further impact on CET1;
- At expiry – 31 December 20X1 – the worthless expiry had no further impact on CET1.

The overall impact on CET1 of the call option, following its worthless expiry, was a decline of EUR 8 million (see Figure 3.63), stemming from the premium paid.

The purchase of the call option limited the negative impact on CET1 of the repurchase to EUR 108 million. The German bank knew that if the call option was exercised, the effect on CET1 was a reduction of EUR 108 million. In contrast, were the call option not to be exercised, the effect on CET1 was a reduction of EUR 8 million. However, it was likely that, following the worthless expiry of the call option, the bank would have purchased the 2.27 million shares in the market, and the consideration paid would have been deducted from CET1 capital. Let us next compare the call option strategy with a strategy in which the German bank acquired the shares in the stock market.

Share Price above the EUR 44.05 Call Strike Price
Imagine that the share price of Deutsche Bank's shares was EUR 55 when the German bank repurchased its 2.27 million own shares.

Under the call option strategy, the German bank would have exercised the call. The impact on CET1 would have been a reduction of EUR 108 million.

Had Deutsche Bank not entered into the call option strategy, it would have acquired the shares in the market, at the share price prevailing at the time of purchase: EUR 55. The treasury shares would have been purchased for a EUR 125 million (= 2.27 million × 55) cash consideration, and the impact on CET1 would have been an equivalent reduction of EUR 125 million.

Consequently, Deutsche Bank would have been better off executing the call option strategy: the negative impact on CET1 would have been EUR 17 million (= 125 mn − 108 mn) lower.

Share Price below (or at) the EUR 44.05 Call Strike Price
Assume that instead the share price of Deutsche Bank's ordinary shares was EUR 39 when the German bank repurchased its own shares.

Under the call option strategy, the German bank would have not exercised the call. Instead, the bank would have purchased the 2.27 million shares in the market for a EUR 89 million (= 2.27 million × 39) cash consideration, and the impact on CET1 would have been a reduction of EUR 97 million (the EUR 8 million premium plus the EUR 89 million consideration paid for the shares).

Had Deutsche Bank not entered into the call option strategy, it would have acquired the shares in the market for a EUR 89 million (= 2.27 million × 39) cash consideration, and the impact on CET1 would have been a corresponding EUR 89 million reduction.

Consequently, the German bank would have been worse off executing the call option strategy: the negative impact on CET1 would have been EUR 8 million (i.e., the premium paid upfront) larger.

Thus, one of the advantages of the call option strategy was the certainty regarding the maximum impact on CET1 of the share repurchase. The main weakness of the call option strategy was the EUR 8 million premium that the German bank had to pay upfront.

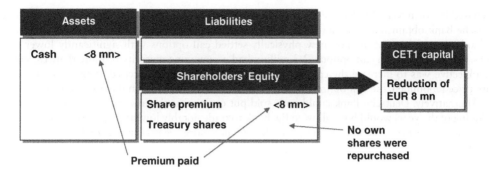

FIGURE 3.63 Overall impact of Deutsche Bank's purchase of call on own shares – option *not* exercised

3.22.5 Accounting and Regulatory Impact of Deutsche Bank's Treasury Shares Activity in 2014

Let us take a look at the impact on Deutsche Bank's CET1 capital of its activity on its own shares during 2014. At the end of 2013, Deutsche Bank reported EUR 13 million of treasury shares at cost in the shareholders' equity section of its statement of financial position.

During 2014 the German bank performed the following transactions on its own shares:

■ It acquired 310.85 million shares, paying a EUR 9,187 million cash consideration;
■ It sold 282.34 million shares, receiving EUR 8,352 million in cash;
■ It distributed 28.42 million shares to beneficiaries of the bank's share-based compensation plans. The cost of these shares was EUR 840 million; and
■ It restructured existing and new call options (to be covered next).

From a regulatory capital perspective, Deutsche Bank was required to calculate the underlying exposure to own CET1 instruments held not only directly, but also indirectly or through synthetic holdings of index securities, and to deduct such exposures from CET1 capital. After applying the netting benefits available under Basel III, the German bank calculated that, synthetically – through stock indices (primarily the Eurostoxx 50 index), the bank had a long position in shares worth EUR 54 million at the end of 2014. In addition, the number of treasury shares held directly by Deutsche Bank at the end of 2014 was only 0.26 million, worth EUR 6.5 million.

Restructuring of Call Options To take advantage of Deutsche Bank's low share price in the third quarter 2014 (see Figure 3.64), the German bank unwound 8.9 million physically-settled call options

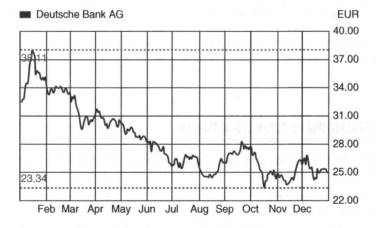

FIGURE 3.64 Deutsche Bank's share price during 2014

purchased between May 2012 and February 2014. Because these options were deep out-of-the-money, Deutsche Bank obtained a premium much lower than the premium it paid originally. Simultaneously, the bank entered into 8.9 million new physically-settled call options with significantly lower strike prices. Of the 8.9 million call options, 2.3 million had a remaining maturity of more than 18 months. The objective was to increase the call options' probability of being exercised. If the German bank's share price rebounded, the call options would be worth notably more than the premium paid.

Alternatively, Deutsche Bank could have sold put options, as the low share price (relative to the beginning of the year) would have allowed the bank to trade notably low strike prices. As we have seen in the previous sections, the sale of put options has a much more negative impact on CET1 capital than call options.

3.23 HOLDINGS OF THE CET1 INSTRUMENTS OF FINANCIAL SECTOR ENTITIES

Holdings of CET1 instruments of other financial sector entities impact a bank's CET1 capital in three different ways:

- Direct, indirect and synthetic holdings of the CET1 instruments of financial sector entities where those entities have **reciprocal cross holdings** with the bank designed to inflate artificially the own funds of the bank;
- Direct, indirect and synthetic holdings by the bank of the CET1 instruments of financial sector entities where the bank does *not* have a **significant investment** in those entities. The impact of these investments on CET1 capital is covered in detail in Chapter 10;
- Direct, indirect and synthetic holdings by the bank of the CET1 instruments of financial sector entities where the bank has a **significant investment** in those entities. The impact of these investments on CET1 capital is covered in detail in Chapter 10.

Pursuant to [CRR 36(1)(g) and 44] direct, indirect and synthetic holdings of the CET1 instruments of financial sector entities, where those entities have reciprocal cross holdings with the bank designed to inflate artificially the own funds of the bank, are deducted from CET1 capital.

The goal of this deduction is to prevent abuse of capital structures purely designed to boost CET1. Any bank disclosing a deduction due to this item is likely to raise special scrutiny as it implies that the regulator has considered that the bank has tried to artificially inflate capital levels.

In Europe some savings and cooperative banks have cross-holdings of ordinary shares and cross-guarantees normally executed as a way to reinforce close alliances between these banks, which may help them to share activities or to jointly offer services. These cross-holdings are typically not intended to artificially inflate CET1 capital levels and, as a result, should not be subject to a CET1 deduction but to the guidelines pertaining to non-significant investments in financial institutions.

3.24 DEDUCTION ELECTION OF 1,250% RW ASSETS

Pursuant to [CRR 36(1)(k)] banks may elect to deduct from CET1 capital certain exposures that otherwise would be applied using a 1,250% risk-weight. These items are:

- Qualifying holdings outside the financial sector, subject to a 1,250% risk-weight;
- Positions related to both traditional and synthetic securitisations, subject to a 1,250% risk-weight. The exposure value of these positions may reflect eligible funded credit protection;

■ Free deliveries. This item refers to the situation in which the bank has paid for securities, foreign currencies or commodities before receiving them or it has delivered securities, foreign currencies or commodities before receiving payment for them. It also refers to cross-border transactions in which one day or more has elapsed since the bank made that payment or delivery;

■ Positions in a basket for which the bank cannot determine the risk weight under the IRB approach, which are subject to a 1,250% risk-weight. Imagine that the bank provides credit protection for a basket of exposures under terms that the nth default among the exposures shall trigger payment and that this credit event shall terminate the contract. In accordance with [CRR 153(8)], if the product is not rated by an ECAI, the risk weights of the exposures included in the basket will be aggregated, excluding n–1 exposures where the sum of the expected loss amount multiplied by 12.5 and the risk-weighted exposure amount shall not exceed the nominal amount of the protection provided by the credit derivative multiplied by 12.5. The n–1 exposures to be excluded from the aggregation shall be determined on the basis that they shall include those exposures each of which produces a lower risk-weighted exposure amount than the risk-weighted exposure amount of any of the exposures included in the aggregation. Positions in the basket for which the bank cannot determine the risk weight under the IRB Approach are applied a 1,250% risk weight and, alternatively, the bank can deduct these positions from CET1.

■ Equity exposures under an internal models approach, subject to a 1,250% risk-weight.

3.25 AMOUNT EXCEEDING THE 17.65% THRESHOLD

Chapters 10 and 13 cover in detail the fact that the following two items are subject to a 10% and a 17.65% threshold, as illustrated in Figure 3.65:

■ Direct and indirect significant investments of the CET1 instruments of unconsolidated financial institutions are subject to a 10% threshold of CET1. Any amount exceeding this 10% threshold is deducted from CET1 capital;

■ DTAs that rely on future profitability and arise from temporary differences are subject to a 10% threshold of CET1. Any amount exceeding this 10% threshold is deducted from CET1 capital

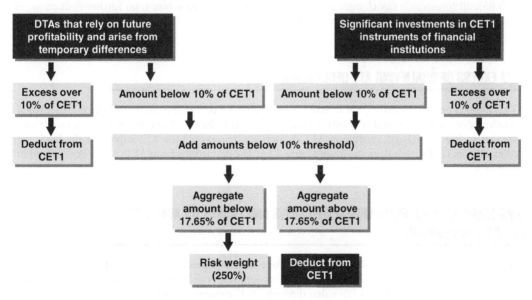

FIGURE 3.65   Amounts exceeding the 17.65% threshold

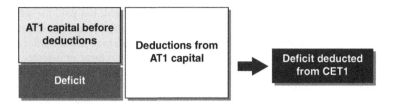

FIGURE 3.66   Excess of qualifying AT1 deductions

The amounts below the 10% threshold of these two items are aggregated and subject to a 17.65% threshold. The portion of the aggregate that exceeds 17.65% of CET1 is excluded from CET1 capital.

3.26 FORESEEABLE TAX CHARGES RELATING TO CET1 ITEMS

Pursuant to [CRR 36(1)(l)] any current and deferred tax charges relating to CET1 items foreseeable at the moment of its calculation are deducted from CET1 capital, except where the bank suitably adjusts the amount of CET1 items insofar as such tax charges reduce the amount up to which those items may be used to cover risks or losses. The estimated amount of deferred tax charges may not be netted against deferred tax assets that are not recognised in the financial statements.

> On the condition that the bank applies accounting framework and accounting policies that provide for the full recognition of current and deferred tax liabilities related to transactions and other events recognised in the balance sheet or the profit or loss account, the bank may consider that foreseeable tax charges have been already taken into account. The competent authority shall be satisfied that all necessary deductions have been made, either under applicable accounting standards or under any other adjustments.
>
> There is a presumption that, when the bank applies the international accounting standards (IFRS), all foreseeable tax charges have been considered and, as a result, no further deduction from CET1 related to such item is required.

3.27 EXCESS OF QUALIFYING AT1 DEDUCTIONS

AT1 capital cannot be negative, but it may happen that AT1 deductions are greater than AT1 capital excluding deductions. When this situation occurs, AT1 has to be equal to zero. As a consequence and pursuant to [CRR 36(1)(j)], qualifying AT1 deductions that exceed the AT1 capital of the bank are deducted from CET1 capital, as shown in Figure 3.66. The deductions from AT1 capital are covered in Chapter 4.

3.28 TEMPORARY FILTER ON UNREALISED GAINS AND LOSSES ON AVAILABLE-FOR-SALE INSTRUMENTS

Under IAS 39 – the financial instruments accounting standard preceding IFRS 9 – there was an asset category called "available-for-sale" ("AFS"). The recognition of debt instruments in this category was notably similar to the current "at fair value through OCI" category under IFRS 9.

Basel III allowed the phase-in of the full recognition of unrealised gains and losses on capital over a five-year period. [CRR 467] provides the option to exclude unrealised gains or losses on exposures to central governments classified in the AFS category if that treatment was applied before 1 January 2014, subject to the discretion of competent authorities. Some EU Member States (e.g., Italy and Spain) applied this filter. This treatment could be applied until the endorsement by the European Community of IFRS 9 replacing IAS 39, although at the time of writing some EU Member States interpreted the provision as still subject to the Basel III-compliant five-year phase-in period.

CHAPTER 4

Additional Tier 1 (AT1) Capital

Although the predominant form of Tier 1 capital must be CET1 capital, Basel III allows instruments other than ordinary shares to be included in a second element of Tier 1 capital called "**Additional Tier 1**" ("**AT1**") capital, if they meet certain requirements.

4.1 AT1 MINIMUM CAPITAL REQUIREMENTS

Tier 1 capital comprises **CET1** and **AT1** capital. As CET1 capital is considered the element of capital that is the highest quality and the most effective in absorbing losses, AT1 capital is a supplementary form of Tier 1 capital. Tier 1 capital is designed to absorb losses on a "going concern" basis (i.e., it helps the bank to avoid insolvency).

According to Basel III requirements, banks are required to hold a minimum CET1 capital (excluding the amounts utilised to meet the buffer requirements) ratio of 4.5%. In addition, banks are required to hold a minimum Tier 1 capital ratio of 6%. As AT1 capital is less costly than CET1 capital, banks have an incentive to hold AT1 capital of 1.5% of RWAs, as shown in Figure 4.1, to meet the Tier 1 capital requirement:

$$\text{Typical level of AT1 capital} = \frac{\text{Additional Tier 1 capital}}{\text{Risk-weighted assets}} \geq 1.5\%$$

4.2 CRITERIA GOVERNING INSTRUMENTS INCLUSION IN AT1 CAPITAL

The criteria governing the inclusion of financial instruments in AT1 capital is set out in [CRR 52(1)]. The EBA published in March 2014 its final draft Regulatory Technical Standards (RTS) and final draft Implementing Technical Standards (ITS) on own funds, aimed at enhancing regulatory harmonisation of capital instruments in the banking sector in Europe.

AT1 capital consists of the sum of the following elements [CRR 51]:

- Instruments issued by the bank that meet the criteria for inclusion in AT1 capital. These instruments shall not qualify as CET1 or Tier 2 items; and
- Share premium (stock surplus) resulting from the issue of instruments included in AT1 capital.

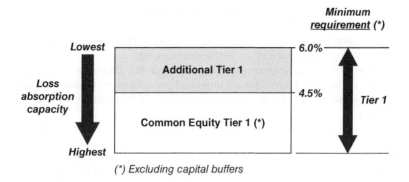

(*) Excluding capital buffers

FIGURE 4.1   Tier 1 minimum capital requirements

4.2.1 Requirements of AT1 Instruments

For an instrument to be included in AT1 capital, it must meet all of the following criteria [CRR 52]:

1. The instruments are issued and paid-in.
2. The instruments are not purchased by any of the following:
   a. The bank or its subsidiaries;
   b. An entity in which the bank has participation in the form of ownership, direct or by way of control, of 20% or more of the voting rights or capital of that undertaking.
3. The purchase of the instruments is not funded directly or indirectly by the bank.
4. The instruments rank below Tier 2 instruments in the event of the insolvency of the bank.
5. The instruments are not secured, or subject to a guarantee that enhances the seniority of the claims by any of the following:
   a. The bank or its subsidiaries;
   b. The parent undertaking of the bank or its subsidiaries;
   c. The parent financial holding company or its subsidiaries;
   d. The mixed activity holding company or its subsidiaries;
   e. The mixed financial holding company or its subsidiaries;
   f. Any undertaking that has close links with entities referred to in points (a) to (e).
6. The instruments are not subject to any arrangement, contractual or otherwise, that enhances the seniority of the claim under the instruments in insolvency or liquidation.
7. The instruments are perpetual and the provisions governing them include no incentive for the bank to redeem them.
8. Where the provisions governing the instruments include one or more call options, the option to call may be exercised at the sole discretion of the issuer.
9. The instruments may be called, redeemed or repurchased only where the conditions laid down in [CRR 77] are met, and not before five years after the date of issuance, except where the conditions laid down in [CRR 78(4)] are met.
10. The provisions governing the instruments do not indicate explicitly or implicitly that the instruments would or might be called, redeemed or repurchased and the bank does not otherwise provide such an indication, except in the following cases:
    a. The liquidation of the bank;
    b. Discretionary repurchases of the instruments or other discretionary means of reducing the amount of AT1 capital, where the bank has received the prior permission of the competent authority in accordance with [CRR 77].
11. The bank does not indicate explicitly or implicitly that the competent authority would consent to a request to call, redeem or repurchase the instruments.

12. Distributions under the instruments meet the following conditions:
    a. They are paid out of distributable items;
    b. The level of distributions made on the instruments will not be amended on the basis of the credit standing of the bank or its parent undertaking;
    c. The provisions governing the instruments give the bank full discretion at all times to cancel the distributions on the instruments for an unlimited period and on a non-cumulative basis, and the bank may use such cancelled payments without restriction to meet its obligations as they fall due;
    d. Cancellation of distributions does not constitute an event of default of the bank; and
    e. The cancellation of distributions imposes no restrictions on the bank (see Section 4.2.2 below).
13. The instruments do not contribute to a determination that the liabilities of a bank exceed its assets, where such a determination constitutes a test of insolvency under applicable national law.
14. The provisions governing the instruments require that, upon the occurrence of a trigger event, the principal amount of the instruments be written down on a permanent or temporary basis or the instruments be converted to CET1 instruments (see Section 4.2.3 below).
15. The provisions governing the instruments include no feature that could hinder the recapitalisation of the bank. According to the EBA, such feature exists, for example when there is a requirement that the bank compensates existing holders of new capital instruments where a new capital instrument is issued;
16. Where the instruments are not issued directly by a bank, both the following conditions shall be met (see Section 4.2.5):
    a. The instruments are issued through an entity within the perimeter of regulatory consolidation;
    b. The proceeds are immediately available to the bank without limitation and in a form that satisfies the conditions laid down above.

Pursuant to [CRR 55], if any of the conditions laid down above ceases to be met, that instrument shall immediately cease to qualify as an AT1 instrument, and the part of the share premium accounts that relates to that instrument shall immediately cease to qualify as an AT1 item.

One of the AT1 eligibility requirements for an instrument is the absence of incentives for the bank to redeem it. In other words, no expectations should be created at the date of issuance that the instrument is likely to be redeemed.

In 2014 the EBA clarified that an expectation that the instrument is likely to be redeemed is created if any of the following provisions are included in the terms and conditions of the capital instrument:
- A call option combined with an increase in the credit spread of the instrument if the call is not exercised;
- A call option combined with a requirement or an investor option to convert the instrument into a CET1 instrument where the call is not exercised;
- A call option combined with a change in reference rate where the credit spread over the second reference rate is greater than the initial payment rate minus the swap rate;
- A call option combined with an increase of the redemption amount in the future;
- A remarketing option combined with an increase in the credit spread of the instrument or a change in reference rate where the credit spread over the second reference rate is greater than the initial payment rate minus the swap rate where the instrument is not remarketed; or
- A marketing of the instrument in a way which suggests to investors that the instrument will be called.

4.2.2 Restrictions on the Cancellation of Distributions AT1 Instruments and Other Features

[CRR 53] sets out the restrictions on the cancellation of distributions on AT1 instruments and features that could hinder the recapitalisation of the bank. For the purposes of points (12) (e) and (15) of Section 4.2.1, the provisions governing AT1 instruments shall *not* include the following:

1. A requirement for distributions on the instruments to be made in the event of a distribution being made on an instrument issued by the bank that ranks to the same degree as, or more junior than, an AT1 instrument, including a CET1 instrument;
2. A requirement for the payment of distributions on CET1, AT1 or Tier 2 instruments to be cancelled in the event that distributions are not made on those AT1 instruments;
3. An obligation to substitute the payment of interest or dividend by a payment in any other form. The bank shall not otherwise be subject to such an obligation.

Dividend Pusher/Stopper

Some financial instruments with discretionary coupons include "dividend stopper/pusher" clauses:

- A **dividend pusher** clause obliges the issuer to pay a discretionary coupon on the financial instrument if a payment is made on another, typically more junior, instrument. Commonly, it means that when a dividend is distributed to ordinary shareholders, the issuer is required to the pay the discretionary coupon.
- A **dividend stopper** clause obliges the issuer to not to make a payment on another, typically more junior, instrument if the discretionary coupon on the financial instrument is not paid. Commonly, it means that while the discretionary coupons are not paid, no dividends can be distributed to ordinary shareholders.

Under Basel III, dividend pushers are prohibited for instrument eligible for AT1 capital. However, it is permitted for AT1 instruments to contain dividend stopper clauses, assuming that the dividend restriction is confined to the immediate distribution period.

4.2.3 Special Requirements for Write-down or Conversion of AT1 Instruments

In line with [CRR 54], the EBA set the following provisions in relation to the write-down or conversion clauses in AT1 instruments:

1. A trigger event occurs when the CET1 ratio of the bank referred to in point (a) of Article 92(1) falls below either of the following:
   a. 5.125%; or
   b. A level higher than 5.125%, where determined by the bank and specified in the provisions governing the instrument.
2. Banks may specify in the provisions governing the instrument one or more trigger events in addition to that referred to in point (1).
3. Where the provisions governing the instruments require them to be **converted** into CET1 instruments upon the occurrence of a trigger event, those provisions shall specify either of the following:
   a. The rate of such conversion and a limit on the permitted amount of conversion; or
   b. A range within which the instruments will convert into CET1 instruments.
4. Where the provisions governing the instruments require their principal amount to be **written down** upon the occurrence of a trigger event, the write down shall reduce all the following:
   a. The claim of the holder of the instrument in the insolvency or liquidation of the bank;
   b. The amount required to be paid in the event of the call or redemption of the instrument;
   c. The distributions made on the instrument.
5. Write down or conversion of an AT1 instrument shall, under the applicable accounting framework, generate items that qualify as CET1 items.

6. The amount of AT1 instruments recognised in AT1 items is limited to the minimum amount of CET1 items that would be generated if the principal amount of the AT1 instruments were fully written down or converted into CET1 instruments.

7. The aggregate amount of AT1 instruments that is required to be written down or converted upon the occurrence of a trigger event shall be no less than the lower of the following:
   a. The amount required to restore fully the CET1 ratio of the institution to 5.125%; and
   b. The full principal amount of the instrument.

8. When a trigger event occurs, banks shall do the following:
   a. Immediately inform the competent authorities;
   b. Inform the holders of the AT1 instruments;
   c. Write down the principal amount of the instruments, or convert the instruments into CET1 instruments without delay, but no later than within one month, in accordance with the requirement laid down in this Article.

9. A bank issuing AT1 instruments that convert to CET1 on the occurrence of a trigger event shall ensure that its authorised share capital is at all times sufficient for converting all such convertible AT1 instruments into shares if a trigger event occurs. All necessary authorisations shall be obtained at the date of issuance of such convertible AT1 instruments. The bank shall maintain at all times the necessary prior authorisation to issue the CET 1 instruments into which such AT1 instruments would convert upon occurrence of a trigger event.

10. A bank issuing AT1 instruments that convert to CET1 on the occurrence of a trigger event shall ensure that there are no procedural impediments to that conversion by virtue of its incorporation or statutes or contractual arrangements.

In 2014 the EBA clarified that for the write-down to be considered temporary, all of the following conditions shall be met:
- Any distributions payable after a write-down shall be based on the reduced amount of the principal;
- Write-ups shall be based on profits after the bank has taken a formal decision confirming the final profits;
- Any write-up of the instrument or payment of coupons on the reduced amount of the principal shall be operated at the full discretion of the bank subject to the constraints arising from the points below and there shall be no obligation for the bank to operate or accelerate a write-up under specific circumstances;
- A write-up shall be operated on a pro rata basis among similar AT1 instruments that have been subject to a write-down;
- The maximum amount to be attributed to the sum of the write-up of the instrument together with the payment of coupons on the reduced amount of the principal shall be equal to (calculated at the moment when the write-up is operated):

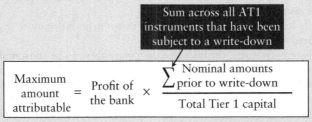

$$\text{Maximum amount attributable} = \text{Profit of the bank} \times \frac{\sum \text{Nominal amounts prior to write-down}}{\text{Total Tier 1 capital}}$$

(Sum across all AT1 instruments that have been subject to a write-down)

- The sum of any write-up amounts and payments of coupons on the reduced amount of the principal shall be treated as a payment that results in a reduction of CET1 and shall be subject, together with other distributions on CET1 instruments, to the restrictions relating to the Maximum Distributable Amount – MDA – (see Section 6.4), as transposed in national law or regulation.

In a full write-down AT1 instrument, the holder of such instrument bears 100% of any loss once the trigger has been breached (e.g., a 5.125% CET1 ratio). At this point, the AT1 holder's position in the hierarchy of the capital structure becomes inverted with CET1 holders of the bank, who in theory should bear the first and greatest share of losses as they arise.

4.2.4 Procedures and Timing for Determining the Occurrence of a Trigger Event

In relation to the write-down or conversion clauses in AT1 instruments, the EBA set that a trigger event occurs when the CET1 ratio of the bank falls below either of the following:

- 5.125%; or
- A level higher than 5.125%, where determined by the bank and specified in the provisions governing the instrument.

The following procedures and timing applies for determining that a trigger event has occurred:

1. Where the bank has established that the CET1 ratio has fallen below the level that activates conversion or write-down of the instrument at the level of application of the requirements as defined under [CRR Title II], the management body or any other relevant body of the bank shall without delay determine that a trigger event has occurred and there shall be an irrevocable obligation to write-down or convert the instrument;
2. The amount to be written-down or converted shall be determined as soon as possible and within a maximum period of one month from the time it is determined that the trigger event has occurred;
3. The competent authority may require that the maximum period of one month referred to in point (2) is reduced in cases where it assesses that sufficient certainty on the amount to be converted or written down is established or in cases where it assesses that an immediate conversion or write-down is needed;
4. Where an independent review of the amount to be written down or converted is required according to the provisions governing the AT1 instrument, or where the competent authority requires an independent review for the determination of the amount to be written down or converted, the management body or any other relevant body of the bank shall see that this is done immediately. Any such review shall be completed as soon as possible and shall not create impediments for the bank to write-down or convert the AT1 instrument and to meet the requirements of points (2) and (3).

4.2.5 Use of Special Purposes Entities for Indirect Issuance of Capital Instruments

Where an instrument is not issued directly by the bank, pursuant to [CRR 83], both the following requirements shall be met for an instrument to qualify as an AT1 instrument (see Section 4.2.1):

- The instrument is issued through an entity within the perimeter of regulatory consolidation; and
- The proceeds are immediately available to the bank without limitation and in a form that satisfies all the other requirements for an instrument to qualify as an AT1 instrument.

According to the EBA, the following treatment shall apply in the use of special purposes entities ("SPEs") for indirect issuance of AT1 and Tier 2 instruments:

- Where the bank or an entity within its regulatory consolidation issues a capital instrument that is subscribed by a SPE, this capital instrument shall not, at the level of the bank or the regulatory consolidated entity, receive recognition as capital of a higher quality than the lowest quality of the capital issued to the SPE and the capital issued to third parties by the SPE. Such requirement applies at the consolidated, sub-consolidated and individual levels of application of prudential requirements;

■ The rights of the holders of the instruments issued by the SPE shall be no more favourable than if the instrument was issued directly by the bank or an entity within its regulatory perimeter of consolidation; and

■ The only asset of the SPE, other than minimal and insignificant assets, is its investment in the own funds of the parent undertaking or a subsidiary thereof that is included fully in the perimeter of regulatory consolidation, the form of which satisfies the relevant conditions for eligibility as an AT1 instrument.

The EBA considers that the assets of a SPE are considered to be minimal and insignificant where both of the following conditions are met:

■ The assets of the SPE which are not constituted by the investments in the own funds of the related subsidiary are limited to cash assets dedicated to payment of coupons and redemption of the own funds instruments that are due; and

■ The amount of assets of the SPE other than the ones mentioned in the previous paragraph are not higher than 0.5% of the average total assets of the SPE over the last three years. The competent authority may permit the bank to use a higher percentage provided that both of the following conditions are met:

   ■ The higher percentage is necessary to enable exclusively the coverage of the running costs of the SPE; and

   ■ The corresponding nominal amount does not exceed EUR 500,000.

4.2.6 Conditions to the Redemption or Repurchase of Capital Instruments

Pursuant to [CRR 77], a bank seeking to repurchase or redeem, including the exercise of a call right, a capital instrument (CET1, AT1 or Tier 2) needs require approval from the competent authority. [CRR 78] sets out that the competent authority shall grant permission if any of the following conditions is met:

■ **First condition:** The bank replaces the capital instruments with other capital instruments of equal or higher quality at terms that are sustainable for the income capacity of the bank. When assessing the sustainability of the replacement instruments for the income capacity of the bank, competent authorities shall consider the extent to which those replacement capital instruments would be more costly for the bank than those they would replace; or

■ **Second condition:** The bank has demonstrated to the satisfaction of the competent authority that the own funds of the bank would, following the action in question, exceed the requirements laid down in [CRR 92(1)] (i.e., a CET1 capital ratio of 4.5%, a Tier 1 capital ratio of 6% and a total capital ratio of 8%) and the combined buffer requirement by a margin that the competent authority may consider necessary.

> The EBA clarified that **"sustainable for the income capacity"** of the bank means that the profitability of the bank, as assessed by the competent authority, continues to be sound or does not see any negative change after the replacement of the instruments with own funds instruments of equal or higher quality, at that date and for the foreseeable future. The competent authority's assessment shall take into account the bank's profitability in stress situations.

Where a bank takes an action to reduce, redeem or repurchase CET1 instruments issued by the bank in a manner that is permitted under applicable national law and the refusal of redemption is prohibited by applicable national law, the competent authority may waive the first condition above provided that the competent authority requires the bank to limit the redemption of such instruments on an appropriate basis.

The competent authorities may permit banks to redeem **AT1 or Tier** 2 instruments before five years of the date of issue only where the first condition above is met and either requirements (1) or (2) below are met:

1. There is a change in the **regulatory classification** of those instruments that would be likely to result in their exclusion from own funds or reclassification as a lower-quality form of own funds, and both the following conditions are met:
   - The competent authority considers such a change to be sufficiently certain; and
   - The bank demonstrates to the satisfaction of the competent authorities that the regulatory reclassification of those instruments was not reasonably foreseeable at the time of their issuance;
2. There is a change in the applicable **tax treatment** of those instruments which the bank demonstrates to the satisfaction of the competent authorities is material and was not reasonably foreseeable at the time of their issuance.

Repurchase of Capital Instruments for Market Making Purposes or Employee Remuneration According to the EBA, competent authorities may give permission in advance to repurchases of CET1, AT1 or Tier 2 instruments for **market making purposes** for a certain predetermined amount which shall not exceed the following:

- For **CET1 instruments,** the lower of the following amounts:
  - 3% of the amount of the relevant issuance; and
  - 10% of the amount by which CET1 capital exceeds the minimum CET1 requirements. Remember that these requirements are the sum of: (i) the CET1 capital requirements pursuant to [CRR 92] (i.e., a CET1 capital ratio of 4.5%), (ii) the capital conservation buffer, (iii) the bank-specific countercyclical capital buffer, (iv) the systemically important institution buffer, (v) the systemic risk buffer and (vi) any additional CET1 requirements set by the competent authority pursuant to [CRD IV 104 (a)];
- For **AT1 instrument or Tier 2 instruments,** the lower of the following amounts:
  - 10% of the amount of the relevant issuance; and
  - 3% of the total amount of outstanding AT1 instruments or Tier 2 instruments, as applicable.

Competent authorities may also give banks permission in advance for repurchases of CET1, AT1 or Tier 2 instruments where the related capital instruments are **passed on to employees** of the bank as part of their remuneration. Banks shall inform competent authorities where own funds instruments are purchased for these purposes and deduct these instruments from own funds on a corresponding deduction approach for the time they are held by the bank. A deduction on a corresponding basis is no longer required, where the expenses related to the repurchase are already included in own funds as a result of an interim or a year-end financial report.

4.3 DEDUCTIONS FROM AT1 CAPITAL

Pursuant to [CRR 56], a substantial number of items are deducted from AT1 capital. The AT1 prudential filters are the following (see Figure 4.2):

- Direct and indirect holdings by the bank of own AT1 instruments;
- Reciprocal cross-holdings of AT1 instruments designed to inflate the AT1 funds artificially;
- The applicable amount of direct, indirect and synthetic holdings by the bank of the AT1 instruments of financial sector entities where the bank does not have a significant investment in those entities (see Section 4.4.2);
- Direct, indirect and synthetic holdings by the bank of the AT1 instruments of financial sector entities where the bank has a significant investment in those entities;
- Qualifying Tier 2 deductions that exceed the Tier 2 capital of the bank; and
- Foreseeable tax charges relating to AT1 items.

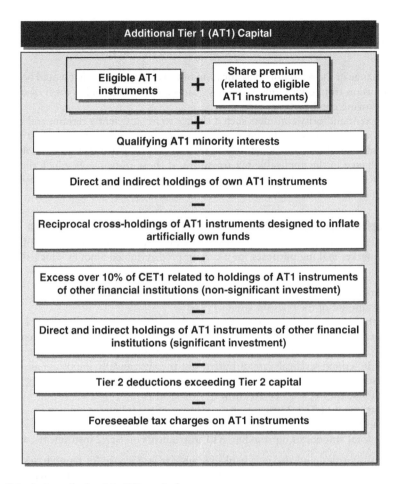

FIGURE 4.2   Calculation of a bank's AT1 capital

4.3.1 Direct and Indirect Holdings of Own AT1 instruments

Pursuant to [CRR 56 (a) and 57], direct, indirect and synthetic holdings by the bank of its own AT1 instruments are deducted from AT1 capital. In addition, any own AT1 instruments that the bank could be contractually obliged to purchase are deducted from AT1 capital as well. This filter applies irrespective of the location of the exposure in the banking book or the trading book.

Banks are required to calculate the underlying exposure to own AT1 instruments through direct, indirect and synthetic holdings of index securities. Section 3.20.1 covers in more detail the general requirements related to indirect holdings arising from index holdings.

Gross long positions may be deducted net of short positions (i.e., only the net long position is deducted) only if both the following conditions are met:

- The long and short positions are in the same underlying exposure and the short positions involve no counterparty risk; and
- Either both the long and the short positions are held in the trading book or both are held in the banking book.

Pursuant to [CRR 75], the maturity requirements for short positions are deemed to be met in respect of positions held where the following conditions are met:

- The bank has the contractual right to sell on a specific future date to the counterparty providing the hedge the long position that is being hedged; and
- The counterparty providing the hedge to the bank is contractually obliged to purchase from the bank on that specific future date the long position referred to in the previous requirement.

The requirement that gross long positions may be deducted net of short positions only if the short positions involve "no" counterparty risk is arguably too restrictive and probably difficult to attain on a practical basis.

From a theoretical perspective, a short position may bear no counterparty credit risk only where all the market value of the AT1 instruments being short is posted upfront and in cash by the counterparty, a notably uncommon situation.

The CRR does not state whether a short position in own AT1 instruments settled against a QCCP is considered to be "counterparty risk-free", although from a theoretical perspective the bank would have some degree of counterparty risk to the QCCP.

Similarly, the CRR remains silent on whether a short position a short position taken through a fully collateralised OTC transaction (which involves a low degree of counterparty risk) is considered to be "counterparty risk-free".

4.3.2 Excess of Qualifying Tier 2 Deductions

Tier 2 capital cannot be negative, but it may happen that Tier 2 deductions are greater than Tier 2 capital excluding deductions. When this situation occurs, Tier 2 capital has to be equal to zero. As a consequence and pursuant to [CRR 56 (e)], qualifying Tier 2 deductions that exceed the Tier 2 capital of the bank are deducted from AT1 capital, as shown in Figure 4.3. The deductions from Tier 2 capital are covered in Chapter 5.

4.3.3 Foreseeable Tax Charges Relating to AT1 Items

Pursuant to [CRR 56 (f)], any current and deferred tax charge relating to AT1 items foreseeable at the moment of its calculation, except where the bank suitably adjusts the amount of AT1 items, insofar as such tax charges reduce the amount up to which those items, may be applied to cover risks or losses.

Although not stated in the CRR, in my view the presumption referred to CET1 instruments that when the bank applies the **international accounting standards** (IFRS), all foreseeable tax charges have been considered, may be applicable to AT1 instruments as well. As a result, when a bank applies IFRS no further deduction from AT1 is required related to foreseeable tax charges.

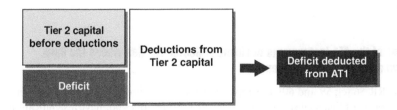

FIGURE 4.3 Excess of qualifying Tier 2 deductions

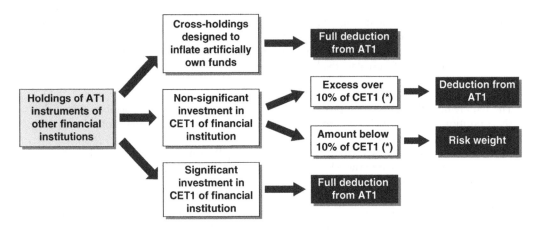

(*) Excess is calculated in combination with holdings of CET1, AT1 and Tier 2 in such financial institutions

FIGURE 4.4   Treatment of investments in AT1 instruments of other financial institutions

4.4 HOLDINGS OF AT1 INSTRUMENTS OF OTHER FINANCIAL INSTITUTIONS

Holdings of AT1 instruments of other financial sector entities impact a bank's AT1 capital in three different ways, as illustrated in Figure 4.4:

- Direct, indirect and synthetic holdings of the AT1 instruments of financial sector entities where those entities have **reciprocal cross-holdings** with the bank designed to inflate artificially the own funds of the bank;
- Direct, indirect and synthetic holdings by the bank of the AT1 instruments of financial sector entities where the bank does *not* have a **significant investment** in those entities; and
- Direct, indirect and synthetic holdings by the bank of the AT1 instruments of financial sector entities where the bank has a **significant investment** in those entities.

4.4.1 Reciprocal Cross-holdings of AT1 Instruments Designed to Artificially Inflate Own Funds

Pursuant to [CRR 56 (b) and 58], direct, indirect and synthetic holdings of the AT1 instruments of financial sector entities where those entities have reciprocal cross-holdings with the bank designed to inflate artificially the AT1 funds of the bank are **fully deducted** from AT1 capital.

When calculating holdings of AT1 instruments of other financial institutions, banks need to take into account the following:

- Holdings of AT1 instruments are calculated on the basis of the gross long positions;
- AT1 own-fund insurance items are treated as holdings of AT1 instruments for the purposes of deduction.

4.4.2 Holdings of the AT1 Instruments of Financial Sector Entities where the Bank does not have a Significant Investment

Pursuant to [CRR 56 (c), 59 and 60], the applicable amount of direct, indirect and synthetic holdings of the AT1 instruments of financial sector entities, where the bank does not have a significant investment in those entities, is deducted from AT1 capital. The calculation of the exposure takes into account the following:

- Holdings of AT1 instruments are calculated on the basis of the gross long positions;
- AT1 own-fund insurance items are treated as holdings of AT1 instruments;
- Underwriting positions held for five working days or fewer are excluded;
- Holdings shall include the underlying long gross exposure to the capital instruments of the financial sector entities – where the bank does not have a significant investment – through direct, indirect and synthetic holdings of index securities. Section 3.20.1 covers in more detail the general requirements related to holdings arising from index holdings.

Gross long positions may be deducted net of short positions (i.e., only the net long position is deducted) in the same underlying exposure only if both the following conditions are met:

- The maturity of the short position matches the maturity of the long position or has a residual maturity of at least one year; and
- Either both the long and the short positions are held in the trading book or both are held in the banking book.

Pursuant to [CRR 75], the maturity requirements for short positions are deemed to be met in respect of positions held where the following conditions are met:

- The bank has the contractual right to sell on a specific future date to the counterparty providing the hedge the long position that is being hedged; and
- The counterparty providing the hedge to the bank is contractually obliged to purchase from the bank on that specific future date the long position referred to in the previous requirement.

The aggregate amount by which the direct, indirect and synthetic holdings by the bank of the CET1, AT1 and Tier 2 instruments of financial sector entities are compared to **10% of the "relevant CET1"** of the bank:

- The amount that exceeds 10% of the "relevant CET1" of the bank is **deducted**; and
- The amount that does not exceed 10% of the "relevant CET1" of the bank is **risk-weighted**.

Applicable Amount to be Deducted from AT1 Capital   The applicable amount to be deducted ("A") is calculated as follows:

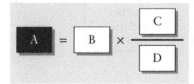

$$A = B \times \frac{C}{D}$$

Where:

A: The amount required to be deducted from AT1 stemming from direct, indirect and synthetic holdings of AT1 instruments of financial sector entities in which the bank does not have a significant investment;

B: The aggregate amount by which the direct, indirect and synthetic holdings by the bank of the CET1, AT1 and Tier 2 instruments of financial sector entities exceeds 10% of the "relevant CET1" of the bank;

C: The amount of direct, indirect and synthetic holdings by the bank of the AT1 instruments of financial sector entities; and

D: The aggregate amount of all direct, indirect and synthetic holdings by the bank of the CET1, AT1 and Tier 2 instruments of those financial sector entities.

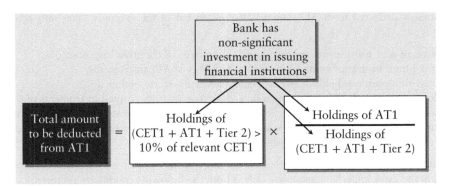

The amount to be deducted is apportioned across each AT1 instrument held. The amount to be deducted from each AT1 instrument ("E") is calculated as follows:

$$ E = A \times \frac{F}{G} $$

Where:

E: The amount to be deducted from AT1 capital allocated to the AT1 instrument;

F: The total amount of the AT1 instrument; and

G: The aggregate amount of direct, indirect and synthetic holdings by bank of the AT1 instruments of financial sector entities in which the bank does not have a significant investment.

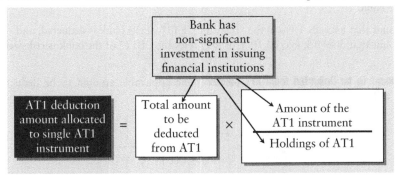

Applicable Amount to be Risk-weighted   The aggregate amount by which the direct, indirect and synthetic holdings by the bank of the CET1, AT1 and Tier 2 instruments of financial sector entities does not exceed 10% of the "relevant CET1" of the bank is not deducted but **risk-weighted**.

The portion of holdings of own funds instruments that is risk-weighted ("H") is calculated as follows:

$$ H = \frac{I}{\dfrac{K}{J}} = I \times \frac{J}{K} $$

Where:

H: Portion of holdings of own fund instruments that is risk-weighted;

I: The aggregate amount by which the direct, indirect and synthetic holdings by the bank of the CET1, AT1 and Tier 2 instruments of financial sector entities does not exceed 10% of the "relevant CET1" of the bank (i.e., the amount to be risk-weighted);

J: The aggregate amount of direct, indirect and synthetic holdings by the bank of the CET1 instruments of financial sector entities in which the bank does not have a significant investment; and

K: The total amount of the CET1 instruments.

Relevant CET1 Capital The "relevant CET1 capital" used to calculate the threshold includes the following filters and deductions:

- The prudential filter related to securitised assets [CRR 32];
- The prudential filter related to cash flow hedges and changes in the value of own liabilities, but maintaining any other unrealised gains and losses measured at fair value [CRR 33 and 35];
- The prudential filter related to additional value adjustments [CRR 34];
- The losses for the current financial year deduction [CRR 36(1)(a)];
- The intangible assets deduction [CRR 36(1)(b)];
- The DTAs that rely on future profitability deduction [CRR 36(1)(c)], excluding the amount of DTAs that rely on future profitability and arise from temporary differences;
- The deduction related to negative amounts resulting from the calculation of expected loss amounts for banks calculating risk-weighted exposure amounts using the Internal Ratings-Based Approach (the IRB Approach) [CRR 36(1)(d)];
- The deduction related to defined benefit pension fund assets on the balance sheet of the bank [CRR 36(1)(e)];
- The deduction related to direct, indirect and synthetic holdings by the bank of its own CET1 instruments, including own CET1 instruments that the bank is under an actual or contingent obligation to purchase by virtue of an existing contractual obligation [CRR 36(1)(f)];
- The deduction related to direct, indirect and synthetic holdings of the CET1 instruments of financial sector entities where those entities have a reciprocal cross-holding with the bank that the competent authority considers to have been designed to inflate artificially the own funds of the bank [CRR 36(1)(g)];
- The deduction related to securitisation positions [CRR 36(1)(k) (ii)];
- The deduction related to free deliveries [CRR 36(1)(k)(iii)];
- The deduction related to positions in a basket for which the bank cannot determine the risk weight under the IRB Approach [CRR 36(1)(k)(iv)];
- The deduction related to equity exposures under the internal models approach [CRR 36(1)(k)(v)];
- The deduction related to foreseeable tax charges relating to CET1 items, except where the bank suitably adjusts the amount of CET1 items insofar as such tax charges reduce the amount up to which those items may be used to cover risks or losses [CRR 36(1)(l)], excluding the amount to be deducted for deferred tax assets that rely on future profitability and arise from temporary differences;
- Cross-holdings of CET1 instruments of financial sector entities designed to artificially inflate own funds [CRR 44];
- The applicable amount of holdings of CET1 instruments of financial sector entities where the bank does not have a significant investment in those entities [CRR 36(h) and 45]; and
- The applicable amount of holdings of CET1 instruments of financial sector entities where the bank has a significant investment in those entities [CRR 36(i) and 45].

4.4.3 Holdings of the AT1 Instruments of Financial Sector Entities where the Bank Has a Significant Investment

Pursuant to [CRR 56 (d) and 59], the underlying exposure to direct, indirect and synthetic holdings of the AT1 instruments of financial sector entities, where the bank has a **significant** investment in those entities, is **fully deducted** from AT1 capital. The calculation of the exposure takes into account the following:

- Holdings of AT1 instruments are calculated on the basis of the gross long positions;
- AT1 own-fund insurance items are treated as holdings of AT1 instruments;
- Underwriting positions held for five working days or fewer are excluded;
- Holdings shall include the underlying long gross exposure to the capital instruments of the financial sector entities – where the bank does has a significant investment – through direct, indirect and synthetic holdings of index securities. Section 3.20.1 covers in more detail the general requirements related to holdings arising from index holdings.

Gross long positions may be calculated net of short positions (i.e., only the net long position is taken into account) only if both the following conditions are met:

- The maturity of the short position matches the maturity of the long position or has a residual maturity of at least one year; and
- Either both the long and the short positions are held in the trading book or both are held in the banking book.

Pursuant to [CRR 75], the maturity requirements for short positions are deemed to be met in respect of positions held where the following conditions are met:

- The bank has the contractual right to sell on a specific future date to the counterparty providing the hedge the long position that is being hedged; and
- The counterparty providing the hedge to the bank is contractually obliged to purchase from the bank on that specific future date the long position referred to in the previous requirement.

4.5 CASE STUDY: LLOYDS BANKING GROUP EXCHANGE OFFER OF TIER 2 FOR AT1 SECURITIES

In March 2014 the British bank Lloyds Banking Group Plc ("Lloyds") launched concurrent GBP, EUR and USD exchange offers for holders of certain series of its Enhanced Capital Notes (ECNs) to exchange them for new AT1 instruments.

4.5.1 Takeover of HBOS

Prior to the 2008–09 credit crisis, the British retail bank HBOS took an aggressive approach to credit risk policies across its retail and commercial lending portfolios and had loose risk management governance and controls. It was willing to lend to significantly risky personal and commercial customers through sub-prime, high loan-to-value and self-certified mortgages. In addition, HBOS expanded into high-risk structured finance. From a funding perspective, HBOS relied heavily on wholesale funding, with retail funding accounting for only 43% of HBOS total funding at the end of 2007.

When the wholesale funding market dried up in September 2008 following the collapse of Lehman Brothers, HBOS faced a liquidity crisis and faced difficulty meeting its liabilities. Moreover, as the economy worsened, the market's attitude to structured finance investments and asset-backed securities soured, causing impairments for HBOS's structured assets portfolio. Finally, as the property market stalled and values started to fall, HBOS's mortgage and commercial loan book also suffered large impairments. The net effect was that by September 2008 HBOS was in urgent need of rescue.

In contrast, in the years preceding the credit crisis, the British retail bank Lloyds TSB had pursued a more prudent strategy than other British banks and as a result its pre-tax income growth between 2003 and 2007 was below the British average. For this reason Lloyds TSB was resilient to the banking crises: in 2008 Lloyds TSB made a profit of GBP 845 million, while in the same period HBOS recorded a loss of GBP 7.4 billion.

As the fifth largest retail bank in Britain, HBOS was of critical importance to the entire British financial system. The UK government decided to facilitate the acquisition of HBOS by Lloyds TSB as a private sector solution. As a result, Lloyds TSB announced the acquisition of its competitor HBOS on 18 September 2008, establishing Lloyds Banking Group ("Lloyds") as the entity resulting from the merger.

Because the takeover offer was conditional upon the receipt of the large government aid necessary to rescue HBOS, on 8 October 2008 the British government announced that it was making available new capital to British banks. On 13 October 2008, it indicated that it was making capital investments in RBS, and, upon successful merger, HBOS and Lloyds TSB, totalling GBP 37 billion. On 19 January 2009 Lloyds received a GBP 17 billion state recapitalisation split into GBP 4 billion of preference shares and GBP 13 billion of ordinary shares. As a result, the UK government acquired a 43.5% stake in Lloyds.

4.5.2 Asset Protection Scheme and its Regulatory Capital Benefits

An Asset Protection Scheme (APS) is a de-risking (often referred to as deleveraging) transaction in which a bank transfers the credit risk on certain illiquid assets to the central government of the bank's jurisdiction. Whilst its main benefit on capital is through a substantial reduction of RWAs, an APS reduces volatility of CET1 capital by reducing volatility of earnings.

Asset Protection Scheme (APS)   Stress tests conducted by the Financial Services Authority (the "FSA", a precursor of the PRA) on the bank showed it had substantially less capital than would be needed should the stress case scenario occur. In order to address the capital shortfall identified by the FSA, in March 2009 it was announced that further aid was available to Lloyds granted by the British government via an Asset Protection Scheme (APS). The APS was an unfunded guarantee scheme whereby the British government committed to cover 90% of the losses, in excess of a first loss tranche of 13% to be borne by the bank, on an initial portfolio of GBP 260 billion of loan assets. The size of the first loss tranche equalled the expected losses of the assets. The initial fee was set at GBP 15.6 billion and was to be payable in B shares and amortised over a seven-year period (see Figure 4.5). The B shares ranked pari passu with ordinary shares but did not carry voting rights and were convertible into ordinary shares. The subscription to the B shares would have taken the government's ownership of Lloyds to 62.0%.

- **Consideration for APS**
- **Qualified as Core Tier 1 equity**
- **Nominal GBP 15.6 bn**
- **Amortising over 7 years**
- **Non-voting**
- **Dividends:**
    - ✓ **Higher of 7% and 125% of dividends paid on ordinary shares; scrip option**
    - ✓ **Discretionary, non-cumulative, must be paid before any ordinary dividend can be declared**
- **Convertible into ordinary shares at a conversion price of 115p per ordinary share**
- **Mandatory conversion at 115p per ordinary share when ordinary share price is or exceeds 150p for 20 out of 30 consecutive trading days**

Issuance of B shares

FIGURE 4.5   Main terms of Lloyds' B shares

The APS served two objectives, with the return to long-term viability as the ultimate target: (i) to provide coverage against losses on the protected assets in particular in case of a continuation of the economic stress period and (ii) to provide regulatory capital relief in the form of an increased Core Tier 1 ratio through the reduction in RWAs. The payment of the fee in the form of B shares would also have contributed to improving this ratio by increasing Tier 1 capital.

Regulatory Capital Benefits At the time the APS was negotiated, Basel II requirements were in force. The best quality of capital under Basel II was called Core Tier 1 capital (see Figure 4.6), relatively different to Basel III's CET1. From a regulatory capital perspective, the benefits were fourfold (see Figures 4.7 and 4.8):

- Firstly, the APS provided a 10% enhancement in Lloyds' Core Tier 1 capital to 35.1 billion. The GBP 3.1 billion [=15.6 bn – 50% × (35 bn – 10 bn)] Core Tier 1 capital improvement comprised the fair value of the GBP 15.6 billion B shares issuance minus 50% of the shortfall in provisions over expected losses. Expected losses were GBP 35 billion, while impairments and write-downs totalled GBP 10 billion;
- Secondly, from a risk-weighted assets perspective, the APS reduced its size by GBP 194 billion, a 39% reduction;
- Thirdly, the enhanced capital position allowed an increase in lending availability to customers; and
- Finally, the APS helped management not be distracted in managing this non-core portfolio.

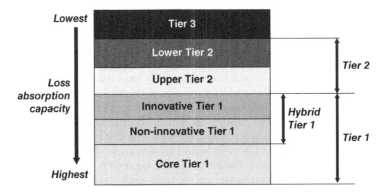

FIGURE 4.6 Basel II regulatory capital categories

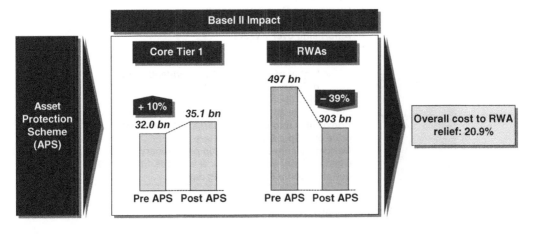

FIGURE 4.7 APS regulatory capital effects

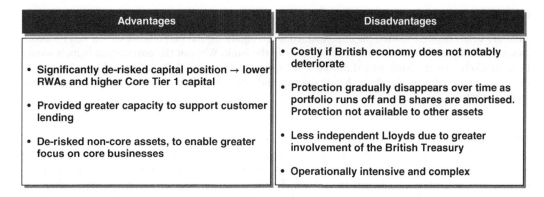

Advantages	Disadvantages
• Significantly de-risked capital position → lower RWAs and higher Core Tier 1 capital • Provided greater capacity to support customer lending • De-risked non-core assets, to enable greater focus on core businesses	• Costly if British economy does not notably deteriorate • Protection gradually disappears over time as portfolio runs off and B shares are amortized. Protection not available to other assets • Less independent Lloyds due to greater involvement of the British Treasury • Operationally intensive and complex

FIGURE 4.8 APS strengths and weaknesses

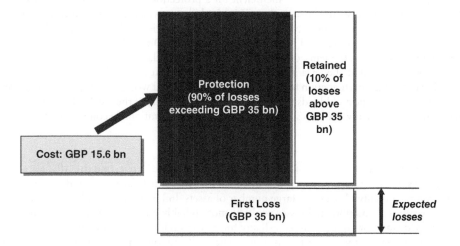

FIGURE 4.9 Share of losses in Lloyds' APS

The APS had several drawbacks, as shown in Figures 4.8 and 4.9:

- The main one was cost. The overall cost of the transaction comprised the GBP 15.6 billion fee in the form of B shares plus the 7% annual dividend (see my comments in box below);
- Secondly, the protection would gradually disappear over time as (i) the protected portfolio runs off and (ii) the B shares are amortized, while not being available to other assets in the bank's whole portfolio;
- Thirdly, the APS would probably increase the amount of intervention of the British government in Lloyds' decision making; and
- Finally, it was operationally intensive and complex.

The protection was arguably costly. The overall cost of the transaction comprised the GBP 15.6 billion fee in the form of B shares plus the 7% annual dividend. It insured 90% of the unexpected losses, while not insuring expected losses. However, the RWA relief was GBP 194 billion that otherwise would have needed to be cushioned with GBP 15.5 billion (=194 bn × 8%) of CET1 capital.

In any case, if Lloyds expected losses in the portfolio were unlikely to exceed the GBP 35 billion first losses, the protection was notably expensive.

4.5.3 Rights Issue and Issuance of the ECNs

APSs are deleveraging transactions implemented when equity capital markets are closed and investors lack confidence on the amount of troubled assets in the bank. Without the government help, it would be quite likely that the bank would not be able to survive. However, APSs are arguably expensive, as the government tries to ascertain that taxpayers and other banks in the same jurisdiction are not treated unfairly.

Redesign of the APS   When Lloyds announced its intention to participate in the APS in March 2009, the financial markets were in turmoil and the economic outlook was highly uncertain. Shortly afterwards, the financial markets and economic outlook became more stable. In particular, the economic environment in Britain had begun to stabilise. Lloyds' margins began to stabilise, cost reductions remained on track and overall impairments had peaked. As a result, over the course of summer 2009, Lloyds started to explore alternative solutions to participation in the APS. Lloyds' management claimed that the impact on capital was relatively inefficient for a protection that would disappear over time.

Under the APS, Lloyds would have made a GBP 15.6 billion payment, for insurance against a significant deterioration in the performance of a specified portfolio of loans. Lloyds believed that the APS would have delivered only a marginal benefit to its shareholders. On the basis of its expectations at the time of future impairments, the bank did not expect to make any claim under the APS. And, even if the British economy declined at the level assumed in the FSA's stress test, Lloyds believed that any claims would be lower than the participation fee. Moreover, the APS capital would not be permanent, given that the fee amortised over time and Lloyds would lose the capital benefits of the RWA relief as the APS assets progressively ran off. Finally, the APS scheme would have been operationally complex and costly to run.

In my view and with the benefit of hindsight, Lloyds was right in rejecting the APS, for several reasons. Firstly, this "rescue scheme" was designed for RBS, which faced a high degree of uncertainty over the potential losses of a large number of assets. In Lloyds, the problematic loans were more concentrated and potential losses could be more reliably estimated. Arguably, what Lloyds really needed was new equity to replenish any future capital losses due to write-downs on those risky loans. Secondly, it was a costly insurance. The GBP 15.6 billion cost, ignoring the 7% dividend, implied a breakeven loss level of 20% [=(35bn+15.6bn/0.9)/260bn], well above the 13% expected loss (see Figure 4.10).

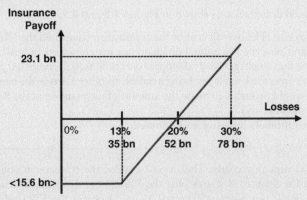

FIGURE 4.10   APS – Benefits vs. cost profile excluding the 7% dividend

In September 2009 it was determined by the British banking regulator that in the absence of any participation in the APS, Lloyds would need to increase its total capital by GBP 21 billion to meet the regulator's requirements. On 3 November 2009, Lloyds announced its final decision not to participate in the APS and its alternative capital raising exercise aimed at increasing the Core Tier 1 capital to meet the regulator requirements. Non-participation in the APS had to be vetted by the regulator as the APS was the key measure to help the bank meet the required capital framework both in base and stress case scenarios.

Although the bank finally decided not to participate in the APS, the British authorities considered that it had benefited from its announced participation in the scheme. For this benefit over the period from March 2009 to September 2009 LBG would need to pay a GBP 2.5 billion exit fee to the government. The exit fee was payable in cash.

The alternative recapitalisation was made up of the following measures:

- A GBP 13.1 billion fully underwritten rights issue. This measure was aimed at raising Lloyds' Core Tier 1 capital;
- A GBP 7.5 billion offer exchanging existing capital securities into either contingent Core Tier 1 instruments (the Enhanced Capital Notes – "**ECN**") and/or ordinary shares. This measure was aimed at meeting the British regulator stress tests;
- An agreement to suspend the payment of coupons for a two-year period from 31 January 2010 to 31 January 2012, unless there was a legal obligation to do so. Therefore, preference shares with discretionary coupons would receive no coupon payments during that period; and
- Other management actions that included cost-cutting measures, securitisation operations and other RWA reductions.

Rights Issue   In the framework of the GBP 13.1 billion rights issue, new shares were issued at a deep discount to the then-prevailing stock market price of Lloyds' ordinary shares. The British treasury participated in the rights issue in order to maintain its shareholding of 43.5% (an additional GBP 5.7 billion investment to GBP 20.4 billion).

Exchange Offer   In the exchange offer, the holders of 52 existing preference shares and undated subordinated bonds, which had a nominal value of approximately GBP 16 billion, were invited to exchange these instruments against ECN and/or new ordinary shares. As a result of the exchange, Lloyds issued a total of GBP 8.55 billion of ECNs, which were eligible Lower Tier 2 instruments.

The ECNs were subordinated debt with maturities ranging from 10 years to perpetual maturities and with non-discretionary coupon payment provisions. The unique feature of the ECNs was that their contingent conversion condition was not linked to Lloyds' share price reaching a certain level nor they could be converted at the discretion of the bondholders. The ECNs automatically converted into Lloyds' common stock if the group's published consolidated Core Tier 1 capital ratio fell to less than 5%. The conversion price was the share price prevailing in December 2009, when the exchange was offered. The ECNs provided an additional buffer of Core Tier 1 capital, which would only materialise in times of stress and allow Core Tier 1 ratio to remain above the minimum requirement under the British regulator stress test scenario by absorbing losses in such scenario. The conversion feature meant that the ECN holders were likely to suffer a material loss upon conversion as it was probable that the share price would have dropped upon the severe deterioration of Lloyds' capital position triggering the conversion.

Table 4.1 shows the principal terms of one of the ECNs issued by Lloyds:

ECNs' Early Redemption Rights   Lloyds could only early redeem the perpetual ECNs in the following three circumstances:

- On each coupon date, commencing on 15 June 2020. This exercise required the prior approval of the British banking regulator.

TABLE 4.1   Main Terms of Lloyds' USD ECN Bond

Lloyds' ECN Bond Terms	
Issuer	LBG Capital No 1 Plc
Guarantor	Lloyds Banking Group Plc
Instrument	Enhanced capital notes (ECN) bond
Rank	Subordinated
Issue date	15 December 2009
Notional amount	USD 1.26 billion
Underlying shares	Lloyds Banking Group Plc shares
Maturity	Perpetual, subject to Call right
Coupon	8% to 15 June 2020; then USD Libor 3-month plus 6.405%, paid quarterly
Conversion price	GBP 0.592093
Call right	Callable at par by issuer on each coupon payment date, commencing on 15 June 2020, Redemption due to taxation and for regulatory purposes
Redemption due to taxation	On occurrence of a tax event
Redemption for regulatory purposes	On occurrence of a capital disqualification event
Mandatory conversion	Bond automatically converts into ordinary shares at the conversion price if the group's published consolidated Core Tier 1 capital ratio falls below 5%
Exercise right by bondholders	None

- When a tax event had occurred and was continuing. A tax event was deemed to have occurred if (i) Lloyds was obliged to pay additional tax as a result of a change in UK tax law which could not be avoided by taking reasonable measures, or (ii) as a result of such change in tax law Lloyds was not entitled to (a) a tax deduction in respect of its financing expenses in relation to the ECNs or (b) have any loss resulting from such deduction taken into account when computing the group's tax liabilities, and in each case Lloyds could not avoid the event by taking reasonable measures.
- When a capital disqualification event had taken place and was continuing. A capital disqualification event was deemed to have occurred if (i) at any time the ECNs no longer qualified for inclusion in the Lower Tier 2 capital of Lloyds, or (ii) at any time the ECNs had ceased to be taken into account for purposes of any "stress test" applied by the British banking regulator in respect of the consolidated Core Tier 1 ratio.

Attractiveness of the ECNs to Lloyds   The advantages of the ECNs issues from Lloyds' perspective were the following:

1. The ECNs were designed to meet the British banking regulator's stress tests, without being dilutive to shareholders at the time of their issue. The ECNs were eligible to be classified as Lower Tier 2 capital. Because the bonds automatically converted if the group's published consolidated Core Tier 1

capital ratio fell below 5%, the ECNs also counted as Core Tier 1 capital for the purposes of the British banking regulator's stress test framework when the stressed projection showed a 5% (or lower) Core Tier 1, which was the trigger for conversion into ordinary shares.

2. Concurrently with the ECNs issue, Lloyds launched a "gigantic" GBP 13.5 billion rights issue in a very difficult market environment. The ECNs allowed Lloyds to reduce the size of the rights offering.
3. The ECNs had embedded countercyclical features at an attractive cost. During the credit crisis of 2007–2008 many banks found themselves with insufficient capital to shield them against the downturn. The ECNs' countercyclical features stemmed from their ability to display loss-absorbing and equity-like qualities if Lloyds reached a low Core Tier 1 capital. Lloyds could put in place countercyclical protection while having an attractive cost of capital in prosperous times.
4. The ECNs' coupon payments were tax-deductible. In other words, the ECNs were treated as debt for tax purposes.
5. The ECNs were issued in exchange for some of Lloyds' Upper Tier 2 capital instruments. The ECNs replaced instruments with high coupon and low regulatory bank capital content.

Attractiveness of the ECNs to Bondholders The attractiveness to the bondholders was the ECNs' high coupon. The coupons were set a large premium above the USD Libor interest rates or Lloyds' dividend yield. For example, the ECN covered above paid a quarterly coupon of 8% to 15 June 2020 and thereafter USD Libor 3-month plus 6.405%.

Another interesting feature to the bondholders was that the ECNs' coupons contained non-discretionary payment provisions. Coupons on other contingent convertible instruments were frequently deferrable and non-cumulative or could be satisfied in ordinary shares. Therefore, Lloyds' ECNs reduced the uncertainty regarding the coupon payments as the bank could not waive them. If Lloyds failed to make payment of an ECN coupon, the bondholders could institute legal proceedings against Lloyds to enforce such payment.

4.5.4 Accounting Impact of the Rights Issue and the ECNs

Prior to analysing the impact of the rights issue and the ECNs in Lloyds' regulatory capital, it is important to understand how these instruments are treated from an accounting perspective.

Rights Issue The 13.1 billion rights issue (net of costs) were recognised in Lloyds' shareholders' equity increasing its share capital and premium accounts, as shown in Figure 4.11.

ECNs A total nominal of GBP 8,554 million of ECNs were issued. According to Lloyds, the ECNs were accounted for as hybrid instruments. A hybrid instrument is an instrument that includes an

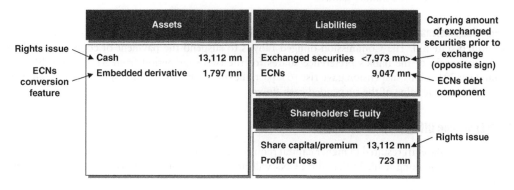

FIGURE 4.11 Accounting impact of exchange offer

embedded derivative. In other words, a hybrid instrument is an instrument that comprises a host contract (i.e., a debt-like component) and an embedded derivative that causes some or all of the contractual cash flows of the host contract to be modified based on a market rate or another variable. In the case of the ECNs the embedded derivative was the conversion feature which was linked to the group's Core Tier capital. According to IFRS, when the embedded derivative is not closely related to the host contract, these two contracts should be accounted for separately.

The ECNs' host contract was recognised as a liability as coupon payments were mandatory. This was the case even for the undated ECNs as it was assumed that the mandatory coupons represented a combination of interest and repayments of principal.

Regarding the equity conversion provision, at the time of writing there is no uniform conclusion in the financial community regarding its accounting treatment. The conversion embedded in the ECNs was for a fixed number of shares for a fixed amount in the entity's functional currency, meeting the "fixed-for-fixed" requirement for equity treatment. However, the conversion into ordinary shares was required if the consolidated Core Tier 1 ratio fell below 5%. According to Lloyds, the conversion feature met the definition of an embedded derivative and was recorded separately as a derivative asset.

The embedded equity conversion feature was valued by comparing the market price of the ECNs with the market price of similar bonds without the conversion feature. The latter was calculated by discounting the expected ECN cash flows in the absence of a conversion using prevailing market yields for similar capital non-convertible securities. The market price of the ECNs was calculated with reference to multiple broker quotes. The initial split between the host contract and the embedded derivative was the following:

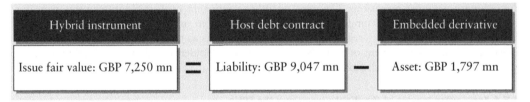

The host contract was recognised at amortised cost using the effective interest rate method. The derivative component was fair valued at each reporting date. Movements in the fair value of the derivative were recorded in profit or loss as net trading income/loss.

Securities Exchanged   Preference shares and undated subordinated liabilities were exchanged for the ECNs. Almost all these instruments were previously recognised as liabilities. The instruments exchanged were assumed to be redeemed, resulting in GBP 7,973 million of liabilities being redeemed, as shown in Figure 4.11.

Additionally, the redemption of these securities resulted, together with coupons suspensions (covered next), in a GBP 723 million gain.

Coupon Suspensions   The restructuring plan required the approval of the European Commission, as it constituted state aid. The Commission obliged Lloyds to suspend the payment of coupons and dividends on certain of the bank's preference shares for the two year period from 31 January 2010 to 31 January 2012. This suspension gave rise to a partial extinguishment of the original liability, equivalent to the present value of the suspended cash flows.

4.5.5 Exchange Offer of ECNs for CoCos

The advent of Basel III resulted in higher capital requirements for banks, including a changed definition of core capital, making it likely that the ECNs will not provide going concern benefit under future stress tests.

During the previous stress test in June 2013, the PRA (the British banking regulator) focused on fully loaded CET1 capital and leverage ratio. As a result of differences in definition, Lloyds' CET1 ratio

(10%) was substantially lower than the Core Tier 1 ratio (14%) on which the conversion trigger of the ECNs was based. As at 31 December 2013, the difference was 4%, as shown in Figure 4.12. As the conversion of the ECNs was triggered when a 5% Core Tier 1 ratio was reached and assuming such 4% difference, it meant that conversion would take place when the fully loaded CET1 ratio of the bank would be 1%, well below the minimum requirements.

Other recent regulatory developments deemed the ECNs rather ineffective, including:

- A requirement in the CRR that with effect from 1 January 2014 convertible AT1capital instruments should have a conversion trigger set at no less than 5.125%;
- Statements by the PRA in late 2013 that a conversion trigger of 5.125% CET1 ratio may not convert in time to prevent the failure of a firm and that it expected major UK firms to meet a 7% fully-loaded CET1 ratio;
- A statement by the EBA in January 2014 that Tier 2 instruments must have a conversion trigger above a 5.5%. CET1 ratio to be recognised in its forthcoming stress tests; and
- An announcement by the PRA that, following a consultation commenced in October 2013, it expected to revise stress testing methodology and pass marks in 2014.

In March 2014 Lloyds launched exchange offers for holders of certain series of its ECNs to exchange them for new contingent convertible instruments ("CoCos"). In addition, Lloyds made a tender offer to eligible retail holders outside the United States to sell their GBP-denominated ECNs for cash. At that time Lloyds had 33 series of ECNs outstanding issued by its subsidiaries LBG Capital No. 1 and LBG Capital No. 2, with a nominal amount of GBP 8.4 billion, an average coupon of 9.3% and a Core Tier 1 conversion trigger of 5%.

ECN holders had an incentive to accept the exchange. The ECNs contained a regulatory call right should, amongst other things, the ECNs cease to be taken into account for the purposes of any "stress test" applied by the PRA in respect of core capital. Given that EBA outlined at the time that the capital hurdle in the adverse scenario was set at 5.5% on a transitional basis, inclusion of old ECNs in the capital buffer by the PRA for stress test purposes was uncertain. Whilst Lloyds could not to exercise the call right yet, the offer provided eligible holders with a means to eliminate the uncertainty around the regulatory call right in the ECNs.

Lloyds targeted a maximum GBP 5 billion nominal amount of CoCos to be issued. Coupons ranged between 6.375% and 7.875%, and the CoCos were convertible into a fixed number of Lloyds' ordinary shares at GBP 0.645 should its reported fully loaded CET1 ratio fall below 7%.

The main terms of one of the CoCos denominated in GBP are outlined in Table 4.2:

The exchange offers were completed in April 2014 and resulted in a total of GBP 5,329 million of CoCos being issued, after issue costs, in exchange for GBP 5.0 billion (nominal) of ECNs.

4.5.6 Regulatory Impact of the Exchange

The offer helped Lloyds in aligning its capital base to the new Basel III capital framework. The impacts on the group's fully loaded Basel III regulatory capital, ignoring grandfathering provisions, were the following (see Figure 4.13):

- As a result of the one-off charge of GBP 1 billion, Lloyds experienced a reduction of approximately 40 basis points in its fully loaded CET1 ratio.
- The offer increased Lloyds' AT1 capital by GBP 5.3 billion, as the CoCos constituted AT1 eligible instruments. The offer helped deliver Lloyds' medium-term AT1 requirement.
- The offer reduced Lloyds' Tier 2 capital by GBP 4.1 billion, as the retired ECNs previously constituted Tier 2 eligible instruments.
- The group's total capital ratio was not materially affected.
- The offer increased Lloyds' leverage ratio by approximately 50 basis points.

Additionally, although not a regulatory capital benefit, the offer benefited the rating agencies' capital measures on Lloyds.

Lloyds' Core Tier 1 (Basel II) (December 2013)

Shareholders' equity per balance sheet	38,989 mn
Non-controlling interests per balance sheet	347 mn
Regulatory adjustments:	
Adjustments to non-controlling interests	<315 mn>
Adjustment for own credit	185 mn
Defined benefit pension adjustment	<78 mn>
Unrealised reserve on AFS debt securities	750 mn
Unrealised reserve on AFS equity invest	<135 mn>
Cash flow hedging reserve	1,055 mn
Other items	452 mn
Less: deductions from core tier 1	
Goodwill	<2,016 mn>
Intangible assets	<1,799 mn>
50% excess of expected losses over impairment provisions	<373 mn>
50% of securitisation positions	<71 mn>
Core Tier 1 capital	36,991 mn

Lloyds' Core Equity Tier 1 (Fully Loaded Basel III) (December 2013)

Shareholders' equity per balance sheet	38,989 mn
Adjustment for insurance equity	<1,917 mn>
Regulatory adjustments:	
Non-controlling interests	—
Other adjustments	1,295 mn
Less: deductions from CET1	
Goodwill and other intangible assets	<1,979 mn>
Excess of expected losses over impairment provisions	<866 mn>
Securitisation deductions	<141 mn>
Significant investments	<3,185 mn>
Deferred tax assets	<5,155 mn>
Core Equity Tier 1 capital	27,041 mn

FIGURE 4.12   Lloyds' Core Tier 1 and CET1 capital as of 31 December 2013

TABLE 4.2   Main Terms of Lloyds' GBP AT1 Instruments

GBP AT1 Securities – Main Terms

ISIN	XS1043545059
Issuer	Lloyds Banking Group Plc (LBG)
Issue date	1 April 2014
Maturity	Perpetual
Coupon	7%, discretionary and non-cumulative, to be reset every five years based on market rates
Call right	Every 5 years commencing at the option of LBG. Any repayments required prior consent of the PRA
Conversion	Into ordinary shares of LBG should the fully loaded CET1 ratio of the group fall below 7%
Conversion price	GBP 0.645, subject to certain anti-dilution adjustments
Call right for regulatory or tax reasons	Issuer may redeem all, but not partially, at their principal amount together with any accrued interest if at any time a "regulatory disqualification event" or a "tax event" occurred, subject to prior consent of the PRA and subject to the issuer being solvent
Ranking (prior to the conversion trigger)	Prior to being converted, the instruments ranked junior to subordinated claims, pari passu to preference shares

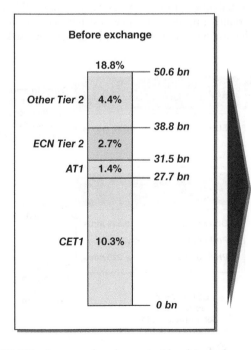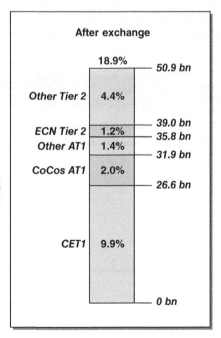

FIGURE 4.13   Impact of exchange in Lloyds' regulatory capital

4.5.7 Accounting Impact of the Exchange

As pointed out previously when the ECNs' equity conversion provision was covered above, at the time of transaction there was no uniform conclusion within the financial community as of the accounting treatment of CoCos. The different interpretations are related to the accounting treatment of the conversion feature linked to the group's CET1 capital, and that also provided for the supervisory authority to require conversion. As in the case of the ECNs, Lloyds assumed that the CoCos were instruments that comprised a host component and an embedded conversion option component, as shown in Figure 4.14.

The host component represented the cash flows of the CoCo as if no conversion clause existed. Under IFRS it was accounted for as an equity instrument (i.e., included in Lloyds' shareholders' equity section) as they were undated, and interest payments made in respect of the CoCos were completely discretionary and non-cumulative. As a result, any interest payments were accounted for as a distribution of profits to equity holders (i.e., as dividends). The CoCos were initially registered at their GBP 5,329 million fair value.

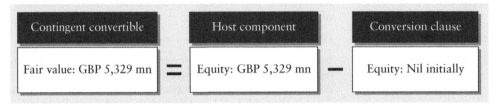

Although the equity conversion feature met the definition of an equity instrument as it provided for a fixed number of shares to be delivered in exchange for a fixed amount (i.e., the conversion price was fixed), its accounting treatment was not clear at the time of the transaction, as mentioned previously. Lloyds estimated that the conversion feature had no value at the time of the exchange.

The exchanged ECNs were classified as debt liabilities prior to the exchange. Under IFRS, an exchange of instruments classified as debt for accounting purposes for new instruments classified as equity for accounting purposes, would result in the original debt instruments being derecognised and

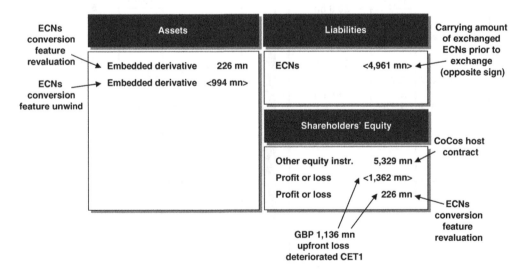

FIGURE 4.14 Accounting impact of Lloyds' exchange offer

the new equity instruments being recognised. A gain or loss would be recognised in the income statement as the difference between the fair value of the new equity instruments issued and the carrying value of the debt instruments derecognised.

As the exchange consideration in the offer was greater than the book value of the ECNs accepted in such offer (including their embedded equity conversion feature), Lloyds recognised a one-off charge of GBP 1,136 million, of which GBP 768 million comprised the accelerated amortisation of the derivative embedded in the ECNs.

The ECNs had non-discretionary coupons which reduced Lloyds' net interest income. As any interest payments made in respect of the CoCos were accounted for as a distribution of profits to equity holders, they did not affect Lloyds' net interest income. Therefore, the exchange offer delivered a benefit to Lloyds' net interest income and net interest margin.

Had the ECNs been classified as equity instruments (which was not the case for Lloyds), the accounting treatment would have been different. Under IFRS an exchange for instruments classified as equity for accounting purposes for new instruments classified as equity for accounting purposes, would result in the original equity instruments being derecognised and new equity instruments being recognised. No gain or loss would be recognised in the income statement.

CHAPTER 5

Tier 2 Capital

Tier 2 capital is a supplementary capital that can absorb losses on a "gone-concern" basis. In other words, Tier 2 capital absorbs losses in insolvency prior to senior creditors (e.g., depositors) losing their claims. Tier 2 is the weakest-quality capital from the regulator's perspective, designed to absorb losses once Tier 1 capital has been deployed (see Figure 5.1). The minimum "total capital" – which comprises CET1, AT1 and Tier2 – required, excluding the capital buffers, is 8% of RWAs. The minimum Tier 1 capital – which comprises CET1 and AT1 – required is 6% of RWAs. As CET1 capital and AT1 capital are more costly than Tier 2 capital, it means that in practice banks are likely to hold Tier 2 capital equal or in excess of 2% of RWAs:

$$\text{Typical level of Tier 2 capital} = \frac{\text{Tier 2 capital}}{\text{Risk-weighted assets}} \geq 2\%$$

5.1 TIER 2 CAPITAL CALCULATION AND REQUIREMENTS FOR INCLUSION

Tier 2 capital is considered the element of capital that is the lowest quality to absorb losses. The calculation of the level of Tier 2 capital that a bank holds is similar to that of AT1 capital.

5.1.1 Tier 2 Capital Calculation

Tier 2 capital consists of the sum of the following elements [CRR 62], as shown in Figure 5.2:

- Capital instruments and subordinated loans issued by the bank that meet the criteria for inclusion in Tier 2 capital and are not included in Tier 1 capital. These instruments shall not qualify as CET1 or AT1 items;
- Share premium (stock surplus) resulting from the issue of instruments included in Tier 2 capital;
- Eligible Tier 2 minority interests;
- For banks calculating RWAs in accordance with the standardised approach to credit risk [CRR Chapter 2 of Title II of Part Three], general provisions can be included in Tier 2 capital subject to the limit of 1.25% of RWAs calculated in accordance with the standardised approach; and

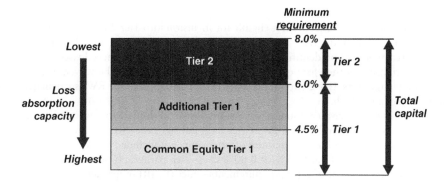

FIGURE 5.1 Tier 2 capital in a bank's regulatory total capital

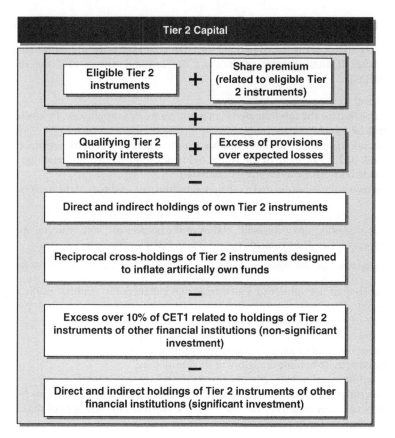

FIGURE 5.2 Components of a bank's Tier 2 capital

- For banks calculating RWAs in accordance with the Internal Ratings-Based (IRB) approach to credit risk [CRR Chapter 3 of Title II of Part Three] and where the total expected loss amount is less than total eligible provisions, banks may recognise the difference in Tier 2 capital up to a maximum of 0.6% of credit RWAs calculated in accordance with the IRB approach.

Specific credit risk adjustments are not eligible for inclusion into Tier 2 capital under the standardised approach for credit risk. Nonetheless, general provisions or loan-loss reserves held against future, presently unidentified, losses are freely available to meet losses which subsequently materialise and therefore qualify for inclusion within Tier 2. However, general provisions are only eligible as Tier 2 capital up to a maximum of 1.25% of RWAs calculated under the standardised approach.

Some banks may have an amount of provisions above this limit. Moreover, some banks may not be able to include general provisions in Tier 2 capital since they would otherwise breach the limit of Tier 2 to Tier 1 capital. The amount of provisions not included in Tier 2 capital (i.e., any amount in excess of one of the 1.25% or 0.60% caps – see paragraph prior to this box) is used to offset the EL-component of capital requirements under the IRB-approach.

5.1.2 Criteria Governing Instruments Inclusion in Tier 2 Capital

Tier 2 instruments are normally issued in bond form but could be issued in subordinated loan formats as well. Under Basel III, an instrument qualifies as a Tier 2 capital instrument if it meets all the following criteria [CRR 63]:

1. It is issued and fully paid-in;
2. It is not purchased (or the subordinated loan is not granted), as applicable, by any of the following:
   a. The bank or its subsidiaries; and
   b. An undertaking in which the bank has participation in the form of ownership, direct or by way of control, of 20% or more of the voting rights or capital of that undertaking;
3. It is not funded directly or indirectly by the bank;
4. Its principal is wholly subordinated to all non-subordinated creditors of the bank (e.g., depositors);

In the case of a winding-up of the bank, claims of the holders of Tier 2 instruments rank above claims in respect of Tier 1 instruments (i.e. CET1 and AT1 instruments).

5. It is neither secured nor subject to a guarantee that enhances the seniority of the claim by any of the following:
   a. The bank or its subsidiaries;
   b. The parent undertaking of the bank or its subsidiaries;
   c. The parent financial holding company or its subsidiaries;
   d. The mixed activity holding company or its subsidiaries;
   e. The mixed financial holding company or its subsidiaries;
   f. Any undertaking that has close links with entities referred to in the previous five points;
6. It is not subject to any arrangement that otherwise enhances the seniority of the claim;
7. It has an original maturity of at least **five** years;

There is no requirement that Tier 2 instruments must have a fixed redemption date. Assuming all other requirements for Tier 2 capital qualification are met, instruments which are perpetual would also qualify as Tier 2 instruments. Economically speaking, a true perpetual instrument is an instrument with an infinite original maturity. Nonetheless, in practice most Tier 2 instruments have a fixed redemption date.

8. It does not include in its provisions any incentive for their principal amount to be redeemed or repaid, as applicable, by the bank prior to their maturity;

9. Where it includes one or more call options or early repayment options, as applicable, the options are exercisable at the sole discretion of the issuer or debtor, as applicable;

10. It may be called, redeemed or repurchased or repaid early only where the conditions laid down in [CRR 77] are met, and not before five years after the date of issuance or raising, as applicable, except where the conditions laid down in [CRR 78(4)] are met. The conditions for the redemption or repurchase of capital instruments set out in [CRR 77 and 78(4)] relate to changes in the regulatory or tax treatment of the instrument, being covered in Section 4.2.6;

11. It does not indicate explicitly or implicitly in its provisions that it would or might be called, redeemed, repurchased or repaid early, as applicable, by the bank other than in the insolvency or liquidation of the bank and the bank does not otherwise provide such an indication;

12. In its provisions, it does not give the holder the right to accelerate the future scheduled payment of interest or principal, other than in the insolvency or liquidation of the bank;

13. The level of due interest or dividend payments, as applicable, on the instrument will not be amended on the basis of the credit standing of the bank or its parent undertaking; and

> No restrictions are set on the coupon payments. Therefore, Tier 2 instruments may pay a mandatory (i.e., non-deferrable) coupon. Tier 2 instruments are "gone concern" instruments, providing loss absorption in an insolvency by way of subordination to senior debt. In other words, because they are *not* "going concern" instruments, they are not required to absorb losses by cancelling payment of coupons or by being converted into equity or written-down.
>
> Nonetheless, Tier 2 instruments may provide for coupon deferral, when the mandatory coupon is not paid. This type of clause does not jeopardise a Tier 2 instrument's eligibility.
>
> Similarly, a Tier 2 instrument which includes terms according to which coupons would be mandatorily deferred and not paid when coupons on AT1 instruments are not paid gets Tier 2 treatment as well. Such clause is commonly aimed at obtaining more equity credit for the Tier 2 instrument by credit rating agencies.

14. Where it is not issued (or raised in the case of a subordinated loan) directly by the bank, both of the following conditions are met:
    a. The issuing entity is part of the perimeter of regulatory consolidation of the bank;
    b. The proceeds are immediately available to the bank in a form that satisfies all the conditions laid down above.

> Pursuant to [CRR 65], if any of the conditions laid down above ceases to be met, that instrument shall immediately cease to qualify as a Tier 2 instrument, and the part of the share premium accounts that relates to that instrument shall immediately cease to qualify as a Tier 2 item.

> One of the Tier 2 eligibility requirements for an instrument is the absence of incentives for the bank to redeem it. In other words, no expectations should be created at the date of issuance that the instrument is likely to be redeemed.
>
> The EBA clarified that an expectation that the instrument is likely to be redeemed is created if any of the following provisions are included in the terms and conditions of the capital instrument:

(*continued*)

- A call option combined with an increase in the credit spread of the instrument if the call is not exercised;
- A call option combined with a requirement or an investor option to convert the instrument into a CET1 instrument where the call is not exercised;
- A call option combined with a change in reference rate where the credit spread over the second reference rate is greater than the initial payment rate minus the swap rate;
- A call option combined with an increase of the redemption amount in the future;
- A remarketing option combined with an increase in the credit spread of the instrument or a change in reference rate where the credit spread over the second reference rate is greater than the initial payment rate minus the swap rate where the instrument is not remarketed; or
- A marketing of the instrument in a way which suggests to investors that the instrument will be called.

Where the instrument is issued by a special purpose vehicle, the conditions laid out in [CRR 83] must be met as well. These criteria is covered in Section 4.2.5 for AT1 instruments, being relevant for Tier 2 instruments as well.

Table 5.1 summarises some of the requirements for Tier 2 instruments:

TABLE 5.1   Template of Tier 2 Instruments' Main Terms

Template of Tier 2 Instruments Termsheet

Term	Minimum 5 years
Call option	Allowed, but no earlier than 5 years from issuance date
Coupons	May be mandatory. May be cumulative
Call right	First call minimum 5 years after issuance. Subject to regulatory permission. No incentive to redeem At any time due to tax or regulatory reasons
Trigger for loss	N/A
Loss absorption	On bail-in
Step-ups	Not permitted (i.e., no incentive to redeem)
Write-up	N/A
Coupon stopper	N/A
Ranking	Rank directly ahead of AT1 instruments and below senior creditors in the capital structure

5.1.3 Amortisation of Tier 2 Instruments

Recognition in regulatory capital in the remaining five years before maturity is amortised on a straight line basis. In other words, the amount of Tier 2 capital recognition is 100%, 80%, 60%, 40%, 20% when the instrument's residual term is five, four, three, two and one years prior to its maturity, respectively.

Although the maturity requirement is a term of at least five years, in practice Tier 2 instruments tend to have a notably longer maturity, as their Tier 2 content is gradually lost during the last 5 years of their life.

As a result, issuers of Tier 2 instruments have a strong incentive to early amortise a Tier 2 instrument when its term to maturity is four years.

5.1.4 Conditions to the Redemption or Repurchase of Tier 2 Instruments

The conditions to the redemption or repurchase of Tier 2 instruments are covered in Section 4.2.6.

5.2 NEGATIVE AMOUNTS RESULTING FROM THE CALCULATION OF EXPECTED LOSS AMOUNTS

At the time of writing, the EU has not yet adapted the CRR to incorporate IFRS 9's provisioning rules. The filter described in this section is based on the rules set out in [CRR 62(c) and (d), 159], which as a result of IFRS 9 being implemented may be subject to changes.

5.2.1 Shortfall of Provisions

It was covered in Section 3.15 that for banks calculating RWAs using the Internal Ratings-Based (IRB) Approach, negative amounts resulting from the calculation of expected loss amounts are deducted from CET1. The objective of such deduction is to eliminate any incentives for under-provisioning.

5.2.2 Excess of Provisions

Unlike a shortfall of provisions, an excess of provisions, gross of tax effects, is *not* added to CET1, but to Tier 2 capital (see Figure 5.3):

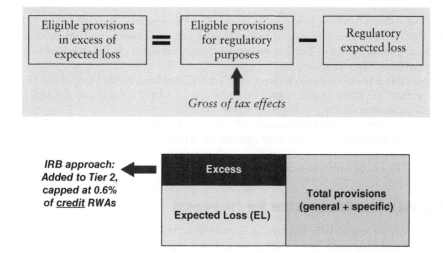

FIGURE 5.3   Treatment of the excess in provisions from expected losses calculated under the IRB approach

This addition is subject to:

- A cap of 1.25% of *credit* RWAs calculated under the standardised approach [CRR Chapter 2 of Title II of Part Three]; or
- A cap of 0.6% of *credit* RWAs calculated under the IRB approach [CRR Chapter 3 of Title II of Part Three].

Banks are not able to reduce the exposure value with the value of general provisions which exceeds the 1.25% or 0.6% cap.

In the case of banks using the IRB approach, they are fully penalised for any shortfall while are partially compensated in the case of an excess. As a result, banks using the IRB approach have no incentives for under-provisioning but at the same time have limited incentives to over-provisioning.

As accounting provisions under IFRS 9 are substantially higher than those under IAS 39, the 1.25% or 0.6% cap (if maintained) will be more likely to be reached, further reducing encouragements for over-provisioning.

In general, except during times of economic downturn, banks generally have substantial provisions in excess of expected losses. Banking supervisors need to carefully assess whether the risks addressed by this filter are already being tackled by the countercyclical buffer. An overlap is likely to unnecessarily impose an additional burden on banks during times of economic weakness, slowing economic recovery.

5.3 DEDUCTIONS FROM TIER 2 CAPITAL

A number of deductions are applied in calculating a bank's Tier 2 capital level pursuant to [CRR 66] (see Figure 5.2):

- Direct and indirect holdings by the bank of own Tier 2 instruments, including own Tier 2 instruments that the bank could be obliged to purchase as a result of contractual obligations;
- Reciprocal cross-holdings of Tier 2 instruments of financial sector entities designed to inflate artificially the bank's Tier 2 funds;
- The applicable amount of direct, indirect and synthetic holdings by the bank of the Tier 2 instruments of financial sector entities where the bank does not have a significant investment in those entities (see Section 5.4.2);
- Direct, indirect and synthetic holdings by the bank of the Tier 2 instruments of financial sector entities where the bank has a significant investment in those entities, excluding underwriting positions held for fewer than five working days; and
- Qualifying Tier 2 minority interests.

5.3.1 Direct and Indirect Holdings of Own Tier 2 Instruments

Pursuant to [CRR 66 (a) and 67], direct, indirect and synthetic holdings by the bank of its own Tier 2 instruments are deducted from Tier 2 capital. In addition, any own Tier 2 instruments that the bank could be contractually obliged to purchase are deducted from Tier 2 capital as well. The amounts to be deducted include the share premium related to the own Tier 2 instruments held. This filter applies irrespective of the location of the exposure in the banking book or the trading book.

Gross long positions may be deducted net of short positions (i.e., only the net long position is deducted) only if both the following conditions are met:

- The long and short positions are in the same underlying exposure and the short positions involve no counterparty risk; and
- Either both the long and the short positions are held in the trading book or both are held in the banking book.

Pursuant to [CRR 75], the maturity requirements for short positions are deemed to be met in respect of positions held where the following conditions are met:

- The bank has the contractual right to sell on a specific future date to the counterparty providing the hedge the long position that is being hedged; and
- The counterparty providing the hedge to the bank is contractually obliged to purchase from the bank on that specific future date the long position referred to in the previous requirement.

Banks are required to calculate the underlying exposure to own Tier 2 instruments through direct, indirect and synthetic holdings of **index securities**. Section 3.20.1 covers in more detail the general requirements related to indirect holdings arising from index holdings.

5.4 HOLDINGS OF TIER 2 INSTRUMENTS OF OTHER FINANCIAL INSTITUTIONS

Holdings of Tier 2 instruments of other financial sector entities impact a bank's Tier 2 capital in three different ways, as shown in Figure 5.4:

- Direct, indirect and synthetic holdings of the Tier 2 instruments of financial sector entities where those entities have **reciprocal cross-holdings** with the bank designed to inflate artificially the own funds of the bank. These holdings are fully deducted from Tier 2 capital;
- Direct, indirect and synthetic holdings by the bank of the Tier 2 instruments of financial sector entities where the bank does *not* have a **significant investment** in those entities. These holdings are aggregated with the bank's holdings of CET1 and AT1 instruments in those entities and compared to 10% of the bank's CET1 capital, resulting in amounts being risk-weighted and, potentially, other amounts being deducted from Tier 2 capital; and
- Direct, indirect and synthetic holdings by the bank of the Tier 2 instruments of financial sector entities where the bank has a **significant investment** in those entities. These holdings are fully deducted from Tier 2 capital.

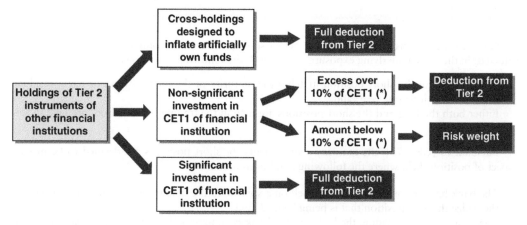

(*) Excess is calculated in combination with holdings of CET1, AT1 and Tier 2 in such financial institutions

FIGURE 5.4 Treatment of investments in Tier 2 instruments of other financial institutions

5.4.1 Reciprocal Cross-holdings of Tier 2 Instruments Designed to Artificially Inflate Own Funds

Pursuant to [CRR 66 (b) and 68], direct, indirect and synthetic holdings of the Tier 2 instruments of financial sector entities where those entities have reciprocal cross-holdings with the bank designed to inflate artificially the AT1 funds of the bank are **fully deducted** from Tier 2 capital.

When calculating holdings of Tier 2 instruments of other financial institutions, banks need to take into account the following:

- Holdings of Tier 2 instruments are calculated on the basis of the gross long positions;
- Holdings of Tier 2 own-fund insurance items and Tier 3 own-fund insurance items are treated as holdings of Tier 2 instruments for the purposes of deduction.

5.4.2 Holdings of Tier 2 Instruments of Financial Sector Entities where the Bank does not Have a Significant Investment

Pursuant to [CRR 66 (c), 69 and 70], the applicable amount of direct, indirect and synthetic holdings of the Tier 2 instruments of financial sector entities, where the bank does not have a significant investment in those entities, is deducted from Tier 2 capital. The calculation of the exposure takes into account the following:

- Holdings of Tier 2 instruments are calculated on the basis of the gross long positions;
- Tier 2 own-fund insurance items and Tier 3 own-fund insurance items are treated as holdings of Tier 2 instruments;
- Holdings shall include the underlying long gross exposure to the capital instruments of the financial sector entities – where the bank does not have a significant investment – through direct, indirect and synthetic holdings of index securities. Section 3.20.1 covers in more detail the general requirements related to holdings arising from index holdings.

> [CRR 66 (c), 69 and 70] do *not* exclude, from the calculations of Tier 2 holdings of financial institutions in which the bank does not have a significant investment, underwriting positions held for five working days or fewer. However, these positions are excluded when a bank calculates Tier 2 holdings of financial institutions in which it has a significant investment. In my view, this opposing treatment is arguably incoherent.

Gross long positions may be deducted net of short positions (i.e., only the net long position is deducted) in the same underlying exposure only if both the following conditions are met:

- The maturity of the short position matches the maturity of the long position or has a residual maturity of at least one year; and
- Either both the long and the short positions are held in the trading book or both are held in the banking book.

Pursuant to [CRR 75], the maturity requirements for short positions are deemed to be met in respect of positions held where the following conditions are met:

- The bank has the contractual right to sell on a specific future date to the counterparty providing the hedge the long position that is being hedged; and
- The counterparty providing the hedge to the bank is contractually obliged to purchase from the bank on that specific future date the long position referred to in the previous requirement.

The aggregate amount by which the direct, indirect and synthetic holdings by the bank of the CET1, AT1 and Tier 2 instruments of financial sector entities are compared to **10% of the "relevant CET1"** of the bank:

- The amount that exceeds 10% of the "relevant CET1" of the bank is **deducted**; and
- The amount that does not exceed 10% of the "relevant CET1" of the bank is **risk-weighted**.

The items that comprise the "relevant CET1" of the bank are disclosed in Section 4.4.2.

Applicable Amount to be Deducted from Tier 2 Capital   The applicable amount to be deducted ("A") is calculated as follows:

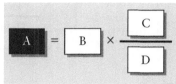

Where:

A: The amount required to be deducted from Tier 2 stemming from direct, indirect and synthetic holdings of Tier 2 instruments of financial sector entities in which the bank does not have a significant investment;

B: The aggregate amount by which the direct, indirect and synthetic holdings by the bank of the CET1, AT1 and Tier 2 instruments of financial sector entities exceeds 10% of the "relevant CET1" of the bank;

C: The amount of direct, indirect and synthetic holdings by the bank of the Tier 2 instruments of financial sector entities; and

D: The aggregate amount of all direct, indirect and synthetic holdings by the bank of the CET1, AT1 and Tier 2 instruments of those financial sector entities.

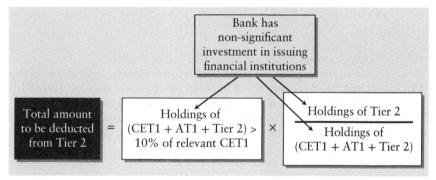

The amount to be deducted is apportioned across each Tier 2 instrument held. The amount to be deducted from each Tier 2 instrument ("E") is calculated as follows:

$$E = A \times \frac{F}{G}$$

Where:

E: The amount to be deducted from Tier 2 capital allocated to the Tier 2 instrument;

F: The total amount of the Tier 2 instrument; and

G: The aggregate amount of direct, indirect and synthetic holdings by bank of the Tier 2 instruments of financial sector entities in which the bank does not have a significant investment.

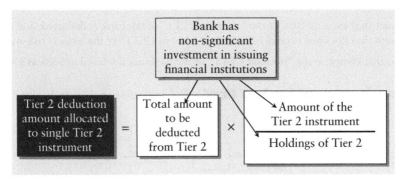

Applicable Amount to be Risk-weighted   The aggregate amount by which the direct, indirect and synthetic holdings by the bank of the CET1, AT1 and Tier 2 instruments of financial sector entities does not exceed 10% of the "relevant CET1" of the bank is not deducted but **risk-weighted**.

The portion of holdings of own funds instruments that is risk-weighted ("H") is calculated as follows:

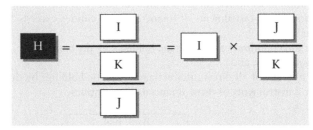

Where:

H: Portion of holdings of own fund instruments that is risk-weighted;
I: The aggregate amount by which the direct, indirect and synthetic holdings by the bank of the CET1, AT1 and Tier 2 instruments of financial sector entities does not exceed 10% of the "relevant CET1" of the bank (i.e., the amount to be risk-weighted);
J: The aggregate amount of direct, indirect and synthetic holdings by the bank of the CET1 instruments of financial sector entities in which the bank does not have a significant investment; and
K: The total amount of the CET1 instruments.

5.4.3 Holdings of Tier 2 Instruments of Financial Sector Entities where the Bank Has a Significant Investment

Pursuant to [CRR 66 (d) and 69], the underlying exposure to direct, indirect and synthetic holdings of the Tier 2 instruments of financial sector entities, where the bank has a **significant** investment in those entities, are **fully deducted** from Tier 2 capital. The calculation of the exposure takes into account the following:

- Holdings of Tier 2 instruments are calculated on the basis of the gross long positions (see below);
- Tier 2 own-fund insurance items are treated as holdings of Tier 2 instruments;
- Underwriting positions held for five working days or fewer are excluded;
- Holdings shall include the underlying long gross exposure to the capital instruments of the financial sector entities – where the bank does has a significant investment – through direct, indirect and synthetic holdings of index securities. Section 3.20.1 covers in more detail the general requirements related to holdings arising from index holdings.

Gross long positions may be calculated net of short positions (i.e., only the net long position is taken into account) only if both the following conditions are met:

- The long and short positions are in the same underlying exposure;
- The maturity of the short position matches the maturity of the long position or has a residual maturity of at least one year; and
- Either both the long and the short positions are held in the trading book or both are held in the banking book.

Pursuant to [CRR 75], the maturity requirements for short positions are deemed to be met in respect of positions held where the following conditions are met:

- The bank has the contractual right to sell on a specific future date to the counterparty providing the hedge the long position that is being hedged; and
- The counterparty providing the hedge to the bank is contractually obliged to purchase from the bank on that specific future date the long position referred to in the previous requirement.

5.5 CASE STUDY: DEUTSCHE BANK'S TIER 2 ISSUE

This case study describes the main terms of a subordinated bond issued by Deutsche Bank in 2013 that qualified as Tier 2 capital.

5.5.1 Main Terms of the Tier 2 Instrument

On 24 May 2013 Deutsche Bank issued a Tier 2 instrument. The subordinated bond had a 15-year maturity, a USD 1.5 billion notional, paid a mandatory fixed coupon of 4.296% to be reset on year 10 and was callable by the issuer on a semiannual basis after 10 years. The bond had no write-down or conversion features. The main terms of the Tier 2 instrument are listed in Table 5.2:

TABLE 5.2   Main Terms of Deutsche Bank's USD Tier 2 Issue

Main Terms of Deutsche Bank's USD Tier 2 Issue	
Issuer	Deutsche Bank AG
Issue date	24-May-2013
Principal	USD 1.5 billion
Eligibility	CRD4/CRR compliant Tier 2 capital
Maturity	24-May-2028 (15 years)
Coupon	Mandatory (i.e., non-discretional)
Coupon rate	4.296% per annum, until the first call date (24 May 2023), with reset on that date at 5-year swap rate + 2.2475%. Payable semiannually each 24 May and 24 November
Call right by Issuer	At par. Callable on each coupon date, commencing on 24 May 2023, subject to regulatory approval. Extraordinary call rights relating to regulatory and tax (at any time)
Applicable law	New York law, except subordination provisions and waiver of set-off-provisions which were governed by German law
Ranking	Insolvency claims junior (i.e., subordinated) to senior claims. Senior to AT1 and CET1 claims

Call Right   Deutsche Bank had the right to early amortise the bond every six months starting on 24 May 2023 (10 years after its issuance), providing not less than 30 nor more than 60 days' notice. On the first call date, the bond will have 5 years' remaining life. The regulatory amortisation will then start to be applied, reducing the bond's regulatory content by 20% per year. As a result, Deutsche Bank will have a strong incentive to call the bond on 24 May 2023.

The bond could also be early amortised by the bank if it failed to qualify as Tier 2 instrument. There was also a call for tax reasons. These provisions are common in AT1 and Tier 2 instruments.

Regulatory Bail-in   Although the terms and conditions of the bond did not contain a write-down or conversion provision, the supervisory authority had a regulatory bail-in power. Under this power, the supervisory authority – were Deutsche Bank to be deemed as **non-viable** and unable to continue its regulated banking activities – could effect a permanent reduction, including to zero, or a conversion into one or more instruments that constitute CET1 capital, such as ordinary shares. In the case of a bail-in the bondholders would have no claim against the bank on the written-down amount, not even for accrued interest.

5.5.2 Accounting Treatment: Recognition at Amortised Cost

On its issue date, the bond was recognised at its fair value less transaction costs directly attributable to the issuance, which equalled the net EUR issue proceeds from the issuance. The USD proceeds were USD 1,491,250,000. On issue date the EUR USD spot exchange rate was 1.2853. Therefore the EUR net proceeds were EUR 1,160.23 million (= 1,491.25 mn/1.2853).

As the bank had an obligation to pay both the coupons and the principal, the bond was recognised as a liability. The bond was measured at amortised cost. The amortisation was calculated using the **effective interest rate** ("EIR"). The EIR was applied to the bond carrying amount to determine the interest expense and ending carrying amount at each reporting period.

Let us assume that the bank reported its financial statements on an annual basis. The effective interest rate was the rate that exactly discounted the USD stream of expected interest and principal cash flows to the initial USD net proceeds. The coupons represented USD 64.44 million (= 1.5 bn × 4.296%) per annum. Because the bond was expected to be called on year 10, the EIR was calculated taking into account the expected cash flows during the first 10 years, as follows (amounts in USD millions):

$$1,491.25 = \frac{64.44}{1+EIR} + \frac{64.44}{(1+EIR)^2} + \ldots + \frac{64.44}{(1+EIR)^9} + \frac{(1,500+64.44)}{(1+EIR)^{10}}$$

According to that expression, the EIR was 4.37%. The interest expense and carrying amounts at each annual period was calculated (in millions) as shown in Table 5.3.

During the first year, Deutsche Bank recognised an interest expense of USD 65.17 million, which was converted into EUR using the average EUR USD spot rate during the accounting period. The carrying amount of the liability at the end of the first year was USD 1,491.98 translated into EUR using the closing rate prevailing on the reporting date. The table highlights that the amortised cost method amortised the USD 8.75 million initial discount over the expected 10 years life of the instrument. In other words, the method gradually brought the initial USD 1,491.25 million carrying amount to the final USD 1,500 million par amount.

Because the bond was denominated in USD while the presentation/functional currency of the bank was the EUR, the USD carrying amount of the bond was translated into EUR using the EUR USD spot exchange rate prevailing on the reporting date. Changes due to changes in the EUR USD rate were recognised in profit or loss. On issue date the EUR USD spot exchange rate was 1.2853.

Let us assume that the bank reported on an annual basis each 24 May – to avoid calculating any accrued interest – and that the average and closing EUR USD FX rates were 1.29 and 1.30 respectively:

TABLE 5.3 Calculation of Interest Expense and Amortised Cost Amounts

Year	Amortised Cost beginning Year (a)	Interest (b)=(a)*4.37%	Cash Flow (c)	Amortised Cost End of Year (d)=(a)+(b)−(c)
1	1,491.25	65.17	64.44	1,491.98
2	1,491.98	65.20	64.44	1,492.74
3	1,492.74	65.23	64.44	1,493.53
4	1,493.53	65.27	64.44	1,494.36
5	1,494.36	65.30	64.44	1,495.22
6	1,495.22	65.34	64.44	1,496.12
7	1,496.12	65.38	64.44	1,497.06
8	1,497.06	65.42	64.44	1,498.04
9	1,498.04	65.46	64.44	1,499.06
10	1,499.06	65.51	64.44	1,500.00 (*)

*Rounded to 1,500

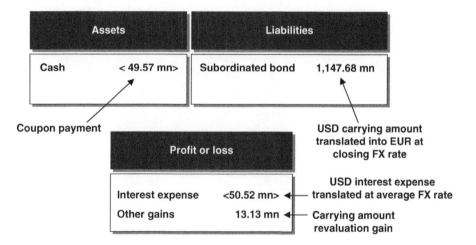

FIGURE 5.5 Effects of the Tier 2 instrument on Deutsche Bank's financials at the end of the first year

■ The carrying amount of the bond was EUR 1,147.68 million (= 1,491.98 mn/1.30), calculated converting the USD 1,491.98 million carrying amount at the end of the first year converted at the closing FX rate;
■ The interest expense, coupon payment and the revaluation gain during the first year were EUR 50.52 million (= 65.17 mn/1.29), EUR 49.57 million (= 64.44 mn/1.30) and EUR 13.13 million (= 1,491.98 mn/1.30 − 1,491.98 mn/1.2853) respectively.

Figure 5.5 depicts the main impacts in the Bank's financial statements at the end of the first year.

From an accounting perspective, the Tier 2 instrument was accounted for as any other debt instrument at amortised cost. Therefore, unless the fair value option is applied, a senior bond and the Tier 2 issued by Deutsche Bank would be treated similarly from an accounting perspective.

Of note is the estimation of the call date. Were Deutsche Bank's call expectations to change, it would need to recalculate the EIR.

CHAPTER 6

Contingent Convertibles (CoCos)

Contingent convertible ("CoCo") bonds are financial instruments that automatically enhance bank capital (commonly, CET1 capital), enabling better absorption of (future) losses when a pre-defined trigger point (such as a specific CET1 capital ratio) is breached.

Most CoCos are designed to qualify as AT1 instruments, although in some jurisdictions Tier 2 CoCos have been issued as well. AT1 CoCos are "going concern" instruments designed to provide new CET1 capital when the bank is still viable. The recapitalisation is provided by the CoCo holders, a private sector solution, without resorting to (or making less likely) government intervention.

It is worth underlining that when the trigger is breached and the conversion/write-down occurs, no fresh cash is raised by the bank. As a result, CoCos do not enhance a bank's liquidity position.

6.1 TYPES OF CoCos

CoCos can take several forms. Most of the differences present in CoCos are due to different combinations of the following structural features:

- **Trigger level:** High or low trigger;
- **Loss absorption mechanism:** Equity conversion or principal write-down;
- **Maturity:** Term maturity or perpetual;
- **Ranking in bankruptcy:** Pari passu with subordinated claims or junior to subordinated claims.

6.1.1 Loss Absorption Mechanisms: Equity Convertible vs. Principal Write-down CoCos

According to their **loss absorption** mechanism, once the trigger level is breached, there are two main types of CoCos (see Figure 6.1):

- **Equity convertible:** A CoCo that is automatically converted into ordinary shares of the bank when a predefined trigger is breached. The amount of shares may be a predetermined amount (i.e., a fixed conversion price), a variable amount or a variable amount with a minimum.
- **Principal write-down:** A CoCo whose principal (i.e., notional) amount is automatically written down when a predefined trigger is breached. Interest is subsequently calculated on the written-down principal. The principal may be reduced, fully or partially. Subsequently, once the principal has been written down, some CoCos provide for a write-up mechanism to partially or totally restore the principal.

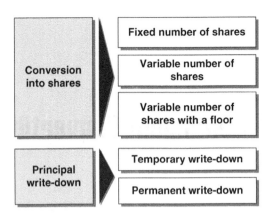

FIGURE 6.1   CoCos classification according to their loss absorption mechanism

TABLE 6.1   Comparative Main Terms of AT1 CoCos and Tier 2 Instruments

Item	AT1 CoCos	Tier 2 Instruments
Term	Perpetual	Minimum 5 years
Call option	Allowed, but no earlier than 5 years from issuance date	Allowed, but no earlier than 5 years from issuance date
Coupons	Full issuer discretion. Coupon payments can be suspended even if the capital ratio is above the trigger level	May be mandatory Non-deferrable
Trigger for loss	Minimum 5.125% of CET1	Not applicable
Loss absorption	Conversion into equity or write-down, upon breach of trigger	On bail-in
Step-ups	Not permitted (i.e., no incentive to redeem)	Not permitted (i.e., no incentive to redeem)
Write-up	Permitted	Not applicable
Coupon stopper	Permitted	Not applicable
Ranking	Rank directly ahead of ordinary share capital in the capital structure	Rank directly ahead of AT1 instruments in the capital structure

6.1.2 Tier 2 vs. AT1 CoCos

From a regulatory capital perspective, CoCos are issued to strengthen AT1 capital and/or to help a bank meet stress tests. Tier 2 instruments do not need to include write-down or conversion features to qualify as Tier 2 capital and, as a result, they are mostly issued as subordinated dated bonds. However, in some jurisdictions (e.g., Switzerland), banks have issued Tier 2 CoCos. The eligibility criteria for AT1 and Tier 2 instruments was covered in Sections 4.2.1 and 5.1.2, which are summarised in Table 6.1.

6.2 TRIGGER LEVELS

CoCos are issued as bonds, commonly with a fixed coupon. In addition, CoCos have a contractual trigger. When the contractual trigger is breached, the CoCo is automatically converted into equity or its principal is written down.

The contractual trigger occurs when the bank determines that its CET1 ratio (which is commonly calculated on a consolidated and fully loaded basis) is less than a pre-specified percentage (e.g., 5.125%).

Because banks publicly report their consolidated fully loaded CET1 ratio at the end of each quarterly period, the trigger is observed at any quarterly financial period end date. Measuring against actual published results on a quarterly basis allows management time to take early and corrective action.

The trigger may also be observed in extraordinary calculation dates. The relevant regulatory body with primary responsibility for the prudential supervision of the bank, as part of its supervisory activity, may instruct the bank to calculate such ratio as of any date, or the bank might otherwise determine to calculate such ratio in its own discretion.

The occurrence of the contractual trigger is inherently unpredictable and depends on a number of factors, some of which may be outside the bank's control.

The calculation could be affected by, among other things, the growth of the bank's business and earnings, dividend payments, regulatory changes, actions that the bank is required to take at the direction of the regulator, and the bank's ability to manage RWAs in both its ongoing businesses and those which it may seek to exit. In addition, the bank has capital resources and RWAs denominated in foreign currencies, and changes in foreign exchange rates will result in changes in the presentation currency equivalent value of foreign currency-denominated capital resources and risk-weighted assets. Actions that the bank takes could also affect its CET1 ratio, including causing it to decline.

The calculation of the CET1 ratio may also be affected by changes in applicable accounting or capital regulatory rules. For example, the definitions and calculations of CET1 capital and RWAs may change. Moreover, even if changes in applicable accounting rules are not yet in force as of the relevant calculation date, the regulator could require the bank to reflect such changes in its CET1 ratio calculation.

The issuing bank has *no* legal obligation to increase its CET1 capital, reduce its RWAs or take mitigating actions in order to prevent its CET1 ratio from falling below the trigger.

6.2.1 High Trigger vs. Low Trigger

An important element of a CoCo is the contractual trigger level, which determines how likely conversion or write-down is. A distinction is made between high and low conversion triggers under CRD IV.

A **high trigger** – defined as a trigger level of 7% or higher – means that the CoCos can be converted relatively quickly when a bank suffers losses. The high trigger is designed to kick in early enough to prevent a bank ever reaching the point at which it can no longer operate as an essentially viable business.

On the other hand, a **low trigger** – defined as a trigger level of 5.125% or higher but lower than 7% – would result in conversion taking place only in an emergency situation, when the bank has suffered severe losses. Probably it would mean that the bank had reached a point at which it could no longer engage in normal business, in which case attention would focus on preventing government funds having to be used to bail it out.

The higher the trigger, the higher the coupon is, because from an investor's point of view a higher trigger implies a greater conversion risk. A low trigger, by contrast, would have the merit of making conversion less likely, and the coupon would therefore be lower.

If, according to [CRR 54] (see Section 4.2.1), the minimum trigger is 5.125% of CET1 for an instrument to qualify as AT1 instrument, why are banks issuing high-trigger CoCos?

Banks are periodically subject to stress tests by their supervisors. In these stress tests the capital levels of banks are assessed in a scenario in which the riskiness of their assets is notably increased. The high trigger of a CoCo may be theoretically breached under a stressed scenario and, as a result, generate CET1 capital that helps the bank pass the stress test.

Regulators may require/recommend a high trigger in the CoCos issued by their supervised banks. For example, in its Policy Statement (PS7/13) of December 2013, the British banking supervisor PRA indicated a preference for a higher CET1 trigger than the CRR minimum of 5.125% on the basis that such a trigger may not allow the AT1 instrument to be written-down or converted in time to prevent a failure of the bank. While that Statement did not suggest a level for the CET1 trigger to be placed, British banks subsequently issued AT1 CoCos with a trigger of 7%.

Some national regulators require capital levels for their supervised banks that are more stringent than the standard Basel III levels, which can be met with high-trigger CoCos. For example, the high-buffer CoCos are especially relevant for Swiss banks. According to the Swiss regulation, there are three categories of regulatory capital that, when fully implemented in 2019, would sum to about 19% of risk-weighted assets:

1. Basic requirement capital (4.5% CET1);
2. Buffer capital (8.5% CET1 or high-trigger CoCos); and
3. Progressive component capital (up to 6% low-trigger CoCos only).

6.3 CoCos' STATUTORY CONVERSION OR WRITE-DOWN – POINT OF NON-VIABILITY

It was mentioned in the previous section that conversion or write-down of a CoCo occurs when the contractual trigger is breached. In addition, CoCos' conversion or write-down may also be triggered by the relevant authority with recovery and/or resolution powers.

6.3.1 European Resolution Regime (BRRD) – Recovery and Resolution

The European Bank Recovery and Resolution Directive ("**BRRD**") – Directive 2014/59/EU – provides an EU-wide framework for the recovery and resolution of credit institutions and investment firms, their subsidiaries and certain holding companies. The BRRD requires all European Economic Area member states to provide their relevant resolution authorities with a set of tools to intervene sufficiently early and quickly in an unsound or failing bank to ensure the continuity of the entity's critical financial and economic functions, while minimising the impact of a bank's failure on the broader economy and financial system.

The aim of the BRRD is to provide resolution authorities with tools and powers to address banking crises pre-emptively in order to safeguard financial stability and minimise taxpayers' exposure to losses.

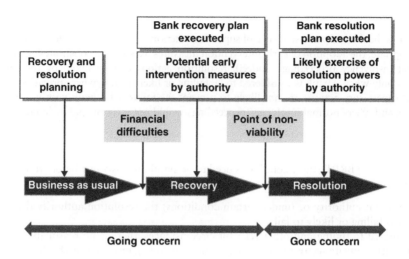

FIGURE 6.2   Stages in a bank financial situation

Business as Usual vs. Recovery vs. Resolution   There are three stages that represent the financial situation of a bank (see Figure 6.2):

- **Business as usual** stage. The bank is a going concern, solvently functioning and meeting the capital and any other requirements set by the banking supervisory authority. The bank has recovery and resolution plans in place.
- **Recovery** stage. The bank is still a going concern but the financial situation of the bank is deteriorating, becoming vulnerable, threatening to reach the point of non-viability, and/or presenting a risk to financial stability.
- **Resolution** stage. The bank has reached its point of non-viability (to be explained below), becoming a "gone concern".

Each bank needs to have in place at all times a recovery plan and a resolution plan, which have to be periodically approved by the banking supervisory authority:

- The **recovery plan** sets out the measures to be adopted by the bank in different scenarios to restore long-term viability in the event of a material deterioration in its financial situation. It gives the resolution authority information to help plan how the essential functions of the bank may be isolated and continued under scenarios of systemic instability, group-wide and entity-specific stress situations. The recovery plan is activated when the competent authority estimates that the bank is in the recovery stage. The supervisory authority may require the bank to implement additional measures – **early intervention measures** – to help the bank return to its "business as usual" stage, including requiring the bank to remove/replace its management.
- The **resolution** plan is a document containing information on actions to be taken in the event of failure (or likely failure) of the bank (or any business of the bank) and that would facilitate planning by the resolution authority. The resolution plan is activated when the competent authority estimates that the bank is in the resolution stage (i.e., when the point of non-viability has been reached). The execution of the recovery plan has failed to restore the viability of the bank. The relevant resolution authority becomes involved exercising the resolution powers given to it by the BRRD.

Resolution is the final step in a sequence of supervisory actions, generally following, where possible and appropriate, the adoption of early intervention measures. Resolution constitutes an alternative to normal insolvency proceedings. Indeed, resolution actions can be taken by the resolution authorities only when a bank is considered to be failing or likely to fail, where private sector solutions and supervisory actions are not likely to prevent the failure of a bank within a reasonable timeframe, and where normal insolvency proceedings would not meet the public interest test.

According to the BRRD, three conditions need to be simultaneously met before resolution actions can be taken by a resolution authority, namely:

1. The competent authority or (under certain conditions) the resolution authority determines that the bank is **failing or likely to fail**;
2. Having regard to timing and other relevant circumstances, there is no reasonable prospect that any alternative private sector or supervisory action (including measures by the deposits protection schemes, or supervisory action, including early intervention measures or the write-down or conversion of capital instruments), would prevent the failure of the bank within reasonable timeframe;
3. A resolution action is necessary in the public interest.

The determination that a bank is **failing or likely to fail** remains the discretionary assessment of the competent authority, after consulting with the resolution authority, or when national legislation so provides. The EBA clarified that, for the purposes of making a determination that a bank is failing or likely to fail, the resolution authority should assess the objective elements relating to the following areas:

- The capital position of the bank;
- The liquidity position of the bank; and
- Any other requirements for continuing authorisation (including governance arrangements and operational capacity).

Where the relevant resolution authority is satisfied that the resolution conditions are met, it may implement resolution measures in the financial institution without requiring the consent of the shareholders or complying with the procedural requirements that would otherwise apply. The stabilisation options available to the relevant resolution authority under the BRRD provide for:

- A bail-in power;
- Directing the sale of the relevant financial institution or the whole or part of its business on commercial terms;
- Transferring all or part of the business of the relevant financial institution to a "bridge bank" (a publicly controlled entity); and
- Transferring the impaired or problem assets of the relevant financial institution to an asset management vehicle to allow them to be managed over time.

6.3.2 Point of Non-viability (PONV) – Write-down and Conversion Power by Resolution Authority

The **point of non-viability** ("PONV") is the point at which the relevant resolution authority determines that either:

- The bank meets the conditions for resolution, but no resolution action has yet been taken;
- The bank will no longer be viable unless the relevant capital instruments are written down or converted; or
- The bank requires extraordinary public support, without which the relevant resolution authority determines that the bank would no longer be viable.

The BRRD provides the resolution authority with the power to permanently write down, or convert into equity, AT1 and/or Tier 2 capital instruments at the PONV of the bank without requiring the consent of the holders of such instruments. Therefore, in the EU, AT1 and/or Tier 2 CoCos can be written down (or converted) because:

- The **contractual CET1 trigger** (e.g., 5.125%) has been reached;
- The resolution authority has exercised its **mandatory write-down or conversion power at the PONV**, before any other resolution action is taken. This power is applicable only to capital instruments, while other more senior liabilities remain unchanged, when the resolution authority determines that, unless the write-down or conversion is applied, the bank will no longer be viable, or if a decision has been made to provide the bank with extraordinary public support without which the bank will no longer be viable.
- The resolution authority has exercised its **bail-in tool**. This power is applicable to all non-secured liabilities, not just to capital instruments.

> In reality it is rather unlikely that the bank reaches its PONV while its CET1 has not breached the contractual trigger. This may be the case whenever the bank still has sufficient capital but is experiencing acute liquidity difficulties.

6.3.3 Bail-in Power

Bail-in power is a resolution tool, also called bail-in tool. It gives national resolution authorities the power to implement measures to the extent necessary to restore the bank to financial viability. More precisely:

- To cancel or modify the terms of the contracts of certain unsecured financial liabilities in order to cancel or reduce all or a portion of their principal amount or interest; and
- To convert certain debt claims into another security, including ordinary shares of the surviving entity, if any.

The bail-in tool enables the relevant resolution authority to recapitalise a financial institution in resolution by allocating losses to its shareholders and unsecured creditors in a manner that (i) reflects the hierarchy of capital instruments under CRD IV and otherwise ought to respect the hierarchy of claims in an ordinary insolvency and (ii) is consistent with shareholders and creditors not receiving a less favourable treatment than they would have received in ordinary insolvency proceedings of the entity (known as the **"no creditor worse off"** safeguard). Figure 6.3 highlights which instruments are considered "bail-inable" within the capital structure based on the BRRD.

Pursuant to [BRRD 44 (d)], certain liabilities are excluded from the scope of the bail-in tool ("explicit exclusions"), as depicted in Figure 6.3. These are:

- Protected (i.e., guaranteed) deposits;
- Secured liabilities including covered bonds and liabilities in the form of financial instruments used for hedging purposes which form an integral part of the cover pool and which according to national law are secured in a way similar to covered bonds;
- Any liability that arises by virtue of the holding by the bank of client assets or client money, including client assets or client money held on behalf of UCITS, provided that such a client is protected under the applicable insolvency law;
- Any liability that arises by virtue of a fiduciary relationship between the bank (as fiduciary) and another person (as beneficiary), provided that such a beneficiary is protected under the applicable insolvency or civil law;

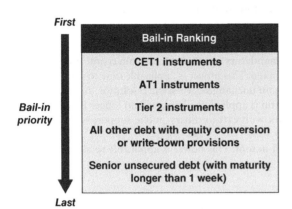

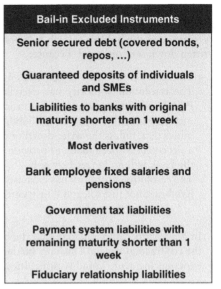

FIGURE 6.3   BRRD – Priority of instruments subject to (and excluded from) bail-in

- Liabilities to a credit institution or investment firm, excluding entities that are part of the same group, with an original maturity of less than seven days;
- Liabilities with a remaining maturity of less than seven days, owed to systems or operators of settlement systems designated or their participants and arising from the participation in such a system;
- A liability to any one of the following:
  - An employee, in relation to accrued salary, pension benefits or other fixed remuneration, except for the variable component of remuneration that is not regulated by a collective bargaining agreement;
  - A commercial or trade creditor arising from the provision to the bank of goods or services (other than financial services) that are critical to the daily functioning of its operations, including IT services, utilities and the rental, servicing and upkeep of premises;
  - Tax and social security authorities, provided that those liabilities are preferred under the applicable law;
  - Deposit guarantee schemes arising from contributions due in accordance with Directive 2014/49/EU;
- Liabilities owed to central counterparties recognised by the European Securities and Markets Authority in accordance with Article 25 of Regulation (EU) 648/2012 (EMIR) of the European Parliament and the Council of 4 July 2012 on OTC derivatives, central counterparties and trade depositaries.

The following list tries to capture the possible reasoning behind the explicit exclusions under [BRRD 44(2)]:

- To avoid run risks (exclusions for covered deposits, liabilities to the deposit guarantee scheme) – depositors lose confidence in other banks and in the reliability of the deposit guarantee scheme;
- To preserve the function of certain transaction types (secured liabilities, covered bonds, client money, fiduciary relationships) – the transactions concerned require a special treatment in insolvency which should be replicated in bail-in;
- To avoid contagion to key financial markets and infrastructure:
  - Financial markets and infrastructure (CCPs);
  - Interbank funding markets (exclusion of certain short-term liabilities);
  - Deposit guarantee schemes (with respect to ex-post contributions);

- To ensure the continuance of the operations of the bank (liabilities to employees, commercial and trade creditors, social authorities), also by avoiding enforcement of security interests, which could reduce the assets of the bank (secured liabilities);
- To state fiscal interest (e.g. tax authorities), where it is protected under national insolvency law; and
- To reflect the insolvency ranking of the liability to ensure consistency with and confidence in the European member state's legal system as a whole, and comply with fundamental rights, also with a view to the no-creditor-worse-off principle (client assets or money, fiduciary relationships, covered bonds, tax and social authorities).

In addition, and in accordance with [BRRD 44(3)], liabilities may be excluded by the resolution authorities on a case-by-case basis in exceptional circumstances (what is called "**exceptional exclusions**"), where:

- It is not possible to bail-in that liability within a reasonable time, notwithstanding the good faith efforts of the resolution authority;
- The exclusion is strictly necessary and is proportionate to achieve the continuity of critical functions and core business lines in a manner that maintains the ability of the bank under resolution to continue key operations, services and transactions;
- The exclusion is strictly necessary and proportionate to avoid giving rise to widespread contagion, in particular as regards eligible deposits held by natural persons and micro-, small and medium-sized enterprises, which would severely disrupt the functioning of financial markets, including of financial market infrastructures, in a manner that could cause a serious disturbance to the economy of a European member state or of the European Union; or
- The application of the bail-in tool to those liabilities would cause a destruction in value such that the losses borne by other creditors would be higher than if those liabilities were excluded from bail-in.

6.4 CoCo's COUPON SUSPENSION – MAXIMUM DISTRIBUTABLE AMOUNT

[CRD IV 141] establishes mandatory restrictions on certain distributions as a way to conserve capital, and include interest payments to AT1 instruments.

6.4.1 Combined Buffer Requirement (CBR)

In Chapter 2 several categories of capital called regulatory buffers were covered. Capital buffers are vital for AT1 holders. Pursuant to [CRD IV 128(6)], the "**combined buffer requirement**" ("**CBR**") is defined as the aggregate of the capital requirements related to the capital conservation buffer, the bank-specific countercyclical capital buffer and, as applicable, the higher of (depending on the bank) of the G-SII buffer, O-SII buffer and/or systemic risk buffer (Figure 6.4).

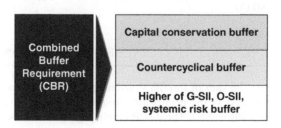

FIGURE 6.4 Composition of the combined buffer requirement

6.4.2 Maximum Distributable Amount (MDA)

Pursuant to [CRD IV 141(1)], banks that meet the CBR are prohibited from making a distribution in connection with CET1 capital to an extent that it would decrease its CET 1 capital to a level where the CBR is no longer met.

A bank that does not meet its CBR faces restrictions on payments that result in a reduction of CET1 capital or in a reduction of profits, and where a suspension of payment or failure to pay does not constitute an event of default or a condition for the commencement of proceedings under the insolvency regime applicable to the bank. The objective of the restrictions is to conserve regulatory capital.

Restrictions are scaled according to the extent of the breach of the CBR. Banks that do not meet their CBR are required to calculate a "**Maximum Distributable Amount**" ("**MDA**") in each relevant period, and notify their MDA to the competent authority.

Pursuant to [CRD IV 141(2)], banks that fail to meet the CBR are prohibited, until the MDA is calculated, from:

- Making a distribution in connection with CET1 capital;
- Creating an obligation to pay variable remuneration or discretionary pension benefits or pay variable remuneration if the obligation to pay was created at a time when the bank failed to meet the CBR; and
- Making payments on AT1 instruments.

Pursuant to [CRD IV 141(3)], while a bank fails to meet (or exceed) its CBR, it is prohibited from making **discretionary distributions** in excess of its MDA. The MDA restrictions came into place in 2016, with a three-year phase-in period (i.e., they will become fully operational from 1 January 2019). Discretionary distributions relate to:

- Making a distribution in connection with CET1 capital:
  - A payment of cash dividends;
  - A distribution of fully or partly paid bonus shares or other CET1 capital instruments;
  - A redemption or purchase by the bank of its own shares or other CET1 capital instruments;
  - A repayment of amounts paid up in connection with CET1 capital instruments;
  - A distribution of share premium accounts related to CET1 instruments, retained earnings, accumulated other comprehensive income or other reserves that qualify as CET1 capital;
- Creating an obligation to pay variable remuneration or discretionary pension benefits or pay variable remuneration if the obligation to pay was created at a time when the bank failed to meet the CBR; or
- Making payments on AT1 instruments.

Pursuant to [CRD IV 141(5)], the MDA is calculated as the bank's distributable profits multiplied by a factor:

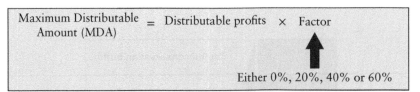

Maximum Distributable Amount (MDA) = Distributable profits × Factor

Either 0%, 20%, 40% or 60%

Distributable profits are the sum of interim year-end profits *not* yet included in CET1 (otherwise a double counting occurred as the profits already included in CET1 are taken into account when assessing whether the CBR is met). The distributable profits of a bank are calculated since its most recent decision on the distribution of profits or any discretionary payment, as follows [CRD IV 144(5)]:

■ Interim profits not included in CET1 – pursuant to [CRR 26(2)] – that have been generated since the most recent decision on the distribution of profits or any discretionary payment;

plus

■ Year-end profits not included in CET1 – pursuant to [CRR 26(2)] – that have been generated since the most recent decision on the distribution of profits or any discretionary payment;

minus

■ Amounts which would be payable by tax if the two previous items were to be retained.

The factor is 0%, 20%, 40% or 60% (dependant on which quartile of its CBR the bank is in). The greater the degree of shortfall of the CBR, the lower the factor. As an example, if the degree of breach of the CBR is such that the bank is in the bottom quartile, the factor would be 0% and, consequently, the bank would not be permitted to pay any discretionary distributions. The lower and upper bounds of each quartile of the CBR shall be calculated as follows:

$$\text{Upper bound of quartile} = \frac{\text{Combined buffer requirement}}{4} \times Q_n$$

$$\text{Lower bound of quartile} = \frac{\text{Combined buffer requirement}}{4} \times Q_{n-1}$$

Where Q_n is the ordinal number of the quartile (1, 2, 3 or 4). The lower bound of quartile 1 is zero.

> The MDA is a percentage of "profits". This means that a bank not meeting the CBR and where the sum of interim and year-end profits since the above decisions is zero or negative, will have an MDA of zero and it will not be able to make any profit distribution or discretionary payments, no matter how much CET1 capital the bank holds in excess of its Pillar 1 capital requirement. This will be the case, for example, where a bank makes a loss that initially causes it to stop meeting its CBR.

Let us assume a bank with a CBR of 4.5% and meeting the 6% minimum Tier 1 capital requirement through a combination of 4.5% CET1 and 1.5% AT1. Let us assume further that the Tier 2 of the bank was 2%, so the 8% minimum total capital requirement was met as well.

An amount of additional CET1 available to meet its CBR below 1.125% (= 4.5% / 4) would imply a 0% factor when calculating the MDA. The upper bound of the second quartile was 2.25% (= 4.5% / 2). Therefore, an excess CET1 capital between 1.125% and 2.25% would imply a 20% MDA factor. Figure 6.5 depicts the boundaries and MDA factors corresponding to each quartile.

In the case of a bank holding 2% of Tier 2 capital, the MDA restriction will not apply as long as:

$$(\text{CET1} + \text{AT1}) - (\text{Min. Tier 1 requirement}) \geq \text{CBR}$$

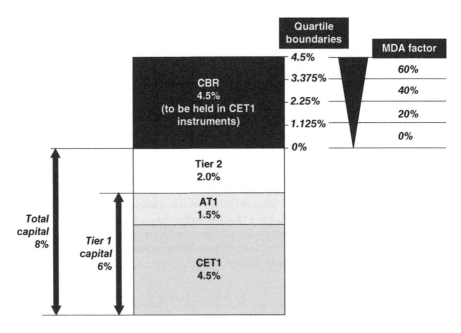

FIGURE 6.5   Bounds of each MDA quartile as a function of excess CET1

Example: MDA Calculation

Let us assume that a bank with a 4.5% CBR held a 7% CET1 capital, a 0.5% AT1 capital and a 2% Tier 2 capital.

The bank's 6% Tier 1 capital minimum requirement was met with a 5.5% CET1 capital and with the 0.5% AT1 capital. The bank's 8% minimum total capital requirement was met with the 6% Tier 1 capital and the 2% Tier 2 capital. Therefore, the bank had a 1.5% (= 7% − 5.5%) CET1 excess capital to meet its CBR.

The upper bound of the second quartile was 2.25% (= 4.5% / 4 × 2) while the lower bound of the second quartile was 1.13% (= 4.5% / 4 × 1). Thus, the bank capital position relative to its CBR was in the second quartile, resulting in a MDA factor of 20%.

Example: Calculation of MDA and Amounts Eligible for Distribution

Let us assume that a bank with a 4.5% CBR held an 8% CET1 capital, a 2% AT1 capital and a 1% Tier 2 capital as illustrated in Figure 6.6.

The 6% Tier 1 capital minimum requirement was met using 1.5% of AT1 (as the maximum AT1 eligible for Tier 1 capital was 1.5%) and 4.5% of CET1. The 8% total minimum capital requirement was met using 1% of Tier 2, 2% of AT1 and 5% of CET1. As a result, the bank utilised 5% of its CET1 capital to meet its total and Tier 1 capital requirements. Therefore, the bank had 3% (= 8% − 5%) CET1 excess capital to meet its CBR, representing 67% (= 3% / 4.5%) or third quartile of its CBR, resulting in a MDA factor of 40%.

Let us assume further that the bank generated a EUR 1 billion net profit which was not part of its CET1 calculation, therefore it had a EUR 400 million MDA (= 1bn × 40%) available to distribute on a discretionary basis. It could for instance, pay a EUR 250 million interest on its AT1 instruments and distribute a EUR 150 million dividend to its ordinary shareholders.

What about implementing a EUR 400 million share buyback programme?

(continued)

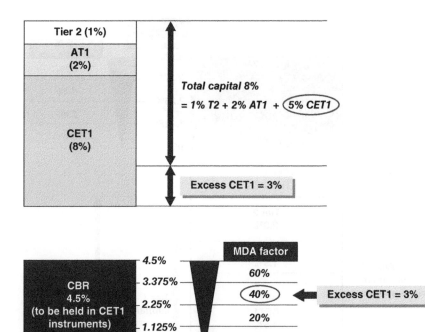

FIGURE 6.6 MDA factor

In theory the bank could execute a share buyback programme amounting to EUR 400 million. However, as the discretionary payment will reduce CET1 capital, it would need to convince the supervisory authority about the merits of buying back CET1 instruments while not fully meeting the CBR.

The MDA shall be reduced by any profit distributions or discretionary payments made.

Pursuant to [CRD IV 141(8)], where a bank fails to meet the CBR and intends to distribute any of its distributable profits or undertake a discretionary distribution, it must notify the designated authority and provide certain prescribed information including the amount of CET1, AT1 and Tier 2 capital it maintains, its interim and year-end profits, its MDA, the amount of profits it intends to distribute and its allocation between the different types of discretionary payments.

Pursuant to [CRD IV 142], a bank which fails to meet its CBR must also prepare a **capital conservation plan** and submit it to the competent authority within five days after it identified that it was failing to meet its CBR (unless the competent authority authorises a longer delay up to 10 days). Upon submission of the plan, the relevant authority will make a decision on whether to approve or reject it. If the capital conservation plan is rejected, the relevant authority shall impose the bank to increase own funds to specified levels within specific time periods and/or exercise its powers under CRD IV to impose more stringent restrictions on distributions than those implied by the bank's MDA. The competent authority will only approve the plan if it considers that it would, if implemented, be reasonably likely to conserve or raise sufficient capital to enable the bank to meet its CBR within an appropriate period.

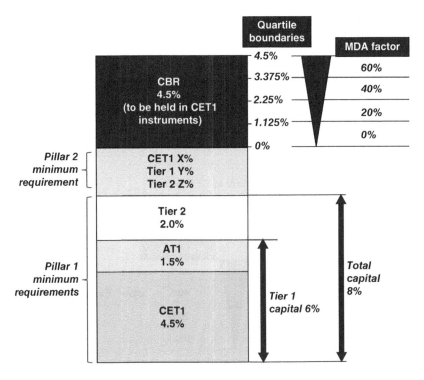

FIGURE 6.7   MDA factor including Pillar 1 and Pillar 2 capital requirements

6.5 ADDING PILLAR 2 CAPITAL REQUIREMENTS TO THE MDA CALCULATION

It was mentioned in Section 2.1.2 that the relevant authority may require a bank to maintain additional regulatory capital (the so-called "Pillar 2 capital requirements"). Pillar 2 capital requirements are in the form of supplementary CET1, supplementary Tier 1 and/or supplementary total capital requirements.

The EBA's document *Opinion of the European Banking Authority on the Interaction of Pillar 1, Pillar 2 and Combined Buffer Requirements and Restrictions on Distributions* (EBA/Op/2015/24) of 16 December 2015 clarifies the interaction between Pillar 1 capital requirements, Pillar 2 capital requirements and the CBR. In the EBA's view, the MDA factor should be calculated with the CET1 capital held in excess of CET1 capital held to meet both Pillar 1 and 2 capital requirements, as shown in Figure 6.7.

6.6 CASE STUDY: BARCLAYS' EQUITY CONVERTIBLE CoCo

In this section an equity convertible CoCo is dissected. An equity convertible CoCo is a bond that is automatically converted into shares of the issuing bank when a predefined trigger is breached. Since this type of bond is transformed into ordinary shares upon conversion, this provides further loss absorption. While the conversion trigger has not occurred, convertible CoCos are simply normal perpetual bonds that are redeemed when called.

TABLE 6.2 Main terms of Barclays Bank's GBP AT1

Main Terms of Barclays Bank's GBP-denominated AT1	
Issuer	Barclays Plc
Rating	B+ (Standard & Poor's), BB+ (Fitch)
Issue date	11 August 2015
Principal	GBP 1 billion
Issue price	99.99% (GBP 999.9 million)
Eligibility	CRD IV/CRR compliant AT1 capital
Maturity	Perpetual, subject to call right
Coupon	Non-cumulative discretionary cancellation of coupon payments; mandatory cancellation as required by the CRR
Coupon rate	7.875% per annum, until the first call date (15 September 2022), with reset every 5 years at 5-year swap rate + 6.099%. Payable quarterly each 15 March, June, September and December
Call right by Issuer	Every 5 years, starting on 15 September 2022 (i.e., 7 years following issuance) at par. Extraordinary call rights relating to regulatory and tax (at any time)
Conversion trigger	A fully loaded consolidated CET1 ratio of less than 7.00%
Conversion price	GBP 1.65, subject to anti-dilution clauses
Applicable law	English law
Ranking	Insolvency claims junior to Tier 2 instruments. Senior to CET1 claims (i.e., to ordinary shares)

6.6.1 Main Terms of Barclays' Contingent Convertible

On 11 August 2015 Barclays Plc – the ultimate holding company of the Barclays group ("Barclays") – issued a GBP-denominated CoCo eligible for AT1 capital. The CoCo had a GBP 1 billion principal amount, and an initial coupon rate of 7.875% paid quarterly. The coupon rate was reset every five years, starting on 15 September 2022, as the sum of the mid-market USD 5-year swap rate plus 6.099%. Barclays had the right, subject to the banking supervisory authority consent, to early amortise the securities at their 7th anniversary (on 15 September 2022) and every five years thereafter at par. The main terms of the AT1 securities are outlined in Table 6.2.

Barclays' CoCo was perpetual and, therefore, had no fixed maturity date or fixed redemption date. Thus CoCo holders had no ability to cash in their investment, except:

- If the bank exercised its early redemption right;
- By selling their CoCo investment in the market or selling the shares in the market following their conversion into ordinary shares;
- Where the trustee instituted proceedings for the winding-up of the bank where the bank had exercised its right to redeem the CoCo but failed to make payment in respect of such redemption when due, in

which limited circumstances CoCo holders would receive some of any resulting liquidation proceeds following payment being made in full to all senior and more senior subordinated creditors; or

■ Upon a winding-up or administration, in which limited circumstances CoCo holders would receive some of any resulting liquidation proceeds following payment being made in full to all senior and more senior subordinated creditors.

6.6.2 Objectives of the Issuance – PRA Capital Requirements

One of the main objectives of the issuance was to enhance Barclays' Tier 1 capital. At the time of issuance, the bank's CET1 was 11.1%, marginally exceeding a 10.6% fully loaded minimum requirement (excluding the countercyclical buffer), while its Tier 1 capital was 12.2%, slightly below its 12.6% fully loaded minimum requirement:

■ Barclays' fully loaded CET1 capital ratio at the time of issuance was 11.1%. Barclays' fully loaded CET1 minimum capital ratio requirement, excluding the countercyclical buffer, was 10.6% comprising a 4.5% Pillar 1, a 1.6% Pillar 2, a 2% G-SIB and a 2.5% capital conservation buffer minimum requirement;

■ Barclays' fully loaded AT1 capital ratio at the time of issuance was 1.1%. The British regulator – PRA – required a Pillar 2 supplementary Tier 1 requirement of 2.1%, which translated into a supplementary AT1 requirement of 0.5% if the 1.6% Pillar 2 CET1 requirement was taken into account;

■ As a result, Barclays' fully loaded Tier 1 capital ratio at the time of issuance was 12.2% (= 11.1% CET1 + 1.1% AT1) and the bank's minimum Tier 1 capital requirement was 12.6% (= 6% Pillar 1 Tier 1 + 2.1% Pillar 2 Tier 1 + 2% G-SIB + 2.5% capital conservation buffer).

The issuance helped Barclays "save" CET1 when trying to meet its 12.6% minimum Tier 1 capital requirement. An efficient Tier capital structure would imply a 2% (= 1.5% Pillar 1 + 0.5% Pillar 2) AT1 level. The AT1 issuance represented almost 0.3% of RWAs, which increased the bank's AT1 holding from 1.1% to 1.4%, as shown in Figure 6.8, still significantly below the 2% optimal.

Another important driver of the issuance was Barclays' leverage ratio, which was 4.1% at the time of issuance. The issuance of the CoCos enhanced this ratio, as AT1 capital was part of the numerator in conjunction with CET1 capital (i.e., the numerator of the leverage ratio was the bank's Tier 1 capital).

6.6.3 Headroom to Contractual Trigger

The contractual trigger was set at 7% of the consolidated fully loaded CET1. As a result, CoCo holders were exposed to changes in Barclays' fully loaded CET1 ratio, especially where such ratio was approaching 7%. Changes in the CET1 ratio could be caused by changes in the amount of the bank's CET1 capital and/or its RWAs, as well as changes to their respective regulatory definition.

Barclays had entities located in foreign countries and, as a result, had CET1 capital and RWAs denominated in foreign currencies. Thus, the bank's CET1 ratio was exposed to changes in the foreign exchange rate of those currencies against the GBP.

Barclays' CET1 ratio was also affected by changes in accounting rules. Moreover, even if changes in applicable accounting rules were not yet in force as of the relevant calculation date, the regulator could require Barclays to reflect such changes in the calculation of the CET1 ratio.

Barclays, as most banks, only publicly reported its CET1 ratio on a quarterly basis as of the period end, and therefore during the quarterly period there was no published updating of the banks' fully loaded CET1 ratio. As a consequence, there could be no prior warning of adverse changes in Barclays' fully loaded CET1 indicating that the bank's fully loaded CET1 ratio was moving towards the 7% trigger level.

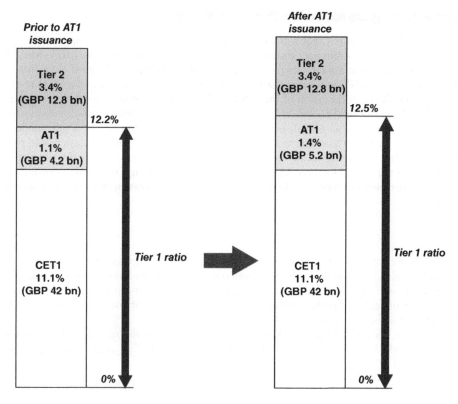

FIGURE 6.8   Barclays' capital levels prior and following the CoCo issuance

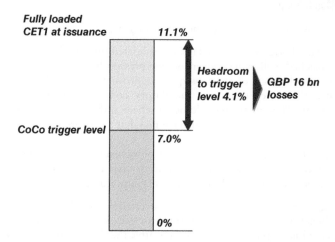

FIGURE 6.9   Barclays' 7.875% CoCo – Headroom to contractual trigger at issuance

At the time of issuance Barclays' fully loaded CET1 capital was GBP 42 billion, representing 11.1% of RWAs. As the contractual trigger was 7%, the headroom for trigger was GBP 16 billion (or 4.1% of RWAs), assuming no change in RWAs, as shown in Figure 6.9. In other words, Barclays had to recognise GBP 16 billion of losses prior to breaching the contractual trigger. At that point, the CoCo would be converted into ordinary shares of the bank.

6.6.4 Coupon Payments and Headroom to Distribution Restrictions

It was mentioned in Section 6.4 that a bank not meeting its combined buffer requirement (CBR) is subject to restrictions on discretionary distributions and is obliged to calculate its MDA, which represents the maximum amount a bank can pay in discretionary distributions. Interest payments to AT1 instruments are considered discretionary distributions and, as such, are subject to the MDA restriction.

Due to the gradual incorporation of the G-SIB and the capital conservation buffer requirements until the end of the transitional period on 1 January 2019, the initial headroom to distribution restrictions was a hefty 5% (= 11.1% − 6.1%), as illustrated in Figure 6.10. However, on a fully loaded basis, that headroom was just 0.50%, meaning that during the next several years Barclays would probably need to issue further CET1 capital to meet its CBR requirement, especially as the countercyclical buffer is added to the CBR. However, let us not forget that in a benign economic environment it is likely that the generation of profits would notably help Barclays increase its headroom to distribution restrictions.

Barclays could cancel (in whole or in part) any interest payment on the CoCo at its discretion and could pay dividends on its ordinary or preference shares. In addition, the bank could without restriction use funds that could have been applied to make such cancelled coupon payments to meet other obligations as they became due. Any cancellation of coupon payments on AT1 CoCos did not amount to an event of default.

In practice, Barclays' Board of Directors took into account the relative ranking of these instruments in the bank's capital structure. However, the Board could at any time depart from this policy at its sole discretion.

6.6.5 Conversion Mechanism

The CoCo could be converted due to any of the following reasons:

- The contractual CET1 trigger (i.e., Barclays' consolidated fully loaded CET1 ratio falling below 7.00%) being breached. Following conversion, the previously CoCo holders were *not* entitled to any compensation in the event of any subsequent improvement in Barclays' CET1 ratio;
- The resolution authority exercising its mandatory conversion power at the point of non-viability of the bank. This situation could occur where, although the bank's fully loaded CET1 was above 7%, the resolution authority determined that a conversion was necessary to stabilise the bank; or
- The resolution authority exercising its bail-in tool powers at the point of non-viability of the bank. As covered in Section 6.3.3, the resolution authority has the right to modify the terms of the CoCo, including the conversion of AT1 instruments into ordinary shares.

Following a trigger event, the CoCo could be converted into ordinary shares, at which point all other contractual obligations under the instrument were irrevocably and automatically released. The conversion period could last up to 40 business days after the delivery of the conversion notice (see "Step 1" below).

The conversion price was fixed at GBP 1.65 per share (i.e., 58% of the bank's GBP share price at the time of issuance), subject to certain anti-dilution adjustments. The conversion price was adjusted if there was a consolidation, reclassification or sub-division of Barclays' ordinary shares, an issuance of ordinary shares in certain circumstances by way of capitalisation of profits or reserves, a rights issue, an extraordinary dividend or certain takeover events.

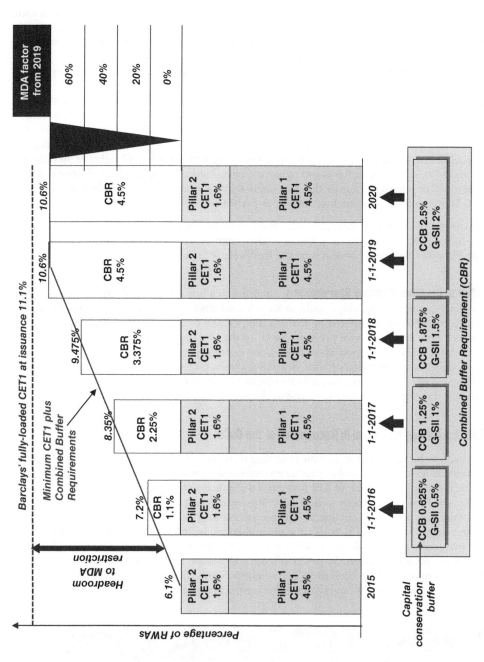

FIGURE 6.10 Barclays' 7.875% CoCo – Headroom to coupon payment restrictions

The timeline of the conversion process was the following:

- **Step 1:** Upon the occurrence of a trigger event, Barclays would inform the CoCo holders (via each of the clearing systems), the trustee, the principal agent and the PRA (the British banking supervisory authority). Any interest falling due between the date of the trigger event and the conversion date would be deemed to have been cancelled.
- **Step 2:** The ordinary shares would be issued, initially registered in the name of a depository (which would hold the shares on behalf of the CoCo holders).
- **Step 3:** The shares would be delivered to the depository within a 10-day period following the communication in Step 1. All of the bank's obligations under the CoCo would be irrevocably discharged and satisfied and under no circumstances would such released obligations be reinstated. The CoCo holders would have recourse only to the depository for the delivery to them of shares. The depositary would have the right to exercise on the behalf of the CoCo holders all rights of an ordinary shareholder (including voting rights and rights to receive dividends), except that holders would not be able to sell or otherwise transfer the shares until they have been delivered to the CoCo holders.
- **Step 4:** The depository would deliver the shares to the CoCo holders.

Upon conversion, Barclays' share price was likely to be significantly below the GBP 1.65 conversion price. As a result, upon conversion CoCo holders were likely to lose part of the value of their investment. However, they could benefit were the bank's share price to recover.

Optional Offer to the Other Ordinary Shareholders In order to allow for shareholders' clawback rights, upon automatic conversion, Barclays could in its sole and absolute discretion elect that the shares issued upon a trigger event be offered by the depositary to all or some of Barclays' ordinary shareholders at such time at a cash price per share equal to the CoCo conversion price. The offer would remain open for a maximum period of 40 days. Upon completion of the offer, CoCo holders would receive cash, shares or combination of both, depending on the take-up of such offer.

In order to maintain liquidity and facilitate investors' exit, during the offer CoCo holders would be able to trade their rights to receive cash and/or shares.

6.6.6 Initial Accounting and Basel III Recognition of the CoCo

The reader needs to be aware that at the time of writing there is no clear guidance from the IASB regarding the conversion feature, in particular whether it constituted a derivative. Despite the unclear accounting guidance, the initial recognition of AT1 instruments is rather uniform across banks. However, at the time of writing no banks have experienced a CET1 ratio approaching their AT1 contractual trigger level, which may raise new accounting challenges. The accounting treatment covered in this chapter is based on the most common recognition by banks and my understanding of the IFRS accounting guidance.

In my view, the best way to determine the accounting recognition of an instrument is to split it into different components and to assess the nature of each component. In the case of a convertible CoCo, there are four components that have to be taken into account: (i) the coupons, (ii) the redemption amount, (iii) the conversion feature and (iv) any other contractual arrangements, as shown in Figure 6.11.

FIGURE 6.11 Convertible CoCo – Suggested split to assess accounting recognition

Coupon and Redemption Cash Flows   From an accounting perspective, Barclays assessed whether the coupons and the redemption amount constituted an equity instrument or a liability. According to IAS 32, a **financial liability** is any liability that is:

- A contractual obligation:
  - To deliver cash or another financial asset to another entity; or
  - To exchange financial assets or financial liabilities with another entity under conditions that are potentially unfavourable to the entity; or
- A contract that will or may be settled in the entity's own equity instruments and is:
  - A non-derivative for which the entity is or may be obliged to deliver a variable number of the entity's own equity instruments; or
  - A derivative that will or may be settled other than by the exchange of a fixed amount of cash or another financial asset for a fixed number of the entity's own equity instruments.

An **equity instrument** is any contract that evidences a residual interest in the assets of an entity after deducting all of its liabilities. An equity instrument is recognised in the "shareholders' equity" section of the balance sheet.

In the case of a CoCo, the key feature of a liability would be the issuer being obliged to deliver either cash or another financial asset to the holder:

- Regarding the **coupons**, the terms governing the CoCo gave Barclays full discretion at all times to cancel the coupons on the instrument for an unlimited period and on a non-cumulative basis. As a result, Barclays had *no* contractual obligation to pay the coupons and, therefore, they had characteristics of an **equity instrument**.
- Regarding the **principal**, as the CoCo was perpetual Barclays had *no* contractual obligation to pay the redemption amount and, therefore, it had the characteristics of an **equity instrument**. The CoCo could be called on certain dates, but the call rights could only be exercised by Barclays, albeit prior consent from the supervisory authority was required. Consequently, the call rights did not change the conclusion that the redemption amount – in isolation – had the characteristics of an equity instrument.

As a result, excluding the conversion right and other contractual arrangements, both the coupons and the redemption amount had the features of equity instruments.

Conversion Feature   Regarding the conversion feature, Barclays assessed whether it constituted a derivative, an equity instrument or another type of asset/liability.

A derivative on own shares is deemed to be an equity instrument if it meets the following two requirements:

- The so-called "fixed-for-fixed" requirement is met (i.e., the exchange of a fixed amount of cash – or another financial asset – in the entity's financial functional currency for a fixed number of the entity's own equity instruments); and
- The derivative is settled gross.

In our case the fixed-for-fixed requirement was met as upon the CoCo conversion its holders would receive a fixed number of shares of Barclays in exchange for a fixed amount – the redemption amount. Anti-dilution features were not taken into account. The second requirement was also met as the conversion could only be settled gross. Thus, the **conversion feature** had the characteristics of an **equity instrument**.

From an accounting perspective, an interesting element of the conversion feature was that neither the issuer nor the holder had the right to exercise the conversion. The conversion was not mandatory either. The conversion could only be triggered automatically upon Barclays' CET1 breaching the contractual trigger or by the resolution authority (or any other relevant authority) provoking the CoCo conversion as a result of the bank reaching its PONV or as part of the authority exercising its bail-in powers. Thus, the conversion could be triggered only by events beyond the control of both the issuer and the holder. This fact did not preclude the equity classification of the conversion feature.

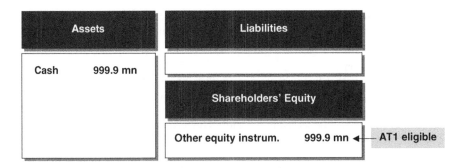

FIGURE 6.12   Initial recognition of Barclays' convertible CoCo

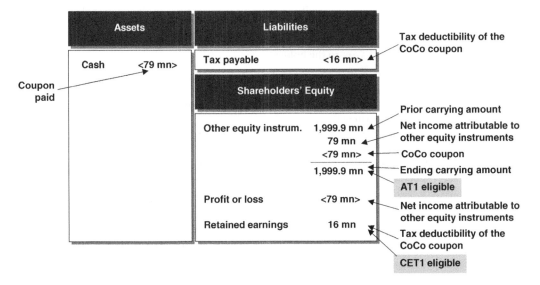

FIGURE 6.13   Barclays' convertible CoCo – Balance sheet impact of a coupon payment

Initial Recognition of the CoCo   The terms of the CoCo implied that it had the characteristics of an equity instrument and, consequently, the issuance net cash proceeds (GBP 999.9 million) were recognised as cash on Barclays' asset side and as "other equity instruments" in its shareholders' equity, as shown in Figure 6.12. From a regulatory perspective, the instrument qualified as an AT1 instrument.

Subsequent Recognition of the CoCo   Subsequent to initial recognition, several accounting entries related to the CoCo impacted Barclays' balance sheet, as shown in Figure 6.13, assuming that the CoCo coupon was paid:

- The carrying amount of the CoCo was *not* fair valued – it was an equity instrument;
- Part of the bank's net income was allocated to the CoCo holders (similar to the allocation to non-controlling interests). The net income amount attributable to the "other equity instruments" was the CoCo 6% coupon, which totalled GBP 79 million (= 1 bn × 7.875%, rounded). This amount increased the "other equity instruments" account by GBP 79 million;

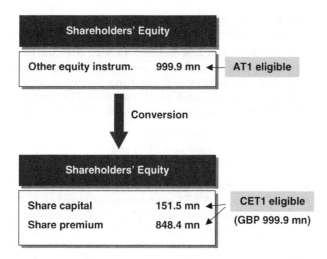

FIGURE 6.14 Recognition of Barclays' convertible CoCo upon conversion

- The GBP 79 million coupon paid to the CoCo holders reduced the British bank's "other equity instruments" account by the coupon amount; and
- Assuming a 20% corporate tax rate, the bank recorded in retained earnings a tax credit of GBP 16 million (= 79 mn × 20%, rounded) and reduced the amount of taxes payable.

After incorporating the impacts of the entries above, the carrying amount of the CoCo in the "other equity instruments" account remained unchanged, which is to say at GBP 999.9 million (= 999.9 mn + 79 mn − 79 mn).

From a regulatory perspective, the AT1 capital related to the CoCo was unchanged, being GBP 999.9 million. The increase in retained earnings stemming from the tax deductibility of the CoCo coupon increased the bank's CET1 by GBP 16 million. Of note is that GBP 79 million of net income was attributable to the CoCo holders, which diminished the bank's profit or loss attributable to ordinary shareholders (a CET1 item).

6.6.7 Accounting and Basel III Effects upon Conversion

Let us assume that the CoCo was converted, either because its contractual trigger was breached or because the corresponding authority exercised its conversion right, into new shares of Barclays. Assuming no anti-dilution adjustments performed to the GBP 1.65 conversion price, upon conversion of the CoCo its holders received 606.06 million (= 1 bn / 1.65) ordinary shares of Barclays. As the share capital per share was GBP 0.25, the share capital related to the new shares was GBP 151.5 million (= 606.06 mn × 0.25) while the GBP 848.4 million (= 999.9 mn − 151.5 mn) remainder was allocated to share premium.

As a result, and upon conversion of the CoCo, Barclays derecognised GBP 999.9 million of "other equity instruments", and recognised GBP 151.5 million of "share capital" and GBP 848.4 million of "share premium", as depicted in Figure 6.14.

From a regulatory capital perspective, the conversion reduced Barclays AT1 holdings by GBP 999.9 million and increased CET1 capital by that amount. Therefore, the conversion generated CET1 capital but maintained the same level of Tier 1 capital.

6.7 CASE STUDY: DEUTSCHE BANK'S WRITE-DOWN CoCo

In this section a principal write-down CoCo is dissected. In May 2014 the German bank Deutsche Bank issued AT1 instruments to further strengthen its capital structure and to support expected future leverage ratio requirements. The transaction was the first step towards reaching an overall targeted volume of approximately EUR 5 billion of CRR/CRD IV-compliant AT1 capital which Deutsche Bank planned to issue by the end of 2015. The issuance consisted of three tranches, totalling EUR 3.5 billion:

- A EUR 1.75 billion tranche with a coupon of 6%;
- A USD 1.25 billion tranche with a coupon of 6.25%; and
- A GBP 650 million tranche with a coupon of 7.125%.

The CoCos were perpetual (i.e., they did not have a maturity date) and had a temporary write-down at a trigger level of 5.125% phase-in CET1 capital ratio, calculated on a consolidated basis. The CoCos constituted unsecured and subordinated notes of Deutsche Bank, ranking just prior to ordinary shares in liquidation of the bank. The interest was fixed and the interest rate was reset at five-year intervals. Payments of interest were subject to cancellation, in whole or in part, and, if cancelled, were non-cumulative (i.e., interest payments in the following years would not increase to compensate for any shortfall in interest payments in any previous year). The EUR-denominated CoCo was redeemable by Deutsche Bank at its discretion on 30 April 2022 and at five-year intervals thereafter (see Figure 6.15) or in other limited circumstances (for certain regulatory or taxation reasons). Any redemption was subject to the prior consent of the competent supervisory authority.

The redemption amount and the nominal amount of the CoCos could be written down upon the occurrence of a trigger event – a contractual trigger being breached. A trigger event occurred if the CET1 capital ratio, determined on phase-in and on a consolidated basis, fell below 5.125%. The CoCos could also be written up, following a trigger event, subject to meeting certain conditions.

The CoCos were issued with attached warrants, excluding shareholders' pre-emptive rights. Each denomination of the bond (EUR 100,000) carried one warrant, entitling the owner to purchase one common share in Deutsche Bank. Prior to the placement of the CoCos via a bookbuilding process, the warrants were detached by the CoCos' initial subscriber. The warrants gave its holders the option to subscribe to a total of 30,250 shares.

The main terms of the EUR tranche CoCo are listed in Table 6.3.

6.7.1 Objectives of the Issuance

Deutsche Bank's minimum fully loaded Tier 1 capital ratio requirement, excluding the countercyclical buffer, was 9.0%, as shown in Figure 6.16. In April 2014, Deutsche Bank had a 9.2% fully loaded Tier 1 capital totally comprised of CET1 capital. Whilst the bank met the fully loaded requirements, it was a rather inefficient way of meeting the Tier 1 capital requirement, due to the lack of AT1 capital instruments

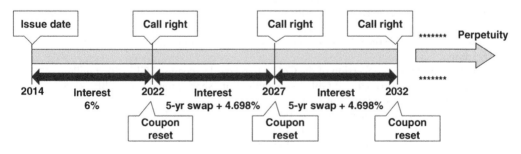

FIGURE 6.15 EUR-denominated CoCo – Call rights and coupon reset dates

TABLE 6.3   Main terms of Deutsche Bank's EUR tranche contingent convertible

Main Terms of Deutsche Bank's EUR Tranche CoCo	
Issuer	Deutsche Bank AG
Issue date	27 May 2014
Principal	EUR 1.75 billion
Eligibility	CRD IV/CRR compliant AT1 capital
Maturity	Perpetual, subject to call right
Coupon	Payable annually on 30 April each year. Non-cumulative discretionary cancellation of coupon payments; mandatory cancellation as required by the CRR
Coupon rate	6% until the first call date (30 April 2022), with reset every 5 years at 5-year swap rate + 4.698%. Payable annually
Call right by Issuer	Every 5 years (unless written-down), starting on 30 April 2022 (i.e., 8 years following issuance) Extraordinary call rights relating to regulatory and tax (any time, including written-down)
Write-down trigger	Temporary write-down, in whole or part, at 5.125% CET1 ratio (phase-in/consolidated). Write-down to restore CET1 ratio back to 5.125%
Write-up mechanism	At full discretion of the issuer, without obligation and based on profits
Applicable law	German law
Ranking	Insolvency claims junior to Tier 2 instruments. Senior to CET1 claims (i.e., to ordinary shares)

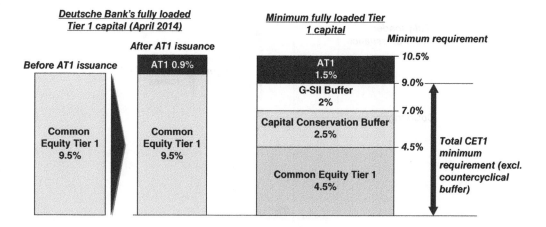

FIGURE 6.16   AT1 issuance effects on Deutsche Bank's Tier 1 capital

(which were notably cheaper than CET1 instruments). The main objective of the issuance was to strengthen the bank's Tier 1 capital using AT1 instruments (see Figure 6.16). The EUR 3.5 billion issuance represented 0.9% of RWAs. This was the first step towards reaching an AT1 capital ratio of 1.5%.

Another important driver was Deutsche Bank's leverage ratio, which arguably was weak at the time of issuance. The issuance of the CoCos enhanced this ratio, as AT1 capital was part of the numerator, in conjunction with CET1 capital.

6.7.2 Headroom to Trigger

One interesting feature of the CoCo was that its contractual trigger was linked to the bank's phase-in (rather than fully loaded) CET1, which gave additional headroom to the CoCo holders.

In April 2014, Deutsche Bank had EUR 50 billion phase-in CET1, representing a 13.2% ratio. The capital headroom, using the bank's phase-in CET1 ratio at the time of issuance, represented 8.075% (= 13.2% − 5.125%) or EUR 30 billion. When taking the bank's fully loaded CET1, the headroom to trigger was a much lower 4.375% or EUR 16.2 billion, as shown in Figure 6.17. In other words, Deutsche Bank had to suffer EUR 16.2 billion of losses for the 5.125% trigger to be breached, assuming that the bank's RWAs remain unchanged.

6.7.3 Coupon Payments and Headroom to Distribution Restrictions

An informed investor focuses not just on the likelihood of the trigger being reached, but the risk of the coupon being cancelled. Deutsche Bank's EUR-denominated CoCo accrued an annual 6% fixed coupon. Starting in April 2022, the interest was reset every five years, at the then-prevailing 5-year swap rate plus 4.698%. The reset periodically protected investors against rising interest rates.

A key requirement of AT1 instruments is that their interest shall be cancellable and non-cumulative. Thus, the CoCo terms included that Deutsche Bank could elect, at its sole discretion, to cancel payment of coupons, in whole or in part, on any coupon payment date. Such cancellation would not constitute an event of default.

Coupon payments were **non-cumulative**. Consequently, coupon payments in following years could not be increased to compensate for any shortfall in coupon payments during a previous year.

If Deutsche Bank exercised its discretion not to pay a coupon on the CoCo on any interest payment date, this would not give rise to any restriction on the bank making distributions or any other payments to the holders of any instruments ranking pari passu with, or junior to, the CoCo.

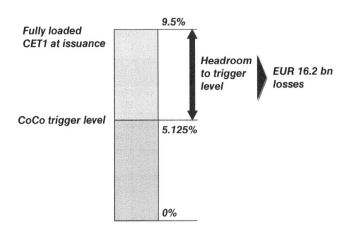

FIGURE 6.17   Deutsche Bank AT1 – Headroom to trigger

Compulsory Cancellation of Interest   Interest payments would mandatorily be cancelled:

- To the extent that such coupon payment, together with any distributions previously made on Tier 1 instruments in the then current fiscal year, exceeded a sum of ADI (to be covered below), increased by the aggregate interest expense relating to Tier 1 instruments reflected in the financial statements for the preceding year, a specific German requirement; or
- To the extent that the restrictions due to CBR/MDA tests were triggered; or
- If and to the extent the competent supervisory authority (the German BaFin or any successor) ordered the bank to cancel a coupon payment in whole or in part or another prohibition of distributions was imposed by law or an authority.

Headroom to the German ADI   A unique feature of the Deutsche Bank CoCo was that coupon payments were subject to an additional local regulatory test known as ADI, a sort of German MDA. Under German law, companies had **"available distributable items"** (**"ADI"**), which represented the sum of included net income, free capital reserves and retained earnings as at the end of the previous financial year. The ADI was adjusted upwards for accrued interest expense on Tier 1 instrument (basically amounts already accrued through profit or loss but not paid yet). Deutsche Bank was not allowed to make a discretionary coupon payment if the payment, together with payments made on other Tier 1 instruments, exceeded its ADI at the parent level (calculated according to German GAAP principles). Under the German commercial code, certain amounts related to intangible assets, deferred tax assets and pension assets could not be distributed, reducing the available distributable items. German accounting standards allowed the issuer to influence the amount of distributable items somewhat (e.g., through dividends up streamed from subsidiaries). Thus, Deutsche Bank needed to manage its parent-only balance sheet profit to ensure that sufficient amounts were available to make interest payments on the AT1 instruments.

Two elements of the ADI trigger added uncertainty to investors. Firstly, having a trigger subject to a somewhat "obscure" variable rather than a yardstick calculated under IFRS guidelines, and secondly, having the ADI-linked trigger applied at a parent-only level rather than at a consolidated level.

Payment capacity for 2014 coupons was EUR 2.7 billion, based on year-end 2013 financials. Payment capacity was consumed on a sequential basis through the year by distributions on AT1 and CET1 instruments. It is relevant to note that the CoCo coupons were paid on 30 April, prior to the distribution of dividends to ordinary shares.

Headroom to the MDA Restrictions   Figure 6.18 depicts the minimum CET1 levels below which the Maximum Distributable Amount ("MDA") restrictions on discretionary distributions (including dividends on ordinary shares, coupon payments on AT1 instruments and variable compensation) would apply. Figure 6.18 also shows Deutsche Bank's CET1 ratio, which was graphed using the reported 13.2% phase-in CET1 and the 9.5% fully loaded CET1 ratios in March 2014. Assuming that RWAs and CET1 capital remained unchanged from April 2014, it can be observed that the headroom before the MDA restrictions applied was very large on the CoCo's issue date, and expected to decline to just 0.5% (the difference between the bank's 9.5% fully loaded CET1 and the 9% requirement) from 2019. Therefore, Deutsche Bank needed to generate a substantial amount of CET1 capital during the years up to 2019 to increase the headroom, for example in the form of undistributed earnings. The minimum level was calculated as the sum of the minimum CET1 capital requirement (4.5%) and the combined buffer requirement ("CBR"). The CBR was applied gradually, with a phase-in period starting in Jan 2016 and completed by January 2019. The CBR in the figure includes the capital conservation buffer and the global systematically important institutions ("G-SII") buffer. The latter was assumed to be 2%, in accordance with the Financial Stability Board publication as per 11 November 2013. The countercyclical capital buffer was not included in these calculations, but Deutsche Bank may need to include it at a later stage.

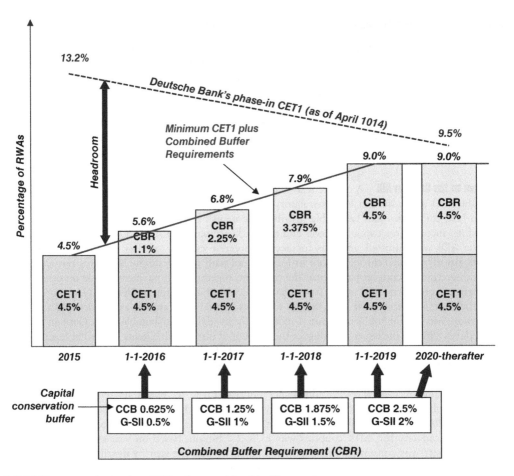

FIGURE 6.18   Deutsche Bank – CET1 plus combined buffer requirement

6.7.4 Write-down Mechanism

The CoCo could be written-down due to any of the following reasons:

- The contractual 5.125% CET1 trigger event occurring;
- The resolution authority exercising its power to write down (and convert) capital instruments at the point of non-viability (PONV); or
- The resolution authority exercising its bail-in tool powers at the PONV of the bank. It was covered in Section 6.3.3 that the resolution authority has the right to modify the terms of a CoCo, including the write-down of AT1 instruments.

A contractual **"trigger event"** occurred when the CET1 ratio of Deutsche Bank, determined on a consolidated and phase-in basis, fell below 5.125%. In reality, it was rather likely that Deutsche Bank's CET1 breached the 5.125% contractual trigger prior to the bank reaching its PONV.

Upon the trigger being breached, the nominal amount of the CoCo was automatically reduced by the amount of the write-down. In addition, and with effect from the beginning of the interest period in which the write-down occurred, coupon payments were calculated on the basis of the reduced nominal amount and, therefore, did not accrue in full.

Any write-down was implemented on a pro-rata basis among all AT1 instruments sharing a trigger-based write-down mechanism in an aggregate amount as required to restore fully the consolidated CET1 ratio of the bank to 5.125%.

> As a write-down only restored Deutsche Bank's CET1 ratio to 5.125%, it could leave the bank close to a second trigger event if during the following quarterly period the bank's CET1 continued to deteriorate.

6.7.5 Regulatory Bail-in

Regarding write-down provisions, the terms and conditions of the CoCo only included the "contractual trigger" provision which stated that the CoCo would be written-down in the event that the bank's CET1 fell below the 5.125% trigger. However, and as a result of the BRRD (see Section 6.3.3), the CoCo was implicitly subject to the competent authority (commonly the resolution authority) writing-down the CoCo (i) upon the bank becoming non-viable (i.e., reaching its PONV) or (ii) as a result of the competent authority exercising its regulatory **bail-in** powers.

A regulatory bail-in would occur if Deutsche Bank became, or was deemed by the competent authority to have become, non-viable and unable to continue its regulated banking activities without a write-off or conversion or without a public sector injection of capital. Therefore, the competent authority could exercise its bail-in powers, writing down the CoCo or converting it into ordinary shares. Following a write-down as a result of regulatory bail-in, the CoCo could not be **written up** subsequently.

Investors bore the risk of losing all of their investment, including the nominal amount plus any accrued interest, if a regulatory bail-in occurred. The extent to which the nominal amount of the CoCo was subject to a regulatory bail-in depended on a number of factors outside Deutsche Bank's control.

6.7.6 Write-up Mechanism

An interesting feature of Deutsche Bank's CoCo was that any contractual write-down (i.e., as a result of the bank's CET1 breaching the 5.125% trigger) was *not* required to be permanent. Following a write-down, the German bank was entitled at its sole discretion to effect a **write-up** of the CoCo (i.e., an increase of the CoCo nominal amount), up to its initial nominal. Any write-ups were effected on a pro rata basis, pari passu with write-ups of other AT1 instruments.

A write-up could not be effected if it would cause the bank to be in breach of any contractual obligations that have been assumed by the bank or with any statutory or regulatory obligations. At the time of a write-up, there shall not exist any trigger event that was continuing. A write-up was also excluded if such write-up gave rise to the occurrence of a trigger event.

Write-ups did not have priority over dividend payments and other distributions on shares and other CET1 instruments of the bank (i.e., such payments and distributions were permitted even if no full write-up had been effected).

> Write-ups commonly can be effected if consolidated net income has been recorded at any time and if the MDA is not exceeded.

The amount of a write-up was limited by the proportion of the annual profit of the bank which represented the share of the initial nominal amount of an individual AT1 Instrument subject to a write-down in the aggregate Tier 1 capital of the bank before a write-up taking effect and was further limited by MDA restrictions. The maximum total amount that could be used for a write-up was calculated in accordance with the following formula:

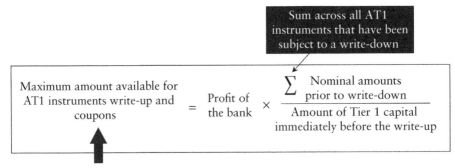

In total, the sum of the amounts of the write-ups of AT1 instruments together with the amounts of any dividend payments and other distributions on shares and other CET1 instruments of Deutsche Bank (including payment of interests and other distributions on AT1 instruments that have been written down) for the relevant financial year could not exceed the Maximum Distributable Amount (MDA), as covered in Section 6.7.3.

6.7.7 Ranking

Any rights under the CoCo ranked behind all creditors of Deutsche Bank in the event of its insolvency or liquidation. Accordingly, in the event of the dissolution, liquidation, insolvency, composition or other proceedings for the avoidance of insolvency of, or against, Deutsche Bank, the obligations under the CoCo were fully subordinated to (i) the claims of senior creditors of the bank, (ii) the claims under Tier 2 instruments, and (iii) other claims specified in the German insolvency laws, as shown in Figure 6.19.

The bank's payment obligations under the CoCo ranked pari passu amongst themselves and with all AT1 claims of the bank and the payment of interest payments thereunder.

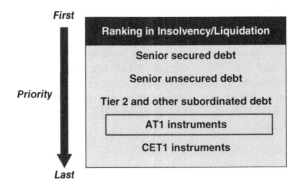

FIGURE 6.19   Ranking of Deutsche Bank's CoCo

6.7.8 Early Amortisation Rights

Whilst Deutsche Bank's CoCo was a perpetual instrument, it incorporated several rights (call rights) to allow for early amortisation.

"Ordinary" Call Right   The CoCo could be early amortised by Deutsche Bank at five-year intervals starting in year eight following issuance, subject to prior consent of the relevant supervisory authority. The bank was interested to early terminate the bonds in a number of situations, including:

- A notably lower funding spread for similar AT1 instruments. The CoCo interest rate was reset every five years at the EUR 5-year swap rate plus 4.698%. A margin (over the 5-year swap rate) at the time of reset notably lower than 4.698% for new AT1 issues would encourage Deutsche Bank to call the CoCo and to issue a new one;
- Ignoring effects on the bank's leverage ratio, a full aggregate amount of AT1 instruments exceeding the 1.5% maximum AT1 eligibility for Tier 1 capital requirement.

> What about exercising the call right following a sharp write-down of the CoCo principal, to avoid having to write-up such principal at a later stage?
>
> Deutsche Bank was *not* compelled to exercise its call right in such a situation as a call right for reasons other than tax and regulatory (see below) could only be effected at the CoCo's **par amount** (i.e., any previously written down amounts would be reimbursed to the CoCo holders).
>
> In the case of an early redemption due to tax or regulatory reasons, the amount reimbursed would be the then written-down amount (i.e., any written-down amounts would not be repaid to the CoCo holders). However, it would not be a simple matter. First of all, it could damage Deutsche Bank's reputation as an issuer, and secondly, the bank had already full discretion to effect a write-up.

Tax and Regulatory Call Rights   In addition to the "ordinary" call right, subject to prior consent of the supervisory authority as well, the CoCo could be early amortised for tax and regulatory reasons. As mentioned previously, the CoCo would be redeemed at its written-down amount.

Early redemption for tax reasons could be exercised if the tax treatment of the CoCo, due to a change in applicable legislation (e.g., any fiscal or regulatory legislation) after issuance and Deutsche Bank in its own discretion determined that such change had a material adverse effect on the Bank. This clause tried to protect the bank against non-deductibility of coupon payments, or a charge of withholding tax.

> A call right for tax reasons is commonly included in the terms and conditions of an instrument to prevent that a newly levied tax (e.g., a withholding tax on coupons) makes the instrument overly expensive for the issuer. In the case of Deutsche Bank's CoCo, the call right for tax reasons was especially important as changes in the tax treatment of the CoCo were particularly relevant.
>
> When the CoCo was issued, the German tax authorities did not tax gains stemming from the write-down of AT1 instruments. It implied that any written down amount was fully eligible as CET1 capital.
>
> Let us imagine that the German tax authorities suddenly decided to levy a 30% tax to AT1 instruments' written-down amounts. It would mean that just 70% of any written-down amount would be eligible as CET1 capital, notably lowering its loss absorption capabilities. In this situation Deutsche Bank would likely exercise its tax call right.

Early redemption for regulatory reasons could be exercised if the CoCo ceased to be eligible for AT1 capital. In the terms and conditions of the CoCo, the call right was rather loosely stated as: "if the Issuer determines, in its own discretion, that it is subject to any other form of a less advantageous regulatory own funds treatment".

6.7.9 Accounting and Basel III Recognition of the CoCo – Write-down Feature not Deemed to be a Derivative

The reader needs to be aware that at the time of writing there is no clear guidance from the IASB regarding the write-down feature, in particular whether the contractual trigger constitutes a derivative. The accounting treatments covered in this chapter are based on the discussions by banks with the auditing community and my understanding of the IFRS accounting guidance.

In my view, the best way to determine the accounting recognition of an instrument is to split it into different components and to assess the nature of each component. In the case of a write-down CoCo, there are four components that have to be taken into account: (i) the coupons, (ii) the redemption amount, (iii) the write-down/up feature and (iv) any other relevant contractual arrangements, as shown in Figure 6.20.

The last item referred to the tax and regulatory calls. These elements are non-financial variables outside the control of Deutsche Bank and as a result are not considered separately to the rest of the terms of the CoCo.

Coupon and Redemption Cash Flows   From an accounting perspective, Deutsche Bank assessed whether the coupons and the redemption amount constituted an equity instrument or a liability. Following the arguments explained in Section 6.6.6:

- Regarding the **coupons**, the terms governing the CoCo gave Deutsche Bank full discretion at all times to cancel the coupons on the instrument for an unlimited period and on a non-cumulative basis. As a result, Deutsche Bank had *no* contractual obligation to pay the coupons and, therefore, they had characteristics of an **equity instrument**.
- Regarding the **principal**, as the CoCo was perpetual, Deutsche Bank had *no* contractual obligation to pay the redemption amount and therefore it had the characteristics of an **equity instrument**. The CoCo could be called on certain dates, but the call rights could only be exercised by Deutsche Bank, albeit obtaining prior permission from the supervisory authority. Consequently, the call rights did not change the conclusion that the redemption amount – in isolation – had the characteristics of an equity instrument.

As a result, excluding the write-down/up right and other relevant contractual arrangements, both the coupons and the redemption amount had features of equity instruments.

Write-down Feature *not* deemed to be a Derivative   Regarding the write-down feature, Deutsche Bank assessed whether this feature needed to be separated from the host contract (i.e., the contract without

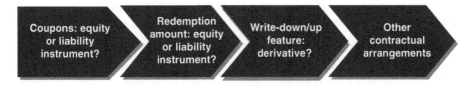

FIGURE 6.20   Write-down CoCo – Suggested split to assess accounting recognition

any embedded features – in our case the coupons and redemption cash flows). The write-down feature had to be separated from the host contract if it met all of the following conditions:

- It was a separate feature with terms that met the definition of a **derivative** according to IFRS 9 (i.e., the feature constituted what is called an "embedded derivative");
- The economic characteristics and risks of the embedded derivative were *not* closely related to the economic characteristics and risks of the host contract. This condition was met; and
- The whole AT1 instrument was *not* accounted for at fair value through profit or loss. As the CoCo was *not* measured at fair value through profit or loss, this condition was met.

Thus, next Deutsche Bank had to assess whether the write-down feature constituted a derivative. Under IFRS 9, a financial instrument is a **derivative** if *all* the following three conditions are met:

- Its value changes in response to the change in a specified interest rate, financial instrument price, commodity price, foreign exchange rate, index of prices or rates, credit rating or credit index, or other variable, provided in the case of a non-financial variable that the variable is not specific to a party to the contract (sometimes called the "underlying");
- It requires no initial net investment or an initial net investment that is smaller than would be required for other types of contracts that would be expected to have a similar response to changes in market factors; and
- It is settled at a future date.

IFRS 9 excluded from the definition of a derivative an instrument whose underlying is a non-market variable specific to a party to the contract. Some argue that the term "non-financial variable specific to a party to the contract" was intended to exclude insurance contracts. However, a substantial number of banks have considered CET1 ratio to be non-financial variable specific to a party to the contract and, as a consequence, subject to the exclusion.

If the write-down feature was *not* deemed to be a derivative, Deutsche Bank did not need to separate the feature and, therefore, the whole CoCo was recognised as an equity instrument (see Figure 6.21). The CoCo in its entirety was recognised in Deutsche Bank's shareholders' equity section as "other equity instruments" with an initial carrying amount equal to the EUR 1.75 billion net proceeds from the CoCo issuance, as shown in Figure 6.22.

From a Basel III perspective, the CoCo fully qualified as AT1 capital as it met the requirements covered in Section 4.2.

Subsequent Recognition Subsequent to initial recognition, several accounting entries related to the CoCo impacted Deutsche Bank's balance sheet, as shown in Figure 6.23, assuming that the CoCo coupon was paid and no write-downs occurred:

- The carrying amount of the CoCo was *not* fair valued as it was an equity instrument;
- Part of the bank's net income was allocated to the CoCo holders (similar to the allocation to non-controlling interests). The net income amount attributable to the "other equity instruments" was the CoCo 6% coupon, which totalled EUR 105 million ($= 1.75\,\text{bn} \times 6\%$). This amount increased the "other equity instruments" account by EUR 105 million;
- The EUR 105 million coupon paid to the CoCo holders reduced the German bank's "other equity instruments" account by the coupon amount; and
- Assuming a 20% corporate tax rate, the bank recorded in retained earnings a tax credit of EUR 21 million ($= 105\,\text{mn} \times 20\%$) and reduced the amount of tax payable.

After incorporating the impacts of the entries above, the carrying amount of the CoCo in the "other equity instruments" account remained unchanged, staying at EUR 1,750 million ($= 1,750\,\text{mn} + 105\,\text{mn} - 105\,\text{mn}$).

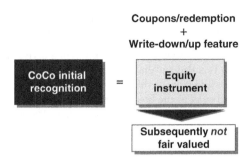

FIGURE 6.21   Deutsche Bank's write-down CoCo – Initial recognition

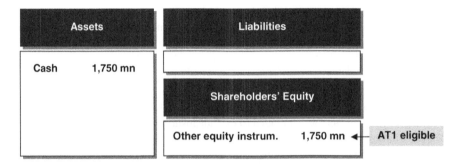

FIGURE 6.22   Deutsche Bank's write-down CoCo – Initial impact on balance sheet

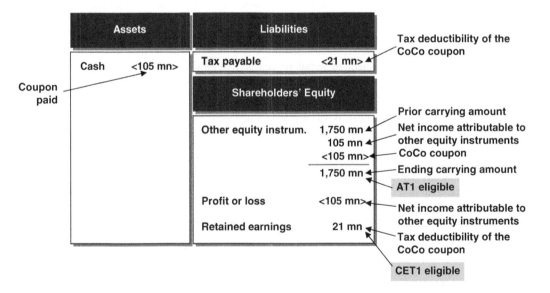

FIGURE 6.23   Deutsche Bank's write-down CoCo – Recognition of a coupon payment

From a regulatory perspective, the AT1 capital related to the CoCo was unchanged, being EUR 1,750 million. The increase in retained earnings stemming from the tax deductibility of the CoCo coupon increased the bank's CET1 by EUR 21 million. Of note is that EUR 105 million of net income was attributable to the CoCo holders, which diminished the bank's profit or loss attributable to ordinary shareholders (a CET1 item).

> Deutsche Bank's net income attributable to its ordinary shareholders was reduced by the amount allocated to the CoCo holders, which was the CoCo coupon.

Write-down Recognition   Let us imagine that a few months later, the German bank's CET1 ratio breached the contractual 5.125% and that in order to bring the CET1 ratio back to 5.125% a write-down of EUR 300 million was effected to the CoCo. From an accounting perspective, the bank's share premium was increased by the EUR 300 million write-down while the carrying amount of the "other equity instruments" account was reduced by that amount, as shown in Figure 6.24. As a result, the carrying amount of the CoCo was EUR 1,450 million (= 1,750 mn – 300 mn).

From a regulatory perspective, the bank's CET1 capital increased by EUR 300 million (as share premium was part of CET1 capital) while the bank's AT1 capital decreased by that amount.

Write-up Recognition   Let us imagine that a EUR 200 million write-up was effected as a result of Deutsche Bank returning to profitability and all other conditions for a write-up being met. The effects on the bank's shareholders' equity were the opposite to those of the previously covered write-down. As a result, the bank's share premium decreased by the EUR 200 million write-up while the carrying amount of the "other equity instruments" account increased by that amount, as shown in Figure 6.25. Thus, the carrying amount of the CoCo was EUR 1,650 million (= 1,450 mn + 200 mn).

From a regulatory perspective, the bank's CET1 capital decreased by EUR 200 million (as share premium was part of CET1 capital) while the bank's AT1 capital increased by that amount.

> Write-up rights are normally at the complete discretion of the issuer, with no pre-established rules. Therefore it is likely that investors would give zero value to it unless the issuer has a consistent past history of write-ups being effected.

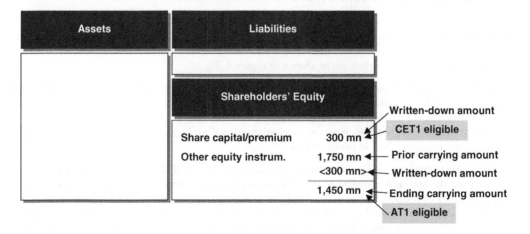

FIGURE 6.24   Deutsche Bank's write-down CoCo – Recognition of a write-down

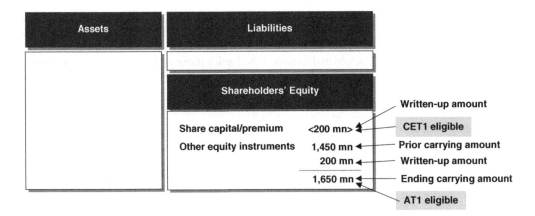

FIGURE 6.25 Deutsche Bank's write-down CoCo – Recognition of a write-up

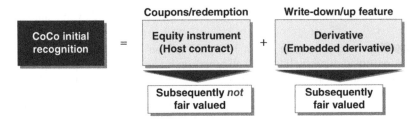

FIGURE 6.26 Deutsche Bank's write-down CoCo – Bifurcation on initial recognition

6.7.10 Accounting and Basel III Recognition of the CoCo – Write-down Feature deemed to be a Derivative

It was mentioned previously that at the time of writing there was no common view in the accounting community regarding the recognition of the write-down feature. A good number of accounting practitioners consider that the write-down feature constitutes a derivative.

Initial Recognition Let us imagine that Deutsche Bank considered the write-down (and write-up) feature to be a derivative (an embedded derivative). The AT1 instrument was bifurcated between a host contract and an embedded derivative, as shown in Figure 6.26:

- A host contract representing the German bank's discretion to pay interest and the redemption amount. The host contract was recognised in Deutsche Bank's shareholders' equity. No fair valuation was effected during the life of the instrument; and
- An embedded derivative which was recognised at fair value. At each reporting date the change in fair value was recognised in profit or loss.

The German bank needed to fair value the derivative on issuance date and at each reporting date by estimating the size and probability of write-downs (and any subsequent write-ups) occurring, a notably complex estimation. Let us assume that the German bank concluded that the embedded derivative initial fair value was nil. As a result, initially Deutsche Bank recognised in its shareholders' equity the EUR 1.75 billion net proceeds from the issuance, while the derivative was *not* recognised on balance sheet due to its nil fair value, as highlighted in Figure 6.27.

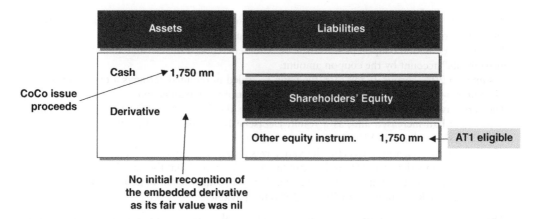

FIGURE 6.27 Deutsche Bank's write-down CoCo – Initial impact on balance sheet

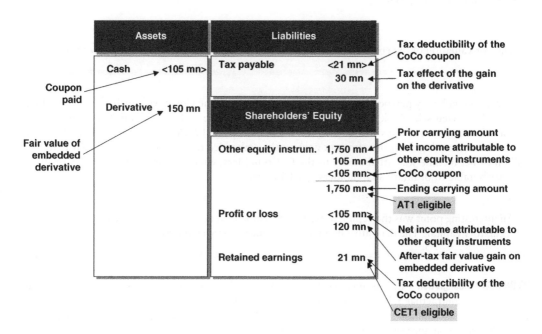

FIGURE 6.28 Deutsche Bank's write-down CoCo – Subsequent recognition

From a regulatory capital perspective, the instrument qualified as AT1 capital. Consequently, Deutsche Bank's AT1 capital strengthened by EUR 1.75 billion.

Subsequent Recognition Subsequent to initial recognition, several accounting entries related to the CoCo impacted Deutsche Bank's balance sheet, as shown in Figure 6.28, assuming that the CoCo coupon was paid:

- The carrying amount of the CoCo was *not* fair valued as it was an equity instrument;
- Part of the bank's net income was allocated to the CoCo holders (similar to the allocation to non-controlling interests). The net income amount attributable to the "other equity instruments" was

the CoCo 6% coupon, which totalled EUR 105 million ($= 1.75\,\text{bn} \times 6\%$). This amount increased the "other equity instruments" account by EUR 105 million;

- The EUR 105 million coupon paid to the CoCo holders reduced the German bank's "other equity instruments" account by the coupon amount;
- Assuming a 20% corporate tax rate, the bank recorded in retained earnings a tax credit of EUR 21 million ($= 105\,\text{mn} \times 20\%$) and reduced the amount of tax payable; and
- The derivative was fair valued. Let us assume that the likelihood of reaching the 5.125% contractual trigger had increased and, as a result, Deutsche Bank estimated that the fair value of the embedded derivative was EUR 150 million. The bank recognised a derivative asset with a EUR 150 million carrying amount. As the derivative was recognised at fair value through profit or loss, the bank recognised a EUR 150 million pre-tax gain. Assuming that the bank's corporate tax rate was 20%, the after-tax gain was EUR 120 million ($= 150\,\text{mn} \times 80\%$). In addition, Deutsche Bank recognised a EUR 30 million ($= 150\,\text{mn} \times 20\%$) tax payable.

After incorporating the impacts of the entries above, the carrying amount of the CoCo in the "other equity instruments" account remained unchanged, which is to say at EUR 1,750 million ($= 1,750\,\text{mn} + 105\,\text{mn} - 105\,\text{mn}$).

> The fair valuation of the embedded derivative added volatility to Deutsche Bank's profit or loss.

From a regulatory perspective, the AT1 capital related to the CoCo was unchanged, being EUR 1,750 million. Deutsche Bank's CET1 capital increased by (i) the EUR 21 million stemming from the increase in retained earnings due to the tax deductibility of the CoCo coupon and (ii) the EUR 120 million stemming from the after-tax gain on the embedded derivative. Of note is that EUR 105 million of net income was attributable to the CoCo holders, which diminished the bank's profit or loss attributable to ordinary shareholders (a CET1 item).

> An interesting point was the capital impact of the embedded derivative. Did it have an impact on regulatory capital? The derivative had no credit counterparty credit risk.

Write-down Recognition   Let us imagine that a few months later, the German bank's CET1 ratio breached the contractual 5.125% and that in order to bring the CET1 ratio back to 5.125% a write-down of EUR 300 million was effected to the CoCo. From an accounting perspective, the impact on Deutsche Bank's balance sheet was the following (see Figure 6.29):

- The derivative was fair valued. Its fair value was the EUR 300 million write-down amount. The change in fair value was EUR 150 million ($= 300\,\text{mn} - 150\,\text{mn}$) recognised in profit or loss, on an after-tax basis. The tax effect was EUR 30 million ($= 150\,\text{mn} \times 20\%$), assuming a 20% corporate tax rate, increasing the amount of taxes payable; and
- The derivative was settled and its fair value became zero, while the carrying amount of the "other equity instruments" was reduced by the EUR 300 million write-down. As a result, the carrying amount of the CoCo was EUR 1,450 million ($= 1,750\,\text{mn} - 300\,\text{mn}$).

From a regulatory perspective, the bank's CET1 capital increased by EUR 120 million, stemming from the after-tax gain on the embedded derivative (as profit or loss was part of CET1 capital). Remember that in the previous period the German bank recognised another EUR 120 million gain in profit or loss, which was also incorporated in CET1 capital. In addition, the bank's AT1 capital decreased by EUR 300 million, the written-down amount.

> If an embedded derivative is recognised, the CET1 effect of a write-down would likely be recognised during different periods. In addition, if the unrealised gain on the embedded derivative is taxed, the effect on CET1 capital would be diminished by the amount of taxes payable.

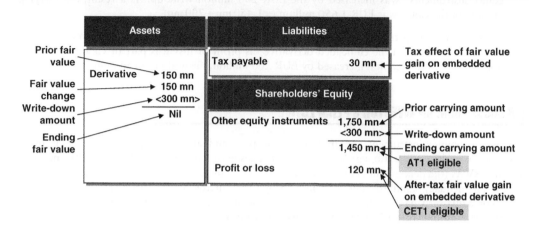

FIGURE 6.29 Deutsche Bank's write-down CoCo – Balance sheet impact of the write-down

Write-up Recognition Let us imagine that a EUR 200 million write-up was effected as a result of Deutsche Bank returning to profitability and all other conditions for a write-up being met. The mechanics would be the opposite to those of a write-down. From an accounting perspective, the impact on Deutsche Bank's balance sheet was the following (see Figure 6.30).

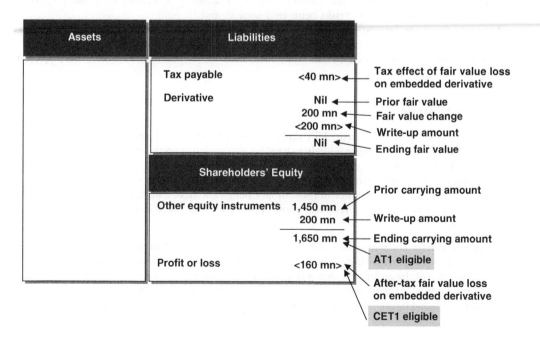

FIGURE 6.30 Deutsche Bank's write-down CoCo – Balance sheet impact of the write-up

- The derivative was fair valued. Its fair value was the EUR 200 million write-up amount. The change in fair value was a EUR 200 million (= nil – 200 mn) loss recognised in profit or loss, on an after-tax basis (EUR 160 million). The tax effect was EUR 40 million (= 200 mn × 20%), assuming a 20% corporate tax rate, decreasing the amount of taxes payable; and
- The derivative was settled and its fair value became zero, while the carrying amount of the "other equity instruments" was increased by the EUR 200 million write-up. As a result, the carrying amount of the CoCo was EUR 1,650 million (= 1,450 mn + 200 mn).

From a regulatory perspective, the bank's CET1 capital decreased by EUR 160 million, stemming from the after-tax gain on the embedded derivative (as profit or loss was part of CET1 capital). In addition, the bank's AT1 capital increased by EUR 200 million, the written-up amount.

6.8 CoCos FROM AN INVESTOR'S PERSPECTIVE

CoCos are complex instruments, notably difficult to price and subject to sharp movements in price. Fluctuations in the CET1 ratio may be caused by changes in the amount of CET1 capital (the numerator) and RWAs (the denominator) of the issuer as well as changes to their respective definitions under the capital adequacy standards and guidelines set by the regulator. Because banks publish their CET1 capital on a quarterly basis, sudden sharp changes in the price of a CoCo may occur if the issuing bank reports a substantial erosion/improvement in its CET1 ratio.

6.8.1 Benefits to Investors

The following are the main advantages of investing in CoCos:

- **High yield:** Due to the conversion/write-down provision and its subordination, CoCos offer high yields;
- **Highly regulated sector:** Exposures taken by banks are under close scrutiny by banking supervisors, reducing the likelihood of risks being over-sought; and
- **Lower sensitivity to interest rates** than other "comparable" instruments (e.g., preference shares). Most CoCos have coupon reset mechanisms that notably reduce their sensitivity to interest rates, especially on the reset dates. In addition, their high yields provide a cushion were interest rates to rise.

6.8.2 Risks to Investors

Any indication that the consolidated CET1 ratio is moving towards the level which would cause the occurrence of the conversion trigger is likely to have an adverse effect on the market price and liquidity of the CoCo. Therefore, investors may not be able to sell their CoCos easily or at prices that will provide them with a yield comparable to other types of subordinated securities. In addition, the risk of conversion could drive down the price of the ordinary shares and have a material adverse effect on the market value of ordinary shares received upon conversion. The main drawbacks of investing in CoCos include:

- **Trigger-level risk:** The main risk in a CoCo is the equity conversion or write-down occurrence as a result of the contractual trigger being breached. An equity conversion is likely to be executed when the price of the underlying shares is well below the conversion price, resulting in a significant loss for investors. If the principal is partially or completely written-down, investors will be losing the amount being written-down, unless the CoCo terms include a write-up clause and this clause is exercised;

- **Coupon partial or complete cancellation risk:** Coupon payments on AT1 instruments are entirely at the discretion of the issuer. This can lead to coupons being partially or totally suspended. Cancelled coupons do not accumulate or are payable at any time thereafter;
- **Discretionary conversion/write-down risk:** Pursuant to the BRRD resolution authorities have the discretionary right to activate the conversion/write-down trigger when they consider the bank's existence is threatened. This may be the case whenever the bank still has sufficient capital but is experiencing acute liquidity difficulties. In principle, this would happen when, according to the relevant authority, the bank has reached its point of non-viability and it is likely that others triggers are about to be breached. The point at which a bank might be considered non-viable is likely to vary by type of bank and by jurisdiction;
- **Early principal redemption risk:** As they are perpetual, CoCos may be cancelled periodically by the issuer, for any reason and for any length of time, at par. An investor that bought a CoCo at a premium to par will realise a loss if the coupons are not enough to compensate for the premium paid;
- **Sector concentration risk:** CoCos have been issued mostly by banks. In addition, it is an asset class notably complex to value. Any financial crisis affecting a number of banks may negatively affect the CoCo market as a whole. Therefore, there is the risk that market values of CoCo may be caught in a downward spiral, resulting in a heavy loss for investors; and
- **Mispricing risk:** CoCos are notably complex to value. Investors risk wrongly estimating the price sensitivity of a CoCo to changes in the numerous variables affecting its pricing.

CHAPTER 7

Additional Valuation Adjustments (AVAs)

[CRR 34] and [CRR 105] require banks, when calculating the amount of their regulatory capital, to apply **prudent valuation** standards to all their financial (and commodities) positions that are measured on the balance sheet at **fair value** and affect **regulatory capital**. Any **additional valuation adjustments** (**AVAs**) necessary to reduce (or increase) the fair value of those asset (or liability) positions, as calculated in accordance with the relevant accounting standards, to the relevant prudent value are deducted from CET1 capital. The objective is to achieve an appropriate degree of certainty having regard to the dynamic nature of fair valued positions.

Financial assets/liabilities (and commodities) at fair value are reported in the financial statements at a "**fair value**" which is calculated according to the relevant accounting standard (IFRS 13 *Fair Value Measurement*). Basel III requires those assets and liabilities to be revalued to arrive at their "**prudent value**".

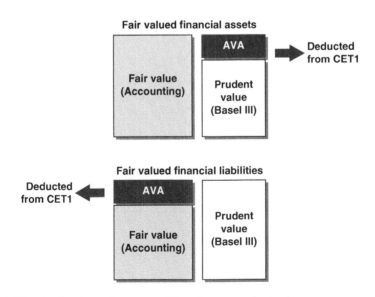

FIGURE 7.1 Additional valuation adjustments: fair value vs. prudent value

In the case of fair valued financial assets (and commodities), an AVA arises when their regulatory "prudent value" is lower than their "accounting fair value" (otherwise *no* AVA arises), as shown in Figure 7.1.

$$\boxed{\text{Additional Valuation Adjustment (AVA)}} = \boxed{\text{Asset fair value}} - \boxed{\text{Asset prudent value}}$$

Conversely, in the case of fair valued financial liabilities (and commodities), an AVA arises when their regulatory "prudent value" is greater than their accounting "fair value" (otherwise *no* AVA arises) (see Figure 7.1).

$$\boxed{\text{Additional Valuation Adjustment (AVA)}} = \boxed{\text{Liability prudent value}} - \boxed{\text{Liability fair value}}$$

7.1 FAIR VALUATION ACCOUNTING FRAMEWORK (IFRS 13)

A bank's balance sheet includes numerous financial instruments that are fair valued (see Figure 7.2):

- On the **asset side**: assets designated at fair value through profit or loss ("FVTPL") and assets designated at fair value through other comprehensive income ("FVTOCI"). The latter is similar to the previous IAS 39 "available for sale" category.
- On the **liability side**: financial liabilities designated at FVTPL.

Assets classified at FVTPL   These typically include:

- Trading assets in the regulatory trading book, primarily debt and equity securities held for trading purposes, commodities and trading loans;
- Financial derivatives with positive market values;
- Some banking book assets which do not fulfil the criteria for being allocated to the regulatory trading book, primarily debt securities as part of a bank's liquidity portfolio as well as traded loans; and
- Loans and commitments reported at FVTPL to significantly reduce profit or loss volatility that results from the accounting mismatch that otherwise would exist when all loans and commitments are reported at amortised cost while derivative hedges are reported at fair value.

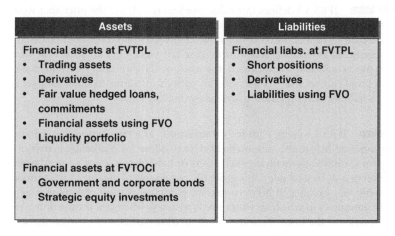

Assets	Liabilities
Financial assets at FVTPL	**Financial liabs. at FVTPL**
• Trading assets	• Short positions
• Derivatives	• Derivatives
• Fair value hedged loans, commitments	• Liabilities using FVO
• Financial assets using FVO	
• Liquidity portfolio	
Financial assets at FVTOCI	
• Government and corporate bonds	
• Strategic equity investments	

FIGURE 7.2   Commonly fair valued financial items in a bank's balance sheet

Assets Classified at FVTOCI   These typically include:

- The bank's portfolio of government, financial institution and corporate bonds;
- Strategic equity investments.

Liabilities Classified at FVTPL   These typically include:

- Short financial positions;
- Financial derivatives with negative market values;
- Financial liabilities, designated at FVTPL under the fair value option ("FVO").

7.1.1 Accounting Fair Valuation Framework (IFRS 13)

All fair valued positions are presented in a bank's financial statements following the accounting guidelines set out in IFRS 13 *Fair Value Measurement*. As mentioned previously, this "accounting fair value" is one of the two components in the calculation of AVAs:

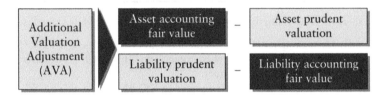

IFRS 13 defines fair value, provides principles-based guidance on how to measure fair value and requires information about those fair value measurements to be disclosed in the financial statements (see Figure 7.3). IFRS 13 applies when another IFRS permits or requires the measurement or disclosure of fair value (e.g. IFRS 9 *Financial Instruments*), or a measure that is based on fair value, except to the following standards:

- Share-based payment transactions within the scope of IFRS 2 *Share-based Payment*;
- Leasing transactions within the scope of IFRS 16 *Leases*; and
- Measurements that have some similarities to fair value but are not fair value, such as net realisable value in IAS 2 *Inventories* or value in use in IAS 36 *Impairment of Assets*.

Definition of Fair Value   IFRS 13 defines fair value (see Figure 7.4) as "the price that would be received to sell an asset or paid to transfer a liability in an orderly transaction between market participants at the measurement date". This definition of fair value emphasises that it is a market-based measurement, not an entity-specific measurement. When measuring fair value, an entity uses the assumptions that market participants would use when pricing the asset or liability under current market conditions, including assumptions about risk. As a result, an entity's intention to hold an asset or to settle or otherwise fulfil a liability is not relevant when measuring fair value.

Orderly Transaction   IFRS 13 defines "orderly transaction" as a transaction that assumes exposure to the market for a period before the measurement date to allow for marketing activities that are usual and customary for transactions involving such assets or liabilities; it is not a forced transaction (e.g., a forced liquidation or a distressed sale). It is generally reasonable to assume that a transaction in which an asset or liability was exchanged between market participants is an orderly transaction. However, there will be circumstances in which an entity needs to assess whether a transaction is orderly, such as when the seller marketed the instrument to a single market participant or when the seller was forced to meet regulatory/legal requirements.

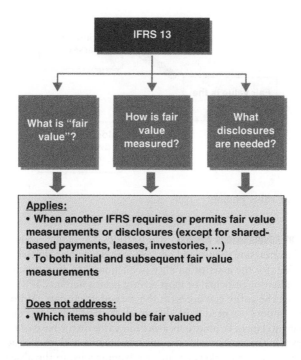

FIGURE 7.3 IFRS 13's framework

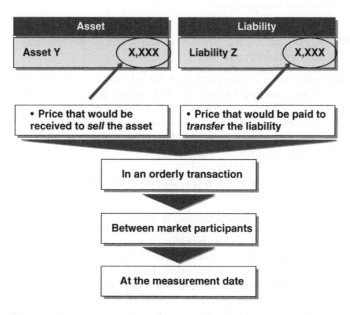

FIGURE 7.4 IFRS 13's fair value definition

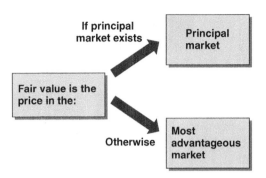

FIGURE 7.5   Market for fair value pricing

Principal Market vs. Most Advantageous Market   Under IFRS 13, management determines fair value based on a hypothetical transaction that would take place in the principal market or, in its absence, the most advantageous market, for the asset or liability (see Figure 7.5). In most cases, these two markets would be the same. In evaluating principal or most advantageous markets, IFRS 13 restricts the eligible markets to only those that the entity can access at the measurement date. Although an entity must be able to access the market, it does not need to be able to sell the particular asset or transfer the particular liability on the measurement date to be able to measure fair value on the basis of the price in that market.

The **principal market** is the market with the greatest volume and level of activity for the asset or liability, even if the prices in other markets are more advantageous. In the absence of evidence to the contrary, the market in which an entity normally transacts is presumed to be the principal market or the most advantageous market in the absence of a principal market.

The **most advantageous market** is the market that maximises the amount that would be received to sell the asset or minimises the amount that would be paid to transfer the liability, after taking into account transaction costs and transport costs.

Market Participants   Market participants are buyers and sellers in the principal (or most advantageous) market for the asset or liability that are:

- **Independent:** The transaction counterparties are not related parties as defined in IAS 24 *Related Party Disclosures*. However, this does not preclude related-party transaction prices from being used as valuation inputs if there is evidence that the transactions were on market terms;
- **Knowledgeable:** Transaction counterparties have a reasonable understanding about the asset or liability, using all available information, including information that might be obtained through due diligence efforts that are usual and customary;
- **Able** to transact in the asset or liability; and
- **Willing** to transact in the asset or liability. Transaction counterparties are motivated but not forced or otherwise compelled to transact.

IFRS 13 explains that a fair value measurement requires an entity to determine the following:

- The particular asset or liability being measured;
- For a non-financial asset, the highest and best use of the asset and whether the asset is used in combination with other assets or on a stand-alone basis;
- The market in which an orderly transaction would take place for the asset or liability; and
- The appropriate valuation technique(s) to use when measuring fair value. The valuation technique(s) used should maximise the use of relevant observable inputs and minimise unobservable inputs. Those inputs should be consistent with the inputs a market participant would use when pricing the asset or liability.

7.1.2 Hierarchy of Financial Assets: Level 1, Level 2 and Level 3

To increase consistency and comparability in fair value measurements and related disclosures, IFRS establishes a fair value hierarchy. IFRS 13 carries over the three-level fair value hierarchy disclosures from IFRS 7 which requires an entity to distinguish between financial asset and financial liability fair values based on how observable the inputs to the fair value measurement are. The hierarchy prioritises the inputs to valuation techniques into three levels: Level 1, Level 2 and Level 3. A fair value measurement is categorised within the hierarchy based on the lowest-level input that has a significant effect on the measure in Figure 7.6.

Figures 7.7 and 7.8 illustrate the decision tree for the Level classification of financial instruments.

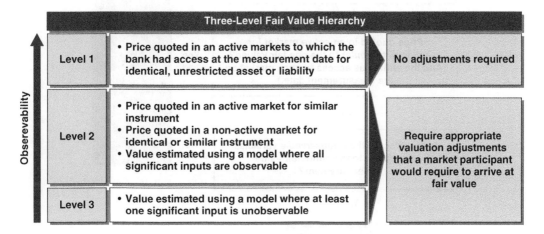

FIGURE 7.6 Three-Level Fair Value Hierarchy

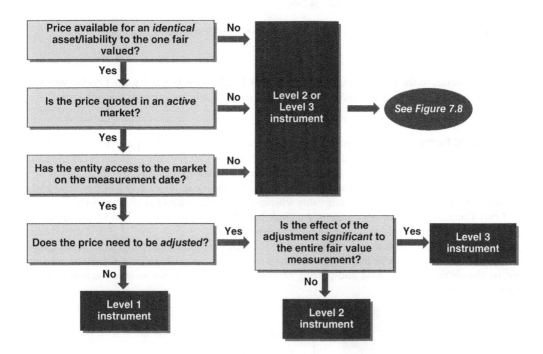

FIGURE 7.7 Decision tree for the Level classification of financial instruments (part one)

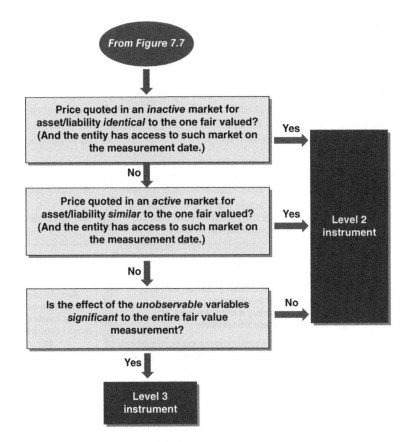

FIGURE 7.8 Decision tree for the Level classification of financial instruments (part two)

When the inputs to the valuation fall within different Levels of the hierarchy, the Level in which the instrument is classified is based on the lowest Level of significant input to the valuation.

Level 1 Financial Assets If an entity holds a position in a single asset or liability and the asset or liability is traded in an active market for identical assets or liabilities that the entity can access at the measurement date, the fair value of the asset or liability is measured within Level 1.

A quoted market price in an active market provides the most reliable evidence of fair value and is used without adjustment to measure fair value whenever available, with limited exceptions.

Level 1 financial instruments commonly include high-liquidity government bonds, and derivative, equity and cash products traded on high-liquidity exchanges.

The fair value is measured as the product of (i) the quantity held by the entity and (ii) the quoted price for the individual asset or liability, even if the market's normal daily trading volume is not sufficient to absorb the quantity held and placing orders to buy/sell the position in a single transaction might affect the quoted price.

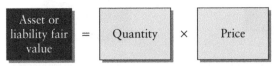

Level 2 Financial Assets Level 2 financial instruments are valued with valuation techniques where **all significant** inputs into the valuation are based on **observable market data,** or where the fair value can be determined by reference to similar instruments trading in active markets.

Level 2 inputs include:

- Quoted prices for similar assets or liabilities in active markets;
- Quoted prices for identical or similar assets or liabilities in markets that are not active. Instruments include, for example, lowly liquid equities;
- Inputs other than quoted prices that are observable (either directly or indirectly) for the asset or liability, for example interest rates and yield curves observable at commonly quoted intervals, implied volatilities and credit spreads. Instruments commonly include most interest rate swaps, FX forwards, cross-currency swaps, FX and interest rate options, and market quoted CDS.

Level 2 and **Level 3** financial **derivatives** are valued using a valuation model. The output of a valuation model is always an estimate or approximation of a fair value that cannot be measured with complete certainty. As a result, valuations are adjusted, where appropriate, to reflect close-out costs, credit exposure, model-driven-valuation uncertainty, trading restrictions and other factors, when such factors would be considered by market participants in measuring fair value:

In the case of Level 2 derivatives, entities typically start by calculating a mid-market fair valuation (i.e., a valuation using mid-market rate and/or price curves) that assumes no counterparty credit risk and then the entity applies different adjustments to this valuation.

In the case of a Level 2 **derivative** recognised as an **asset,** these adjustments reduce the mid-market fair value of the derivative by deducting other elements that would be taken into account by market participants were the entity to sell the derivative in the market (i.e., its exit price). These adjustments, which reduce the value of the asset, typically include:

- Mid-market to bid adjustment;
- Non-performance adjustment (CVA – credit valuation adjustment); and
- Funding valuation adjustment (FVA).

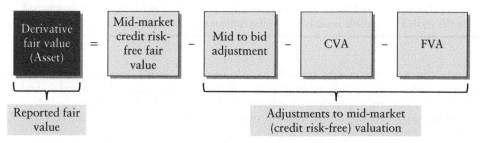

In the case of a Level 2 **derivative** recognised as a **liability,** the adjustment to the credit-risk free mid-market fair valuation would commonly include the following elements:

- Mid-market to offer adjustment. This term increases the value of the liability;
- Non-performance adjustment (DVA – debit valuation adjustment). This adjustment reduces the value of the liability; and

■ Funding valuation adjustment (FVA). This term increases the value of the liability.

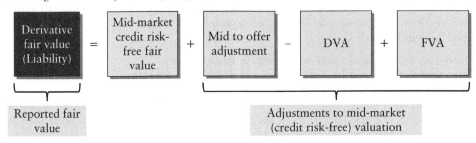

Level 3 Financial Instruments   Financial instruments are classified as Level 3 if their valuation incorporates significant inputs that are not based on observable market data or data that can be corroborated using observable market data (unobservable inputs). A valuation input is considered observable if it can be directly observed from transactions in an active market, or if there is compelling external evidence demonstrating an executable exit price. In other words, the fair valuation of the financial asset/liability requires the estimation of at least one input variable that has a **significant** impact in the valuation, because such variable price/rate is **unobservable** in the market. IFRS 13 does not specify where an input is deemed to be significant, but generally it is assumed that an input variable is significant if it contributes more than 10% (although some more conservative banks use a lower percentage) to the valuation of a financial instrument. An entity develops unobservable inputs using the best information available in the circumstances, which might include the entity's own data, taking into account all information about market participant assumptions that is reasonably available.

Whilst there may be some significant inputs that are readily observable, the existence of at least one unobservable variable that has a significant impact in the fair valuation triggers the classification of an instrument into the Level 3 category. Level 3 instruments indicate that there is a significant degree in subjectivity in the fair valuation. Unobservable inputs are determined based on the best information available, for example by reference to similar assets, similar maturities or other analytical techniques.

The availability of observable inputs may change over time. For instance, a deep market turmoil may cause some markets to become illiquid, thus reducing the availability of certain observable data used by the bank's valuation techniques. This may cause the classification of an instrument to change from Level 2 (or Level 1) to Level 3. When liquidity returns to these markets, the valuations will revert to using the related observable inputs and the instrument will revert to Level 2 (or Level 1).

Level 3 financial instruments typically include correlation-based derivatives (e.g., basket and spread options) for which underlying correlations are unobservable, illiquid bonds and illiquid loans, and CDSs for which credit spreads are unobservable. Level 3 financial instruments include, as well, interest swaps, cross-currency swaps, inflation swaps, FX forwards and options with very long-dated maturities.

The fair value of a Level 3 derivative, recognised as an **asset** or **liability**, is calculated applying the adjustments to its credit-risk free mid-market fair valuation as if it were a Level 2 derivative, but adding an additional adjusting element. This element addresses the inherent valuation uncertainty associated with the forecasting process, primarily uncertainty in estimating unobservable valuation input parameters and uncertainty in the output provided by the valuation model. For example, in the case of a Level 3 derivative recognised as an asset, the fair value would be calculated as follows:

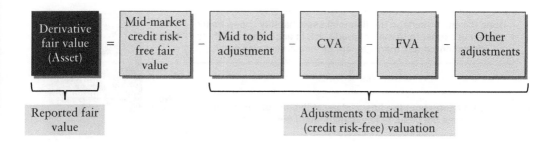

7.1.3 Adjustments to the Fair Valuation of Financial Derivatives

In this section I cover some of the adjustments applied to Level 2 and Level 3 derivatives when calculating their fair value.

Mid-to-bid or Mid-to-offer Adjustments   Instruments that are measured as part of a portfolio of combined long and short derivatives positions are valued at mid-market levels to ensure consistent valuation of the long and short component risks. A valuation adjustment ("mid-to-offer" or "mid-to-bid") is then made to the overall net long or short exposure to move the fair value to bid or offer as appropriate, reflecting current levels of market liquidity. The bid-to-offer spreads used in the calculation of the valuation adjustment are obtained from market and broker sources.

An operational complexity of this approach is the allocation of the mid-to-bid or mid-to-offer adjustment to the individual derivative positions in the portfolio. IFRS 13 requires that an entity should allocate a portfolio-level adjustment to the individual financial assets and liabilities in the portfolio on a reasonable and consistent basis using a methodology appropriate in the circumstances.

Portfolio Exception to the Application of Mid-to-offer or Mid-to-bid Adjustments   IFRS 13 allows an exception whereby if an entity manages a group of financial assets and financial liabilities on the basis of its net exposure to either market risks or counterparty risks, it can opt to measure the fair value of that group on the basis of the net position (i.e., without having to perform the mid-to-offer or mid-to-bid adjustment). This exception is permitted only if an entity (see Figure 7.9):

- Manages the financial asset/liability group based on its net exposure to market/credit risk in accordance with its documented risk management or investment strategy;
- Provides information about the financial asset/liability group on a net basis to key management personnel as defined in IAS 24; and
- Measures those financial assets and liabilities at fair value in the statement of financial position on a recurring basis.

Other conditions on the use of the exception are that it:

- Applies only to financial assets and liabilities within the scope of IFRS 9;
- Applies only to financial assets and liabilities that are exposed to identical, or at least substantially similar, market risks. If the risks are not identical, the differences should be considered when allocating the group's fair value to component assets and liabilities; and
- Applies only to exposures of a similar duration. IFRS 13 provides the following example: ". . . an entity that uses a 12-month futures contract against the cash flows associated with 12 months' worth of interest rate risk exposure on a five-year financial instrument within a group made up of only those financial assets and financial liabilities measures the fair value of the exposure to 12-month interest rate risk on a net basis and the remaining interest rate risk exposure (i.e., years 2–5) on a gross basis."

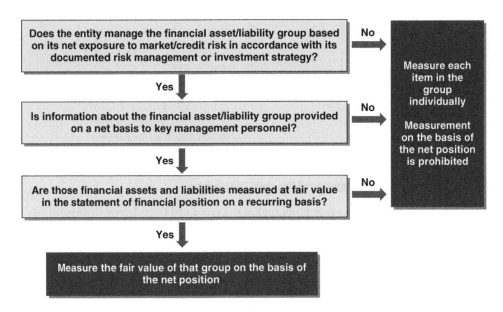

FIGURE 7.9   Fair valuation on the basis of net position: decision tree

If the exception is applied, the fair value of the net position is measured using IFRS 13 principles. For example:

- For **market risks**, fair value of the net position is the price within the bid-ask spread that is most representative of fair value in the entity's circumstances;
- For **credit risk**, fair value of such a group should consider credit enhancements (such as master netting agreements and collateral requirements) and expectations about the legal enforceability of such enhancements.

Credit Valuation Adjustment (CVA)/Debit Valuation Adjustment (DVA)   An important element of IFRS 9 is the requirement, when determining the fair value of a financial **derivative**, to include **non-performance risk**. This risk quantifies the possibility that the counterparty to the financial derivative or the entity will default before the maturity/expiration of the transaction and will be unable to meet all contractual payments, thereby resulting in a loss for the entity or the counterparty.

Let us assume that an entity bought a six-month option and paid an upfront premium. The option was, therefore, recognised as an asset. The entity was exposed to the credit risk of the counterparty to the option during the option's six-month term. When fair valuing the option, the entity was required to adjust the option's fair value to incorporate the risk that the counterparty to the option could default before its expiration. This adjustment is referred to as **"credit valuation adjustment"** (CVA), and it is based on the rationale that a market participant would include it when determining the price it would pay to acquire the option. This valuation adjustment for credit reflects the estimated fair value of protection required to hedge the counterparty credit risk embedded in such instrument.

Conversely, let us assume that an entity sold a six-month option in exchange for an upfront premium. The option was recognised as a liability. The counterparty to the option would be exposed to the credit risk of the entity during the next six months. When fair valuing the option, the entity would be required to adjust the option's fair value to incorporate the risk that the entity will default before its expiration. This adjustment is referred to as **"debit valuation adjustment"** (DVA).

IFRS 9 does not provide guidance on how CVA or DVA is to be calculated beyond requiring that the resulting fair value must reflect the credit quality of the instrument. Quantifying CVA adjustments is a complex exercise due to the substantial number of assumptions involved and the interaction among these assumptions. There is a variety of ways to determine CVA and judgement is required to assess the appropriateness of the method used.

Funding Valuation Adjustment (FVA) Banks include FVAs in the pricing and fair valuation of uncollateralised derivatives. Some of the key drivers of FVA include the market implied cost of funding spread over LIBOR, expected term of the trade and expected average exposure by counterparty. FVA is further adjusted to account for the extent to which the funding cost is incorporated into observed traded levels and to calibrate to the expected term of the trade.

Whilst FVA applies to both derivative assets and liabilities, FVA adjustments largely relate to uncollateralised derivative assets given the impact of the bank's own credit risk, which is a significant component of the funding costs, is already incorporated in the valuation of uncollateralised derivative liabilities through the application of debit valuation adjustments (DVAs).

Imagine an uncollateralised swap between Megabank (our entity) and ABC (a corporate client) whose fair value (excluding FVA) was a EUR 10 million unrealised gain from Megabank's perspective (i.e., the derivative was recognised in Megabank's statement of financial position as an asset). As the derivatives agreement between Megabank and ABC was uncollateralised, ABC was not required to post any collateral to reduce Megabank's credit exposure to ABC. As a result, were ABC to become insolvent, Megabank would suffer a EUR 10 million loss.

Imagine further that, in turn, Megabank hedged its market risk exposure by entering into another derivative that mirrored the terms of the derivative with another bank – Hedgebank – with which a cash collateral agreement was in place (see Figure 7.10). As a result, Megabank had to post EUR 10 million in cash collateral to mitigate Hedgebank's exposure to Megabank, incurring a funding cost stemming from the financing of such cash collateral.

Alternatively, had the derivative between ABC and Megabank showed a EUR 10 million unrealised gain, Hedgebank would have posted EUR 10 million cash collateral with Megabank. Megabank would have placed that cash earning a yield or reducing its funding needs.

Therefore, when Megabank quoted the derivative pricing to ABC on trade date, it should have taken into account the potential funding costs stemming from future potential favourable movements (from Megabank's perspective) in the derivative's fair value. Additionally, Megabank should have incorporated in the pricing the potential funding benefits stemming from future potential unfavourable movements in the derivative's fair value. The net adjustment is termed "**Funding Valuation Adjustments**" or FVA.

Thus, FVA incorporates the cost or benefit of unsecured funding into the fair valuation of a derivative to ensure an accurate exit price.

Model Uncertainty Adjustment Uncertainties associated with the use of model-based valuations are incorporated into the measurement of fair value through the use of model reserves. These reserves reflect the amounts that an entity estimates should be deducted from valuations produced directly by models to incorporate uncertainties in the relevant modelling assumptions, in the model and market

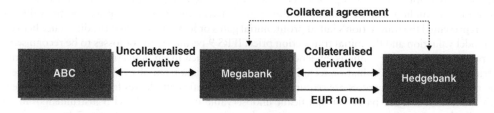

FIGURE 7.10 Derivative hedge process

inputs used, or in the calibration of the model output to adjust for known model deficiencies. Model valuation adjustments are dependent on the size of portfolio, the complexity of the model, whether the model is market standard and to what extent it incorporates all known risk factors. In arriving at these estimates, an entity considers a range of market practices, including how it believes market participants would assess these uncertainties. Model reserves should be reassessed periodically in light of information from market transactions, consensus pricing services and other relevant sources.

Day One Profit (or Loss)   For new transactions, the financial instrument is initially recognised at fair value, which on initial recognition is normally the transaction price. In general, two situations may arise:

- *No* **day one profit/loss:** Where the fair value is evidenced by a quoted price in an active market for an identical instrument (i.e., Level 1 instrument) or based on a valuation technique that uses only data from observable markets, no "day one gain" or loss arises. The bank recognises the difference between the fair value at initial recognition and the transaction price as a gain or loss in profit or loss.
- **Day one profit/loss:** In all other circumstances a "day one profit" or loss arises. The bank recognises the instrument at fair value and defers the difference between the fair at initial recognition and the transaction price. A day one profit or loss is recognised subsequently only to the extent that it arises from a change in a factor (including time) that market participants would consider in setting a price.

> In theory if an input is entity-specific (i.e., not observable), day one gain profit cannot be recognised upfront unless "there is a quoted price in an active market for an identical instrument". Most banks defer day one profit when significant unobservable parameters are used, which is equivalent to the instrument being classified as a Level 3 asset/liability. In practice, day one profit is recognised in the income statement over the life of the transaction (commonly amortised on a linear basis) until the transaction matures, is closed out or the valuation inputs become observable.
>
> Most banks also recognised a day one profit if the bank enters into an offsetting transaction that substantially eliminates the instrument's risk. For example, most banks argue that when the transaction is back-to-backed then "there is a quoted price in an active market for an identical instrument", but this is a rather "particular" although widespread interpretation.
>
> In the rare circumstances that a day one loss arises, it would be recognised at inception of the transaction to the extent that it is probable that a loss has been incurred and a reliable estimate of the loss amount can be made.

Let us assume that an option was bought from a client in exchange for the payment of an upfront premium of EUR 11 million. At the closing of the trade date, the option was revalued using the entity's valuation model for that type of options. Let us assume that the valuation indicated that the option was worth EUR 13 million. The EUR 2 million difference between the transaction price and the valuation price represented the transaction's initial profit. **Initial gains or losses** result from the difference between the model valuation and the initial transaction price. IFRS 9 permits gains or losses to be recognised at inception only when fair value is evidenced by a quoted price in an active market for an identical instrument or based on a valuation technique that uses only data from observable markets by observable market data. Thus, entities are required to defer initial gains and losses for financial instruments with fair values that are based on significant unobservable inputs (i.e., Level 3 instruments). In our example, the recognition of the transaction's initial profit was as follows (see Figure 7.11):

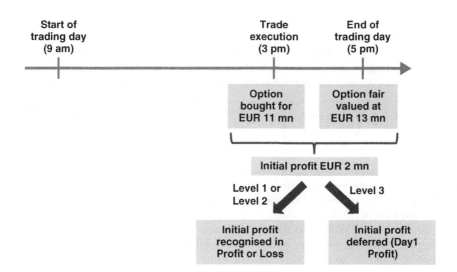

FIGURE 7.11   Derivative initial profit recognition

- If the derivative was classified as a **Level 1** or **Level 2** instrument, the initial profit was recognised immediately in profit or loss. In this case, the entity recognised a EUR 2 million gain in profit or loss at the end of trade date and, in theory, the counterparty to the option recognised a EUR 2 million loss;
- If the derivative was classified as a **Level 3** instrument, the initial profit was *not* immediately recognised, but rather deferred (unless at least one of the two requirements for upfront recognition of day one profit was met). The initial profit for Level 3 derivatives is termed "**Day one profit**". The counterparty to the derivative would recognise a "Day one loss".

In the case of financial assets, deferred day one profit is recognised as a liability and amortised (typically on a straight-line basis) over the term of the instrument or over the period until the instrument is closed out or all model inputs will become observable.

7.2 CASE STUDY: GOLDMAN SACHS INVESTMENT IN INDUSTRIAL AND COMMERCIAL BANK OF CHINA

In January 2006, Goldman made an important strategic investment in Industrial and Commercial Bank of China ("ICBC"), China's largest commercial bank. It did so through a strategic cooperation agreement in which Goldman committed to advise ICBC in developing further ICBC's corporate governance, risk management and internal controls, as well as providing expertise to enhance ICBC's capabilities in treasury, asset management, corporate and investment banking, non-performing loans disposal and product innovation. In turn, ICBC committed to help Goldman identify new clients and opportunities in the key Chinese market. Goldman invested USD 2.58 billion, directly and through several investment funds managed by the firm, in exchange for 7% of ICBC's ordinary share capital.

Goldman's investment in ICBC was subject to transfer restrictions by contract that, among other things, prohibited any sale, disposition or other transfer until 28 April 2009, and that from 28 April 2009 to 20 October 2009 it could transfer up to 50% of the aggregate ordinary shares of ICBC that it owned as of 20 October 2006. Goldman could transfer any remaining shares after 20 October 2009.

The investment in ICBC was carried at fair value. The first thing Goldman determined was whether the shares should be categorised as a Level 1 or a Level 2 asset. Although ICBC shares traded on the Hong Kong stock exchange, the transfer restrictions required the investment to be classified within the Level 2 category. As a consequence, the stake in ICBC was fair valued using quoted market prices and taking into account the transfer restrictions and the HKD USD exchange rate, as follows:

$$\begin{array}{c}\text{Fair value of ICBC} \\ \text{ordinary shares}\end{array} = \left(\begin{array}{c}\text{Number of} \\ \text{shares}\end{array} \times \begin{array}{c}\text{Share price in} \\ \text{Hong Kong} \\ \text{exchange}\end{array} - \begin{array}{c}\text{Restriction} \\ \text{adjustment}\end{array} \right) \times \begin{array}{c}\text{HKD/USD} \\ \text{exchange} \\ \text{rate}\end{array}$$

The second element that Goldman determined was whether the transfer restrictions were imposed to Goldman or to the ordinary shares. Under IFRS 13, consideration of the restriction in the valuation is allowed only if it is an attribute of the security and does *not* arise from an agreement or condition that is *not* an attribute of the security itself.

ICBC did *not* permit Goldman to transfer the shares; however, if they were to do so, they likely would require the transferee to accept a similar or identical restriction. Therefore Goldman believed the restriction was specific to the shares and *not* to the holder. The records of the share registrar, Computershare Hong Kong Investor Services Limited, reflected this restriction.

When a restriction is an attribute of a financial instrument, the restricted financial instrument should be valued based on the observable quoted price for an otherwise identical unrestricted instrument of the same issuer that trades in the public market, adjusted to reflect the effect of the restriction. Therefore, Goldman performed an adjustment to the share's quoted market price to reflect a discount for the contractual restrictions a transferee would have to accept as a condition of the transfer. The adjustment reflected the discount market participants would demand because of the risk relating to the inability to access a public market for the security for the specified period. The adjustment took into account:

- The nature and duration of the restriction;
- The extent to which buyers were limited by the restriction; and
- Factors specific to both the security and the issuer (qualitative and quantitative).

Goldman determined the valuation adjustment for its restricted ICBC shares by using a model that incorporated the remaining duration of the transfer restriction and observed volatility levels, as well as a block discount factor to adjust for the fact that its position size was too large to be absorbed by regular market activity levels. The block discount factor was not required by IFRS 13, but Goldman performed it because it was required under US GAAP. The remaining duration of its transfer restriction was based on the contractual restriction period, while volatility levels were derived from observed trading activity.

Goldman updated the inputs to its model at the end of each reporting period to reflect the declining contractual restriction period and any changes in volatility levels, as well as any additional evidence related to block discount factors based on observable market dispositions of comparable stakes in other Chinese banks.

After 20 October 2009, Goldman could transfer the remaining shares, but it was not until the second quarter of 2010 that Goldman's investment in ICBC became unrestricted. As a consequence, the fair valuation of the stake did not include the adjustment due to the transfer restriction:

In addition, the investment bank transferred the ordinary shares investment into Level 1 of the fair value hierarchy. The absence of the restriction adjustment resulted in Goldman recognising a USD 905 million gain in its 2010 second quarter profit or loss statement.

7.3 PRUDENT VALUATION VS. FAIR VALUATION

[CRR 34] requires banks to apply prudent valuation standards to all financial and commodity positions that are measured at fair value and that impact regulatory capital. Any **additional valuation adjustments (AVAs)** necessary to reduce (or increase) the fair value of those asset (or liability) positions as calculated in accordance with the relevant IFRS accounting standard (IFRS 13), to the relevant prudent value are deducted from CET1 capital. The objective is to set valuations at a level that achieves an appropriate degree of certainty that the valuation used for regulatory purposes is not higher than the true realisable value.

7.3.1 Fair Value vs. Prudent Value

Why accounting and regulatory valuations differ? As mentioned in Section 7.1, IFRS aims at arriving at a best estimate of the amount that market participants would be willing to pay for the financial asset or to receive for the financial liability on the reporting date. Basel III is, on the other hand, more concerned with the uncertainty regarding such an exit price (see Figure 7.12).

7.3.2 The Principles Underlying EBA's Prudent Valuation Methodology

As mentioned previously in this chapter, the prudent valuation of a fair valued financial asset or liability is one of the two components in the determination of the AVA for such asset or liability, the other component being the reported fair value amount in the balance sheet:

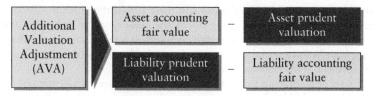

Prudent valuation is dealt with in [CRR 34 and 105] and EBA's Final Draft RTS on Prudent Valuation (EBA RTS/2014/06). Not only are guidelines for the calculation of prudent valuations addressed in these two documents but also systems, controls and procedures that support the prudent valuation process, as shown in Figure 7.13.

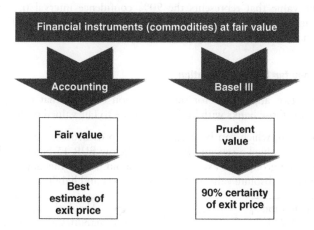

FIGURE 7.12 Accounting vs. regulatory valuations

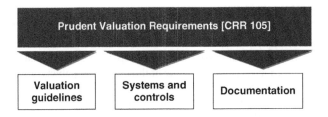

FIGURE 7.13   Prudent valuation framework

Confidence Level   A robust calculation of a bank's regulatory capital levels relies, among other variables, on fair valued assets and liabilities on its balance sheet being valued at their "**true realisable value**" – the value at which a bank can exit a position. However, there is no certainty regarding a position's true realisable value. A prudent value is estimated instead.

For positions where there is extensive independent and reliable data available, EBA's **prudent valuation** uses a statistical approach based on a threshold **confidence level**: in other words, a probability that the bank can exit a position (i.e., the true realisable value) without a loss against the estimated prudent value. For other positions where there is less independent and reliable data available, the threshold level of confidence is used as guidance for a more judgemental approach.

The aim of setting up a level of confidence is to ensure homogeneity and level playing field between banks. Nonetheless, establishing a required level of confidence by regulators is a delicate decision. As level of confidence becomes too high, so the less risk there is that the prudent valuation would be in excess of the true realisable value of the asset, but at the same time the higher the amount of AVAs being deducted from CET1 capital. Consequently, a too-high level of confidence may discourage a bank from offering high AVAs financial instruments demanded by its customers/clients and may require an unrealistic deployment of operational resources.

Conversely, a level of confidence that is too low is likely to create a small amount of AVA but may result in a bank holding capital levels too low to sustain losses realised when selling financial assets or buying back financial liabilities.

EBA assumed that the appropriate confidence interval is **90%**. As shown in Figure 7.13 for an asset position, an AVA is required where the fair value (i.e., the balance sheet accounting value) represents a probability lower than 90% that the bank would realise such fair value if it sells the asset. Therefore, a position does not require an AVA where the fair value implies a valuation equal or more conservative than the value that represents the 90% confidence interval (i.e., its prudent value). Figure 7.14 depicts an example financial asset that requires an AVA of 2 million as its fair value (100 million) is materially greater than its prudent value (98 million).

7.3.3 EBA's Methodology for Prudent Valuation

The EBA put forward two approaches for the calculation of AVAs that take proportionality into account, in particular for those banks with limited exposure to fair valued positions (see Figure 7.15):

- A **simplified approach**, which can be used by banks, provided their absolute value of on- and off-balance sheet fair valued assets and liabilities is below EUR 15 billion and provided they are not part of a banking group that exceeds this threshold. Under this approach the AVA is set at 0.1% of the aggregate absolute value of fair-valued assets and liabilities:

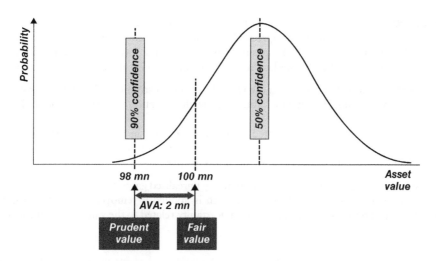

FIGURE 7.14 Confidence interval and AVAs

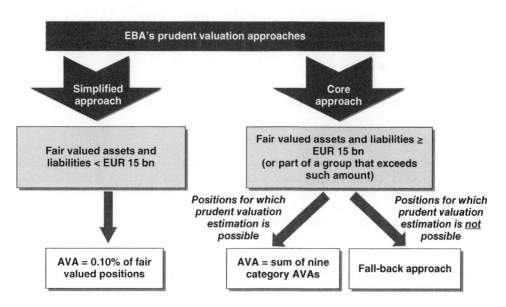

FIGURE 7.15 EBA's prudent valuation approaches

- A **core approach**, which is compulsory for banks that are above the EUR 15 billion threshold of the simplified approach or subsidiaries that are part of a banking group for which such threshold is surpassed. The remainder in this section relates to the core approach. Under the core approach, for positions for which prudent values can be estimated, their AVA is calculated as the aggregate of the AVAs associated with nine categories. Positions for which the estimation of their prudent values is *not* possible, have their AVA calculated following a fall-back approach.

Fall-back Approach   Where the application of the core approach is not possible for a position, its AVA is calculated according to a **"fall-back approach"**. The objective of this approach is to provide a penal treatment to deal with the risk posed by positions where the bank has no data available to have any view on the prudent value. The AVA under the fall-back approach is calculated as the sum of:

- 100% of the net unrealised profit on the related financial instruments. Unrealised profit refers to the change, where positive, in fair value since trade inception, determined on a first-in-first-out basis;
- 10% of the notional value of the related financial instruments in the case of derivatives; and
- 25% of the absolute value of the difference between the fair value and the unrealised profit of the related financial instruments in the case of non-derivatives.

The first element of the sum above implies that any unrealised gains recognised in the balance sheet related to positions for which the fall-back approach is applied is removed from CET1 capital. The rationale behind such removal is that the notable uncertainty related to the valuation of those positions.

> When issuing the Final Draft on AVAs, the EBA expected that for most banks the fall-back approach would only be necessary on a very small number of positions. On this basis the identification and exclusion of unrealised gains from capital was not expected to be overly burdensome.

7.3.4 Positions Subject to AVAs

A **position** is any **single** instrument measured at fair value which may be subject to prudent valuation. Positions are subject to the standards for prudent valuation if both the following conditions are met:

- Financial assets and liabilities, and commodities recognised at fair value; and
- Their fair valuation impacts regulatory capital.

Management intent regarding the positions does not affect their prudent valuation requirement. As a result, positions in both the **banking book** and **trading book** may be subject to prudent valuation.

The second condition is key to determine whether a fair valued position is subject to prudent valuation. For fair-valued assets and liabilities for which a change in accounting valuation has a partial or zero impact on regulatory capital, AVAs shall only be calculated based on the proportion of the accounting valuation change that impacts regulatory capital.

7.3.5 Derivatives Designated as Hedging Instruments in Cash Flow Hedges

Cash flow hedges were covered in detail in Section 3.14. It was highlighted that the fair valuation of a derivative being designated as hedging instrument in a cash flow hedge impacted CET1 in two steps:

- Firstly, the changes in the fair value of the derivative impacted CET1 capital either through OCI (the effective part of the hedge) or profit or loss (the ineffective part of the hedge or the reclassification from OCI);
- Secondly, the impact in CET1 due to the previous paragraph was offset by requiring changes in fair value to be deducted from CET1.

Because the overall impact in CET1 of derivatives designated as hedging instruments in cash flow hedges is zero, they are *not* subject to prudent valuation. Therefore, there is *no* need to calculate prudent values of derivatives designated as hedging instruments in cash flow hedges, and as a result, no AVA will result from such derivatives.

7.3.6 Derivatives Designated as Hedging Instruments in Fair Value Hedges

IFRS prescribes the use of **fair value** hedge accounting to avoid a distorted impact on earnings for derivatives which serve to hedge the risk of changes in the fair value of recognised assets and/or liabilities, or unrecognised firm commitments.

Fair value hedges are dealt with by **IFRS 9** *Financial Instruments*. For qualifying fair value hedges of **debt instruments**, the change in the fair value of the hedging instrument (i.e., the derivative hedging the risk) is recognised in profit or loss along with the change in the fair value of the hedged item (i.e., the debt instrument being hedged) that is attributable to the hedged risk (e.g., interest rate), as shown in Figure 7.16. In fair value hedges of interest rate risk, the fair value change of the hedged item attributable to the hedged risk is reflected in a separate line adjusting the carrying value of the hedged item.

If the hedge accounting relationship is terminated for reasons other than the derecognition of the hedged item, the difference between the carrying value of the hedged item at that point and the value at which it would have been carried had the hedge never existed (the "unamortised fair value adjustment") is amortised to the profit or loss statement over the remaining term to maturity of the hedged item.

Fair value hedges of **equity instruments** recognised at "fair value through OCI", both the changes in fair value of the hedging instrument and the hedged item are recognised in OCI.

Banks enter into fair value hedges, using primarily interest rate swaps and options, in order to protect themselves against movements in the fair value of fixed-rate debt instruments due to movements in market interest rates. In banking, fair value hedges are typically applied to:

- Fixed-rate debt assets, normally fixed-rate government and covered bonds, classified at fair value through OCI (or "available for sale" under IAS 39, the standard preceding IFRS 9). When subject to a fair value hedge, these instruments are carried at fair value with the changes in fair value resulting from the risk being hedged reported in profit or loss.
- Fixed-rate debt issued (normally senior, covered and subordinated bonds) or fixed-rate debt assets (normally fixed-rate commercial and mortgage loans) carried at amortised cost. When fair value hedge accounting is applied to these instruments, their carrying amount is adjusted for changes in fair value related to the hedged exposure.

As the fair valuation of the hedged item (for the risk being hedged) and the hedging instrument affect CET1 (through profit or loss or through OCI), *both* are subject to the prudent valuation adjustments.

7.3.7 General Credit Risk Adjustments

Pursuant to [CRR 159], expected loss amounts are subtracted from the general and specific credit risk adjustments and additional value adjustments. Discounts on balance sheet exposures purchased when in default in accordance with [CRR 166(1)] are treated in the same manner as specific credit risk

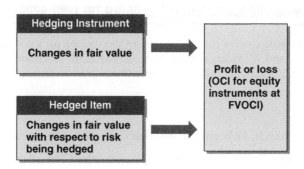

FIGURE 7.16   Fair value hedge accounting

adjustments. Specific credit risk adjustments on exposures in default shall not be used to cover expected loss amounts on other exposures.

> [CRR 159] does not provide for a treatment of discounts on balance sheet exposures purchased when *not* in default in the same manner as specific credit risk adjustments. Furthermore, such discounts do not qualify as credit risk adjustments. Hence, such discounts are not allowed to be included in the calculation according to [CRR 159].
>
> However, according to [CRR 166(1)], if the discount on these exposures purchased is reflected in the balance sheet, the discount is also reflected in the exposure value when calculating credit risk RWAs.

The adjustment to AVAs are restricted to expected loss amounts calculated for corporate, central government and central bank, financial institutions, retail, specialised lending and purchased receivables exposures. Expected loss amounts for securitised exposures and general and specific credit risk adjustments related to these exposures are not included in this calculation.

The intention behind [CRR 159] is to ensure that expected loss amounts calculated under the IRB approach are only deducted from regulatory capital to the extent they have not already been reflected through either:

- General and specific credit risk provisions within in the financial statements, which are the starting point of the regulatory capital calculation; or
- Adjustments to these general and specific credit risk provisions, deducted from own funds to meet prudent valuation requirements of Article 105 of the CRR.

Conversely, if expected loss amounts calculated under the IRB approach are already being deducted from regulatory capital, they should not be included in the AVA calculation.

> Credit and counterparty risk RWAs on assets, including the expected loss amount, are calculated using the higher accounting values, not the AVA adjusted values. As a result, without an adjustment to the capital requirements on those assets, there is a double negative impact on regulatory capital. The offset against expected losses in [CRR 159] is a means of mitigating that double impact.

7.4 ADDITIONAL VALUATION ADJUSTMENTS (AVAs) UNDER THE CORE APPROACH

As noted above, banks (themselves or the banking group they belong to) whose absolute value of fair valued assets, liabilities and off-balance sheet items exceed EUR 15 billion must apply the **core approach** when estimating additional valuation adjustments.

7.4.1 The Nine AVAs

Under the EBA's core approach, AVAs are split into nine categories, as shown in Figure 7.17:

- **Market price uncertainty.** This AVA estimates valuation uncertainty stemming from mid-market prices;
- **Close-out costs.** This AVA estimates valuation uncertainty stemming from bid-offer spreads;

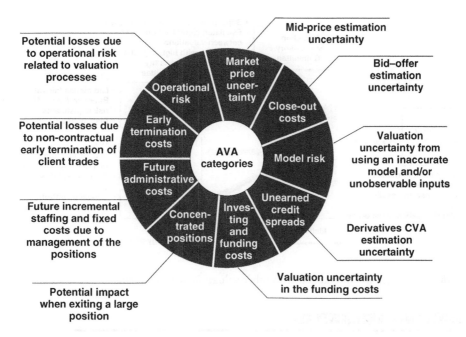

FIGURE 7.17 AVA categories under the EBA's core approach

- **Model risk** (where relevant). This AVA estimates valuation uncertainty stemming from the use of inaccurate models and/or unobservable calibration parameters;
- **Unearned credit spreads.** This AVA estimates valuation uncertainty stemming from CVA in derivatives;
- **Investing and funding costs.** This AVA estimates valuation uncertainty stemming from funding costs;
- **Concentrated positions.** This AVA estimates valuation uncertainty stemming from a position size when exiting such position;
- **Future administrative costs.** This AVA estimates future incremental staffing and fixed costs associated with the management of the position;
- **Early termination costs.** This AVA estimates potential losses stemming from non-contractual early termination of client trades; and
- **Operational risk.** This AVA estimates potential losses arising from operational risk related to the valuation processes.

The overall AVA figure that is deducted from CET1 is the aggregate of the nine individual AVAs.

$$AVA = \sum_{Nine\,categories} [Category\,AVA] = MPU\,AVA + Close\text{-}out\,costs\,AVA + \cdots + Operational\,risk\,AVA$$

7.4.2 The Independent Price Verification Function

[CRR 105(8)] requires a bank to perform, at least monthly, an independent price verification ("IPV") in addition to daily marking-to-market or marking-to-model. The IPV must be performed by a unit independent from units that benefit from the position (the front office and its supporting middle office). The IPV function is at the heart of the AVA calculations, as shown in Figure 7.18.

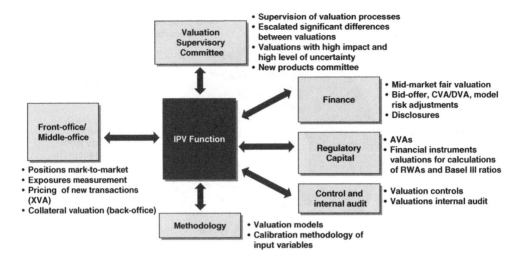

FIGURE 7.18   IPV function – Interaction with other valuation areas in a bank

7.5 MARKET PRICE UNCERTAINTY AVA

The market price uncertainty AVA ("MPU AVA") is an adjustment to the fair value of a position due to uncertainty regarding the mid-price of the positions.

7.5.1 Sources of Market Data Hierarchy

The calculation of AVAs shall consider the same market data used in the IPV. The following sources of market data are considered, ordered in terms of reliability (see Figure 7.19):

- Exchange prices in a liquid market;
- Trades in the exact same or very similar instrument, either from the bank's own records or, where available, trades from across the market;
- Tradable quotes from brokers and other market participants;
- Consensus service data;
- Indicative broker quotes; and
- Counterparty collateral valuations.

7.5.2 Steps in the Calculation of Market Price Uncertainty AVAs

AVAs are calculated at valuation exposure level ("individual market price uncertainty AVAs").

For those positions for which the bank concludes that their MPU AVA is relevant, the calculation of the MPU AVA is performed following the flowchart shown in Figure 7.20.

7.5.3 Step 1: Selection of Valuation Positions

The first step in the calculation of the MPU AVA is to group all the individual items subject to prudent valuation (i.e., those items *not* assumed to have a zero AVA) into a set of portfolios. Each portfolio constitutes what is called a "**valuation position**".

This step is in practice relatively straightforward, as the bank is likely to have already divided its market risk management/trading activities into different books that are valued on the basis of the same risks. Remember that the AVA calculation process has to be consistent with the IPV process. As an example, imagine that Megabank has several hundred of portfolios grouped into books, as shown in Figure 7.21:

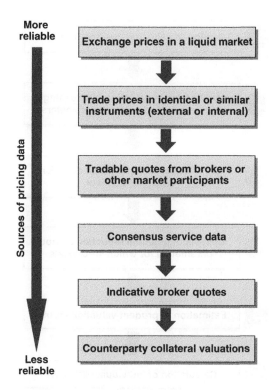

FIGURE 7.19   Reliability hierarchy of market data sources

Valuation positions are then split between:

- Positions that are marked-to-market; and
- Positions that are marked-to model.

Marked-to-market positions (i.e., as opposed to marked-to-model) are those for which their fair value is based on a directly observable market price. These positions comprise non-derivative valuation positions (e.g., government bonds held by the bank) and some derivative positions (e.g., exchange-traded futures).

Marked-to-model positions (i.e., as opposed to marked-to-market) are those for which their fair value is obtained by putting a set of valuation parameters in a pricing model. These positions comprise a substantial part of derivative positions. No non-derivative positions are assumed to be marked-to-model.

7.5.4 Step 2: Identification of Valuation Inputs

The second step in the estimation of the MPU AVA is the identification of the inputs needed to prudent value each valuation position.

Marked-to-Market or Non-Derivative Valuation Positions   In the case of marked-to-market or non-derivative valuation positions, the granularity of the inputs to be used to estimate AVAs is either:

- The price of the instrument; or
- Decomposed into more than one valuation inputs, such that all inputs required to calculate an exit price for the position are treated separately.

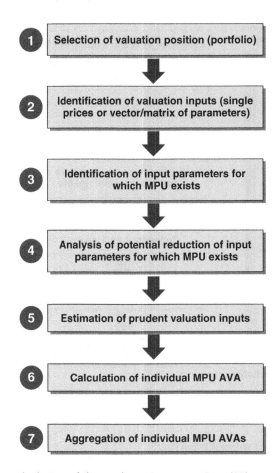

FIGURE 7.20 Steps in the calculation of the market price uncertainty AVA

Example

As an example imagine that a European bank – Megabank – whose presentation currency was the EUR, held 10 million ordinary shares of Littlebank which were quoted in EUR as well. The position was relatively small, not requiring Megabank to recognise Littlebank as an associate or subsidiary. On the reporting date, the shares of Littlebank closed at EUR 5.20. Megabank fair valued its position in Littlebank as follows:

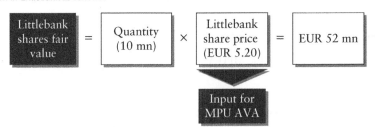

In this case, the quoted price in EUR of the Littlebank shares was the only input required to assess the MPU AVA of the position. In reality, it was quite likely that Megabank would deem the position to have zero AVA if the market in Littlebank shares was sufficiently liquid.

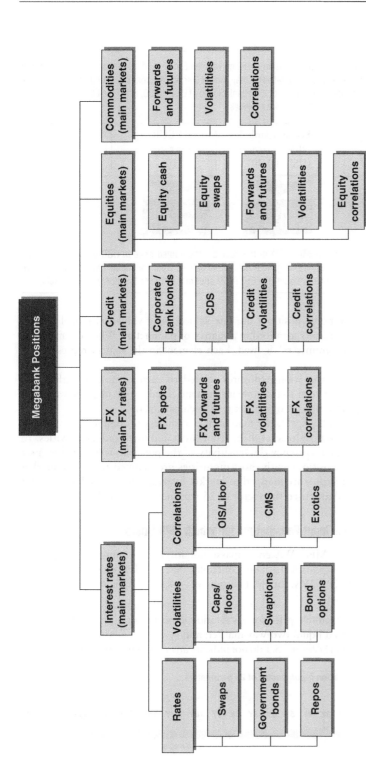

FIGURE 7.21 Megabank portfolios subject to prudent valuation

Example

In another example imagine that Megabank – whose presentation currency was the EUR – held 10 million ordinary shares of Foreignbank which were quoted in USD. The position was relatively small, *not* requiring Megabank to recognise Foreignbank as an associate or subsidiary. On the reporting date, the shares of Littlebank closed at USD 10.30, when the EUR/USD exchange rate was 1.10. Megabank fair valued its position in Foreignbank as follows:

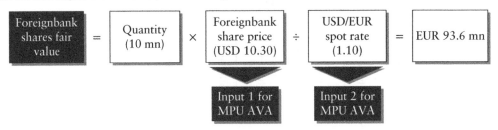

In this case, two inputs were required to assess the MPU AVA of the position: the quoted price in USD of the Foreignbank shares and the EIR USD spot FX rate. Again, in reality it was quite likely that Megabank would deem the position to have zero AVA if the market in Foreignbank shares was sufficiently liquid (the EUR/USD spot rate is one of the most liquid markets).

Marked-to-Model Positions   Market-to-model positions are fair valued using valuation models. These models use inputs which can be systematically arranged in a **matrix of parameters**. When the matrix is one-dimensional, the term "vector of parameters" is used. Each element in the matrix represents an input to the model.

AVAs are calculated based on the valuation exposures related to each parameter within that matrix. Where a valuation input does not refer to tradable instruments, banks shall map the valuation input and the related valuation exposure to a set of market tradable instruments.

In the case of interest rate swaps ("swaps"), the matrix of parameters is commonly consistent with the way the bank manages its swap positions resulting from client and own trading activities. To risk manage the swaps portfolio, for each currency the sensitivity of the portfolio is mapped to a set of tradable interest rate instruments. Positions with short maturities are mapped to money market rates and to futures, while longer maturities are mapped to market interest rate swaps. Imagine that regarding the EUR swaps book, Megabank used the vector of 25 parameters depicted in Figure 7.22.

7.5.5 Step 3: Identification of Valuation Input Parameters for which MPU Exists

The third step in the calculation of the MPU AVA encompasses identifying the input parameters for which MPU exists. Input parameters for which the bank concludes that no MPU exists will result in their related exposures having a zero MPU AVA. An input parameter is assessed to have no MPU where both of the following conditions are met:

- The bank has firm evidence of a tradable price for a valuation exposure or a price can be determined from reliable data based on a **liquid two-way market**; and
- The sources of market data set out in Section 7.5.1 do not indicate any material valuation uncertainty.

Valuation input: vector of 25 parameters

ON 1D 1W 1M 2M 3M 6M 1Y 18M 2Y 3Y 4Y 5Y 6Y 7Y 8Y 9Y 10Y 12Y 15Y 20Y 25Y 30Y 40Y 50Y

Money market   *Futures*   *Swaps*

FIGURE 7.22   Megabank – Vector of parameters used to risk manage the EUR interest rate swap book

Pursuant to [CRR 338], a two-way market is deemed to exist where there are independent bona fide offers to buy and sell so that a price reasonably related to the last sales price or current bona fide competitive bid and offer quotations can be determined within one day and settled at such price within a relatively short time conforming to trade custom.

In reality, banks are interested not only in justifying that MPU AVA is not relevant for a position, but also all the other eight AVAs (i.e., no AVAs are necessary for that position). Such positions are called **"zero AVA"** positions.

Banks would need to demonstrate that the level of valuation uncertainty is not material. To achieve this, banks would need to show that there is strong evidence of actual trades or readily-tradable quotes at the balance sheet date and time (meaning this could only be applied to very liquid positions) for sizes of trade that indicate the position could be closed in its entirety at the fair value on the balance sheet. Banks should have policies and controls in place to identify positions where no AVAs are required.

In the case of Megabank's EUR swaps book, the bank concluded that the money market and futures parameters met the two requirements above. As a result, only the 15 parameters from the 3-year swap rate to the 50-year swap rate indicated market price uncertainty, as shown in Figure 7.23.

7.5.6 Step 4: Analysis of Potential Reduction of Valuation Input Parameters for which MPU Exists

EBA allows the reduction of valuation input parameters. A lower number of inputs is likely to reduce the corresponding MPU adjustment as exposures are more probable to offset.

Valuation Exposures A **valuation exposure** is the amount of a valuation position which is sensitive to the movement in a valuation input parameter.

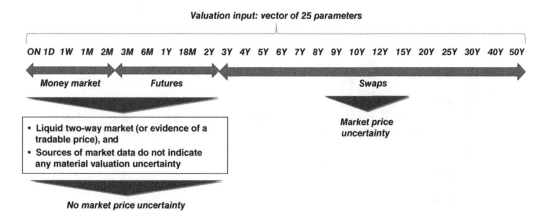

FIGURE 7.23 Megabank – Vector of parameters identified as lacking or having market price uncertainty

In the example covered in Section 7.5.4, a bank held 10 million ordinary shares of Littlebank. On the reporting date, the shares of Littlebank closed at EUR 5.20. Megabank fair valued its position in Littlebank as follows:

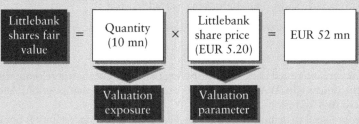

In this case, the 10 million shares was the **valuation exposure**. Each EUR 1 change in the price of Littlebank shares exposed the valuation of the stake to a EUR 10 million change. Littlebank's share price was the only **valuation input**.

In the case of swaps, the valuation exposure is a vector of exposures. Each exposure represents the sensitivity of the valuation position (i.e., the swaps portfolio) to each valuation input parameter. Each valuation input parameter represents the swap instrument rate used to build the swaps curve. Commonly exposures are calculated as the sensitivity of the position to one basis point change in the input parameter. Figure 7.24 illustrates Megabank's exposures of its EUR swap portfolio. For example, the exposure to a one basis point change in the 5-year swap rate was EUR 720,000, meaning that if the 5-year swap rate rises by one basis point, the swap book would experience a EUR 720,000 gain.

Reduction of Input Parameters   Banks may reduce the number of parameters of the valuation input for the purpose of calculating market price uncertainty and close-out costs AVAs using any appropriate methodology, provided the reduced parameters satisfy *all* of the following requirements:

Input parameter	3Y	4Y	5Y	6Y	7Y	8Y	9Y	10Y	12Y	15Y	20Y	25Y	30Y	40Y	50Y
Exposure (EUR '000)	120	170	720	390	–450	–160	–280	–670	110	–180	120	–20	30	40	20

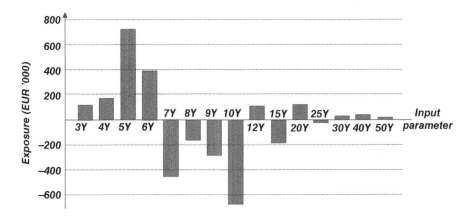

FIGURE 7.24   Megabank – EUR swap book exposures (amounts in EUR thousands)

- The total value of the reduced **valuation exposure** is the **same** as the total value of the original valuation exposure;
- The reduced set of parameters can be **mapped** to a set of **market tradable instruments**; and
- The **ratio of variance** measure 2 over variance measure 1, based on historical data from the most recent 100 trading days, is **less than 10%**:

$$\text{Ratio of variance measures} = \frac{\text{Var}_2}{\text{Var}_1} \leq 10\%$$

Where,

Var_1: Profit or loss variance of the valuation exposure based on **unreduced** valuation input (over the last 100 trading days); and

Var_2: Profit or loss variance of the (i) valuation exposure based on the **unreduced** valuation input, minus (ii) valuation exposure based on the **reduced** valuation input (over the last 100 trading days).

> The parameter reduction process is a complex exercise, subject to independent control function review of the netting methodology and internal validation on at least an annual basis.

Megabank tried to reduce the size of the vector of input parameters by assessing whether the three requirements were met for a potential vector of seven parameters (3Y, 5Y, 7Y, 10Y, 20Y, 30Y, 50Y EUR swap rates).

Allocation of Exposures of Eliminated Input Parameters to those of the Reduced Input Parameters   The valuation exposures corresponding to the eliminated input parameters were allocated to those of the two closest remaining input parameters. For example, the valuation exposure corresponding to the 4Y input parameter was EUR 170,000. The present value of a basis point change ("**PV01**") of the 4Y bucket was 3.82, while those of the 3Y and 5Y buckets were 2.91 and 4.67 respectively. Megabank allocated EUR 112,000 to the 3Y bucket and EUR 69,000 to the 5Y bucket. The bank ascertained that the EUR 649,000 (=170,000 × 3.82) exposure to a one basis point change in the 4Y swap rate was equal to the EUR 649,000 aggregate of the EUR 326,000 (=112,000 × 2.91) and the EUR 322,000 (=69,000 × 4.67) exposures to a one basis point change in the 3Y and 5Y swap rates respectively (the difference was due to rounding):

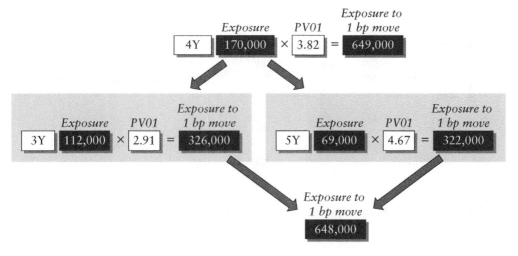

After that allocation, the new exposures regarding the 3Y and 5Y buckets were the following:

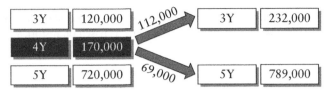

Megabank performed a similar allocation to each eliminated input parameter resulting in the valuation exposures vector depicted in the following table (see Figure 7.25).

Requirement 1: Same Total Value of Exposures   The first requirement was that the total value of the valuation exposures based on the unreduced (i.e., original) vector of input parameters had to be equal to the total value of the valuation exposures based on the reduced vector of input parameters.

The aggregate sensitivity of the unreduced valuation exposures to a one basis point parallel change was EUR <3,345,000>, calculated as the aggregate of each exposure multiplied by its PV01, as shown in Table 7.1.

Similarly, the aggregate sensitivity of the reduced valuation exposures to a one basis point parallel change was EUR <3,358,000> as shown in Table 7.2.

Megabank concluded that the first requirement was met as the EUR <3,345,000> total value of the **unreduced valuation exposure** was the **same** as the EUR <3,358,000>total value of the **reduced valuation exposure** (the difference was due to rounding errors).

Requirement 2: Reduced Set of Parameters Mapped to Market Tradable Instruments   The third requirement was that the reduced set of parameters had to be **mapped** to a set of **market tradable instruments**.

Input parameter	3Y	5Y	7Y	10Y	20Y	30Y	50Y
Exposure (EUR '000)	232	1,017	−539	−924	73	41	40

FIGURE 7.25   Megabank – EUR swap book exposures reduced to seven parameters

TABLE 7.1 Calculation of unreduced valuation exposure

Input Parameter	3Y	4Y	5Y	6Y	7Y	8Y	9Y	10Y	12Y	15Y	20Y	25Y	30Y	40Y	50Y
Exposure (EUR '000)	120	170	720	390	-450	-160	-280	-670	110	-180	120	-20	30	40	20
PV01	2.91	3.82	4.67	5.47	6.24	6.96	7.64	8.26	9.43	10.95	13.07	14.26	14.86	15.92	16.25
Unreduced Valuation Exposure (EUR'000)	349	649	3,362	2,133	-2,808	-1,114	-2,139	-5,534	1,037	-1,971	1,568	-285	446	637	325

Total Unreduced Valuation Exposure (EUR'000)	<3,345,000>

TABLE 7.2   Calculation of reduced valuation exposure

Input parameter	3Y	5Y	7Y	10Y	20Y	30Y	50Y
Exposure (EUR '000)	232	1,017	−539	−924	73	41	40
PV01	2.91	4.67	6.24	8.26	13.07	14.86	16.25
Unreduced Valuation Exposure (EUR'000)	675	4,749	−3,363	−7,632	954	609	650

Total Unreduced Valuation Exposure (EUR '000)	<3,358,000>

Megabank justified that swaps with the maturities for the first six parameters could be traded directly in the EUR swaps market, and justified that the seventh parameter (the 50Y EUR swap rate) was traded being priced as (i) the 30-year swap rate plus (ii) a relatively constant 50-year versus 30-year spread. Thus, Megabank concluded that the second requirement was met.

Requirement 3: Variance Test   The third requirement was that the **ratio of variance measure 2 over variance measure 1,** based on historical data from the most recent 100 trading days, had to be **less than 10%:**

$$\text{Ratio of variance measures} = \frac{\text{Var}_2}{\text{Var}_1} \le 10\%$$

Var₁: P&L Variance using Unreduced Input Parameters   In order to calculate the profit or loss variance (Var$_1$) of the valuation exposure based on **unreduced** valuation input parameters over the last 100 trading days, Megabank performed the following tasks:

1. Took the "unreduced" vector of exposures of the EUR swap book:

Input Parameter	3Y	4Y	5Y	6Y	7Y	8Y	9Y	10Y	12Y	15Y	20Y	25Y	30Y	40Y	50Y
Exposure (EUR '000)	120	170	720	390	−450	−160	−280	−670	110	−180	120	−20	30	40	20

2. Took the closing rates for each of the fifteen unreduced input parameters (3Y, 4Y, 5Y, 6Y, 7Y, 8Y, 9Y, 10Y, 12Y, 15Y, 20Y, 25Y, 30Y, 40Y and 50Y EUR swap rates) during the previous 101 trading sessions;
3. Calculated the daily profit or loss ("PL$_i$") during each trading session as follows:

$$PL_i = \sum_{j=1}^{15} \text{Exposure}_j \times \left(\text{Input}_{i,j} - \text{Input}_{i-1,j}\right)$$

Where:

Exposure$_j$: The exposure j of the vector of exposures (j varied from 1 to 15);

Input$_{i,j}$: The closing swap rate for day i corresponding to input parameter j; and
PL$_i$: Daily gain or loss on day i.

4. Calculated the variance of the daily profit or loss during the previous 100 trading sessions:

$$\text{Variance of unreduced inputs} = Var_1 = \sqrt{\frac{\sum_{i=1}^{n}(X_i - M)^2}{n-1}} = \sqrt{\frac{\sum_{i=1}^{100}(PL_i - M)^2}{100}}$$

Where:

PL$_i$: Daily gain or loss on day i; and
M: Sample mean.

This variance was **Var$_1$**, the profit or loss variance (over the last 100 trading days) of the valuation exposure based on the **unreduced** vector of input parameters.

Var$_2$: P&L Variance using Reduced Input Parameters In order to calculate the profit or loss variance Var$_2$, the profit or loss variance of the (i) valuation exposure based on the **unreduced** valuation input, minus (ii) valuation exposure based on the **reduced** valuation input (over the last 100 trading days), Megabank performed the following tasks:

1. Took the "unreduced" vector of exposures of the EUR swap book:

Input Parameter	3Y	4Y	5Y	6Y	7Y	8Y	9Y	10Y	12Y	15Y	20Y	25Y	30Y	40Y	50Y
Exposure (EUR '000)	120	170	720	390	–450	–160	–280	–670	110	–180	120	–20	30	40	20

2. Took the closing rates for each of the fifteen unreduced input parameters (3Y, 4Y, 5Y, 6Y, 7Y, 8Y, 9Y, 10Y, 12Y, 15Y, 20Y, 25Y, 30Y, 40Y and 50Y EUR swap rates) during the previous 101 trading sessions;
3. Took the "reduced" vector of exposures of the EUR swap book (see Figure 7.25):

Input Parameter	3Y	5Y	7Y	10Y	20Y	30Y	50Y
Exposure (EUR '000)	232	1,017	–539	–924	73	41	40

4. Took the closing rates for each of the seven reduced input parameters (3Y, 5Y, 7Y, 10Y, 20Y, 30Y and 50Y EUR swap rates) during the previous 101 trading sessions;
5. Calculated the daily profit or loss ("PL$_i$") during each trading session as follows:

$$PL_i = \sum_{j=1}^{15} \text{Unreduced Exposure}_j \times \left(\text{Input}_{i,j} - \text{Input}_{i-1,j}\right) - \sum_{k=1}^{7} \text{Reduced Exposure}_k \times \left(\text{Input}_{i,k} - \text{Input}_{i-1,k}\right)$$

Where:

Unreduced Exposure$_j$: The exposure j of the vector of exposures based on the vector of unreduced input parameters (j varied from 1 to 15);

Reduced Exposure$_k$: The exposure k of the vector of exposures based on the vector of reduced input parameters (k varied from 1 to 7);
Input$_{i,j}$: The closing swap rate for day i corresponding to the original input parameter j;
Input$_{i,k}$: The closing swap rate for day i corresponding to reduced input parameter k; and
PL$_i$: Daily gain or loss on day i.

6. Calculated the variance of the daily profit or loss during the 100 trading sessions:

$$\text{Variance of reduced inputs} = \text{Var}_2 = \sqrt{\frac{\sum_{i=1}^{n}(X_i - M)^2}{n-1}} = \sqrt{\frac{\sum_{i=1}^{100}(PL_i - M)^2}{100}}$$

Where:

PL$_i$: Daily gain or loss on day i; and
M: Sample mean.

This variance was **Var$_2$**, the profit or loss variance (over the last 100 trading days) of the difference between the valuation exposure based on the **unreduced** vector of input parameters and that based on the **reduced** vector of input parameters.

Let us assume that the **ratio of variance measure 2 over variance measure** was **less than 10%**, and as a result the third requirement was met:

$$\text{Ratio of variance measures} = \frac{\text{Var}_2}{\text{Var}_1} \leq 10\%$$

7.5.7 Step 5: Estimation of Prudent Mid-market of Valuation Inputs

Under the EBA's core approach, individual market price uncertainty AVAs are determined as follows:

1. Where sufficient data exists to construct a range of plausible values for a valuation input:
   - For a valuation input where the **range of plausible values** is based on **exit prices**, banks shall estimate a point within the range where they are **90% confident** they could exit the valuation exposure at that price or better; or
   - For a valuation input where the **range of plausible values** is created from **mid-prices**, banks shall estimate a point within the range where they are **90% confident** that the mid-value they could achieve in exiting the valuation exposure would be at that price or better.
2. Where insufficient data exists to construct a plausible range of values for a valuation input (i.e., the number or quality of data is too small to inform a statistical estimation), banks use an **expert-based approach** using qualitative and quantitative information available to achieve a level of certainty in the prudent value of the valuation input that is equivalent to that targeted under the approach covered in 1). Banks shall notify competent authorities of the valuation exposures for which this approach is applied, and the methodology used to determine the AVA.

According to the EBA, where an expert-based approach is applied alternative methods and sources of information shall be considered, including each of the following, where relevant:

- The use of proxy data based on similar instruments for which sufficient data is available;
- The application of prudent shifts to valuation inputs; and
- The identification of natural bounds to the value of an instrument.

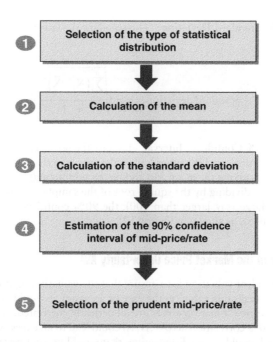

FIGURE 7.26   Steps in the calculation of the prudent mid-price

Calculation of the Volatility (Standard Deviation)   For a valuation input where the **range of plausible values** (i.e., where there is sufficient data of a good quality such that a range can be statistically estimated) is created from **mid-prices** (or **exit prices**), banks shall estimate a point within the range where they are **90% confident** that the mid-value (or exit price) they could achieve in exiting the valuation exposure would be at that price or better.

The process to arrive at the 90% confident mid-value (or exit price) is calculated following the steps highlighted in Figure 7.26:

1. A type of statistical distribution is assumed for the data;
2. The mean of the data is calculated;
3. The standard deviation (i.e., the volatility) of the data is calculated;
4. The 90% interval of mid-prices (or mid-rates) is estimated; and
5. The prudent mid-price (or mid-rate) is calculated.

Calculation of the Prudent Values Assuming a Normal Distribution   Next the steps in Figure 7.26 are followed, assuming a normal distribution.

Step 1: Calculation of the Mean   A type of statistical distribution is assumed for the data. Normally there are three types of distribution considered: normal, log-normal or t-statistic distributions. I assume that the bank selected the normal distribution as the type of distribution that best represented the series of mid-prices.

Step 2: Calculation of the Mean   Mean and expected value are used synonymously to refer to the central tendency of the input variable. The mean is calculated as follows:

$$\text{Mean} = \overline{X} = \frac{X_1 + X_2 + X_3 + \cdots + X_{n-1} + X_n}{n} = \frac{\sum\limits_{i=1}^{n} X_i}{n}$$

Step 3: Calculation of the Standard Deviation   The standard deviation of the observations is calculated as follows:

$$\text{Standard deviation} = \sigma = \sqrt{\frac{\sum_{i=1}^{n}\left(X_i - \bar{X}\right)^2}{n-1}}$$

Step 4: Estimation of the 90% Confidence Interval   Because the normal curve is symmetric, half of the area is in the left tail of the curve, and the other half of the area is in the right tail of the curve. A 90% interval implies is calculated, taking the mean and adding (or subtracting) the product of 1.645 and the standard deviation and then dividing by the square root of the sample size, as shown in Figure 7.27.

If the sample size is large (say larger than 100), the 90% confidence interval is 3.29 standard errors wide (3.29 = 2 × 1.645), as shown in Figure 7.28.

7.5.8 Step 6: Calculation of the Market Price Uncertainty AVA

Even if the objective of prudent valuation is to ensure that the valuation used for regulatory purposes is not higher than the true realisable value (in the case of an asset), it would be excessively prudent to suppose that adverse valuation estimation errors are all perfectly correlated. Not recognising diversification (i.e., assuming a 100% correlation across AVAs) could lead to an excessive overestimation of the deductions to CET1, which could create disincentives that would prevent certain otherwise profitable transactions from being made.

Diversification in the core approach is allowed for the AVAs calculated regarding market price uncertainty, close-out costs and model risk. In order to arrive at the total category AVA for these AVAs, the aggregation of the individual AVAs is allowed a 50% reduction to account for the benefit of diversification. Two methods are available for the aggregation:

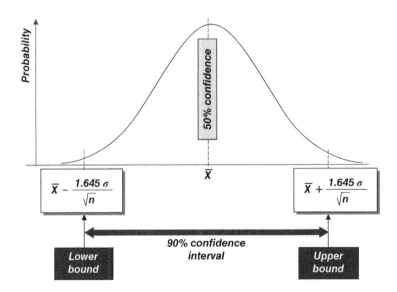

FIGURE 7.27   Upper and lower boundaries with a 90% confidence interval in a normal distribution – Small sample size

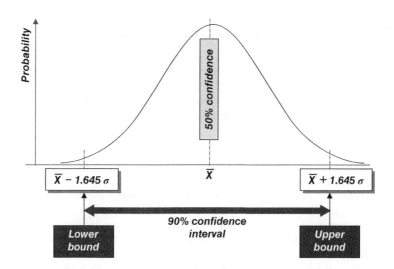

FIGURE 7.28 Upper and lower boundaries with a 90% confidence interval in a normal distribution – Large sample size

- **Method 1:** The 50% reduction is performed as the difference between fair value and prudent value. For example, in the case of assets:

$$\text{Market Price Uncertainty AVA} = \sum_{\text{Within category}} \left[\underbrace{\frac{50\% \times (\text{Fair value} - \text{Prudent value})}{\text{At valuation exposure level}}} \right]$$

- **Method 2:** The individual AVA is calculated as the difference between: (i) the fair value and (ii) the average of the expected value and prudent value. For example, in the case of assets:

$$\text{Market Price Uncertainty AVA} = \sum_{\text{Within category}} \left[\underbrace{\frac{\text{Max}\{0, \text{Fair Value} - 50\%(\text{Expected value} + \text{Prudent value})\}}{\text{At valuation exposure level}}} \right]$$

Imagine an asset with an expected value of 100, a fair value of 98 and a prudent value of 95. The **first method** would result in an AVA of 1.5, calculated as follows:

$$\text{Individual Market Price Uncertainty} = 50\% \times (\text{Fair Value} - \text{Prudent Value}) = 50\% \times (98 - 95) = 1.5$$

The **second method** would result in an AVA of 0.5, calculated as follows:

$$\text{Individual Market Price Uncertainty} = \text{Max}\{0, \text{Fair value} - 50\%(\text{Expected value} + \text{Prudent value})\}$$
$$\text{Individual Market Price Uncertainty} = \text{Max}\{0, 98 - 50\%(100 + 95)\} = 0.5$$

Therefore, the second method was more beneficial for the bank than the first method as it resulted in a lower amount of AVA. In practice a good number of banks have adopted the second method, but it requires keeping track of the expected values.

7.6 CLOSE-OUT COSTS AVA

Uncertainty in the exit price of a position arises from uncertainty in the mid-price of the position and from uncertainty in the bid-offer spread. The close-out costs AVA measures potential valuation uncertainty arising from **bid-offer spreads**.

The impact of the bid-offer spread on an instrument's fair value is incorporated either by the use of a direct mark-to-exit price or through the use of a bid-offer adjustment to the valuation input parameter:

- When the bank has calculated a market price uncertainty AVA for the valuation exposure based on an **exit price**, the **close-out cost AVA** for the valuation input parameter is assumed to have **zero** value. In other words, the calculation of the uncertainties regarding mid-price and bid-offer spreads were already taken into account when calculating the uncertainty regarding the exit price;
- When the bank can close out the valuation exposure at mid-market the close-out cost AVA for such exposure are assumed to have zero value, pursuant to [CRR 105(5)]. In other words, when the bank provides evidence that it is 90% confident that sufficient liquidity exists to support the exit of the valuation exposure at mid-price, the close-out costs AVA are assumed to have zero value. Where a bank makes use of this derogation, it shall every six months inform their competent authorities of the positions concerned and furnish evidence that it can close out at mid-market; or
- Otherwise, the bank needs to calculate the close-out costs AVA for each valuation input parameter by taking into account the more prudent side of the bid and the offer.

Steps in the Calculation of Close-out Costs AVA   For valuation exposures that cannot be assumed to have a zero close-out costs AVA, the calculation of this AVA follows steps similar to those to arrive at the calculation of market price uncertainty AVA, as covered in Section 7.5:

1. Selection of the valuation positions. The selection performed when calculating the market price uncertainty AVA should remain valid;
2. Identification of valuation input parameters. The selection performed when calculating the market price uncertainty AVA should remain valid;
3. Identification of valuation input parameters for which close-out costs exists. The identification and mapping to a set of market tradable instruments performed when calculating the market price uncertainty AVA should remain valid;
4. Analysis of potential reduction of valuation input parameters for which close-out costs exists. The reduction in the valuation input parameters performed when calculating the market price uncertainty AVA should remain valid;
5. Estimation of the prudent bid-to-mid (or mid-to-offer) of the valuation inputs;
6. Calculation of the individual close-out costs AVAs; and
7. Calculation of the category close-out costs AVA.

Estimation of the Prudent Bid-to-Mid (or Mid-to-Offer) of the Valuation Inputs   Under the EBA's core approach, individual market price uncertainty AVAs are determined as follows:

- Where sufficient data exists to construct a range of plausible bid-offer spreads for a valuation input, banks shall estimate a point within the range where they are **90% confident** that the spread they could achieve in exiting the valuation exposure would be at that price or better.
- Where insufficient data exists to construct a plausible range of bid-offer spreads for a valuation input, banks use an **expert-based approach** using qualitative and quantitative information available to achieve a level of certainty in the prudent value of the valuation input that is equivalent

to that targeted where a range of plausible values is available. Banks shall notify competent authorities of the valuation exposures for which this approach is applied, and the methodology used to determine the AVA.

The individual close-out costs AVA is calculated applying 50% of the estimated bid-offer spread to the valuation exposures related to the valuation inputs.

The calculation of the category (i.e., total) close-out costs AVA is perfumed by applying to the individual close-out costs AVAs the formulae for either Method 1 or Method 2 covered in Section 7.5.8.

7.7 MODEL RISK AVA

The model risk AVA is an adjustment to the fair value of a position due to the uncertainty regarding the use of a model to determine such fair value.

Valuation models are employed by banks to value, risk manage and monitor certain financial instruments which cannot otherwise be valued using quoted prices. Model risk assesses whether the model accurately reflects:

- The characteristics of the instrument being fair valued and its significant risks;
- The selection and reliability of model inputs;
- The consistency with models for similar instruments;
- The appropriateness of any model-related adjustments; and
- The sensitivity to input parameters and assumptions that cannot be observed from the market.

A model risk AVA is estimated for each valuation model ("individual model risk AVA") by considering valuation model risk which arises due to the potential existence of a range of different models or model calibrations, which are used by market participants, and the lack of a firm exit price for the specific product being valued. Banks shall not consider valuation model risk which arises due to calibrations from market derived parameters, which shall be captured by the market price uncertainty AVA.

The model risk AVA is calculated using one of the two following approaches:

- Estimating a 90% confidence interval; or
- Using an expert-based approach.

90% Confidence Interval Approach   Where possible, banks shall calculate the model risk AVA by determining a range of plausible valuations produced from alternative appropriate modelling and calibration approaches. In this case, banks estimate a point within the resulting range of valuations where they are 90% confident they could exit the valuation exposure at that price or better.

Expert-based Approach   Where banks are unable to estimate a 90% confidence interval, they shall apply an expert-based approach to estimate the model risk AVA. The expert-based approach shall consider all of the following:

- Complexity of instruments relevant to the model;
- Diversity of possible mathematical approaches and model parameters, where those model parameters are not related to market variables;
- The degree to which the market for relevant products is "one-way";
- The existence of unhedgeable risks in relevant products; and
- The adequacy of the model in capturing the behaviour of the pay-off of the products in the portfolio.

Banks are required to notify competent authorities of the models for which this approach is applied, and the methodology used to determine the model risk AVA.

Where a bank uses the expert-based approach, the prudence of the method shall be confirmed annually by comparing the following:

1. The AVAs calculated using the expert-based approach, if it were applied to a material sample of the valuation models for which the bank applies the 90% confidence interval approach; and
2. The AVAs produced by the 90% confidence interval approach for the same sample of valuation models.

> In practice most individual model risk AVAs are estimated using the expert-based approach. A scoring system is a popular way to assign the AVA to each model.
>
> Individual model risk AVAs are mostly related to Level 3 instruments. Banks should be aware that a model risk adjustment may be already effected to the fair valuation of such instruments to avoid double counting.

Determination of the Model Risk AVA

Once each individual model risk AVA has been estimated, the total category level AVA for model risk is calculated by applying the formulae for either Method 1 or Method 2, as covered in Section 7.5.8.

7.8 UNEARNED CREDIT SPREADS AVA

Unearned credit spreads AVA reflects the valuation uncertainty in the adjustment necessary according to the applicable accounting framework to include the current value of expected losses due to counterparty default on derivative positions.

> This element of the AVA relates to counterparty credit risk (**Counterparty Valuation Adjustment – CVA**) of derivatives which was covered in Section 7.1.3. Where a derivatives portfolio is fully collateralised, the bank may be able to justify that the fair valuation of the portfolio incorporates CVA to a 90% level of confidence without the need for an unearned credit spread AVA. If the portfolio is weakly collateralised or uncollateralised then the bank will need to assess both its CVA model and the CVA model input parameters to a 90% level of confidence. The bank would include the difference between any fair value CVA held against the portfolio and the prudent value CVA as an unearned credit spread AVA.
>
> As mentioned previously, own debt valuation adjustments are recognised on a bank's liabilities (other than non-recourse and similar liabilities) for which the fair value option has been elected and in derivatives with negative fair values. The fair value of these liabilities is impacted by the narrowing or widening of a bank's credit spreads. **Debit Valuation Adjustment – DVA** (the adjustment to derivative liabilities due to a bank's own credit quality) is not included in the calculation of regulatory capital. Therefore, DVA does not need to be assessed for prudent valuation purposes. DVA was covered in Section 7.1.3.

The unearned credit spreads AVA is allocated to three other AVAs, namely market price uncertainty, close-out costs and model risk AVAs. The allocation allows the unearned credit spreads AVA to benefit from the 50% diversification benefit applicable to those three AVAs (see Section 7.5.8), as shown in Figure 7.29.

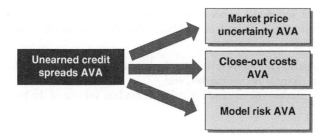

FIGURE 7.29 Allocation to other AVAs of unearned credit spreads AVA

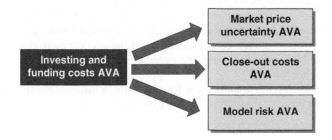

FIGURE 7.30 Allocation to other AVAs of investing and funding costs AVA

7.9 INVESTING AND FUNDING COSTS AVA

The **investing and funding costs AVA** reflects the valuation uncertainty in the funding costs used when assessing the exit price according to the accounting framework (IFRS 13). It was discussed in Section 7.1.3 that funding valuation adjustments or FVA incorporate in the fair valuation of a derivative the potential funding cost or benefits stemming from future potential unfavourable movements in the derivative's fair value.

Similar to the unearned credit spreads AVA, the investing and funding costs AVA is allocated to three other AVAs, namely market price uncertainty, close-out costs and model risk AVAs. This allocation allows the investing and funding costs AVA to benefit from the 50% diversification benefit applicable to those three AVAs (see Section 7.5.8), as shown in Figure 7.30.

7.10 CONCENTRATED POSITIONS AVA

Concentrated positions AVA reflects the valuation uncertainty regarding positions with a large size relative to the liquidity of the market. A concentrated position is defined as any position that requires more than **10 trading days** to be closed, assuming current market conditions.

Concentration reserves are not allowable under IFRS accounting standards. In other words, size of a position is not taken into account when financial instruments are fair valued under IFRS 13 guidelines. Therefore, banks using the AVA core approach need to establish and document a methodology applied to identify positions for which a concentrated positions AVA is calculated.

No diversification benefits are allowed when aggregating individual concentrated positions AVAs. Consequently, the total AVA level for concentrated positions is calculated as the sum of individual concentrated positions AVAs:

$$\text{Concentrated positions AVA} = \sum \text{Individual concentrated positions AVA}$$

The calculation of individual concentrated positions AVA follows the flowchart depicted in Figure 7.31. In the first step in the process the bank identifies the concentrated valuation positions considering the following:

- The size of all valuation positions relative to the liquidity of the related market;
- The bank's ability to trade in that market; and
- The average daily market volume and typical daily trading volume of the bank.

One of the elements to be taken into account when identifying concentrated positions is the bank's typical trading volume in the financial instrument being assessed for concentration position AVA. This element is arguably more relevant than the average daily market volume as the bank can gather first-hand information on the capacity of the market to absorb positions of the traded sizes. Therefore, a bank that regularly trades positions of similar size is more likely to conclude that the position is not a concentrated one. If the average daily market volume is significant, there would be numerous counterparties with which to exit the position, regardless of how often the bank trades.

In practice banks develop a matrix that for each type of instrument category identifies the size threshold above which a position is deemed to be concentrated.

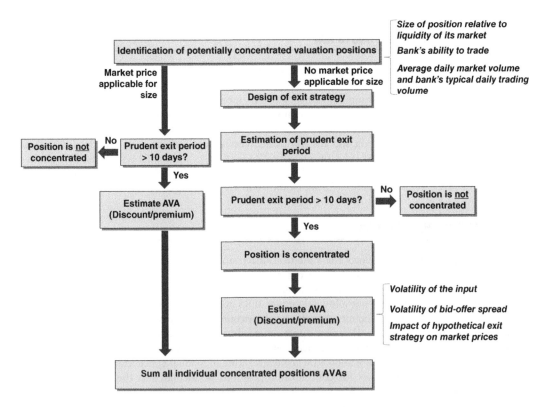

FIGURE 7.31   Calculation of concentrated positions AVAs – Flowchart

The subsequent steps depend on whether there is a market price for the position in its entirety.

Positions with Market Price Applicable for Size   For each identified concentrated valuation position (i.e., it requires more than 10 trading days to exit the position), where a market price applicable for the size of the valuation position is available, the bank estimates the individual concentrated position AVA as the discount (in the case of assets) or the premium (in the case of liabilities) to exit such position.

> In general the discount/premium will depend on the volatility of the price/rate and the daily market volume. The existence of recent block trades executed in the instrument's market may provide a realistic indication of the discount/premium for the concentrated position.

Positions without Market Price Applicable for Size   For each identified valuation position which may be concentrated and where a market price applicable for the size of the valuation position is unavailable, the following steps are followed to estimate the concentrated position AVA:

1. A prudent exit strategy is devised;
2. Based on the prudent strategy devised, a prudent exit period is estimated;
3. If the prudent exit period exceeds 10 trading days, the individual concentrated positions AVA is estimated taking into account the volatility of the valuation input, the volatility of the bid-offer spread and the impact of the hypothetical exit strategy on market prices.

> The calculation of the discount/premium, where no market price is applicable for size, commonly utilises an approach similar to the calculation of VaR for market risk. The horizon of variation of the market price/rate is the prudent exit period and the confidence interval is 90%.

7.11 FUTURE ADMINISTRATIVE COSTS AVA

Recognition of future administrative costs is not allowable under IFRS accounting standards. Therefore, banks need to quantify their future administrative costs AVA when determining the amount of AVAs to be deducted from CET1 capital. No diversification benefit is assumed when aggregating individual future administrative costs AVA. As a result, the total AVA level for future administrative costs is calculated as the sum of individual future administrative costs AVAs:

$$\text{Future administrative costs AVA} = \sum \text{Individual future administrative costs AVA}$$

The individual **future administrative costs AVA** takes into account the administrative costs and future hedging costs over the expected life of a valuation exposure, discounted using a rate which approximates the risk free rate. The administrative costs includes all incremental staffing and fixed costs that will be incurred in managing the portfolio but a reduction in these costs may be assumed as the size of the portfolio reduces.

Future administrative costs AVAs are arguably incongruent with the notion of AVAs being designed to estimate a prudent exit value. Consequently, where a bank calculates market price uncertainty and close-out cost AVAs for a valuation exposure, which imply fully exiting the exposure (i.e., a direct exit price), it may assess a zero AVA for future administrative costs. In other words, market participants are likely to incorporate the expected future administrative costs in the exit price. Banks need to identify whether, when calculating market price uncertainty and close-out costs AVAs, future administrative costs are already included. Otherwise double counting of costs may occur.

Future administrative costs AVA is especially relevant for hard-to-exit portfolios, like for example defaulted trading loans that are in a work-out process. However, the future administrative costs that a market participant may charge for taking and managing that position may differ from the administrative costs expected to be incurred by the bank for managing such position.

Arguably an incongruent situation may potentially occur as future administrative costs of an instrument are deducted from CET1 capital through their AVA while the expected future net income stemming from that instrument is not yet recognised in CET1 capital.

7.12 EARLY TERMINATIONS COSTS AVA

Early termination AVA considers the potential losses arising from non-contractual early terminations of client transactions. The early termination AVA is calculated taking into account the frequency of client trades that have historically terminated early and the losses that the bank incurred in those cases.

No diversification benefits are allowed when aggregating individual early termination costs AVAs. Consequently, the total AVA level for early termination costs is calculated as the sum of individual early termination costs AVAs:

$$\text{Early termination costs AVA} = \sum \text{Individual early termination costs AVA}$$

Normally clients need to pay a fee for early termination to compensate the bank for the market price and a foregone future profit. Banks need to assess whether such fee is sufficient to cover early termination costs, whether there is a significant amount of early terminated transactions in which such fee has been waived or whether there is a history of transactions in which the right to terminate has been rarely exercised.

Break-out clauses in OTC derivatives are included to reduce counterparty credit exposure. Commonly both parties to the instrument have the right to early terminate at certain dates, but the exit is made at market values. Banks need to assess whether there is a history of incurring in costs not covered by such market values.

7.13 OPERATIONAL RISK AVA

Operational risk AVA takes into account the potential losses that may be incurred as a result of operational risk related to valuation processes. Provisioning for operational risk is not allowable under IFRS. Therefore banks need to quantify their operational risk AVA when determining CET1 capital.

7.13.1 Operational Risk Capital Charges under Basel III

Operational risk is defined in [CRR 4(52)] as "the risk of loss resulting from inadequate or failed internal processes, people and systems or from external events, and includes legal risk". Under the Basel III requirement, an operational loss event is associated with the following seven operational loss event categories: (i) internal fraud, (ii) external fraud, (iii) employment practices, (iv) clients, products and business practices, (v) damage to physical assets, (vi) business disruption and systems failures and (vii) execution, delivery and process management. Basel III provides a continuum of three approaches

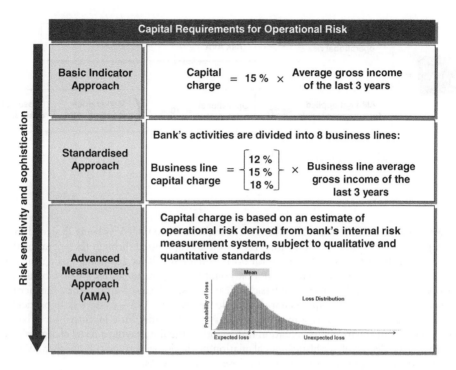

FIGURE 7.32 Basel III approaches to operational risk

of increasing sophistication and risk sensitivity for the calculation of the minimum capital requirements necessary to cover operational risk (see Figure 7.32):

- **Basic Indicator Approach:** Capital charge is calculated as 15% of the average of gross income over the previous three years;
- **Standardised Approach:** Capital charge is calculated as the sum across eight business lines of a percentage (either 12%, 15% or 18%) of the business line average of gross income over the previous three years; and
- **Advanced Measurement Approach** (AMA): This is covered in [CRR Title III Chapter 4]. The capital charge is calculated using an internally generated measure based on internal loss data, external loss data, scenario analysis, business environment and internal control factors.

By providing these three approaches, Basel III (as Basel II) allows banks and their regulators to select the one most appropriate to a bank's size, the complexity of its operations, and the nature of its risks.

7.13.2 Operational Risk AVA

Operational risk AVA takes into account the potential losses that may be incurred as a result of operational risk related to valuation processes. The estimate includes an assessment of valuation positions judged to be at-risk during the balance sheet substantiation process, including those due to legal disputes. Operational risk AVA is calculated as follows (see Figure 7.33):

- Where a bank applies **AMA** for operational risk it may report a **zero** operational risk AVA on condition that it provides evidence that the operational risk AVA is fully accounted for by the AMA calculation.
- Otherwise, the operational risk AVA is calculated as **10%** of the sum of the aggregated category level AVAs for market price uncertainty and close-out costs.

FIGURE 7.33   Approaches to operational risk AVA

Operational risk AVAs are arguably incongruent with the notion of AVAs being designed to estimate a prudent exit value. Arguably, this risk should be capitalised through the operational risk capital charge. In fact, this is the case with operational risk RWAs determined using the AMA approach. However, there is a potential double counting of operational risk where a bank calculates operational risk RWAs using the basic indicator or standardised approaches. Furthermore, it is inconsistent with other capital charges that do not bear an AVA – credit risk in particular.

Finally, the 10% charge is somewhat arbitrary and provides little incentive for a bank to spend resources in enhancing its valuation framework. Arguably, having a fixed charge is incongruent with the degree of sophisticated calculation methodologies to calculate other AVAs – in particular, the market price uncertainty and close-out costs AVAs.

CHAPTER 8

Accounting vs. Regulatory Consolidation

This section covers the accounting consolidation mechanics of investments in non-structured entities (i.e., entities that have sufficient equity and provide the equity investors with voting rights that enable them to make significant decisions relating to the entity's operations) and the interaction between accounting and regulatory consolidation. Understanding the accounting impact of an acquisition or disposal is crucial to understand the regulatory impact of the transaction.

8.1 ACCOUNTING RECOGNITION OF INVESTMENTS IN NON-STRUCTURED ENTITIES

The accounting standard that sets out the guidance for consolidation is IFRS 10 *Consolidated Financial Statements*. The accounting treatment of unconsolidated equity investments in other entities is covered in IFRS 9 *Financial Instruments* and IAS 28 *Investments in Associates*. An investment in equity securities of another company is recognised according to the degree of influence over the investee (see Figure 8.1) as follows:

1. The group has **control** over the investee. Control is regarded as the power to govern the operating and financial policies of the investee so as to obtain benefits from its activities. Usually, control is presumed if the investor holds more than 50% of the voting rights of the investee. The existence and effect of potential voting rights are also considered when assessing whether the group controls the investee. Companies that are controlled by the group are called **subsidiaries**. Subsidiaries are **fully consolidated**.

2. The group has interests in a **joint venture**. A joint venture is a contractual arrangement whereby the group and other parties undertake an economic activity that is subject to joint control, that is when the strategic operating and financial policies require the unanimous consent of the parties sharing control. Joint ventures are accounted for using the **equity consolidation method** (see below). In addition, under IFRS there is another type of joint arrangement called "joint operation" that is proportionally consolidated.

3. The group has **significant influence** over an investee but it is neither a subsidiary nor a joint venture. In this case, the investee is called an **associate**. Significant influence is the power to participate the operating and financial policies of the investee, but without control or joint control over those decisions. Usually significant influence is presumed when the group holds at least 20%, but no more than 50%, of the actual and potential voting rights of the investee. An associate is accounted for in the consolidated financial statements using the **equity method**. Under the equity method the

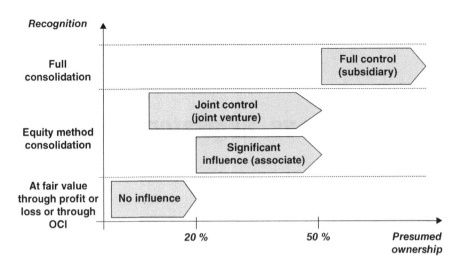

FIGURE 8.1   Accounting recognition of equity investments

investment is originally accounted for at cost. The investment carrying amount increases (decreases) with the profits (losses) of the associate, decreases with the dividends received from the associate and increases (decreases) with the increase (decrease) in the associate's other comprehensive income.

4. The group does not exercise significant influence or control over the investee. This is the usual case when the group holds less than 20% of the actual and potential voting rights of the investee. The investment is then classified under IFRS 9 as held at either **fair value through profit or loss (FVTPL)** or **fair value through other comprehensive income (FVTOCI)**. This is an irrevocable choice on investment date.

   a. The equity investment is classified at FVTPL if it is acquired for the purpose of selling it in the near term (i.e., investment is held for trading). The investment is measured at fair value. Gains and losses arising from changes in fair value are included in profit or loss.

   b. The equity investment is classified at FVTOCI if it is acquired for the purpose of not holding it for trading. The investment is measured at fair value. Gains and losses arising from changes in fair value are included in other comprehensive income (OCI). Dividends received from the investment are recognised in profit or loss.

8.2 ACCOUNTING FOR FULL CONSOLIDATION

Full consolidation purports that the assets and liabilities of the investee will not be combined with the assets and liabilities of the investor, presenting a single economic entity.

8.2.1 Control

The financial information in the consolidated financial statements of a banking group includes the parent company together with its **subsidiaries**. A group's subsidiaries are those entities which it directly or indirectly controls.

Where voting rights are relevant, a group is deemed to have control where it holds, directly or indirectly, more than half of the voting rights – including potential voting rights that are deemed to be substantive – over an entity unless there is evidence that another investor has the practical ability to unilaterally direct the relevant activities, as indicated by one or more of the following factors:

- Another investor has the power over more than half of the voting rights by virtue of an agreement with the group; or
- Another investor has the power to govern the financial and operating policies of the investee under a statute or an agreement; or
- Another investor has the power to appoint or remove the majority of the members of the board of directors or equivalent governing body and the investee is controlled by that board or body; or
- Another investor has the power to cast the majority of votes at meetings of the board of directors or equivalent governing body and control of that entity is by this board or body.

Likewise, a group also assesses existence of control where it does not control the majority of the voting power but has the practical ability to unilaterally direct the relevant activities. This may arise in circumstances where the size and dispersion of holdings of the shareholders give the group the power to direct the activities of the investee.

In other cases, where an entity is *not* governed by voting rights (e.g., an SPV), the assessment of control is more complex and requires greater use of judgment. Control over an SPV is evidenced by a group's power over the relevant activities, its exposure to variable returns from the investee and its ability to affect those returns through its power over the investee:

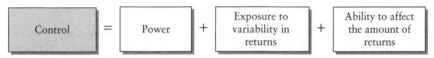

The assessment of control is based on all facts and circumstances and the conclusion is reassessed if there is an indication that there are changes in facts and circumstances. When assessing whether to consolidate an entity, a group evaluates a range of control factors, namely:

- The purpose and design of the entity;
- The relevant activities and how these are determined;
- Whether the group's rights result in the ability to direct the relevant activities;
- Whether the group has exposure or rights to variable returns; and
- Whether the group has the ability to use its power to affect the amount of its returns.

8.2.2 Initial Recognition

Subsidiaries are consolidated from the date on which control is transferred to the group and are deconsolidated from the date that control ceases. On the date the group obtains control of an investee, the following items are calculated:

- The **consideration transferred** for the new subsidiary is measured, including any previously held interest;
- The **identifiable assets and liabilities** of the new subsidiary are identified and fair valued;
- The **non-controlling interest** is calculated; and
- **Goodwill** is calculated.

Consideration Transferred   The consideration transferred is the cost of the acquisition. It is measured at the fair value of the consideration given, including:

- Any cash or non cash (e.g., equity instruments) transferred;
- Any **contingent consideration**. It is recognised and measured at fair value on acquisition date, irrespective of the probability of payment. A contingent consideration is remeasured at every balance sheet date, with any changes recognised in profit or loss;
- Any previously held equity interest in the acquiree; and
- Any liabilities incurred or assumed.

Acquisition-related **transaction costs** are not part of the consideration transferred, and are expensed in the period in which they are incurred and the related services are received. Commonly these costs relate to transaction advisory fees paid to the investment banks, lawyers and accountants.

Identifiable Assets and Liabilities   An asset or liability, to qualify for recognition, should meet the following IFRS definitions:

- An **asset** is a "resource controlled by the entity as a result of past events and from which future economic benefits are expected to flow to the entity";
- A **liability** is a "present obligation of the entity arising from past events, the settlement of which is expected to result in an outflow from the entity of resources embodying economic benefits".

In addition, an asset is **identifiable** if it either:

- Is separable: that is, capable of being separated or divided from the entity and sold, transferred, licensed, rented or exchanged, either individually or together with a related contract, identifiable asset or liability, regardless of whether the entity intends to do so; or
- Arises from contractual or other legal rights, regardless of whether those rights are transferable or separable from the entity or from other rights and obligations.

Some assets and liabilities are identified as an exception to the recognition and fair value measurement principles. These include contingent liabilities, income taxes, employee benefits and indemnification assets.

Non-controlling Interest and Goodwill   IFRS 10 defines a non-controlling interest ("NCI") as "equity in a subsidiary not attributable, directly or indirectly, to a parent". IFRS allows the buyer to value a NCI at either the minority's proportionate share of the net identifiable assets (**"partial goodwill"**), or at fair value – recognising goodwill on the non-controlling share (**"full goodwill"**).

The excess of the aggregate of the cost of an acquisition and any non-controlling interests in the acquiree over the group's share of the fair value of the identifiable net assets acquired is recorded as goodwill. If the aggregate of the acquisition cost and the non-controlling interest is below the fair value of the identifiable net assets and the fair value of previously held equity interests (i.e., **negative goodwill**), a gain is reported in profit or loss by the acquirer.

Goodwill is an indefinite life asset, and as such, is tested annually for impairment. It is measured as the excess of (A) over (B), where (A) is the sum of:

- The fair value of consideration transferred to gain control over the acquiree; and
- Any recognised amount of NCI

and (B) is the recognised amount of the acquiree's identifiable net assets.

Goodwill	=	Fair value of consideration transferred	+	Amount of NCI	−	Fair value of identifiable net assets

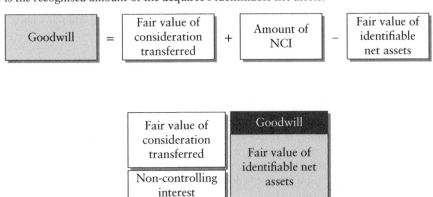

Example: Goodwill and Non-controlling Interests

This example illustrates how goodwill is determined when a non-controlling interest ("NCI") is present in an acquisition. Assume Bank A acquires 75% of Bank B for EUR 1.3 billion. The fair value of the identifiable net assets and liabilities is determined to be EUR 1.2 billion.

Goodwill resulting from a business combination is calculated by comparing the consideration paid plus the value of the NCI to the fair value of the identifiable net assets, as follows:

$$\boxed{\text{Goodwill}} = \boxed{\begin{array}{c}\text{Consideration}\\\text{paid}\end{array}} + \boxed{\begin{array}{c}\text{Value of non-}\\\text{controlling}\\\text{interest}\end{array}} - \boxed{\begin{array}{c}\text{Fair value of}\\\text{identifiable net}\\\text{assets}\end{array}}$$

When determining the value attributed to the NCI in an acquiree, IFRS 3 provides the acquirer with a choice: to measure it either at the non-controlling interests' proportionate share of the acquiree's identifiable net assets ("partial goodwill" or "proportionate share method") or at fair value ("full goodwill" or "fair value method"). This election is made on a transaction-by-transaction basis. The elected choice in turn affects the value attributed to goodwill, a residual amount.

The acquirer – Bank A – can choose to measure the NCI based on the fair value of the identifiable net assets acquired (**partial goodwill**), or EUR 300 mn (= 1.2 bn × 25%). In our case, this would result in goodwill of EUR 400 million (= 1.3 bn + 300 mn − 1.2 bn) being recognised.

Alternatively, Bank A can measure the NCI at fair value (**full goodwill**), that is, EUR 433 million (= 1.3 bn / 75% × 25%). This method recognises goodwill on the NCI. This would result in goodwill of EUR 533 mn (= 1.3 bn + 433 mn − 1.2 bn) being recognised. The fair value measurement of the NCI may require the use of complex valuation techniques, an important drawback.

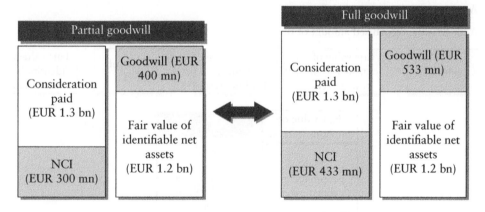

Accounting Perspective

From an accounting perspective and compared to the partial goodwill method, the full goodwill method results in a larger shareholders' equity at the acquisition date, implying a lower level of leverage. However, any subsequent goodwill impairment charge would be higher than under the partial goodwill method, with a negative impact on reported profit or loss.

In jurisdictions where goodwill is tax-deductible, electing the full goodwill method results in a larger deductibility, a remarkable advantage.

Finally, the full goodwill method would reduce any potential decrease in bank A's shareholders' equity resulting from a subsequent buyout of the NCI.

Regulatory Perspective

Goodwill is deducted from CET1 capital. As the partial goodwill method results in a lower amount of goodwill than the full goodwill method, in theory it is a more advantageous method from a regulatory capital perspective. Albeit I agree with this conclusion, this is only part of the story. The NCI would be eligible for consolidated CET1 capital, but recognition may be limited

(continued)

(in Chapter 9 it is explained that surplus capital of a subsidiary related to the NCI does not receive recognition on regulatory consolidation).

The use of the full goodwill method exposes the banking group to larger goodwill impairment charges. Whilst an impairment would have a negative impact in consolidated CET1 through consolidated profit or loss, this impact would be offset with a corresponding lower deduction of goodwill from CET1 capital. Thus, from a CET1 perspective, goodwill impairment charges have a neutral effect. However, the negative impact on profit or loss of a large impairment charge may limit the capacity of the bank to distribute dividends if, for instance, the statutory laws of the bank contain a limitation on dividend distributions in the case of a reported loss.

Step Acquisitions   In business combinations achieved in stages ("**step acquisitions**"), a previously held equity interest in the acquiree is remeasured to its acquisition-date fair value and the resulting gain or loss, if any, is recognised in profit or loss. In other words, it is as if the previously held interest was sold at fair value and bought back at such fair value. Amounts recognised in prior periods in other comprehensive income associated with the previously held investment would be recognised on the same basis as would be required if the group had directly disposed of the previously held equity interest.

In a step acquisition, goodwill is measured as the excess of (A) over (B):

Where (A) is the sum of:

- The fair value of consideration transferred to gain control over the acquiree;
- The fair value of any previously held investment; and
- Any recognised amount of NCI.

And (B) is the recognised amount of the acquiree's identifiable net assets.

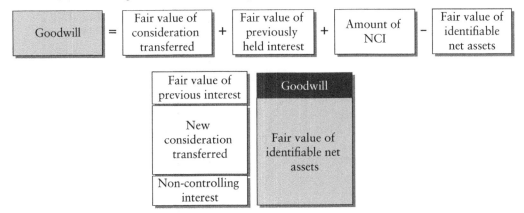

8.2.3 Subsequent Recognition: Consolidation

Subsidiaries should be consolidated from the date control is obtained to the date control is lost. The objective of consolidated financial statements is to present the information for a parent and its subsidiaries as if they were the financial statements of a single economic entity. The process of consolidation of subsidiaries comprises the following key steps:

1. Because the consolidated accounts are prepared under uniform accounting policies, the subsidiaries' financial statements are adjusted to conform to IFRS guidelines and group accounting policies;
2. Financial statements of subsidiaries are adjusted so they are drawn up to the same reporting date;
3. All the assets, liabilities, equity, income, expenses and cash flows of the parent and its subsidiaries are combined, line by line. Foreign subsidiaries are translated into the group's presentation currency;

4. The carrying amount of the parent's investment in each subsidiary and the parent's portion of equity of each subsidiary are eliminated. Any related goodwill and other business combination-related adjustments are recognised;
5. Profit or loss and OCI are allocated between the parent and the non-controlling interests (NCIs). NCIs are shown in the consolidated balance sheet as a separate component of equity, which is distinct from the group's shareholders' equity;
6. Changes in the ownership interest in subsidiaries which do not result in a loss of control are treated as transactions between equity holders and are reported in share premium (i.e., additional paid-in capital); and
7. All intragroup assets, liabilities, equity, income, expenses and cash flows relating to transactions between group entities are eliminated in full.

Uniform Accounting Policies For consolidation purposes, the financial statements of each group entity must be adjusted so they are fully IFRS-compliant and prepared using the parent's (or group's) accounting policies.

Same Reporting Date The basic requirement of IFRS 10 is that the financial statements of each group entity are drawn up to the same reporting date for consolidation purposes. Where reporting dates differ, additional financial information is prepared for consolidation purposes, unless it is impractical to obtain the additional information.

Elimination of Investment in Subsidiary The single entity concept requires that the parent's investment in each subsidiary is eliminated on consolidation. The following steps are implemented simultaneously:

- The investment in subsidiary is offset against the subsidiary's share capital and pre-acquisition reserves;
- Goodwill is recognised net of impairment. Goodwill is tested annually for impairment, by applying the requirements of IAS 36 *Impairment of Assets*;
- Fair value adjustments to assets, liabilities and contingent liabilities made in the business combination are reflected, including their income statement effects;
- Non-controlling interests are recognised; and
- Changes in ownership without loss of control are reflected.

Allocation of Comprehensive Income and Equity to Non-controlling Interests As discussed above, the basic consolidation process involves the aggregation of the assets and liabilities, income and expenses if the individual group entities. Therefore, when the group does not hold the whole of the share capital of a subsidiary, an adjustment is required to take account of the interests of the outside shareholders. NCIs are represented in the consolidated balance sheet and profit or loss, as shown in Figure 8.2.

NCI is included as a separate item in consolidated shareholders' equity, representing the equity in subsidiaries not attributable, directly or indirectly, to the parent. It comprises the part attributed to third parties of each subsidiary share capital, retained earnings and other comprehensive income (OCI). As a highly simplified example, imagine that a subsidiary bank is 60% owned by its parent bank, and that the subsidiary shareholders' equity comprises EUR 10 billion of share capital (including share premium), EUR 6 billion of retained earnings and EUR 3 billion of OCI. The carrying amount of the NCI in consolidated shareholders' equity would be EUR 7.6 billion [= 40% × (10 bn + 6 bn + 3 bn)], as shown in Figure 8.3.

Consolidated profit or loss is split between the shareholders of the parent entity and the NCI. The net income attributable to NCIs is separately disclosed on the face of the consolidated profit or loss

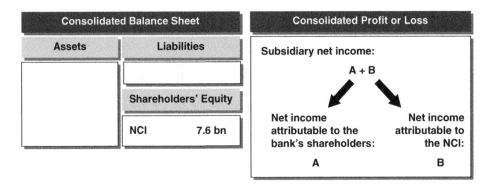

FIGURE 8.2   Representation of a non-controlling interest in a group's financial statements

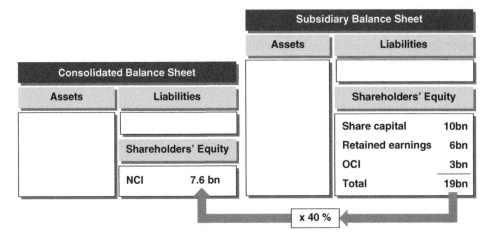

FIGURE 8.3   Simplified calculation of a non-controlling interest

statement. IFRS 10 does not specify any particular method for attributing net earnings between these two parties. If there are contractual arrangements that determine the attribution of earnings, such as a profit-sharing agreement, the attribution specified by the arrangement should be considered if it is determined to be substantive. If there are no such contractual arrangements, the relative ownership interests in the subsidiary should be used if the parent's ownership and the NCI ownership in the assets and liabilities are proportional. For example, if the controlling interest owns 60% of the entity and the NCI owns 40%, then 60% of the earnings should be allocated to the controlling interest and 40% to the NCI.

Elimination of Intercompany Items   One important step in the consolidation process is to eliminate in full intragroup assets, liabilities, equity, income, expenses and cash flows relating to transactions between group entities. Gains or losses resulting from intragroup transactions that are included in the carrying amount of assets are also eliminated. Intragroup losses may indicate an impairment that requires recognition in the consolidated financial statements.

As consolidated financial statements are based on the assumption that they represent the financial position and operating results of a single economic entity, such statements shall not include items among the entities in the consolidated group. Figure 8.4 shows the main items eliminated on

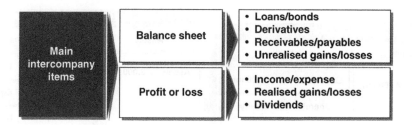

FIGURE 8.4 Main intercompany items in banking

consolidation of banking entities. For example, a liability due by one group entity to another is set off against the corresponding asset in the other group entity's financial statements; income generated by one group entity from another is excluded both from income and expense in the consolidated profit or loss; dividends received from a subsidiary should be excluded from consolidated profit or loss and set off against the corresponding movement in equity. IFRS provides for no distinction between wholly owned and partially owned entities with respect to the need for the elimination of intercompany transactions. In both cases, all transactions with members of the consolidated group are considered internal transactions that must be eliminated fully, regardless of the percentage ownership.

The treatment of tax requires substantial care, especially on temporary differences that arise from the elimination of profits and losses resulting from intragroup transactions. In addition, some intragroup transactions may be classified and measured differently on consolidation.

8.3 WORKING EXAMPLE ON CONSOLIDATION

The purpose of this simple example is to review, from an accounting perspective, the full consolidation process.

8.3.1 Consolidation on Gain of Control

Let us assume that Megabank acquired 70% of the ordinary shares of Trustbank for EUR 1.4 billion, gaining control of Trustbank, which became its only subsidiary, as shown in Figure 8.5. A subsidiary is an entity that is controlled by another entity and, as a result, is fully consolidated.

The book value of Trustbank's net assets on the day control was achieved by Megabank was EUR 1.4 billion, comprising EUR 4.7 billion of assets and EUR 3.3 billion of liabilities. Trustbank's

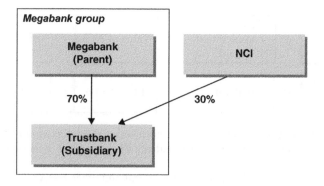

FIGURE 8.5 Structure of the Megabank group

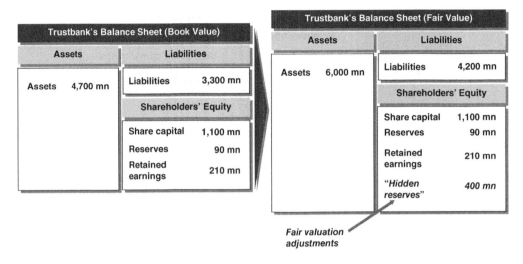

FIGURE 8.6 Book vs. fair values of Trustbank's net assets

shareholders' equity comprised EUR 1.1 billion of share capital and EUR 300 million of reserves (including retained earnings), as shown in Figure 8.6.

Pursuant to IFRS 3, Megabank performed a fair valuation of Trustbank's identifiable assets and liabilities, estimating that their net fair value was EUR 1.8 billion, split between EUR 6 billion of assets and EUR 4.2 billion of liabilities. Therefore, fair value adjustments totalled EUR 400 million (= 1.8 bn − 1.4 bn), as shown in Figure 8.6.

The non-controlling interest (NCI) was the equity in Trustbank (the subsidiary) not attributable, directly or indirectly, to Megabank (the parent). In our case, the NCI was the 30% interest in Trustbank not owned by Megabank. Entities have the option of measuring the NCI at fair value or at its proportionate share of the recognised amount of the acquiree's identifiable net assets at the acquisition date. This election can be chosen on a transaction-by-transaction basis and cannot be changed subsequently.

Non-controlling Interest Measured Using the Full Goodwill Method   Imagine that Megabank chose to measure the NCI at fair value for this acquisition (the full goodwill method). The value of the NCI amounted to EUR 0.6 billion (= 1.4 bn / 70% × 30%). Since the NCI was recorded at fair value, goodwill was effectively recognised for both the controlling and non-controlling interest. Goodwill was calculated as follows:

Goodwill	=	Fair value of consideration paid	+	Value of NCI	−	Fair value of 100% of identifiable net assets
Goodwill = EUR 0.2 bn	=	EUR 1.4 bn	+	EUR 0.6 bn	−	EUR 1.8 bn

Assuming that the fair value of the identifiable net assets was split between EUR 6 billion of assets and EUR 4.2 billion of liabilities, the effect on Megabank's balance sheet of the acquisition can be seen in Figure 8.7.

An interesting fact was that Trustbank's share capital and other reserves were not recognised in the consolidated balance sheet.

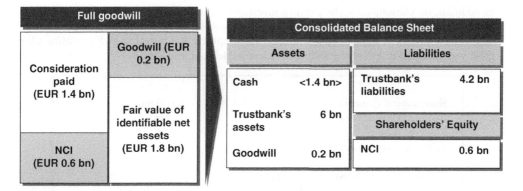

FIGURE 8.7 Megabank's balance sheet after acquisition

Non-controlling Interest Measured Using the Partial Goodwill Method Imagine that Megabank chose instead to measure the NCI at its proportionate share of the recognised amount of the acquiree's identifiable net assets for the acquisition (the partial goodwill method). Under the partial goodwill method, the proportionate share of the NCI – EUR 540 million – was calculated by multiplying (i) the fair value of 100% of the net identifiable assets (EUR 1.8 bn) and (ii) the share of the NCI (30%):

$$
\boxed{\begin{array}{c}\text{NCI}\\ \text{(EUR 540 mn)}\end{array}} = \boxed{\begin{array}{c}\text{Percentage}\\ \text{ownership}\\ (30\%)\end{array}} \times \boxed{\begin{array}{c}\text{Fair value of 100\%}\\ \text{of identifiable net}\\ \text{assets (EUR 1.8 bn)}\end{array}}
$$

Goodwill was calculated as follows:

$$
\boxed{\begin{array}{c}\text{Goodwill}\\ \text{(EUR 140 mn)}\end{array}} = \boxed{\begin{array}{c}\text{Fair value of}\\ \text{consideration}\\ \text{paid}\\ \text{(EUR 1.4 bn)}\end{array}} + \boxed{\begin{array}{c}\text{NCI}\\ (540\ \text{mn})\end{array}} - \boxed{\begin{array}{c}\text{Fair value of 100\%}\\ \text{of identifiable net}\\ \text{assets}\\ \text{(EUR 1.8 bn)}\end{array}}
$$

Next I cover the accounting entries necessary to record the acquisition on a consolidated basis.

1. To record the acquisition on Megabank's stand-alone financial statements:

Investment in Trustbank (Asset)	1,400 mn
Cash (Asset)	1,400 mn

2. Trustbank's assets, liabilities and equity were added to those of Megabank (Trustbank's assets and liabilities have been aggregated in one entry for simplicity, but in reality each net identifiable asset and liability was individually recognised):

Trustbank's assets and liabilities (Assets & Liabilities)	1,400 mn
Share capital (Equity)	1,100 mn
Retained earnings (Equity)	210 mn
Reserves (Equity)	90 mn

3. In addition, on consolidation the parent's investment was eliminated against Trustbank's share capital and reserves, and fair value adjustments, goodwill and NCI were recognised (fair value adjustments have been aggregated in one entry for simplicity, but in reality each fair value adjustment was allocated to its corresponding net identifiable asset and liability):

Share capital (Equity)	1,100 mn
Retained earnings (Equity)	210 mn
Reserves (Equity)	90 mn
Fair value adjustments (Assets & Liabilities)	400 mn
Goodwill	140 mn
Investment in Trustbank (Asset)	1,400 mn
Non-controlling interest (Equity)	540 mn

The elimination of Trustbank's share capital implied that only Megabank's share capital showed up in the consolidated balance sheet. Trustbank's pre-acquisition retained earnings and other reserves were eliminated in full. NCI was recognised to incorporate the fact that 30% of the net assets of Trustbank were not owned by Megabank. The investment in Trustbank was recognised in Megabank's stand-alone balance sheet and had to be eliminated as Megabank's share of the net assets of Trustbank were consolidated.

Assuming that the fair value of the identifiable net assets was split between EUR 6 billion of assets and EUR 4.2 billion of liabilities, the effect on Megabank's consolidated balance sheet is shown in Figure 8.8.

As mentioned above, Trustbank's share capital and other reserves were not recognised in the consolidated balance sheet, as they were eliminated on consolidation.

8.3.2 Subsequent Consolidation

Let us assume that a year elapsed following the gain of control and that the Megabank group had to prepare its consolidated financial statements. Let us assume that the financial statements of both Megabank and Trustbank were produced following uniform accounting policies and had identical reporting dates.

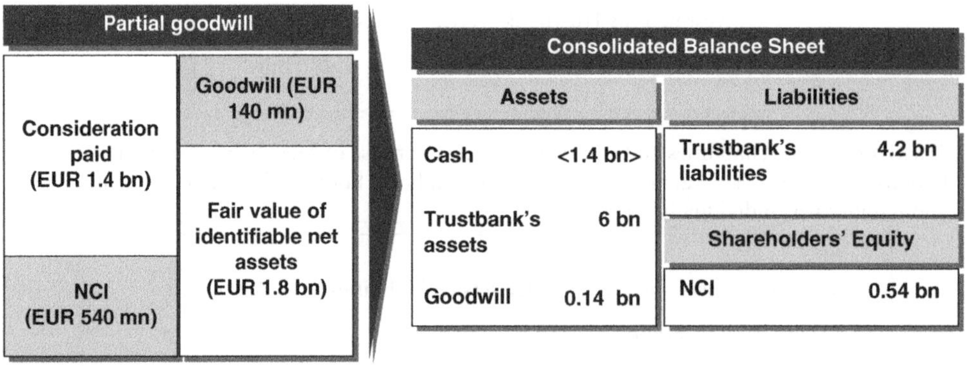

FIGURE 8.8   Megabank's consolidated balance sheet

Aggregation of Like-items   The first step in the consolidation process was to combine 100% like items of assets, liabilities, equity, income, gains, expenses, losses and cash flows from the financial statements of Megabank and Trustbank, resulting in the statement of financial position outlined in Table 8.1.

TABLE 8.1   Aggregation of Megabank's and Trustbank's financial statement items

Financial Statement Item	Megabank (EUR mn)	Trustbank (EUR mn)	Total (EUR mn)
Profit or loss:			
Net interest and fee income	26,300	4,238	30,538
Net trading income	2,050	310	2,360
Operating expenses	−26,700	−4,300	−31,000
Tax expenses	−496	−110	−606
Total profit or loss	**1,154**	**138**	**1,292**
Assets:			
Derivatives	7,450	410	7,860
Investment in Trustbank	1,400		1,400
Fair value adjustments			
Goodwill			
Other assets	76,612	4,790	81,402
Total assets	**85,462**	**5,200**	**90,662**
Liabilities:			
Derivatives	7,350	430	7,780
Other liabilities	36,650	3,222	39,872
Total liabilities	**44,000**	**3,652**	**47,652**
Shareholders' equity:			
Share capital	22,400	1,100	23,500
Retained earnings	10,300	210	10,510
Other reserves	7,608	100	7,708
Profit or loss	1,154	138	1,292
Total Shareholders' Equity	**41,462**	**1,548**	**43,010**

Let us assume that the following events occurred during the year:

- Megabank and Trustbank entered into an interest rate swap whose fair value (excluding accrual of settlement amounts) at the end of the year was EUR 10 million, a positive amount for Megabank and, thus, a negative amount for Trustbank. The accrual of the swap's next settlement amount was EUR 2 million to be paid by Trustbank.
- Trustbank's net earnings during the year were EUR 138 million. Trustbank suffered a double loss stemming from the derivative: a EUR 10 million loss due to its mark-to-market and a EUR 2 million loss due to the accrual of the settlement amount. The effects of the swap on Megabank's financials were the opposite.
- Trustbank distributed a EUR 60 million cash dividend, of which Megabank received EUR 42 million while other investors received EUR 18 million.

Elimination of Investment, and Recognition of NCI and Goodwill   The second step in the consolidation process was to eliminate the investment in subsidiary, by replicating the entries performed on the date control was achieved. The entries eliminated the parent's investment and recognised the NCI against Trustbank's share of initial capital and reserves, fair value adjustments and goodwill:

Share capital (Equity)	1,100 mn
Retained earnings (Equity)	210 mn
Other reserves (Equity)	90 mn
Fair value adjustments (Assets & Liabilities)	400 mn
Goodwill	140 mn
Investment in Trustbank (Asset)	1,400 mn
Non-controlling interest (Equity)	540 mn

The entries were recorded on the consolidation worksheet as shown in Table 8.2.

TABLE 8.2   Elimination entries performed to the combined financial statements

Financial Statement Item	Megabank (EUR mn)	Trustbank (EUR mn)	Initial Elimination Entries
Profit or loss:			
Net interest and fee income	26,300	4,238	
Net trading income	2,050	310	
Operating expenses	<26,700>	<4,300>	
Tax expenses	<496>	<110>	
Total profit or loss	1,154	138	
Assets:			
Derivatives	7,450	410	
Investment in Trustbank	1,400		<1,400>

Financial Statement Item	Megabank (EUR mn)	Trustbank (EUR mn)	Initial Elimination Entries
Fair value adjustments			400
Goodwill			140
Other assets	76,612	4,790	
Total assets	**85,462**	**5,200**	
Liabilities:			
Derivatives	7,350	430	
Other liabilities	36,650	3,222	
Total liabilities	**44,000**	**3,652**	
Shareholders' equity:			
Share capital	22,400	1,100	<1,100>
Retained earnings	10,300	210	<210>
Other reserves	7,608	100	<90>
Profit or loss	1,154	138	
Non-controlling interest			540
Total Shareholders' Equity	**41,462**	**1,548**	

Calculation of the NCI   The third step in the consolidation process involved calculating the new carrying amount of the NCI. Because the financial statements were fully aggregated, in order to show Megabank's real ownership, the amount of Trustbank's net assets not owned by Megabank was calculated and reported as NCI.

The NCI was not remeasured to fair value following initial recognition. Initially, the NCI – EUR 540 million – represented 30% of the fair value of Trustbank's equity:

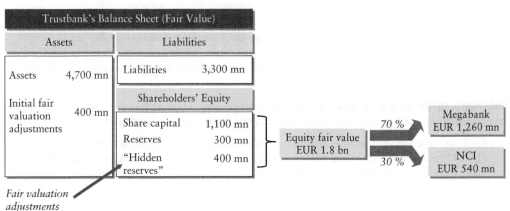

At the end of the first year, the NCI was allocated its 30% share of Trustbank's shareholders' equity, including its share of the initial fair valuation adjustments, as follows:

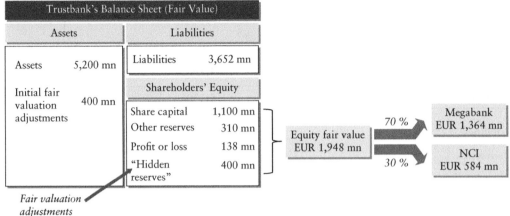

NCI's carrying amount – EUR 584 million (= 330 mn + 41 mn + 93 mn + 120 mn) – comprised: (i) its EUR 330 million (= 30% × 1,100 mn) share of Trustbank's share capital plus (ii) its EUR 41 million (= 30% × 138 mn) share of Trustbank's profit or loss plus (iii) its EUR 93 million (= 30% × 310 mn) share of Trustbank's OCI plus (iv) its EUR 120 million (= 30% × 400 mn) share of the initial fair value adjustments.

NCI's carrying amount could be calculated as well, as the sum of: (i) the EUR 540 million original NCI plus (ii) its EUR 41 million share of Trustbank's profit or loss plus (iii) its EUR 21 million (= 30% × 70 mn) share of the change in OCI less (iv) its EUR 18 million (= 30% × 60 mn) share of distributed dividends, or EUR 584 million (= 540 mn + 41 mn + 21 mn – 18 mn).

The change in the NCI since the date when control was achieved was EUR 44 million (= 584 mn – 540 mn), of which EUR 3 million and EUR 41 million were allocated to "other reserves" and "profit or loss" respectively.

NCI was shown as a separate line in the consolidated shareholders' equity section of the consolidated balance sheet. Additionally in consolidated profit or loss, the amount of Trustbank's profit or loss attributed to the NCI was reported as a separate line.

The journal entries to adjust the NCI were as follows:

Other reserves (Equity)	3 mn
Profit or loss (Equity)	41 mn
Non-controlling interest (Equity)	44 mn

The adjustment had the following effects on the consolidation worksheet as shown in Table 8.3.

Elimination of Intragroup Transactions   The next step in the consolidation process was to eliminate in full the intragroup transactions (assets and liabilities, equity, income, expenses and cash flows), as follows:

- Earnings were adjusted on consolidation to eliminate the effects of the intragroup dividend. The EUR 42 million cash dividend was unwound: Trustbank's retained earnings were increased by EUR 42 million while Megabank's dividend income was reduced by that amount.

■ The financial statements were adjusted on consolidation to eliminate the effects of the intragroup swap. Megabank's EUR 10 million swap position on its asset side were eliminated against Trustbank's equivalent position on its liability side. In addition, Megabank's earnings were reduced by EUR 12 million, while Trustbank's earnings were increased by that amount.

TABLE 8.3 Non-controlling interest adjustment

Financial Statement Item	Megabank (EUR mn)	Trustbank (EUR mn)	NCI Adjustment
Profit or loss:			
Net interest and fee income	26,300	4,238	
Net trading income	2,050	310	
Operating expenses	<26,700>	<4,300>	
Tax expenses	<496>	<110>	
Total profit or loss	**1,154**	**138**	
Assets:			
Derivatives	7,450	410	
Investment in Trustbank	1,400		
Fair value adjustments			
Goodwill			
Other assets	76,612	4,790	
Total assets	**85,462**	**5,200**	
Liabilities:			
Derivatives	7,350	430	
Other liabilities	36,650	3,222	
Total liabilities	**44,000**	**3,652**	
Shareholders' equity:			
Share capital	22,400	1,100	
Retained earnings	10,300	210	
Other reserves	7,608	100	<3>
Profit or loss	1,154	138	<41>
Non-controlling interest			44
Total Shareholders' Equity	**41,462**	**1,548**	

The accounting entries to recognise the elimination of the intragroup transactions:

Dividend income (Profit or Loss)	42 mn
Retained earnings (Equity)	42 mn
Swap (Asset)	10 mn
Trading gain (Profit or Loss)	12 mn
Swap (Liability)	10 mn
Trading loss (Profit or Loss)	12 mn

The resulting consolidation worksheet is shown in Table 8.4.

TABLE 8.4 Consequent consolidation worksheet

Financial Statement Item	Megabank (EUR mn)	Trustbank (EUR mn)	Initial Elimination Entries	NCI Adjustment	Intragroup Dividend	Intragroup Swap	Total (EUR mn)
Profit or loss:							
Net interest & fee income	26,300	4,238			<42>		30,496
Net trading income	2,050	310				<10> + 10	2,360
Operating expenses	<26,700>	<4,300>					<31,000>
Tax expenses	<496>	<110>					<606>
Total profit or loss	**1,154**	**138**			**<42>**		**1,250**
Assets:							
Derivatives	7,450	410				<10>	7,850
Investment in Trustbank	1,400		<1,400>				0
Fair value adjustments			400				400
Goodwill			140				140
Other assets	76,612	4,790					81,402
Total assets	**85,462**	**5,200**	**<860>**			**<10>**	**89,792**
Liabilities:							
Derivatives	7,350	430				<10>	7,770
Other liabilities	36,650	3,222					39,872
Total liabilities	**44,000**	**3,652**				**<10>**	**47,642**

Financial Statement Item	Megabank (EUR mn)	Trustbank (EUR mn)	Initial Elimination Entries	NCI Adjustment	Intragroup Dividend	Intragroup Swap	Total (EUR mn)
Shareholders' equity:							
Share capital	22,400	1,100	<1,100>				22,400
Retained earnings	10,300	210	<210>		42		10,342
Other reserves	7,608	100	<90>	<3>			7,615
Profit or loss	1,154	138		<41>	<42>		1,209
Non-controlling interest			540	44			584
Total Shareholders' Equity	41,462	1,548	<860>				42,150

TABLE 8.5 Consolidated profit or loss statement

Financial Statement Item	(EUR mn)
Profit or loss:	
Net interest & fee income	30,496
Net trading income	2,360
Operating expenses	<31,000>
Tax expenses	<606>
Net income	**1,250**
Net income attributable to non-controlling interests	**41**
Net income attributable to Megabank's shareholders	**1,209**

Trustbank's profit or loss was attributed to Megabank and to the NCI. The relative ownership interests of Megabank and the NCI in Trustbank were used as the parent's ownership (70%) and the NCI ownership (30%) in the assets and liabilities were proportional. As a result, the profit or loss attributable to Megabank was EUR 97 million (= 138 mn × 70%) while the EUR 41 million remainder was attributed to the NCI. As a result the consolidated profit or loss statement had the profile outlined in Table 8.5.

8.4 LOSS OF CONTROL

An investee ceases to be to be consolidated in a group as a result of the investor losing control over the investee. This section covers the accounting implications of consolidation discontinuance.

8.4.1 Recognition of Loss of Control

A group may lose control of a subsidiary as a result of a transaction that changes its ownership level. Commonly control is lost because the parent bank sells ordinary shares of the subsidiary or because the subsidiary issues new ordinary shares not subscribed by the parent bank. On the date that control of a subsidiary is lost, the group performs the following accounting actions:

- Derecognises the assets (including attributable goodwill) and liabilities of the subsidiary at their carrying amounts;
- Derecognises the carrying amount of any non-controlling interests in the former subsidiary (including any components in accumulated other comprehensive income attributable to them);
- Recognises the fair value of the consideration received and any distribution of the shares of the subsidiary to owners in their capacity as owners;
- Recognises any investment retained in the former subsidiary at its fair value;
- Recognises any resulting difference of the above items as a gain or loss in the profit or loss statement; and
- Reclassifies to the consolidated profit or loss (or transferred directly to retained earnings if required by other IFRSs) any amounts recognised in prior periods in other comprehensive income in relation to that subsidiary.

8.4.2 Working Example of Loss of Control

Let us assume that Megabank originally owned 60% of the ordinary shares in Banktrust. Imagine further that, at a later stage, Megabank disposed of a 15% interest in Banktrust in exchange for a EUR 1.5 billion cash consideration and, thus, lost control over Banktrust.

At the date control was lost, the fair value of the remaining 45% investment was estimated to be EUR 4 billion, and the carrying amount of the net assets of the subsidiary, including goodwill, was 7 billion. Other comprehensive income included the following amounts related to the subsidiary (net of amounts allocated to NCI):

- Foreign currency translation reserve of EUR 240 million; and
- Other reserves of EUR 90 million.

The amount of NCI in the consolidated financial statements of Megabank was EUR 2.8 billion (= 7 bn × 40%). The carrying amount of NCI included the following amounts that were recognised in OCI before being allocated to NCI:

- Foreign currency translation reserve of EUR 160 million (= 240 mn / 60% × 40%); and
- Other reserves of EUR 60 million (= 90 mn / 60% × 40%).

Megabank recorded the following entries to reflect the loss of control over Banktrust on the day control was lost:

Cash (Asset)	1,500 mn
NCI (Equity)	2,800 mn
Foreign currency translation reserve (Equity)	240 mn
Other reserves (Equity)	90 mn
Investment in Banktrust (Asset)	4,000 mn
Net assets of Banktrust, including goodwill	7,000 mn
Gain on disposal (Profit or loss)	1,630 mn

The EUR 1,630 million recognised in profit or loss represented (i) the increase in the fair value of the retained 45% of EUR 850 million ($= 4\,\text{bn} - 7\,\text{bn} \times 45\%$), plus (ii) the gain on the disposal of the 15% interest of EUR 450 million ($= 1.5\,\text{bn} - 7\,\text{bn} \times 15\%$), plus (iii) the reclassification from OCI of the two reserves of EUR 330 million ($= 240\,\text{mn} + 90\,\text{mn}$). It was as if Megabank had sold all its investment in Trustbank at fair value and repurchased its remaining 45% holding.

Assuming that subsequently the remaining interest in Banktrust was treated as an associate, the fair value of EUR 4 billion represented the initial carrying amount of the investment in Banktrust as an associate. Figure 8.9 depicts Megabank's balance sheet after the loss of control.

8.5 THE EQUITY METHOD – ASSOCIATES

This section covers the accounting recognition in an investor's financial statements of an investee categorised as an associate.

8.5.1 Equity Method of Consolidation – Associates

Equity accounting is the method that is used to reflect investors' interests in "**associates**" or in joint ventures. An associate is an entity in which a group has significant influence, but not a controlling interest, over the operating and financial management policy decisions of the entity. Significant influence is generally presumed when a group holds between 20% and 50% of the investee's voting rights.

Consolidated Balance Sheet			
Assets		**Liabilities**	
Assets of Banktrust	36.3 bn	Liabilties of Banktrust	30.0 bn
Goodwill	0.7 bn	**Shareholders' Equity**	
		NCI	2.8 bn
		OCI of Banktrust	0.33 bn

Consolidated Balance Sheet			
Assets		**Liabilities**	
Cash	1.5 bn		
Investment in Banktrust (associate)	4.0 bn	**Shareholders' Equity**	
		P&L	1.63 bn

FIGURE 8.9 Megabank's balance sheet after loss of control over Banktrust

The existence and effect of potential voting rights that are currently exercisable or convertible are considered in assessing whether a group has significant influence. Among the other factors that are considered in determining whether a group has significant influence are representation on the board of directors and material intercompany transactions. The existence of these factors could require the application of the equity method of accounting for a particular investment even though a group's investment is less than 20% of the investee's voting stock.

Initial Recognition   IFRS requires that an investment in an associate is initially recognised at **cost,** stated as one line item. Cost is the fair value of consideration paid by the acquirer – commonly the purchase price and other costs directly attributable to the acquisition or issuance of the asset such as professional fees for legal services, transfer taxes and other transaction costs.

IFRS requires that when an entity acquires an associate, fair values are attributed to the investee's identifiable assets and liabilities. These fair values are ascertained in accordance with the principles of IFRS 3 *Business Combinations.*

On the acquisition date any difference between the cost of the investment and the bank's share of the fair values of the associate's identifiable assets and liabilities acquired is recognised as goodwill and is accounted for as follows:

- Goodwill (i.e., positive goodwill) relating to an associate is included in the carrying amount of the investment. In other words, goodwill is not separately recognised and forms part of the cost of the investment.
- **Negative goodwill** is included as income as part of the investor's share of the associate's profit or loss in the period in which the investment is acquired. Negative goodwill does not form part of the cost of the investment.

> If a group previously held an equity interest in an entity (for example, recognised at fair value through OCI) and subsequently gained significant influence, the previously held equity interest is remeasured to fair value and any gain or loss is recognised in consolidated profit or loss. Any amounts previously recognised in other comprehensive income associated with the equity interest would be reclassified to the consolidated profit or loss at the date the group gains significant influence, as if the group had disposed of the previously held equity interest.

Subsequent Recognition   Adjustments similar to those made generally on the consolidation of subsidiaries are made when the associates are incorporated into the group's consolidated financial statements. The types of adjustments that may be necessary include:

- Recognising goodwill and dealing with fair value adjustments arising on the associate's acquisition;
- Making adjustments to conform the associate's financial statements to IFRS guidelines; and
- Eliminating the effects of transactions with the associate. For example, eliminating the group's share in the associate's profits and losses resulting from intragroup financial instruments.

Under the equity method:

- The carrying amount of the investment is increased or decreased to recognise the group's share of the profit or loss of the associate after the date of acquisition;
- Any distributions (e.g., dividends) received from the associate reduce the investment's carrying amount;
- The bank's share of the profit or loss of the associate is adjusted for the effect of any fair value adjustments recognised upon initial recognition and is recognised in the group's profit or loss statement;

■ Adjustments to the associate's carrying amount may also be necessary for changes in the group's proportionate interest in the associate that arises from changes in the associate's other comprehensive income (OCI), that have not been recognised in the associate's profit or loss. Such changes will include those arising, for example, from the revaluation of investments at fair value through OCI and from foreign exchange translation differences. The bank's share of such changes is recognised directly in the bank's OCI.

At each balance sheet date, the group assesses whether there is any objective evidence that the investment in the associate is **impaired**. As goodwill is not reported separately, it is not specifically tested for impairment. Rather, the entire equity method investment is tested for impairment. The impairment test is performed by comparing the investment's recoverable amount, which is the higher of its value in use and fair value less costs to sell, with its carrying amount.

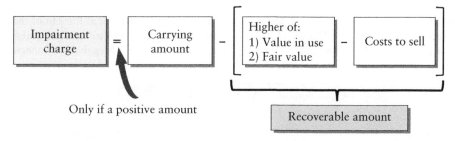

Only if a positive amount

Recoverable amount

An impairment loss recognised in prior periods is only reversed if there has been a change in the estimates used to determine the investment's recoverable amount since the last impairment loss was recognised. In this case the carrying amount of the investment is increased to its higher recoverable amount.

8.5.2 Working Example of Equity Method Consolidation

Imagine that Megabank acquired a 30% interest in Trustbank and achieved significant influence. The cost of the investment was EUR 3 billion. The associate had net assets of EUR 5 billion at the date of acquisition. Megabank estimated that the fair value of those net assets was EUR 8.33 billion.

Initially the investment was recognised at its EUR 3 billion cost. Part of the initial recognition included the transaction's EUR 0.5 billion (= 3 bn − 30% × 8.3 bn) goodwill. Megabank's balance sheet included the following one line item related to its investment in Trustbank:

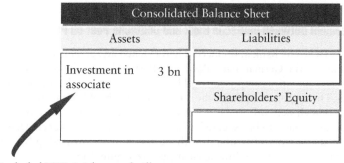

Included EUR 0.5 bn goodwill

In the year following the acquisition, Trustbank recognised a profit after tax of EUR 900 million and paid a dividend out of these profits of EUR 400 million. Trustbank also recognised losses of 100 million in OCI.

Megabank's share of Trustbank's after-tax profit was EUR 270 million (= 900 mn × 30%) and its share of the change in reserves during the period represented a EUR 30 million (= 100 mn × 30%) reduction, while it received EUR 120 million (= 400 mn × 30%) dividends. Megabank tested the whole investment in Trustbank for impairment, resulting in a EUR 60 million charge. Megabank's interest in Trustbank at the end of the year was calculated as follows:

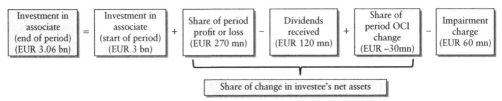

Therefore, the carrying amount of Megabank's investment in Trustbank at the end of the period was EUR 3.06 billion (= 3 bn + 270 mn – 120 mn – 30 mn – 60 mn). The goodwill amount embedded in the investment was EUR 440 million (= 500 mn – 60 mn). The effects on Megabank's financial statements of its investment in Trustbank were the following:

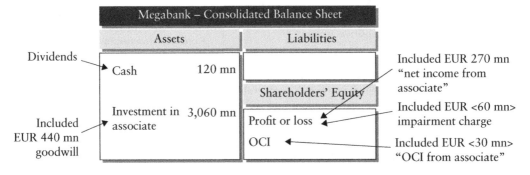

8.6 CASE STUDY: DEUTSCHE BANK'S ACQUISITION OF POSTBANK

The purpose of this real-life case is to review the application of the equity method and the process of initial recognition when control is achieved.

8.6.1 Initial Agreement between Deutsche Bank and Deutsche Post on Postbank

In September 2008 Deutsche Bank announced it had reached an agreement to acquire from Deutsche Post a minority stake in the German bank Postbank. Postbank was one of the largest retail banks in Germany. Its business activities comprised retail banking, business with corporate clients and capital markets activities. The aggregate of Deutsche Bank's and Postbank's retail networks was at the time by far the biggest branch network in Germany, opening opportunities for cross-selling of financial products. Were the agreement to be executed, which in reality did not happen, Deutsche Bank would become the largest shareholder of Postbank with a 29.75% share ownership (see Figure 8.10).

The agreement comprised the following elements (see Figure 8.11):

- Deutsche Bank was to acquire **29.75% of Postbank** for EUR 2.79 billion (EUR 57.25 per share) in cash. The stake included a right to receive Postbank's dividend related to 2008;
- Deutsche Post would have a **lock-up** obligation regarding the sale of its remaining 20.25% stake in Postbank. The lock-up period would expire in 24 months;

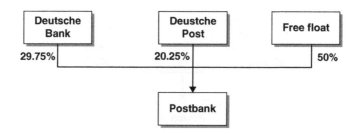

FIGURE 8.10 Ownership structure of Postbank were the initial acquisition to materialise (it did not happen)

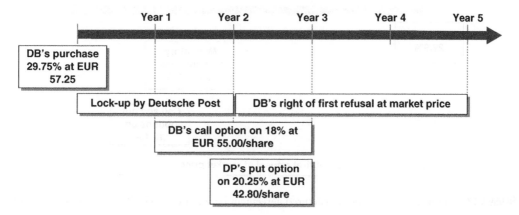

FIGURE 8.11 Main clauses of the initial agreement between Deutsche Bank (DB) and Deutsche Post (DP)

- Deutsche Post would grant Deutsche Bank a **call option** to acquire an additional 18% of Postbank for EUR 55.00 per share (i.e., EUR 1.62 billion). This option could be exercised between 12 months and 36 months after the initial acquisition. The option could be settled in cash and/or Deutsche Bank shares, at Deutsche Bank's discretion;
- Deutsche Bank would grant Deutsche Post a **put option** on 20.25% of Postbank for EUR 42.80 per share (i.e., EUR 1.42 billion). The option could be exercised after 21 months and up to 36 months. The option could be settled in cash and/or Deutsche Bank shares, at Deutsche Bank's discretion; and
- Deutsche Post would grant Deutsche Bank a **right of first refusal** for its remaining Postbank shares until the end of 5 years from closing.

The agreement was expected to be closed in the first quarter of 2009. Deutsche Bank funded the acquisition through an equity raising of EUR 2.2 billion in September 2008. Deutsche Bank placed 40 million new registered shares without par value with institutional investors by way of an accelerated book-built offering at EUR 55 per share. There was no public offering. The main objective of the equity raising was to offset the capital deduction and risk-weighted assets resulting from the investment.

8.6.2 Restructuring of the Initial Terms

In November 2008 (i.e., before the initial agreement between Deutsche Bank and Deutsche Post was executed) Postbank implemented a capital increase, resulting in gross proceeds of approximately EUR 1 billion and the issuing of 54.8 million new shares, 99.2% of which were acquired by Deutsche Post,

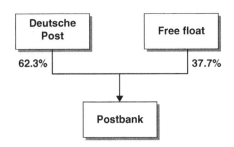

FIGURE 8.12   Ownership structure of Postbank after its capital increase

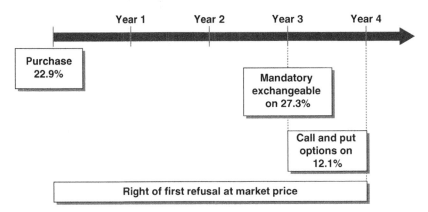

FIGURE 8.13   Main elements of the restructured agreement between Deutsche Bank and Deutsche Post

increasing its interest in Postbank to approximately 62.3%. Figure 8.12 summarises Postbank's shareholder structure following the capital increase. The transaction aimed at strengthening Postbank's capital base against the backdrop of the 2007–08 financial market crisis.

Before the initial agreement was implemented, Deutsche Bank and Deutsche Post restructured its terms in February 2009. The new contract comprised four elements (see Figure 8.13):

- As a first element, Deutsche Bank **acquired** 50 million **Postbank shares** – corresponding to a stake of **22.9%** – from Deutsche Post in an in-kind (i.e., non-cash) capital increase of EUR 958 million excluding subscription rights. As a result, Deutsche Post acquired a shareholding of approximately 8% in Deutsche Bank. Deutsche Post could dispose of half of this holding in Deutsche Bank from the end of April 2009, the other half could be disposed of from mid-June 2009. It was agreed that mechanisms designed to avoid market disturbances would be applied to any such sales. During the interim a certain amount of hedging was permissible, and some measures were planned.
- As a second element, Deutsche Bank underwrote a **mandatory exchangeable bond** ("MEB") issued by Deutsche Post of EUR 3.0 billion. After three years (in February 2012), the bond – including interest payments accrued – would be exchanged for 60 million Postbank shares, or a 27.3% stake. The bond was a zero-coupon bond with a 4% accrued interest per year. Deutsche Post pledged the underlying shares to Deutsche Bank until conversion.
- As a third element, Deutsche Bank bought a **call option** and sold a **put option** on the remaining 26.4 million shares – equal to a 12.1% stake in Postbank. The options were exercisable between the 36th and 48th month after the closing (i.e., between February 2012 and February 2013). Deutsche Bank paid cash collateral of EUR 1.1 billion, equivalent to the present value of the two options.

Deutsche Post pledged Postbank shares to Deutsche Bank as security for repayment of the cash collateral.

■ Finally, Deutsche Post granted Deutsche Bank a **right of first refusal** for its remaining Postbank shares until the end of 4 years from closing. In addition, both banks were obliged to participate in potential Postbank capital increases on a pro-rata basis for a period of 3 years.

If the call or put options were exercised, Deutsche Bank would end up owning all Deutsche Post's shares in Postbank, becoming a majority shareholder with a 62.3% stake (see Figure 8.14).

Accounting Treatment As a result of its initial investment in February 2009, Deutsche Bank directly held 22.9% of the shares and voting rights of Postbank, giving it the ability to **significantly influence** Postbank's financial and operating policies. Accordingly, this investment was accounted for using the **equity method** and, thus, Postbank became an associate of Deutsche Bank.

The MEB was to be fully exchanged in 2012 for 60 million Postbank shares, or a 27.42% stake. For accounting purposes, the MEB constituted an equity investment with risk and reward characteristics substantially similar to an ownership interest in the Postbank shares and therefore was included as part of the equity method investment.

The MEB contained an additional cash component related to a profit sharing agreement with Deutsche Post on Deutsche Bank shares issued which were received as consideration by Deutsche Post. This component represented an embedded derivative. The embedded derivative was bifurcated as the risks and rewards from the profit sharing were not clearly and closely related to the host contract. The initial fair value of the embedded derivative was EUR 0.2 billion which reduced the cost of the equity method investment in Postbank.

The call and put options were recognised as a single derivative. The initial fair value of the derivative was a negative EUR 1.1 billion. At each reporting date the derivative was fair valued, and its change in fair value recognised in profit or loss.

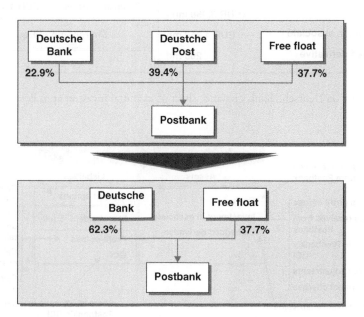

FIGURE 8.14 Ownership structure of Postbank assuming full implementation of the restructured agreement

The initial investment in Postbank was recognised as the sum of the three items, as follows (see Figure 8.15):

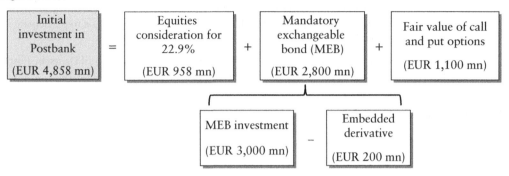

Subsequent to initial recognition, Deutsche Bank's financial statements were impacted by several items related to its investment in Postbank (see Figure 8.16):

■ The carrying amount of the investment in Postbank, on the asset side of Deutsche Bank's balance sheet, was impacted by four items: plus (i) Deutsche Bank's share (22.9%) of Postbank's net earnings, less (ii) any distributions (e.g., dividends) received from Postbank, less (iii) any impairment charges, plus/less (iv) Deutsche Bank's share (22.9%) of the change in Postbank's OCI. Any fair value adjustments also adjusted the carrying amount of the investment.

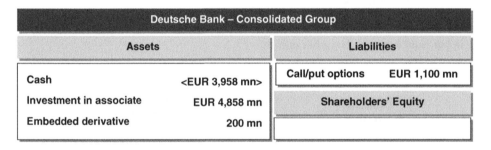

FIGURE 8.15   Impact on Deutsche Bank's balance sheet of its initial investment in Postbank

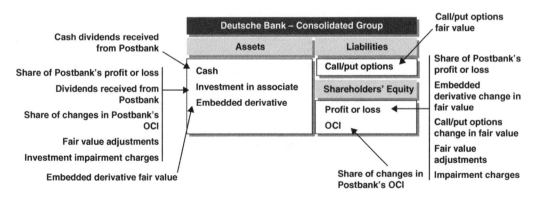

FIGURE 8.16   Impact on Deutsche Bank's balance sheet related to the Postbank transaction

■ Profit or loss was impacted by four items: (i) Deutsche Bank's share (22.9%) of Postbank's net earnings, (ii) any changes in the fair value of the derivative embedded in the MEB, (iii) any changes in the fair value of the call and put options, and (iv) any impairment charges. Any fair value adjustments also adjusted consolidated profit or loss.

■ The cash position was enhanced by any cash dividends distributed by Postbank.

■ The carrying amount of the embedded derivative equalled its fair value. It was recognised on the asset side.

■ The carrying amount of the call and put options represented their fair value. It was originally recognised on the liability side of Deutsche Bank's balance sheet, and would remain as a liability as long as the put was worth more than the call. Conversely, were the fair value of the call to exceed the fair value of the call, the net fair value would be recognised on the asset side.

■ Consolidated OCI was impacted by Deutsche Bank's share of Postbank's changes in OCI.

Deutsche Bank performed an impairment test on its investment in Postbank each year based on its recoverable amount which was defined as the higher of the fair value less costs to sell and the value in use. The value in use of the investment was derived from future cash flows expected to be generated by Postbank discounted to their present value. The future cash flows were derived from the estimate as to the development of the future capital requirements and the expected corresponding annual return on that future capital base. The assessment of the capital development and the corresponding profitability was based on publicly available information issued by Postbank, such as its annual and quarterly financial reports, management and investor relations announcements as well as broker reports on Postbank. This information was further substantiated by internal analysis. In addition, the expected benefits of the signed cooperation agreement between Deutsche Bank and Postbank were taken into account further contributing to the value in use. Deutsche Bank did not recognise any impairment charges on its investment in Postbank while it was recognised as an associate.

8.6.3 Impact on Regulatory Capital of the Initial Investment

This section covers the impact of the initial investment in Postbank on Deutsche Bank's regulatory capital. Whilst in 2009 Deutsche Bank was subject to Basel II guidelines, I have assumed that Basel III rules were already in place, which has required a substantial number of assumptions. In any case, the objective of this section is to explain the application of Basel III to significant investments in financial entities.

The recognition of Postbank as an associate under the equity method comprised Deutsche Bank's initial 22.9% direct investment and the 27.3% future investment implied in the MEB. From a regulatory perspective, several elements of this investment impacted Deutsche Bank's regulatory capital calculations:

■ The goodwill arising from the investment;

■ The carrying amount of the investment (excluding goodwill);

■ The embedded derivative in the MEB;

■ The call and put options; and

■ Any subsequent change in Deutsche Bank's proportionate share of Postbank's retained earnings and reserves.

Goodwill   On the asset side of Deutsche Bank's statement of financial position, the EUR 4,858 million initial investment in Postbank was recognised in one line item: "Investment in associate", which included goodwill. Goodwill represented the excess of the initial investment over the fair value of Postbank's individually identifiable assets and liabilities. In other words, Deutsche Bank did not recognise the goodwill related to its Postbank investment separately in its financial statements, but kept track of the outstanding goodwill for capital purposes.

According to Basel III goodwill and all other intangibles must be deducted in the calculation of CET1. This deduction is also required for any goodwill included in the valuation of significant investments in the capital of banking, financial and insurance entities that are outside the scope of consolidation. In our case, let us assume that goodwill was estimated to be **EUR 972** million which, consequently, reduced CET1 by that amount. The reduction was calculated net of deferred tax effects.

Any future impairment would lower the amount of goodwill. It was covered previously in Section 8.5 that when an investment is accounted for using the equity method, the whole investment is tested for impairment. Any impairment charges on the investment in Postbank would reduce the amount of outstanding goodwill, reducing the size of the deduction from CET1. However, impairment charges would be recognised in profit or loss, reducing the amount of CET1. If from a tax perspective an impairment charge would be tax-deductible, then impairment charges may have a positive impact in CET1, equal to the amount of taxes being saved.

Carrying Amount of the Investment (Excluding Goodwill)   Because (i) Postbank was a bank, (ii) Deutsche Bank did not consolidate Postbank and (iii) Deutsche Bank owned in excess of 10% of Postbank's ordinary share capital, its investment in Postbank was considered a "significant investment in the capital of banking, financial and insurance entities that are outside the scope of regulatory consolidation". Following the flowchart in Figure 8.17, Deutsche Bank's investment in ordinary shares was added to other investments in CET1 instruments deemed to be significant as well.

The initial carrying amount of Deutsche Bank's investment in Postbank was EUR 4,858 million. After deducting the EUR 972 million goodwill (as it was already deducted from CET1), the amount subject to the capital treatment of significant investments thresholds was EUR 3,886 million.

Besides its investment in Postbank, Deutsche Bank's other significant investments comprised mainly its investment in the Chinese bank Hua Xia. Let us assume that the overall investment in these unconsolidated entities deemed to be significant was EUR 2,344 million, excluding EUR 586 million of goodwill.

The aggregate of the significant investments in unconsolidated financial institutions subject to the thresholds was EUR 6,230 million (= 3,886 mn + 2,344 mn). This amount was compared to 10% of Deutsche Bank's CET1 prior to the calculation of this deduction. Let us assume that Deutsche Bank's CET1 prior to this deduction was EUR 32 billion. The excess of the aggregate of the significant investments in unconsolidated financial institutions over 10% of that CET1 amount represented EUR 3,030 million (= 6,230 mn − 10% × 32,000 mn). As the investment in Postbank represented 62.4% of the aggregate of significant investments in unconsolidated financial institutions, an amount of **EUR 1,891** (= 62.4% × 3,030 mn) was deducted from CET1 related to the investment in Postbank (excluding goodwill). The amount not subject to deduction – EUR 1,995 million (= 3,886 mn − 1,891 mn) – was subject to a 15% aggregate threshold.

The 15% threshold was incorporated by Basel III to allow limited recognition of three asset items when calculating CET1. These items are:

- Significant investments in the CET1 instruments of non-consolidated financial institutions. In our case, this amount was the aggregate of the amounts not already subtracted from CET1 capital, or EUR 3,200 million (of which EUR 1,995 million (= 3,886 mn − 1,891 mn) corresponded to the Postbank investment);
- Deferred tax assets relating to temporary differences. I assume that this item amounted to EUR 3,760 million; and
- Mortgage servicing rights. I assume that this item was negligible.

Therefore, the aggregate of these three items was EUR 6,960 million (= 3,200 mn + 3760 mn). The balance of CET1 prior to this deduction was EUR 28,970 million (= 32,000 mn − 3,030 mn). The 15% threshold represented EUR 5,112 million (= 28,970 mn × 15% / 85%). Consequently, Deutsche

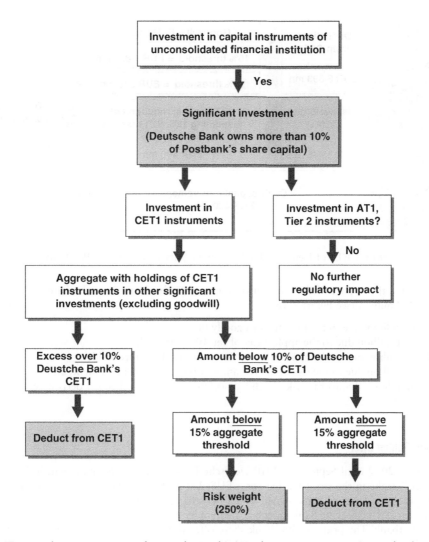

FIGURE 8.17   Regulatory treatment of Deutsche Bank's initial equity investment in Postbank

Bank had to deduct from CET1 EUR 1,848 million (= 6,960 mn − 5,112 mn) related to the 15% threshold, of which **EUR 530 million** (= 1,848 mn × 1,995 / 6,960 mn) corresponded to its investment in Postbank.

The amount related to the investment in Postbank not subject to deduction was EUR 1,465 million (= 4,858 mn − 972 mn − 1,891 mn − 530 mn). This amount was risk-weighted at 250%, or EUR 3,663 million (= 1,465 mn × 250%) of risk-weighted assets. Assuming that Deutsche Bank's CET1 target was a 12% CET1 ratio, the bank had to raise EUR 440 million (= 12% × 3,663 mn) of CET1 capital related to the risk-weighted amount.

The call and put options and the embedded derivative consumed CET1 capital as well. The impact was EUR 400 million.

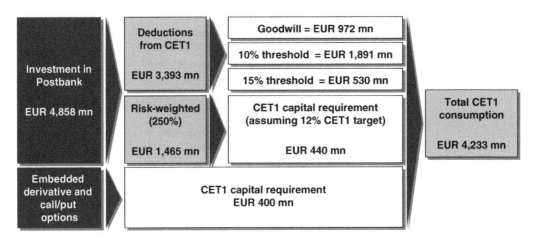

FIGURE 8.18   Impact on CET1 of Deutsche Bank's initial equity investment in Postbank

In summary, the impact of the initial investment in Postbank on Deutsche Bank's CET1 capital was EUR 4,233 million (see Figure 8.18):

- EUR 972 million, due to the investment's goodwill;
- EUR 1,891 million due to the application of the 10% threshold;
- EUR 530 million due to the application of the aggregate 15% threshold;
- EUR 440 million due to the risk-weighted amount related to the investment; and
- EUR 400 million due to the risk weights associated with the embedded derivative and the call/put options.

8.6.4 Public Tender Offer

From February 2009 until September 2010 Deutsche Bank increased its investment in Postbank by buying a 7.1% stake in the stock market for a EUR 231 million total cash consideration. After this additional purchase Deutsche Bank owned 30% of Postbank's ordinary share capital.

In October 2010 Deutsche Bank launched a voluntary public takeover offer ("PTO") to the shareholders of Postbank. The price per Postbank share offered in the PTO amounted to EUR 25.00, the three-month average share price prior to the PTO. The offer was accepted for 48.2 million Postbank shares, corresponding to 22.03% of the Postbank share capital and voting rights. The total cash consideration paid for the Postbank shares acquired in the PTO amounted to EUR 1,205 million. Together with the already held before the PTO, Deutsche Bank held 113.7 million shares of Postbank, equal to 52.03% of all voting rights in Postbank. When added to the MEB underlying shares, Deutsche Bank controlled 79.33% (= 52.03% + 27.30%) of Postbank:

Deusche Bank's equity interest		Previous direct stake		Mandatory exchangeable		Public tender offer
79.33%	=	30.00%	+	27.30%	+	22.03%

In order to finance the PTO and to offset its capital impact, Deutsche Bank launched a rights issue. Shareholders could purchase one new share for every two shares they owned (2:1 subscription ratio) through so-called indirect subscription rights. Deutsche Bank issued a total of 308.6 million new reg-

TABLE 8.6   Fair valuation of Postbank's identifiable assets and liabilities

Balance Sheet Item	Fair Value (EUR mn)
Cash and cash equivalents	8,752
Financial assets at fair value through profit or loss	37,811
Financial assets at fair value through OCI	33,732
Loans	129,877
Intangible assets	1,357
All other assets	27,788
Deposits	<139,859>
Financial liabilities at fair value through profit or loss	<32,840>
Long-term debt	<39,331>
All other liabilities	<24,450>
Total identifiable net assets	2,837

istered no par value ordinary shares (common shares) in public offerings in Germany and the United States using authorised capital, resulting in gross proceeds from the issuance of EUR 10.2 billion and in net proceeds of EUR 10.1 billion (after expenses of about EUR 0.1 billion net of tax). The share capital of Deutsche Bank was increased by EUR 790.1 million, from EUR 1,589.4 million to EUR 2,379.5 million, corresponding to a volume of 49.7% of the then share capital.

8.6.5 Accounting for the Gain of Control

Following the settlement of the PTO Deutsche Bank was deemed to control Postbank, and as a result, commenced its consolidation. On 3 December 2010, the date when control over Postbank was obtained, Deutsche Bank performed a fair valuation of the identifiable assets acquired and liabilities assumed as shown in Table 8.6.

As part of the identifiable assets, Deutsche Bank recognised intangible assets of EUR 1,357 million, which represented both intangible assets included in the balance sheet of Postbank as well as those intangible assets which were ultimately identified in the acquisition. The intangible assets mainly comprised customer relationships (EUR 588 million), the Postbank trademark (EUR 411 million) as well as software (EUR 282 million).

In addition, Deutsche Bank remeasured to fair value its existing equity method investment in Postbank in accordance with IFRS. The fair value of the equity method investment was determined on the basis of the offer price of EUR 25.00, totalling an acquisition-date fair value of EUR 3,139 million. It excluded the embedded derivative and the call and put options.

Before the business combination, Deutsche Bank and Postbank were parties to certain transactions considered as pre-existing relationships. Among these transactions were various financial instruments included in the course of the parties' regular interbank and hedging activities, certain bonds issued by Deutsche Bank or by Postbank which were held by the other party, and specific payment services provided to Deutsche Bank by Postbank. All of these instruments were eliminated upon consolidation of Postbank. The aggregated acquisition-date fair value of the financial instruments totalled EUR 103 million, which was considered as a deduction in the determination of the consideration transferred and its allocation to Postbank's net assets acquired. The settlement of certain of these finan-cial instruments issued by Deutsche Bank and held by Postbank resulted in an extinguishment loss of EUR 1 million, which was included in Deutsche Bank's consolidated profit or loss statement.

The aggregate of the cost of the acquisition – EUR 4,241 million – was calculated as follows:

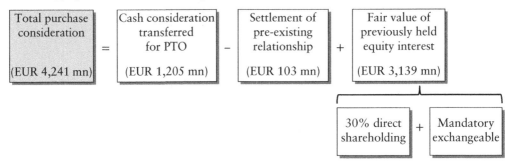

The consolidation of Postbank was based on Deutsche Bank's 79.33% total equity interest. Non-controlling interest (NCI) was included as a separate item in the consolidated shareholders' equity, representing the equity in Postbank not attributable to Deutsche Bank. NCI was calculated using the "partial goodwill" method, based on the fair value of the identifiable net assets acquired. As the NCI represented 20.67% (= 100% − 79.33%) of Postbank's ordinary shares, it amounted to EUR 586 million (= 20.67% × 2,837 mn).

Goodwill arising from the acquisition of Postbank was determined pursuant to IFRS 3. The goodwill – EUR 2,093 million – largely reflected the value from revenue and cost synergies expected from the acquisition of Postbank. It was calculated as the excess of the cost of the acquisition and the non-controlling interest over Deutsche Bank's share of the fair value of the net identifiable assets:

On the date when control over Postbank was achieved, several items impacted Deutsche Bank's consolidated profit or loss:

- The previously held interest (i.e., the equity method investment) was fair valued and compared to its carrying amount. The difference between these two values was recognised in **profit or loss**. The previously held interest in Postbank was valued at a price per share equal to the EUR 25.00 offered by Deutsche Bank in the PTO, resulting in a EUR 3,139 million fair valuation. The carry-ing amount of the previously held interests as of the date when control was achieved was EUR 5,060 million (my assumption), resulting in a EUR 1,921 million (= 3,139 mn − 5,060 mn) pre-tax loss recognised in consolidated profit or loss.
- The amounts in Deutsche Bank's consolidated other comprehensive income related to the equity method investment were reclassified to consolidated profit or loss.
- The embedded derivative was fair valued and the change in fair value since the previous fair valu-ation (30 September 2010) was recognised in consolidated profit or loss.
- The call and put options were fair valued and the change in fair value since the previous fair valu-ation (30 September 2010) was recognised in consolidated profit or loss.

Regarding the call and put options, they remained in place for the remaining 26.4 million shares (or 12.1% of Postbank's ordinary share capital). The terms of the options were renegotiated to provide for physical settlement only (i.e., if exercised Deutsche Bank would receive shares in exchange for cash). Upon consolidation, the put and call option structure with Deutsche Post on Postbank shares was reclassified to an equity instrument due to the fact that it became a physically settled derivative on shares in a consolidated subsidiary settled for a fixed amount of cash. On the date when control over Postbank was obtained, the net fair value of the options was EUR 560 million. The options were reclassified from a derivative liability into equity (share premium). Correspondingly, for the respective shares under the put and call option structure, a liability was recognised at the present value of the expected purchase price, due to the requirement to purchase these shares under the put option agreement. The liability to purchase of EUR 1,286 million was recognised with a corresponding debit to equity (share premium).

Subsequent Conversion/Exercise of the mandatory Exchangeable and Call/Put Options On 27 February 2012 the MEB was converted and, as a result, Deutsche Bank further increased its direct interest in Postbank by 60 million shares or 27.3% of Postbank's ordinary share capital. Because the MEB had already been considered as an equity investment in the first place, its conversion did not result in any change in Deutsche Bank's consolidated Postbank stake and therefore had no impact on Deutsche Bank's total equity and profit or loss. In addition, the embedded derivative was settled, resulting in a EUR 677 million cash inflow.

On 28 February 2012, Deutsche Post exercised its put option and, consequently, Deutsche Bank's direct interest and consolidated stake in Postbank further increased by 26.4 million shares or 12.1% of Postbank's ordinary share capital. Upon exercise, the recognised liability to purchase Postbank shares was settled. The exercise of the option did not have a material impact on Deutsche Bank's total equity.

8.7 IFRS CONSOLIDATION VS. REGULATORY CONSOLIDATION

The calculation of a banking group regulatory capital is performed at the regulatory consolidated level. [CRR Chapter 2 of Title II of Part One] sets out the guidelines for regulatory consolidation. Interestingly, consolidation perimeters for regulatory and accounting purposes are often different. In a banking group, the entities consolidated under IFRS comprise all the companies **controlled** by the ultimate parent company.

The aim of regulatory consolidation, by contrast, is to prevent multiple use of capital that in fact exists only once by subsidiary companies in the financial sector.

8.7.1 Entities Consolidated for Regulatory Purposes

[CRR 18(1)] requires banks to carry out a full consolidation of all financial institutions which are its subsidiaries for the application of prudential requirements on a consolidated basis. Undertakings, other than financial institutions which neither acquire holdings nor pursue any of the activities listed in [CRD IV Annex I points 2 to 12 and point 15], are excluded from the scope of prudential consolidation irrespective of whether or not these undertakings are directly or indirectly held by the parent entity. The activities listed in [CRD IV Annex I points 2 to 12 and point 15] are the following:

- Lending including, inter alia: consumer credit, credit agreements relating to immovable property, factoring, with or without recourse, financing of commercial transactions (including forfeiting);
- Financial leasing;
- Payment services as defined in Article 4(3) of Directive 2007/64/EC;
- Issuing and administering other means of payment (e.g., travellers' cheques and bankers' drafts) insofar as such activity is not covered by the previous paragraph;
- Guarantees and commitments;

- Trading for own account or for account of customers in any of the following: money market instruments (cheques, bills, certificates of deposit, etc.), foreign exchange, financial futures and options, exchange and interest rate instruments, and transferable securities;
- Participation in securities issues and the provision of services relating to such issues;
- Advice to undertakings on capital structure, industrial strategy and related questions and advice as well as services relating to mergers and the purchase of undertakings;
- Money broking;
- Portfolio management and advice;
- Safekeeping and administration of securities; and
- Issuing electronic money.

As a result, when a bank controls subsidiaries whose activities are different to the ones listed above, the basis of consolidation for the purpose of financial accounting under IFRSs differs from that used for regulatory purposes. Commonly, the main differences in the basis of consolidation for IFRS and regulatory capital purposes occur in the following cases, regardless of the bank's level of control:

- Interests in associates and joint ventures that are financial in nature, and that accounted under the **equity method,** are consolidated in *proportion* to the participation for regulatory calculations. This follows line-by-line (accounting) consolidation based on the ownership share in the particular entity. In certain circumstances, participations are deducted from capital rather than proportionally consolidated (e.g., private equity investments treated as associates are commonly deducted from capital for regulatory calculations).
- **Real estate** and commercial companies as well as **investment schemes** are *not* consolidated for regulatory capital purposes, but are risk-weighted.
- Subsidiaries and associates engaged in **insurance** are *not* consolidated for regulatory capital purposes, but are risk-weighted based on applicable threshold rules. Chapter 11 covers the regulatory treatment of investments in insurers.
- **Special purpose entities** – SPEs – (e.g., securitisation vehicles) where **significant risk has been transferred** to third parties are *not* consolidated for regulatory capital purposes. Exposure to these SPEs are risk-weighted as securitisation positions under the securitisation framework.
- **Joint ventures** controlled by two ventures are fully consolidated for regulatory capital purposes, and are accounted for under the equity method for IFRS.
- Subsidiaries and associates engaged in **non-financial** activities are *not* consolidated for regulatory capital purposes, but are risk-weighted.

Additionally, banks could face the opposite situation: there could be entities which are consolidated for regulatory capital purposes but not consolidated under IFRS. For example, banks may set up entities for the sole purpose of issuing preferred securities. These entities hold bonds issued by the bank which are eliminated in the consolidated regulatory capital accounts. These entities commonly do not have material third-party asset balances and equity is attributable to non-controlling interests.

> Insurance entities are excluded from the calculation of consolidated capital requirements and consolidated capital resources. Investments in insurance entities are, instead, subject to threshold rules.
>
> Insurance entities are themselves required to maintain capital adequacy under Solvency II.

8.7.2 Making Adjustments for Regulatory Consolidation

Adjusting the scope of consolidation for prudential purposes is a highly complex and costly undertaking, especially in large groups where hundreds of entities are assessed for consolidation. In general, there are three possible scenarios, each posing its own challenges.

- Firstly, units consolidated for both accounting and regulatory purposes do not pose any key challenges with the exception of associates. From a regulatory consolidation perspective a banking group needs to proportionally consolidate the assets and liabilities of associates. This may be particularly challenging when granular data is not available to the banking group, for example when the associate is reluctant to share sensitive information with the banking group.
- Secondly, a unit may have to be consolidated for accounting, but not for prudential purposes. In this case, the financials of the unit have to be filtered out from the banking group accounts. The deconsolidation process affects not only the unit that needs to be removed, but also any other subsidiaries which, though remaining in the scope of consolidation for prudential purposes, have conducted intercompany transactions with the segregated unit.
- Finally, should a unit have to be consolidated for prudential but not for accounting purposes, no IFRS measurements exist. IFRS valuation rules have to be used to calculate figures purely for the purpose of regulatory reporting. Intercompany transactions with other subsidiaries need to be identified and the entire consolidation process has to be carried out.

8.7.3 Exemption to Regulatory Consolidation

[CRR 19] allows the exclusion of small entities in the regulatory scope of application from consolidated regulatory reporting if either their total assets (including off-balance sheet items) are below EUR 10 million or below 1% of the group's total assets.

From a regulatory perspective, these regulatory unconsolidated entities have to be included in the deduction treatment for significant investments in financial sector entities.

CHAPTER **9**

Treatment of Minority Interests in Consolidated Regulatory Capital

Minority interests arise in many situations, like for example the use of local partners or the partial flotation of locally incorporated subsidiaries. This chapter covers the impact on consolidated regulatory capital of capital instruments issued by a subsidiary to third-party investors (i.e., a subsidiary's minority interest). Capital instruments – CET1, AT1 and Tier 2 – issued by a subsidiary to these investors may partially/totally qualify as capital instruments for the banking group.

9.1 MINORITY INTERESTS INCLUDED IN CONSOLIDATED CET1

In the Basel III regulatory framework the term "**minority interests**" is used rather than its accounting equivalent "**non-controlling interests**" (NCI). Chapter 8 covers in detail how minority interests are recognised from an accounting perspective. In this chapter I use the term "minority interest" when referring to both the accounting and the regulatory concepts.

> Remember from Chapter 8 that from an **accounting** perspective, a minority interest represents the equity in a subsidiary not attributable, directly or indirectly, to a parent entity. In other words, a minority interest includes the third parties' interest in the issued capital instruments (i.e., instruments that are recognised as equity instruments from an accounting perspective), retained earnings and other reserves of the consolidated subsidiaries. Thus, CET1 and AT1 instruments are normally taken into account when calculating accounting minority interests. Tier 2 instruments are not included in the calculation of minority interests if they are recognised as liabilities.
>
> From a **regulatory** capital perspective CET1, AT1 and Tier 2 instruments are taken into account when calculating the impact on regulatory capital of minority interests.

9.1.1 Minority Interests that Qualify for Inclusion in Consolidated CET1 Capital

Minority interests that qualify for inclusion in consolidated CET1 are covered in [CRR 81], and refer to minority interests that comprise:

- CET1 instruments of a subsidiary. In other words, the instrument giving rise to the minority interest would, if issued by the bank, meet all the criteria for classification as CET1 instrument;
- The share premium accounts related to those CET1 instruments; and
- Retained earnings and other reserves of the subsidiary.

Regarding the subsidiary the following conditions must be met:

- The subsidiary is a credit institution or an investment firm (or an undertaking that is subject by virtue of applicable national law to the requirements of CRD IV);
- The subsidiary is included fully in the regulatory consolidation perimeter; and
- The CET1 items are owned by persons other than the undertakings included in the regulatory consolidation.

Minority interests that are funded directly or indirectly, through an SPE (i.e., special purpose entity) or otherwise, by the parent undertaking of the entity or its subsidiaries do *not* qualify as consolidated CET1 capital.

> Minority interests of subsidiaries that are not banks (i.e., a credit institution or an investment firm) do *not* add regulatory capital to the group. In other words, only minority interests of institutions that are subject to the same minimum prudential standards and level of supervision as a bank may be eligible for inclusion in the consolidated CET1 capital.

9.1.2 Minority Interests Included in Consolidated CET1

This section covers the Basel III treatment of minority interests in the CET1 capital ratio calculations.

General Treatment of Minority Interests   Minority interests arising from the issue of CET1 instruments by the subsidiaries of a bank may receive limited recognition. In particular, Basel III requires the excess capital above the minimum capital requirement of a subsidiary (i.e., the surplus CET1 of the subsidiary) that is a bank to be deducted in proportion to the minority interest share.

> Although minority interest absorbs losses within the subsidiary to which it relates, this exclusion is based on the premise that this capital is not fully available to support risks in the group as a whole, and that it may represent an interest in a subsidiary with little or no risk.

For each minority interest of a subsidiary that qualifies for inclusion in consolidated CET1 capital, [CRR 84] sets out the method for calculating the amount of minority interests to be included in CET1 at consolidated level (what I have called the "General Treatment").

This calculation is undertaken on a sub-consolidated basis for each subsidiary in the regulatory consolidation perimeter. However, a bank may choose *not* to undertake this calculation for a subsidiary. Where a bank takes such a decision, the minority interest of that subsidiary may *not* be included in consolidated CET1 capital.

The amount of a subsidiary's CET1 attributable to its minority interest that can be recognised in consolidated CET1 is calculated as the difference between (i) the total minority interest that qualify as CET1 capital (as covered in the previous Section 9.1.1) and (ii) the amount of **surplus CET1** of the subsidiary attributable to the minority interest:

| Recognised CET1 in consolidation attributable to minority interest | = | CET1 of subsidiary attributable to minority interest | − | Surplus CET1 attributable to minority interest |

The amount of **surplus CET1** of a subsidiary **attributable to the minority interest** is calculated by multiplying (i) the percentage of the subsidiary's CET1 that is held by the minority interest (i.e., the percentage that the minority interest represents of all CET1 instruments of the subsidiary plus the related share premium accounts, retained earnings and other reserves, but prior to regulatory adjustments) by (ii) the subsidiary's surplus CET1.

The amount of a subsidiary's **surplus CET1** is calculated as the CET1 capital of the subsidiary minus the lower of: (i) the minimum CET1 requirement of the subsidiary and (ii) the portion of the consolidated minimum CET1 requirements that relates to the subsidiary.

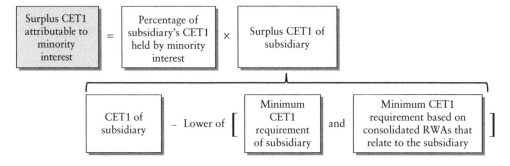

To calculate the portion of the consolidated minimum CET1 requirements that relates to the subsidiary, the bank calculates the minimum CET1 requirements imposed on the subsidiary but taking the consolidated RWAs that relate to the subsidiary. When performing this calculation:

- All intra-group transactions between entities included in the prudential scope of consolidation of the bank are eliminated;
- The subsidiary shall not include capital requirements arising from its entities which are not included in the prudential scope of consolidation of the bank for which the eligible minority interests are calculated.

The RWAs of the subsidiary and the consolidated RWAs of the subsidiary do not coincide when there are intercompany transactions between the parent bank and the subsidiary (or between entities within the consolidation perimeter). An example of intercompany transactions would be a loan from the parent bank to the subsidiary.

The subsidiary's minimum CET1 capital requirement includes all the following (as set by the supervisory authority of the subsidiary):

- The 4.5% minimum pursuant to [CRR 92(1)(a)];
- The **combined buffer requirement** pursuant to [CRD IV 128(6)]. Remember from Section 6.4.1 that the combined buffer included the capital conservation buffer, the countercyclical capital buffer and the higher of the G-SII buffer, the O-SII buffer and the systemic risk buffer;
- Any extraordinary CET1 requirements set by a member state or the EU to address changes in the intensity of microprudential and macroprudential risks which arise from market developments affecting the member state or affecting all member states of the EU as covered in [CRR 458, 459];
- The transitional provisions (until 31 December 2017) stated in [CRR 500]; and
- Any additional CET1 requirements set by local supervisory regulations in third countries.

CET1 capital arising from minority interests receives limited recognition. The excess over the minimum capital requirements of a subsidiary that is included in the regulatory consolidation perimeter, calculated on the basis of its local reporting as well as its contribution to the parent consolidated requirements, is not allowable in the consolidated CET1 capital to the extent it is attributable to minority shareholders.

Arguably, the minority interest deduction reduces the incentive of banks to overcapitalise banking subsidiaries, which is against Basel III's spirit of having a resilient financial system. It also creates an asymmetry between the numerator and the denominator of the capital ratio because Basel III ignores the excess capital of the subsidiary representing the minority interest at group level while the risks exposures related to this excess are fully recognised in the consolidated accounts. In other words, a bank does not deduct from consolidated RWAs the quota corresponding to the excess capital related to the minority interest. This asymmetry contrasts with the symmetrical treatment in the calculation of the leverage ratio which permits deduction of an appropriate portion of the affected subsidiaries' risk-weighted assets: "where a bank has a subsidiary that is included in the accounting consolidation, but not in the regulatory consolidation, then the treatment is to deduct the holding in the subsidiary from capital and not to include the subsidiary's assets in the total exposure measure".

Exceptions to the General Treatment on Minority Interests Pursuant to [CRR 7], a banking supervisor in the EU may derogate from the application of prudential requirements to a subsidiary if a set of requirements are met, which includes that both the subsidiary and the bank are subject to authorisation and supervision by the EU member state concerned and that the subsidiary is included in the supervision on a consolidated basis of the parent bank. In such case minority interest within the subsidiaries to which the waiver is applied cannot be recognised in total capital at the sub-consolidated or at the consolidated level, as applicable. However, any parent undertaking of the subsidiary benefiting from the waiver may include in its CET1 capital minority interests arising from subsidiaries of the subsidiary itself benefiting from the waiver, provided that the "General Treatment" calculations have been made for each of those subsidiaries.

Also, banking supervisors may grant a waiver from the application of the general rule to a parent financial holding company that satisfies all the following conditions:

- Its principal activity is to acquire holdings;
- It is subject to prudential supervision on a consolidated basis;
- It consolidates a subsidiary bank in which it has only a minority holding by virtue of the control relationship defined in Article 1 of Directive 83/349/EEC; and
- More than 90% of the consolidated required CET1 capital arises from the subsidiary bank calculated on a sub-consolidated basis.

Where a parent financial holding company that meets the conditions laid down above becomes a "parent mixed financial holding company", competent authorities may grant the waiver to that parent mixed financial holding company provided that it meets these conditions.

Where credit institutions permanently affiliated in a network to a central body and institutions established within an institutional protection scheme subject to the conditions laid down in [CRR 113(7)] have set up a cross-guarantee scheme that provides that there is no current or foreseen material, practical or legal impediment to the transfer of the amount of total capital above the regulatory requirements from the counterparty to the bank, these banks are exempted from the provisions of the "General Treatment" regarding deductions and may recognise any minority interest arising within the cross-guarantee scheme in full.

9.2 MINORITY INTERESTS INCLUDED IN CONSOLIDATED AT1, TIER 1, TIER 2 AND QUALIFYING TOTAL CAPITAL

This section covers the treatment of AT1 and Tier 2 instruments issued by a subsidiary, and their aggregate with CET1 instruments, owned by third-party investors. Unlike CET1 instruments, most of the investments in AT1 and Tier 2 instruments issued by a subsidiary are commonly owned by third-party investors. Beware that the term "minority interest" relates to CET1 instruments only.

9.2.1 Qualifying AT1, Tier 1, Tier 2 Capital and Qualifying Total Capital

Pursuant to [CRR 82], qualifying AT1, Tier 1, Tier 2 capital and qualifying total capital (also called "own funds") comprise the minority interest, AT1 or Tier 2 instruments, as applicable, plus the related retained earnings and share premium accounts, of a subsidiary where the following conditions are met:

- The subsidiary is a credit institution or an investment firm (or an undertaking that is subject by virtue of applicable national law to the requirements of CRD IV);
- The subsidiary is included fully in the regulatory consolidation perimeter; and
- Those instruments are owned by persons other than the undertakings included in the regulatory consolidation perimeter.

9.2.2 Qualifying AT1 and Tier 2 Capital Issued by an SPE

Pursuant to [CRR 83], AT1 and Tier 2 instruments, and their related share premium accounts, issued by an SPE are included in qualifying AT1, Tier 1 or Tier 2 capital or qualifying total capital, only where the following conditions are met:

- The SPE issuing those instruments is included fully in the regulatory consolidation perimeter;
- The instruments, and their related share premium accounts, are included in qualifying AT1 capital only where the instruments meet the requirements for qualification as AT1 instruments;
- The instruments, and the related share premium accounts, are included in qualifying Tier 2 capital only where the instruments meet the requirements for qualification as Tier 2 instruments;
- The only asset of the SPE is its investment in the total capital of the parent undertaking or a subsidiary thereof that is included fully in the regulatory consolidation perimeter. Other assets may be owned by the SPE if they are considered by the relevant regulatory supervisor to be minimal and insignificant.

According to the EBA, the assets of a SPE are considered to be minimal and insignificant where both of the following conditions are met:

- The assets of the SPE (the "other assets") which are not constituted by the investments in the total capital of the related subsidiary are limited to cash assets dedicated to payment of coupons and redemption of the total capital instruments that are due; and
- The amount of other assets of the SPE is not higher than 0.5% of the average total assets of the SPE over the last three years. The relevant regulatory supervisor may permit a higher percentage provided that both of the following conditions are met: (i) the higher percentage is necessary to enable exclusively the coverage of the running costs of the special purpose entity and (ii) the corresponding nominal amount does not exceed EUR 500,000.

There is an understandable concern in the regulators' minds that banks may use SPEs to artificially inflate capital levels. The rules mentioned above try to ascertain that consolidated capital is strictly available where all minority investments in a bank subsidiary solely represent genuine third-party common equity contributions to the subsidiary.

9.2.3 Qualifying Tier 1 Instruments Included in Consolidated Tier 1 Capital

The partial derecognition of capital issued to third-party investors by subsidiaries affects CET1 as well the AT1 and Tier 2 provided to third parties by all such subsidiaries. The methodology for calculating the amount of minority interests to be included in CET1 at consolidated level is applied by analogy for the calculation of the amount of qualifying AT1 and Tier 2 instruments. This calculation is undertaken on a sub-consolidated basis for each subsidiary in the regulatory consolidation perimeter. However, when a bank chooses not to undertake the calculation of minority interests of a subsidiary for their inclusion in consolidated CET1 capital, the qualifying Tier 1 capital of that subsidiary may not be included in consolidated Tier 1 capital.

Pursuant to [CRR 85], the amount of qualifying Tier 1 capital of a subsidiary that is included in consolidated Tier 1 is calculated as follows:

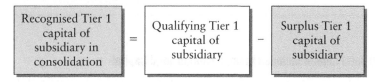

The amount of surplus Tier 1 of a subsidiary is calculated by multiplying (i) the percentage that the subsidiary qualifying Tier 1 represents of all Tier 1 instruments of the subsidiary (plus the related share premium accounts, retained earnings and other reserves) by (ii) the subsidiary surplus Tier 1 capital.

The amount of a subsidiary surplus Tier 1 is calculated as the Tier 1 capital of the subsidiary minus the lower of: (i) the minimum Tier 1 requirement of the subsidiary and (ii) the portion of the consolidated minimum Tier 1 requirements that relates to the subsidiary.

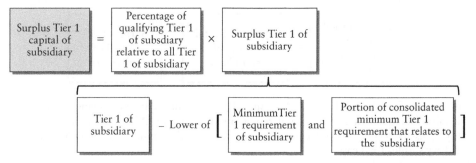

The subsidiary and the consolidated (as the case may be) minimum Tier 1 capital requirement include all the following (as set by the supervisory authority of the subsidiary or the consolidated group, as applicable):

- The 6% minimum Tier 1 capital ratio pursuant to [CRR 92(1)(b)];
- The **combined buffer requirement** pursuant to [CRD IV 128(6)]. Remember from Section 6.4.1 that the combined buffer included the capital conservation buffer, the countercyclical capital buffer and the higher of the G-SII buffer, the O-SII buffer and the systemic risk buffer;
- Any extraordinary Tier 1 requirements set by a member state or the EU to address changes in the intensity of microprudential and macroprudential risks which arise from market developments affecting the member state or affecting all member states of the EU as covered in [CRR 458, 459];
- The transitional provisions (until 31 December 2017) stated in [CRR 500]; and
- Any additional Tier 1 requirements set by local supervisory regulations in third countries.

Where a competent authority derogates from the application of prudential requirements on an individual basis, as laid down in [CRR 7], Tier 1 instruments within the subsidiaries to which the waiver is applied shall *not* be recognised in total capital at the sub-consolidated or at the consolidated level, as applicable.

9.2.4 Qualifying Tier 1 Capital Included in Consolidated AT1 Capital

Pursuant to [CRR 86], and without prejudice to the waivers from the application of prudential require-ments to a subsidiary mentioned above (granted by the supervisory authorities pursuant to [CRR 84(5) and (6)]), the amount of qualifying Tier 1 capital of a subsidiary that is included in consolidated AT1 capital is determined by subtracting from the qualifying Tier 1 capital of that undertaking included in consolidated Tier 1 capital the minority interests of that undertaking that are included in consolidated CET1 capital:

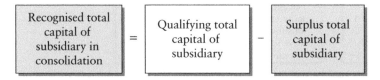

9.2.5 Qualifying Total Capital Included in Consolidated Total Capital

The calculation of the amount of qualifying total capital of a subsidiary that is included in consolidated total capital is undertaken on a sub-consolidated basis for each subsidiary in the regulatory consolida-tion perimeter. However, when a bank chooses not to undertake the calculation of minority interests of a subsidiary for their inclusion in consolidated CET1 capital, the qualifying total capital of that subsidiary may *not* be included in consolidated total capital.

Pursuant to [CRR 87], the amount of qualifying total capital of a subsidiary that is included in consolidated total capital is calculated as follows:

The amount of surplus total capital of the subsidiary is calculated by multiplying (i) the percentage that the subsidiary qualifying total capital represents of all CET1, AT1, Tier 2 instruments of the subsidiary (plus its related share premium accounts, retained earnings and other reserves) by (ii) the subsidiary surplus total capital.

The amount of a subsidiary surplus total capital is calculated as the total capital of the subsidiary minus the lower of: (i) the minimum total capital requirement of the subsidiary and (ii) the portion of the consolidated total capital requirements that relates to the subsidiary.

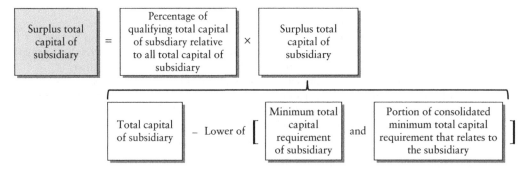

The subsidiary and the consolidated (as the case may be) minimum total capital requirement includes all the following (as set by the supervisory authority of the subsidiary or the consolidated group, as applicable):

- The 8% minimum total capital ratio pursuant to [CRR 92(1)(c)];
- The **combined buffer requirement** pursuant to [CRD IV 128(6)]. Remember from Section 6.4.1 that the combined buffer included the capital conservation buffer, the countercyclical capital buffer and the higher of the G-SII buffer, the O-SII buffer and the systemic risk buffer;
- Any extraordinary total capital requirements set by a member state or the EU to address changes in the intensity of microprudential and macroprudential risks which arise from market developments affecting the member state or affecting all member states of the EU as covered in [CRR 458, 459];
- The transitional provisions (until 31 December 2017) stated in [CRR 500]; and
- Any additional total capital requirements set by local supervisory regulations in third countries.

Where a competent authority derogates from the application of prudential requirements on an individual basis, as laid down in [CRR 7], total capital within the subsidiaries to which the waiver is applied cannot be recognised in total capital at the sub-consolidated or at the consolidated level, as applicable.

9.2.6 Qualifying Total Capital Included in Consolidated Tier 2 Capital

Pursuant to [CRR 88], and without prejudice to the waivers from the application of prudential requirements to a subsidiary mentioned above (granted by the supervisory authorities according to [CRR 84(5) and (6)]), the amount of qualifying total capital of a subsidiary that is included in consolidated Tier 2 capital is determined by subtracting from (i) the qualifying total capital of that subsidiary included in consolidated total capital (ii) the qualifying Tier 1 capital of that subsidiary that is included in consolidated Tier 1 capital:

$$\text{Qualifying Tier 2 of subsidiary} = \text{Qualifying total capital of subsidiary} - \text{Qualifying Tier 1 of subsidiary}$$

9.3 ILLUSTRATIVE EXAMPLE 1: CALCULATION OF THE IMPACT OF MINORITY INTERESTS ON CONSOLIDATED CAPITAL

This example covers how capital related to minority interests is allocated to the capital of the consolidated bank. This example is based on a notably similar one provided in the Annex 3 of the document published by the Basel Committee on Banking Supervision: *Basel III: A Global Regulatory Framework for More Resilient Banks and Banking Systems*. Whilst this example is highly simplified, it provides an introduction to how a subsidiary contributes to regulatory consolidated capital.

Let us assume that a banking group comprised Bank P – the parent bank – and a sole subsidiary – Bank S. Bank P and Bank S were included in the group's regulatory consolidation parameter. Bank P owned 75% of the ordinary shares issued by Bank S (i.e., minority interests were attributed 25% of Bank S's share capital and reserves), as shown in Figure 9.1. Bank S issued 8 and 9 of AT1 and Tier 2 instruments respectively, of which 5 and 5 were owned by third-party investors respectively.

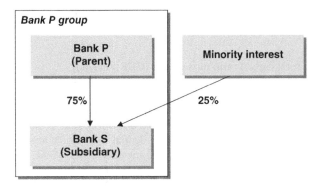

FIGURE 9.1   Structure of the Bank P group

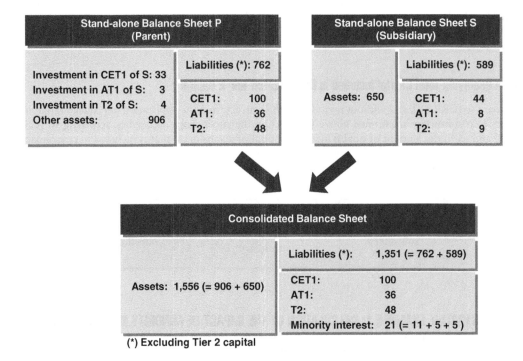

(*) Excluding Tier 2 capital

FIGURE 9.2   Bank P and Bank S, stand-alone and consolidated balance sheets

Figure 9.2 highlights the stand-alone balance sheets of each bank and the consolidated balance sheet (note that CET1 is Common Equity Tier 1, AT1 is Additional Tier 1 and T2 is Tier 2). Beware that from an accounting perspective Tier 2 capital is commonly recognised as a liability, but from a regulatory perspective it is a component of the total regulatory capital.

The first step was to calculate the minimum capital requirements, including its "combined buffer requirement" (CBR), for Bank S on a sub-consolidated basis (i.e., on an individual basis in this case as Bank S had no subsidiaries of its own). Let us assume that Bank S's RWAs were 400. In this example, the minimum requirements of Bank S and the subsidiary's contribution to consolidated requirements were the same as there were no intercompany items. In other words, the RWAs of Bank S on a sub-consolidated level coincided with the RWAs of the consolidated group related to Bank S.

TABLE 9.1　Capital position of Bank S

Capital Component	Minimum Requirement (a)	RWAs (b)	Minimum Requirement (c) = (a) × (b)	Bank S Capital (d)	Bank S Surplus (e) = (d) − (c)
CET1	8%	400	32	44	12
Total Tier 1	9.5%	400	38	52	14
Total Capital	11.5%	400	46	61	15

Note: the CET1 minimum requirement included the subsidiary's CBR

TABLE 9.2　Calculation of the qualifying consolidated capital attributable to minority interests

Capital Component	Bank S Capital (d)	Amount Issued to Minority Interest (f)	Bank S Surplus (e)	Surplus Attributable to Minority Interest (g) = (e) × (f)/(d)	Amount Included in Consolidated Capital (h) = (f) − (g)
CET1	44	11	12	3	8
Total Tier 1	52	16	14	4	12
Total Capital	61	21	15	5	16

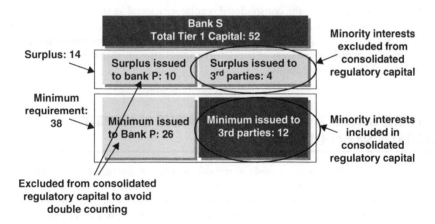

FIGURE 9.3　Bank S's Tier 1 capital and its contribution to consolidated Tier 1 capital

The CET1, Tier 1 and total capital (i.e., own funds) ratio requirements of Bank S were 8%, 9.5% and 11.5% respectively. Table 9.1 summarises the capital position of Bank S.

　　The second step was to calculate the amount of the capital issued by Bank S to the minority interest (i.e., to third parties) that could be included in consolidated capital as shown in Table 9.2.

　　Thus, if we look at Bank S's total Tier 1 capital, we can see that only the minimum requirement attributed to third parties was included in the consolidated total Tier 1 capital (see Figure 9.3). In other words, the surplus total Tier 1 capital issued to third parties was excluded from consolidated total Tier 1 capital.

TABLE 9.3   Calculation of consolidated regulatory capital

Capital Component	Bank P Capital (i)	Added From Bank S (j)	Consolidated Capital (k) = (i) + (j)
Common Equity Tier 1	100	8	108
Additional Tier 1	36	4	40
Tier 2	48	4	52

The third step was to calculate the components of Bank S's capital to be included in the consolidated regulatory capital (all data taken directly from column (h) in Table 9.2). AT1 was calculated as the difference between Tier 1 and CET1, while Tier 2 was the difference between total capital and Tier 1:

$$\text{Common Equity Tier 1(CET1)} = 8$$

$$\text{Additional Tier 1 (AT1)} = \text{Total Tier 1} - \text{CET1} = 12 - 8 = 4$$

$$\text{Tier 2} = \text{Total capital} - \text{Total Tier 1} = 16 - 12 = 4$$

The last step was to calculate the consolidated regulatory capital as shown in Table 9.3.

Therefore, the components of Bank S's capital that were added to the consolidated capital were those placed with third-party investors that were utilised to meet the subsidiary's minimum capital requirements. In other words, any excess of regulatory capital attributed to third parties was excluded from the consolidated regulatory capital.

9.4 ILLUSTRATIVE EXAMPLE 2: CALCULATION OF THE IMPACT OF MINORITY INTERESTS ON CONSOLIDATED CAPITAL

The following is another illustrative example of the calculation for determining the amount of capital issued out of subsidiaries to third parties that can be included in consolidated capital.

Let us assume that Megabank owned 75% of Trustbank's ordinary shares, which were deemed to be eligible CET1 instruments if they were issued by Megabank. Trustbank's share capital plus reserves were 2,160, of which 540 (i.e., 25%) was attributed to minority interests. Additionally, Trustbank had to deduct 160 of regulatory adjustments (e.g., goodwill) resulting in a 2,000 (= 2,160 – 160) CET1 capital.

In addition, Trustbank had outstanding 320 in qualifying AT1 instruments (i.e., they were deemed to be eligible AT1 instruments if they were issued by Megabank) and 480 in qualifying Tier 2 instruments, fully owned by third parties (i.e., no AT1 or Tier 2 instruments of Trustbank were issued to Megabank). There were no regulatory adjustments to AT1 or Tier 2 capital.

Trustbank's minimum capital requirements were a 7.5% CET1 (including the combined buffer requirement), a 9% Tier 1 and an 11% total capital, as shown in Figure 9.4. Trustbank's risk-weighted

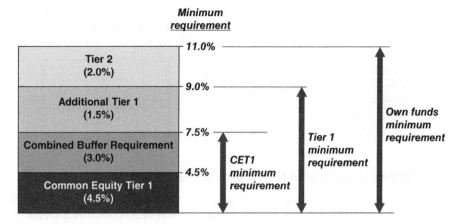

FIGURE 9.4 Trustbank's minimum capital requirements

assets (at the sub-consolidated level) represented 16,800, while the risk-weighted assets of the consolidated group that related to Trustbank were 18,000.

9.4.1 Minority Interests Included in Consolidated CET1 Capital

Let us calculate the amount of the minority interest of Trustbank that was included in consolidated CET1 capital, step by step.

Trustbank's minimum CET1 requirement was 1,260 (= 7.5% × 16,800), calculated as the product of (i) the 7.5% minimum CET1 ratio requirement and (ii) its risk-weighted assets (16,800).

The minimum CET1 requirement based on the consolidated risk-weighted assets that related to Trustbank was 1,350 (= 7.5% × 18,000), calculated as the product of (i) the 7.5% minimum CET1 ratio requirement and (ii) the risk-weighted assets of the consolidated group attributable to Trustbank (18,000).

The lower of these two minimum CET1 requirements was 1,260 (i.e., the lower of 1,260 and 1,350). Next, the surplus CET1 of Trustbank was 740, calculated as the difference between (i) the CET1 capital of Trustbank (2,000) and (ii) that lower CET1 requirement (1,260):

$$\begin{array}{c} \text{Surplus CET1 of} \\ \text{Trustbank} \\ (740) \end{array} = \begin{array}{c} \text{CET1 of} \\ \text{Trustbank} \\ (2,000) \end{array} - \text{Lower of} \left[\begin{array}{c} \text{Minimum} \\ \text{CET1} \\ \text{requirement} \\ \text{of Trustbank} \\ (1,260) \end{array} \text{ and } \begin{array}{c} \text{Minimum CET1} \\ \text{requirement based on} \\ \text{consolidated RWAs that} \\ \text{relates to Trustbank} \\ (1,350) \end{array} \right]$$

The surplus CET1 capital of Trustbank attributable to the minority interest was 185, calculated as the product of (i) the percentage of Trustbank's share capital and reserves held by minority interest (25% = 540/2,160) and (ii) the surplus CET1 of Trustbank (740).

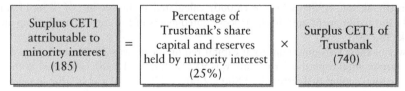

The amount of the minority interest of Trustbank that was included in consolidated CET1 capital was 355 (= 540 – 185), calculated as the difference between (i) the amount of the minority interest of Trustbank (540) and (ii) Trustbank's surplus CET1 attributable to the minority interest (185):

$$
\begin{array}{c}
\boxed{\begin{array}{c}\text{Recognised CET1}\\\text{in consolidation}\\\text{attributable to}\\\text{minority interest}\\(355)\end{array}}
\;=\;
\boxed{\begin{array}{c}\text{CET1 of subsidiary}\\\text{attributable to minority}\\\text{interest}\\(540)\end{array}}
\;-\;
\boxed{\begin{array}{c}\text{Surplus CET1}\\\text{attributable to}\\\text{minority interest}\\(185)\end{array}}
\end{array}
$$

9.4.2 Amounts Included in Consolidated AT1 and Tier 2 Capital

The methodology for calculating the amount of minority interests to be included in CET1 at consolidated level is applied by analogy for the calculation of the amount of AT1 and Tier 2 capital attributable to the minority interest to be included in consolidated AT1 and Tier 2 capital.

Calculation of Amount related to Minority Interest Included in Consolidated AT1   Trustbank's minimum Tier 1 requirement was 1,512 (= 9% × 16,800), calculated as the product of (i) its 9% minimum Tier 1 ratio requirement and (ii) its risk-weighted assets (16,800).

The minimum Tier 1 requirement based on the consolidated risk-weighted assets that related to Trustbank was 1,620 (= 9% × 18,000), calculated as the product of (i) its 9% minimum Tier 1 ratio requirement and (ii) risk-weighted assets of the consolidated group attributable to Trustbank (18,000).

The lower of these two minimum Tier 1 requirements was 1,512 (i.e., the lower of 1,512 and 1,620). The surplus Tier 1 capital of Trustbank was 808, calculated as the difference between (i) the Tier 1 capital of Trustbank (2,320 = 2,000 + 320) and (ii) that lower Tier 2 requirement (1,512).

The surplus Tier 1 capital of Trustbank attributable to the minority interest was 280, calculated as the product of (i) the percentage of Trustbank's Tier 1 capital held by minority interest (34% = (540 + 320)/(2,160 + 320)) and (ii) the surplus Tier 1 of Trustbank (808).

The amount of the minority interest of Trustbank that was included in consolidated Tier 1 capital was 580 (= 860 – 280), calculated as the difference between (i) the amount of Trustbank's Tier 1 capital attributable to the minority interest of Trustbank (860 = 540 + 320) and (ii) Trustbank's surplus Tier 1 attributable to the minority interest (280).

Finally, the amount of AT1 capital attributable to minority interests to be included in AT1 capital at consolidated level was 225 (= 580 – 355), calculated as the difference between (i) the amount of Trustbank's Tier 1 capital attributable to the minority interest to be included in consolidated Tier 1 capital (580) and (ii) the amount of Trustbank's CET1 attributable to the minority interest to be included in consolidated CET1 capital (355).

Calculation of Amount related to Minority Interest Included in Consolidated Tier 2   Trustbank's minimum total capital requirement was 1,848 (= 11% × 16,800), calculated as the product of (i) its 11% minimum total capital ratio requirement and (ii) its risk-weighted assets (16,800).

The minimum total capital requirement based on the consolidated risk-weighted assets that related to Trustbank was 1,980 (= 11% × 18,000), calculated as the product of (i) its 11% minimum total capital ratio requirement and (ii) the risk-weighted assets of the consolidated group attributable to Trustbank (18,000).

The lower of these two minimum total capital requirements was 1,848 (the lower of 1,848 and 1,980). The surplus total capital of Trustbank was 952 (= 2,800 – 1,848), calculated as the difference between (i) the total capital of Trustbank (2,800 = 2,000 + 320 + 480) and (ii) that lower total capital requirement (1,848).

The surplus total capital of Trustbank attributable to the minority interest was 431 (= 45% × 952), calculated as the product of (i) the percentage of Trustbank's total capital held by minority interest (45% = (540 + 320 + 480)/(2,160 + 320 + 480)) and (ii) the surplus total capital of Trustbank (952).

The amount of the minority interest of Trustbank that was included in consolidated total capital was 909 (= 1,340 − 431), calculated as the difference between (i) the amount of Trustbank's total capital attributable to the minority interest of Trustbank (1,340 = 540 + 320 + 480) and (ii) Trustbank's surplus total capital attributable to the minority interest (431).

Finally, the amount of Tier 2 attributable to minority interests to be included in Tier 2 at consolidated level was 329 (= 909 − 580), calculated as the difference between (i) the amount of Trustbank's total capital attributable to the minority interest to be included in consolidated total capital (909) and (ii) the amount of Trustbank's Tier 1 attributable to the minority interest to be included in consolidated Tier 1 capital (580).

9.5 CASE STUDY: ARTIFICIAL CREATION OF MINORITY INTERESTS

An interesting way to create capital under Basel II was to add minority interests that were not deducted from Core Tier 1 capital (see Figure 9.5). Although feasible under Basel II, the transaction described herein does not work under Basel III. However, I have included it to show an interesting technique, albeit obsolete, to enhance regulatory capital.

Let us assume that a bank called SmallBank had a stake in a corporate, called ABC, worth EUR 500 million. The transaction was implemented along the following steps:

1. SmallBank created an SPV. SmallBank provided the stake in ABC in exchange for the equity capital of the SPV. At this stage, SmallBank owned 100% of the SPV.
2. SmallBank sold 40% of the equity capital of the SPV to Gigabank in exchange for EUR 200 million. At this stage SmallBank owned 60% of the SPV.
3. Because after implementing Step (2) SmallBank reduced its economic exposure from 100% to 60% to the ABC stake, SmallBank and Gigabank entered into an equity derivative. The derivative underlying shares were 40% of the ABC shares.

The strategy just covered was a very preliminary version of the transaction. It faced the following drawbacks:

1. The derivative was probably booked in SmallBank's trading book. This meant that SmallBank was likely to be required to fair value the derivative through profit or loss, increasing the volatility of its profit or loss statement.

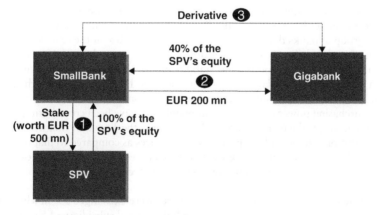

FIGURE 9.5 Creating non-deductible minority interests

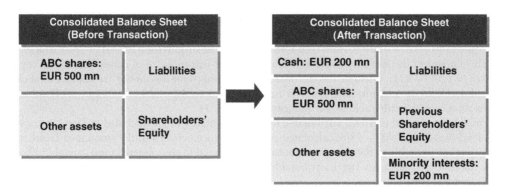

FIGURE 9.6   SmallBank's consolidated balance sheet, ignoring the derivative fair valuing

2. The derivative consumed capital as it bore market risk.
3. Gigabank needed to hedge its exposure to ABC's shares. To hedge its exposure, Gigabank needed to sell ABC shares in the market. Therefore, a sufficiently liquid stock lending market for ABC shares was required.

Figure 9.6 illustrates the consolidated balance sheet of SmallBank after implementing the transaction, ignoring the fair valuing of the derivative. The transaction generated EUR 200 million of minority interests.

9.6 CASE STUDY: BANCO SANTANDER REPURCHASE OF MINORITY INTERESTS IN SANTANDER BRASIL

This case study covers the regulatory capital initiatives taken by the Spanish bank Banco Santander ("Santander") related to its Santander Brasil subsidiary.

9.6.1 Acquisition of Banco Real by Banco Santander

In August 2008, Santander acquired majority control of the Brazilian Banco Real through its Brazilian subsidiary Banco Santander Brasil ("Santander Brasil") as a result of the acquisition of the Dutch Bank ABN Amro by a group of banks that included Santander. Banco Real at the time was the fourth largest non-government owned Brazilian bank as measured by assets. Since the mid-1990s, Brazil had benefited from political, social and macroeconomic stability coupled with improvements in real income and a resulting high rate of upward social and economic mobility. During this period, the Brazilian financial services industry experienced substantial growth, as economic stability, increased employment rates and rising purchasing power of the Brazilian population have been contributing to an increase in penetration of financial products and services. Nonetheless, the Brazilian financial market still presented a low penetration rate of banking products and services as compared to that of other developed and emerging markets, offering further growth opportunities. The acquisition offered significant opportunities for the creation of operating, commercial and technological synergies by preserving the best practices of each bank.

In a share exchange transaction, Banco Real's shares were exchanged for newly issued shares of Banco Santander. As a result, Banco Real became a wholly-owned subsidiary of Santander.

The acquisition of Banco Real resulted in a substantial amount of goodwill – BRL 27.6 billion. Potential impairments of goodwill relating to Banco Real could have a significant future impact on profit or loss of both Santander and Santander Brasil. Note that under IFRS, entities are required to test goodwill for impairment on an annual basis and that any impairment in goodwill is reflected in profit or loss. Note as well that from a regulatory capital perspective the only effect of a goodwill impairment charge is its tax effect. As goodwill was amortised over a 10-year period under the Brazilian tax code, the deduction of goodwill from CET1.

On Santander's financial statements the goodwill related to Banco Real was denominated in BRL. At each reporting date Santander had to translate the BRL amount (BRL 27.6 billion) into EUR. Any translation gains and losses were recognised in consolidated other comprehensive income – OCI – (i.e., in the translation differences reserve). From a regulatory capital perspective, retranslation gains and losses on goodwill had no impact on Santander's CET1 capital, as two opposing effects fully offset each other:

- Retranslation gains and losses were recognised in OCI. As OCI is an element of CET1 capital, any retranslation gains positively impacted Santander's CET1 capital, while any retranslation losses had a direct negative impact on Santander's CET1 capital; and
- Goodwill was deducted from CET1 capital. Thus, any retranslation gains meant a larger deduction from CET1 capital and, conversely, any retranslation losses meant a larger deduction from CET1 capital.

Although goodwill was amortised from a tax perspective, its IFRS accounting carrying amount was not influenced by such amortisation. As a result, prior to any impairment charge, Santander recognised a BRL 27.6 billion goodwill in its balance sheet under IFRS. Thus, prior to any goodwill impairment and from a regulatory capital perspective, the Spanish bank deducted BRL 27.6 billion from its CET1 capital, regardless of the tax amortisation.

Because it generated sufficient taxable profit, the goodwill amortisation benefited Santander as it paid less taxes. In other words, the Spanish bank's profit or loss was aided from a lower tax expense. As profit or loss is a component of CET1 capital, the tax amortisation helped the Spanish bank to generate CET1 capital more rapidly.

9.6.2 IPO of Santander Brasil and Mandatory Convertible Issuance to Qatar Holding

In October 2009 Santander Brasil raised BRL 14.1 billion (approximately USD 8.05 billion) in an initial public offering. The Brazilian bank 600 million shares at a BRL 23.5 price per share. The offering benefited from a growing appetite for emerging market securities that helped push the benchmark Bovespa index 68% higher in 2009. As a result of the IPO, Santander's ownership of Santander Brasil was reduced from 98.5% to 83.1%. Figure 9.7 illustrates the shareholding structure of Santander Brasil before and after the IPO.

The bankruptcy of Lehman Brothers in September 2008 triggered a worldwide funding crisis. The acquisition of Banco Real required heavy investment by Santander Brasil to integrate operations and modernise the infrastructure. The IPO aimed at raising funding to meet the acquisition objectives.

In 2009 capital was a secondary, albeit important, concern. Basel II's capital requirements were notably less stringent than those of Basel III.

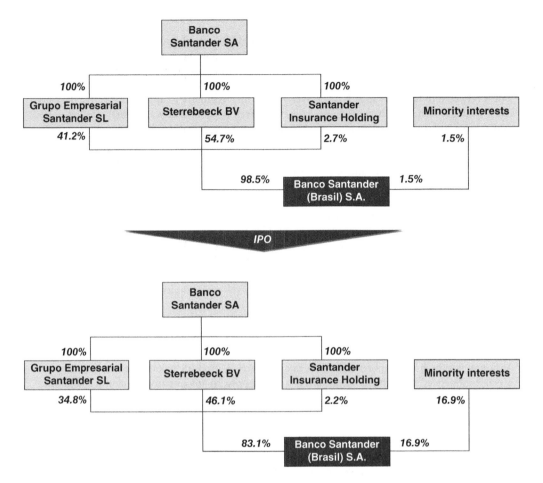

FIGURE 9.7   Banco Santander (Brasil) – Shareholding prior and after the IPO

In August 2010, Santander Insurance Holding sold in the market 2.2% of the capital of Santander Brasil. As a result, minority interests held 19.1% of the ordinary shares of the Brazilian bank. The sale price amounted to EUR 867 million, which gave rise to increases of EUR 162 million in reserves and EUR 790 million in non-controlling interests, and a decrease of EUR 85 million in the translation differences reserve.

9.6.3 Mandatorily Convertible Issuance to Qatar Holding

As part of the IPO, the Spanish bank to comply with securities regulations which required Santander Brasil to have at least 25% of its shares traded on the São Paulo stock exchange by the end of 2014. In order to meet that requirement, in October 2010 Santander sold bonds mandatorily convertible into Santander Brasil shares to Qatar Holding amounting to USD 2.8 billion.

Qatar Holding was the investment arm of the Qatar Investment Authority, the Persian Gulf country's sovereign wealth fund. It owned stakes in several of the world's largest banks, including Agricultural Bank of China, Barclays Plc and Credit Suisse Group. The underlying shares represented 5% of Santander Brasil's share capital. The bond was denominated in USD, had a maturity of three years (29

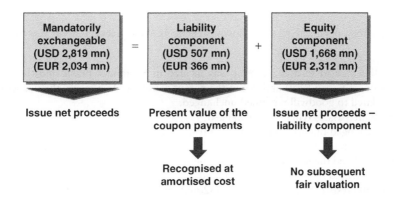

FIGURE 9.8 Initial recognition of the mandatorily convertible bond into Banco Santander (Brasil) shares

October 2013), a 6.75% coupon and a conversion price of BRL 23.75 per share. At conversion, Santander had the right to deliver to Qatar Holding either existing or new shares.

The mandatorily convertible sale also raised much-needed funding for Santander, following an acquisition spree that saw it buy assets in the UK, Poland, Germany and the US.

Initial Accounting Recognition   From an accounting perspective the mandatorily convertible bond was recognised as a compound instrument. The instrument was split between (see Figure 9.8):

- A liability component of USD 507 million (EUR 366 million) relating to the present value of the interest payable. This component was recognised at amortised cost; and
- An equity component of USD 2,312 million (EUR 1,668 million) representing the conversion feature. This component was recognised in Santander's shareholders' equity in "other equity instruments". The EUR amount was not subsequently fair valued.

Transfer of the Mandatorily Convertible Underlying Shares   In 2012, Santander decided to meet the conversion of the mandatorily convertible bond through the delivery of Santander Brasil shares owned by the Spanish bank. In January and March 2012 Santander transferred shares representing 4.41% and 0.77% of Santander Brasil to two leading international banks that undertook to deliver these shares to the holder of the mandatorily convertible bond upon their maturity and under the terms of the bond.

From an accounting perspective, under IFRS disposals (and acquisitions) not giving rise to a change in control are recognised as equity transactions, and no gain or loss is recognised in the profit or loss statement and the initially recognised goodwill is not remeasured. The difference between the consideration received (or transferred) and the increase (or decrease) in non-controlling interests is recognised in reserves.

In our case, the transfer eliminated the EUR 1,668 million equity component previously recognised. As a result, "other equity instruments" in Santander shareholders' equity section was reduced by EUR 1,668 million. In addition, translation differences in equity were reduced by EUR 26 million. Santander recognised as well an increase in reserves of EUR 162 million corresponding to the difference between the consideration received and the increase in non-controlling interests, and an increase in non-controlling interests of EUR 1,532 million. Accordingly, there was no substantial overall impact on Santander's shareholders' equity.

From a regulatory perspective, the following elements were relevant upon the transfer (see Figure 9.9):

- Goodwill remained unchanged as it was located in Santander Brasil (mostly due to the acquisition of Banco Real) and not in the parent company. As a result, the deduction from CET1 related to goodwill remained unchanged;
- Risk-weighted assets remained unchanged;
- Reserves changed due to the reduction in translation differences (EUR 26 million) and the increase in retained earnings (EUR 162 million) due to the difference between the consideration received and the increase in non-controlling interests. As a result, CET1 related to these reserves increased by EUR 136 million; and
- Minority interests increased by EUR 1,532 million. Let us assume that all this increase was related only to CET1 instruments (i.e., ordinary shares) of Santander Brasil. The amount that met the minimum CET1 capital requirements of Santander Brasil was recognised in consolidated CET1. The amount exceeding the minimum CET1 capital requirements of Santander Brasil was excluded from consolidated CET1 capital.

Thus, overall, the transfer had a positive impact on Santander's consolidated CET1 capital.

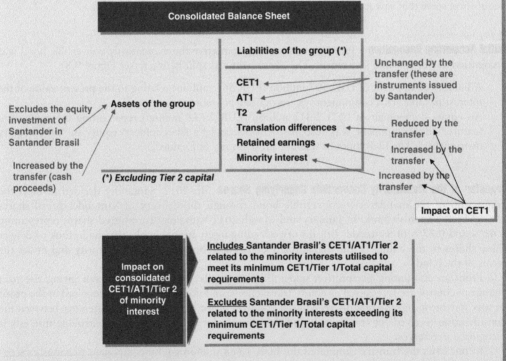

FIGURE 9.9 Impact on CET1 capital of the transfer of the Banco Santander (Brasil) shares by Banco Santander S.A

9.6.4 Capital Reduction of Santander Brasil

In September 2013 Santander announced a capital reduction in its Brazilian subsidiary to be replaced by hybrid instruments. In November 2013 Santander Brasil's shareholders approved:

- A BRL 6 billion (approximately EUR 2 billion) ordinary share capital reduction. 75% of the capital reduction was effected to the shares owned by the parent bank and 25% to those owned by the minority shareholders. This action was economically similar to an extraordinary dividend paid to Santander Brasil's shareholders.
- The issuance of Tier 1 and Tier 2 capital instruments in a total amount equivalent to BRL 6 billion. The parent bank committed to take its 75% share of the hybrid capital and offer retail shareholders to take their corresponding stake, subscribing any notes not subscribed by minority shareholders. The distribution of the Tier 1 and Tier 2 capital instruments was finalised in January 2014. Santander Brasil issued USD 1.25 billion of Tier 1 subordinated perpetual securities with a coupon of 7.375% and USD 1.25 billion of Tier 2 10-year subordinated securities with a coupon of 6%.

Prior to the capital reduction, Santander Brasil had 21.5% total capital under Basel II, well exceeding its minimum capital requirements. At the same time, Santander Brasil had 25% of its ordinary shares held by minority interests. Note that according to Basel III any excess capital associated with minority interests was not recognised in consolidated regulatory capital. In the case of Santander Brasil, it meant that 25% of the substantial surplus was not included in Santander's consolidated regulatory capital, a rather inefficient situation.

Additionally, Santander Brasil had almost no AT1 and Tier 2 capital, implying that the total capital requirements were met largely with CET1 instruments (i.e., with ordinary shares), another inefficient situation.

The main objective of the transaction was to relocate regulatory capital to regions with stronger credit growth than Brazil, probably Mexico although at that time Santander did not provide any guidance on where exactly the capital would be deployed.

The transaction consisted of a replacement of CET1 by hybrid capital and distribution of a special dividend in an amount approximately equivalent to the issue of the two subordinated debt with the aim to optimise their regulatory capital structure. The amount of total capital at Santander Brasil remained unchanged, but its proportion of CET1 was notably reduced. As a result, the surplus CET1 associated with the minority interests was reduced.

9.6.5 Repurchase of Minority Interests

In April 2014 Santander announced a public offer to acquire the minority interests of Santander Brasil, to be implemented in September 2014 (see Figure 9.10). Prior to the offer, the minority interests owned 25% of the share capital of Santander Brasil. The offer was voluntary in that the minority interests were not obliged to participate and it was not conditional upon a minimum acceptance level.

The offer was valued at BRL 15.31 per share (or USD 6.86), a 20% premium over the closing price on the day prior to the announcement. The main terms of the offer were the following:

- All the shares accepted in the offering would be acquired by Santander. Santander Brasil shareholders would receive 0.7152 newly issued Santander ADRs (American Depositary Receipts) or BDRs (Brazilian Depositary Receipts). Up to approximately 665 million shares of Banco Santander would be issued and listed in the São Paulo stock exchange, denominated in BRL through BDRs;
- Shareholders accepting the offer would receive Santander dividends after completion of the transaction;

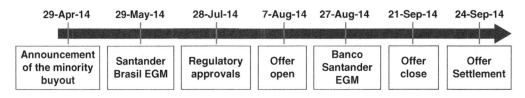

FIGURE 9.10   Planned timetable of Santander Brasil minority buyout at the time of its announcement

- Shares not tendered in the offering would continue to be listed in the São Paulo and New York stock exchanges (i.e., there would be no squeeze-out);
- The offer was not subject to a minimum acceptance requirement; and
- The offer was subject to approval by the São Paulo and New York stock regulators, and Santander Brasil and Santander shareholders.

UBS provided a fairness opinion to the board of directors of Santander and NM Rothschild prepared a customary "laudo" valuation report for Santander Brasil.

In October 2014, Santander disclosed that minority shareholders representing 13.65% of the ordinary share capital of Santander Brasil had accepted the offer. Accordingly, Santander owned 88.30% of Santander Brasil's ordinary share capital. As consequence of the offer, Santander Brasil's shares were no longer listed on Level 2 of BM&F Bovespa, and were trading on the notably more illiquid traditional listing segment.

9.6.6 Rationale, Strengths and Weaknesses of the Minority Buyout

According to Banco Santander the main objective of the transaction was to fully capture the long-term growth potential in its Brazilian unit. Despite the economic downturn in Brazil, Santander was optimistic about Santander Brasil's long-term prospects. Therefore, Santander was prepared to further invest in Santander Brasil and enhance long-term value.

Strengths   The main strength of the transaction was the repurchase of the minority interests at a price much lower than the IPO price.

Another relevant strength of the transaction was its positive impact on the group's regulatory capital. The impact in CET1 capital was an increase of EUR 1,458 million, as follows (see Figure 9.11):

- The newly issued shares by Santander gave rise to an increase of EUR 185 million in share capital and EUR 2,375 million in share premium, both elements of CET1 capital. Consequently, the share issuance increased the group's CET1 capital by EUR 2,560 million (= 2,375 mn + 185 mn);
- The difference between the decrease in non-controlling interests and the consideration paid (i.e., the fair value of the Santander shares delivered) was recognised in retained earnings, an element of CET1 capital. This amount totalled EUR 15 million, increasing the carrying amount of retained earnings and, as a consequence, CET1 capital; and

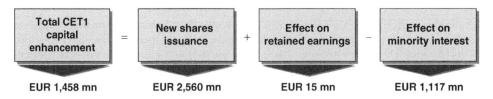

FIGURE 9.11   Effect on the group's CET1 capital of Santander Brasil minority buyout

■ The reduction in minority interests of EUR 2,572 million reduced the level of Santander's CET1 capital. Interestingly, the reduction from CET1 capital was notably lower than the EUR 2,572 million amount of accounting reduction. Prior to the repurchase, the excess regulatory capital at Santander Brasil related to the purchased minority interests was *not* included in consolidated regulatory capital. At the time of the repurchase Santander Brasil had a 15.2% CET1 capital ratio, no AT1 capital and 1.4% Tier 2 capital ratio. The Brazilian bank's CET1, Tier 1 and total capital requirements were 4.5%, 6% and 8% respectively. Santander Brazil met its 8% total capital requirement using 6.6% of CET1 capital and 1.4% of Tier 2 capital. It met its 6% Tier 1 capital requirement using 6% of CET1 capital. Thus, it employed 6.6% of CET1 capital to meet its minimum capital requirements. As the bank had a 15.2% CET1 capital ratio, it held a notably large 8.8% (= 15.2% − 6.6%) excess CET1 capital level. The reduction of CET1 capital at Santander due to the reduction of the minority interests was approximately EUR 1,117 million (= 2,572 mn × 6.6%/15.2%).

The second strength of the transaction was its accretive nature. The minority buyout had a positive impact on Santander's Price/Earnings ("P/E") and Earnings-per-Share (EPS). For example, Santander Brasil was trading at a P/E multiple of 8.8 in 2014. By paying the 20% premium, this multiple was increased to 10.5, a multiple notably lower than Santander's 14.7 at the time.

Weaknesses   The main weakness of the strategy was the potential creation of a deep sense of frustration in Santander Brasil minority shareholders. Whilst Banco Santander offered a 20% premium relative to then current share price, investors that took part in the flotation of Santander Brasil back in October 2009 were experiencing large losses (35%, assuming that the offer was valued at BRL 15.31) as the IPO price was BRL 23.50. These investors faced a challenging dilemma: take a substantial loss by accepting Santander's offer or risk holding an illiquid stock if a majority of shareholders accepted the buyback offer. Especially relevant was the position of the top shareholder after Santander, Qatar Holding which prior to the offer owned 5.17% of Santander Brasil.

This was not the first time Santander bought minorities at a price notably lower than its IPO price. For example, in December 2012 Santander offered to buy the 10.26% stake in Banco Español de Credito that it didn't own for a price well below its IPO pricing level. However, Santander had no trouble in January 2014 in placing with a strong demand the flotation of its U.S. consumer finance unit.

Investors with a buy-and-hold investment philosophy are very important to the success of IPOs. At that time, the market was expecting Santander to list its British subsidiary Santander UK (an IPO still not materialised at the time of writing). Any investor interested in making an investment in a future IPO of a Santander subsidiary would look very carefully at the parent's record with regard to their treatment of minority shareholders.

CHAPTER 10

Investments in Capital Instruments of Financial Institutions

This chapter covers the Basel III treatment of investments in capital instruments of financial institutions that are not consolidated from a regulatory capital perspective. Broadly, the calculations of the impact on regulatory capital are based on the type of investment and on comparisons of the investment amount relative to the bank's CET1 levels. There are two types of investment in unconsolidated financial institutions:

- **Non-significant investments** in CET1 instruments of unconsolidated financial institutions: direct, indirect and synthetic holdings by the bank of the CET1 instruments of financial sector entities where the bank does *not* have a significant investment in those entities; and
- **Significant investments** in CET1 instruments of unconsolidated financial institutions: direct, indirect and synthetic holdings by the bank of the CET1 instruments of financial sector entities where the bank has a significant investment in those entities.

The objective of this chapter is to shed more light on how a bank calculates those items as well as the amounts to be risk-weighted.

The regulatory treatment of these investments, when unconsolidated, follows three main lines (see Figure 10.1): (i) to deduct the investment from capital (CET1, AT1 or Tier 2), (ii) to risk weight the investment like any other investment in such instruments and (iii) a combination thereof. On the one hand, a deduction of a capital investment in a financial institution from a bank's capital is the most conservative way to deal with double leverage: the bank is holding enough capital to absorb a full loss in its investment in the financial institution. On the other hand, a risk weighting of the investment is the less conservative approach as the risk weight applied is typically notably lower than 1,250%.

Whist national supervisors are allowed some flexibility when setting guidelines to allow banks avoid fully deducting equity investments in financial institutions through the incorporation of thresholds, most supervisors are applying a rather common approach.

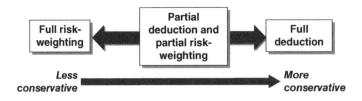

FIGURE 10.1 Main regulatory approaches on investments in capital instruments of financial institutions

10.1 BASEL III TREATMENT OF INVESTMENTS IN CAPITAL INSTRUMENTS OF FINANCIAL INSTITUTIONS

This section covers the Basel III treatment of equity investments in financial institutions as guided in the general framework (i.e., the BCBS document titled *Basel III: A Global Regulatory Framework for More Resilient Banks and Banking Systems*) regarding these investments. Particular clauses incorporated by the CRR are covered where relevant.

10.1.1 Reciprocal Cross-holdings Designed to Artificially Bolster Capital Positions

Reciprocal cross-holdings of capital, designed to artificially inflate the capital position of the bank, are deducted in full. For this purpose, a holding is considered to be a cross-holding if the investee entity has also invested in any type of the bank's capital instruments, which may not be the same type of instrument as the bank is holding.

Banks must apply a "corresponding deduction approach" (to be explained below) to such investments in the capital of other banks, other financial institutions and insurance entities. This means the deduction is applied to the same component of capital for which the capital would qualify if it was issued by the bank itself.

10.1.2 Regulatory Consolidation of Investments in Capital Instruments of Financial Entities

Basel III's objective of its treatment regarding investments in capital instruments of financial institutions is to prevent double leverage (i.e., the double counting of capital), or in other words to ensure that banks do not bolster their own capital with capital that is also used to support the risks of other financial sector entities.

The Basel III treatment of these investments depends on their size and their nature. The starting point is to assess whether the financial sector investee is consolidated from a regulatory perspective. Investments in entities that are outside of the scope of regulatory consolidation refers to investments in entities that have not been consolidated at all or have not been consolidated in such a way as to result in their assets being included in the calculation of consolidated risk-weighted assets of the group.

Investments in Capital Instruments of Banking Entities In principle, the basis of the regulatory consolidation is the accounting consolidation. I assume that the reader is familiar with the fundamentals of accounting consolidation, which were covered in Chapter 8. Let us undertake a simple situation in which a parent bank holds an investment in the capital instruments of a bank investee. Whether the investment is in the scope of regulatory consolidation is driven by its accounting recognition (see Figure 10.2):

- If the bank investee is **fully consolidated** into the group's financial statements (i.e., the investee is a **subsidiary**), the parent bank's investment in the shareholders' equity of the subsidiary is eliminated upon accounting consolidation and is substituted with the assets and liabilities of the banking subsidiary. Therefore, from an accounting perspective, the assets of the banking subsidiary are incorporated upon consolidation into the assets of the consolidated banking group. From a regulatory perspective, the subsidiary's assets are **risk-weighted** in conjunction with the other assets of the banking group. The subsidiary is **in the scope of the regulatory consolidation** and, therefore, the guidelines in this chapter do *not* apply.
- If the bank investee is consolidated under the **equity method** (i.e., the investee is an **associate** or a **jointly controlled** entity) from an accounting point of view, the investment is initially recognised at cost and adjusted thereafter for the post-acquisition change in the investor bank's share of the

investee's net assets. From a regulatory perspective, the investee is consolidated on a pro-rata basis (i.e., the assets of the investee are incorporated to the consolidated assets in proportion to the ownership). The subsidiary is **in the scope of the regulatory consolidation** and, therefore, the guidelines in this chapter do *not* apply.

■ If the banking investee is *not* consolidated (i.e., it is not a subsidiary, associate or jointly controlled entity), from an accounting point of view the investment is recognised at either "fair value through profit or loss" or "fair value through OCI". The investment in the banking investee is **outside the scope of the regulatory consolidation** and, therefore, the guidelines in this chapter *do* apply.

Investments in Capital Instruments of Insurance Entities As explained in detail in Chapter 11, investments in the capital instruments of insurance entities are **outside the scope of regulatory consolidation**. Therefore, the guidelines in this chapter *do* apply.

Insurance companies are subject to the regulatory requirements of Solvency II, which takes into account the special characteristics of insurers' assets and liabilities. Therefore, insurance entities that

Accounting recognition	Example	Regulatory consolidation
Investment at FVTPL or FVTOCI (*)	Bank holds less than 10% in the share capital of the investee bank	Investment likely to be non-significant • If so, investment is added to other non-significant investments in financials ✓ Amounts exceeding 10% CET1 threshold are deducted ✓ Amounts below are risk weighted
	Bank holds more than 10% but less than 20% in the share capital of the investee bank	Investment likely to be significant • If so, investment is added to other significant investments in financials ✓ Amounts exceeding 10%/15% CET1 threshold are deducted ✓ Amounts below are risk-weighted
Associate (equity method)	Bank holds more than 20% and less than 50% in the share capital of another bank	Bank consolidates on a pro-rata basis → all assets and off-balance sheet positions are added to the other positions of the bank based on share of ownership
Joint control (equity method)	Bank enters into a contractual arrangement to exercise joint control over another bank	
Subsidiary (full consolidation)	Bank holds more than 50% of the issued share capital of the investee bank	Bank fully consolidates its subsidiary → all assets and off-balance sheet positions are added to the other positions of the bank Minority interests are recognised

(*) Investment recognised at FVTPL (fair value through profit or loss) or at FVTOCI (fair value through other comprehensive income)

FIGURE 10.2 General framework of the regulatory treatment of investments in capital instruments of banks

Accounting recognition	Example	Regulatory consolidation

Investment at FVTPL or FVTOCI	Bank holds less than 10% in the share capital of the insurer	**Investment likely to be non-significant**
		
		• If so, investment is added to other non-significant investments in financials
		  ✓ Amounts exceeding 10% CET1 threshold are deducted
		  ✓ Amounts below are risk weighted

	Bank holds more than 10% but less than 20% in the share capital of the insurer	

Associate (equity method)	Bank holds more than 20% and less than 50% in the share capital of another insurer	**Investment likely to be significant**
		
		• If so, investment is added to other significant investments in financials
		  ✓ Amounts exceeding 10%/15% CET1 threshold are deducted
		  ✓ Amounts below are risk-weighted

Joint control (equity method)	Bank enters into a contractual arrangement to exercise joint control over the insurer	
Subsidiary (full consolidation)	Bank holds more than 50% of the issued share capital of the insurer	

(*) Investment recognised at FVTPL (fair value through profit or loss) or at FVTOCI (fair value through other comprehensive income)

FIGURE 10.3 General framework of the regulatory treatment of investments in capital instruments of insurance companies

are consolidated from an accounting point of view (i.e., subsidiaries and associates) are deconsolidated for regulatory purposes. The capital treatment is based on whether the investment is deemed to be significant or non-significant, as shown in Figure 10.3. Thus, the accounting consolidation of the insurer investee does *not* affect the regulatory treatment.

10.1.3 Significant Investments

The regulatory treatment of investments in the capital of banking, financial and insurance entities that are **outside** the scope of regulatory consolidation depends on their size and their nature. In particular, Basel III distinguishes between investments on the basis of significance.

The general Basel III framework defines a **significant investment** as an investment that:

- Is more than 10% of the issued common share capital of the non-consolidated financial institution (in both the banking book and trading book); or
- The investee controls, or is controlled by, or is under common control with, the bank. Control of a company is defined as (i) ownership, control or holding with power to vote 20% or more of a class of voting securities of the company; or (ii) the company is consolidated for accounting purposes.

> If a bank has a significant investment in common equity, then any other capital instruments investment (e.g., in subordinated debt) in the unconsolidated investee is significant as well.

The CRR's definition of significant investment is similar to the one in the Basel III general framework. Pursuant to [CRR 43], a **significant investment** of a bank in a financial sector entity arises where any of the following conditions is met:

- The bank owns more than **10%** of the CET1 instruments issued by that entity;
- The bank has close links with that entity and owns CET1 instruments issued by that entity; or
- The bank owns CET1 instruments issued by that entity and the entity is not included in its regulatory consolidation but is included in its accounting consolidation.

> According to the third criterion, an investment in a fully or equity consolidated insurance entity is deemed to be a significant investment.
> An investment in a financial institution is consolidated as an associate (i.e., using the equity consolidation method) from an accounting perspective if the bank has significant influence over the financial institution, irrespective of the bank's holding of the common share of the institution. Therefore, a bank may hold less than 10% of the common share capital of a financial institution and be required to treat the investment as a significant investment.

The ownership of capital investments extends to **indirect** and **synthetic** holdings (such as through the holdings of **index** securities). Indirect holdings are exposures or parts of exposures that, if a direct holding losses its value, will result in a loss to the bank substantially equivalent to the loss in value of the direct holding. If a bank finds it operationally burdensome to look through and monitor their exact exposure to the capital of other financial institutions as a result of its holding of index securities, national authorities may permit the bank, subject to prior supervisory approval, to use a conservative estimate.

When a bank holds both long and short positions in the same underlying exposure where the maturity of the short position either matches the maturity of the long position or has a residual maturity of at least one year, it is the net long position that is to be included.

Nevertheless, pursuant to [CRR 47], owned instruments shall exclude underwriting positions held for five working days or fewer. Underwriting positions held for longer than five working days must be included.

Furthermore, national supervisors may allow banks, with prior supervisory approval, to exclude temporarily certain investments where these have been made in the context of resolving or providing financial assistance to reorganise a distressed institution.

10.1.4 Basel III Treatment of Non-significant Investments in Capital Instruments of Financial Entities

Hereinafter I will refer to an investment which is not deemed to be significant as "**non-significant**" (or "not significant" according to the CRR). I am aware that grammatically the term "**insignificant**" is more precise, but I am afraid that such term denotes a risk too small to be taken into account, a potentially misleading meaning when referred to financial assets.

Under Basel III and pursuant to [CRR 46], non-significant investments in non-consolidated financial institutions are added together and subject to a threshold treatment (see Figure 10.4).

1. The bank aggregates the investment amounts in CET1, AT1 and Tier 2 instruments of all non-significant investments. This aggregate amount is compared to 10% of the "relevant CET1 capital" of the bank (the 10% threshold);
2. The amount exceeding the 10% threshold is deducted applying the corresponding deduction approach (i.e., to the same component of capital for which the investment would qualify if it was issued by the bank itself). Any shortfall is deducted from the next higher tier of capital.

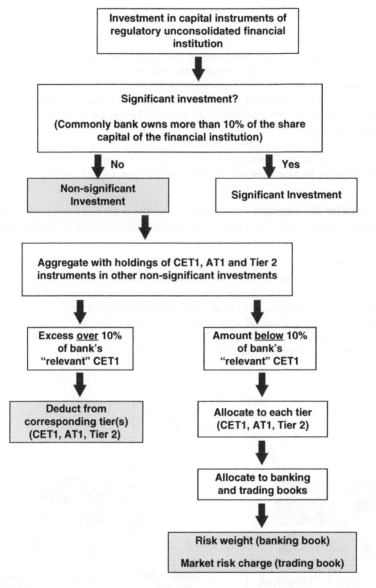

FIGURE 10.4 Basel III's treatment of non-significant investments in the capital instruments of unconsolidated financial institutions

> The amount to be deducted from CET1 is calculated as the total of all holdings which in aggregate exceed 10% of a bank's CET1 multiplied by the CET1 holdings as a percentage of the total capital holdings. This results in a CET1 deduction which corresponds to the proportion of total capital holdings held in CET1. Similarly, the amount to be deducted from AT1 or Tier 2 capital is calculated as the total of all holdings which in aggregate exceed 10% of the bank's CET1 multiplied by the AT1 or Tier 2 capital holdings as a percentage of the total capital holdings.

3. The amount below the 10% threshold is allocated, on a pro rata basis, between those below and those above the threshold, to the three tiers of capital (i.e., CET1, AT1 or Tier 2) and assigned to be risk-weighted taking into account whether the investment is located in the banking book or in the trading book:
   - Instruments in the **banking book** are treated as per the standardised approach or the Internal Ratings-Based Approach (as applicable), as shown in Figure 10.5. Where a bank uses the standardised approach for credit risk, [CRR 133] applies and the investments in the regulatory capital instruments are classified as equity claims and receive a risk weight of 100%, unless they are treated as high-risk items in accordance with [CRR 128]; and
   - Instruments in the **trading book** are treated as per the market risk rules.

Relevant CET1 Capital for 10% Threshold   [CRR 46(1)(a)] sets out the elements comprising the "**relevant CET1**" used to calculate the 10% threshold. It includes the items that qualify for CET1 capital and the following filters and deductions (see Figure 10.6):

- The prudential filter related to **securitised assets** [CRR 32];
- The prudential filter related to **cash flow hedges and changes in the value of own liabilities**, but maintaining any other unrealised gains and losses measured at fair value [CRR 33 and 35];
- The prudential filter related to **additional value adjustments** [CRR 34];
- The **losses for the current financial year** deduction [CRR 36(1)(a)];
- The **intangible assets** deduction [CRR 36(1)(b)];
- The **DTAs that rely on future profitability** deduction [CRR 36(1)(c)];

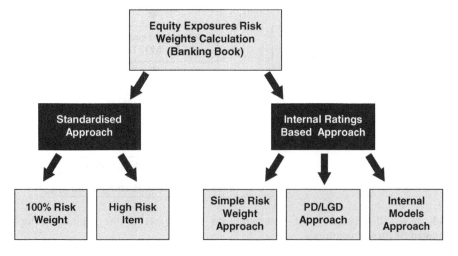

FIGURE 10.5   Basel III treatment of risk-weighted capital investments in the banking book

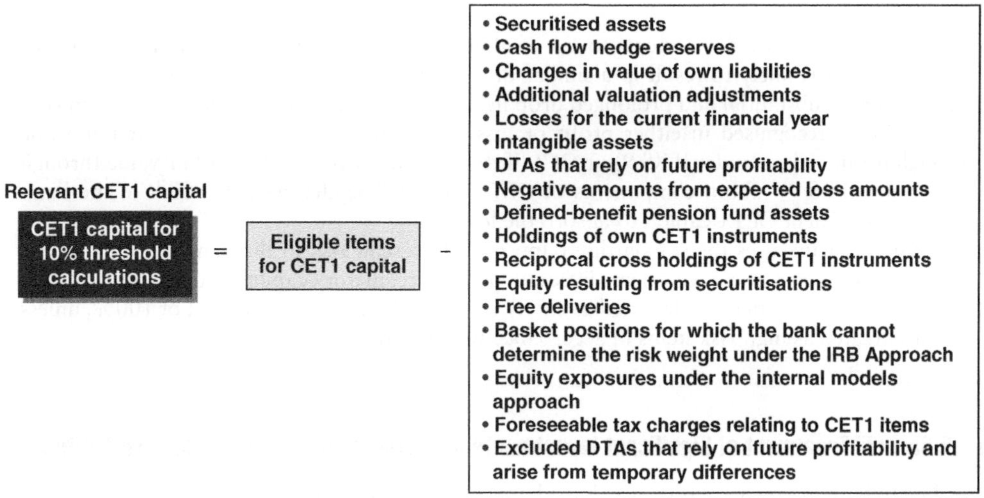

Relevant CET1 capital

$$
\boxed{\begin{array}{c}\text{CET1 capital for}\\\text{10\% threshold}\\\text{calculations}\end{array}} = \boxed{\begin{array}{c}\text{Eligible items}\\\text{for CET1 capital}\end{array}} -
$$

- Securitised assets
- Cash flow hedge reserves
- Changes in value of own liabilities
- Additional valuation adjustments
- Losses for the current financial year
- Intangible assets
- DTAs that rely on future profitability
- Negative amounts from expected loss amounts
- Defined-benefit pension fund assets
- Holdings of own CET1 instruments
- Reciprocal cross holdings of CET1 instruments
- Equity resulting from securitisations
- Free deliveries
- Basket positions for which the bank cannot determine the risk weight under the IRB Approach
- Equity exposures under the internal models approach
- Foreseeable tax charges relating to CET1 items
- Excluded DTAs that rely on future profitability and arise from temporary differences

FIGURE 10.6   Relevant CET1 for 10% threshold

- The deduction related to **negative amounts resulting from the calculation of expected loss amounts** for banks calculating risk-weighted exposure amounts using the Internal Ratings-Based Approach (the **IRB** Approach) [CRR 36(1)(d)];
- The deduction related to **defined benefit pension fund** assets on the balance sheet of the bank [CRR 36(1)(e)];
- The deduction related to direct, indirect and synthetic **holdings by the bank of its own CET1 instruments,** including own CET1 instruments that the bank is under an actual or contingent obligation to purchase by virtue of an existing contractual obligation [CRR 36(1)(f)];
- The deduction related to direct, indirect and synthetic holdings of the CET1 instruments of financial sector entities where those entities have a **reciprocal cross-holding** with the bank that the competent authority considers to have been designed to inflate artificially the total capital of the bank [CRR 36(1)(g)];
- The deduction related to **securitisation positions** [CRR 36(1)(k)(ii)];
- The deduction related to **free deliveries** [CRR 36(1)(k)(iii)];
- The deduction related to **positions in a basket for which the bank cannot determine the risk weight under the IRB Approach** [CRR 36(1)(k)(iv)];
- The deduction related to **equity exposures under the internal models approach** [CRR 36(1)(k)(v)];
- The deduction related to **foreseeable tax charges relating to CET1 items,** except where the bank suitably adjusts the amount of CET1 items insofar as such tax charges reduce the amount up to which those items may be used to cover risks or losses [CRR 36(1)(l)]; and
- It is *excluded* from the relevant CET1 the amount to be deducted for **deferred tax assets** that rely on **future profitability** and arise from **temporary differences.**

The idea behind this deduction from CET1 capital is to take into account concentration of positions in the financial sector that, albeit considered to be "non-significant" individually, may cause the capital level of a bank to erode substantially.

Let us assume that a bank has a large exposure to several financial services entities which are deemed to be non-significant. Imagine a crisis hitting the financial sector that causes the

(continued)

correlation between the investments to rise to almost 100%, meaning that a fall in the value of one investment is likely to result in a similar drop in the value of the other investments in the same sector. A substantial and prolonged drop in the value of the investments may result in substantial losses recognised in either profit or loss (if the investment is classified at fair value through profit or loss under IFRS 9) or OCI (if the investment is classified at fair value through OCI under IFRS 9) – both components of CET1 capital. The charges may result in the bank holding insufficient CET1 capital to absorb the losses.

Where a bank uses the standardised approach for credit risk in the banking book, [CRR 133] applies. In that case, investments in equity or other regulatory capital instruments issued by financial services entities are classified as equity claims and receive a risk weight of 100%, unless they are treated as high-risk items in accordance with [CRR 128].

10.1.5 Basel III Treatment of Significant Investments in Capital Instruments of Financial Entities

According to Basel III's general framework if a bank holds a **significant** investment in the capital instrument of an unconsolidated financial entity then the bank must deduct (from the bank's CET1) any amounts exceeding 10% of the bank's "relevant CET1" capital (see Figure 10.7). The deducted amount is based on the cost of the investment. However, amounts below this 10% threshold and above a 15% threshold are deducted from CET1 capital as well, while the remainder may receive recognition (i.e., being risk-weighted at 250%) when calculating CET1.

Relevant CET1 Capital for 10% Threshold Calculations   Pursuant to [CRR 48], the "relevant CET1 capital" used to calculate the 10% threshold includes the items that qualify for CET1 capital and **excludes** the amount of DTAs that rely on future profitability and arise from temporary differences but **includes** the following filters and deductions (see Figure 10.8):

- The prudential filter related to **securitised assets** [CRR 32];
- The prudential filter related to **cash flow hedges and changes in the value of own liabilities**, but maintaining any other unrealised gains and losses measured at fair value [CRR 33 and 35];
- The prudential filter related to **additional value adjustments** [CRR 34];
- The **losses for the current financial year** deduction [CRR 36(1)(a)];
- The **intangible assets** deduction [CRR 36(1)(b)];
- The **DTAs that rely on future profitability** deduction [CRR 36(1)(c)], **excluding** the amount of DTAs that rely on future profitability and arise from temporary differences;
- The deduction related to **negative amounts resulting from the calculation of expected loss amounts** for banks calculating risk-weighted exposure amounts using the Internal Ratings-Based Approach (the IRB Approach) [CRR 36(1)(d)];
- The deduction related to **defined benefit pension fund assets** on the balance sheet of the bank [CRR 36(1)(e)];
- The deduction related to direct, indirect and synthetic **holdings by the bank of its own CET1 instruments,** including own CET1 instruments that the bank is under an actual or contingent obligation to purchase by virtue of an existing contractual obligation [CRR 36(1)(f)];
- The deduction related to direct, indirect and synthetic holdings of the CET1 instruments of financial sector entities where those entities have a **reciprocal cross-holding** with the bank that the competent authority considers to have been designed to inflate artificially the total capital of the bank [CRR 36(1)(g)];
- The deduction related to the applicable amount of direct, indirect and synthetic holdings by the bank of **CET1 instruments of financial sector entities** where the institution does *not* have a significant investment in those entities [CRR 36(1)(h)];

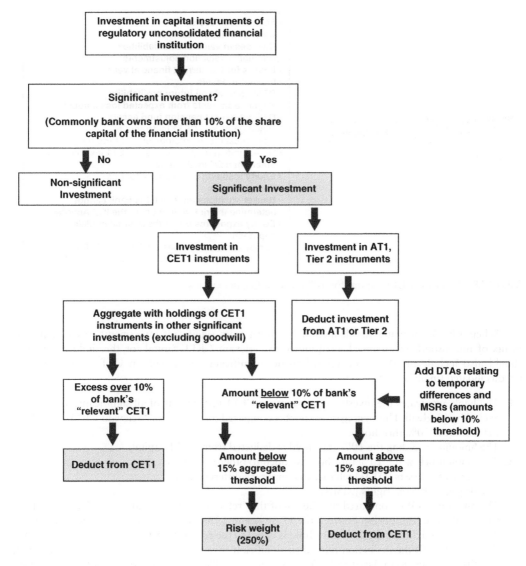

FIGURE 10.7 Basel III's treatment of significant investments in capital instruments of unconsolidated financial entities

- The deduction related to **securitisation positions** [CRR 36(1)(k)(ii)];
- The deduction related to **free deliveries** [CRR 36(1)(k)(iii)];
- The deduction related to **positions in a basket for which the bank cannot determine the risk weight under the IRB Approach** [CRR 36(1)(k)(iv)];
- The deduction related to **equity exposures under the internal models approach** [CRR 36(1)(k)(v)]; and
- The deduction related to **foreseeable tax charges relating to CET1 items**, except where the bank suitably adjusts the amount of CET1 items insofar as such tax charges reduce the amount up to which those items may be used to cover risks or losses [CRR 36(1)(l)].

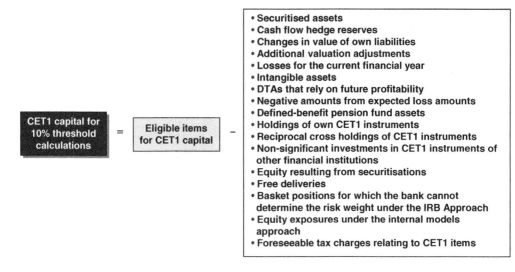

FIGURE 10.8   Relevant CET1 capital for 10% threshold calculations

When a bank calculates the deduction stemming from **significant** investments in CET1 instruments of unconsolidated financial institutions, the relevant CET1 capital for threshold deductions should also include the deduction related to **non-significant** investments in CET1 instruments of unconsolidated financial institutions.

1. The bank aggregates the investment amounts in CET1 instruments of all significant investments, excluding goodwill. This aggregate amount is compared to 10% of the "relevant CET1 capital" of the bank (the 10% threshold);
2. The amount exceeding the 10% threshold is deducted from CET1 capital;
3. The amount below the 10% threshold is added to other two items:
   - Deferred tax assets (DTAs) relating to temporary differences; and
   - Mortgage servicing rights (MSRs).
4. The amount in (3) is compared to 17.65% of the "relevant CET1 capital" of the bank (the 15% threshold). The relationship between the 17.65% and 15% factors is explained in Section 10.2.2. The relevant CET1 for the 15% threshold is equal to the relevant CET1 capital used for the 10% threshold less (i) the deduction related to significant investments exceeding the 10% threshold, less (ii) the deduction related to DTAs exceeding the 10% threshold and less (iii) the deduction related to DTAs exceeding the 10% threshold:

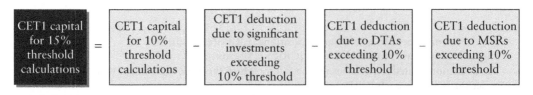

5. Amounts below the 15% threshold are risk-weighted, while amounts above the threshold are deducted from CET1 capital. In accordance with [CRR 48(4)], where the bank uses the standardised approach for credit risk, the risk weight to be assigned to these exposures is 250%.

The existence of the 10% threshold allowance mitigates the impact of the deduction by allowing a significant portion of investments in financial sector entities to be risk-weighted. In practice, this threshold gives some allowance for diversification within the financial system and the fact that the financial sector entity would normally maintain capital above its minimum requirements.

Example: 10% vs. 15% Thresholds

Let us assume that a bank owns 12% of the ordinary share capital of a financial institution. This investment does not exceed 10% of the bank's CET1. Whilst the investment is deemed to be a significant investment, no deduction from the bank's CET1 capital is required. Thus, the investment is in principle risk-weighted. However, this investment would be subject to the 15% aggregate threshold, which may require part of it be deducted.

National supervisors are given discretion to apply the threshold (i.e., to allow recognition of significant investments up to 10% of the bank's CET1). Interestingly, a good number of national supervisors have not adopted the 10% threshold on the bank's CET1. For example, the British PRA and the Australian APRA require significant investments in CET1 instruments in financial institutions to be deducted from the bank's CET1.

As explained in the ING case study in Section 11.2, the logic behind the deduction is that there is a danger that losses in the investee financial institution would lead directly to losses in the equity of the investor bank. That is because the investor bank would incur a loss on its investment in the financial institution. The deduction rule ensures that when capital absorbs a loss at one financial institution, this does not immediately result in a loss of regulatory capital in a bank that has invested that capital. For this reason, every EUR 1 of equity claim on the financial institution is backed by EUR 1 of equity held by the bank, making certain that the investing bank has sufficient equity to sustain potential losses in the financial institution.

If, in addition to holding the CET1 instruments of the unconsolidated financial institution that trigger the classification of the investment as significant (normally 10% or more of the financial institution's CET1 instruments), the bank holds any AT1 or Tier 2 capital instruments of the financial institution, then the full amount of the bank's holdings in that AT1 or Tier 2 capital instrument must also be deducted from the bank's regulatory capital using the "**corresponding deduction approach**". Pursuant to this approach, deduction is applied to the corresponding tier of capital for which the capital investment, subject to deduction, would qualify if it were issued by the investing bank itself.

If the capital instrument of the unconsolidated financial institution in which the bank has invested does not meet the criteria for CET1, AT1 or Tier 2 capital of the bank, the capital is considered common shares. However, if the investment is issued out of a regulated financial entity and not included in regulatory capital in the relevant sector of the financial entity, it is not required to be deducted.

Furthermore, if the bank is required to make a deduction from a particular tier of capital and it does not have enough of that tier of capital to satisfy that deduction, the shortfall will be deducted from the next higher tier of capital. For example, if a bank does not have enough AT1 capital to satisfy the deduction, the shortfall will be deducted from CET1.

Example: Significant Investment Coupled with Investment in AT1 Instruments

Let us assume that a bank owns 12% of the ordinary share capital of a regulatory unconsolidated financial institution. As this percentage exceeds 10%, it is deemed to be a significant investment. In addition, the bank invests in CoCos of the financial institution which represent 5% of the AT1 capital of the institution.

The bank must deduct the ordinary shares investment that exceeds 10% of the bank's CET1 from the bank's CET1 and the full 5% of its holdings in the institution's CoCos from its AT1 capital. Therefore, whilst there is a 10% threshold applicable to significant investments in CET1 instruments, additional investments in AT1 and Tier 2 do not benefit from any threshold.

10.1.6 Temporary Exemption from Deduction of Equity Holdings in Insurance Entities

The CRR allows EU member states to adopt a separate and more advantageous treatment for equity holdings in insurance entities. Pursuant to [CRR 471], by way of derogation from [CRR 49(1)], during the period from 1 January 2014 to 31 December 2022, EU member states may permit banks to not deduct equity holdings in insurance entities, and instead risk weight those investments at **370%**, where *all* the following conditions are met:

- The entity is an insurance undertaking, reinsurance undertaking or insurance holding company;
- The holdings in the insurance entity belong to one of the following: (i) the parent credit institution; (ii) the parent financial holding company; (iii) the parent mixed financial holding company; or (iv) the bank;
- The equity holdings of the bank in the insurance entity do not exceed **15%** of the CET1 instruments issued by that insurance entity as at 31 December 2012 and during the period from 1 January 2013 to 31 December 2022;
- The supervisory authorities are satisfied with the level of risk control and financial analysis procedures specifically adopted by the bank in order to supervise the investment in the undertaking or holding company; and
- The amount of the equity holding which is *not* deducted does *not* exceed the amount held in the CET1 instruments in the insurance entity as at 31 December 2012.

Example: Exemption from CET1 Deduction of Equity Holdings in Insurers

This is an example based on an EBA consultation related to the exemption from deduction of equity holdings in an insurance company from CET1.

Assume that as at 31 December 2012 a bank holds 13% share of the insurance company's ordinary share capital which is recognised as an associate using the equity method with a carrying amount of EUR 3 billion. As at 31 December 2016 the percentage of the equity investment in the insurance company remains at 13% and the investment's carrying amount increases to EUR 2.3 billion just because of the application of the equity method (without any further investment). The bank is reporting its capital position as of 31 December 2016.

If any of the conditions of [CRR 471] is not met then the equity holding of the bank in the insurance company shall be deducted from CET1. Let us take a look to such conditions, assuming that the supervisory authorities have approved the application of [CRR 471]:

- The entity is an insurance undertaking, reinsurance undertaking or insurance holding company. This condition is met.
- The holdings in the insurance entity belong to one of the following: (i) the parent credit institution; (ii) the parent financial holding company; (iii) the parent mixed financial holding company; or (iv) the bank. This condition is met as it is owned by the bank itself.
- The equity holdings of the bank in the insurance entity do not exceed 15% of the CET1 instruments issued by that insurance entity as at 31 December 2012 and during the period from 1 January 2013 to 31 December

2022 (i.e., to 31 December 2016 in our case). This condition is met as the bank holds 13% of the ordinary share capital of the insurance entity since 31 December 2012. Thus, this condition is met.

- The amount of the equity holding which is not deducted does not exceed the amount held in the CET1 instruments in the insurance entity as at 31 December 2012. In our case, the carrying amount of the equity holding in the insurance company on 31 December 2012 was EUR 2 billion, while that on 31 December 2015 was EUR 2.3 billion. Therefore, EUR 2 billion of the investment is risk-weighted at 370% while the EUR 0.3 billion excess is deducted from the bank's CET1.

10.2 WORKED EXAMPLES OF INVESTMENTS IN CAPITAL INSTRUMENTS OF UNCONSOLIDATED FINANCIAL INSTITUTIONS

In this section several examples are included with the objective of shedding more light on the mechanics of Basel III's treatment of capital investments in unconsolidated financial institutions.

10.2.1 Significant Investments Worked Example

In this section an example is covered in which a bank owned significant investments in capital instruments of two unconsolidated financial institutions.

Let us assume that Megabank was a regulated bank supervised under the Basel III rules. The regulatory capital structure of the bank was the following:

Regulatory Capital Structure Megabank	
Share capital	450
Other CET1 items	20
Relevant CET1 (*)	470
AT1	4
Tier 2	30

(*) After application of all adjustments
prior to this adjustment

Megabank owned investments in capital instruments of two financial institutions: FinA and FinB. From a regulatory standpoint, Megabank did not consolidate any of these two entities. The regulatory capital structure of each investee was the following:

Capital Structure FinA		Capital Structure FinB	
Share capital	300	Share capital	200
Other reserves and profit	12	Other reserves and profit	8
AT1	60	AT1	50
Tier 2	15	Tier 2	10

Megabank held in each FinA and FinB the following capital instruments:

Megabank's Investment in Capital of FinA		Megabank's Investment in Capital of FinB	
CET1	36	CET1	29
AT1	8	AT1	6
Tier 2	4	Tier 2	2
Total	48	Total	37

The first step in calculating the regulatory impact of such investments was to determine whether each investment constituted a "significant investment". Because Megabank owned more than 10% of FinA's issued share capital, its investment in this entity was considered to be significant. The same held for the investment in FinB:

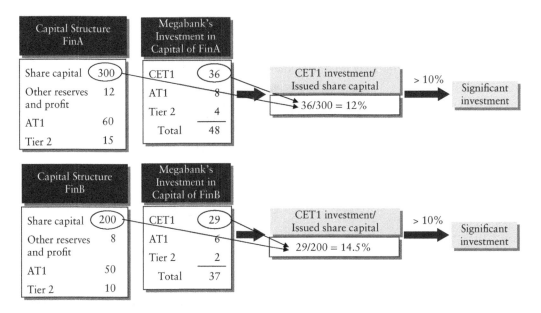

The second step in calculating the regulatory impact of the investments was to fully deduct from Tier 2 and AT1 Megabank's investments in these types of capital instruments. Any shortfall was deducted from the next higher tier of capital. In our case:

- Megabank invested $6 (= 4 + 2)$ in Tier 2 capital instruments of FinA and FinB, therefore it had to deduct 6 from its Tier 2 capital. As a result, the bank had $24 (= 30 - 6)$ of Tier 2 capital after incorporating the deduction.
- Megabank invested $14 (= 8 + 6)$ in AT1 capital instruments of FinA and FinB, therefore it had to deduct 14 from its AT1. Because Megabank had only 4 of AT1 instruments, there was a $10 (= 14 - 4)$ shortfall that had to be deducted from CET1. As a result, the bank had no AT1 capital and $460 (= 470 - 10)$ of CET1 capital after incorporating these deductions.

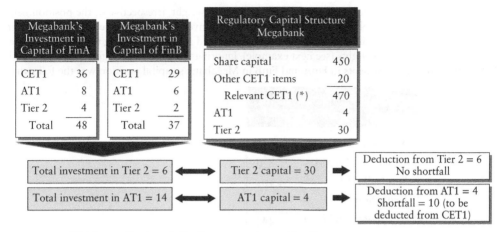

(*) After application of all adjustments prior to this adjustment

The third step in calculating the regulatory impact of the investments was to compare the aggregate of all significant investments in CET1 instruments with 10% of Megabank's CET1 (adjusted for all items prior to this deduction). In our example, the sum of all significant investments in CET1 was $65 (= 36 + 29)$, while 10% the eligible CET1 capital was $46 (= 10\% \times 460)$. As a result, $19 (= 65 - 46)$ were required to be deducted from CET1 while 46 were eligible to receive limited recognition (i.e., to be risk-weighted):

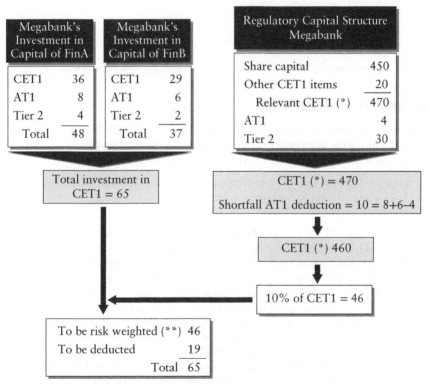

(*) After application of all adjustments prior to this adjustment
(**) Subject to 15% aggregate threshold

The amount to be risk-weighted was subject to a 250% weight, irrespective of the position being in the banking or trading book. Nonetheless, the part of the investments that were risk-weighted were subject to an aggregate 15% limit in conjunction with deferred tax assets relating to temporary differences and mortgage servicing rights (see next example). Ignoring the effect of the aggregate 15% threshold, the impact of the investments in FinA and FinB in Megabank's capital position was the following:

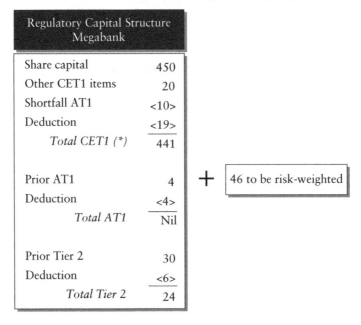

(*) After application of all adjustments, including this adjustment

10.2.2 Aggregate 15% Threshold Example

This example is taken from an example provided in the general Basel III framework that is meant to clarify the calculation of the aggregate 15% limit. Remember Basel III that allows limited recognition of three asset items when calculating CET1. These items – the specified items – are:

- Significant investments in the CET1 instruments of non-consolidated financial institutions;
- Deferred tax assets relating to temporary differences; and
- Mortgage servicing rights.

Imagine a bank with 85 CET1 (calculated net of all deductions, including the deduction of the specified items in full). To determine the maximum amount of the specified items that can be recognised (i.e., risk-weighted as opposed to deducted), the bank multiplies the amount of CET1 by 17.65% (the "**15% threshold**"). This number is derived from the proportion of 15% to 85% (that is, 15%/85% = 17.65%). At this point the threshold is a "hypothetical" amount of CET1 in that it is used only for the purposes of determining the deduction of the specified items.

The maximum amount of specified items that can be recognised by this bank in its calculation of CET1 capital is 15 (= 85 × 17.65%). The actual amount that would be recognised may be lower than this maximum, either because the sum of the three specified items are below the aggregate 15% threshold, or due to the application of the 10% threshold applied to each item. Any excess above 15 must be deducted from CET1. If the bank has specified items (excluding amounts deducted after applying the individual 10% thresholds) that in aggregate sum up to the 15% threshold, CET1 after inclusion of the specified items amounts to 85 + 15 = 100. The percentage of specified items to total CET1 would equal 15%.

10.2.3 Non-significant Investments Worked Example

In this section an example is covered in which a bank owned **non-significant** investments in capital instruments of two unconsolidated financial institutions.

Let us assume that Megabank was a regulated bank supervised under the Basel III rules. The regulatory capital structure of the bank was the following:

Regulatory Capital Structure Megabank	
Share capital	450
Other CET1 items	20
Relevant CET1 (*)	470
AT1	4
Tier 2	30

(*) After application of all adjustments prior to this adjustment

Megabank owned investments in capital instruments of two financial institutions: FinA and FinB. From a regulatory standpoint, Megabank did not consolidate any of these two entities. The regulatory capital structure of each investee was the following:

Capital Structure FinA		Capital Structure FinB	
Share capital	400	Share capital	300
Other reserves and profit	12	Other reserves and profit	8
AT1	60	AT1	50
Tier 2	15	Tier 2	10

Megabank held in each FinA and FinB the following capital instruments:

Megabank's Investment in Capital of FinA		Megabank's Investment in Capital of FinB	
CET1	36	CET1	29
AT1	8	AT1	6
Tier 2	4	Tier 2	2
Total	48	Total	37

The first step in calculating the regulatory impact of the two investments was to determine whether each investment constituted a "significant investment". Because Megabank owned *less* than 10% of FinA's issued share capital, its investment in this entity was considered to be non-significant. The same held for the investment in FinB:

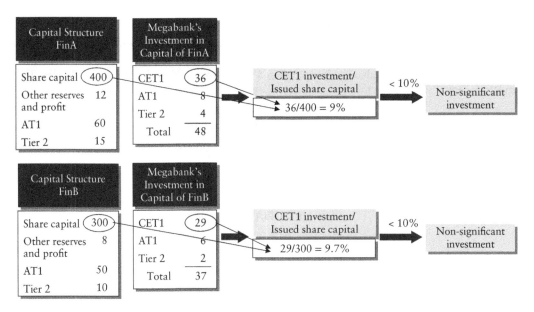

The second step in calculating the regulatory impact of the two investments was to determine whether their aggregate (including the investments in AT1 and Tier 2 instruments) exceeded 10% of the bank's CET1 (after applying all other regulatory adjustments in full prior to this one) – the relevant CET1. The total amount of investments were $85 (= 48 + 37)$ and 10% of the bank's relevant CET1 was $47 (= 10\% \times 470)$. The amount above the 10% threshold $(38 = 85 - 47)$ was required to be deducted, while the remainder 47 was risk-weighted:

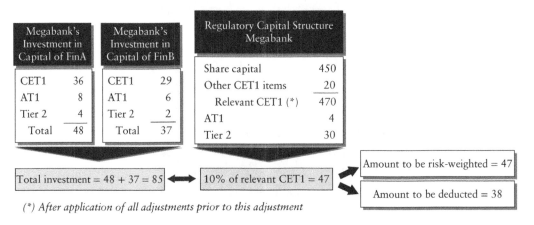

(*) After application of all adjustments prior to this adjustment

The third step in calculating the regulatory impact of the investments was to allocate the amount to be deducted (38 in our case) among the three tiers of capital (CET1, AT1 and Tier 2). This allocation was performed according to the corresponding deduction approach, based on the proportion of the investment in each tier relative to the total investment. For example, Megabank's investment in CET1 instruments was 65 $(= 36 \text{ in FinA} + 29 \text{ in FinB})$, representing 76% (rounded for simplicity) of its 85 total investment in capital instruments of FinA and FinB. Similarly, Megabank's investment in AT1 and Tier 2 instruments of FinA and FinB represented $17\% (= 14 / 85, \text{rounded for simplicity})$ and $7\% (= 6 / 85, \text{rounded for simplicity})$ respectively of its total investment in capital instruments of these two entities:

Megabank's Investment in Capital of FinA		Megabank's Investment in Capital of FinB		Megabank's Total Investment		Megabank's Total Investment	
CET1	36	CET1	29	CET1	65	CET1	76%
AT1	8	AT1	6	AT1	14	AT1	17%
Tier 2	4	Tier 2	2	Tier 2	6	Tier 2	7%
Total	48	Total	37	Total	85	Total	100%

Therefore, the 38 deduction was allocated $29 (= 76\% \times 38)$ to CET1, $6 (= 17\% \times 38)$ to AT1 and $3 (= 7\% \times 38)$ to Tier 2:

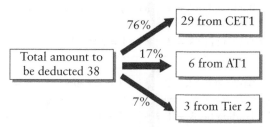

The fourth step in calculating the regulatory impact of the investments was to allocate the amount to be risk-weighted (47 in our case) between the banking and trading books. Let us assume that Megabank held the investments in each book, as follows:

Megabank's Total Investment		Held in Banking Book		Held in Trading Book		Held in Banking Book		Held in Trading Book	
CET1	65	CET1	40	CET1	25	CET1	62%	CET1	38%
AT1	14	AT1	10	AT1	4	AT1	71%	AT1	29%
Tier 2	6	Tier 2	4	Tier 2	2	Tier 2	67%	Tier 2	33%
Total	85	Total	54	Total	31				

The allocation was performed according to the percentage of each tier of instruments held in each book, as follows:

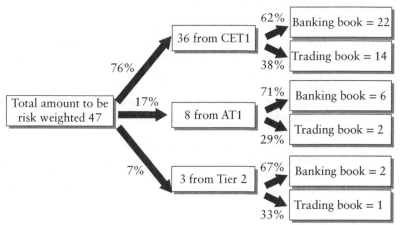

The exposures to be risk-weighted in the banking book were subject to credit risk, while those in the trading book were subject to market risk.

The final step in calculating the regulatory impact of the investments was to allocate the amounts in each tier/book to be risk-weighted between the instruments of FinA and FinB, according to the amounts of each instrument of FinA and FinB held by Megabank, as follows:

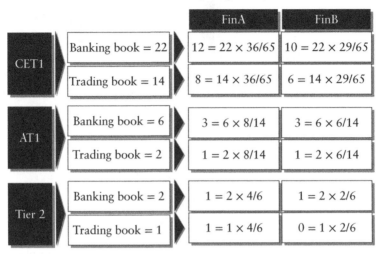

		FinA	FinB
CET1	Banking book = 22	12 = 22 × 36/65	10 = 22 × 29/65
	Trading book = 14	8 = 14 × 36/65	6 = 14 × 29/65
AT1	Banking book = 6	3 = 6 × 8/14	3 = 6 × 6/14
	Trading book = 2	1 = 2 × 8/14	1 = 2 × 6/14
Tier 2	Banking book = 2	1 = 2 × 4/6	1 = 2 × 2/6
	Trading book = 1	1 = 1 × 4/6	0 = 1 × 2/6

Because the investments were categorised as non-significant, they were not subject to the aggregate 15% threshold.

If the bank was using the standardised approach for credit risk, the investments belonging to the banking book were risk-weighted using a 100% risk weight pursuant to [CRR 133] unless treated as high-risk items pursuant to [CRR 128].

10.3 CASE STUDY: BBVA'S ACQUISITION OF GARANTI

This case study describes the accounting and regulatory impact of the acquisition by the Spanish bank BBVA of a stake in the Turkish bank Garanti. The acquisition was executed in two steps: in the first step, BBVA acquired an initial stake and entered into a joint controlled arrangement, and several years later it acquired a second stake, gaining control of the Turkish bank.

10.3.1 Initial Investment and Call Option on Garanti

In March 2011, the Spanish bank BBVA acquired 24.9% of the share capital of Turkey's second largest private bank (in terms of assets), Turkiye Garanti Bankasi ("Garanti"), for a USD 5.84 billion consideration (equivalent to EUR 4.20 billion) in cash from the Turkish group Dogus and the North American company General Electric. The purchase price – TRY 8.00 per share – represented a 10% discount relative to the then-prevailing trading market price. The purchase was financed through a EUR 5 billion rights issue, with the new shares priced at a 29% discount relative to BBVA's prior share price. After the investment, BBVA and Dogus held identical ownership of Garanti's ordinary share capital, with the remainder being publicly traded, as shown in Figure 10.9.

The objective of the transaction was to increase BBVA's exposure to emerging markets. At the time, Turkey experienced high economic growth, held one of the largest and youngest populations in Europe (75 million inhabitants) and had an underpenetrated financial system in terms of the amount of loans relative to GDP. Garanti had the equivalent of EUR 60 bn of assets, 837 branches and 9.5 million customers.

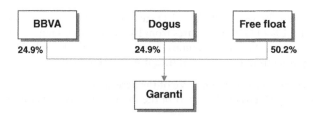

FIGURE 10.9 Garanti's ownership structure following BBVA's initial investment

Shareholders' Agreement   The transaction included a shareholders' agreement signed by BBVA and Dogus. The agreement provided for the joint management of Garanti by both shareholders, BBVA and Dogus, which together at the time of the agreement held 49.8% of Garanti's share capital. The agreement distinguished two phases ("Phase I" and "Phase II") in the management of the bank, with a step-up in rights for BBVA in Phase II.

In **Phase I** the two shareholders would have the same number of voting rights in the share capital of Garanti Bank, and the corporate bodies would operate as follows:

- The **board of directors** of Garanti would be composed of nine members, four appointed by each party and the ninth member would be the CEO, jointly designated from among the candidates proposed by Dogus. The chairman of the board would be elected from among the directors appointed by Dogus. The quorum necessary to convene the board meetings would be six directors and decisions would require the favourable vote of at least six directors.
- The **credit committee** would be composed of four board members (in addition to the CEO), with each party appointing two members.
- The **audit committee** would be composed of two board members with each party appointing one member.
- The agreement provided that prior mutual consent was necessary for the approval of **material decisions** relating to Garanti, either at board or general assembly of shareholders level.
- In the event that one of the parties **acquired further shares** during Phase I, such party would be obliged to offer to the other party the option to acquire, at the same price, half of the shares it had acquired. If the other party chose not to acquire them, the acquiring party would nevertheless be obliged to grant the other party voting rights over 50% of the shares acquired until the end of this phase. This was intended to ensure that the voting rights of both parties remained equal during Phase I.

The objective of Phase I was to allow BBVA to become familiar with the Turkish banking market, in collaboration with a strong local partner, prior to a potential gain of control.

Phase II would be commencing only when any of the following triggering events occurred: (i) BBVA exercising its call option to purchase 1% of Garanti, (ii) Dogus selling to BBVA any of the shares in Garanti that it held at the time of the agreement, or (iii) the difference between the shareholding of BBVA and Dogus in Garanti exceeding 15% of the Turkish bank's capital for reasons other than the purchase by BBVA of shares of Garanti from Dogus. In Phase II, BBVA would be granted broader rights in the appointment of board members and in the management of Garanti, while Dogus would maintain certain rights according to the level of the stake it maintained in Garanti. Phase II was designed for BBVA to gain control of Garanti.

Subsequently to the initial acquisition, BBVA bought from the open market an additional 0.12% stake for approximately USD 38 million, increasing its total stake in the ordinary shares of Garanti to 25.01%. The total cost of the 25.01% stake was USD 5,876 million (approximately EUR 4,222 million).

Call Option   The agreement between BBVA and Dogus also provided for a call option available to BBVA to enable it to buy 1% of Garanti's shares from Dogus and to nominate a majority of the members of the board of directors, effectively gaining control of the Turkish bank. The call option could be exercised by BBVA any time from the earlier of (i.e., it was a perpetual right):

- The fifth anniversary of the entry into force of the agreement; or
- Sale to a third party by Dogus of all or part of the shares it owned in Garanti as of the date of the agreement.

The strike price for the call would be the weighted average market price of Garanti's shares over the 30 trading days immediately prior to the delivery by BBVA of the call option exercise notice.

The call option gave the right to gain decision making control of Garanti in five years' time or when Dogus decided to sell all or part of its stake to a third party, without having to launch a tender offer for the remaining shares of the Turkish bank.

10.3.2 Accounting Treatment of the Initial Investment in Garanti including the Call Option

Phase I of the shareholders' agreement provided for a joint management of Garanti between BBVA and Dogus. From an accounting perspective, BBVA recognised the investment as a joint controlled arrangement under the equity method. This accounting treatment was applicable while Phase I was in force.

Fair Valuation of Garanti's Identifiable Assets and Liabilities   On the acquisition date BBVA performed a fair valuation of 25.01% of Garanti's identifiable assets and liabilities. An independent expert applied different valuation methods (i.e., discounted value of future cash flows, comparable market transactions and the cost method) on the basis of each asset and liability. The results of the fair valuation are summarised in Table 10.1 (amounts were denominated in TRY and converted into EUR).

TABLE 10.1   Fair valuation of Garanti's identifiable assets and liabilities

Balance Sheet Item	Carrying Amount (EUR mn)	Fair Value (EUR mn)
Cash	536	536
Loans and receivables	9,640	9,558
Financial assets	4,051	4,103
Tangible assets	176	243
Intangibles assets obtained from previous business combinations	4	0
Intangible assets identified at the date of the business combination	0	528
Other assets	837	836
Financial liabilities	<12,466>	<12,474>
Other liabilities	<967>	<967>
Deferred tax	28	<83>
Total (EUR mn)	1,840	2,280

Thus, the net fair value of 25.01% of Garanti's identifiable assets and liabilities was EUR 2,280 million, EUR 440 million in excess of their book values. The amount of intangible assets mainly corresponded to the Garanti name and its core deposits.

Fair Valuation of the Call Option A complex issue when determining the cost of the investment was the fair valuation of the call option. It was mentioned previously that BBVA was granted a call option on 1% of Garanti's ordinary share capital and that its exercise would give BBVA a majority of Garanti's board of directors, triggering control. Because the strike price was the market share price of Garanti at the time of exercise, in theory the option was worthless. However, in reality an exercise of the call option would give BBVA control of the decision making. An informed seller would require a premium ("**control premium**") for granting such option. The control premium represented the amount paid by BBVA to have the right to become a controlling shareholder, and as a result, to gauge the benefits resulting from synergies and other potential benefits derived from controlling Garanti. Therefore, it was clear that the consideration paid included the call's control premium. Now, what was the fair value of the control premium?

Fair valuing the control premium required substantial judgement and a careful analysis of all facts and circumstances. BBVA did not disclose how it fair valued the control premium. I can think of three approaches that may have provided indicative valuations of the call option:

- **Approach 1:** To calculate the premium paid to Dogus relative to the consideration which was paid to General Electric;
- **Approach 2:** To calculate the premium paid to Dogus relative to the then-prevailing share price of Garanti in its most active publicly traded market (i.e., the Istanbul stock exchange); and
- **Approach 3:** To calculate the premium based on the premium paid on comparable transactions.

Next I discuss the first two approaches. Regarding the first approach (i.e., to value the call option based on the premium paid to Dogus relative to the consideration paid to General Electric), it was mentioned previously that BBVA acquired its initial stake from Dogus and General Electric. The option was granted by Dogus, so the difference between the per share prices paid to Dogus and General Electric gave an indication of the control premium:

- BBVA purchased from Dogus 264,188,400 shares representing 6.2902% of the share capital of Garanti for a total amount of USD 2,062 million, equivalent to USD 7.8050 per share (approximately TRY 11.18 per share);
- BBVA purchased from General Electric 781,200,000 shares representing 18.60% of the share capital of Garanti Bank for a total amount of USD 3,776 million, equivalent to USD 4.8336 per share (approximately TRY 6.92 per share).

BBVA paid a 61.5% (= 7.8050/4.8336 − 1) premium, totalling USD 785 million [= 264,188,400 × (7.8050 − 4.8336)]. Using the EUR/USD exchange rate at the time of the agreement (1.3916), the premium amounted to EUR 564 million (= 785 mn/1.3916). However, it may be argued that BBVA would have required a discount to purchase the stake from General Electric, and as a result, not all the EUR 564 million amount comprised the control premium. In fact, the average price per share – TRY 8.00 – represented a discount to the then-prevailing market share price, corroborating my argument that **EUR 564 million** was arguably too high an estimate for the control premium.

Regarding the second approach (i.e., comparing the consideration paid to Dogus with Garanti's share price at the time of the agreement), let us assume that Garanti's ordinary shares were trading at TRY 8.89 at the time. Because BBVA paid TRY 11.18 per share, the premium over the market value of the shares purchased from Dogus was TRY 605 million [= 264,188,400 × (11.18 − 8.89)], or USD 422 million using a TRY USD 1.4327 exchange rate. Using the EUR/USD exchange rate at the time of the agreement (1.3916), the premium amounted to **EUR 303 million** (= 422 mn/1.3916).

BBVA disclosed that it valued the control premium at **EUR 425 million**, notably close to the average of the fair valuations resulting from those two approaches (i.e., EUR 433 million). The call option was recognised as a separate asset on BBVA's balance sheet.

A very relevant question is what type of asset constituted the call option. Its categorisation may have a profound impact in the regulatory capital consumption (i.e., risk weight) of the asset. For example, it would be deducted from CET1 (net of any related deferred tax liability) if it were recognised as an intangible. In our case, BBVA concluded that the call option was a financial asset. However, it was not recognised as a financial derivative. According to IFRS 9, a financial instrument is a derivative if it meets all the following three requirements:

1. Its value changes in response to changes in a specified "underlying" interest rate, financial instrument price, commodity price, foreign exchange rate, index of prices or rates, credit rating or credit index, or other variable, provided in the case of a non-financial variable that the variable is not specific to a party to the contract;
2. It requires no initial investment, or an initial net investment that is smaller than would be required for other types of contracts that would be expected to have a similar response to changes in market factors; and
3. It is settled at a future date.

The second requirement was clearly *not* met. The option gave BBVA the right to acquire 1% of the share capital of Garanti. At the price paid by BBVA (EUR 4,222 million for a 25.01% shareholding), a 1% stake was worth EUR 168 million, while the value of the options was EUR 422 million. Therefore, the call option was *not* deemed to be a derivative.

The call option was subject to an impairment test at each reporting date. Any indication that this financial instrument was *not* going to be exercised would likely trigger an impairment charge. For example, if after 5 years following the agreement (i.e., the first date in which the option could be exercised) BBVA did *not* exercise the call, the value assigned (EUR 425 million) to the option would be reassessed.

Calculation of the Consideration Transferred   BBVA paid for the Garanti shares an amount in USD equivalent to EUR 4,222 million. However, in order to arrive at the consideration transferred (i.e., the cost of entering into the joint venture agreement) the amount paid had to be adjusted by several items:

- From the date of the agreement to the time of payment BBVA was exposed to a strengthening of the USD relative to the EUR. The bank entered into a hedging agreement in the market which eliminated the bank's exposure to the EUR/USD exchange rate. When the hedging arrangement was settled, at the time of the payment, BBVA received EUR 82 million, which decreased the consideration being transferred;
- Garanti had already declared a dividend at the time of the agreement. BBVA would be receiving the equivalent to EUR 65 million in cash, which reduced the consideration being transferred;
- The control premium (i.e., the call option) (EUR 425 million), which reduced the consideration being transferred.

As a result, the consideration being transferred was estimated to be EUR 3,650 million:

Consideration transferred (EUR 3,650 mn)	=	Consideration agreed (EUR 4,222 mn)	−	Hedging gain (EUR 82 mn)	−	Dividends declared (EUR 65 mn)	−	Control premium (EUR 425 mn)

Calculation of Goodwill   The transaction goodwill (an equivalent to EUR 1,370 million) was calculated as the difference between the consideration transferred and the net fair value of the identifiable assets and liabilities acquired, as follows (note that the goodwill was denominated in TRY):

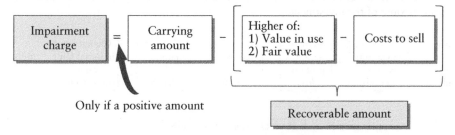

Goodwill arising on the acquisition of the jointly controlled Garanti was included in the carrying value of the investment (i.e., it was not reported separately).

At each balance sheet date subsequent to initial recognition the Group assessed whether there was any objective evidence that the investment in the joint venture was impaired. Goodwill was not specifically tested for impairment. Rather, the entire equity method investment was tested for impairment. If there was objective evidence of impairment, an impairment test would be performed by comparing the investment's recoverable amount (which was the higher of (i) its value in use and (ii) its fair value less costs to sell) with its carrying amount. If an impairment charge was recorded, the carrying amount of the investment would then be registered net of any accumulated impairment loss.

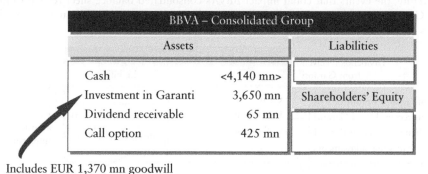

An impairment loss recognised in prior periods was only reversed if there was a change in the estimates used to determine the investment's recoverable amount since the last impairment loss was recognised. If this was the case, then the carrying amount of the investment would be increased to its higher recoverable amount.

Recognition of the Initial Investment on Acquisition Date   The initial investment in Garanti was recognised on BBVA's consolidated statement of financial position as follows:

BBVA – Consolidated Group		
Assets		**Liabilities**
Cash	<4,140 mn>	
Investment in Garanti	3,650 mn	Shareholders' Equity
Dividend receivable	65 mn	
Call option	425 mn	

Includes EUR 1,370 mn goodwill

The investment in the jointly controlled Garanti was recognised as a one line item on the asset side of BBVA's statement of financial position. The initial carrying value of the investment (EUR 3,650 million) included the goodwill (EUR 1,370 million) arising on the acquisition.

Subsequent Recognition of the Joint-controlled Venture   Like any other investment accounted for under the equity method the initial cost was subsequently increased (or decreased) to reflect BBVA's pro-rata share of the post-acquisition net assets of Garanti.

Assuming that no intercompany transactions took place between BBVA and Garanti, the investment the Turkish bank was adjusted as follows:

- BBVA's proportionate interest in the net profit (or loss) of Garanti during the reporting period increased (or decreased) the carrying amount of the investment;
- Any distributions (e.g., dividends) declared by Garanti during the reporting period reduced the investment's carrying amount;
- BBVA's proportionate share of the net profit or loss of Garanti was adjusted for the changes during the reporting period in any fair value adjustments recognised upon initial recognition, being recognised in BBVA's profit or loss statement, decreasing BBVA's carrying amount of the investment;
- BBVA's proportionate interest in the changes of Garanti's other comprehensive income (OCI) during the reporting period was recognised in BBVA's OCI and increased (or decreased) BBVA's carrying amount of the investment;
- Any impairment charge during the reporting period on the investment in Garanti reduced BBVA's carrying amount of the investment.

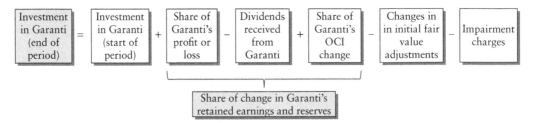

In addition, because the functional currency of Garanti (TRY) was different to the presentation currency of the BBVA group (EUR), the financial statements of Garanti were translated into EUR (see Section 3.5.1 for a more detailed description on how the translation of foreign operations is performed). The exchange differences arising from the conversion to EUR of the financial statements of Garanti were recognised in BBVA's OCI under the heading "exchange differences" (or the equivalent "foreign currency translation").

Therefore, the events that could impact BBVA's consolidated balance sheet related to its investment in Garanti, while being accounted for using the equity method and assuming no additional purchases or disposals of shares, were the following:

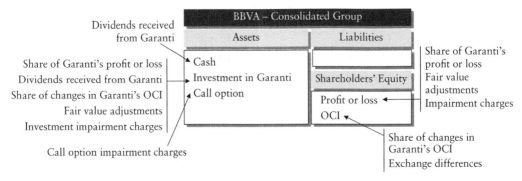

10.3.3 Regulatory Capital Treatment of the Initial Investment in Garanti

From a regulatory perspective, there were several elements of its initial 25.01% investment that impacted BBVA's regulatory capital calculations (as shown in Figure 10.10):

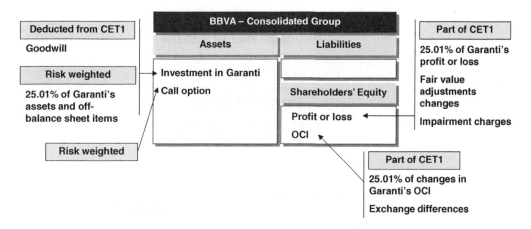

FIGURE 10.10 Regulatory capital effects of BBVA's equity investment in Garanti

- The goodwill arising from the investment;
- The carrying amount of the investment (excluding goodwill). From a regulatory point of view, the pro-rata share of Garanti's assets and liabilities, and off-balance sheet items;
- Any subsequent change in BBVA's proportionate share of Garanti's retained earnings and reserves; and
- Any exchange differences arising from converting the TRY-denominated investment in Garanti into EUR.

Goodwill According to Basel III goodwill and all other intangibles must be deducted in the calculation of CET1. This deduction is also required for any goodwill included in the valuation of significant investments in the capital of banking, financial and insurance entities that are outside the scope of regulatory consolidation. In our case, goodwill was estimated to be EUR 1,370 million and, consequently, CET1 was reduced by that amount assuming no tax effects on such goodwill.

Remember that on the asset side of BBVA's statement of financial position, the investment was represented in one line: "Investment in Garanti", which included goodwill. In other words, BBVA did *not* recognise goodwill separately in its financial statements, but kept track of the outstanding goodwill for regulatory capital purposes.

Any future impairment would lower the amount of goodwill. It was mentioned previously that when an investment is accounted for using the equity method, the whole investment is tested for impairment. Any impairment charges on the investment in Garanti would reduce the amount of outstanding goodwill, reducing the size of the deduction from CET1. However, impairment charges would be recognised in profit or loss, reducing the amount of CET1. If from a tax perspective a goodwill impairment charge is tax-deductible, then impairment charges may have a positive impact in CET1, equal to the amount of taxes being saved. Otherwise, any goodwill impairment charges would have a neutral effect on CET1 capital.

Carrying Amount of the Investment (excluding Goodwill) – Regulatory Treatment in Reality Due to the fact that Garanti was consolidated from an accounting perspective as a jointly controlled entity using the equity method, from a regulatory capital perspective BBVA consolidated Garanti on a **pro-rata basis**. In other words, BBVA calculated the risk-weighted assets corresponding to 25.01% of Garanti's assets and off-balance sheet items, and translated them into EUR from TRY.

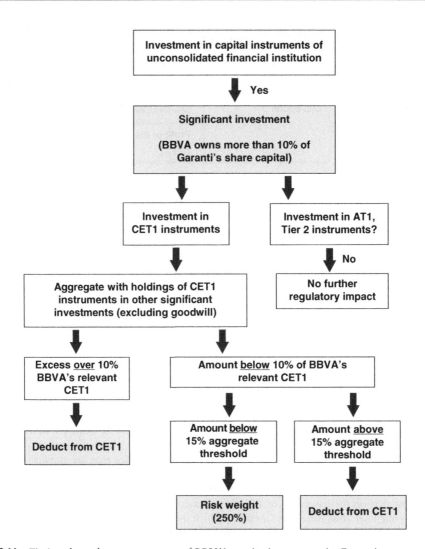

FIGURE 10.11 Fictional regulatory treatment of BBVA's equity investment in Garanti

In addition, the call option was risk-weighted. The estimated impact on CET1 of the transaction was a EUR 4.1 billion consumption. The EUR 5 billion rights issue fully offset that impact. Therefore, from a CET1 point of view, the transaction did not have a negative impact.

Carrying Amount of the Investment (excluding Goodwill) – Fictional Regulatory Exercise   Next as an exercise to review the mechanics of the regulatory capital calculations related to significant investments in financial institutions, I will assume that BBVA did *not* consolidate Garanti from a regulatory perspective. Instead, let us assume that because BBVA owned in excess of 10% of Garanti's ordinary share capital, its investment in the Turkish bank was considered a "significant investment in the capital of banking, financial and insurance entities that are outside the scope of regulatory consolidation". Following the flowchart in Figure 10.11, BBVA's investment in ordinary shares of Garanti was added to other investments in CET1 instruments of financial institutions deemed to be significant as well.

The initial carrying amount of BBVA's investment in Garanti was EUR 3,650 million. After deducting the EUR 1,370 million goodwill (as it was already deducted from CET1), the amount subject to the capital treatment of significant investments thresholds was EUR 2,280 million.

Besides its investment in Garanti, BBVA's other significant investments comprised mainly investments in the group's insurance companies (most of them were consolidated for accounting purposes, albeit not for regulatory purposes – as explained in Chapter 11, insurance entities are deconsolidated for regulatory purposes). The overall investment in these unconsolidated entities deemed to be significant was EUR 3,421 million. I assume that because these entities were not acquired that no goodwill was associated with these other significant investments.

The aggregate of the significant investments in unconsolidated financial institutions subject to the 10% and 15% thresholds was EUR 5,701 million (= 2,280 mn + 3,421 mn), of which 40% (= 2,280 mn / 5,701 mn) was related to its investment in Garanti. This amount was compared to 10% of BBVA's relevant CET1 (i.e., CET1 capital after applying all deductions prior to this deduction stemming from significant investments in financial institutions). Let us assume that BBVA's CET1 prior to this deduction was EUR 35,800 million. The excess of the aggregate of the significant investments in unconsolidated financial institutions over 10% of that CET1 amount represented EUR 2,121 million (= 5,701 mn − 10% × 35,800 mn). As the investment in Garanti represented 40% of the aggregate of significant investments in unconsolidated financial institutions, EUR 848 (= 40% × 2,121 mn) was deducted from CET1 related to the investment in Garanti (excluding goodwill). The amount not subject to deduction – EUR 1,432 million (= 2,280 mn − 848 mn) – was subject to the 15% aggregate threshold.

The 15% threshold was incorporated by Basel III to allow limited recognition of three asset items when calculating CET1. These items are:

- Significant investments in the CET1 instruments of non-consolidated financial institutions below the 10% threshold, or EUR 3,580 million (= 5,701 mn − 2,121 mn) of which 40% (EUR 1,432 million) was related to the investment in Garanti;
- Deferred tax assets (DTAs) relating to temporary differences (EUR 2,406 million). All this amount was subject to the 15% threshold; and
- Mortgage servicing rights (MSRs). I assume that BBVA had no MSRs.

The aggregate of the three items subject to the 15% threshold was EUR 5,986 million (= 3,580 mn + 2,406 mn + nil). The relevant CET1 capital for the calculation of the 15% threshold was EUR 33,679 million, calculated as follows:

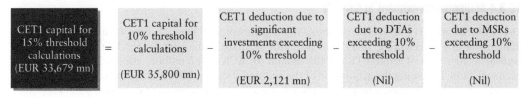

CET1 capital for 15% threshold calculations (EUR 33,679 mn)	=	CET1 capital for 10% threshold calculations (EUR 35,800 mn)	−	CET1 deduction due to significant investments exceeding 10% threshold (EUR 2,121 mn)	−	CET1 deduction due to DTAs exceeding 10% threshold (Nil)	−	CET1 deduction due to MSRs exceeding 10% threshold (Nil)

The 15% threshold was EUR 5,944 million (= 17.65% × 33,679 million). Therefore, the excess of the aggregate of the three items over the 15% aggregate of the three items was EUR 42 million (= 5,986 mn − 5,944 mn) and was deducted from CET1 capital. The deduction from CET1 capital related to the investment in Garanti was EUR 10 million (= 42 mn × 1,432 mn / 5,986 mn). The amount of significant investments below the 15% threshold were risk-weighted. In the case of the investment in Garanti, EUR 1,422 million (= 1,432 mn − 10 mn) of exposure was risk-weighted.

In conclusion, regarding the EUR 3,650 million investment in Garanti assuming that it was treated as a significant investment in a financial institution, the effect on CET1 capital was the following (see Figure 10.12):

- EUR 1,370 million related to the goodwill of the acquisition was deducted from CET1 capital;
- EUR 848 million related to the excess over the 10% threshold was deducted from CET1 capital;

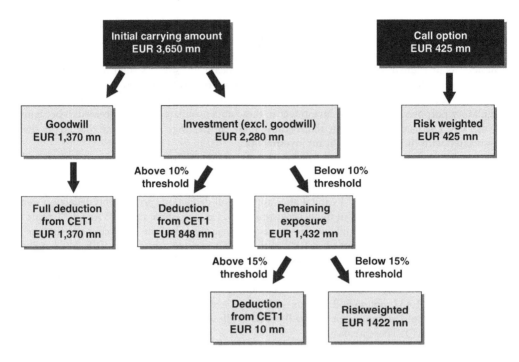

FIGURE 10.12   Capital impact of fictional regulatory treatment of BBVA's equity investment in Garanti

- EUR 10 million related to the excess over the 15% threshold was deducted from CET1 capital;
- EUR 1,422 million related to the amount below the 15% threshold was risk-weighted; and
- EUR 425 million related to the call option was risk-weighted.

The decrease in CET1 capital was offset with BBVA's EUR 5 billion capital increase.

10.3.4 Additional Investment in Garanti

On 19 November 2014 BBVA entered into a new agreement with Dogus for the acquisition of 625,380 million shares – representing 14.89% of Garanti's ordinary share capital – for TRY 8.764 per share, equivalent to a total of around TRY 5,481 million (or EUR 1,882 million, using a 2.9116 TRY/EUR exchange rate). Following the acquisition of the additional shares, BBVA's stake in Garanti was 39.9%. In addition, BBVA obtained a majority representation in Garanti's board of directors.

From an accounting and regulatory perspectives raising its ownership in the Turkish bank had a key consequence: BBVA was required to fully consolidate Garanti (see Figure 10.13). Interestingly, BBVA achieved control not by owning a majority of the ordinary shares of Garanti, but by getting a majority of the seats in Garanti's board of directors.

10.3.5 Accounting Impact of the Additional Investment – Gaining Control

Because BBVA already held a stake (25.01%) in Garanti prior to it gaining control, the transaction was treated from an accounting perspective as a **"step acquisition"**. A step acquisition occurs when a shareholder obtains control over an entity by acquiring an additional interest in that entity. IFRS 3 *Business Combinations* treats a step acquisition as two separate transactions. In the case of BBVA:

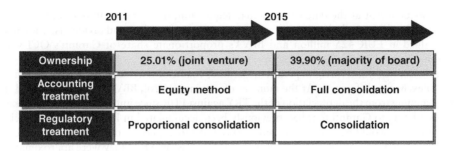

FIGURE 10.13   Accounting and regulatory impact of BBVA's stake increase in Garanti

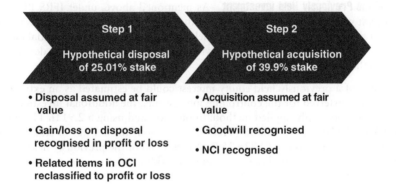

FIGURE 10.14   Two-step acquisition

- In a first step, the previously held 25.01% in Garanti was hypothetically sold at the price per share implied in the acquisition of the additional stake; and
- In a second phase, all the resulting 39.9% stake was hypothetically acquired at the price per share implied in the acquisition of the additional stake. Figure 10.14 summarises these two transactions.

> The "sale" of the previously held 25.01% equity stake and the simultaneous "purchase" of the 39.9% stake was only hypothetical, having no effect on BBVA's cash flow other than the consideration paid to acquire the additional 14.89% stake.

First Step: Hypothetical Sale of the Previous Stake   In a first transaction, a hypothetical disposal of the previously held equity interest was assumed to have occurred, leading to the recording of a gain/loss in BBVA's profit or loss statement. In our case, it would be as if BBVA sold its 25.01% stake. In other words, the previously held equity interest in the acquiree had to be remeasured to fair value and the resulting gain/loss recognised in the profit or loss statement. This treatment was applicable irrespective of whether the previously owned shares were accounted for under the equity method or as at fair value through profit or loss. However, if the previously owned shares were recognised at fair value through other comprehensive income (OCI), the resulting remeasurement gain/loss would have been recognised in OCI. In our case, because BBVA recognised the previously held stake under the equity method, the remeasurement gain/loss was recognised in its profit or loss.

Let us assume that at the date of the actual acquisition, the carrying amount of the investment was EUR 3,853 million (including any effects of Garanti's profit or loss and dividends), the call option was fair valued at EUR 425 million and BBVA's proportionate share of Garanti's OCI was EUR 609 million.

Because Garanti was a foreign operation, Garanti's financial statements were translated into EUR resulting in exchange differences. At the moment of gaining control, BBVA had an unrealised translation loss stemming from the depreciation of the TRY against EUR since initial acquisition. The exchange differences relating to Garanti that had previously been accumulated in BBVA's OCI were reclassified to profit or loss, as would be required for any disposal of a foreign operation. BBVA did not separately disclosed the exchange differences related to Garanti, but I assume that they were approximately EUR 1.1 billion, net of tax.

Fair Valuation of the Previously Held Investment   As mentioned above, under IFRS BBVA's previously held equity interest was remeasured to fair value at the date the controlling interest was acquired. The determination of the fair value of the previously held investment required substantial judgement of all facts and circumstances, as IFRS does not prescribe a specific method for such determination. I can think of three methods:

- The fair value of a previously held equity interest could be estimated as an **extrapolation** of the **consideration transferred** for the controlling interest (i.e., the additional investment). In practice this is the most commonly applied method. In our case and using a 2.9116 TRY/EUR exchange rate, BBVA paid EUR 1,882 million (TRY 5,481 million) for a 14.89% stake, implying a fair value of EUR 3,161 million (= 1,882 × 25.01% / 14.89%) of the previously held stake. When the previously held interest is notably small while the additional investment is close to 100%, this alternative provides an accurate estimate, which was not BBVA's case. However, this was a relevant method.
- The fair value of the previously held equity interest could be estimated using the **quoted share price** of Garanti at the time when control was obtained. Garanti shares were trading TRY 9.42 per share, implying a fair value of the previous 25.01% stake of EUR 3,398 million.
- The fair value of the previously held equity interest could be estimated using ratios (e.g., price-to-book value, price-to-earnings) of **comparable transactions**. Ideally transactions in which control was obtained by the acquirer in the banking sector and in emerging markets were analysed.

Taking into account all these elements, BBVA concluded that the fair value of the previously held interest was EUR 3,161 million. BBVA took the estimate using the first method – interpolation based on the consideration transferred for the controlling interest.

The following items impacted profit or loss, related to the first transaction:

- The difference between the fair value of the previously held interest (EUR 3,161 million) and the aggregate of the carrying amount of the previously held interest (EUR 3,853 million) and the fair value of the call option (EUR 425 million). This item represented a EUR 1,117 million pre-tax loss, the difference between EUR 3,161 million and EUR 4,278 million (= 3,853 mn + 425 mn). Assuming a 30% tax rate, such loss was EUR 782 million [= 1,117 mn × (1 – 30%)] on an after-tax basis.
- The reclassification of the exchange differences, a EUR 1.1 billion after-tax loss.

Thus, the recognition of this accounting impact did not entail any additional cash divestment for BBVA. A significant part of this impact consisted of conversion differences due to the depreciation of the TRY against the EUR in the period from the initial acquisition by BBVA of 25.01% of Garanti to the gain of control.

Second Step: Purchase of the Entire Stake   In a second step, a hypothetical purchase of the subsequent acquisition of control over the target company is assumed. In our case, it would be as if BBVA acquired 39.9% of Garanti in one purchase: 25.01% at its EUR 3,161 million fair value (as determined in the first step) and the 14.09% remainder acquired for EUR 1,882 million. Thus, the total cost of the hypothetical acquisition of the 39.9% stake was EUR 5,043 million (= 3,161 mn + 1,882 mn).

Pursuant to IFRS 3, BBVA first calculated the fair value of the net identifiable assets (EUR 10,852 million) and subsequently calculated the non-controlling interest using the partial goodwill method as follows:

$$
\begin{array}{|c|}\hline \text{NCI}\\ \text{(EUR 6,522 mn)}\\\hline\end{array}
= \begin{array}{|c|}\hline \text{Percentage}\\ \text{ownership}\\ \text{(60.10\%)}\\\hline\end{array}
\times \begin{array}{|c|}\hline \text{Fair value of 100\% of}\\ \text{identifiable net assets}\\ \text{(EUR 10,852 mn)}\\\hline\end{array}
$$

Finally, the goodwill related to the Garanti acquisition was calculated by comparing the fair values assigned to the acquired identifiable assets and assumed liabilities of Garanti, the fair value of the consideration paid and the non-controlling interest:

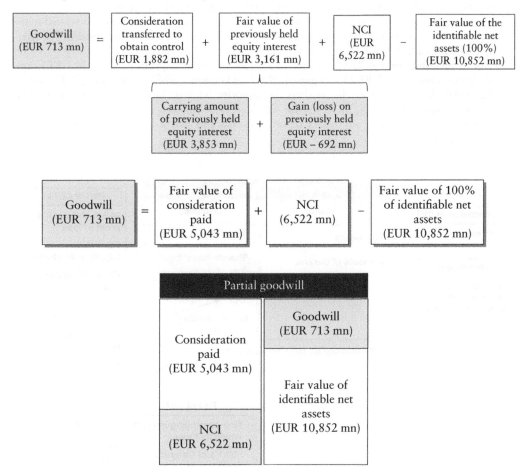

10.3.6 Regulatory Impact of the Assumption of Control

The following were the impacts on BBVA's CET1 ratio upon the acquisition of control of Garanti:

- **Goodwill** was deducted from CET1 capital. Prior to the stake increase, BBVA deducted the EUR equivalent amount of the TRY-denominated goodwill. Initially it was EUR 1,370 million. Following the stake increase, goodwill was remeasured and its TRY amount translated into EUR totalled EUR 713 million. Thus, related to goodwill BBVA deducted a lower amount from CET1 capital after assuming control.
- Prior to taking control, BBVA risk-weighted 25.01% of Garanti's **assets** and **off-balance sheet items**. After assuming control, BBVA risk-weighted 100% of Garanti's assets and its off-balance sheet items. Thus, the risk-weighted assets of BBVA increased notably.
- Prior to taking control, BBVA did not recognise any minority interests related to Garanti as it was recognised from an accounting perspective under the equity method. After taking control, BBVA recognised a **minority interest** in TRY that totalled EUR 6,522 million when converted into EUR. In CET1 BBVA recognised this minority interest but excluded the portion of Garanti's excess CET1 capital attributable to the minority interest. Consequently, the CET1 capital of BBVA increased notably as a result of the recognition of Garanti's minority interests.
- Upon the acquisition of control, BBVA recognised a EUR 1,117 million pre-tax loss related to the difference between the **fair value of the previously held interest** and its **carrying amount**. The after-tax loss reduced BBVA's CET1 capital.
- Prior to assuming control, BBVA recognised 25.01% of Garanti's **profit or loss** in its CET1 capital. After taking control, BBVA recognised 39.9% of Garanti's profit or loss in its CET1 capital. The remainder 60.1% was allocated to the minority interest. In the reporting periods that Garanti recognised a profit, BBVA's profit was increased and, as a result, BBVA's CET1 capital strengthened. Conversely, any losses reported by Garanti had a negative impact on BBVA's CET1 capital.

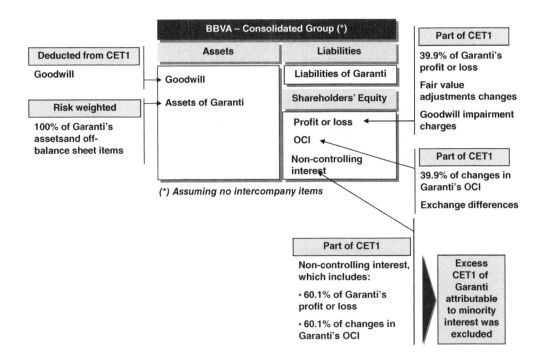

FIGURE 10.15   Effect on BBVA's CET1 of its investment in Garanti after assuming control

■ At each reporting date, BBVA retranslated its share of Garanti's net assets. Any differences were recognised in the **exchange differences** account of BBVA's OCI. Any strengthening (weakening) of the TRY relative to the EUR triggered an exchange difference gain (loss), strengthening (weakening) BBVA's CET1 capital. This effect was offset by a greater (lower) amount of **risk-weighted assets** when translated into EUR.

■ Any changes in BBVA's share of Garanti's **OCI** were recognised in the Spanish bank's OCI. As a result of the control assumption, BBVA's OCI became more sensitive to changes in Garanti's OCI and, as OCI is an element of CET1 capital, BBVA's CET1 capital became more sensitive to changes in Garanti's OCI.

■ Any capital increases to finance the acquisition enhanced BBVA's CET1 capital.

Figures 10.10 and 10.15 summarise the impact on BBVA's CET1 of its investment in Garanti prior and following the assumption of control, assuming no intercompany transactions between the two banks and no investment of BBVA in Garanti's AT1 and Tier 2 instruments.

CHAPTER 11

Investments in Capital Instruments of Insurance Entities

This chapter covers the Basel III treatment of investments in capital instruments of insurance entities. These entities comprise insurance undertakings, reinsurance undertakings and insurance holding companies (which I am going to refer to as "insurance entities" hereinafter). Most of the Basel III guidelines regarding investments in the capital instruments of insurance entities are common to those of other types of financial institutions. Therefore, rather than repeating the contents of the previous chapter, I have focused only on the peculiarities of investments in insurers.

One of the key characteristics of banks and insurers is their power to leverage their balance sheets. One of the main concerns of the Basel Committee when dealing with capital investments in insurance entities (or financial institutions in general) was the possibility of using the leverage in a bank parent to increase the leverage in an insurance subsidiary – what is termed "**double leverage**".

11.1 THE CONCEPT OF DOUBLE LEVERAGE

The concept of double leverage is a key element behind the regulatory rules on investments in financial services entities. Let us shed more light on this concept with a simple example. Imagine that a bank with 12 billion of assets holds 100% of the ordinary share capital of an insurance company – a 2 billion investment. The insurer total assets are 7 billion. Figure 11.1 depicts the stand-alone balance sheet of the parent bank and its fully-owned insurance subsidiary, as well as the consolidated balance sheet of the group.

Observing the parent bank's balance sheet, it appears that there is 3 billion of equity supporting banking risks. Nevertheless, in reality this is not the case as the bank has an investment of 2 billion in the insurer's equity. In other words, the 2 billion of equity on the bank's balance sheet is not only supporting 10 billion of non-insurance risks, but also supporting 7 billion of insurance risks (i.e., a total of 17 billion). There is a danger that losses suffered by the insurer will lead directly to losses in the bank's equity. Imagine that the insurer suffers losses exceeding its capital buffer: the bank will probably be inclined to inject funds in the insurer. Unless the parent bank has sufficient equity to absorb potential losses in both the bank and the insurance subsidiary, it may not be able to sustain these losses.

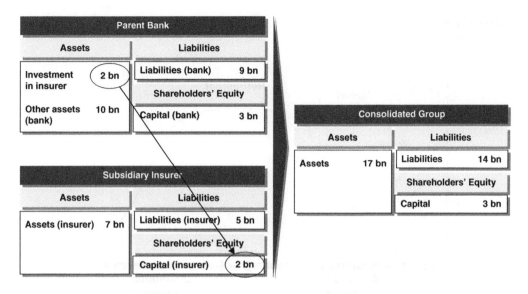

FIGURE 11.1 Individual and consolidated balance sheets – double leverage

The Lloyds case study in Section 11.4, covered the fact that an alternative to prevent the multiple use of the same capital resources in different parts of the financial system is to deduct significant investments in insurance entities from a bank's CET1 capital. The deduction of significant investments made by the bank in the insurer helps to ensure that both regulated entities are properly capitalised and limits the risk of contagion and reliance on free transfer of capital, which may not be possible in practice. Deduction is arguably the most effective way to ensure that for banks with significant investments in insurance companies there is sufficient capital of the right quality to support risks in both the bank and the insurer.

11.2 CASE STUDY: ING'S DOUBLE LEVERAGE

This case study covers the restructuring of the Dutch group ING Groep N.V. ("ING Group"), to depict the challenges posed by double leverage in financial services groups. An interesting element that this case points out is that a bank is *not* an isolated entity which with a certain level of capital ratios is able to withstand risk. It is important to take into account the way a holding company, a bank (or group of banks) is part of, is structured. Recovery plans and multiple points of entry set-ups and banking supervision at the holding level are tools to isolate banks from damaging events in other parts of a financial services group.

11.2.1 ING's Business Model Prior to its Bail-out

ING Group, one of the largest financial services group in Europe, was the holding company of a broad spectrum of companies offering banking, life insurance and retirement services to meet the needs of a broad customer base. Prior to 2009, ING had a proud history as a global financial services

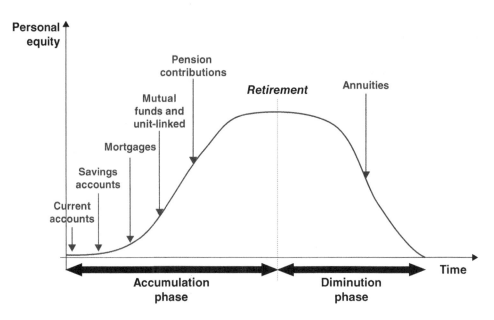

FIGURE 11.2   Customer financial life cycle

leader, being a strong advocate for combining banking and insurance in one company, what is referred to as **bancassurance**.

The main advantage of the bancassurance business model was to allow the distribution of insurance products through the banking channel for mass-market clients looking for simple and low-cost products available from a trusted financial institution. Banking offered opportunities for early customer acquisition and insurance provided opportunities for maintaining customer relationships (see Figure 11.2). Globally, bancassurance emerged as an important insurance distribution channel that not only allowed insurance companies to expand their geographical presence but also enabled banks to expand their overall product portfolio. The combination provided the bancassurance group with advantages of scale, capital efficiency and earnings stability through a diversified portfolio of businesses.

Additionally, and in a benign economic environment, bancassurance gave ING a material capital benefit, as its diversification allowed the group to utilise **double leverage** at its holding company. The rationale behind double leverage was the assumption that the required amount of capital for a bancassurance group was smaller than the sum of the stand-alone (i.e., individual) capital requirements for the bank and insurer. This was due to the implied diversification between both lines of business.

11.2.2 Effects of the 2008–09 Financial Crisis

The rapidly worsening market conditions following the summer of 2008, especially after the collapse of Lehman Brothers, caused the price of structured assets to plummet. The financial crisis raised doubts regarding ING's credit portfolio position and fuelled a belief that capital levels for ING had to be raised, but the equity capital markets were closed. As a result, ING received two instances of emergency government support to strengthen its capital position and to mitigate risk. In November 2008 the Dutch State purchased from ING Group EUR 10 billion of Core Tier 1 securities and in the first quarter of 2009 the Dutch State provided a so-called "Illiquid Asset Back-up Facility" to protect ING from a substantial deterioration in its asset portfolio (see Case Study in Section 14.1). The financial crisis brought to light the drawbacks of the bancassurance model.

Firstly, ING's double leverage turned into a detrimental capital structure that added risk to the profile of the bank. During the crisis, ING faced substantial headwinds in both lines of business: its banking arm suffered high impairment charges on its assets while its insurance arm witnessed its assets decline in value due to historically low interest rates. Due to doubts regarding the capital position of ING Group, it was very difficult for it to recapitalise or refinance itself in the market. This forced the Group to resort to its banking and insurance arms for its funding. This in turn led to further entanglement of the Group as a whole, through an increase in intra-group positions. It thereby weakened the position of the policy and deposit holders in the regulated entities as they were funding part of the equity that was meant precisely for their protection.

Secondly, and due to its rapid growth in previous years, managing the group became increasingly complex, as banking and insurance not only had different drivers in their business models, but they also faced different challenges in managing and pricing risk as well as in managing balance sheet exposures and capital needs.

11.2.3 Agreement with the European Union – Strategic Initiatives

As a condition to receiving approval from the European Union (EU) for the Dutch State aid, ING Group was required in 2009 to develop and submit a restructuring plan demonstrating its long-term viability and detailing actions to prevent undue distortions of competition. The restructuring plan was approved by the EU in November 2009 (it was restructured in November 2012).

A key goal of that plan was to reduce complexity by operating the bank and insurer separately under one group umbrella. To achieve that goal, ING Group committed to divest its insurance and investment management businesses across the world.

In addition, ING committed to eliminate its double leverage. To that end, the bank agreed with the EU to use the insurance businesses divestments proceeds to reduce and ultimately fully eliminate its double leverage at the latest in 2018, including the repayment of the CT1 instruments issued to the Dutch State. Separately, to the extent that surplus capital was being generated in excess of what is needed to satisfy Basel III or Solvency II needs, dividends to ING Group would be used to help accelerate the elimination of double leverage.

Finally, the EU imposed certain restrictions on the ING group, including with respect to its price leadership in EU banking markets and its ability to make acquisitions of financial institutions and other businesses.

Prior to the agreement with the EU, ING had already started a strategic change programme to stabilise the group, restore credibility and regain trust, with the ultimate objective of sharpening focus and creating a more coherent set of activities. ING set four priorities to comply with its agreement with the EU (see Figure 11.3):

- Legal and operational separation of banking and insurance;
- Implementation of a series of measures to strengthen the group's financial position through cost containment, reductions of risk and capital exposures, and deleveraging the balance sheet by reducing asset exposures and preserving equity;
- Divestment of the insurance companies;
- Repayment of the state aid; and
- Reduction and subsequent elimination of double leverage.

11.2.4 Separating Banking and Insurance

As part of the agreement with the EU, ING decided to legally and operationally separate its banking and insurance businesses under the umbrella of the ING Group. The process towards separation comprised five steps, as summarised in Figure 11.4. The main hurdle in the process was to identify and take the actions to separate the interdependencies between the businesses. The identified interdependencies were evaluated in terms of how complex it would be to achieve separation.

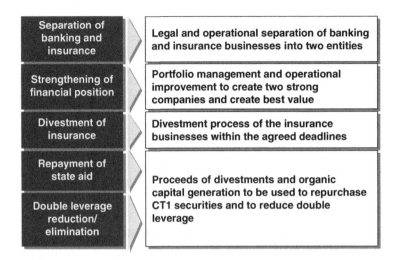

FIGURE 11.3   ING's strategic priorities following its agreement with the EU

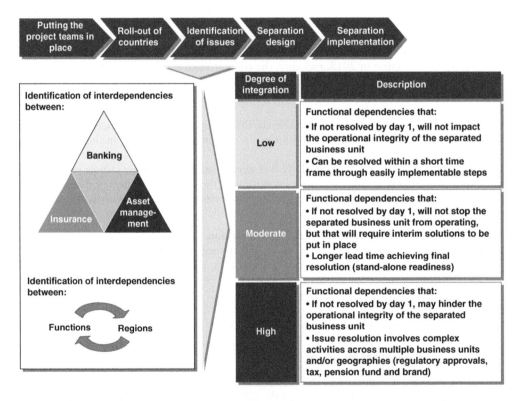

FIGURE 11.4   Steps in the separation of ING's banking and insurance/asset management businesses

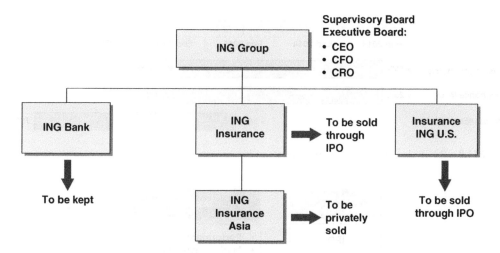

FIGURE 11.5   ING Group's new structure

One of the key goals of the separation of ING's banking and insurance was to reduce the complexity of the group. However, in order to maximise the value of the disposal of the insurance business, it was split into ING Insurance (ING Verzekeringen) and Insurance ING U.S. (as shown in Figure 11.5), clearing the way to two IPOs targeted to a European and an American investor base respectively. The transfer of ING U.S. was done as a dividend upstream to the Group.

An operational split of the ING Group's corporate governance was in effect since 1 June 2009 when a separate Management Board Banking and Management Board Insurance were created. At the holding level – ING Group – a two-tier board system was implemented, consisting of a Supervisory Board and an Executive Board. The task of the Supervisory Board was to supervise the policy of the Executive Board and the general course of events in the company and to assist the Executive Board by providing advice. The Executive Board was responsible for the daily management of the company. The Executive Board was limited to the chief executive officer, chief financial officer and chief risk officer positions.

The insurance and investment management businesses of ING Group were operationally separated as of 31 December 2010.

11.2.5 Divestment of Insurance

As shown in Figure 11.6, ING committed to divest more than 50% of ING Insurance Asia and US operations before the end of 2013 (and a full disposal by the end of 2016) and more than 50% of ING Insurance Europe operations before the end of 2015 (and a full disposal by the end of 2018). The agreement with the EU did not include any decision regarding the method of disposal of the different insurance businesses. ING considered several disposal options (see Figure 11.7), including:

- An initial public offering (IPO); and/or
- A spin-off; and/or
- A private sale.

By divesting more that 50% of all insurance entities by the end of 2015 and losing control of the board of the legal entities of ING Insurance, ING's strategic decision-making would only take place in the banking market and no longer in the insurance market.

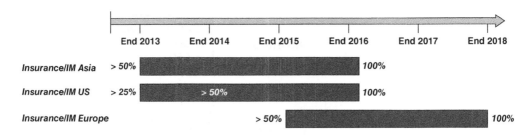

FIGURE 11.6   ING's deadlines for the divestments of its insurance businesses

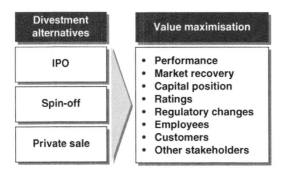

FIGURE 11.7   Alternatives to dispose of ING's insurance businesses

In line with the restructuring plan, ING Group divested a number of businesses around the world from 2011 to 2013, including divestments of insurance and investment management businesses in the United States, Latin America and Asia/Pacific (other than Japan). ING Group indicated in 2012 that the intended base case for divestment of its European insurance and investment management businesses was through an Initial Public Offering (IPO), while keeping all other options open. In May 2013 took place the IPO of ING Insurance U.S. under the new name Voya, which upon completion reduced ING Group's stake in Voya to 71%. In November 2013, ING Group expanded the scope of this intended base case IPO with the inclusion of the Japan Life and Japan Closed Block VA businesses. In early June 2014, ING announced it would proceed with the IPO of NN Group (the new entity comprising the European and Asian insurance businesses). The offering consisted solely of existing shares of NN Group owned by ING.

11.2.6 Effects on Double Leverage

By fully divesting its insurance subsidiaries, ING intended to pay back the Dutch State aid and to eliminate its double leverage. ING's accounting capital structure as of the end of 2011 is shown in Figure 11.8. The double leverage is represented by the difference between the EUR 46 billion (sum of ING bank and ING insurance equity) and the Group's EUR 34 billion equity, resulting in EUR 12 billion double leverage (EUR 7 billion were the Group's CT1 securities be counted as equity). In other words, the common shareholders of the Group did not own all the equity of the bank and the insurance businesses. This was because the external debt and hybrids, and government CT1 securities were raised to increase the equity of the underlying businesses.

The main advantage of the double leverage capital structure was the possibility to magnify returns. Whilst at the end of 2011 ING Group shareholders had invested EUR 34 billion, they had an equity position in both the banking and insurance businesses totalling EUR 46 billion.

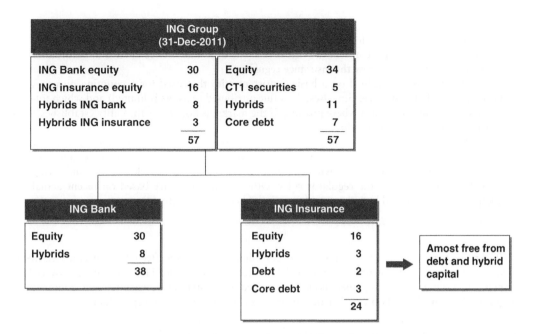

FIGURE 11.8 ING Group's capital position as of 31 December 2011

The main weakness of such a capital structure is the dependency on dividend income from subsidiaries, the only possible income, to pay interest on the debt, hybrids and CT1 instruments at the group level. At the height of the crisis, the Group's subsidiaries stopped paying dividends in order to protect their dwindling capital levels. ING Group's other potential sources of cash – to issue more debt/hybrids or to issue new capital – were prohibitively expensive, instigating the group to request the aid from the Dutch state.

Each time part of the insurance business was sold or IPOed, the proportional part of the double leverage was reduced. At the end of 2011, the insurance business had a EUR 16 billion of pure equity capital, meaning that a full disposal of this business at book value (assuming that the buyer takes all the debt) would allow ING Group to repay the EUR 5 billion of CT1 securities (a very expensive item), EUR 7 billion of core debt and EUR 4 billion of hybrids. As a result, EUR 7 billion would remain, to be gradually repaid through dividends from the bank business.

11.3 REGULATORY PECULIARITIES OF INVESTMENTS IN INSURANCE ENTITIES

The Basel III framework is applied on a consolidated basis to capture the risks of a whole banking group. As mentioned in Section 8.1, from an accounting perspective an insurance entity is either fully or equity consolidated when the investor bank controls or exerts significant influence over the insurer respectively, irrespective of the percentage in the ordinary share capital of the insurance company that the bank holds. A fully consolidated insurance entity is called subsidiary, while an equity method consolidated insurance entity is called associate or jointly controlled entity.

Subsidiaries and associates engaged in insurance activities are **excluded** from the regulatory consolidation by excluding assets, liabilities and post-acquisition reserves, leaving the investment of these insurance subsidiaries to be recorded at cost. This is due to two reasons: (i) to avoid double leverage and (ii) to take into account that insurance entities are subject to different capital requirements – under the Solvency II regime – which differ notably from those of Basel III.

The regulatory capital of life insurance businesses is based on available capital resources. Available capital resources represent the excess of assets over liabilities calculated in accordance with regulatory rules set out by the insurance regulator.

Assets are generally valued on a basis consistent with that used for accounting purposes (with the exception that, in certain cases, the value attributed to assets is limited) and which follows a market value approach where possible. If the market is not active, the entity establishes a fair value by using valuation techniques.

Liabilities are calculated using a projection of future cash flows after making prudent assumptions about variables such as investment return, expenses and mortality. Discount rates used to value the liabilities are set with reference to the risk adjusted yields on the underlying assets in accordance with the regulator rules. Other assumptions are based on recent actual experience, supplemented by industry information where appropriate.

The regulatory treatment once regulatory deconsolidation has been effected follows the treatment for investments in capital instruments in financial institutions (see Figure 11.9), which was covered in Chapter 10. In summary, an investment is either deducted from capital, risk-weighted or a combination thereof. Deductions depend on whether the investment is significant or non-significant.

11.3.1 Conglomerates Exception: Consolidation of Equity Holdings in an Insurance Entity

CRD IV/CRR permits national authorities to apply an alternative risk weighting approach to deduction where the bank and insurer are supervised as part of a conglomerate. Precisely, [CRR 49] allows jurisdictions to permit or require banks the regulatory consolidation of banking and insurance entities in a group subject to conglomerate consolidation, as an alternative to the deduction approach, subject to prior regulatory approval. This alternative is an updated version of the Financial Conglomerates Directive (FICOD) approach. FICOD is a specific legal mechanism that addresses the risk of double counting of capital across the banking and insurance sectors.

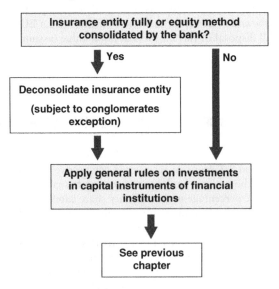

FIGURE 11.9   Regulatory treatment of investments in capital instruments of insurance entities

If the consolidation option is applied, Basel III requires that the bank demonstrates in each reporting period that consolidation results in a regulatory capital outcome that is at least as conservative as deduction, thereby preventing double counting of capital. Interestingly, the CRR does not mandate the critical additional requirement that any consolidation method must not produce a capital ratio benefit compared to a deduction approach.

11.4 CASE STUDY: LLOYDS BANKING GROUP'S CAPITAL ENHANCEMENT INITIATIVES RELATED TO ITS INSURANCE SUBSIDIARIES

This case study covers the initiatives taken by the British Bank Lloyds Banking Group ("Lloyds") to enhance its CET1 capital related to its insurance businesses.

11.4.1 Lloyds' Initiatives to Reduce Deductions from CET1 Related to its Insurance Subsidiaries

In 2013 the insurance division of Lloyds' was one of the United Kingdom's largest insurers, providing long-term savings, protection and investment products, and general insurance products to customers in the UK and Europe. These products were distributed through the bancassurance, intermediary and direct channels of the Lloyds Bank, Halifax, Bank of Scotland, TSB and Scottish Widows brands. The insurance division comprised several insurance entities fully consolidated from an accounting perspective by the Lloyds Bank Plc, all of which were excluded from the regulatory scope of consolidation (see Figure 11.10). As a result of the accounting consolidation (or holding more than 10% of the ordinary share capital) of these entities, the investments were deemed to be significant. As explained in Chapter 10, Lloyds' significant investments in financial institutions (not just insurance entities) were aggregated and the excess over 10% of the relevant CET1 capital (the 10% threshold) was deducted from Lloyds' CET1 capital. The amount below the 10% threshold was added to the amounts of deferred tax assets relating to temporary differences (below the 10% threshold) and the amounts of mortgage servicing rights (below the 10% threshold). The aggregate of these three amounts were compared to 17.65% of the relevant CET1 capital (the 15% threshold). The amount above the 15% threshold was deducted from Lloyds' CET1 capital (see Figure 11.11).

While the regulators concern over double leverage has its logic, arguably the Basel III treatment of investments in insurance entities penalises the bancassurance business model.

Basel III assumes that there is a high correlation between the risks in an investee insurer and the risks in its investor bank by requiring a full deduction from CET1 the investment amounts (deemed to be significant), exceeding the 10% and 15% thresholds, in insurance entities. In other words and looking for simplicity at the 10% threshold only, Basel III's treatment implies that if an insurer faces financial stress and once the bank has consumed 10% of its CET1 capital, the value of the investment in the insurer is likely to be almost zero.

In practice, the nature and time horizon of insurance and banking risks notably differ, so there is a significant diversification in financial risks. As shown in the ING case, the bank was in a delicate financial situation but was able to extract substantial value from the disposals of its insurance business.

As covered in Section 13.3.1, the financial conglomerates exception provides an alternative to financial groups with large bank and insurance businesses.

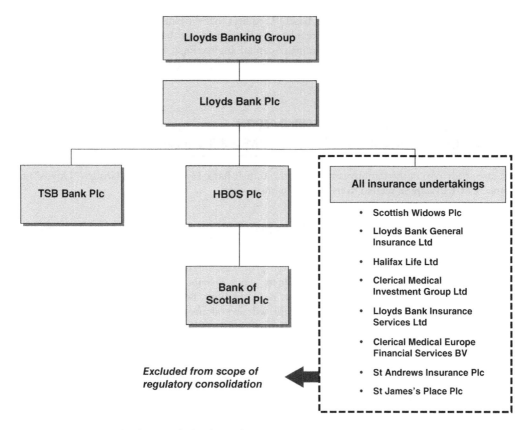

FIGURE 11.10   Main subsidiaries of Lloyds Banking Group

In 2013, the British financial regulator determined that Lloyds had a GBP 8.6 billion capital deficit and, as a result, the bank embarked into a process to bolster its capital levels. Three were the initiatives taken in 2013 by Lloyds to reduce the capital impact of its insurance and asset management businesses:

■ The distribution of dividends by the insurance businesses to the banking group totalling GBP 2,155 million;
■ The disposal of Lloyds' holding in its insurer/asset manager St. James's Place; and
■ The partial repayment of the Lloyds' subordinated debt holdings in the insurance businesses following the issuance of external subordinated debt.

These three initiatives were primarily aimed at reducing the significant holdings deduction from CET1 capital, resulting in a GBP 2,978 million CET1 enhancement, or 104 basis points.

Dividend from Lloyds' Insurance Businesses   A significant portion of the carrying amounts of Lloyds' investments in the insurance businesses were deducted from the bank's CET1 capital, as they were categorised as significant investments and well exceeded the 10% and 15% thresholds. In 2013 Lloyds had little incentive to keep these businesses overcapitalised, as their excess capital did not permeate to the bank's regulatory capital.

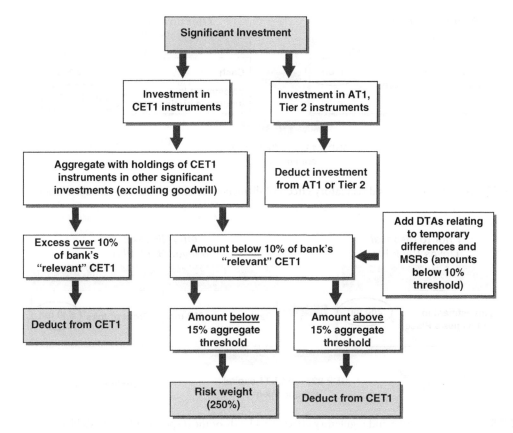

FIGURE 11.11   Basel III's treatment of significant investments in unconsolidated financial entities

There were no material, practical or legal impediments to such transfers or repayments, other than the constraints imposed over the available capital resources of the group's assurance businesses. The legal and regulatory structure of the group provided a capability for the prompt transfer of surplus capital resources over and above regulatory requirements or repayment of liabilities when due throughout the group. As a result, Lloyds decided to reduce the overcapitalisation of the insurance undertakings through the distribution of a GBP 2,155 million cash dividend to their parent company Lloyds Bank Plc. The effect (see Figure 11.12) was an equivalent reduction of the carrying amounts of the investments of Lloyds Bank Plc in these insurance entities, thus reducing the CET1 deduction by GBP 2,155 million (assuming that the deduction from Lloyd Bank Plc's CET1 capital related to significant investments in financial institutions exceeded that amount).

Disposal of Asset Manager St James's Place   Prior to March 2013, Lloyds owned 57% of the London-based long-life insurer/wealth manager St James's Place plc ("St James's"). This entity was regulated by the insurance arm of the British PRA. Whilst Lloyds fully consolidated St James's from an accounting perspective, the assets and liabilities of the asset manager were excluded from the calculation of consolidated regulatory capital requirements and resources. Rather, this investment was deemed to be a significant investment in a financial institution and, as a result, compared to the 10% and 15% thresholds, as shown in Figure 11.11.

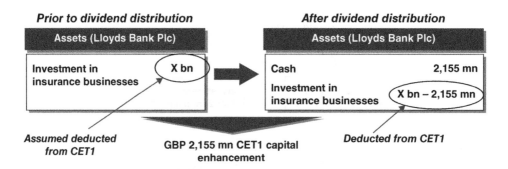

FIGURE 11.12 Accounting and regulatory effects of dividend from Lloyds' insurance subsidiaries

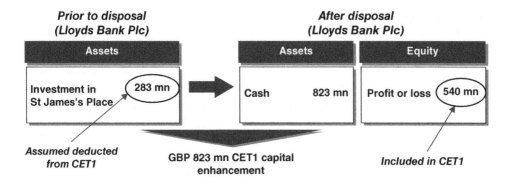

FIGURE 11.13 Accounting and regulatory effects on Lloyds of the disposal of St James's Place

On 15 March 2013 Lloyds completed the sale of 102 million shares in St James's for GBP 520 million, reducing the bank's holding in that company to approximately 37%. As a result of that reduction in ownership, Lloyds ceased to fully consolidate St James's Place Plc in its accounts, instead accounting for the residual investment as an associate. Lloyds realised a gain of GBP 394 million on the sale of those shares and the fair valuation of the bank's residual stake. Subsequently, on 29 May 2013 Lloyds completed the sale of a further 77 million shares, generating a profit of GBP 39 million. Following the expiry of a 180-day unwaivable lock-up period agreed between Lloyds and the sole bookrunner of the previous placement, on 13 December 2013 completed the sale of its remaining 21% holding – 109 million shares – generating a profit of GBP 107 million.

Therefore, the total gain from the full disposal was GBP 540 million (=394 mn + 39 mn + 107 mn), recognised in profit or loss. As Lloyds Bank Plc owned a large amount of deferred tax assets, no tax was levied on this gain, resulting in a GBP 540 million after-tax gain, which enhanced the bank's CET1 capital by that same amount.

Let us assume that the carrying cost of the investment – GBP 283 million – was fully deducted from Lloyds' CET1 capital, following the process depicted in Figure 11.11. The disposal of St James's also eliminated the deduction from CET1 caused by the significant investment in the wealth manager/insurer. Because the carrying amount of the investment was GBP 283 million, the total effect of the disposal on Lloyds' CET1 capital was GBP 823 million (= GBP 540 million gain on disposal + GBP 283 million deduction savings), as shown in Figure 11.13, a 28 basis points (0.28%) improvement.

Partial Repayment of Subordinated Debt Basel III requires deduction of investments in the capital of other financial entities to be made on a "corresponding deduction approach". Deduction is consequently applied to the corresponding tier of capital for which the capital investment, subject to deduction, would qualify if it were issued by the investing bank itself. In our case, Lloyds held subordinated debt issued by its insurance entities. Therefore, as the debt would have qualified as a Tier 2 instrument if it were issued by Lloyds, the group deducted from its Tier 2 capital its investment in the subordinated debt.

If the corresponding tier was insufficient to satisfy the required deduction, the shortfall was deducted from the next higher tier of capital. For example, if Lloyds did not have enough Tier 2 capital to satisfy the deduction, the shortfall would be from its AT1 capital and, should that also be insufficient, then from the bank's CET1 capital.

The repayment of subordinated debt by Lloyds' insurance entities freed up an equivalent amount of Tier 2 capital.

Final Considerations

The main advantage of the capital enhancement measures implemented by Lloyds was the reduction of the deduction from CET1 of its significant investments in financial institutions. This deduction was likely to be reduced further over the subsequent years for two reasons:

Firstly, the insurance entities were likely to continue paying dividends to the bank, reducing the equity investment.

Secondly, the 10% and 15% thresholds allowance was likely to raise appreciably as Lloyds increased its CET1 capital levels. For example, for every extra GBP 1 billion of capital generated by Lloyds, the 10% threshold would increase by GBP 100 million and the investments in financial institutions deduction would decrease by the same amount (although non-deducted amounts would be risk-weighted).

The main drawback of the disposal was the decrease in Lloyds' future net fee and commission income.

CHAPTER 12

Equity Investments in Non-financial Entities

Whilst this book dissects the numerator of the regulatory capital ratio (i.e., the capital figure), this chapter is an exception as it relates to the effects on the denominator – the RWAs – due to equity exposures to non-financial entities held in the banking book. In the previous two chapters, investments in capital instruments of financial institutions were covered and I thought that a chapter devoted to equity investments in non-financial entities would be a necessary addition to understand the capital impact of such investments.

12.1 BASEL III AND EQUITY EXPOSURES TO NON-FINANCIAL ENTITIES IN THE BANKING BOOK

The treatment of equity exposures to non-financial entities is an addition to that of other exposures – mainly to debt instruments – in the banking book. Thus, equity exposures to non-financial entities are approached from a credit risk perspective, resulting in a risk weight that takes into account the likelihood of the bank not being able to recover the amount recognised in the balance sheet. Therefore, potential future appreciation of an equity investment is ignored from a regulatory capital perspective.

> **Equity exposures** are defined in [CRR 133(1) and 147(6)] as either:
>
> 1. Non-debt exposures conveying a subordinated, residual claim on the assets or income of the issuer; or
> 2. Debt exposures and other securities, partnerships, derivatives or other vehicles, the economic substance of which is similar to the exposures specified in 1).

> Certain instruments which are held as debt investments on the IFRS balance sheet, mainly investment fund units, are treated as equity instruments for regulatory capital purposes.
>
> Certain instruments which are held as trading portfolio assets on the IFRS balance sheet, but which are not part of the regulatory VaR framework, are included in the banking book for regulatory capital purposes.

Like any other credit risk in the banking book, the risk weight of equity exposures in this book is determined according to either the standardised approach or the Internal Ratings-Based (IRB) Approach. The simplest approach – the standardised approach – is used by most small banks. The IRB approach is a more risk-sensitive approach, but permission is needed from the relevant supervisory authority to use it.

12.2 EQUITY EXPOSURES UNDER THE STANDARDISED APPROACH

Under the standardised approach, RWAs related to an equity exposure are determined using the supervisor's determined risk weights for every type of exposure.

12.2.1 Risk-Weighted Assets under the Standardised Approach

The RWAs of an equity exposure to a non-financial entity under the standardised approach are calculated by multiplying (i) the exposure value of the asset by (ii) the risk weight of the asset (expressed as a percentage):

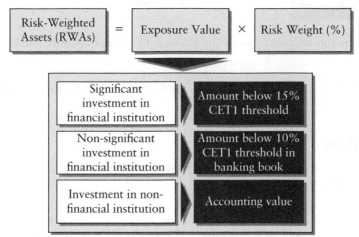

The exposure value is either:

■ The amount below the 15% CET1 threshold, in the case of a significant investment in a financial institution;
■ The amount below the 10% CET1 threshold and allocated to the banking book, in the case of a non-significant investment in a financial institution; or
■ The accounting value, otherwise. This is the case for equity investments in non-financial entities.

According to [CRR 133], under the standardised approach equity exposures held in the banking book are assigned a risk weight of either (see Figure 12.1):

■ **100%**, for equity exposures not treated as high-risk items, in the case of non-significant investments in financial institutions (see Section 10.1.4) or investments in non-financial entities (non-qualifying holdings);
■ **150%** for equity exposures treated as high-risk items (see section 12.2.2);
■ **250%**, in the case of non-significant investments in financial institutions (see Section 10.1.5); or
■ **1,250%** for qualifying holdings in non-financial institutions above the 15% threshold (see Section 12.4).

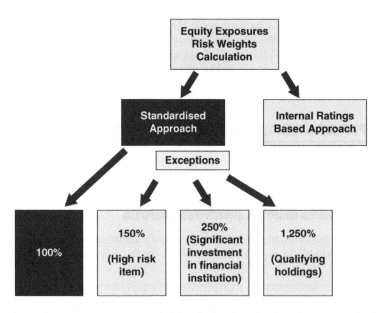

FIGURE 12.1   Risk weights of equity exposures held in the banking book under the standardised approach

Sections 10.1.4 and 10.1.5 described how investments in financial institutions below specific CET1 thresholds are deducted from CET1 capital.

12.2.2 High-Risk Items

[CRR 128] sets out the risk weight for high-risk items. Exposures with particularly high risks include any of the following exposures:

- Investments in venture capital firms;
- Investments in Alternative Investment Funds as defined in [Directive 2011/61/EU 4(1)(a)] except where the mandate of the fund does not allow a leverage higher than that required under [Directive 2009/65/EC 51(3)];
- Investments in private equity;
- Speculative immovable property financing;
- Exposures in the form of shares or units in a Collective Investment Undertaking that are associated with particularly high risks; and
- Other exposures in which there is (i) a high risk of loss as a result of default of the obligor or (ii) it is impossible to assess adequately whether the exposure falls under (i).

Exposures on items categorised as **high-risk items** are assigned a **150% risk weight**.

12.3 EQUITY EXPOSURES UNDER THE IRB APPROACH

The IRB approach provides banks with a more risk-sensitive approach to determining the capital charges for equity positions in non-financial entities held in the banking book. Permission is needed from the relevant supervisory authority to use the IRB approach.

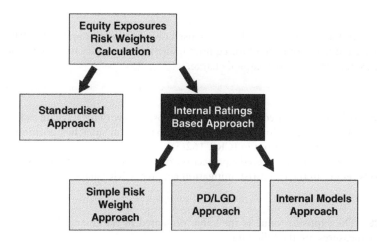

FIGURE 12.2   Methods available under the IRB approach for equity exposures in the banking book

Pursuant to [CRR 151(4) and 155], risk-weighted assets for equity exposures held in the banking book under the IRB approach are calculated in accordance with one of the following methods (see Figure 12.2):

- The simple risk weight approach;
- The PD/LGD approach; and
- The internal models approach.

Banks need permission from the competent authorities to apply either the PD/LGD or the internal models approaches.

In addition, a bank may apply different approaches to different equities portfolios where the bank itself uses different approaches for internal risk management purposes. Where a bank uses different approaches, the choice of the PD/LGD approach or the internal models approach shall be made consistently, including over time and with the approach used for the internal risk management of the relevant equity exposure, and shall not be determined by regulatory arbitrage considerations.

12.3.1 The Simple Risk Weight Approach

Pursuant to [CRR 155(2)], under the simple risk weight approach, the RWAs of an equity exposure are calculated by multiplying (i) the exposure value of the asset by (ii) the risk weight of the asset (expressed as a percentage):

$$\boxed{\text{Risk-Weighted Assets (RWAs)}} = \boxed{\text{Exposure Value}} \times \boxed{\text{Risk Weight (\%)}}$$

Short cash positions and derivative instruments held in the banking book are permitted to offset long positions in the same individual stocks, provided that these instruments have been explicitly designated as hedges of specific equity exposures and that they have remaining maturities of at least one year (i.e., they provide a hedge for at least another year).

The offset rule in the above paragraph may be used only for equities under the IRB simple risk weight approach. It may not be used for equities under the standardised approach nor for equities that are exempt from the IRB capital charge.

Other short positions are treated as if they are long positions with the relevant risk weight assigned to the absolute value of each position. In the context of maturity mismatched positions, the method is that for corporate exposures as set out in [CRR 162(5)].

Banks may recognise unfunded credit protection obtained on an equity exposure in accordance with the methods set out in the credit risk mitigation chapter [CRR Chapter 4].

Exposure Values   The exposure value is the value presented in the financial statements. Admissible equity exposure measures are the following:

- For investments held at **fair value through profit or loss** (i.e., at fair value with changes in value flowing directly through income), the exposure value is the **fair value** presented in the balance sheet (i.e., the accounting fair value). These changes in value flow into CET1 capital resources;
- For investments held at **fair value at fair value through other comprehensive income** (i.e., at fair value with changes in value not flowing through income but into a tax-adjusted separate component of equity) the exposure value is the **fair value** presented in the balance sheet (i.e., the accounting fair value); and
- For investments held at cost or at the lower of cost or market value, the exposure value is the cost or market value presented in the balance sheet, excluding goodwill. Typically, these investments are consolidated either fully or under the equity method from an accounting perspective.

Risk Weights   The simple risk weight approach [CRR 155(2)] prescribes a set of risk weights depending on the composition of the equities portfolio:

- **190%** risk weight for private equity exposures in sufficiently diversified portfolios;
- **290%** risk weight for exchange-traded equity exposures; and
- **370%** risk weight for all other equity exposures.

12.3.2 The PD/LGD Approach

Pursuant to [CRR 155(3)], banks using the IRB approach for credit risk may use the PD/LGD approach, following permission from competent authorities to apply the PD/LGD approach.

Conceptually the PD/LGD approach is based on the IRB approach to measuring credit risk on debt instruments held in the banking book and issued by sovereigns, financial institutions and corporates. The IRB approach calculates a "value-at-risk" (VaR) amount which represents the loss amount over the time horizon with a certain probability. In the Basel III framework the time horizon is a one-year period and the probability is 99.9%. The regulatory framework assumes that, while banking book positions are difficult to exit, the bank has sufficient time in a year to raise capital if needed. This confidence interval means that if all the assumptions in the IRB supervisory model for credit risk were correct for a bank, there would be less than a 0.1% probability that credit losses at the bank in any year would exceed the IRB risk-based capital requirement. In other words, the bank is expected to suffer losses that exceed its level of capital on average once in a thousand years. This confidence level might seem rather high. However, the high confidence level is also set to protect against errors that

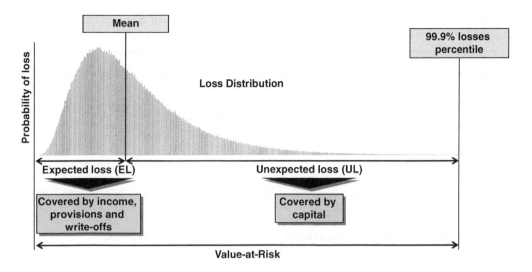

FIGURE 12.3 Thinking behind Basel III's credit risk approach

might occur from the bank's internal PD, LGD and EAD estimation, as well as other model uncertainties. The VaR amount is split between (see Figure 12.3):

- The **expected loss** (EL) amount represents the amount of loss that is "expected" over the time horizon. Mathematically, the EL is the statistical mean of the loss distribution. Under the Basel III framework, the expected loss in a debt instrument is assumed to be covered by the income paid by the borrower, provisions and write-offs.
- The **unexpected loss** (UL) amount represents the potential losses over and above the EL. Under the Basel III framework ULs are covered by regulatory capital. The UL amount is equal to (i) the 99.9% VaR amount less (ii) the amount of expected losses.

$$\boxed{\text{Unexpected Loss Amount}} = \boxed{\text{VaR Amount}} - \boxed{\text{Expected Loss Amount}}$$

Risk-weighted assets of an exposure are calculated by multiplying (i) the exposure value of the asset by (ii) the risk weight:

$$\boxed{\text{Risk Weighted Assets (RWAs)}} = \boxed{\text{Exposure Value}} \times \boxed{\text{Risk Weight (\%)}}$$

$$\text{Risk Weight} = \left[N\left(\sqrt{\frac{1}{1-R}} \times N^{-1}(PD) + \sqrt{\frac{R}{1-R}} \times N^{-1}(0.999) \right) \times LGD - PD \times LGD \right] \times MF \times 12.5 \times 1.06$$

The risk weight is calculated according to the formula in [CRR 153(1)] (i.e., the formula to calculate the risk weights related to credit risk for debt instruments held in the banking book and issued by sovereigns, financial institutions and corporates). The formula requires the bank to estimate certain risk parameters, which the bank may do using a variety of techniques. These risk parameters are probability of default (PD), expected loss given default (ELGD), loss given default (LGD), exposure at default (EAD) and effective remaining maturity (M).

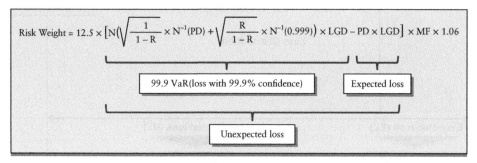

Where:

b: The maturity adjustment factor, calculated according to the following formula:

$$b = \left[0.11852 - 0.05478 \times Ln(PD)\right]^2$$

M: The instrument's effective maturity;

MF: Maturity factor, which is calculated as:

$$MF = \frac{1 + (M - 2.5) \times b}{1 - 1.5 \times b}$$

N(X): The cumulative distribution function for a standard normal random variable (i.e., the probability that a normal random variable with mean zero and variance of one is less than or equal to X);

N⁻¹(X): The inverse cumulative distribution function for a standard normal random variable;

PD: Probability of default;

R: The coefficient of correlation, which is defined as:

$$R = 0.12 \times \frac{1 - e^{-50 \times PD}}{1 - e^{-50}} + 0.24 \times \left(1 - \frac{1 - e^{-50 \times PD}}{1 - e^{-50}}\right)$$

The last component of the formula (i.e., the **1.06 multiplier**) is called the **scaling factor** which was included by the Basel II framework to take into account the disparities in provisioning among banks of their expected credit losses. The 1.06 scaling factor was established following a quantitative study was performed, meaning a slight under-provisioning of expected losses.

If a bank does not have sufficient information to use the definition of default set out in [CRR 178] a scaling factor of 1.5 is assigned to the risk weights.

At the individual exposure level the sum of the expected loss amount multiplied by 12.5 and the risk-weighted assets shall not exceed the exposure value multiplied by 12.5.

Banks may recognise unfunded credit protection obtained on an equity exposure in accordance with the methods set out in [CRR Chapter 4]. This is subject to an LGD of 90% on the exposure to the provider of the hedge. For private equity exposures in sufficiently diversified portfolios an LGD of 65% is used. For these purposes M is five years.

The **probability of default** (PD) is estimated as the one year probability of default on the non-financial entity company (whether or not the bank itself had a holding of debt of the entity and regardless of situations where the entity may have no debt in its capital structure).

A **loss given default** (LGD) of 90% would be assumed in deriving the appropriate risk weight. In other words, if the entity defaults the equity investment is assumed to be worthless.

With regard to the **maturity adjustment** of the derived risk weight, the implied 3 year average maturity embodied in the corporate debt risk weights sits uneasily with the conceptually potentially infinite "maturity" of equity interests. Consequently, the maturity adjustment is normally the maximum used in the IRB framework (i.e., 5 years).

Baseline risk-weighted assets for the entire equities portfolio equal the simple aggregate of the capital requirements on each investment. Equity positions are included in the granularity adjustment.

12.3.3 The Internal Models Approach

Banks need permission from competent authorities to apply the internal models approach, which is subject to meeting the requirements laid down in [CRR Section 6 Subsection 4]. As set out in [CRR 155(4)], under the internal models approach, the risk-weighted assets are the potential losses on a bank's equity exposures held in the banking book. Potential losses are derived using internal value-at-risk models subject to the 99th percentile, one-tailed confidence interval of the difference between quarterly returns and an appropriate risk-free rate computed over a long-term sample period, multiplied by 12.5 (i.e., the inverse of the minimum 8% risk-based capital requirement).

Banks may recognise unfunded credit protection (i.e., eligible credit risk mitigation – CRM) obtained on an equity position.

The risk-weighted assets at the equities portfolio level are subject to a floor. They shall not be less than the total of the sums of the following:

- The RWAs required under the PD/LGD approach; and
- The corresponding expected loss amounts multiplied by 12.5.

These two amounts are calculated on the basis of the PD and LGD values set out next.

Probability of Default (PD)   Pursuant to [CRR 165(1)], the probability of default (PD) is determined according to the methods for corporate exposures. The following minimum PDs apply:

- 0.09% for exchange-traded equity exposures where the investment is part of a long-term customer relationship;
- 0.09% for non-exchange-traded equity exposures where the returns on the investment are based on regular and periodic cash flows not derived from capital gains;
- 0.40% for exchange-traded equity exposures including other short positions as set out in [CRR 155(2)] (see short positions covered in Section 12.3.1 on the simple risk weight approach); and
- 1.25% for all other equity exposures including other short positions as set out in [CRR 155(2)].

Loss Given Default (LGD)   Pursuant to [CRR 165(2)], loss given default (LGD) is assigned as follows:

- 65% for private equity exposures in sufficiently diversified portfolios; and
- 90% for all other such exposures.

12.3.4 Use of the Standardised Approach by IRB-approved Banks

> The use of the standardised approach for equity exposures held in the banking book is likely to result in a lower capital consumption than that under the IRB simple risk weight approach. Thus, banks with permission to use the IRB approach have a strong incentive to switch to the standardised approach for equity exposures they were freely allowed to choose between both approaches. In order to eliminate this capital arbitrage opportunity, the CRR establishes conditions for such change.

Pursuant to [CRR 149], a bank that uses the IRB approach for credit risk can apply the standardised approach for specific exposures (including equity exposures) if the following two conditions are met:

- The bank has demonstrated to the satisfaction of the competent authority that the use of the standardised approach is not proposed in order to reduce the capital consumption of the exposure, but it is necessary on the basis of nature and complexity of the bank's total exposures of this type and would not have a material adverse impact on the solvency of the bank or its ability to manage risk effectively;
- The bank has received the prior permission of the competent authority.

12.4 EXPECTED LOSSES FROM EQUITY EXPOSURES UNDER THE IRB APPROACH

For banks calculating RWAs using the IRB approach, negative amounts resulting from the calculation of expected loss amounts are deducted from CET1, as covered in Section 3.15.

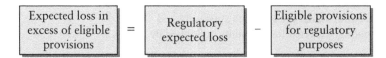

The objective of this deduction is to eliminate any incentives for under-provisioning.

Expected Losses

Non-qualifying investments in equity instruments of non-financial entities held in the banking book consume capital in the form of RWAs. These represent unexpected losses which are supposed to be covered with regulatory capital.

If a bank applies the IRB approach to calculate RWAs (either under the simple risk weight or the PD/LGD approach), there will be an expected loss attributable to the equity instrument. The portion of expected losses not covered by existing provisions shall be deducted from CET1 capital.

Investments (both non-significant and significant) in equity instruments of financial institutions held in the banking book do not follow the IRB approach and, thus, their expected losses do not affect CET1 capital. This is the case as well of investments in equity instruments of non-financial entities held in the banking book for which their RWAs are calculated using the standardised approach or the internal models IRB approach.

12.4.1 Expected Losses under the Simple Risk Weight Approach

Pursuant to [CRR 158(7)], **expected loss amounts** for equity exposures where the risk-weighted assets are calculated according to the simple risk weight approach are calculated according to the following formula:

$$
\boxed{\text{Expected Loss Amount}} = \boxed{\text{Exposure Value}} \times \boxed{\text{Expected Loss (\%)}}
$$

The expected loss values are the following:

- **0.8%** for private equity exposures in sufficiently diversified portfolios;
- **0.8%** for exchange-traded equity exposures; and
- **2.4%** for all other equity exposures.

12.4.2 Expected Loss Amounts under the PD/LGD Approach

Pursuant to [CRR 158(8)], the **expected loss amounts** for equity exposures where the risk-weighted assets are calculated according to the PD/LGD approach are calculated according to the following formula:

$$
\boxed{\text{Expected Loss Amount}} = \boxed{\text{Exposure Value}} \times \boxed{\text{Expected Loss (EL)}}
$$

$$
\boxed{\text{PD}} \times \boxed{\text{LGD}}
$$

12.4.3 Expected Loss Amounts under the Internal Models Approach

Pursuant to [CRR 158(9)], **expected loss amounts** for equity exposures where the risk-weighted assets are calculated according to the internal models approach are zero. It was covered in Section 12.3.3 that RWAs under the internal models approach represent potential losses, which include both expected and unexpected losses.

12.5 QUALIFIED HOLDINGS OUTSIDE THE FINANCIAL SECTOR EXCEEDING THE 15% THRESHOLD

[CRR 89] discourages large equity exposures to non-financial entities. The total amount of the qualifying holdings of a bank in non-financial sectors entities are subject to a special treatment.

> **Qualified holdings** are defined in [CRR 4(36)] as "a direct or indirect holding in an undertaking which represents 10% or more of the capital or of the voting rights or which makes it possible to exercise a significant influence over the management of that undertaking".
>
> A **non-financial sector** entity is defined in [CRR 89(1)] as "an entity that is not: (i) a financial sector entity; or (ii) a direct extension of banking; or (iii) ancillary to banking; or (iv) leasing, factoring, the management of unit trusts, the management of data processing services or any other similar activity".

[CRR 89(3)] requires that competent authorities choose between two options with respect to "qualifying holdings" that exceed the greater of two threshold criteria (see below), and publish their choice:

- To apply a risk weight of 1,250% to the excess qualifying holdings above the greater of the two threshold criteria (see below). Under this option banks may also choose to deduct from CET1 the excess above the greater of the two threshold criteria, rather than risk weighting it at 1,250%; or
- To prohibit firms from having qualifying holdings above the greater of these two criteria.

The two threshold criteria referred to above are the following:

1. The amount that a qualifying holding exceeds 15% of the bank's eligible capital; and
2. The aggregate of all qualifying holdings exceeds 60% of its eligible capital.

Commonly national supervisors have chosen the first alternative as its level of risk weighting adequately discourages high concentration in a single firm and excessive equity exposures to non-financial sectors.

Eligible capital is defined in [CRR 4(71)] as the sum of the following:

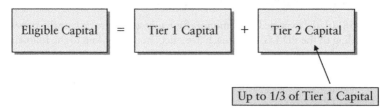

According to [CRR 24(1)], the valuation of assets shall be effected in accordance with the applicable accounting framework, which in the European Union means the IFRS standards. According to IFRS 9, an equity investment *not* consolidated (either fully or under the equity method) is recognised at its fair value.

According to [CRR 91], the following shares are not included in calculating the qualifying holdings outside the financial sector:

1. Shares held temporarily during a financial assistance operation;
2. Shares held in an underwriting position held for five working days or fewer; and
3. Shares held in the own name of the bank and on behalf of others.

12.6 TEMPORARY EXEMPTION FROM THE IRB TREATMENT OF CERTAIN EQUITY EXPOSURES

[CRR 495(3)] allowed competent authorities temporarily to exempt from the Internal Ratings-Based (IRB) Approach treatment certain equity exposures held by banks as at 31 December 2007. The provision was temporary, its application ending on 31 December 2017.

The main guidance for European banks is the EBA's document EBA/RTS/2014/13 issued on 5 August 2014 and titled *EBA Final Draft Regulatory Technical Standards on the Treatment of Equity Exposures under the IRB Approach According to Article 495(3) of Regulation (EU) No 575/2013 (Capital Requirements Regulation – CRR)*. The EBA imposed a condition on competent authorities that must be met for the exemption to be granted: if it was being applied on the last day of application of CRD.

Equity exposures subject to the exception were treated using the **standardised approach**. The exempted position was measured as the number of shares as at 31 December 2007 and any additional share arising directly as a result of owning those holdings, provided they did not increase the proportional share of ownership in the investee company.

If an acquisition increased the proportional share of ownership in a specific holding, the part of the holding which constituted the excess was not subject to the exemption. Nor the exemption applied to holdings that were originally subject to the exemption, but were sold and then bought back.

> This exception allowed banks to avoid part of the increase in the capital requirement of the equity exposure class under the IRB approach. It was particularly relevant for some banks with significant equity holdings, given the higher capital requirement of the equity exposure class under the IRB approach compared to the standardised approach.
>
> However, in practice this exemption was immaterial to most banks due to the requirement that the equity exposures had to be held as at December 2007. The notably more stringent capital requirements under Basel III relative to Basel II triggered the disposal of most of the strategic corporate shareholdings held by European banks.

12.7 CASE STUDY: CAIXABANK'S MANDATORY EXCHANGEABLE ON REPSOL

In November 2013 CaixaBank, a Spanish bank, had a 12% stake in the Spanish oil and gas company Repsol, being its largest shareholder. Since it was created, CaixaBank had always held a relevant position in Repsol's shareholder structure and on its board of directors. The stake had a market value of approximately EUR 2.86 billion and was recognised in accounting terms as an associate using the equity consolidation method.

On 12 November 2013, CaixaBank issued a 3-year mandatorily exchangeable bond into Repsol shares for a total principal amount of EUR 594.3 million. The bonds, which were issued at par, bore a nominal annual fixed interest rate of 4.50%, payable annually. The main terms of the mandatory exchangeable are outlined in Table 12.1.

TABLE 12.1   Main terms of CaixaBank's mandatory exchangeable into Repsol

CaixaBank's Mandatory Exchangeable into Repsol – Main Terms	
Issuer	CaixaBank, S.A.
Closing date	22-Nov-2013
Maturity date	22-Nov-2016 (3 years)
Principal amount	EUR 594.3 mn
Underlying	Ordinary shares of Repsol S.A.
Coupon	4.5%
Status	Senior unsecured
Rating	BBB – (S&P), Baa3 (Moody's), BBB (Fitch)
Minimum exchange price	EUR 18.25 (100% of share price at issuance)
Maximum exchange price	EUR 22.815 (125% of share price at issuance)
Structure	Full dividend pass-through
Cash settlement	CaixaBank had the right to deliver cash to redeemed the bond
Bookrunners	Morgan Stanley, Citigroup

12.7.1 Structural Features of the Transaction – Conversion Mechanism

At maturity, CaixaBank could elect to repay the exchangeable's nominal amount in shares of Repsol (physical settlement), in cash (cash settlement) or a combination thereof.

Physical Settlement   In the case of physical settlement, the bond would mandatorily exchange at maturity into a number of Repsol shares. Such number was variable, being a function of Repsol's stock price at maturity. Bondholders would receive a number of shares of Repsol calculated by dividing the principal amount of the bonds by the exchange price. The exchange price of the bond varied according to the level of the underlying stock price at the date of conversion, being limited by the lower and the upper conversion prices. The lower conversion price – EUR 18.25 – was set at the stock price prevailing at issuance. The upper conversion price – EUR 22.8125 – was set at a 25% premium to the stock price at issue. Figure 12.4 shows the number of shares of Repsol to be received by the bondholders, were CaixaBank to elect physical settlement, which would be calculated as (i) the mandatory exchange principal amount divided by (ii) the average share price:

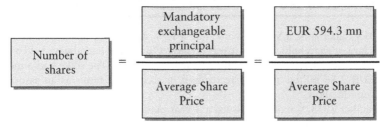

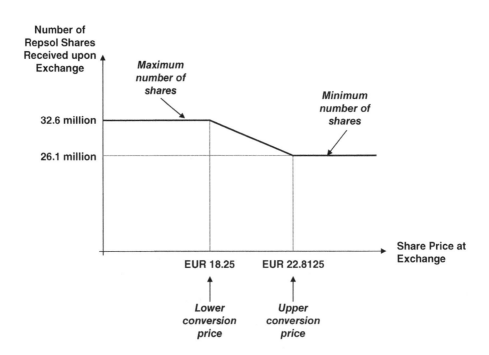

FIGURE 12.4   Number of shares to be received in the case of physical settlement

The **average share price** was arithmetic average of the Daily Share Price in the period of 20 consecutive trading days (the "averaging period") commencing on the third trading day after the cash election exercise date. Each trading day in the averaging period, CaixaBank observed the VWAP Share Price which was the volume-weighted average price (VWAP) of the Repsol shares on each trading say in the period. The VWAP was based on the Repsol share trading prices on the Spanish Stock Exchanges as published on Bloomberg. The Daily Share Price was calculated as follows:

1. If on that trading day Repsol's VWAP Share Price was below the EUR 18.25 minimum exchange price:

$$\text{Daily Share Price} = \text{Minimum exchange price} = \text{EUR } 18.25$$

2. If on that trading day Repsol's VWAP Share Price was between the minimum and the maximum exchange prices:

$$\text{Daily Share Price} = \text{VWAP Share Price}$$

3. If on that trading day Repsol's VWAP Share Price at maturity was above the EUR 22.8125 maximum exchange price:

$$\text{Daily Share Price} = \text{Maximum exchange price} = \text{EUR } 22.8125$$

It meant that if the average share price was below the EUR 18.25 minimum exchange price, investors would receive the maximum number of shares – 32.6 million – representing 2.5% of Repsol's issued share capital.

$$\text{Maximum number of shares} = \text{ME principal/Minimum exchange price}$$
$$\text{Maximum number of shares} = \text{EUR } 594.3\,\text{mn/EUR } 18.25 = 32.6\,\text{million shares}$$

Similarly, if the average share price at maturity was above the EUR 22.8125 maximum conversion price, investors would receive the minimum number of shares (26.1 million, representing 2% of Repsol's issued share capital).

$$\text{Minimum number of shares} = \text{ME principal/Maximum exchange price}$$
$$\text{Minimum number of shares} = \text{EUR } 594.3\,\text{mn/EUR } 22.8125 = 26.1\,\text{million shares}$$

Cash Settlement   CaixaBank could elect to pay the exchangeable bondholders a settlement amount in cash, calculated by multiplying (i) the average share price and (ii) the number of shares that, had a settlement election been made, would fall to be delivered to the investors:

Mean Share Price was the arithmetic average of the VWAP Share Price on each trading in the averaging the period:

$$\text{Mean Share Price} = \frac{\sum_{i=1}^{20} \text{VWAP Share Price}_i}{20}$$

It meant that if the Mean Share Price was equal to the average share price (i.e., each VWAP Share Price was between the minimum and maximum exchange prices), investors would receive the exchangeable principal:

$$\text{Cash settlement amount} = \text{ME principal} = \text{EUR } 594.3 \text{ million}$$

12.7.2 Mandatory Exchangeable from an Investor's Perspective

Let us analyse the ME from an investor's point of view. Let us assume that the whole issue was acquired by one investor and that he/she held the exchangeable until maturity. The investor invested EUR 594.3 million in the bond on issue date, received a 4.50% annual coupon and the dividends during the 3-year life of the bond, got the underlying shares upon exchange and sold the shares immediately after. The graph in Figure 12.5 depicts the value of the investment at maturity as a function of Repsol's share price at maturity, taking into account coupons (which totalled EUR 80.2 million during the three year term) and ignoring dividends. The coupons received during the 3-year term, ignoring any reinvestment proceeds, amounted to EUR 80.2 million (= $3 \times 4.5\% \times 594.3$ mn, rounded). The graph also compares the investment in the ME with a EUR 594.3 million direct investment in the underlying stock (i.e., an investment in 32.6 million Repsol shares), ignoring dividends. We can split the graph into three different areas:

- An **outperformance** area, in which the investment in the ME yielded EUR 80.2 mn more than the direct investment in Repsol shares. In this area, Repsol's share price at maturity was below the lower conversion price (or the share price at issuance). A share price below EUR 15.79 (= $18.25 - 80.2$ mn / 32.6 mn) implied the investor generating a loss, as the value of its investment would be below its initial EUR 594.3 million (ignoring dividends and time value of money).

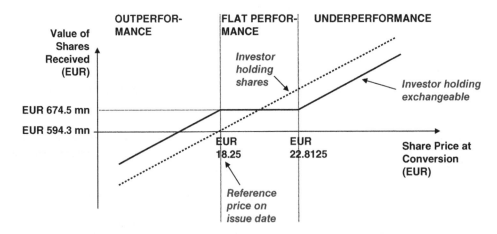

FIGURE 12.5 Value of the instrument at maturity, ignoring dividends, as a function of Repsol's share price

■ A **flat performance** area, in which the investment in the ME was rather similar to the direct investment in Repsol shares. In this area, the share price at maturity was between the lower and upper conversion prices. The investment would be worth EUR 674.5 million (= 594.3 mn + 80.2 mn).

■ An **underperformance** area, in which the investment in the ME yielded less than the direct investment in Repsol shares. In this area, the share price at maturity was above the upper conversion price. The underperformance was constant, amounting to EUR 69.2 mn (= 32.6 mn × 22.8125 − 594.3 mn − 80.2 mn). Therefore, the coupons received under the ME helped diminished the underperformance.

Initial Accelerated Bookbuilding   In general two types of investors acquired the mandatory exchangeable:

■ Long-only institutional investors. These investors were primarily investment funds that wanted to be long Repsol share price and invested in mandatory exchangeable attracted by the payout profile; and

■ Hedge funds. These funds did not want to take an exposure to Repsol share price, but were attracted by the 4.5% coupon.

In order to almost fully eliminate the exposure to the underlying shares, hedge funds sold short Repsol shares at issuance. The placing banks offered an **accelerated bookbuilding** in which they lent a number of shares of Repsol to the hedge funds and these funds sold the borrowed shares at the accelerated bookbuilding price, which was at a discount relative to the then trading share price. The minimum exchange price was then set at the accelerated bookbuilding price. The number of shares sold was calculated using the initial delta of the exchangeable. The initial delta was 77%, meaning that a hedge fund investing EUR 18.25 million needed to sell 770,000 shares (= 18.25 mn investment/18.25 bookbuild × 77%) at issuance. Apparently, 55% of the total initial delta was sold, implying that 55% of the issue was placed with hedged funds.

12.7.3 Other Features of the Mandatory Exchangeable

This section covers other relevant terms in CaixaBank's mandatory exchangeable on Repsol.

Voting Rights   After the issuance of the exchangeable bonds, CaixaBank retained the voting rights attached to the exchangeable's underlying 26.1 million Repsol shares. Therefore, CaixaBank maintained the same significant influence in Repsol.

Dividend Pass-through   CaixaBank's exchangeable included a dividend pass-through mechanism, in which all ordinary and extraordinary dividends in cash (or where the recipient may elect to receive such dividend in specie or in cash), were passed directly to the bondholders. The bondholders, proportionately to their bondholding, received an amount equivalent to the dividend gross amount distributed to the underlying 26.1 million Repsol shares. CaixaBank was required to pay such amount within five Barcelona business days following the date on which the dividend was distributed.

The inclusion of the dividend pass-through mechanism resulted in CaixaBank paying a lower fixed coupon than with a transaction without such mechanism because during the life of the investment bondholders expected to receive dividends in addition to the coupons. In addition, the pass-through mechanism helped the investment in the mandatory exchangeable to be more similar to a direct investment in the underlying shares.

12.7.4 Accounting Impact of the Mandatory Exchangeable

The rationale of the transaction was simply to enhance CaixaBank's regulatory capital levels. As mentioned throughout the book, before addressing the regulatory capital it is important to understand the accounting impact of any capital enhancement transaction.

Accounting Treatment Prior to the Mandatory Exchangeable Issuance   Prior to the issuance of the mandatory exchangeable, in the consolidated financial statements of CaixaBank the investment is shares of Repsol was treated as an associate, and thus, accounted for using the "equity method". An investee is treated as an associate if the investor has significant influence in the investee. Although the share ownership (12.2%) was well below the 20% that IFRS assumes for significant influence, the presence of CaixaBank's executives in Repsol's board of directors, delegate committee, and nomination and compensation committee implied that CaixaBank had a significant influence in Repsol. In applying the equity method of accounting (see Figure 12.6):

- Initially its investment in Repsol was originally accounted for at cost. Goodwill relating to this acquisition was included in the carrying amount of the investment.
- Goodwill was not amortised but was tested for impairment as part of the overall investment in Repsol (i.e., goodwill was not separately tested for impairment but the investment in its entirety). CaixaBank determined at each reporting date whether there was any objective evidence that the investment in Repsol was impaired. If this was the case, the bank calculated the amount of impairment as the difference between the recoverable amount of Repsol and its carrying value. Any impairment charges were recognised in profit or loss.
- The carrying amount of the investment decreased with distributions (e.g., dividends) received from Repsol.
- The carrying amount of the investment increased (decreased) with the bank's share of the profits (losses) of Repsol. Its share of Repsol's profits or losses was recognised in the bank's profit or loss. The profits and losses arising from transactions between the bank and Repsol were eliminated, upon consolidation, to the extent of CaixaBank's interest in the share capital of Repsol.
- Its share of the changes in Repsol's equity (e.g., OCI) that had not been recognised in Repsol's profit or loss was recognised in the bank's equity according to its share of such movements in equity.

Accounting Recognition of the Mandatory Exchangeable   For accounting purposes, the issue was treated as a hybrid financial instrument, decomposed into two components: a financial liability (the host contract) and an embedded derivative (see Figure 12.7). The host contract represented the bond coupon payments and was recognised at amortised cost using the effective interest rate method. The embedded derivative included a combination of an equity call and an equity put to ensure the maximum and minimum exchange prices.

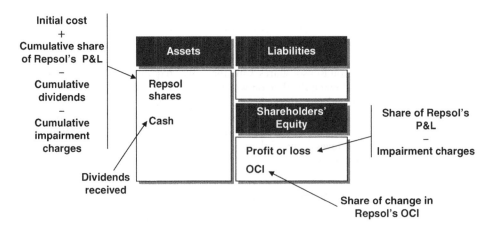

FIGURE 12.6   CaixaBank's stake in Repsol – equity method recognition

FIGURE 12.7 Initial recognition of the mandatory exchangeable

According to IFRS 9, the embedded derivative had to be separated from the host contract as its risk and characteristics were not closely related to those of the instrument or host contract. CaixaBank allocated EUR 491.3 million and EUR 103.0 million to the host contract and the embedded derivative respectively, as shown in Figure 12.7.

The embedded derivative was fair valued at each reporting date. Unless cash flow hedge accounting was applied period changes in the fair value of the embedded derivative would be recognised in profit or loss, which could add substantial volatility to CaixaBank's profit or loss. To minimise the impact in profit or loss due to the revaluation of the embedded derivative, it was designated as the hedging instrument in a cash flow hedge of 2.5% of the bank's investment in Repsol shares. As a result of applying cash flow hedge accounting, the effective part of the change in fair value of the embedded derivative was temporarily recognised in OCI in equity, being reclassified to profit or loss upon sale of the Repsol shares through the exchangeable.

Accounting Treatment of the Stake in Repsol Following the Mandatory Exchangeable Issuance As CaixaBank retained the voting rights from its stake after the issue of the exchangeable bonds, as well as significant influence, it continued to classify Repsol as an associate (i.e., Repsol was recognised under the equity method of accounting consolidation). Consequently, the mandatory exchangeable issuance did not change the manner CaixaBank recognised the stake.

Overall Accounting Impact The issuance of the mandatory exchangeable impacted on several items of CaixaBank's balance sheet, as shown in Figure 12.8:

- The investment in Repsol was unchanged by the issuance. It continued to be classified as an associate on the asset side;
- Cash was positively affected by the EUR 594.3 million issue proceeds. However, CaixaBank had to pay the 4.5% coupons and could not keep any cash dividends corresponding to 2.5% of Repsol as these had to be passed through to the exchangeable investors;
- An embedded derivative was recognised on the asset side, with an initial fair value of EUR 103 million. This item was recognised at fair value;
- The host contract representing the future coupon payments and principal amount was recognised on the liability side. This item was recognised at amortised cost using the effective interest rate method;
- Profit or loss was impacted, although CaixaBank continued to recognise its share of Repsol's profit or loss and any impairment charges on the investment. The Spanish bank had to recognise the interest expense related to the 4.5% coupons. Thus, the exchangeable had a negative impact on the bank's net interest margin due to the interest expense stemming from the coupon payments. In addition, the ineffective part of the change in the fair value of the embedded derivative was recognised in profit or loss as well; and
- Other comprehensive income (OCI) was impacted, although CaixaBank continued to recognise its share of Repsol's OCI. The effective part of the change in the fair value of the embedded derivative was recognised in OCI temporarily in the cash flow hedge reserve. The effective part would be reclassified to profit or loss upon the exchange at maturity of the exchangeable (or on early termination).

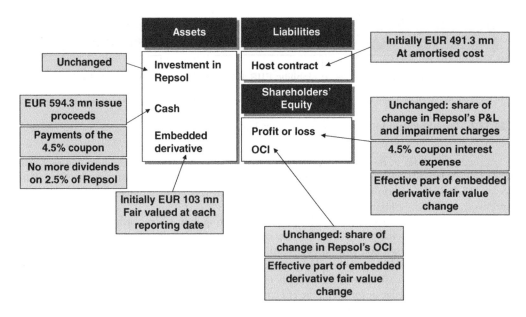

FIGURE 12.8 Impact of the mandatory exchangeable on CaixaBank's balance sheet

12.7.5 Regulatory Capital Impact of the Mandatory Exchangeable

As mentioned previously, the rationale of the transaction was to enhance CaixaBank's regulatory capital levels. Let us analyse the impact on the Spanish bank's regulatory capital by comparing the effects on its CET1 prior and after the issuance.

Capital Regulatory Treatment Prior to the Mandatory Exchangeable Issuance   Prior to the issuance of the mandatory exchangeable, CaixaBank's investment in Repsol was part of its banking book and treated as a **qualified holding** for two reasons: (i) Repsol was a non-financial entity and (ii) CaixaBank had a significant influence in Repsol. In addition, CaixaBank's ownership (voting rights) exceeded 10% of Repsol's capital which, were Repsol not to have significant influence, would have caused the investment to be treated as a qualified holding. CaixaBank calculated the following two thresholds:

- **The 15% threshold:** The amount representing 15% of the bank's eligible capital. The **eligible capital** was the sum of its Tier 1 and Tier 2 capital, with the Tier 2 capital capped at 1/3 of the Tier 1 capital. As CaixaBank had EUR 18,094 million of CET1 capital and EUR 4,365 million of Tier 2 capital (it held no AT1 capital), its eligible capital was EUR 22,449 million (= 18,094 mn + 4,365 mn). The 15% threshold was then EUR 3,367 million (= 22,449 mn × 15%).
- **The 60% threshold:** The amount representing 60% of the bank's eligible capital. The 60% threshold was EUR 13,469 million (= 22,449 mn × 60%).

CaixaBank's investment in Repsol consumed EUR 855 million of CET1 capital, assuming an 8% minimum CET1 capital ratio requirement, split between (i) a EUR 418 million amount due to the RWAs stemming from an excess over the 15% threshold, (ii) a EUR 431 million amount due to RWAs stemming from the unexpected loss and (iii) a EUR 6 million amount deduction from CET1 capital stemming from the expected loss amount, as shown in Figure 12.9.

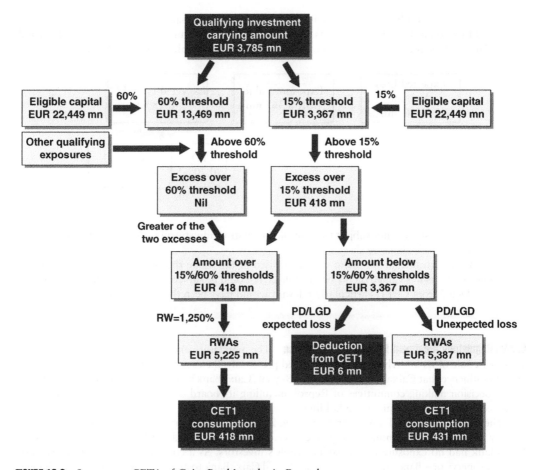

FIGURE 12.9 Impact on CET1 of CaixaBank's stake in Repsol

- CaixaBank had to compare the carrying value of its investment in Repsol with the EUR 3,367 million 15% threshold. The carrying value of its investment in Repsol was EUR 3,785 million and, consequently, the excess over the 15% threshold was EUR 418 million (= 3,785 mn − 3,367 mn).
- The carrying value of its investment in Repsol was added to other qualifying holdings and compared with the 60% threshold. This aggregate was below the EUR 13,469 million 60% threshold. Thus, the excess over the 60% threshold was zero.
- The greater of (i) the excess over the 15% threshold (EUR 418 million) and (ii) the excess over the 60% threshold (zero) was EUR 418 million. This amount was risk-weighted at 1,250%, resulting in EUR 5,225 million (= 418 mn × 1,250%) of RWAs. These RWAs consumed EUR 418 million (= 5,225 mn × 8%) of CET1 capital
- The exposure not risk-weighted at 1,250% (EUR 3,367 million) was risk-weighted using the PD/LGD approach. CaixaBank applied the formula depicted in Section 12.3.2 to estimate unexpected losses and appraised a risk weight of 160% on its investment in Repsol. As a result, the RWAs were EUR 5,387 million (= 3,367 mn × 160%), which consumed EUR 431 million (= 5,387 mn × 8%) of CET1 capital.

■ Finally, and as a result of applying the PD/LGD approach, CaixaBank had to calculate the expected loss (EL) amount. The EL amount was deducted from CET1 capital. Assuming a PD of 0.20% and a LGD of 90%, the expected loss amount was EUR 6 million, calculated as follows:

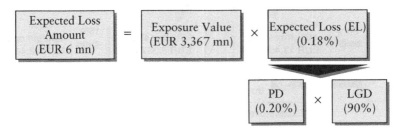

> The stake in Repsol was not subject to additional valuation adjustments (AVAs) as it was not fair valued on the bank's balance sheet.
>
> Imagine instead that the stake was recognised at fair value through other comprehensive income. As it was fair valued on the balance sheet, it would be subject to AVAs which would have been deducted from CET1. Particularly relevant would have been the concentration AVA.

Capital Regulatory Treatment Following the Issuance   The mandatory exchangeable can be thought of as a synthetic sale of its underlying shares. As noted previously, the exchangeable did not change the significant influence that CaixaBank exerted over Repsol (CaixaBank's executives retained their positions in key decision making committees of Repsol, including its board of directors) and, thus, the stake remained categorised as a qualifying holding.

The structure provided a price protection on 2.5% of the ordinary share capital of Repsol delivered by the EUR 18.25 minimum exchange price. This protection did not have counterparty risk as CaixaBank had no exposure to the exchangeable's investors. As a consequence, should the Spanish banking supervisor – Banco de España – have allowed CaixaBank to avoid risk weighting the exchangeable's underlying shares (i.e., 2.5% of the ordinary share capital of Repsol)? Not quite. CaixaBank valued the stake in its balance sheet at EUR 21.48 per share. In other words, regarding the 2.5% of Repsol's ordinary share capital, CaixaBank was exposed to a fall from EUR 21.48 to EUR 18.25, a potential loss of EUR 105 million. Prior to the issuance of the exchangeable, the pro rata CET1 capital consumption of the 2.5% stake was EUR 178 million (= 855 mn × 2.5% / 12%). Thus, it was reasonable for CaixaBank to claim a capital benefit of at least EUR 73 million (= 178 mn − 105 mn).

> The EUR 73 million savings represented 40 basis points (= 73 mn / 18,094 mn) enhancement in CaixaBank's CET1 capital. These savings were obtained by the bank while keeping its 12% stake and its related voting rights.
>
> The exchangeable represented a synthetic sale of between a 2% and a 2.5% stake in Repsol, as inferred by the maximum and minimum exchange prices respectively. As CaixaBank held a 12% stake, the physical delivery of the shares at maturity of the exchangeable would likely cause the bank to own less than 10% of the ordinary share capital of Repsol. Could CaixaBank claim that, as a result of the exchangeable issuance, the investment ceased to be categorised as a qualified holding? The answer is no, as the bank would still maintain a significant influence in Repsol.

(continued)

CaixaBank could have sold the stake, but it would have recognised a pre-tax loss in earnings of EUR 105 million – based on the EUR 18.25 minimum exchange price which represented market prices. The after-tax loss would have had a one-to-one negative impact in CET1. In addition, such a large block being sold in the market would need to be executed at a discount to market prices, generating a larger loss.

The exchangeable bond improved the liquidity position of CaixaBank by the EUR 594.30 million raised proceeds.

On 28 January 2016, the CaixaBank Board resolved to fully redeem the bond issuance early on 10 March 2016 by delivering Repsol shares representing 2.07% of this company's share capital.

12.8 CASE STUDY: MITSUBISHI UFJ FINANCIAL GROUP'S CORPORATE STAKES

This case study covers a rather contrasting situation of Japanese banks relative to their European peers at the end of 2014. In Japan, the biggest banks held large stakes in non-financial companies, while European banks had been disposing of most of their corporate strategic stakes in the previous years due to the advent of Basel III. For example, the large Japanese banks held more that 10% of the share capital of several Japanese publicly traded railway companies. Similarly, global Japanese banks were outliers relative to their U.S. competitors: unrealised gains on Mitsubishi UFJ's corporate equities portfolio represented 24% of its CET1 capital while those at JP Morgan represented approximately 1% of its CET1 capital. As a result, Japanese banks were exposed to a sudden decline in Japanese stock prices, which could be caused by, for instance, increasing concerns over the deterioration of domestic listed companies' earnings.

12.8.1 Background of the Strategic Equity Holdings

In March 2015, the Japanese bank Mitsubishi UFJ Financial Group ("MUFG") reported that it held exposures to publicly traded equities worth JPY 5,913 billion (approximately USD 42 billion), comprising JPY 5,722 billion and JPY 191 billion worth of Japanese and non-Japanese equities respectively. Japanese banks held substantial strategic equities portfolios issued by their corporate clients for strategic purposes, in particular to maintain long-term relationships with these clients. These investments had the potential to increase business revenue and appreciate in value.

Since the start of 2013, the Nikkei 225 index had soared by 52% as a result of the aggressive quantitative easing implemented by Shinzo Abe's government, as shown in Figure 12.10.

From an IFRS 9 accounting point of view, let us assume that these stakes were recognised "at fair value through other comprehensive income" (FVTOCI). As a result, the change in the fair valuation since their acquisition was recognised in other comprehensive income (OCI). Because as of 31 March 2015 the carrying amount of the listed equities held by the bank was JPY 5,913 billion and the acquisition cost of these equities was JPY 2,924, MUFG reported in OCI JPY 2,989 billion (= 5,913bn − 2,924bn) of unrealised gains related to these equities.

MUFG reported a JPY 12,467 billion CET1 capital as of 31 March 2015. Unrealised gains on instruments at FVTOCI were included in MUFG's CET1 capital. Thus the bank's unrealised gain on its corporate equities portfolio represented 24% of its CET1 capital. In fact, much of the improvement in MUFG's CET1 capital ratio since 1 January 2013 had come from unrealised gains in its equity and Japanese government bond portfolios.

Nonetheless, this was just one part of the story. Equity holdings carried a high capital charge and, as a result, MUFG's risk-weighted assets were unfavourably affected by the equity holdings.

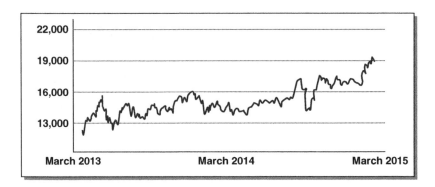

FIGURE 12.10   Nikkei 225 index spot price (1-Jan-13 to 31-Mar-15)

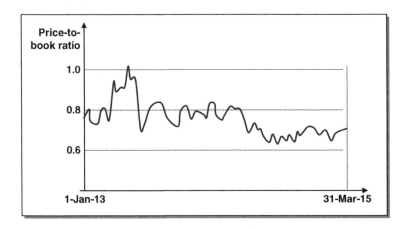

FIGURE 12.11   MFUG's price-to-book value (1-Jan-13 to 31-Mar-15)

Interestingly, investors in MUFG's ordinary shares took into account the potential volatility of its equity holdings. For example MUFG's price-to-book value, rather than rising as the portfolio's market value rose, exhibited a falling trend, as shown in Figure 12.11. The price-to-book discount was a symptom that investors did not regard MUFG's capital as high-quality given how susceptible it was to market volatility.

MUFG faced an interesting dilemma: whether to dispose of its equities portfolio. Compared to 2002, the Japanese bank had in March 2011 a notably lower domestic equities portfolio. However, since March 2011 the bank's domestic equity holdings had been rather stagnant, as shown in Figure 12.12.

A disposal would enhance MUFG's capital levels by reducing the bank's risk-weighted assets. In addition, a disposal would realise the gains on the equities portfolio, reducing the volatility of the bank's CET1 capital stemming from the volatility of its OCI. Thus, a disposal would

(continued)

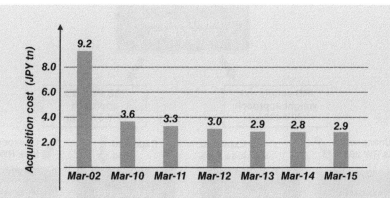

FIGURE 12.12   MFUG's acquisition cost of its domestic equity holdings

bolster capital ratios and ensure thatg capital was of higher quality. MUFG would then have the option to return some of the cash to shareholders, either through buybacks or higher dividend payouts. That, in turn, would be positive for its return on equity.

However, a disposal would likely alienate its corporate clients, which may direct their banking business to MUFG's competitors. A substantial portion of its equity holdings allowed the Japanese bank to establish close corporate banking relationships with the issuers of the shares. Thus, disposing of the shares could affect future profitability of the bank.

12.8.2 Capital Benefits and Other Impacts of a Potential Disposal

Let us try to quantify the impact on MUFG's regulatory capital of a full disposal of its equity holdings, assuming that all of them were issued by corporates (i.e., non-financial entities) and that no shares were categorised as qualifying holdings.

Impact on RWAs   The exposure value of MUFG's equities portfolio was JPY 5,913 bn, which was its market value as it was recognised at FVTOCI. Interestingly, an increase in the market value of the shareholdings pushed up exposure values and, as a consequence, RWAs. Let us calculate next the impact on RWAs of a potential disposal of the portfolio:

- JPY 436 billion were risk-weighted using IRB's **simple risk weight approach**. As these shares traded over an exchange, MUFG applied a 290% risk weighting (note that in reality the Japanese FSA required Basel II's 300% risk weights for publicly traded equities, but I am using instead Basel III CRR's risk weights). Thus, the RWAs were JPY 1,264 billion ($= 436\,\text{bn} \times 290\%$); and
- JPY 5,477 billion were risk-weighted using IRB's **PD/LGD approach**. The average PD was 0.15%, which applying the formula depicted in Section 12.3.2 resulted in a 129% risk weight. Thus, the RWAs were JPY 7,065 billion ($= 5,477\,\text{bn} \times 129\%$).

Therefore, the total RWAs savings from a potential disposal of the equities portfolio were JPY 8,329 billion ($= 1,264\,\text{bn} + 7,065\,\text{bn}$). These RWAs stemmed from the **unexpected losses** on the equities portfolio. Figure 12.13 depicts the calculations to arrive at the RWAs savings.

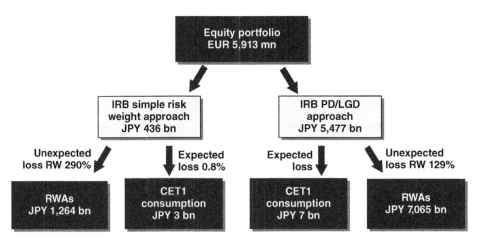

FIGURE 12.13 Calculations of MUFG's CET1 capital of the potential disposal of its equity holdings

Impact on CET1 Capital The expected losses on the equities portfolio were deducted from CET1 capital. Let us calculate next the expected losses of the portfolio:

- JPY 436 billion were risk-weighted using IRB's **simple risk weight approach**. As these shares traded over an exchange, MUFG applied a 0.8% to the exposure to arrive at the expected losses. Thus, the expected losses were JPY 3 billion (= 436 bn × 0.8%); and
- JPY 5,477 billion were risk-weighted using IRB's **PD/LGD approach**. The expected losses were calculated by multiplying (i) the JPY 5,477 billion exposure value by (ii) the 0.15% average PD and by (iii) the 90% LGD, resulting in a JPY 7 billion amount (= 5,477 bn × 0.15% × 90%).

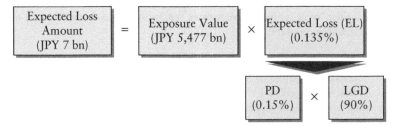

Therefore, and related to the **expected losses** on the equities portfolio, the total CET1 savings from a potential disposal of the equities portfolio were JPY 10 billion (= 3 bn + 7 bn).

There were two other impacts on CET1 capital that I have not quantified:

- An adverse impact on CET1 due to lower future income from the issuers of the shares in the equities portfolio; and
- A positive impact from the utilisation of deferred tax assets (DTAs). The disposal would trigger the realisation of gains, which are taxable and, as covered in Chapter 13, would use DTAs. If prior to the disposal these DTAs were deducted from CET1 capital, then the disposal would reduce the amount of such deduction from CET1 capital.

As both unrealised gains and realised gains were part of CET1 capital, excluding the effect on DTAs, the realisation of gains would have no impact on MUFG's CET1 capital.

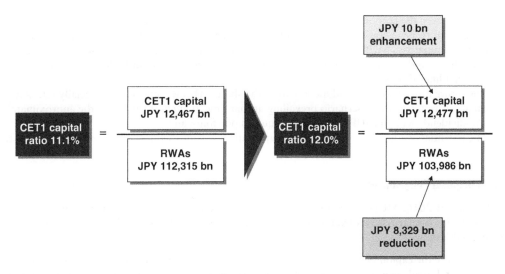

FIGURE 12.14 Impact on MUFG's CET1 capital of the potential disposal of its equity holdings

Overall Impact on CET1 Capital Ratio   Figure 12.14 depicts the calculations to arrive at the CET1 capital savings. Prior to the potential disposal, MUFG had JPY 12,467 billion of CET1 capital and JPY 112,315 billion of RWAs as of 31 March 2015. Therefore, MUFG's CET1 capital ratio was 11.1% (= 12,467 bn / 112,315 bn).

Following the assumed disposal, MUFG would have JPY 12,477 billion (= 12,467 bn + 10 bn) of CET1 capital and JPY 103,986 billion (= 112,315 bn − 8,329 bn) of RWAs. Thus, following the disposal of the equities portfolio MUFG's CET1 capital ratio would be 12.0% (= 12,477 bn / 103,986 bn), implying a 90 basis points (= 12% − 11.1%) boost in its CET1 capital ratio.

Benefits and Drawbacks of the Potential Disposal   The main **benefits** of the potential disposal were:

- The capital enhancements covered above;
- The reduction of the potential volatility of the bank's capital levels, improving capital quality, an intangible benefit. By locking in the unrealised gains MUFG would eliminate its equities portfolio exposure to a share price fall;
- The potential utilisation of deferred tax assets. Chapter 13 covers that some of this type of assets are deducted from CET1 capital;
- The likely greater focus of MUFG's on embarking in capital optimisation initiatives. One major drawback of holding such a substantial equity holding was the reduced attention of MUFG's management in optimising capital usage across the bank. In fact the improvement in MUFG's capital ratios during the previous years was largely due to the stock market rally; and
- The greater options with regard to MUFG's capital strategy. An improvement in the capital ratios would allow MUFG to invest in new businesses, acquire other financial institutions, increase its dividend and/or expand its share buyback programme.

The main **drawbacks** of the potential disposal were:

- The possible reduction in interest and fee income from clients switching to other banks as a result of the reduced strategic ties of MUFG with these clients. As earnings is a key ingredient of CET1 capital, a reduction in future earnings would imply lower levels of organic capital generation. The reaction from the corporates was significantly difficult to quantify, although MUFG expected the impact not to be excessively large as all the major Japanese banks planned to undertake similar disposal initiatives. MUFG needed to take the earnings attributable to the companies in which it held shares and estimate the percentage of these earnings that would be lost as a result of the shareholdings disposals;

- The future absence of dividend income from the shares. This weakness was especially relevant in the negative interest rate scenario prevailing at that time, that contrasted with the approximately 2% dividend yield on MUFG's corporate equities portfolio; and
- The potential overhang caused by all the major Japanese banks selling their shares simultaneously.

12.8.3 Disposal Programme

At the start of 2016, MUFG announced its intention to reduce its equity holdings. This disclosure coincided with similar releases from other large Japanese banks. The disposal plan was triggered by two main drives:

- To achieve the capital benefits outlined above, following institutional investor criticism; and
- To meet Japan's new governance code, which required stronger corporate governance. Cross-shareholdings have been thought to insulate Japanese companies, to a degree, from market pressures.

To reduce the impact on business relationships, MUFG held in-depth discussions with the shares' issuers to gradually dispose of the strategic stakes, trying to minimise potential stock overhangs. These discussions tried to obtain permission in principle from the issuers and to agree with them on the disposal execution plan (periods, amount of shares and prices). One potential solution was for the issuers of the shares to repurchase the shares sold by MUFG. For companies with substantial cash levels and low debt-to-equity ratios, a share buyback was an interesting tool to boost returns on their equities.

The target announced by MUFG was the reduction of the ratio of (i) the book value of its corporate equities portfolio divided by (ii) MUFG's Tier 1 capital (including the unrealised gains on the portfolio) from 19% to 10% over 5 years. At the moment of the announcement, the ratio reduction target implied a reduction of approximately 30% of the total portfolio. Thus, the sales to be executed depended partly on changes in Tier 1 capital. In addition, the use of the book value of the portfolio in the numerator while using its market value (i.e., the unrealised gains) in the denominator meant that a further appreciation of the shares reduced the speed of the disposals.

CHAPTER**13**

Deferred Tax Assets (DTAs)

Deferred tax assets that rely on future profitability negatively impact CET1 capital. For example, tax loss carry forwards are deducted from CET1 capital.

[CRR 4(106)] provides that the term "deferred tax assets" must be interpreted on the basis of the "applicable accounting standard". Thus, deciding whether a deferred tax asset should be deducted from CET1 capital requires prior understanding on how deferred taxes are generated, a process that is not intuitive, requiring a thorough knowledge of accounting rules and relevant tax laws. This chapter seeks to help readers to understand (i) why deferred tax assets ("**DTAs**") and liabilities ("**DTLs**") arise, (ii) how to account for DTAs and DTLs under IFRS and (iii) how DTAs are treated for regulatory capital purposes.

It is important to note that, while the application of Basel III and IFRS rules across the EU is relatively uniform, tax practice varies within the EU. The tax aspects discussed in this chapter are based on the most common tax treatments in the EU.

13.1 TAXES FROM AN ACCOUNTING PERSPECTIVE

From a regulatory capital perspective, DTAs and DTLs have the same meaning as under IFRS. Therefore, it is important to understand how these assets are recognised from an accounting perspective.

Accounting wise, deferred tax is dealt with, in conjunction with current taxes, by **IAS 12** *Income Taxes*. Income taxes are represented in the financial statements of a bank, seeking to give a true reflection of future tax consequences of assets and liabilities, as follows (see Figure 13.1):

- In the asset and liability sides of the balance sheet are recognised taxes receivable and payable related to current taxes, in addition to deferred tax assets and liabilities;
- In the profit or loss statement, the amount of current taxes related to the reporting period taxable earnings are represented. The changes in deferred taxes associated with items recognised in profit or loss are also recognised in profit or loss;
- In other comprehensive income (OCI), tax expected to be paid or received related to items which are temporarily recognised in OCI that would be subsequently reclassified to profit or loss are also represented; and
- In equity, tax related to transactions on own shares such as share-based plans and share buybacks.

The amount of tax payable on the pre-tax amount of earnings is often notably different to the tax charge that would be expected from applying a tax rate to all income/gain and expense/loss amounts

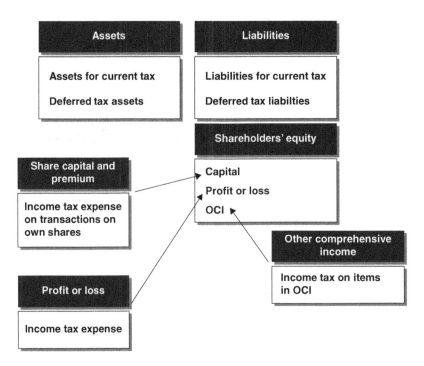

FIGURE 13.1   Recognition of taxes in the balance sheet and profit or loss statements

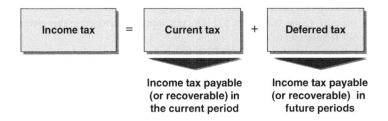

FIGURE 13.2   Income taxes overview

in a bank's profit or loss statement. Differences occur due to the dissimilarities between tax laws and accounting rules. For example, in a bank's profit or loss statement, some income/gains items are taxable during the reporting year, some income/gains are taxable in future accounting periods and some items are expensed but are not tax-deductible.

Income tax comprises **current tax** and **deferred tax** (see Figure 13.2).

13.1.1 Accounting Recognition of Current Tax

A **current tax** liability (or asset) is the amount of income taxes payable (or recoverable) in respect of the taxable profit (or loss) for the *current* financial period. In other words, current tax is based on the taxable and deductible amounts that will be reported in the current year's tax return (see Figure 13.3). Moreover, current tax includes any adjustment to tax payable in respect of previous years, for example,

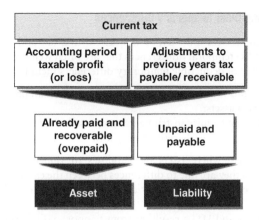

FIGURE 13.3   Current income tax recognition

if the tax payable for a year agreed with the tax authorities is expected to differ from the amount previously reflected in the accounts.

A bank recognises its current tax in profit or loss. In addition, a bank recognises unpaid current tax expense for the current and prior periods as a liability in the balance sheet. In contrast, it recognises any tax overpayment of current and prior periods as an asset.

Current tax liabilities (assets) for the current and prior periods shall be measured at the amount expected to be paid to (recovered from) the taxation authorities, using the tax rates (and tax laws) that have been (substantively) enacted by the balance sheet date.

Current tax assets and liabilities are **offset** when the bank intends to settle on a net basis and the legal right to offset exists.

13.1.2 Deferred Taxes

Deferred tax is the amount of income taxes that a bank may recover or pay in future financial periods. Deferred tax is normally calculated by reference to the year-end balance sheet amounts of assets and liabilities, which are compared to the year-end tax base amounts of the same assets and liabilities.

- **Taxable deferred taxes** represent the amounts that may be added in the future to other taxable profit for the calculation of payable taxes or used against future tax-deductible economic benefits, and that serve as the base for the calculation of **deferred tax liabilities** ("DTLs").
- **Deductible deferred taxes** represent the amounts that may be recoverable against future taxable economic benefits and that serve as the base for the calculation of **deferred taxes assets** ("DTAs").

Deductible deferred taxes arise from a diversity of sources which vary across tax jurisdictions. According to IAS 12, deductible deferred taxes can be grouped in the following three categories:

- **Deductible temporary differences:** expenses recognised in the profit or loss, or unrealised losses in OCI, or tax effects in own capital, that are not deductible until at a later date, normally when the associated cash flows occur;
- **Tax loss carry forwards:** past tax losses that can be carried forward to be utilised against taxable profits in future years; and
- **Tax credits carry forwards:** unused tax credits that can be carried forward to be utilised against taxable profits in future years.

13.1.3 Deferred Tax Arising from Temporary Differences

The nature of the financial services industry, as well as existing tax and accounting rules, generally result in substantial deductible temporary differences that are often well in excess of taxable temporary differences. Common sources of deductible temporary differences include:

- Allowances and provisions for credit risk and insolvency, and loan impairment;
- Impairment of foreclosed assets;
- Unrealised gains of debt and equity instruments recognised at fair value; and
- Allowances or contributions to early retirement plans.

Temporary differences arise where assets and liabilities are valued differently for accounting and tax purposes. In other words, they are due to differences between the carrying amount of the assets and liabilities in the balance sheet and the temporary amounts attributed to such assets and liabilities for tax purposes.

The calculation of DTAs and DTLs resulting from temporary differences is covered in detail in Section 13.2.

Ultimately, the purpose of deferred taxes on taxable and deductible temporary differences is to reconcile taxable income with accounting profits.

The reversal of such temporary differences occurs either (i) when the asset is sold or the liability is settled, or (ii) in the period in which tax law requires/allows to apply the carrying amount in the balance sheet for tax purposes, or (iii) the carrying amount converges with the tax base.

13.1.4 Deferred Tax Arising from Tax Loss Carry Forwards

The carry forward of past and current losses may reduce tax liabilities of future years. The amount of tax losses that, based on the evidence available the bank expects to recover against future taxable income generated by the business, are recognised as DTAs. The related DTAs are calculated as follows:

$$\boxed{\text{DTA}} = \boxed{\begin{array}{c}\text{Negative tax} \\ \text{base} \\ \text{(sign reversed)}\end{array}} \times \boxed{\text{Tax rate}}$$

Where:

- The **tax base** is the aggregate of part years and current year losses that the bank may carry forward and that the bank expects to recover against future taxable income.
- The **tax rate**(s) is the rate(s) expected to apply to the period(s) when the tax loss carry forward will be utilised, based on tax rates and laws enacted, or substantially enacted, by the reporting date.

13.1.5 Deferred Tax Arising from Tax Credit Carry Forwards

Tax credits not used in previous periods and not applied to reduce the taxes payable in the current period, and that can be carried forward, generate DTAs if likely to be utilised against future taxable profits. Many countries permit a carry forward of such unused tax credits into future years. The calculation of DTAs arising from tax credit carry forwards is similar to that of DTAs arising from tax loss carry forwards.

Tax Credits

Tax credits are amounts that can normally be established with certainty and are not subject to revisions once they are known. They can be fixed for a single amount, fixed for different amounts or tranches, or they may depend on a variable or a group of variables. They can be fully recovered (or not) according to their payable (or non-payable) nature, but, regardless of the effective use of the tax credit to reduce taxes, the initial amount can be fixed. Tax credits are not based on assumptions, but on facts.

13.2 ACCOUNTING FOR DEFERRED TAXES ARISING FROM TEMPORARY DIFFERENCES – APPLICATION TO EQUITY INVESTMENTS AT EITHER FVTPL OR FVTOCI

This section covers in detail how deferred taxes (DTAs and DTLs) arising from temporary differences are accounted for under IAS 12. The concepts are emphasised using an example of two simultaneous investments in equity instruments, one recognised at fair value through profit or loss (FVTPL) and the other recognised at fair value through OCI (FVTOCI).

The process to account for deferred taxes arising from temporary differences can be split into seven steps, as shown in Figure 13.4.

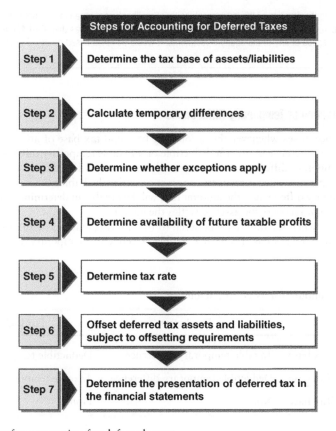

Steps for Accounting for Deferred Taxes

Step 1	Determine the tax base of assets/liabilities
Step 2	Calculate temporary differences
Step 3	Determine whether exceptions apply
Step 4	Determine availability of future taxable profits
Step 5	Determine tax rate
Step 6	Offset deferred tax assets and liabilities, subject to offsetting requirements
Step 7	Determine the presentation of deferred tax in the financial statements

FIGURE 13.4   Steps for accounting for deferred taxes

13.2.1 Step 1: Determination of the Tax Base

The first step in the accounting for deferred taxes entails the bank determining the tax base. The tax base of an asset or liability is the amount attributed to that asset or liability for tax purposes.

The **tax base of an asset** is the amount that will be deductible for tax purposes against any taxable economic benefits that will flow to the entity when it recovers the carrying amount of the asset. If those economic benefits will not be taxable, the tax base of the asset is equal to its carrying amount.

The **tax base of a liability** is its carrying amount, less any amount that will be deductible for tax purposes in respect of that liability in future periods. In the case of revenue received in advance, the tax base of the resulting liability is its carrying amount less any amount of the revenue that will not be taxable in future periods.

The tax base is determined based on how the tax authorities will tax the entity when it recovers the asset or settles the liability. In the case of investments in equity instruments, the tax base is commonly their original cost (unless taxable dividends that constitute a partial/total redemption of capital are distributed).

Example: Determination of the Tax Base of an Equity Investment

As an example, let us assume that on 1 January 20X0 Megabank invested EUR 400 million in ordinary shares of Smallbank and another EUR 400 million in ordinary shares of Largebank. In accordance with IFRS 9, Megabank's classified its investment in Smallbank shares at "fair value through OCI" (FVTOCI), while its investment in Largebank was classified at "fair value through profit or loss" (FVTPL).

Assuming that, during the duration of the investment, neither Smallbank nor Largebank distributed dividends that represented a partial redemption of their ordinary shares, the **tax base** of each investment was their **EUR 400 million** original cost. If Megabank decided to dispose of any of the equity investments, it would be taxed based on the difference between the sale proceeds and the tax base.

13.2.2 Step 2: Calculation of Temporary Differences

A temporary difference arises whenever the accounting base and tax base of an asset or liability are different. A temporary difference is either a deductible or a taxable temporary difference.

A **deductible temporary difference** is the amount that an entity will deduct in determining its taxable profit for future periods when it recovers the asset or settles the liability.

A **taxable temporary difference** is the amount that will be taxable in determining its taxable profit fir future periods when it recovers the asset or settles the liability.

Table 13.1 details when the difference between (i) the carrying amount of an asset or liability on the balance sheet and (ii) its tax base result in a taxable or deductible temporary difference.

TABLE 13.1 Carrying amount for assets and liabilities

	For Assets	For Liabilities
Carrying amount > Tax base	Taxable temporary difference	Deductible temporary difference
Carrying amount < Tax base	Deductible temporary difference	Taxable temporary difference
Carrying amount = Tax base	None	None

Example: Deductible Temporary Differences Arising from Equity Investments

Let us assume that at 31 December 20X0 Megabank's stakes in Largebank and Smallbank were worth EUR 340 million and EUR 500 million respectively. These stakes were fair valued without an equivalent adjustment being made for current tax purposes. Consequently:

- The position in Largebank gave rise to a **deductible temporary difference** as its carrying amount (EUR 340 million) was lower than its tax base (EUR 400 million). The size of this temporary difference was EUR 60 million (= 400mn – 340mn); and

- The position in Smallbank gave rise to a **taxable temporary difference** as its carrying amount (EUR 500 million) was greater than its tax base (EUR 400 million). The size of this temporary difference was EUR 100 million (= 500mn – 400mn).

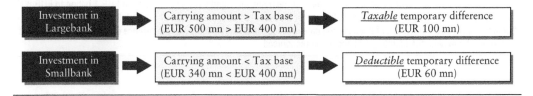

13.2.3 Step 3: Determination of Exceptions

There are situations where even though a temporary difference exists, no DTA or DTL is recognised. IAS 12 prohibits the recognition of a **DTA** on deductible temporary differences that arise from:

- The initial recognition of an asset or a liability in a transaction that:
  - Is not a business combination; and
  - At the time of the transaction, affects neither accounting profit nor taxable profit (tax loss); or
- Investments in subsidiaries, branches and associates, and interests in joint arrangements to the extent that any of the following conditions is satisfied:
  - Taxable profit will *not* be available against which the temporary difference can be utilised; or
  - It is probable that the temporary difference will *not* reverse in the foreseeable future.

IAS 12 prohibits the recognition of a **DTL** on taxable temporary differences that arise from:

- The initial recognition of goodwill in a business combination; or
- The initial recognition of an asset or liability in a transaction which:
  - Is not a business combination; and
  - At the time of the transaction, affects neither accounting profit nor taxable profit (tax loss); or
- Investments in subsidiaries, branches and associates, and interests in joint arrangements to the extent that both of the following conditions are satisfied:
  - The parent, investor, joint venturer or joint operator is able to control the timing of the reversal of the temporary difference; and
  - It is probable that the temporary difference will *not* reverse in the foreseeable future.

Example: Deferred Tax Exception from Goodwill

As an example, let us assume that Megabank acquired another bank and goodwill amounting to EUR 1 billion arose on the acquisition. In the jurisdiction where Megabank was domiciled, no tax deduction was available in the future for this goodwill because it only arose in the consolidated financial statements of Megabank and tax was assessed on the basis of Megabank's separate financial statements. There was a taxable difference of EUR 1 billion, the difference between the EUR 1 billion carrying amount of goodwill and its tax base of nil. However, in accordance with the initial recognition exception in IAS 12, a

(*continued*)

DTL was not recognised on that taxable difference. The effect of this was goodwill being recognised at it its full EUR 1 billion amount and no DTL arose.

The underlying rationale for this exception is that if a DTL were recognised in respect of the goodwill at the time of the business combination, this would decrease the total for the net assets being recognised. Because goodwill is a residual, the recognition of a DTL would increase the carrying amount of goodwill and the increase would also need to be tax-effected.

Many taxation authorities do not allow reductions in the carrying amount of goodwill as a deductible expense in determining taxable profit. Moreover, in such jurisdictions, the cost of goodwill is often not deductible when a subsidiary disposes of its underlying business. Let us assume that, subsequently, the goodwill was impaired by EUR 300 million, resulting in a reduction in the taxable temporary difference from EUR 1 billion to EUR 700 million. The decrease is also regarded under IAS 12 as relating to the initial recognition of goodwill and, consequently, the DTL was still not recognised.

There are, however, situations in which a DTL is recognised for taxable temporary differences relating to goodwill to the extent they do not arise from the initial recognition of goodwill. In the previous example, let us assume that the EUR 1 billion of goodwill is deductible for tax purposes at a rate of 20% per annum starting in the year of acquisition. At the end of the first year following the acquisition, the tax base of the goodwill would have decreased from EUR 1 billion to EUR 800 million. If the carrying amount of goodwill at the end of that year remains unchanged at EUR 1 billion, a taxable temporary difference of EUR 200 million would arise on that date. Because that taxable temporary difference did not relate to the initial recognition of goodwill, the resulting DTL would be recognised.

In the case of Megabank's investments in Largebank and Smallbank, no exceptions to the recognition of DTAs and DTLs were applicable.

13.2.4 Step 4: Availability of Future Profits and Recognition of DTA and DTLs

A taxable temporary difference may originate a DTL, while a deductible temporary difference may originate a DTA.

- A **DTA**, subject to the exceptions in Section 13.2.3, is recognised to the extent that it is *probable* that future taxable profits will be available against which the deductible temporary difference can be utilised.
- A **DTL**, subject to the exceptions in Section 13.2.3, is recognised for all taxable temporary differences.

"Probable" is not defined in IAS 12, but it is generally agreed to mean at least "more likely than not" (i.e., a probability of greater than 50%).

General Framework for the Accounting Treatment of Deductible Deferred Taxes   Not necessarily a deductible deferred tax (i.e., a deductible temporary difference, a tax loss carry forward or a tax credit carry forward) will end up being recognised on the balance sheet of a bank. The process in which a deductible deferred tax is fully/partially transformed into a DTA can be split into the following steps (see Figure 13.5):

1. The bank would determine the deductible deferred tax amount;
2. The deductible deferred tax would be assessed for recognition. The portion that is expected to be utilised using probable future taxable profits would be recognised, constituting the tax base for the calculation of the gross DTA (i.e., the DTA prior to offsetting benefits). The remainder would become a valuation allowance (i.e., the unrecognised portion of the deductible deferred tax amount);

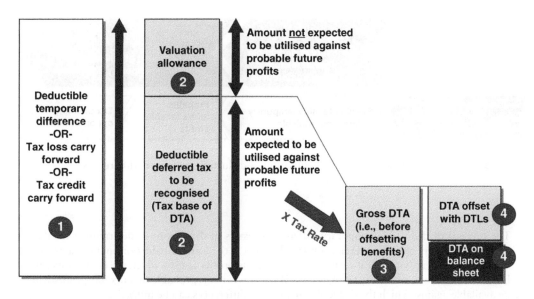

FIGURE 13.5 Deductible deferred assets: DTA vs. valuation allowance

3. The gross DTA is calculated as the product of (i) its tax base and (ii) its tax rate. The tax rate is calculated using the tax rates expected to apply to the periods when the assets will be realised or the liabilities settled, based on tax rates and laws enacted, or substantially enacted, by the reporting date;
4. The gross DTA is then assessed for offsetting with available DTLs, subject to meeting IAS 12's offsetting requirements. DTAs and DTLs are offset when they arise in the same tax reporting group and relate to income taxes levied by the same taxation authority, and when the bank has a legal right and intention to offset. The DTA amount not set off with DTLs is then recognised in the balance sheet.

For deductible temporary differences associated with investments in subsidiaries, branches and associates, and interests in joint arrangements, a DTA is recognised.

Assessment of Utilisation of Deductible Temporary Differences IAS 12 identifies three sources of taxable profits against which an entity can utilise deductible temporary differences (beyond this extent, no DTA is recognised):

- Future reversal of existing taxable temporary differences;
- Taxable profit in future periods; and
- Tax planning opportunities.

Accordingly, IAS 12 requires an assessment of the utilisation of deductible temporary differences in two successive steps (see Figure 13.6):

- In a **first step: Recovery of deductible temporary differences against taxable temporary differences**. The bank assesses whether there are sufficient taxable temporary differences relating to the same taxation authority and the same taxable entity, which are expected to reverse:
  - In the same period as the expected reversal of the deductible temporary difference; or
  - In periods into which a tax loss arising from the DTA can be carried back or forward; and

In such circumstances, the DTA is recognised in the period in which the deductible temporary differences arise.

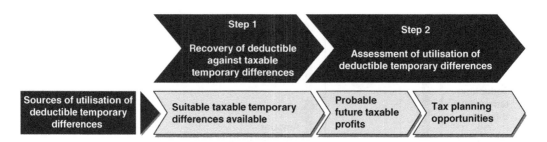

FIGURE 13.6   Steps in the assessment of the utilisation of deductible temporary differences

The reversal of deductible temporary differences results in deductions in determining taxable profits of future periods. However, economic benefits in the form of reductions in tax payments will flow to the entity only if it earns sufficient taxable profits against which the deductions can be offset. Therefore, and entity recognises DTAs only when it is probable that taxable profits will be available against which the deductible temporary differences can be utilised.

- In a **second step: Assessment of utilisation of deductible temporary differences** (only when the first step does not result in the full utilisation in the period of all deductible temporary differences). A DTA is recognised to the extent that:
  - It is probable that the bank will have sufficient taxable profit relating to the same taxation authority and the same taxable entity, in the same period as the reversal of the deductible temporary difference (or in the periods into which a tax loss arising from the DTA can be carried back or forward); or
  - Tax planning opportunities are available to the entity that will create taxable profit in appropriate periods.

Estimating Probable Future Taxable Profit   The estimation of probable future taxable profit relies primarily on projected earnings. These earnings have to be consistent with the financial budgets approved by the bank's top management and the estimations used in other assessments (e.g., the cash generating units' earnings used to assess goodwill impairment).

When estimating future taxable profit, it is important to make appropriate adjustments for past non-recurring items which are not expected to recur. Examples of non-recurring items that should be excluded are one-time restructuring charges, one-off litigation settlements for misconduct and one-off profits on the sale of a subsidiary.

Projections of future taxable profit are commonly based on approved business plans/forecasts, requiring careful judgement based on the facts and circumstances available.

Caution should be exercised upon the existence of certain indicators. For example, if the entity has incurred in net losses during recent years or the entity has a recent history of tax loss carry forwards that have expired unused. In particular IAS 12 points out that "the existence of unused tax losses is strong evidence that future taxable profit will *not* be available".

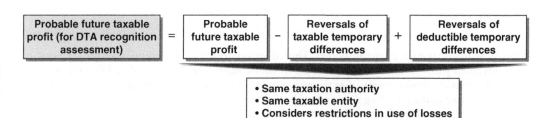

FIGURE 13.7 Steps in the assessment of the utilisation of deductible temporary differences

Adjusting Probable Future Taxable Profit Intuitively "future taxable profit" relates to the amount on the tax return on which income taxes are paid (i.e., the bottom line). However, under IAS 12 **future taxable profit** for the recognition test is the bottom line amount adjusted for the reversal of any temporary differences relating to the **same taxation authority** and the **same taxable entity**. In other words, in evaluating whether it will have sufficient taxable profit in future periods, the entity ignores taxable amounts arising from deductible temporary differences that are expected to generate in future periods, because the DTA arising from these deductible temporary differences will itself require future taxable profit in order to be utilised, as shown in Figure 13.7.

Allocation of Future Profits to Deferred Taxes The allocation of forecast profits to deferred taxes is also judgemental. In the case of deductible deferred taxes associated with temporary differences, the bank considers whether tax law restricts the sources of taxable profits against which the bank may make deductions on the reversal of that deductible temporary difference:

- If tax law imposes no such restrictions, the bank assesses the deductible temporary difference in combination with all its other deductible temporary differences; or alternatively
- If tax law restricts the utilisation of losses to deduction against income of a specific type, the deductible temporary difference is assessed in combination only with other deductible temporary differences of the appropriate type.

The accounting estimate related to DTAs is a critical accounting estimate because the underlying assumptions can change from period to period and requires significant management judgment. For example, tax law changes or variances in future projected operating performance could result in a change of the DTA amounts.

DTAs are reassessed at each reporting date in order to ascertain whether any adjustments need to be made on the base of the findings of the analyses performed.

If a bank will not able to realise all or part of its net DTAs in the future, an adjustment to its DTAs would be charged to income tax expense, OCI or directly to equity in the period such determination was made.

If a bank was to recognise previously unrecognised deferred tax assets in the future, an adjustment to its deferred tax asset would be credited to income tax expense, OCI or directly to equity in the period such determination was made.

Reversal of Temporary Differences on Equity Investments

Ordinary shares do not have a maturity date. Thus, there is uncertainty regarding when the tax benefits from unrealised gains or losses on investments in equity instruments measured at fair value will be realised. Commonly, banks assume that the recovery of the investment's carrying amount (i.e., its fair value) takes place at the reporting date and at the instrument's fair value.

In our case, Megabank had a EUR 100 million **taxable temporary difference**. As a DTL is recognised when a taxable temporary difference exists and no exceptions are available, Megabank recognised a DTL associated with the EUR 100 million. This taxable temporary difference was assumed to be reversed at the reporting date.

In addition, Megabank had a EUR 60 million **deductible temporary difference**, which was assumed to be reversed at the reporting date. To assess whether the temporary difference was expected to be utilised against taxable profits, Megabank applied the two-step process mentioned above:

- In the **first step**, Megabank assessed whether there were sufficient taxable temporary differences relating to the same taxation authority and the same taxable entity, which were expected to reverse either (i) in the same period as the expected reversal of the deductible temporary difference, or (ii) in periods into which a tax loss arising from the DTA could be carried back or forward. In our case, Megabank had EUR 100 million of taxable temporary differences that met these requirements. Thus, the bank recognised a DTA associated with the EUR 60 million deductible temporary difference (i.e., the EUR 60 million amount constituted the investment's tax base for the recognition of its related DTA).

- As the first step resulted in the **full** utilisation in the period of all deductible temporary differences, there was *no* need to apply the second step.

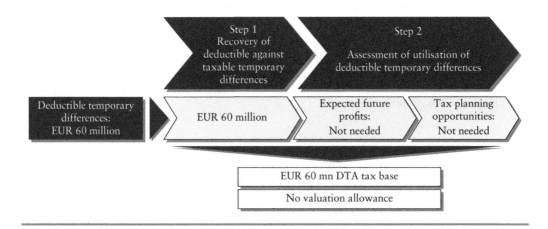

Example: Application of the Deferred Tax Two-step Process

In a different situation, let us assume that Megabank held the same equity investments but faced an opposite situation: it had a EUR 60 million taxable temporary difference and a EUR 100 million deductible temporary difference. Let us assume further that both temporary differences related to the same taxation authority and the same taxable entity.

- Megabank recognised a DTL associated with the EUR 60 million taxable temporary difference; and
- Megabank had to apply the two-step process to determine the amount of the deductible temporary difference to be recognised as a DTA.

The two-step process was applied as follows:

- In the first step, Megabank determined that EUR 60 million of the deductible temporary difference would be utilised against the EUR 60 million taxable temporary difference. As a result, EUR 60 million of the deductible would be recognised as a DTA;
- In the second step, Megabank had to assess the utilisation of the remaining EUR 40 million deductible temporary difference. Let us assume that Megabank expected to generate EUR 18 million of future taxable profits against which deductible temporary differences could be utilised, and a further EUR 5 million would be available through tax planning initiatives. As a result, Megabank expected EUR 23 million (=18mn+5mn) of temporary differences to be recognised, when multiplied by the appropriate tax rate, as a DTA.

In summary, Megabank recognised the following:

- A DTL associated with the EUR 60 million taxable temporary difference;
- A DTA associated with the EUR 83 million deductible temporary difference. This amount represented the aggregate of the EUR 60 million amount recognised under the first step and the EUR 23 million amount recognised under the second step.
- A EUR 17 million (=100mn−83mn) valuation allowance (i.e., unrecognised deductible temporary difference).

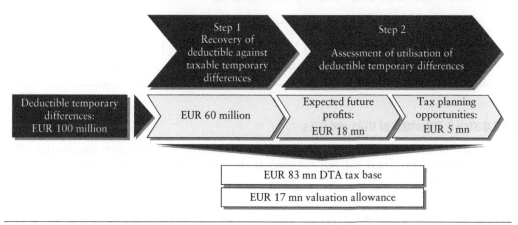

13.2.5 Step 5: Determination of the Tax Rate

DTAs (DTLs) are measured based on the **tax rates** that are expected to apply to the period when the asset is realised (or the liability is settled), based on tax rates and tax laws that have been enacted or substantively enacted at the balance sheet date.

Enacted means that the tax rate is part of tax law, while **substantively enacted** means that the government has announced changes in tax rates/laws at or before balance sheet date, but the formalities of the enactment process have yet to be finalised (and future steps in the enactment process will not change the outcome).

When different tax rates apply to different levels of taxable income, DTAs and DTLs are measured using the average rates that are expected to apply to the taxable profit (tax loss) of the periods in which the temporary differences are expected to reverse.

The measurement of DTAs and DTLs shall reflect the tax consequences that would follow from the manner in which the entity expects, at the balance sheet date, to recover or settle the carrying amount of its assets and liabilities.

In some jurisdictions, the manner in which an entity recovers (settles) the carrying amount of an asset (liability) may affect either or both of:

- The tax rate applicable when the entity recovers (settles) the carrying amount of the asset (liability); and
- The tax base of the asset (liability).

In such cases, an entity measures DTAs and DTLs using the tax rate and the tax base that are consistent with the expected manner of recovery or settlement.

Example: Calculation of Resulting Deferred Tax from Equity Investments

The tax rate to be used in the calculation of the DTAs and DTLs would be the rate to be applied to the period when the equity investments would be realised. It was mentioned above that because ordinary shares had no maturity date, Megabank assumed reversal of the temporary differences in the reporting period. As there were sufficient taxable temporary differences to offset the deductible temporary difference, for tax purposes Megabank expected the utilisation of the DTA and DTL in the reporting period.

In our case, let us assume that Megabank was subject to a 30% income tax rate on the reporting date. The resulting DTL amounted to EUR 30 million, calculated as follows:

The resulting DTA amounted to EUR 18 million, calculated as follows:

$$
\boxed{\begin{array}{c}\text{DTA}\\\text{EUR 18 million}\end{array}} = \boxed{\begin{array}{c}\text{Recognised }\textit{deductible}\\\text{temporary difference}\\\text{EUR 60 million}\end{array}} \times \boxed{\begin{array}{c}\text{Tax rate}\\30\%\end{array}}
$$

13.2.6 Step 6: Offsetting of DTAs and DTLs

This section covers the offsetting of deferred taxes. From an accounting perspective, it means that DTA and DTL amounts are netted and only the residual amount is presented in the entity's statement of financial position.

Current Tax   Pursuant to IAS 12, **current tax** assets and liabilities are **offset** from an accounting perspective in the statement of financial position (i.e., in the balance sheet) when *all* the following conditions are met:

- The entity has a legally enforceable right to set off the recognised amounts. An entity will normally have this right when they relate to income taxes levied by the same taxation authority and the taxation authority permits the entity to make or receive a single net payment; and
- The entity intends either to settle on a net basis or to realise the asset and settle the liability simultaneously.

In **consolidated** financial statements, a current tax asset of one entity in a group is offset against a current tax liability of another entity in the group if, and only if, the entities concerned have a legally enforceable to make or receive a single net payment and the entities intend to make or receive such a net payment or to recover the asset and settle the liability simultaneously.

Deferred Tax   Pursuant to IAS 12, **DTAs and DTLs** are **offset** if, and only if:

- The entity has a legally enforceable right to set off current tax assets against current tax liabilities; and
- The DTAs and the DTLs relate to income taxes levied by the same taxing authority on either:
  - The same tax reporting entity; or
  - Different taxable entities which intend either to settle current tax liabilities and assets on a net basis, or to realise the assets and settle the liabilities simultaneously, in each future period in which significant amounts of DTLs or DTAs are expected to be settled or recovered.

When a bank assesses whether to set off DTAs and DTLs, there is no need for detailed scheduling of the timing of the reversal of each temporary difference, if the previous requirements are met.

However, in rare circumstances a bank may have a legally enforceable right of set off, and an intention to settle net, for some periods but not for others. In such rare circumstances, detailed scheduling may be required to establish reliably whether the DTL of one taxable entity will result in increased tax payments in the same period in which a DTA of another taxable entity will result in decreased payments by that second taxable entity.

In our case, the EUR 30 million DTL and the EUR 18 million DTA were **offset** as:

- Megabank AG – the investing entity – had a legally enforceable right to set off current tax assets against current tax liabilities; and
- The DTAs and the DTLs related to income taxes levied by the same taxing authority on the same tax reporting entity – Megabank AG.

As a result, Megabank AG (and the consolidated group) disclosed in its balance sheet a DTL totalling EUR 12 million (=30 mn – 18 mn).

Albeit similar, the requirements for offsetting DTAs and DTLs from an accounting perspective do not necessarily coincide with those from a regulatory capital perspective.

13.2.7 Step 7: Presentation of Deferred Tax in the Financial Statements

The final step in the deferred tax recognition process is to determine in which balance sheet section the deferred tax is recognised. The underlying principle is that the deferred tax effects of a transaction (or other event) should follow the accounting for the transaction (or event).

Items Recognised in Profit or Loss   Deferred (and current) tax is recognised in profit or loss for the period where income or expense (or gain or loss) is included in accounting profit or loss in the period but is included in taxable profit (or tax loss) in a different (or the same) period. Thus, deferred (and current) taxes are recognised in profit or loss *except* to the extent that the tax arises from:

- A transaction or event which is recognised, in the same or a different period, outside profit or loss, either in OCI or directly in equity; or
- A business combination (other than the acquisition by an investment entity – as defined in IFRS 10 – of a subsidiary that is required to be measured at fair value through profit or loss).

Items Recognised in Other Comprehensive Income (OCI)   Deferred (and current) tax is recognised in OCI if the tax relates to items that are recognised, in the same or a different period, in OCI. Examples of such items are:

- Unrealised gains and losses on financial assets recognised at fair value through OCI (FVTOCI);
- Exchange differences arising on the translation of the financial statements of a foreign operation;
- Changes in the fair value of hedging instruments (i.e., derivatives) in cash flow hedges;
- Actuarial gains and losses relating to defined benefit pension plans; and
- Changes in the carrying amount arising from the revaluation of property, plant and equipment.

Items Recognised Directly in Equity   Certain types of deferred (and current) tax are required or permitted to be recognised directly in equity, for instance:

- The expected tax deduction for an equity-settled, share-based remuneration (e.g., a stock options plan on shares of the bank). For example, when the tax deduction is not received until the shares are delivered (or the options are exercised) to the beneficiaries while the bank recognises during the life of the award, an expense in profit or loss expense recognised in respect of that share-based payment;
- The tax effects related to the initial recognition of the equity component of a compound financial instrument (e.g., a convertible bond which may result in the delivery to the bondholders of a fixed number of shares upon conversion);
- The withholding tax charged on dividend distributions to the entity's shareholders; or
- The tax effects related to an adjustment to the opening balance of retained earnings resulting from a change in accounting policy that is accounted for retrospectively or the correction of an error.

Megabank's investment in Largebank resulted, on 31 December 20X0, in a pre-tax unrealised gain of EUR 100 million and a EUR 30 million DTL. As this investment was recognised at fair value through profit or loss (FVTPL), the tax effects were recognised in profit or loss as well. Consequently, and related to its investment in Largebank, Megabank disclosed the following items in its balance sheet and profit or loss statements:

- The fair value of the investment (EUR 500 million) on the asset side of the balance sheet;
- A DTL totalling EUR 30 million on the liability side of the balance sheet. EUR 18 million of this amount would set off against EUR 18 million of DTAs at a later stage of the accounting process;
- A pre-tax trading gain totalling EUR 100 million in profit or loss. This item represented the unrealised pre-tax gain on the investment; and
- A deferred tax effect totalling EUR 30 million, reducing the amount of the gain and representing the tax effects on such gain. This amount was equal to the DTL.

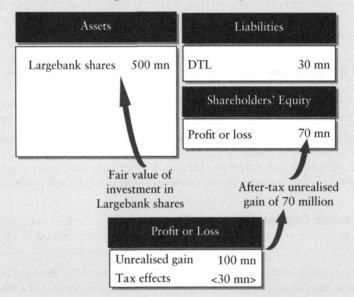

Megabank's investment in Smallbank resulted, on 31 December 20X0, in a pre-tax unrealised loss of EUR 60 million and a EUR 18 million DTA. As this investment was recognised at fair value through OCI (FVTOCI), the tax effects were recognised in OCI as well. Consequently, and related to its investment in Smallbank, Megabank disclosed the following items in its balance sheet:

- The fair value of the investment (EUR 340 million) on the asset side of the balance sheet;
- A DTA totalling EUR 18 million on the asset side of the balance sheet. This amount would set off against EUR 18 million of DTLs at a later stage of the accounting process;
- A pre-tax unrealised loss totalling EUR 60 million in OCI. This item represented the difference between the EUR 340 million fair value of the Smallbank shares and the EUR 500 million investment; and
- A deferred tax effect totalling EUR 18 million, reducing the amount of the loss and representing the tax effects on such loss. This amount was equal to the DTA.

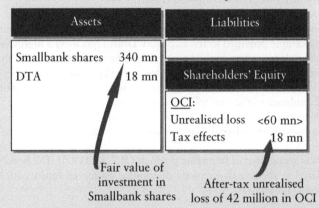

It was mentioned in the previous section that the EUR 18 million DTA was set off against an equal amount of DTLs. As a result of the offset, Megabank recognised a EUR 12 million (= 30 mn − 18 mn) DTL in its balance sheet. The combined presentation of the investments in Largebank and Smallbank in Megabank's balance sheet as of 31 December 20X0 was the following:

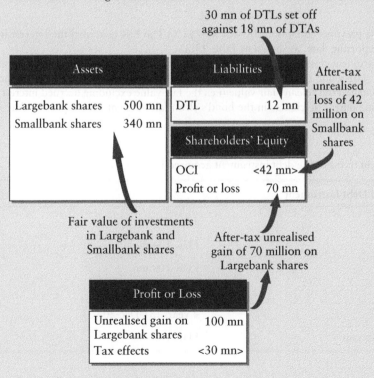

13.3 WORKED EXAMPLE: TEMPORARY DIFFERENCES STEMMING FROM DEBT INSTRUMENTS RECOGNISED AT FAIR VALUE

This section covers how deferred taxes (DTAs and DTLs) arising from temporary differences are generated and accounted for under IAS 12 in the case of bonds classified at fair value. The assessment of the utilisation of their temporary differences using probable taxable future profits is rather different to the general approach covered in the previous section. A numerical example of a bond classified at fair value through OCI (FVTOCI) is covered to illustrate the main issues stemming from deferred taxes arising from temporary differences of such financial instruments.

A helpful reference for the accounting treatment of financial assets recognised at FVTOCI is the IASB's Exposure Draft *Recognition of Deferred Tax Assets for Unrealised Losses* published in August 2014. In my view the example provided in the Exposure Draft represents a highly simplified situation that provides insufficient clarity when applied to other more real situations, notably in circumstances where probable future taxable profits are available for partially deferred taxes beyond the period in which temporary differences reverse. Therefore, I had to make my own assumptions regarding the application of IAS 12 guidance to the example I provide next.

Let us assume that on 1 January 20X0 Megabank invested EUR 104 million (i.e., 104% of its nominal amount) in a bond with a 4-year maturity on its issue date with the main terms outlined in Table 13.2.

The instrument was recognised at fair value through OCI (FVTOCI). The bond's effective interest rate (EIR) was calculated as the rate that exactly discounted estimated future cash flows through the expected life of the bond, as follows:

$$104\,mn = \frac{6\,mn}{1+EIR} + \frac{6\,mn}{\left(1+EIR\right)^2} + \frac{6\,mn}{\left(1+EIR\right)^3} + \frac{106\,mn}{\left(1+EIR\right)^4}$$

Solving the previous equation, EIR was 4.8752%. The EIR governed the interest income recognised at each reporting date, as shown in Table 13.3.

A debt instrument classified at FVTOCI may result in the recognition of unrealised gains or losses in OCI as the fair value of the instrument changes over the contractual term of the investment. Megabank calculated the "clean" fair value (i.e., the fair value excluding accrued interest) of the bond at each reporting date. The change in the bond's clean fair value at each reporting date is outlined in Table 13.4.

TABLE 13.2   Main terms of the debt instrument acquired by Megabank

Main Terms of Debt Instrument	
Purchase date	1-Jan-20X0
Purchase price	EUR 104 mn
Nominal	EUR 100 mn
Coupon	6%
Maturity	4 years (31-Dec-20X3)
Redemption amount	EUR 100 mn

TABLE 13.3 Calculation of each period interest income and amortised cost amounts

Year	Amortised Cost Beginning Year (a)	Interest Income (b) = (a) × EIR	Cash Flow (c)	Amortised Cost End of Year (d) = (a) + (b) − (c)
1	104,000,000	5,070,000	6,000,000	103,070,000
2	103,070,000	5,025,000	6,000,000	102,095,000
3	102,095,000	4,977,000	6,000,000	101,072,000
4	101,072,000	4,927,000	6,000,000	100,000,000

TABLE 13.4 Calculation of the period change in the debt's fair value

Year	Clean Fair Value (a)	Previous Clean Fair Value (b)	Change (c) = (a) − (b)
1	102,500,000	104,000,000	<1,500,000>
2	101,000,000	102,500,000	<1,500,000>
3	101,400,000	101,000,000	400,000
4	100,000,000	101,400,000	<1,400,000>

TABLE 13.5 Calculation of amounts in OCI related to the debt investment

Year	Clean Fair Value (a)	Amortised Cost End of Year (b)	FVOCI Reserve (c) = (a) − (b)	Previous FVOCI Reserve (d)	New FVOCI Entry (c) − (d)
1	102,500,000	103,070,000	<570,000>	0	<570,000>
2	101,000,000	102,095,000	<1,095,000>	<570,000>	<525,000>
3	101,400,000	101,072,000	328,000	<1,095,000>	1,423,000
4	100,000,000	100,000,000	0	328,000	<328,000>

In order to account for the bond, the bank had to keep track of both the bond's amortised cost and its fair value. Any difference between the bond's clean fair value and its amortised cost was recognised in the FVOCI reserve of OCI as shown in Table 13.5.

Let us assume further that at each reporting date:

- Megabank expected the issuer to perform. In other words, it was probable that Megabank would receive all the contractual cash flows (i.e., the remaining coupons and the redemption amount) if it held the bond until maturity;
- Megabank had the ability and intention to hold the bond until any decrease in value reversed (which could be at its maturity);
- The tax base of the bond remained at amortised cost until the debt instrument was sold or until maturity; and
- The tax base of the bond was not reduced by an impairment charge, because the criteria for recognising an impairment loss for tax purposes was not met.

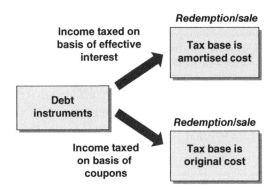

FIGURE 13.8 Tax base determination – Debt instruments

13.3.1 Step 1: Determination of the Tax Base of Debt Instruments

The first step in the accounting for deferred taxes entails the bank determining the tax base. The **tax base of an asset** is the amount that will be deductible for tax purposes against any taxable economic benefits that will flow to the entity when it recovers the carrying amount of the asset. If those economic benefits will not be taxable, then the tax base of the asset is equal to its carrying amount.

The determination of a tax base takes into account the manner the tax authorities will tax the entity when it recovers the asset or settles the liability. Commonly, debt instruments (i.e., bonds and loans) are taxed either based on its amortised cost or its original cost (i.e., its purchase price), as highlighted in Figure 13.8.

In the case of Megabank's bond, there were two tax bases: (i) a tax base related to the redemption or sale amounts and (ii) a tax base related to the interest/coupons received (i.e., the economic benefits flowing to the bank). The tax base related to the bond's redemption or disposal depended on the manner the tax authority would tax Megabank upon the bond's redemption or disposal.

Taxation Based on Amortised Cost   Were the tax authority to tax Megabank on the basis of the instrument's **amortised cost**, the bond's tax base, for purposes of the redemption amount, at each reporting date was its amortised cost on that date as shown in Table 13.6.

Interest income was taxed when recognised in profit or loss. The tax bases related to interest income for each year are summarised in Table 13.7.

Taxation based on Original Cost   Alternatively, were the tax authority to tax Megabank on the basis of the **original cost** of the financial instrument, the original cost of the bond was deductible against total redemption proceeds. Consequently, the bond's tax base related to the redemption amount at each

TABLE 13.6 Calculation of the debt's tax base related to its amortised cost balances

Year	Amortised Cost (End of Year)	Tax Base
1	103,070,000	103,070,000
2	102,095,000	102,095,000
3	101,072,000	101,072,000
4	100,000,000	100,000,000

TABLE 13.7 Calculation of the debt's tax base related to its interest income

Year	Interest Income Tax Base
1	5,070,000
2	5,025,000
3	4,977,000
4	4,927,000

reporting date was its EUR 104 million initial cost. In addition, if the tax law did not explicitly specify any tax consequences resulting from the repayment of the nominal amount, the tax base would be the cost of the financial instrument as well.

Coupons were taxed when received, being such tax part of the current tax. The tax base related to the coupons at each year would be, therefore, the bond's EUR 6 million annual coupon.

13.3.2 Step 2: Calculation of Temporary Differences

A temporary difference arises whenever the accounting and tax bases of an asset or liability are different. A temporary difference stemming from the unrealised gain/loss on a debt investment accounted for at fair value can be either a deductible or a taxable temporary difference, depending on the difference between (i) the carrying amount of the debt on the balance sheet (i.e., its "clean" fair value) and (ii) its tax base, as shown below.

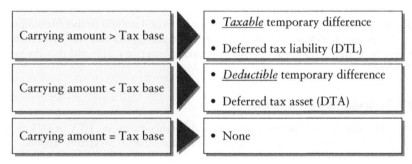

In the case of Megabank's bond, the temporary differences depended on the manner the tax authority would tax the bank upon the bond's redemption or disposal. Let us calculate next the temporary differences arising from Megabank's bond investment.

Taxation based on Amortised Cost Were the tax authority to tax Megabank on the basis of the instrument's **amortised cost** and taking into account that the bond's tax base at each reporting date was its amortised cost, the temporary differences at the end of each year are outline Table 13.8.

Thus for example, at the end of year 3, Megabank would record a EUR 328,000 taxable temporary difference. Upon redemption, in year 4, the deferred tax would completely reverse, and no current tax would stem from the investment in the bond.

Taxation Based on Original Cost Alternatively, were the tax authority to tax Megabank on the basis of the **original cost** of the financial instrument and taking into account that the bond's tax base at each reporting date was its EUR 104 million initial cost, the temporary differences are outlined in Table 13.9.

TABLE 13.8 Temporary differences arising from the debt investment where taxation is based on its amortised cost

Year	Clean Fair Value	Tax Base	Temporary Difference	Deductible/Taxable
1	102,500,000	103,070,000	<570,000>	Deductible
2	101,000,000	102,095,000	<1,095,000>	Deductible
3	101,400,000	101,072,000	328,000	Taxable
4	100,000,000	100,000,000	Nil	—

TABLE 13.9 Temporary differences arising from the debt investment where taxation is based on its original cost

Year	Clean Fair Value	Tax Base	Temporary Difference	Deductible/Taxable
1	102,500,000	104,000,000	<1,500,000>	Deductible
2	101,000,000	104,000,000	<3,000,000>	Deductible
3	101,400,000	104,000,000	<2,600,000>	Deductible
4	100,000,000	104,000,000	<4,000,000>	Deductible

Thus, at the end of year 4, Megabank would record a EUR 4 million deductible temporary difference. Upon redemption, the deferred tax would be released and would help Megabank set off current tax payable (assuming that Megabank had sufficient available tax payable and that the tax authority allowed such offset).

13.3.3 Step 3: Determination of Exceptions

There are situations where even though a temporary difference exists, no DTA or DTL is recognised. These exceptions were covered in Section 13.2.3. In our bond case *no* exceptions applied.

13.3.4 Step 4: Determination of Availability of Future Profits and Recognition of DTA and DTLs

Let us assume that at the end of year 3, which corresponded to 31 December 20X0, Megabank assessed the recognition of DTAs and DTLs related to its bond portfolio. Megabank intended to hold its bond portfolio until maturity and it expected the portfolio to be fully performing. A taxable temporary difference, not subject to the exceptions covered in Section 13.2.3 necessarily becomes a DTL, while a deductible temporary difference may or not become in its entirety a DTA.

- A **DTA** is recognised, subject to the exceptions covered in Section 13.2.3, to the extent that it is *probable* that future taxable profits will be available against which the deductible temporary difference can be utilised;
- A **DTL** is recognised, subject to the exceptions covered in Section 13.2.3, when a taxable temporary difference exists.

IAS 12 required an assessment of the utilisation of deductible temporary differences into two successive steps, as covered in Section 13.2.4 (see Figure 13.9). Let us apply the two-step process in our

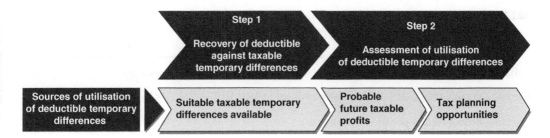

FIGURE 13.9 Steps in the assessment of the utilisation of deductible temporary differences

case at 31 December 20X0, assuming that the taxable entity was Megabank's parent company – Megabank AG – and that it expected the following reversal of temporary differences and probable future tax profit/loss (in EUR) for the year 20X1, as shown in the following table:

Year End	Reversal of Deductible Temp.Diffs	Reversal of Taxable Temp.Diffs	Probable Future Profit/Loss
20X1	104 mn	15 mn	<40 mn>

Thus, the EUR 328,000 taxable temporary difference related to the bond at the end of year 3, calculated in Section 13.3.2, was aggregated to other taxable differences reversing in the year 20X1 associated with the bond portfolio, resulting in a EUR 15 million total.

Step 1: Recovery of Deductible Temporary Differences against Taxable Temporary Differences   In applying Step 1, Megabank assessed the availability of taxable temporary differences relating to the same taxation authority that were expected to reverse in the same period, or in periods into which an ordinary tax loss arising from the deferred tax asset could be carried back or forward. The application of this step to the taxable differences relating to the year 20X1 is shown in Table 13.10.

Step 2: Assessment of Utilisation of Deductible Temporary Differences   In applying Step 2, Megabank assessed the availability of future taxable profit relating to Megabank AG and its taxation authority, in the same period as the reversal of the deductible temporary difference. Let us assume that in that year Megabank expected to incur in a EUR 40 million loss.

TABLE 13.10   Calculation of reversing temporary differences requiring further assessment of utilisation

Item	Amount (EUR)
Reversal of deductible temporary differences (a)	104 mn
Reversal of taxable temporary differences (b)	15 mn
Utilisation in the period (c) [min. of (a) and (b)]	15 mn
Reversing temporary differences requiring further assessment of utilisation (Step 2(d)) {max. [0 ; (a) – (b)]}	89 mn

TABLE 13.11   Calculation of the adjusted taxable profit (or loss) for utilisation assessment

Item	Amount (EUR)
Probable loss for 20X1	<40 mn>
Reversing taxable temporary differences considered in Step 1(b)	<15 mn>
Reversing deductible temporary differences (a)	104 mn
Adjusted taxable profit (loss) for utilisation assessment	**49 mn**

In order to avoid double counting, the bank's estimate of future taxable profit excluded any reversal of deductible temporary differences, as shown in Table 13.11 for the year ending 20X1.

Thus, EUR 49 million were expected to be utilised of deductible temporary differences on unrealised losses on debt instruments being held to maturity. Let us assume that Megabank did not expect to implement any tax planning strategies, concluding, as a result, that the utilisation of these deductible deferred taxes totalled EUR 64 million, comprising a EUR 15 million utilisation resulting from the application of Step 1 and a EUR 49 million utilisation resulting from the application of Step 2, as shown in Figure 13.10. In addition, Megabank recorded a valuation allowance of EUR 40 million which was *not* disclosed in Megabank's balance sheet.

Why was it possible to expect the utilisation of EUR 49 million of deductible temporary differences against future profits when Megabank expected a loss for the year?   Imagine that Megabank AG did expect just a EUR 1 gain for 20X1, then all the deductible temporary difference would be recognised as a DTA (i.e., no valuation allowance would exist). The presumption for any non-credit losses was that the debt instrument will recover its fair value to its amortised cost basis (as of the reporting date). This was the case because Megabank expected to recover the carrying amount of the debt instruments by holding them to maturity and collecting all the contractual cash flows. Accordingly, Megabank AG did not need any further source of taxable income to demonstrate realisation of this specific deductible temporary difference. Any unrealised loss recorded in OCI would reverse over the contractual term of the instrument without affecting the entity's profit or loss or taxable income.

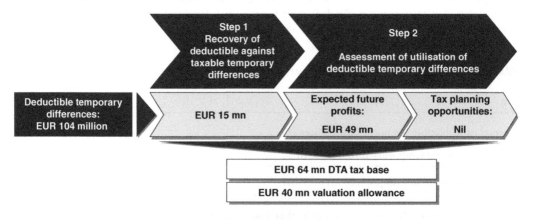

FIGURE 13.10   Resulting utilisation of deductible temporary differences through the two-step process

Why do temporary differences arising from unrealised losses of debt instruments recognised at fair value follow a different DTA recognition treatment relative to other types of temporary differences? Because Megabank (i) had the intent and ability to hold the debt instruments until recovery of its amortised cost and (ii) expected to collect all the instruments' contractual cash flows, decreases/increases in the instrument's fair value up to its amortised cost basis would reverse out of OCI on redemption of the instruments, resulting in no cumulative change in Megabank's future taxable income. In other words, temporary differences would reverse in full, resulting in *no* actual deduction or taxable amount recorded in Megabank's tax return.

In this respect, temporary differences associated with unrealised gains and losses on debt instruments that meet the previous two conditions are unlike other types of temporary differences (or unlike deductible deferred taxes arising from tax loss and credit carry forwards) because they do not affect profit or loss or the tax return if held until recovery (i.e., until maturity) of the instruments' amortised cost. Thus, according to the IASB, this differentiated treatment better reflects the actual behaviour of DTAs.

13.3.5 Measurement of the DTA

The DTA was measured based on the tax rate that was expected to apply in the period that the debt instruments were realised, based on tax rates and tax laws that have been enacted or substantively enacted at the balance sheet date. For the measurement of the resulting DTA, Megabank used the then-prevailing tax rate for ordinary gains of 25% because that was the tax rate that applied to gains and losses resulting from recovering debt instruments by holding them to maturity and collecting their contractual cash flows. As a result, Megabank recognised a EUR 16 million DTA:

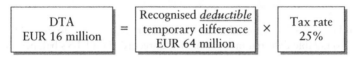

The bond portfolio was recognised at "fair value through OCI" ("FVTOCI"). Deferred tax related to fair value remeasurement of debt investments classified at FVTOCI is also credited or charged directly to OCI and subsequently recognised in consolidated profit or loss once the underlying transaction or event to which the deferred tax relates is recognised in profit or loss. As a result, Megabank recognised the EUR 16 million in OCI, reducing the unrealised loss pertaining to the bond portfolio. However, before recognising the DTA in OCI, Megabank had to take into account the following:

- Whether any of the bonds in the portfolio were subject to fair value hedges, in which case changes in fair value resulting from the risk being hedged were recorded in profit or loss. This could jeopardise the presumption that Megabank planned to hold the hedged bonds until maturity; and
- Whether the changes in carrying amounts related to changes in foreign exchange rate, in which case they were recognised in profit or loss.

Finally, the DTA was assessed for offsetting with other DTLs, following the guidelines covered in Section 13.2.6.

13.4 CASE STUDY: UBS'S DEFERRED TAX ASSETS

This case study illustrates that DTAs may have a significant influence in the financial results of a bank. The case analyses the nature of the deferred taxes being reported by the Swiss bank UBS in 2014, highlighting that DTAs may be notably influenced by exchange rates and critical assumptions by the bank.

As of 31 December 2014, UBS's DTAs amounted to CHF 11.1 billion while DTLs amounted to only CHF 80 million (see Figure 13.11). DTAs were reported net of DTLs where the requirements for offset were met. It can be inferred from the low level of DTLs on UBS's consolidated balance sheet that most DTLs were set off against DTAs.

> From an accounting perspective, DTAs and DTLs of the same type (current or deferred) are offset when they arise from the same tax reporting group, they relate to the same tax authority, the legal right to offset exists, and they are intended to be settled net or realised simultaneously.

As detailed in Figure 13.12, while disclosed (in UBS's consolidated balance sheet) DTAs totalled CHF 11.1 billion, UBS had 34.6 billion of deductible deferred taxes. Thus, UBS had CHF 23.5 billion of deductible deferred taxes unrecorded on its balance sheet (i.e., recorded as valuation allowances).

> The portion of a deductible deferred tax, not subject to the exceptions covered in Section 13.2.3, for which it is probable that sufficient taxable profits will be available against which this deferred tax can be utilised, is recognised in the balance sheet as a **DTA**.
>
> The portion of a deductible deferred tax that is not recognised as a DTA becomes a **valuation allowance**, an off-balance sheet item.

As detailed in Figure 13.13, reported taxable deferred tax amounted to just CHF 80 million, recognised as DTLs. No taxable deferred taxes remained unrecorded on UBS's balance sheet.

> All taxable deferred taxes, not subject to the exceptions covered in Section 13.2.3, are recognised as DTLs (the amounts not offsetting DTAs), independently of whether it is probable that sufficient losses will be available against which the DTLs can be utilised.

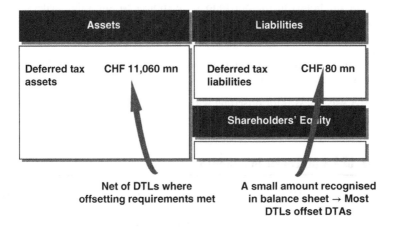

FIGURE 13.11 UBS's reported DTAs and DTLs, as of 31 December 2014

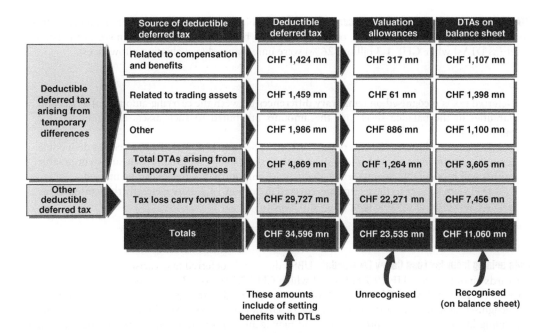

FIGURE 13.12 Items in UBS's deductible deferred taxes, as of 31 December 2014

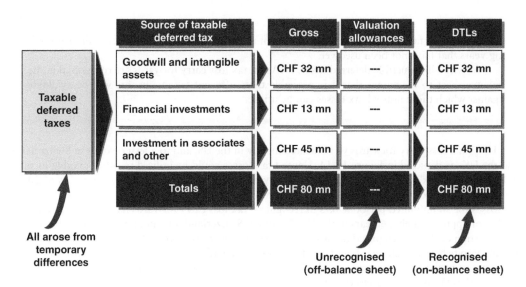

FIGURE 13.13 Items in UBS's taxable deferred taxes, as of 31 December 2014

13.4.1 Composition of UBS's Deferred Tax Assets

Reported DTAs (see Figure 13.12) comprised (i) CHF 3.6 billion in respect of temporary differences and (ii) CHF 7.5 billion in respect of tax loss carry forwards. Let us next take a closer look at the nature of these DTAs.

DTAs Arising from Temporary Differences   UBS's deductible deferred tax arising from temporary differences amounted to CHF 4.9 billion, of which CHF 3.6 billion (74%) were recognised in the balance sheet (as DTAs) while CHF 1.3 billion (26%) were unrecognised (as valuation allowances).

> Deferred tax is recognised on **temporary differences** between the carrying amounts of assets and liabilities in the balance sheet and the amounts attributed to such assets and liabilities for tax purposes.
>
>   **DTAs** not subject to the exceptions covered in Section 13.2.3 are recognised for deductible temporary differences in the balance sheet to the extent that it is probable that sufficient taxable profits will be available against which deductible temporary differences can be utilised.
>
>   **DTLs** not subject to the exceptions covered in Section 13.2.3 are generally recognised in the balance sheet for all taxable temporary differences.

DTAs arising from Tax Loss Carry Forwards   UBS's deductible deferred taxes arising from tax loss carry forwards amounted to CHF 29.7 billion, of which CHF 7.5 billion (25%) were recognised in the balance sheet (as DTAs) while CHF 22.3 billion (75%) remained unrecognised (as valuation allowances). Unrecognised amounts were the consequence of UBS's expectation, based on the evidence available (including historical levels of profitability and management projections of future income), that there will be not sufficient taxable income generated by the corresponding business to recover the losses carried forward.

> Deferred tax on tax loss carry forwards represent incurred losses in either the current or preceding years that have not been used yet.
>
>   As with all deductible deferred taxes, DTAs on **tax loss carry forwards** are recognised in the balance sheet to the extent that it is probable that sufficient taxable profits will be available against which those unused tax losses can be utilised.

UBS's tax loss carry forwards were located mainly in the US, and to a lesser extent in Switzerland and the UK, as depicted in Figure 13.14. Unused tax losses could be utilised to offset taxable income in future years. Tax authorities often set temporary limits on the utilisation of tax losses. As of 2014, US federal tax losses could be carried forward for 20 years, Swiss tax losses for seven years, and UK tax losses for an unlimited period. UBS's unrecognised tax loss carry forwards had an average remaining life of approximately 16 years in the US, 2 years in Switzerland and an indefinite life in the UK. A large portion of the unrecognised tax loss carry forwards corresponded to the US (CHF 16.8 billion), which, despite having a 20-year limit for future utilisation, had a probability lower than 50% of being used against probable future profit. Table 13.12 details the expiries of the tax loss carry forwards not recognised as DTAs, as of 31 December 2014.

Wait a minute! Why is the total figure in the table above CHF 68,969 million, while the amounts in Figure 13.12 show a total of CHF 22,271 million of valuation allowances related to tax loss carry forwards? The CHF 68,969 million represented the total amount of unrecognised losses available to offset taxable future profits, while the CHF 22,271 million valuation allowance figure was a tax amount (i.e., 22,271 million = CHF 68,969 million × 32.3% tax rate), as shown in Figure 13.15. I assume that UBS used the tax rate applied in the calculation of the DTAs.

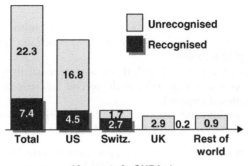

(Amounts in CHF bn)

FIGURE 13.14   Location of UBS's tax loss carry forwards (pre-tax amounts), as of 31 December 2014

TABLE 13.12   Expiries of UBS's unrecognised tax loss carry forwards

Expiries of UBS's Unrecognised Tax Loss Carry Forwards (in CHF)	
Within 1 year	9,341 mn
From 2 to 5 years	43 mn
From 6 to 10 years	613 mn
From 11 to 20 years	39,899 mn
No expiry	18,973 mn
Totals	68,869 mn

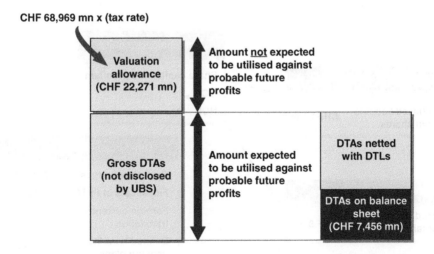

FIGURE 13.15   Recognition of UBS's tax loss carry forwards, as of 31 December 2014

The DTAs that UBS recognised on its balance sheet as of 31 December 2014 in respect of prior years' tax losses reflected the probable recoverable level based on future taxable profit as informed by its business plan forecasts.

Existing assessments were reviewed and, if necessary, revised to reflect changed circumstances. This review was conducted annually, in the second half of each year, but adjustments could be made at other times, if required.

If the business plan earnings and assumptions in future periods substantially deviated from current forecasts, the amount of recognised DTAs could need to be adjusted in the future.

- If UBS performance was expected to improve, particularly in the US, the UK or Switzerland, the bank could potentially recognise additional DTAs as a result of that assessment;
- Conversely, if UBS performance in those countries was expected to produce diminished taxable profit in future years, the bank could be required to write down all or a portion of the currently recognised DTAs through profit or loss.

13.4.2 Deferred Tax Assets and Liabilities Recognised in Equity

Certain deferred tax expenses and benefits were recognised directly in shareholders' equity, primarily in other comprehensive income (OCI), as the items generating such deferred taxes were recognised in equity. Most of the taxes recognised in OCI will be reclassified at a later stage to profit or loss.

UBS's deferred tax recognised in shareholders' equity comprised (see Figure 13.16):

- An expense of CHF 195 million for cash flow hedges, recognised in OCI. Therefore, UBS recognised an unrealised profit in the derivatives designated as hedging instruments in cash flow hedges and the deferred tax reduced such unrealised profit. In the periods during which the hedged cash flows of the financial asset or liability are recognised in profit or loss, both the unrealised gain on the derivative and its related deferred tax are simultaneously reclassified from OCI to profit or loss;
- An expense of CHF 51 million for financial investments at FVTOCI (in reality related to assets recognised as available for sale under the previous IAS 39 accounting standard, as UBS had not at

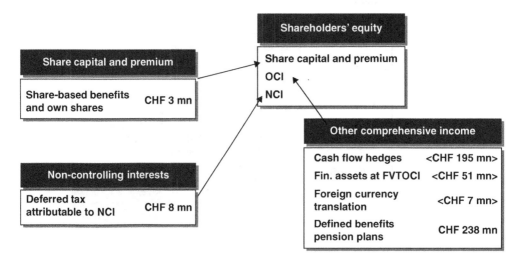

FIGURE 13.16   Deferred tax items recognised in UBS's shareholders' equity, as of 31 December 2014

the reporting date adopted IFRS 9 yet). This amount was recognised in OCI. Therefore, UBS recognised an unrealised gain in its financial assets at FVTOCI and the deferred tax reduced such unrealised gain. In the period during which the gain or loss on the financial instrument is reclassified to profit or loss (i.e., upon its sale or redemption), its related deferred tax is simultaneously reclassified from OCI to profit or loss;

- An expense of CHF 7 million for foreign currency translation gains and losses, recognised in OCI. When the foreign operation translation gains or losses (i.e., upon the foreign operation's sale or liquidation) are reclassified to profit or loss, its related deferred tax is simultaneously reclassified from OCI to profit or loss;
- A benefit of CHF 238 million for defined benefit pension plans, recognised in OCI;
- A benefit of CHF 8 million related to the previous items, but attributable to non-controlled interests; and
- A benefit of CHF 3 million recognised in share premium. This tax was related to share-based employee benefits and to gains and losses on the sale of treasury shares, and is not to be reclassified from share premium.

13.4.3 Factors Influencing the Recognition of UBS's Deferred Tax Assets

Changes in the recognition of DTAs can have a very significant effect on a bank's reported results. In the case of UBS, these changes could be influenced by several factors, including:

- Changes in the future profitability of the operations in the countries where the DTAs were located. If UBS performance was expected to improve, particularly in the US, the UK or Switzerland, the bank could potentially recognise additional DTAs as a result of that assessment. Conversely, if UBS performance in those countries was expected to produce diminished taxable profit in future years, the bank could be required to write down all or a portion of previously recognised DTAs through profit or loss.
- Changes in statutory tax rates. DTAs and DTLs are measured at the tax rates that are expected to apply in the period in which the asset will be realised or the liability will be settled based on enacted rates. Changes in tax rates have the effect of changing the future tax saving that is expected from tax losses or deductible tax differences and therefore the amount of DTAs recognised or, alternatively, changing the tax cost of additional taxable income from taxable temporary differences and, therefore, the amount of DTLs. For example, reductions in the statutory tax rate could cause the expected future tax benefit from tax loss carry forwards in the affected locations to diminish in value. This in turn would cause a write-down of the associated DTAs;
- Changes in exchange rates. For example, in 2014 the Swiss National Bank ended its support for a minimum exchange rate against the EUR, causing a substantial appreciation of the CHF. The appreciation of the CHF led to a reduction in recognised DTAs, mainly related to the US, of approximately CHF 0.4 billion (of which CHF 0.2 billion related to temporary differences DTAs), which were recognised in other comprehensive income (in the translation differences account);
- Changes to the way in which courts and tax authorities interpreted tax laws could cause the amount of taxes ultimately paid by the bank to materially differ from the amount accrued.

Particularly in a situation where recent losses have been incurred, IAS 12 requires convincing evidence that there will be sufficient future profitability. UBS relied on management business plans to substantiate such future profitability and its confidence level in assessing the probability of taxable profit beyond the current outlook period. An interesting initiative that the Swiss bank took to increase expected future profitability was to extend the horizon of its business plans.

Consistent with past practice, UBS expected to revalue its overall level of DTAs in the second half of 2015 based on a reassessment of future profitability taking into account updated business

(continued)

plan forecasts, including consideration of a possible further extension of the forecast period used for US DTA recognition purposes to seven years from the six years used at 31 December 2014.

This extension followed an extension implemented in 2014 from five to six years in the bank's business plans. The higher profitability forecast resulted in a net increase of recognised DTAs of CHF 685 million.

13.5 DEFERRED TAX ASSETS FROM A REGULATORY CAPITAL PERSPECTIVE

The impact on regulatory capital of tax assets depends on its nature, and in the particular case of DTAs, whether they arise from temporary differences and whether they rely on future profits.

13.5.1 Accounting vs. Regulatory DTAs

The amount of DTAs that a bank discloses in its balance sheet differs from the amount of DTAs that serve as a basis for the calculations of RWAs and deductions from regulatory capital. Several adjustments are made to the amount of accounting DTAs:

- Firstly, offsetting benefits between DTAs and DTLs achieved under IAS 12 are unwound (i.e., the DTAs and DTLs are grossed up). Therefore, the amount of DTAs for regulatory purposes is independent of the offsetting rules under the relevant accounting framework (IAS 12 or national GAAP);
- Secondly, DTAs and DTLs related to entities not consolidated for regulatory purposes (e.g., insurance and real estate entities) are excluded from the amount of regulatory DTAs and DTLs;
- Thirdly, any DTLs that have been used to reduce the deductions from CET1 capital stemming from intangible assets and defined benefit pension plans assets are excluded (see box below); and
- Finally, DTAs (that rely on future profitability) and DTLs that meet the regulatory netting requirements stated in [CRR 38(3)] are netted out.

Intangible Assets   Pursuant to [CRR 37 (a)], the amount of intangibles (including goodwill) to be deducted from CET1 capital is reduced by the amount of associated DTLs that would be extinguished if the intangible assets became impaired or were derecognised under the applicable accounting framework.

In the case of business acquisitions, DTLs only may arise when badwill has been recognised. A case study has been provided in Section 3.12 illustrating the acquisition by Barclays of Lehman Brothers N.A.

Defined Benefit Pension Plans   Pursuant to [CRR 41 (a)], the amount of defined benefit pension fund assets to be deducted from CET1 capital is reduced by the amount of any associated DTLs which could be extinguished if the assets became impaired or were derecognised under the applicable accounting framework.

Consequently, and pursuant to [CRR 38(4)], DTLs that reduce the amount of intangible assets and/or defined benefit pension fund assets required to be deducted cannot be used to reduce the amount of DTAs that rely on future profitability.

Other Tax Items that Impact Regulatory Capital   Other tax items have an impact on regulatory capital. Pursuant to [CRR 36(1)(l)], any tax charge relating to CET1 items, foreseeable at the moment of its calculation, are deducted from CET1 capital, except where the bank suitably adjusts the amount of CET1 items insofar as such tax charges reduce the amount up to which those items may be used to cover risks or losses.

13.5.2 Netting of Deferred Tax Assets and Deferred Tax Liabilities

The amounts of DTAs that rely on future profitability are calculated **net of related DTLs** where the following conditions are met [CRR 38(3)]:

1. The bank has a legally enforceable right under applicable national law to set off those current tax assets against current tax liabilities; and
2. The DTAs and the DTLs relate to taxes levied by the same taxation authority and on the same taxable entity.

DTLs used for the purposes of reducing the deduction related to the amount of intangible assets or defined benefit pension plan assets cannot be used for the netting with DTAs that rely on future profitability.

The amount of associated DTLs (which meet the two previous requirements) available to net DTAs is allocated on a pro rata basis between the following [CRR 38(5)]:

1. DTAs that rely on future profitability and arise from temporary differences that are not deducted according to [CRR 48(1)]; and
2. All other DTAs that rely on future profitability and do *not* arise from temporary differences. It is covered in the next several sections that these DTAs are deducted in full from CET1 and comprise carry forwards of unused tax losses and credits.

Regarding DTAs that rely on future profitability and arise from temporary differences, netting with DTLs are restricted to the amounts to be risk-weighted (i.e., not deducted from CET1 capital). The amounts of these DTAs that are deducted are those that exceed the 10% or the 17.65% thresholds (this treatment is covered in the next several sections).

In my view, it is not intuitive why the CRR discriminates for netting purposes between the amounts of DTAs exceeding the thresholds and those that do not. Moreover, it obliges the banks to calculate the amounts above the thresholds before applying the netting benefits.

The allocation of associated DTLs is performed according to the proportion of DTAs that rely on future profitability that these two items represent. For example, the allocation to DTAs that rely on future profitability and arise from temporary differences is calculated as follows:

$$\text{DTLs allocated to DTAs that rely on future profitability and arise from temporary differences} = \text{Available DTLs} \times \frac{A}{A+B}$$

Where:

A: Amount of DTAs that rely on future profitability and arise from temporary differences not subject to deductions from CET1 capital; and
B: Amount of DTAs that rely on future profitability and do *not* arise from temporary differences

13.5.3 Regulatory Treatment of DTAs

It was mentioned above that on the balance sheet a bank may report two types of income tax assets: (i) current tax assets and (ii) DTAs. Next, let us take a look at the Basel III (CRR) treatment of each type of income tax assets (see Figure 13.17).

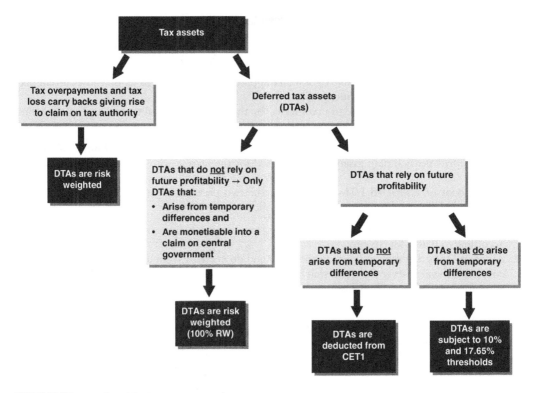

FIGURE 13.17   Basel III (CRR) treatment of tax assets

13.5.4 Regulatory Treatment of Current Tax Assets

Remember that current tax assets represent estimated tax refundable for the current year. Current tax assets comprise: (i) tax overpayments and (ii) tax loss carry backs.

Tax overpayments represent payments of taxes in excess of the bank's tax obligations for the year. Tax loss carry backs represent current year losses of the bank carried back to previous years' positive earnings that give rise to a claim on, or receivable from, a central government, regional government or local tax authority.

The corresponding tax authorities are expected to refund the bank such overpayments and tax loss carry backs in the short term. As a result, the bank is exposed from a credit risk perspective to non-performance of the tax authorities. Pursuant to [CRR 39], tax overpayments and tax loss carry backs are *not* deducted from CET1 capital, but *risk-weighted* in accordance with the capital requirements for credit risk [CRR Chapter 2 or 3 of Title II of Part Three]. Therefore, these tax items affect the denominator (i.e., the RWAs) of the capital ratios.

13.5.5 Regulatory Treatment of Deferred Tax Assets

Remember that DTAs represent the amounts of income taxes recoverable in future years. Remember as well that DTAs are only recognised on the asset side of the balance sheet if the bank expects that there will be sufficient future taxable profits against which the DTAs would be utilised.

DTAs that do *not* Rely on Future Profitability   DTAs that do *not* rely on future profitability are limited to DTAs arising from temporary differences, where all the following conditions are met [CRR 39(2)]:

1. They are automatically and mandatorily replaced without delay with a tax credit in the event that the bank reports a loss when the annual financial statements of the bank are formally approved, or in the event of liquidation or insolvency of the bank;
2. The bank shall be able under the applicable national tax law to offset a tax credit referred to in point (1) against any tax liability of the bank or any other undertaking included in the same consolidation as the bank for tax purposes under that law or any other undertaking subject to the supervision on a consolidated basis in accordance with [CRR Chapter 2 of Title II of Part One]; and
3. Where the amount of tax credits referred to in point (2) exceeds the tax liabilities referred to in that point, any such excess is replaced without delay with a direct claim on the central government of the EU member state in which the institution is incorporated.

The case study in Section 13.6 covered the application of [CRR 39(2)] in the case of Spanish banks. DTAs that do *not* rely on future profitability are applied a risk weight of 100%. Therefore, these DTAs affect the denominator (i.e., the RWAs) of the capital ratios.

DTAs that Rely on Future Profitability and do *not* Arise from Temporary Differences   Pursuant to [CRR 36(1)(c) and 38], deferred tax assets that rely on future profitability, but do *not* arise from temporary differences, are **completely deducted from CET1** and thus are not subject to any threshold. These DTAs are calculated **net of related DTLs** (see Section 13.5.2).

Therefore, the carry forward of unused tax losses, or unused tax credits, are to be deducted in full from CET1, net of related DTLs.

> An interesting item for debating is whether DTAs have value when a bank is facing a loss-making situation or even when it is in an insolvency situation. A bank acquiring other bank with substantial amounts of DTAs will take into account in its valuation of the acquiree the potential future utilisation of these DTAs. Thus, even though Basel III does not provide any capital credit for some DTAs, they have some inherent equity value which often can be monetised when sold to solvent acquirers.

> A criticism of the deduction of DTAs from CET1 capital is that it contributes to **procyclicality**. DTAs would be expected to rise in downturns as banks take more provisions and begin to make losses. It is then, when DTAs deductions from CET1 capital would kick in, resulting in a double negative effect on CET1 capital. Conversely, as the economy recovers, provisions are unwound and DTAs are utilised, resulting in a double positive effect on CET1 capital.

DTAs that Rely on Future Profitability and *Arise* from Temporary Differences   Pursuant to [CRR 36(1)(c), 38 and 48], DTAs that rely on future profitability and arise from temporary differences are partially deducted from CET1 capital if they exceed two thresholds:

- A 10% threshold; and
- A 17.65% threshold. Sometimes this threshold is referred to as the "15% threshold", but in reality it is a $17.65\% (= 15\%/85\%)$ threshold.

The DTA amounts subject to the thresholds are calculated **net of related DTLs** (see Section 13.5.2).

Pursuant to [CRR 48], DTAs that are dependent on future profitability and arise from temporary differences are compared to the relevant CET1 capital of the bank (see Figure 13.18):

- The amounts above the 10% threshold are deducted from CET1 capital; and
- The amounts below or at the 10% threshold are subject to the 17.65% threshold (see next).

The (i) amounts of DTAs, dependent on future profitability and arising from temporary differences, which are equal to or less than 10% of the relevant CET1 capital are added to the (ii) amounts of significant investments in the CET1 instruments of financial sector entities (the amount above or equal 10% of its relevant CET1 capital). The aggregate of (i) and (ii) is compared to 17.65% of the relevant CET1 capital (see Figure 13.18):

- The amounts above the 17.65% threshold are deducted from CET1 capital; and
- The amounts below or at the 17.65% threshold are subject to a risk weight of 250%. Thus, these amounts are exempted from deduction, but affect the denominator of the capital ratios calculations.

> The existence of the 10% threshold allowance mitigates the impact of the deduction by allowing a significant portion of DTAs that rely on future profitability and arise from temporary differences to be risk-weighted (250% risk weight).

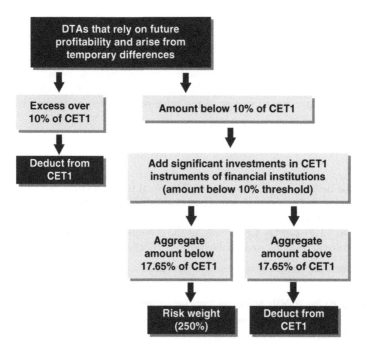

FIGURE 13.18 Regulatory treatment of DTAs that rely on future profitability and arise from temporary differences

The "relevant CET1 capital" used to calculate the 10% threshold **excludes** the amount of DTAs that rely on future profitability and arise from temporary differences but **includes** the following filters and deductions (see Figure 13.19):

- The prudential filter related to **securitised assets** [CRR 32];
- The prudential filter related to **cash flow hedges and changes in the value of own liabilities**, but maintaining any other unrealised gains and losses measured at fair value [CRR 33 and 35];
- The prudential filter related to **additional value adjustments** [CRR 34];
- The **losses for the current financial year** deduction [CRR 36(1)(a)];
- The **intangible assets** deduction [CRR 36(1)(b)];
- The **DTAs that rely on future profitability** deduction [CRR 36(1)(c)], **excluding** the amount of DTAs that rely on future profitability and arise from temporary differences;
- The deduction related to **negative amounts resulting from the calculation of expected loss amounts** for banks calculating risk-weighted exposure amounts using the Internal Ratings-Based Approach (the IRB Approach) [CRR 36(1)(d)];
- The deduction related to **defined benefit pension fund** assets on the balance sheet of the bank [CRR 36(1)(e)];
- The deduction related to direct, indirect and synthetic **holdings by the bank of its own CET1 instruments**, including own CET1 instruments that the bank is under an actual or contingent obligation to purchase by virtue of an existing contractual obligation [CRR 36(1)(f)];
- The deduction related to direct, indirect and synthetic holdings of the CET1 instruments of financial sector entities where those entities have a **reciprocal cross-holding** with the bank that the competent authority considers to have been designed to inflate artificially the total capital of the bank [CRR 36(1)(g)];
- The deduction related to the applicable amount of direct, indirect and synthetic holdings by the bank of **CET1 instruments of financial sector entities** where the institution does *not* have a **significant investment** in those entities [CRR 36(1)(h)];

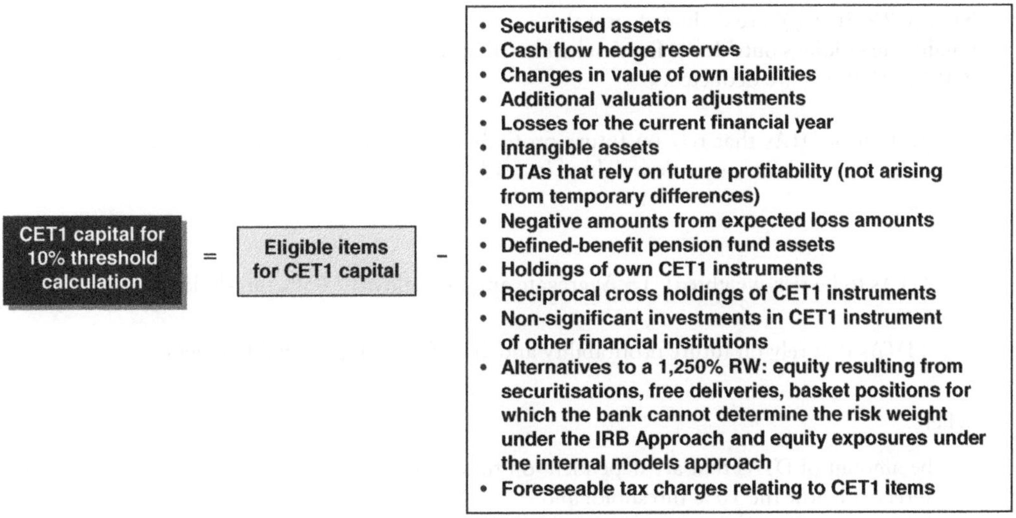

| CET1 capital for 10% threshold calculation | = | Eligible items for CET1 capital | − | • Securitised assets
• Cash flow hedge reserves
• Changes in value of own liabilities
• Additional valuation adjustments
• Losses for the current financial year
• Intangible assets
• DTAs that rely on future profitability (not arising from temporary differences)
• Negative amounts from expected loss amounts
• Defined-benefit pension fund assets
• Holdings of own CET1 instruments
• Reciprocal cross holdings of CET1 instruments
• Non-significant investments in CET1 instrument of other financial institutions
• Alternatives to a 1,250% RW: equity resulting from securitisations, free deliveries, basket positions for which the bank cannot determine the risk weight under the IRB Approach and equity exposures under the internal models approach
• Foreseeable tax charges relating to CET1 items |

FIGURE 13.19 Relevant CET1 for DTAs' 10% threshold calculations

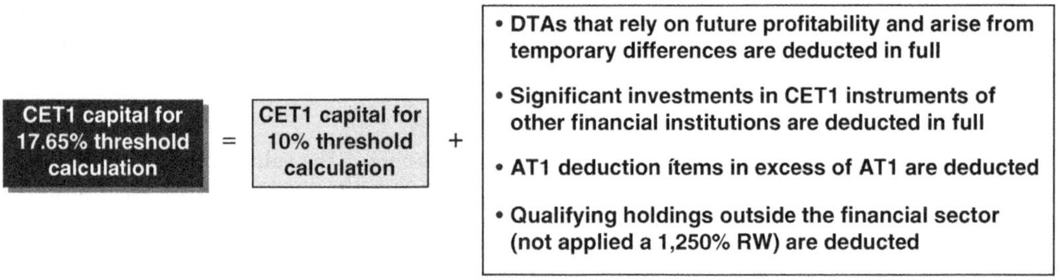

FIGURE 13.20   Relevant CET1 for 17.65% threshold calculations

- The deduction (rather than the application of a 1,250% risk weight) related to **securitisation positions** [CRR 36(1)(k)(ii)], **free deliveries** [CRR 36(1)(k)(iii)], **positions in a basket for which the bank cannot determine the risk weight under the IRB Approach** [CRR 36(1)(k)(iv)] and **equity exposures under the internal models approach** [CRR 36(1)(k)(v)]; and
- The deduction related to **foreseeable tax charges relating to CET1 items**, except where the bank suitably adjusts the amount of CET1 items insofar as such tax charges reduce the amount up to which those items may be used to cover risks or losses [CRR 36(1)(l)].

The "relevant CET1 capital" used to calculate the 17.65% threshold is different to that for the 10% threshold calculation, as shown in Figure 13.20:

- The amount of DTAs that rely on future profitability and arise from temporary differences is applied (i.e., deducted) in full;
- The amount related to **significant investments in CET1 instruments of financial sector entities** [CRR 36(1)(i)] is applied (i.e., deducted) in full;
- The amount of items required to be **deducted from AT1 items** that exceed the AT1 capital of the bank [CRR 36(1)(j)] are deducted; and
- **Qualifying holdings outside the financial sector** (that the bank did not apply a 1,250% risk weight) [CRR 36(1)(k)(i)] are deducted.

The portion of DTAs that rely on future profitability and arise from temporary differences not required to be deducted (i.e., are risk-weighted instead) is calculated as:

$$\text{DTAs to be risk weighted}(*) = \text{Aggregate amount below 17.65\% threshold} \times \frac{A}{A+B}$$

(*) DTAs that rely on future profitability and arise from temporary differences

Where:

A: The amount of DTAs that are dependent on future profitability and arise from temporary differences below the 10% threshold; and
B: The amount of significant investments in the CET1 instruments of other financial institutions below the 10% threshold.

13.6 CASE STUDY: SPANISH BANKS CONVERSION OF DTAS INTO TAX CREDITS, IMPROVING THEIR CET1 POSITIONS

As mentioned above, DTAs that rely on future profitability and that do *not* arise from temporary differences are deducted from CET1 capital. In addition, the amount of DTAs – that rely on future profitability and arise from temporary differences – exceeding the 10% or 17.65% thresholds are deducted from CET1 capital. [CRR 39] provides an exception to such deductions when several conditions are met. This case study covers the application of the exception provided in [CRR 39].

In 2009 the economic environment in South European countries and in Ireland sharply deteriorated. During subsequent years, levels of non-performing loans dramatically increased obliging banks to recognise substantial impairment charges in profit or loss. These impairments were not tax-deductible and, as a result, generated notably large holdings of DTAs which were deducted from CET1 capital as there was generally no guarantee that the banks would be able to generate sufficient taxable profits to offset them.

This situation induced several countries (including Brazil, Greece, Italy, Portugal and Spain) to enact specific changes in legislation to help their banks pass Basel III CET1 ratio scrutiny. This was achieved through sovereign guarantees or deferred tax credits being made available for domestic DTAs, particularly relating to loan loss provisions.

13.6.1 Spanish Banks' DTAs vs. Core Capital Positions

Spanish banks' DTAs mainly arose from losses and loan impairment charges, which were particularly pronounced in 2012. The deduction from CET1 capital of DTAs that rely on future profitability had a substantial impact on Spanish banks capital levels, especially for three reasons:

Firstly, when a bank reported losses (i.e., negative earnings) in its profit or loss, unlike other countries in which the tax authority returns part of the taxes paid in previous years, the bank had to wait to report positive earnings in its profit or loss statement to compensate previous years' losses.

Secondly, the Spanish tax law did not recognise as tax-deductible several expenses recognised for accounting purposes. An important item of these DTAs comprised impairments of loans assessed collectively (what the Spanish banks called "generic provisions") which were not tax-deductible when the provisions were recognised. These provisions were tax-deductible only when they became allocated to specific risks/individual loans (what the Spanish banks called "specific provisions").

Thirdly, the Spanish authorities promoted the acquisition by banks with a strong capital position of troubled banks (commonly banks that had been previously bailed out by the Spanish government). A deterrent for such acquisitions was the large stock of DTAs that the investees held (DTAs that relied on future profitability) and, as a result, would be deducted from the acquiree's CET1 capital.

> At that time, Bank of Spain was notoriously conservative, requiring Spanish banks to recognise "generic provisions" well in excess what other European central banks required. The cautious provisioning policies applied by the Spanish banks created a contradiction: the more conservative a bank was in covering its loans with provisions, the more it was penalised from a regulatory capital perspective. In other words, there could be a situation in which the more solvent banks could report lower capital ratios, due to the deduction of its DTAs stemming from provisions.

As a result, as of 31 December 2013 DTAs represented a large proportion of these banks' Basel II core capital (prior to any DTAs deduction), as illustrated in Figure 13.21.

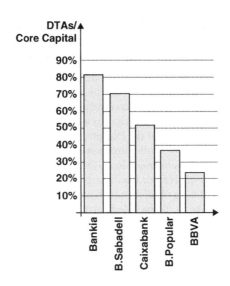

FIGURE 13.21   Spanish banks' DTAs as a percentage of Basel II's core capital, end of 2013

13.6.2 The Spanish Royal Decree

In November 2013 Spain approved a Royal Decree-Law (14/2013 of 29 November 2013) on new tax rules applicable not just to banks but to all corporate tax payers (although banks were by far the main beneficiaries). For fiscal years starting in 2014, DTAs corresponding to the impairment of loans or of assets acquired in payment of loans, and contributions to certain pensions schemes would be converted into an effective credit against the Spanish tax administration. The conversion would take place at the time of filling the corporate tax return corresponding to the fiscal year in which either of the following circumstances occurred:

- The taxpayer registered accounting losses in its annual accounts, which were audited and approved by the corresponding body. In this case, the amount of DTAs converted would be the result of multiplying the total amount by the percentage that the accounting losses represented with respect to the sum of capital plus reserves; or
- The entity was liquidated or declared insolvent by a court.

DTAs corresponding to tax losses which had been generated through the reversal of the above-mentioned DTAs from the year 2014 were also covered by the conversion.

The credit could be directly claimed or offset against any tax liability generated after the conversion. After 18 years, counted from the date on which the DTAs were recorded for accounting purposes (or from the date of the Royal Decree became into force with respect to DTAs registered before), such DTAs could be converted into government bonds if not refunded or offset earlier.

Special rules were defined for the application of the same principle to tax groups and to the incorporation or exclusion of companies from said groups.

> In a nutshell, the Royal Decree allowed banks with operations in Spain to mandatorily and compulsorily covert some DTAs (those arising from temporary differences related to credit loss provisions, provisions for foreclosed assets and pension and pre-retirement obligations) into a tax credit in the case of loss, insolvency or liquidation that could be offset against any tax liability, and in the case of excess tax credit, converted into a direct claim against the Spanish state.

For the Spanish government the Royal Decree had no impact in the short term: generic provisions continued to be non-deductible from a tax perspective, and past negative earnings continued to be applied only to offset future positive earnings.

Only if the temporal differences were not reversed in a period of 18 years, or in the case of liquidation or insolvency of the entity, would the cash position of the Spanish government be affected.

13.6.3 Regulatory Impact of the Royal Decree

The Royal Decree followed the exceptions foreseen in [CRR 39], as shown in Figure 13.22, removing their reliance on future profits. Thus, it helped banks with Spanish operations to avoid deducting significant amounts of DTAs for their calculations of CET1 capital.

For example, on 31 December 2014 the Spanish bank Banco Santander had EUR 16.5 billion of DTAs arising from temporary differences. Due primarily to the Brazilian and Spanish decrees, the bank was able to avoid deducting 51% of these DTAs (or EUR 8.4 billion), as shown in Figure 13.23.

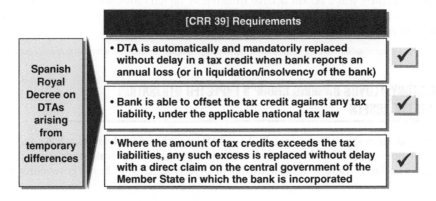

FIGURE 13.22 Spanish Royal Decree and [CRR 39] requirements

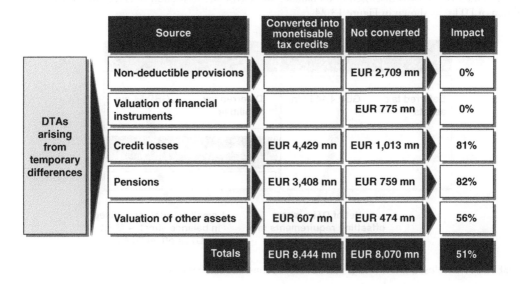

Source	Converted into monetisable tax credits	Not converted	Impact
Non-deductible provisions		EUR 2,709 mn	0%
Valuation of financial instruments		EUR 775 mn	0%
Credit losses	EUR 4,429 mn	EUR 1,013 mn	81%
Pensions	EUR 3,408 mn	EUR 759 mn	82%
Valuation of other assets	EUR 607 mn	EUR 474 mn	56%
Totals	EUR 8,444 mn	EUR 8,070 mn	51%

FIGURE 13.23 Impact of the changes in DTA laws on Banco Santander, as of year-end 2014

13.6.4 Review by the European Commission

In 2015 the European Commission examined whether certain EU members' treatment of bank's DTAs constituted illegal state aid. The review involved Greece, Italy, Portugal and Spain. Because the capital positions of several banks in these countries was rather precarious, a EU decision to turn down the conversion into deferred tax credits had to be careful analysed. For example, it could slow the ongoing consolidation process in the South European banking sectors.

The countries involved argued that main issue was their changes in DTA laws brought a more even treatment of DTAs across the EU. South European countries had stricter tax rules than other EU member states, resulting in an unlevel paying field. For example, in France, banks could carry back losses to previous periods, whereas in the four countries involved this was not possible.

> The main issue was whether the new tax regime for DTAs really strengthens the capital at the banks involved, or is a clever way to exploit the loophole in [CRR 39] without substantial costs to the taxpayer.
>
> In any case, there was a benefit derived from higher capital ratios in boosting investor confidence in banks' solvency, which could ultimately improve banks' access to funding and their liquidity profiles.

13.7 CASE STUDY: LLOYDS BANKING GROUP'S EXPECTED UTILISATION OF DEFERRED TAX ASSETS

This case study illustrates the nature of the DTAs and DTLs of the British bank Lloyds Banking Group ("Lloyds") and their impact on the bank's regulatory capital. In addition, the case study covers the effects of the changes in tax laws regarding future utilisation of DTAs enacted by the British government in 2015.

13.7.1 Nature of Lloyds' DTAs and DTLs

At year-end 2014, Lloyds disclosed in its balance sheet GBP 4,145 million of DTAs and just GBP 50 million of DTLs, as shown in Figure 13.24.

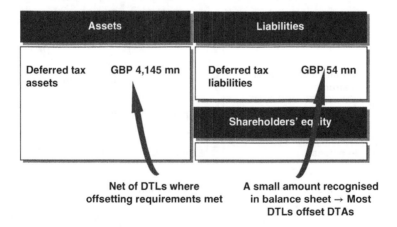

FIGURE 13.24   Disclosed DTAs and DTLs in Lloyds' consolidated balance sheet, as of year-end 2014

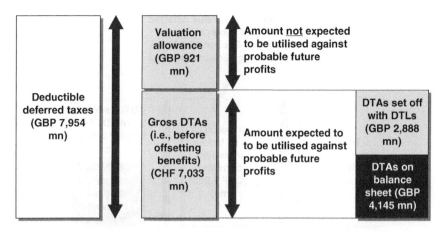

FIGURE 13.25 Structure of Lloyds' deductible deferred tax assets, as of year-end 2014

Lloyds held a large amount of deductible deferred taxes – GBP 7,954 million – stemming from the losses generated by the group in the aftermath of the HBOS acquisition, of which valuation allowances (i.e., the amounts *not* expected to be realised through future taxable profits) totalled GBP 921 million while gross DTAs (i.e., the amounts expected to be realised through future taxable profits) totalled 7,033 million. After setting off GBP 2,888 million of DTAs and DTLs, Lloyds disclosed in its consolidated balance sheet GBP 4,145 million of DTAs, as shown in Figure 13.25. The vast majority (82%) of Lloyds' gross DTAs arose from tax losses being carried forward (GBP 5,758 million), as shown in Table 13.13.

Valuation allowances stemming from deductible deferred taxes totalled GBP 921 million, comprising:

- GBP 614 million in respect of trading losses carried forward, mainly in certain overseas companies and in respect of other temporary differences in the insurance businesses. Trading losses could be carried forward indefinitely, except for losses in the US which expired after 20 years;
- GBP 190 million in respect of capital losses carried forward as there were no predicted future capital profits. Capital losses could be carried forward indefinitely; and
- GBP 117 million in respect of unrelieved foreign tax carried forward, as there were no predicted future taxable profits against which the unrelieved foreign tax credits could be utilised. These tax credits could be carried forward indefinitely.

TABLE 13.13 Main sources of Lloyds' gross deferred tax assets

Sources of Lloyds' Gross DTAs (in GBP)	
Tax losses carried forward	5,758 mn
Accelerated capital allowances	682 mn
Allowances for impairment losses	5 mn
Other provisions	15 mn
Other temporary differences	573 mn
Total gross DTAs	7,033 mn

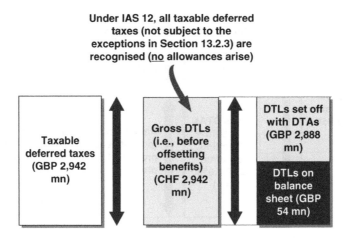

FIGURE 13.26 Structure of Lloyds' taxable deferred tax assets, as of year-end 2014

TABLE 13.14 Main sources of Lloyds' gross deferred tax liabilities

Sources of Lloyds' Gross DTLs (in GBP)	
Tax on fair value of acquired assets	1,072 mn
Long-term assurance business	944 mn
Derivatives (mostly cash flow hedges)	421 mn
Pensions and other post-retirement benefits	87 mn
Available-for-sale assets unrealised gains	13 mn
Effective interest rates	10 mn
Other temporary differences	395 mn
Total gross DTAs	2,942 mn

Lloyds' taxable deferred taxes totalled GBP 2,942 million. After setting off GBP 2,888 million of DTLs, the bank Lloyds disclosed in its consolidated balance sheet just GBP 54 million of DTLs, as shown in Figure 13.26. The sources of Lloyds' taxable deferred taxes is shown in Table 13.14.

13.7.2 Reconciliation of Accounting vs. Regulatory DTAs

It was mentioned in the previous section that Lloyds disclosed GBP 4,145 million of DTAs in its balance sheet. This was an accounting figure that had to be adjusted for regulatory purposes (see Figure 13.27). Lloyds performed the following adjustments from the accounting DTAs:

- Firstly, EUR 2,888 million of offsetting benefits between DTAs and DTLs achieved under IAS 12 were unwound. This resulted in GBP 7,033 million ($= 4,145\,mn + 2,888\,mn$) of accounting gross DTAs;

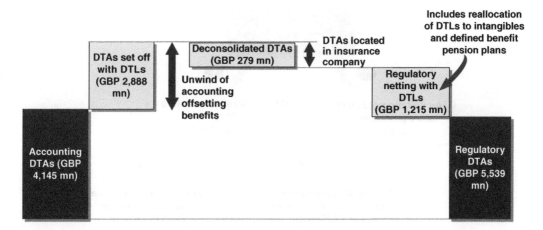

FIGURE 13.27 Reconciliation of Lloyds' accounting vs. regulatory DTAs, as of year-end 2014

- Secondly, DTAs and DTLs related to entities deconsolidated for regulatory purposes (primarily Lloyds' insurance business) were excluded from the amount of regulatory DTAs and DTLs. This adjustment reduced the amount of DTAs by GBP 279 million;
- Thirdly, any DTLs that have been used to reduce the deductions from CET1 capital stemming from intangible assets and defined benefit pension plans assets were excluded; and
- Finally, DTAs (that rely on future profitability) and DTLs that met the following regulatory netting requirements were netted out:
  - The bank had a legally enforceable right under applicable national law to set off those current tax assets against current tax liabilities; and
  - The DTAs and the DTLs related to taxes levied by the same taxation authority and on the same taxable entity.

As a result, for regulatory purposes, after performing these adjustments, Lloyds' DTAs totalled GBP 5,539 million.

13.7.3 Impact on CET1 Capital of Lloyds' DTAs

In order to determine the impact on CET1 capital of the GBP 5,539 million of regulatory DTAs, Lloyds followed the decision trees depicted in Figures 13.28 and 13.29.

1. Lloyds analysed whether any regulatory DTAs did *not* rely on future profitability. Commonly, these are DTAs monetisable into tax credits (see case study in Section 13.6). Lloyds concluded that it had no DTAs of this type and, thus, that all regulatory DTAs relied on future profitability;
2. Lloyds split the DTAs that relied on future profitability between DTAs that did *not* arise from temporary differences (GBP 4,533 million) (these DTAs arose from tax losses being carried forward) and those that *arose* from temporary differences (GBP 1,006 million);
3. The GBP 4,533 million of DTAs that did *not* arise from temporary differences were fully deducted from CET1 capital;
4. The GBP 1,006 million of DTAs that arose from temporary differences were subject to the 10% and 17.65% thresholds, which are covered next;
5. Lloyds calculated the relevant CET1 capital for the 10% threshold. Let us assume that the bank determined this CET1 capital to be GBP 33,240 million. The 10% threshold was, therefore, GBP 3,324 million (= $33,240 \text{ mn} \times 10\%$). As the amount of DTAs arising from temporary differences was GBP 1,006 million, the 10% threshold was not exceeded and, as a result, no amount of DTAs was required to be deducted in connection with the 10% threshold.

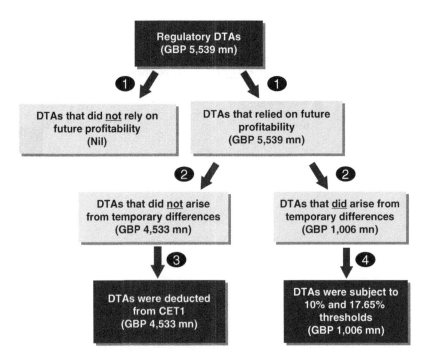

FIGURE 13.28   Calculation of regulatory impact of Lloyds' DTAs, as of year-end 2014 (part I of II)

6. Lloyds had GBP 5,870 million invested in CET1 instruments of other financial institutions, of which 2,546 million exceeded their 10% threshold (and, therefore, were deducted from CET1 capital) and GBP 3,324 million were below the 10% threshold (and, therefore, subject to the 17.65% threshold). From (5), the amount of DTAs that relied on future profitability that arose from temporary differences below the 10% threshold (i.e., the full GBP 1,006 million) was subject to the 17.65% threshold in conjunction with the amount of significant investments in CET1 instruments of other financial sector entities below their 10% threshold (GBP 3,324 million). Therefore, the aggregate amount subject to the 17.65% threshold was GBP 4,330 million (= 3,324 mn + 1,006 mn). Let us assume that the CET1 capital that's relevant for the 17.65% was GBP 26,364 million (basically, (i) the CET1 capital for the 10% threshold calculations (GBP 33,240 million), less (ii) the amount of DTAs that rely on future profitability and arise from temporary differences (GBP 1,006 million), less (iii) the amount of significant investments in CET1 instruments of other financial sector entities – GBP 5,870 million). The 17.65% threshold was at GBP 4,653 million (= 26,364 mn × 17.65%). Consequently, the full aggregate amount subject to the 17.65% threshold – GBP 4,330 million – was below the 17.65% threshold.

7. As a consequence of (6), all the GBP 1,006 million of DTAs that relied on future profitability and arose from temporary differences were risk-weighted. The risk weight was 250%, resulting in GBP 2,515 million (= 1,006 mn × 250%) of RWAs.

8. As the 17.65% threshold was not exceeded, no amount of DTAs that relied on future profitability and arose from temporary differences was deducted from CET1 capital.

In summary the effects of Lloyds' DTAs in the bank's CET1 capital ratio were the following (see Figure 13.30):

■ CET1 capital was reduced by GBP 4,533 million, stemming from DTAs that relied on future profitability excluding those arising from temporary differences (i.e., in the case of Lloyds, due to tax losses being carried forward); and

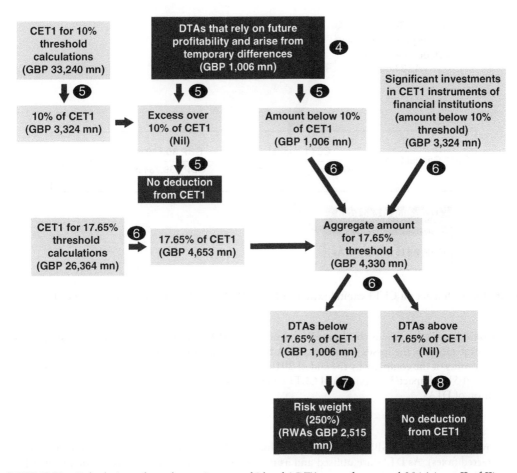

FIGURE 13.29 Calculation of regulatory impact of Lloyds' DTAs, as of year-end 2014 (part II of II)

■ RWAs were increased by GBP 2,515 million, representing just 1% of Lloyds' GBP 239,734 million RWAs.

The overall impact of Lloyds' DTAs on its CET1 capital ratio was a 205 basis points [= (30,689 mn + 4,533 mn) / (239,734 mn − 2,515 mn) − 12.8%] reduction, a notably relevant impact.

13.7.4 Analysis of Double Effect on CET1 Capital of DTAs Utilisation

As noted above, Lloyds reported GBP 30,689 million of fully loaded CET1 capital and a CET1 capital ratio of 12.8% at the end of 2014. Prior to the 50% restriction introduced by the British government in 2015 and assuming a 21% corporate tax rate, for every GBP 100 of taxable income generated the bank was able to utilise GBP 21 (= 100 × 21%) of previous years' tax losses. The overall effect on the CET1 capital would be a GBP 121 enhancement due to the following:

■ The GBP 100 income would be incorporated into CET1 capital through the profit or loss statement; and
■ The GBP 21 reduction in tax loss carry forwards would cause the deduction from CET1 capital, stemming from DTAs that rely on future profitability and that do not arise from temporary differences, to diminish by GBP 21.

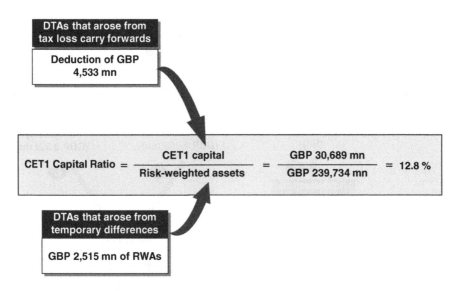

FIGURE 13.30   Impact on CET1 capital ratio of Lloyds' DTAs, as of year-end 2014 (part II of II)

Consequently, for Lloyds the degree of utilisation of DTAs was an important matter. Based on the bank's strategic plan, the losses on which a DTA had been recognised would be utilised against future taxable profits of the company by the end of 2019 (i.e., in 5 years). It meant that on average a 41 basis points (= 205 bps impact/5 years) annual CET1 enhancement was expected, which would stem from the utilisation of DTAs.

> However, Lloyds had GBP 921 million of valuation allowances (i.e., unrecognised deductible deferred taxes). As DTAs are utilised and as under UK rules tax losses can be carried forward indefinitely, valuation allowances may convert into DTAs as their probability of being utilised rises above 50%. In the case of Lloyds, it would be likely that, when the existing DTAs are utilised, those GBP 921 million of valuation allowances would become DTAs, which would be fully deducted from CET1 as they arose from tax loss carry forwards. Consequently, the CET1 benefits mentioned in the previous paragraph would be lower than the estimated 205 basis points.

13.7.5 Impact of British Government Changes in DTAs Utilisation Laws

In a plan to raise GBP 4 billion taxes from the banking sector over the following five years, in December 2014 the UK government announced a 50% restriction on the amount of a bank's annual taxable profit that could be offset by carried forward tax losses for the purposes of calculating income tax liabilities. In other words, only 50% of the income taxes could be paid using these DTAs. The restriction took effect in periods from 1 April 2015 onwards.

Given Lloyds' increasing profit generation capacity and the fact that tax losses could be carried forward indefinitely in the UK, the bank still expected to fully utilise, against probable future taxable profits, its British DTAs arising from tax loss carry forwards. Therefore, from an accounting perspective the new tax legislation did not have any impact on the amount of DTAs recognised.

The new legislation only slowed down the pace at which these DTAs would be used. Lloyd estimated that the new proposal would increase the period over which it expected to fully utilise its UK tax losses from 2019 to 2025. However, because DTA amounts are undiscounted, the slower pace did not change the amounts of these DTAs recognised in the balance sheet. In addition, as the level of DTAs recognised remained unchanged, Lloyds did not have to write off any portion of its DTAs.

As a result, from a regulatory capital perspective the new legislation had a neutral effect. However, it slowed the pace of generation of CET1 capital stemming from the utilisation of DTAs.

Interestingly, at that time the British government was Lloyds' largest shareholder. By implementing the new law, the government increased its tax revenues but, at the same time, reduced Lloyds' ability to distribute a hefty dividend to its shareholders. However, the British government was at the time gradually reducing its Lloyds holding, aiming at fully disposing its shareholding by 2015–2016.

Prior to the new law, investment banks were recommending Lloyds to negotiate with the British government the repurchase of the bank's shares held by the government, at a substantial discount to the market price, in exchange for surrounding its DTAs. The cancellation of the repurchased shares would immediately increase Lloyds' return on equity, raising the attractiveness of the bank among investors.

13.8 INITIATIVES TO REDUCE IMPACTS OF DEFERRED TAX ASSETS ON BANK CAPITAL

DTAs may have a substantial impact in the regulatory capital of banks. This section describes a general framework to identify initiatives to reduce such impact. The framework is illustrated using examples of initiatives taken by banks to address the impact of DTAs in regulatory capital.

13.8.1 Tax Planning Opportunities

It was mentioned in Section 13.1.2 that deductible deferred taxes arise from the following three types of sources:

- Those arising from temporary differences;
- Those arising from tax loss carry forwards; and
- Those arising from tax credit carry forwards.

Deductible Deferred Taxes Arising from Temporary Differences   Regarding deductible deferred taxes arising from temporary differences and following their "netting" with suitable taxable temporary differences and their utilisation of probable future taxable profits, **tax planning opportunities** are taken into account when a bank determines the extent to which an existing deductible temporary difference will be utilised (as shown in Figure 13.31). I am using the term "netting" rather than "offsetting" because both the DTAs and DTLs are presented separately in the bank balance sheet, rather than just being presented the excess of one over the other.

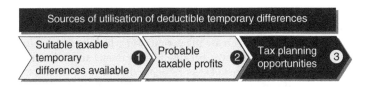

FIGURE 13.31   Sources of utilisation of deductible temporary differences

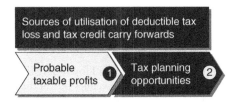

FIGURE 13.32   Sources of utilisation of deductible tax loss and tax credit carryforwards

Deductible Deferred Taxes Arising from Tax Loss and Tax Credit Carry Forwards   In the case of deductible deferred taxes stemming from tax loss and tax credit carry forwards, the assessment of their utilisation is simpler: tax planning opportunities are taken into account once the bank has concluded that probable future taxable profits are not enough to fully utilise these deductible deferred taxes, as shown in Figure 13.32.

Tax Planning Opportunities   A tax planning opportunity is an action that the bank would not normally take, except to prevent unused tax losses from expiring. The feasibility of a tax planning opportunity is assessed based on the individual facts and circumstances. In addition, management should be capable of undertaking and implementing them, and should have the expectation that it will implement them.

Tax planning opportunities are only considered to determine the extent to which an existing deductible temporary difference will be utilised (i.e., to determine whether a DTA or a valuation allowance should be recognised). They may not be used:

- To create a new DTA; or
- To reduce the recognition of DTLs.

In addition, consideration of tax-planning strategies is not optional: a bank cannot recognise the effect of only certain tax-planning strategies and postpone recognising the effect of other qualifying tax-planning strategies until later years if the valuation allowance still has a balance.

13.8.2 A General Framework for Identification of Initiatives

A first step on this journey is often the review of the bank's tax strategy and key tax objectives. Whilst highly dependent on each bank's particular facts and circumstances, potential initiatives to enhance the impact of DTAs on banking regulatory capital can be grouped into three types of initiatives (see Figure 13.33):

- First, initiatives to optimise the expected reversal of temporary differences;
- Second, initiatives to maximise the utilisation of deductible deferred taxes; and
- Third, initiatives to increase the setoff of DTAs and DTLs.

The first group of initiatives target deferred taxes arising from temporary differences only. The second and third groups are aimed at all three types of deferred taxes.

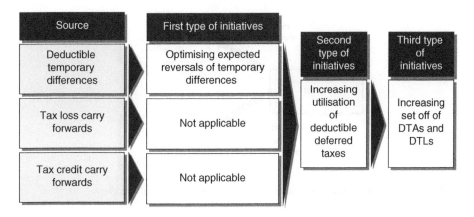

FIGURE 13.33 Types of initiative to enhance impact of deferred taxes on regulatory capital

Initiatives to Optimise the Expected Reversal of Temporary Differences It is highly recommended that prior to devising initiatives to optimise the expected reversal of temporary differences, the bank performs a thorough review of the differences between the income tax basis and the accounting reporting basis to gain comfort about the completeness and accuracy of such differences.

Once the true position of the pattern and timing of future reversals is determined, the bank implements initiatives to optimise the expected future reversal of temporary differences by shifting the estimated pattern and timing of such differences. For example, the sale of appreciated or depreciated financial instruments, classified as either at fair value through profit or loss or at fair value through OCI, may impact the timing of reversal of deferred taxes and/or type of income. With respect to timing of reversal of deferred taxes, the sale of appreciated (depreciated) financial instruments immediately reverses the taxable (deductible) deferred tax related to the instrument.

A better matching between deductible and taxable temporary differences may result in a higher amount of deductible temporary differences being recognised as DTAs.

Initiatives to Maximise the Utilisation of Deductible Deferred Taxes The initiatives to maximise the utilisation of deductible deferred taxes commonly aim at generating an extraordinary profit, or accelerating ordinary profit, against which such taxes can be utilised. These initiatives include:

- Sale and leaseback transactions. An example is covered in the case study in Section 13.8.6.
- Sale of non-strategic assets or businesses which are notably undervalued in the balance sheet.

Initiatives to Increase the Regulatory Netting of DTAs and DTLs It was covered in Section 13.5.2 that, from a regulatory capital perspective, the amounts of DTAs that rely on future profitability are calculated **net of related DTLs** where the following conditions are met [CRR 38(3)]:

1. The bank has a legally enforceable right under applicable national law to set off those current tax assets against current tax liabilities; and
2. The DTAs and the DTLs relate to taxes levied by the same taxation authority and on the same taxable entity.

Remember that DTLs used to reduce the deductions related to intangible assets and defined benefit pension plans cannot be used for netting with DTAs that rely on future profitability.

Most of the initiatives to optimise the regulatory netting of DTAs and DTLs involve corporate reorganisations in which entities with substantial DTLs are merged – from a tax perspective – with entities with substantial DTAs.

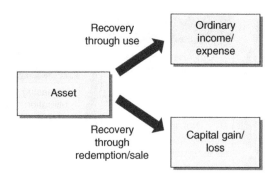

FIGURE 13.34 Recovery of an asset: ordinary income/expense vs. capital gain/loss

Other Initiatives Other initiatives typically aim at reducing the tax rate. Examples of these opportunities are:

- Changing the character of taxable or deductible amounts; and
- Changing the nature of the income.

13.8.3 Changing the Character of Taxable/Deductible Amounts

In some tax jurisdictions ordinary income (e.g., interest) is taxed differently to capital gains (e.g., sale of the asset at a price higher than its cost or settlement of a liability at a price lower than its issuance amount) (see Figure 13.34). When ordinary income is taxed at rates notably greater than those for capital gains, an initiative consists in changing the character of taxable amounts from ordinary gains to capital gains, or vice versa for ordinary losses.

13.8.4 Corporate Reorganisations

Corporate reorganisation initiatives consist in implementing changes in the legal structure in the countries where the DTAs have been originated. Tax losses incurred in one legal entity may be transferred to newly organised or reorganised subsidiaries or affiliates.

Imagine a Swiss bank that wholly owns a holding bank in the US that, in turn, wholly owns two US subsidiaries. Despite being in the same jurisdiction, these subsidiaries file different tax returns. Historically one of the subsidiaries has generated losses and has significant tax loss carry forwards. The other subsidiary has generated profits in the past, which are expected to continue in the foreseeable future.

The Swiss bank may consider whether to merge both subsidiaries or just to consolidate them for tax purposes. If the merged entity is expected to be profitable, it would utilise the tax loss carry forwards. In addition, any excess DTLs generated by the profitable subsidiary may be net against excess DTAs generated by the other subsidiary.

However, tax laws or the tax authorities in some jurisdictions prevent the transfer of tax losses or impose limitations on the utilisation of tax losses that are expected to carry on businesses formerly conducted by the transferor.

13.8.5 Case Study: HSBC's Reduction of Deductible Amounts through Retention of Capital Offshore

In 2014, HSBC implemented a **tax planning strategy** in the US, where a substantial part of its DTAs were located. The net DTAs relating to HSBC's operations in the US – HSBC USA – were USD 4.1 billion at year-end 2014. These DTAs stemmed from previous years' tax losses being carried forward which were caused by large losses in the bank's CDO portfolio during the 2008/09 financial crisis.

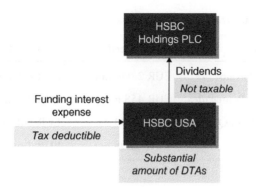

FIGURE 13.35 HSBC USA funding vs. dividends distributions

HSBC USA operations were funded by a large amount of external borrowings, while a substantial amount of dividends were regularly distributed to the parent bank. Interest on external borrowings was tax-deductible, as summarised in Figure 13.35.

The main problem with the DTAs at HSBC USA was that, at the time, US federal tax losses could be carried forward for a maximum period of 20 years. HSBC's tax planning strategy involved generating future taxable profits through the retention of capital in HSBC USA in excess of normal regulatory requirements in order to reduce deductible funding expenses or otherwise deploy such capital to increase levels of taxable income. HSBC expected that, with this strategy, the US operations would generate sufficient future profits to support the recognition of the DTAs. If HSBC Holdings were to decide not to provide this ongoing support, the full recovery of the DTA may no longer be probable and could result in a significant reduction of the DTA which would be recognised as a charge in the profit or loss statement. HSBC's projections of profits from the US operations indicated that tax losses and tax credits were to be fully recovered by 2017.

This type of initiative has to be carefully designed to make sure that the subsidiary retaining capital does not provoke an unwanted deduction from consolidated capital of the excess capital allocated to minority interests (see Chapter 9 for a detailed discussion on this Basel III deduction related to minority interests).

13.8.6 Case Study: Santander's Sale and Leaseback of its Headquarters

This case study illustrates a sale and leaseback transaction, an initiative that, although typically it aims at offsetting the impact of provisions in the profit or loss statement, it may help a bank to increase its utilisation of deductible deferred taxes.

In September 2008 the Spanish bank Santander completed the sale and leaseback of its head offices (Ciudad Financiera), at the time one of the largest real estate assets in Europe. The transaction was part of a strategy that commenced in 2007 to monetise hidden values of operating assets – mostly real estate – through their sale and simultaneous leaseback, generating a net profit for Santander of EUR 1,662 million, as shown in Table 13.15.

The sale and leaseback transactions undertaken by Santander were also implemented by a good number of banks. For example, Deutsche Bank in 2013 entered into a 15-year sale and leaseback arrangement on its global headquarters in Frankfurt am Main and HSBC did the same with its headquarters building in London, receiving GBP 1.09 billion cash through a 15-year transaction.

The disposal and leaseback of the Ciudad Financiera was structured as follows (see Figure 13.36):

1. Santander and Marme Inversiones 2007 SLU ("Marme") entered into a sale and leaseback agreement under which the bank sold Ciudad Financiera to Marme for a EUR 1.9 billion consideration.

TABLE 13.15   Sale and leaseback transactions undertaken by Santander

Real Estate Asset	Buyer	Sale Proceeds	After-tax Gain	Term
1,152 branches	Pearl Group	EUR 2,040 mn	EUR 860 mn	45–47 years
10 buildings	Grupo Pontegadea	EUR 458 mn	EUR 216 mn	40 years
Headquarters	Mr Maud/Quinlan	EUR 1,900 mn	EUR 586 mn	40 years
	Totals	EUR 4,398 mn	EUR 1,662 mn	

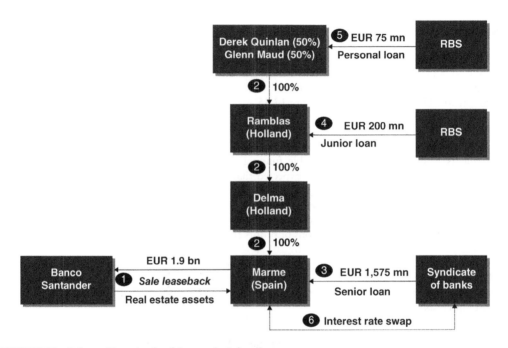

FIGURE 13.36   Sale and leaseback of Santander's headquarters

2. Marme was 100% owned by Delma Projectotwinkkeling ("Delma"), a Dutch SPV. Delma was in turn owned by Ramblas Investments BV, another Dutch SPV. Ramblas was owned on an equal basis by two investors, Glenn Maud and Derek Quinlan.

3. A five-year senior loan of EUR 1.6 billion was provided to Marme through a syndicate of banks headed by Royal Bank of Scotland (RBS). The senior loan could be accelerated on the occurrence of certain events. The main banks in the syndicate were RBS, Bayerische Landesbank, HSH Nordbank, Deutsche Postbank, ING and CaixaBank.

4. A EUR 200 million junior loan from RBS was provided to Ramblas. This was secured by, amongst other things, (i) a pledge executed by Mr Maud and Mr Quinlan over their shares in Ramblas in favour of RBS; (ii) a pledge executed by Ramblas over its shares in Delma; and (iii) a limited personal guarantee from Mr Maud and Mr Quinlan. This personal guarantee from Mr Maud and Mr Quinlan was secured by a number of instruments, the most relevant one being a charge given by Mr Quinlan in favour of RBS over shares and loan stock that he owned (directly or indirectly) in Coroin Ltd.

5. A EUR 75 million personal loan made to Mr Maud and Mr Quinlan by RBS and then loaned on by them to Marme. Mr Maud and Mr Quinlan were jointly and severally liable on this loan. This loan was also secured by a number of instruments, again the most relevant one being the charge given by Mr Quinlan in favour of RBS over his Coroin Ltd stake.
6. A 15-year interest rate swap between a group of banks (most notably RBS) and Marme. The purpose of this swap was to fix the Euribor interest payments under the senior loan. Of note is the substantially longer maturity of the swap (15 years) compared to that of the senior loan (5 years).

Santander could have structured the transaction as a securitisation. However, the credit crisis prevailing at that time made this alternative unfeasible at reasonable levels. There are three main drawbacks of traditional securitisation structures. Firstly, in a securitisation, rating agencies commonly require the selling bank to incorporate substantial equity tranches (or reserve funds) in the structure to credit enhance the more senior tranches, an expensive feature. Secondly, accounting derecognition of the assets being securitised is in practice challenging to achieve. Finally, regulatory retention rules reduce the capital relief attractiveness of these transactions.

A lease is an agreement whereby the lessor (Marme in our case) conveys to the lessee (Santander in our case) in return for a payment or series of payments the right to use an asset (Ciudad Financiera in our case) for an agreed period of time, a stream of cash flows that is essentially equivalent to the combination of principal and interest payments under a loan agreement. The main terms of the Ciudad Financiera sale and leaseback transaction are outlined in Table 13.16.

TABLE 13.16 Main terms of Santander's sale and leaseback transaction on its headquarters building complex

Ciudad Financiera Sale and Leaseback

Agreement date	12 September 2008
Lessor	Marme Inversiones 2007, SL
Lessee	Banco Santander SA
Asset	Ciudad Financiera
Term	40 year
Rent	Initially EUR 82.7 mn per annum, payable quarterly, subject to an annual inflation adjustment
Inflation adjustment	Annually, based on the variation in the preceding 12 months of the Eurozone Harmonised Consumer Price Index multiplied by 1.74 with a minimum of 2.20% (first 10 years only) and a maximum of 6% (whole term)
Call option	Santander had the right to repurchase the asset at the end of the 40-year term at its market value (to be determined by independent appraisers)
Other options	Right of first refusal by the Lessee if the Lessor wished to sell the Asset
Additional clause	The Lessee could require the Lessor to construct additional buildings in the campus or acquire additional land (from the third year onwards) with a maximum total cost of EUR 296 mn which would be subsequently included in the lease

There were four noteworthy additional features of the leaseback agreement, which helped the transaction to be categorised as an operating lease:

- Firstly, it did *not* provide for the mandatory transfer of ownership of the property back to Santander on expiry thereof;
- Secondly, although Santander had the right to buy back the property, its exercise at fair value made it reasonably uncertain its exercise;
- Thirdly, although Santander had the right to extend the lease, the bank was entitled to *not* to renew the rentals beyond the minimum compulsory term; and
- Finally, Santander did *not* grant any guarantee to the buyers for any losses that might arise from the early termination of the agreements or for possible fluctuations in the residual value of the property.

> Banco Santander recognised a EUR 586 million after-tax gain (EUR 836 million pre-tax gain) in the profit or loss statement on the sale of its headquarters. Under the international accounting standard for leases prevailing at that time, IAS 17 Leases, the gain or loss resulting from the difference between the sale price (if executed at fair market value) and the book value of an asset in a operating lease was recognised at the time of sale in profit or loss.
>
> - A lease was classified as a **finance lease** when it substantially transferred all the risks and rewards incidental to ownership of the asset forming the subject-matter of the contract.
> - A lease was classified as **operating lease** when it was not a financial lease.
>
> Operating leases did not result in a recognition of an asset. In other words, the leased asset was fully derecognised from Santander's balance sheet. Thus, from a regulatory capital perspective, the sale and leaseback transaction was notably beneficial for Santander: it recognised a substantial profit while avoiding having to recognise RWAs associated with the leased asset.

Leases under the Current IFRS Accounting Standard

Leases under the current international accounting standards are accounted for as either Type A or Type B leases. Leases of **property** (land and buildings) are presumed to qualify for **Type B**. **Type A** applies only if:

- The lease is for the major part of the asset's remaining economic life; or
- The present value of payments accounts for substantially all of the asset's fair value.

  For all non-property assets, the Type A recognition pattern applies. Type B is only permitted when:

- The lease is for an insignificant part of the economic life of the underlying asset; or
- The present value of future lease payments is insignificant relative to the asset's fair value.

  In our case, the Ciudad Financiera would have been classified as a Type B lease. Santander would have recognised:

- An asset representing the right-of-use asset and a lease liability. The asset would have been amortised over the life of the lease;
- A liability representing Santander's obligation to make lease payments; and
- The amortisation of the asset and interest expense on the financial liability would have been recognised in profit or loss, as to achieve an annual constant lease charge.

Therefore, from a capital perspective, the old accounting treatment of leases was notably more advantageous as no asset was recognised. Under the current lease standard, Santander would have to risk-weight the asset.

Sales and leaseback strategies generate taxable income which may be utilised, for example to accelerate the utilisation of tax loss carry forwards before they expire.

13.8.7 Case Study: Citigroup's Purchase of Credit Card Loan Portfolio and Agreement with Costco

This case study illustrates how a bank may increase its utilisation of DTAs through the purchase of income producing assets. In addition, the case study highlights that a substantial holding of DTAs can be a strategic weapon.

Acquisition of Best Buys' Credit Card Portfolio   In February 2013, Citi Retail Services – a subsidiary of Citigroup – agreed to buy a portfolio of USD 7 billion in credit card loans to Best Buy – a leader in consumer electronics – customers from Capital One Financial.

Citi Retail Services provided consumer and commercial credit card products, services, and retail solutions to national and regional retailers across North America. The business serviced nearly 90 million accounts for a number of iconic brands, including The Home Depot, Macy's, Sears, Shell and ExxonMobil. The purchase of the credit card loan portfolio significantly expanded the entity's already strong position as a market leader in private label and co-branded credit cards.

Agreement with CostCo   In 2015 Citigroup won the exclusive right to issue credit cards for Costco Wholesale Corporation ("Costco"). Several months prior to the agreement, American Express announced that it would not renew its deal with Costco because the retailer was demanding terms that were not economic, an indication that the profit margins for anyone taking on the business were likely to be notably thin.

Author's Comments on this Case Study   Citigroup held a very large amount of DTAs which stemmed from the USD billions of losses it generated during the 2008–09 financial crisis. Citigroup was rescued three times by the US government during that period, and one of the rescues threatened to wipe out some of the bank's DTAs. However, the US Treasury and the Internal Revenue Service – which were concerned about the stability of the banking system – relaxed the rules governing such assets to help Citigroup and other banks during the crisis.

Even though the American bank had been using DTAs in the years following the financial crisis, it created new ones through provisions mainly stemming from mortgage litigation settlements. For example, Citigroup's DTA's grew by about USD 3.8 billion in 2012. At the end of 2014, following the utilisation of about USD 3 billion of DTAs to reduce tax liability during that year, Citigroup still had USD 49.5 billion in DTAs. Citigroup's two most important source of taxable domestic income at that time were its investment banking and its credit card businesses.

For Citigroup, utilising such a large amount of DTAs was not an easy task. Assuming a 30% tax rate, the bank had to generate USD 165 billion (= 49.5bn / 30%) in taxable domestic income in order to use all of its DTAs and buying US assets was one way to achieve that goal. Furthermore, some of the DTAs would expire after a certain period. For example, the US federal and New York state and city net operating losses could be carried forward for a period of 20 years.

Tax planning strategies available to Citigroup, especially to prevent tax loss carry forwards from expiring, included:

- Repatriating low-taxed foreign source earnings for which an assertion that the earnings have been indefinitely reinvested has not been made;
- Accelerating US taxable income into, or deferring US tax deductions out of, the latter years of the carry-forward period (e.g., selling appreciated assets, electing straight-line depreciation);
- Accelerating deductible temporary differences outside the US;

- Selling certain assets that produce tax-exempt income, while purchasing assets that produce fully taxable income; and
- Selling or restructuring of certain businesses that could produce significant US taxable income within the relevant carry-forward periods.

DTAs gave Citigroup a strategic advantage: the bank's DTAs allowed it to offer Capital One Financial and Costco better terms than competitors could. Banks without sufficient deductible deferred tax balances could pay as much as 35% of their US income in federal tax. In contrast, Citigroup was likely to eliminate its federal income tax liability by utilising deductible deferred taxes.

Despite their advantage resulting from the potential utilisation of DTAs, these two transactions were not without risks for Citigroup, especially in the event of an economic downturn that would cause more cardholders to default on payments. However, the short-to-medium term maturity of credit card loans could allow the bank to adjust its credit eligibility standards down the road.

In addition, the urge to utilise DTAs could lead Citigroup to overpay or to embark in transactions that made inadequate strategic sense.

CHAPTER 14

Asset Protection Schemes and Bad Banks

This chapter covers in detail two asset protection schemes (APSs): one between the Dutch bank ING and the Dutch state and a second one between the British bank RBS and the British state. APSs are de-risking (often referred to as deleveraging) transactions in which banks transfer the credit risk on certain assets. This book is about the numerator of the capital ratios, so why devote a chapter to APSs? Whilst their main benefit on capital is through a substantial reduction of RWAs, APSs reduce volatility of CET1 capital by reducing volatility of earnings. Furthermore, APSs are often accompanied by capital raising transactions.

In addition, this chapter covers the set-up of bad banks by covering the Spanish bad bank, SAREB, and compares this type of solution with APSs.

> An interesting element of APSs is that they usually take place when equity capital markets are closed (or prohibitively expensive) and asset prices are trapped in a downward spiral. Through APSs desperate banks tap their governments to protect particularly risky assets and raise much-needed capital.
>
> The main objective of the arguably high requirements of capital under Basel III, the conversion or write-down of AT1 instruments and other measures is to keep banks solvent, avoiding the need for future state aid. However, and I hope I am mistaken, a bank in a difficult financial situation (e.g., breaching AT1 conversion trigger levels) may face liquidity problems and deteriorating operating results. As future prospects suffer, its credit ratings may drop, its ability to lend and access funding will be further limited and its cost of funding may increase.
>
> In such a precarious situation only state intervention may restore trust from banking counterparts and customers. Thus, I am afraid that APSs are not obsolete tools.

14.1 ING'S ILLIQUID ASSET BACK-UP FACILITY WITH THE DUTCH STATE

This case study covers in detail the mechanics, and the accounting and regulatory impacts of a set of initiatives undertaken by the Dutch bank ING Groep N.V. ("ING") to protect it from a credit deterioration of certain assets and to strengthen its capital levels.

14.1.1 Overview

After the unprecedented shockwave that hit financial markets in 2008, ING undertook several transactions with the Dutch state to strengthen its capital base and reduce its credit risk exposure:

- In November 2008, a issuance of EUR 10 billion of capital securities to the Dutch state, aimed at strengthening ING's regulatory capital;
- In January 2009, as prices for structured assets plummeted, an agreement between ING and the Dutch state on an Illiquid-Assets Back-up Facility with respect to 80% of ING's Alt-A residential mortgage-backed securities; and
- In December 2009, an execution of a EUR 7.5 billion rights issue. ING used part of the proceeds to repurchase EUR 5 billion of the capital securities from the Dutch state.

14.1.2 Issuance of Capital Securities – Terms, Accounting and Regulatory Impacts

On 12 November 2008, ING issued capital securities for a total consideration of EUR 10 billion to the Dutch state, with the following main terms:

- Nominal and issue proceeds: EUR 10 billion;
- Maturity: perpetual;
- Voting rights: non-voting (i.e., they did not carry voting rights at ING's general shareholders meetings);
- Rank: pari-passu with ordinary shares in a winding up of ING;
- Coupon: the higher of: (a) 8.5% per security, payable annually in arrears, with a first coupon of EUR 4.25% paid on 12 May 2009; and (b) 110% of the dividend paid on each ordinary share over 2009 (payable in 2010), 120% of the dividend paid on each ordinary share over 2010 (payable in 2011), and 125% of the dividend paid on each ordinary share over 2011 onwards (payable from 2012 onwards). Since ING had already paid an interim dividend of EUR 0.74 per ordinary share in August 2008, ING recognised a coupon payable of EUR 425 million to the Dutch state as of 31 December 2008. This coupon was paid out on 12 May 2009. Further coupons were to be paid on 12 May of each year (the coupon date) in cash if the dividend on ordinary shares was paid in cash or in scrip securities (in the event of a scrip dividend on ordinary shares). Coupons were only due and payable, on a non-cumulative basis and if a dividend was paid on ordinary shares over the financial year preceding the coupon date, either on an interim or a final dividend basis, provided that ING's capital adequacy position was and remained satisfactory both before and after payment in the opinion of the Dutch central bank. Coupon was non-tax-deductible;
- Call right: ING had the right to repurchase all or some of the capital securities at 150% of the issue price, together with the pro-rata coupon, accrued to such date. ING and the Dutch state agreed in October 2009 that up to EUR 5 billion of the EUR 10 billion securities could be repurchased at any time until 31 January 2010 at 100% of the original issue price, plus a repurchase premium and accrued interest. Repurchase of the securities needed approval by the Dutch Central Bank;
- Conversion right: ING had the right to convert all or some of the securities into ordinary shares on the basis of one security for 1.335 ordinary shares or bearer depositary receipts from three years after the issue date onwards, subject to certain conditions. The Dutch state in that case had the right to demand a cash redemption payment per security of 100% of its issue price, together with the pro-rata coupon, if due, accrued to such date. Conversion of the securities needed approval by the Dutch Central Bank;
- Other: the securities were non-transferable.

Due to ING's discretion over the payment of coupons and their perpetual maturity the capital securities were classified as equity instruments from an accounting perspective. The accounting entries to recognise the issuance of the securities on 12 November 2008 (in EUR million):

Cash (Asset)	€ 10,000
Capital securities (Equity)	€ 10,000

Thus, the capital securities issuance strengthened ING's shareholders' equity.

A full coupon (i.e., dividend) amount of EUR 425 million was recognised as a liability on 12 November 2008 (entries in EUR million):

Retained earnings (Equity)	€ 425
Coupon payable (Liability)	€ 425

The coupon was paid on 12 May 2009 (entries in EUR million):

Coupon payable (Liability)	€ 425
Cash (Asset)	€ 425

The main objective of the issuance was to strengthen ING's capital levels. The regulatory regime prevailing at the time was Basel II. The Dutch central bank allowed the issue to be recognised as Basel II's Core Tier 1 capital. Thus this type of capital increased by the EUR 10 billion proceeds.

Under the Basel III regime, the equity securities would not have qualified as CET1 or AT1 instruments, but as Tier 2 instruments. Thus, were Basel III to be applicable at the time, it is highly likely that the terms of the securities under Basel III would have probably been different, probably in the form of non-voting ordinary shares.

The declared coupon/dividend would have reduced ING's CET1 capital as retained earnings diminished by an amount equivalent to the declared amount.

14.1.3 Illiquid Asset Back-up Facility (IABF) – Terms, Accounting and Regulatory Impacts

In the fourth quarter of 2008 market conditions deteriorated even further, making it the worst quarter for equity and credit markets in over half a century. Market prices for residential mortgage-backed securities (RMBSs, including Alt-A classified RMBSs), collateralised debt obligations (CDOs) and collateralised loan obligations (CLOs) fell sharply as liquidity dried up. Because ING held a large portfolio of Alt-A RMBSs classified at fair value through other comprehensive income (in reality the bonds were classified in a similar category under IAS 39 called available for sale), ING shareholders' equity was negatively impacted by (i) large impairment charges in profit or loss related to the portfolio and (ii) large reductions in other comprehensive income due to the enormous reduction in the portfolio's fair value not being impaired.

These negative effects in profit or loss and other comprehensive income had a knock-on effect on ING's regulatory capital position. In addition, the sharp credit rating downgrades on the portfolio increased the bank's RWAs, deteriorating further ING's regulatory capital levels.

With the objective of protecting the bank from a credit deterioration of its Alt-A portfolio, on 26 January 2009 ING reached an agreement with the Dutch state on an Illiquid Asset Back-up Facility ("IABF"). The transaction closed on 31 March 2009. Under the IABF, ING transferred 80% of the economic ownership of its Alt-A portfolio, with a par value of approximately EUR 30 billion, to the

FIGURE 14.1   Transfer pricing of 80% of ING's Alt-A portfolio

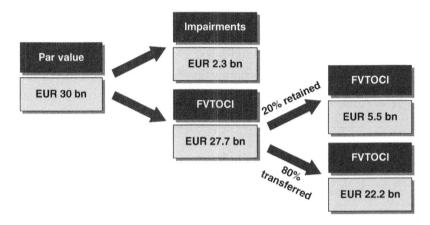

FIGURE 14.2   Recognition of 80% of ING's Alt-A portfolio

Dutch state. As a result, an undivided 80% interest in the risk and rewards on the portfolio was transferred to the Dutch state. Nonetheless, ING retained 100% of the legal ownership of its Alt-A portfolio.

The transaction price was EUR 21.6 billion, 90% of the EUR 30 billion par value with respect to the 80% proportion of the portfolio of which the Dutch state had become the economic owner, as shown in Figure 14.1. The Dutch state also acquired certain consent rights with respect to the sale or transfer of the 20% proportion of the Alt-A portfolio that was retained by ING.

The IABF included an early exit mechanism. Each year ING and the state could discuss whether the parties wished to terminate the IABF agreement. Upon voluntary termination ING was obliged to pay to the Dutch state an amount equal to the fair market value of the remaining part of the 80% Alt-A portfolio.

Although the transferred Alt-A portfolio was previously included in the old IAS 39 available-for-sale category, I have assumed that it was recognised at fair value through other comprehensive income (FVTOCI). The carrying amount, after prior impairments at the transaction date was approximately EUR 22.2 billion (see Figure 14.2).

The cash flows of the IABF transaction during its life are shown in Figure 14.3:

1. ING being the legal owner of the Alt-A securities, received the interest and principal paid by the Alt-A securities issuers;
2. ING passed through 80% of the cash flows received to the Dutch state;
3. The Dutch state did not pay upfront to ING, but during the life of the transaction. As a result, ING recognised two receivables to be redeemed over the remaining life. The Dutch state paid interest and principal on the receivables. The first receivable initially had a funding fee of 3.5% and the second receivable initially had a funding fee of Libor plus 50 basis points;
4. ING received a management fee from Dutch state;
5. ING paid a guarantee fee to the Dutch state.

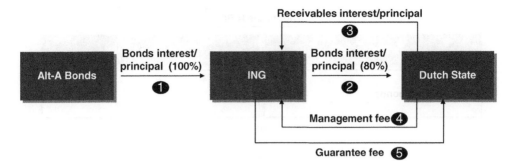

FIGURE 14.3 Main flows of ING's IABF during its life

The net present values of the management and guarantee fees were EUR 700 million and EUR 600 million, respectively.

As a result of the transaction ING derecognised 80% of the Alt-A portfolio from its balance sheet and recognised a receivable from the Dutch state. The transaction resulted in a pre-tax loss in the first quarter of 2009 of EUR 500 million. The accounting entries to recognise the IABF on its 31 March 2009 closing date (entries in EUR million):

Loans and advances to customers (Asset)	€ 21,600
Management fee (Asset)	€ 700
Other financial expense (P&L)	€ 500
Alt-A bonds (Asset)	€ 22,200
Guarantee fee (Liability)	€ 600

The recognition of the remaining 20% Alt-A portfolio remained in ING's balance sheet, unaltered by the IABF. ING's balance sheet situation prior and after the IABF is summarised in Figure 14.4, showing that ING replaced the 80% Alt-A portfolio with mainly Dutch state risk.

14.1.4 Adjustments Required by the EU – Accounting Treatment

Under European state-aid rules, all state-supported financial institutions needed to demonstrate their long-term viability and take actions to prevent undue distortions of competition. ING was required to submit a restructuring plan, pursuant to which ING was required to divest by the end of 2013 all of its insurance businesses and its investment management business, as well as ING Direct US and certain portions of its retail banking business in the Netherlands. The EC's approval of the restructuring plan was issued on 18 November 2009.

In connection with the overall agreement with the EC, ING agreed to make additional IABF payments to the Dutch state in the form of a reduction of 50 basis points on the monthly funding fee received by ING and an increase of 82.6 basis points on the annual guarantee fee paid by ING. In total, these annual extra payments amounted to a net present value of EUR 1.3 billion pre-tax, which was recognised as a one-off charge in the fourth quarter of 2009, shown in the entries below (in EUR million):

Other financial expense (P&L)	€ 1,300
IABF additional fee (Liability)	€ 1,300

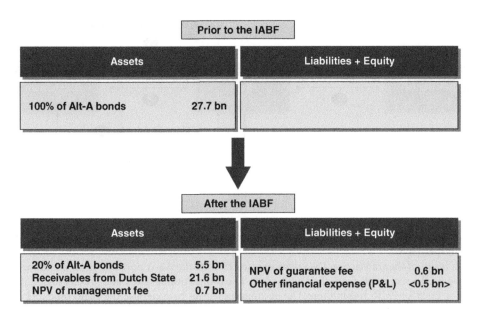

FIGURE 14.4   ING's balance sheet before and after the IABF

Also in connection with the overall agreement with the EC, the fair value of the transferred 80% Alt-A portfolio was estimated. ING's internal models came up with a EUR 15.2 billion valuation, an amount accepted by the EC. The difference between the total sales proceeds of EUR 20.4 billion (EUR 21.6 billion plus the EUR 700 million management fee minus the EUR 600 million guarantee fee minus the EUR 1.3 billion additional charge) and the EUR 15.2 billion fair value represented a "government grant" under IAS 20. This government grant was considered to be an integral part of the transaction and was therefore accounted for as part of the result on the transaction.

Under IFRS, government grants were recognised where there was reasonable assurance that the grant will be received and all attached conditions will be complied with. When the grant related to an expense item, the grant was recognised over the period necessary to match the grant on a systematic basis to the expense that it was intended to compensate. In such case, the grant was deducted from the related expense in the profit and loss account.

14.1.5 Rights Issue and Repurchase of Capital Securities – Accounting Treatment

In November 2009, ING's board of directors and shareholders approved a EUR 7.5 billion rights issue. Its main objectives were to raise funds to repay half of the capital securities held by the Dutch state, to mitigate the capital impact of the EUR 1.3 billion additional payments for the IABF and to further strengthen ING's capital position. The rights issue was successfully completed on 21 December 2009. Eligible rights holders could subscribe for 6 new ordinary shares in relation to every 7 subscription rights that they held. The issue price was set at EUR 4.24 per share. This represented a discount of 37.3% to the Theoretical Ex-Rights Price (TERP), based on the closing price of EUR 8.92 of ING's shares on 26 November 2009. A total of 1,768,412,544 ordinary shares were offered and sold. As a result, ING received EUR 7,276 million in proceeds, net of fees and expenses. The accounting entries to recognise the issuance of the new shares (in EUR million):

Cash (Asset)	€ 7,276
Share capital (Equity)	€ 424
Share premium (Equity)	€ 6,852

ING repurchased half of the capital securities. The total payment amounted to EUR 5,605 million and comprised (i) a repayment of the EUR 5 billion principal amount plus (ii) an accrued coupon of EUR 259 million and (iii) a premium of EUR 346 million.

Capital securities (Equity)	€ 5,000
Retained earnings (Equity)	€ 259
Other reserves (Equity)	€ 346
Cash (Asset)	€ 5,605

14.1.6 Final Remarks

Asset protection programmes commonly try to achieve a series of benefits. As shown in Figure 14.5. ING's IABF achieved most of these benefits:

- ING's earnings were significantly de-risked by reducing the uncertainty regarding the impact on ING of any future losses in the Alt-A securities portfolio. The Dutch state took an 80% share of any future impairment and potential write-backs on the portfolio. The transaction resulted in a significant reduction of earnings volatility;
- On the balance sheet, 80% of ING's Alt-A portfolio was derecognised from an accounting perspective. In other words, the IABF was equivalent to a synthetic sale of the portfolio;
- ING did not raise new funding through the IABF. The derecognised assets were replaced with two receivables from the Dutch state, a much stronger credit. Nonetheless, the issuance of capital securities and the rights issue provided ING with new funding;

FIGURE 14.5 ING's IABF – summary of potential benefits (excluding capital securities and rights issues)

- The IABF transaction, excluding the rights issue, had a negative effect ING's CET1 capital ratio. The IABF transaction reduced RWAs by approximately EUR 13 billion, which resulted in a EUR 1,040 million (=13 bn × 8%) CET1 benefit, assuming an 8% minimum CET1 capital ratio requirement. This benefit was eclipsed by the loss of EUR 500 million and the one-off charge of EUR 1.3 billion which reduced CET1 capital. As mentioned above, the design of the capital securities was aimed at strengthening Basel II's Core Tier 1 capital but did not qualify as Basel III CET1 instruments while its costly dividend had a negative impact on CET1 when declared. Nonetheless, the rights issue provided ING with new CET1 capital; and
- The IABF allowed ING to early exit the transaction, albeit at market value.

The IABF limited ING's decision making, especially regarding dividends, commitments to lend to Dutch corporates and top management compensation. The coupon paid to the Dutch state was not fixed as it was a function of normal dividends, floored at 8.5%. Any time ING distributed a dividend to its shareholders, it was obliged to pay a coupon to the Dutch state, non-tax-deductible, which impaired the bank's ability to pay or increase the dividend. Also, as long as the Dutch state held at least 25% of the capital securities, the IABF was in place or any of the government guaranteed senior unsecured bonds issued by ING under the Credit Guarantee Scheme of the Netherlands were outstanding, ING was prohibited from issuing or repurchasing any own ordinary shares (other than as part of regular hedging operations and the issuance of shares according to employment schemes) without the consent of the Dutch state's nominees on ING's supervisory board.

14.2 ROYAL BANK OF SCOTLAND'S ASSET PROTECTION SCHEME

In this section another real-life asset protection scheme is covered. In contrast with ING's, RBS's scheme did not achieve accounting derecognition of the protected portfolio of assets.

14.2.1 Overview of the UK Government's Assistance

During the credit crisis of 2008–09, the UK government provided assistance to the British bank Royal Bank of Scotland Group ("RBS") through several actions. The aid started in 2008 after RBS experienced large impairment losses and write-downs (in 2008 RBS reported a net loss of GBP 7.2 billion, which included goodwill write-downs of GBP 16.2 billion) and continued during 2009 as the challenging financial market and economic conditions remained. Several times RBS sought help from the UK government to enable it to weather the very testing environment and to achieve the higher capital ratios that markets demanded, as summarised in Figure 14.6:

- Firstly, in October 2008 RBS issued to the UK government non-cumulative preference shares for a total consideration of GBP 5 billion;
- Secondly, in December 2008 RBS issued 22.9 billion ordinary shares ("A shares") raising GBP 14.7 billion. The UK government acquired 22.9 billion of these shares and as a result held 57.9% of RBS's ordinary share capital;
- Thirdly, in April 2009 RBS redeemed the GBP 5 billion preference shares held by the UK government and financed it by issuing ordinary shares. In total, the UK government acquired approximately 16.8 billion new ordinary shares at 31.75p per share. Following the conversion, the UK government owned 70.3% of RBS's issued ordinary share capital. This move increased RBS's Basel II's Core Tier 1 capital by GBP 5 billion and saved an annual GBP 0.6 billion cost of preference dividends; and
- Finally, in December 2009 RBS and UK government agreed to an additional state aid in which the latter:
  - Subscribed for GBP 26.5 billion of B shares at a subscription price of 50p;
  - Acceded to an Asset Protection Scheme ("APS"), providing loss protection against potential losses arising from a pool of assets;

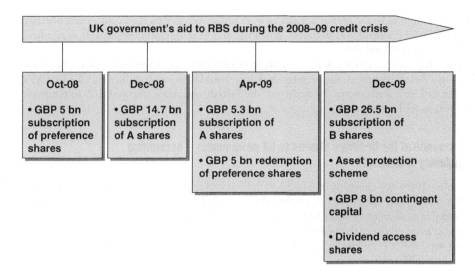

FIGURE 14.6 UK government's aid to RBS during the 2008–09 credit crisis

- Provided a further GBP 8 billion of capital in the form of B shares, potentially available as contingent capital; and
- Received dividend access shares.

In October 2012 RBS exited the APS, the earliest date at which that was possible.

14.2.2 Issuance of the Preference Shares to the UK government – Accounting and Regulatory Treatment

Pursuant to an agreement effective as of 13 October 2008 between RBS and the UK government, RBS issued to the UK government 5 million non-cumulative preference shares for a total consideration of GBP 5 billion. The preference shares entitled the UK government to receive periodic non-cumulative cash dividends at a 12% fixed rate payable out of RBS's distributable profits. From 2 December 2013 RBS had the right to redeem at any time, in whole or in part, at par plus dividends otherwise payable for the then current dividend period accrued to the date of redemption.

On a winding-up or liquidation of RBS, the holders of the non-cumulative preference shares ranked prior to ordinary shareholders. Therefore, as regards the participation in the surplus assets of the company available for distribution, their holders (and the holders of other instruments ranking pari passu with the non-cumulative preference shares) were entitled to receive (after payment of arrears of dividends on the cumulative preference shares up to the date of repayment), before any distribution or payment could be made to ordinary shareholders, a liquidation distribution per share equal to their redemption price together with an amount equal to dividends for the then current dividend period accrued to the date of payment.

The preference shares were classified as equity instruments because their maturity was perpetual and their dividend distributions were discretionary and non-cumulative. The accounting entries to recognise the issuance of the preference shares (in GBP million):

Cash (Asset)	5,000
Preference shares (Equity)	5,000

Any distributions to the preference shares were recognised as a payable and a reduction of retained earnings when the dividend was declared. When the dividend was paid the payable was cancelled and the cash account was credited.

From a regulatory capital perspective, the issue of preference shares took place when Basel II was in effect. In a Basel III context, the preference shares would have not qualified as CET1 or AT1 instruments, but as Tier 2 instruments. Nonetheless, the British supervisor allowed RBS to temporarily recognise them as AT1 instruments.

14.2.3 Issuance of the Ordinary Shares to UK government – Accounting and Regulatory Treatment

In December 2008, the company issued 22.91 billion ordinary shares of 25p each at 65.5p per share through a placing and open offer. This offer, which was fully underwritten by the UK government, was made available to shareholders on 31 October 2008. The related placing expenses were EUR 265 million. The net proceeds were then GBP 14.7 billion (= 22.91 bn shares × 0.655 − 265 mn). The share capital issued was GBP 5.73 billion (= 22.91 bn shares × 0.25). The accounting entries to recognise the share placement (in GBP million):

Cash (Asset)	14,700
Share capital (Equity)	5,723
Share premium (Equity)	8,977

From a regulatory capital perspective the ordinary shares would have qualified as CET1 instruments and, as a result, RBS's CET1 capital would have increased by GBP 14.7 billion.

14.2.4 Issuance of New Ordinary Shares and Redemption of the Preference Shares – Accounting and Regulatory Treatment

In April 2009, RBS issued 16.8 billion ordinary shares of 25p by way of a placing and open offer to their existing shareholdings at a fixed price of 31.75p on the basis of three new shares for every seven existing shares, raising GBP 5.33 billion. Any shares not taken up by shareholders in the open offer (or otherwise placed on behalf of the company) were subscribed for by UK government at 31.75p per share. This resulted in the UK government's shareholding increasing by 16.8 billion ordinary shares to 70.3% of RBS's ordinary share capital. The accounting entries to recognise the issuance of the ordinary shares (in GBP million):

Cash (Asset)	5,334
Share capital (Equity)	4,200
Share premium (Equity)	1,134

Following the ordinary shares placement, on 14 April 2009 RBS redeemed the GBP 5 billion preference shares held by the UK government at 101% of their issue price (i.e., GBP 5.05 billion) and paid a GBP 171 million (= 5 bn × 12% × 104 days / 365 days) representing the dividend accrued on these shares from 1 December 2008 to the date of redemption. The accounting entries to recognise the redemption of the preference shares (in GBP million):

Preference shares (Equity)	5,000
Retained earnings (Equity)	171
Share premium (Equity)	50
Cash (Asset)	5,221

From a Basel III perspective, the issuance of ordinary shares strengthened RBS's CET1 capital by GBP 5,334 million. The repurchase of the preference shares reduced RBS's CET1 capital by GBP 221 million, comprising a GBP 171 million reduction in retained earnings and a GBP 50 million reduction in share premium. As mentioned above, the preference shares were at the time recognised as AT1 instruments following a temporary permission by the British supervisor and, as a consequence, the repurchase reduced RBS's AT1 capital by GBP 5 billion.

14.2.5 Terms of the Asset Protection Scheme and Issuance of the B Shares

The UK government provided protection against potential credit losses arising from a pool of approximately GBP 282 billion par value of assets, including approximately 39 billion of credit derivatives (see Table 14.1). The portfolio included historic impairments as at 31 December 2008 of GBP 21.3 billion.

The protection was subject to a first loss of 21.3% of the portfolio par value (i.e., GBP 60 billion) and covered 90% of any subsequent losses (see Figures 14.7 and 14.8). Therefore, receipts from the UK government, over time, would amount to 90% of cumulative losses (net of cumulative recoveries) on the portfolio of covered assets less the first loss amount. Trigger events on the covered assets were:

- Failure to pay: the counterparty to the covered asset failed (subject to specified grace periods) to pay an amount due under the terms of its agreement with RBS;
- Bankruptcy: the counterparty was subject to a specified insolvency or bankruptcy-related event; or
- Restructuring: a covered asset which was individually impaired and was subject to a restructuring.

TABLE 14.1 Asset types covered by RBS's asset protection scheme

Asset type	Covered Amount (GBP Billion)
Residential mortgages	15.4
Consumer finance	54.5
Commercial real estate	39.9
Leveraged finance	27.7
Lease finance	2.4
Project finance	2.2
Structured finance	19.3
Loans	80.0
Bonds	1.6
Derivatives	39.0
Total	**282.0**

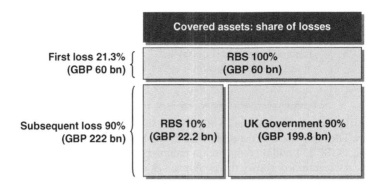

FIGURE 14.7   RBS's APS – Share of losses

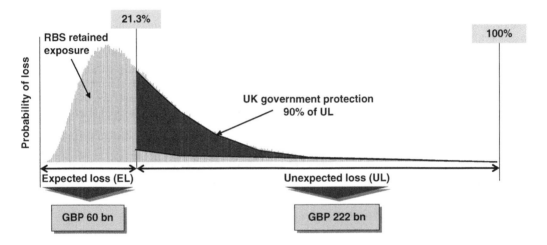

FIGURE 14.8   RBS's APS – Share of losses split between expected and unexpected losses

First Loss   The UK government set the 21.3% first loss (i.e., GBP 60 billion) equal to its estimate of the losses likely to be incurred by RBS under the most likely economic scenario. In other words, the 21.3% first loss was set at the expected losses level of the portfolio, as shown in Figure 14.8. Therefore, the APS only provided protection against further losses if the economy performed below expectations. Setting the first loss at or above the expected loss was crucial in providing the right incentive to the bank to manage the protected assets effectively: up to the first loss, all losses were borne by the bank. The UK government conducted extensive due diligence on the assets proposed by RBS for the APS and designed a series of stress scenarios which were used to calculate the expected losses. As graphed in Figure 14.9, the UK government estimated that expected losses would peak between 2012 and 2013, slightly exceeding the first loss, but subsequent recoveries were expected to keep the life-time expected net loss at GBP 57 billion, just below the agreed GBP 60 billion first loss.

Second Loss   The UK treasury covered 90% of losses net of recoveries incurred in excess of the first loss (the "second loss"). The objective of the 10% share of the second loss retained by RBS was to encourage RBS to manage the assets to minimise further losses, although the bank considered it still had a legal and moral obligation to manage the assets as best it could. The UK government decided

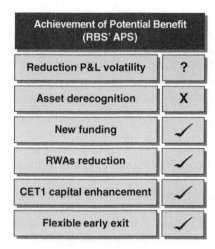

FIGURE 14.9   RBS's APS – Summary of potential benefits

against RBS bearing a higher percentage of second losses as this would have required a higher injection of capital upfront to strengthen the bank's position.

Any payments by the UK government for second losses were delayed by two years from the point at which the loss was realised, providing time for any recoveries on assets to be offset. More significantly, second loss payments had to be repaid by RBS if it wished to exit the APS before December 2099, the latest maturity date of the covered assets.

> In the U.S., the Asset Guarantee Program, which pre-dated the announcement of the UK's APS by two months, also used a 10:90 split between Citigroup and the US government, respectively, for losses beyond the first loss.

Fees   The costs of participating in the APS incurred by RBS to the UK government included a fee of GBP 700 million, paid in advance for the first three years of the APS, and GBP 500 million per annum thereafter until the earlier of (i) the date of termination of the APS and (ii) 31 December 2099. Subject to the UK government's consent, RBS could satisfy all or part of the annual fee in respect of the APS, the payments related to the GBP 8 billion contingent B shares (to be covered below), the dividend payments (if made) on the GBP 25.5 billion of B shares and the exit fee payable in connection with any termination of RBS's participation in the APS, in cash or by waiving the right to certain UK tax reliefs that were treated as deferred tax assets or by issuing a further issue of B shares to the UK government.

RBS could exit the APS at any time, subject to the British banking supervisor approval, and pay an exit fee which was an amount equal to (a) the larger of (i) the cumulative aggregate fee of GBP 2.5 billion and (ii) 10% of the annual aggregate reduction in Pillar 1 capital requirements in respect of the assets covered by the APS up to the time of exit (i.e., 10% of the actual capital relief provided) less (b) the aggregate of the annual fees paid up to the date of exit. In the event that RBS had received payments from the UK government under the APS in respect of losses on the covered assets, it had to either negotiate a satisfactory exit payment to exit the APS, or absent such agreement, refund to the UK government any net payments made by the UK government under the APS in respect of losses on the covered assets.

The UK government, in setting the fee at GBP 2.5 billion, aimed to charge the maximum fee possible, consistent with leaving RBS well-capitalised and securing the primary objective of financial stability, and to ensure that the pricing structure maintained an incentive on RBS to exit as quickly as possible.

The UK government estimated that, up to about GBP 73 billion, RBS had a financial incentive to exit the APS long before December 2099, taking account of the annual fees that it would have to pay to stay in.

If losses were, however, to exceed about GBP 73 billion, RBS would have an incentive to stay in the APS until the end, rather than incur a large and immediate repayment to the UK government. After this point, the remaining incentives on RBS to stem any further losses were unlikely to be effective. Losses of this magnitude would only occur in seriously stressed economic circumstances.

Issuance of the B shares   Included in the APS agreement, the UK government committed to subscribe a capital increase. This new capital took the form of B shares. As a result, in December 2009 RBS issued a further GBP 25.5 billion of new capital to UK government with the following terms:

- **Number of shares:** 51 billion new B shares, with a nominal value of 1p each;
- **Subscription price:** 50p per share;
- **Subscription amount:** GBP 25.5 billion;
- **Voting rights:** no voting rights at general meetings of ordinary shareholders;
- **Dividends:** each share was entitled to one tenth of the cash dividend of an ordinary share (subject to anti-dilution adjustments);
- **Conversion right:** the shares were convertible into ordinary shares, at the option of the holder at any time, subject to anti-dilution adjustments, at an initial conversion price of 50p per ordinary share (i.e., at the rate of 10 B shares for each ordinary share). The UK government agreed not to convert its B shares into ordinary shares to the extent that its holding of ordinary shares following the conversion represented more than 75% of RBS's issued ordinary share capital; and
- **Issue proceeds:** GBP 25.1 billion, net of expenses.

Following the issuance of the B shares, the UK government's holding of ordinary shares of the company remained at 70.3% although its economic interest rose to 84.4%.

The decision to convert the B shares into ordinary shares ("A shares") was highly dependent on the market value of the A shares, as shown in Table 14.2:

- If the A shares were trading below 50p, the conversion right was out-of-the-money. Optimally, the UK government would not exercise this right;
- If the A shares were trading between 50p and 60p, the UK government had a preferential right to a dividend through the "dividend access share" (to be covered later), which was set at the higher of 7% or 2.5x the dividend on the A shares. Although the conversion right was in-the-money, it was likely that the UK government would prefer to have access to a potentially attractive dividend, although payment of this dividend was at RBS's discretion; and
- If the A shares were trading above 60p, the UK government would convert the B shares into A shares and in turn sell them into the market at a healthy premium to its 50p entry level.

TABLE 14.2   Scenarios of potential conversion of RBS's B shares

Ordinary Share Price	B Share's Conversion Right Status	Likely Outcome
"A" < 50p	Out-of-the-money	No conversion
50p < "A" < 60p	In-the-money	Conversion unlikely. Potential dividend attractive, if paid
"A" > 60p	In-the-money	Conversion likely

However, RBS had a strong incentive to redeem the B shares because it would:

- Eliminate their potential dividend burden; and
- Avoid the potential dilution if the B shares were converted into A shares.

Dividend Access Share   Also included in the state aid, the UK government received a "dividend access share". The dividend access share entitled the holder (i.e., the UK government) to dividends equal to the greater of 7% of the aggregate issue price of B shares issued to the UK government and 250% times the ordinary dividend rate multiplied by the number of B shares issued, less any dividends paid on the B shares and on ordinary shares issued on conversion.

Dividends on the dividend access share were discretionary unless a dividend had been paid on the ordinary shares, in which case dividends became mandatory. The dividend access share did not carry voting rights at general meetings of ordinary shareholders and was not convertible into ordinary shares.

The combined effect of the dividend access share and the B shares was that UK government enjoyed preferential but non-transferable dividend rights on the new capital it provided.

Contingent B Shares   Also included in the state aid and in the event that the RBS's Basel II Core Tier 1 capital ratio declined to below 5%, the UK government was committed to subscribe for up to an additional GBP 8 billion of capital in the form of 16 billion B shares – the contingent B shares – if certain conditions were met. If such conditions were not met and were not waived by the UK government, and RBS was unable to issue the B Shares, RBS would be required to find alternative methods for achieving the requisite capital ratios. The contingent B shares agreement expired at the end of five years from 22 December 2009 or, if earlier, until the occurrence of a termination event or until the company decided (with the regulatory supervisor consent) to terminate such agreement.

RBS was required to pay an annual fee respect of the contingent capital of GBP 320 million less 4% per annum of the value of any B shares subscribed for under the contingent B shares agreement. Such fee was payable in cash or, with the UK government's consent, by waiving certain UK tax reliefs that were treated as deferred tax assets or through a further issue of B shares to UK government. The present value of the contingent capital fees was estimated to be GBP 1.2 billion at inception.

The contingent capital commitment agreement could be terminated in whole or in part by RBS, with the British supervisor's consent, at any time.

14.2.6 Accounting Recognition of the Asset Protection Scheme and Issuance of the B Shares

From an accounting perspective, the APS was a single contract providing credit protection in respect of the portfolio of financial assets: the unit of account was the contract as a whole. Under IFRS, credit protection was either treated as a financial guarantee contract ("FGC") or as a derivative depending on the terms of the agreement and the nature of the protected assets and exposures.

The portfolio contained more than an insignificant element of derivatives and limited recourse assets, and hence the contract did not meet the definition of an FGC. The APS contract was therefore treated as a derivative and was recognised at fair value, with changes in fair value recognised in profit or loss.

The fair value of the APS derivative in theory represented the payment of the minimum level of fees in return for protection receipts which were in excess of both the first loss and the total future premiums. The fair value of the credit protection at inception was GBP 1.46 billion, representing the initial premium paid at 31 December 2009.

B Shares and Contingent B Shares   From an accounting perspective, the B shares (without a conversion right), their conversion right and the contingent B shares were equity instruments. Thus, there was no need to separate the conversion right from the rest of the B shares. The accounting entries to recognise the issuance of the B shares (in GBP million):

Cash (Asset)	25,100
B share capital (Equity)	510
B share premium (Equity)	24,590

The contingent B shares were recognised as reduction of shareholder's equity in the form of a negative reserve.

Protected Assets   There was no change in the recognition and measurement of the covered assets as a result of the APS. Impairment provisions on the covered assets measured at amortised cost were assessed and charged in accordance with RBS's accounting policy.

Initial Accounting Entries   The accounting entries to initially recognise the APS, the B shares and the contingent B shares were the following (in GBP million):

Cash (Asset)	22,440
Contingent capital reserve (Equity)	1,200
APS derivative (Asset)	1,460
B share capital (Equity)	510
B share premium (Equity)	24,590

14.2.7 Basel III Impact of the Asset Protection Scheme and Issuance of the B Shares

An interesting element of the APS was that the misalignment between its accounting recognition and its regulatory capital recognition:

- From an accounting perspective, there was no change in the recognition and measurement of the covered assets as a result of the APS. The protection was recognised as a derivative and fair valued through profit or loss at each reporting date; and
- From a regulatory perspective, the RWAs on the protected assets benefited from the APS. Basel III (similarly to Basel II) provide for a protection relief under the credit risk mitigation framework. The second loss covered by UK government were risk-weighted at 0%, which resulted in a RWAs benefit of GBP 128 billion in 2009. The first loss and the remaining 10% share of second losses borne by RBS was risk-weighted, unaffected by the APS.

The fair valuation of the APS through profit or loss added significant volatility to RBS's CET1. For example in 2010 RBS recognised a pre-tax charge of GBP 1,550 billion due to the reduced fair value of the APS.

B Shares and Contingent B Shares   The B shares qualified as Basel II's core tier one capital. From a Basel III perspective, the B shares qualified as CET1 capital instruments. As a result, RBS's CET1 capital was enhanced by the GBP 25.1 billion issue proceeds.

The contingent B shares were treated as a call option on B shares contingent to the 5% Core Tier 1 capital trigger being reached. This right was similar to the conversion right embedded in convertible CoCos. The accounting recognition of a negative reserve of GBP 1.2 billion in equity offset in part the CET1 benefit stemming from the issuance of the B shares.

14.2.8 Main Benefits and Weaknesses of the State Aid

Following the large impairment losses and write-downs experienced in 2008 and the continuing challenging financial market and economic conditions during 2009, prompted RBS to request a state aid from the UK government. Although the aid achieved most of the potential benefits targeted by this type of transactions (see Figure 10.9), it had key implications for RBS and its shareholders.

Main Benefits of the State Aid   The main benefit of the state aid for RBS and its shareholders was that it allowed the bank to restore the viability of the bank. Otherwise, it would have been very difficult for RBS to generate sufficient capital to meet its regulatory capital requirements or to offset losses. Capital deterioration could potentially have triggered a cascade of credit rating downgrades, making it more expensive for RBS to raise funding in the wholesale markets.

A second benefit for RBS was the substantial reduction in the likelihood of reporting large impairment and write-down losses in its income statement related to the covered assets, once the first loss on these assets was recognised. However, the recognition in profit or loss of the changes in the fair valuation of the APS' protection could add volatility to the income statement. The overall reduction in profit or loss volatility in turn reduced the volatility of RBS's CET1 capital.

A third benefit for RBS was the notable enhancement of its regulatory capital. The issuance of the B shares and the APS increased CET1 capital.

Main Weaknesses of the State Aid   Ordinary A shareholders paid a hefty premium to assure the viability of the bank. This was the main weakness of the state aid: the huge dilution of the interests of existing shareholders as a consequence of the successive capital raising exercises with the UK government. From the beginning of 2008, RBS's share count increased more than 10-fold, from 10 billion shares to 107 billion after the B shares issuance, as shown Table 14.3. By way of example, for RBS shares to reach half of their pre-crisis peak (300p), RBS market capitalisation had to be five times its pre-crisis peak.

A second weakness of the state aid was its large cost through the combination of the APS insurance fee, contingent capital fees and, if paid, the B share dividend enhanced by the dividend access share.

A third weakness was the potential conflict of interest within RBS's capital structure: the interests of the UK government could be misaligned with the interests of the A shareholders. It also presented RBS with a dilemma, in that, while paying a dividend would provide a good short-term outcome for the B shareholder (i.e., the UK government), it could represent a longer-term negative for the A shareholders. Therefore, the best outcome for the A shareholders was for RBS not to pay a dividend at all.

A fourth weakness of the state aid was the prohibition on the making of discretionary dividend or coupon payments on existing hybrid capital instruments (including preference shares and B shares) for a two-year period commencing no later than 30 April 2010, which impaired RBS's ability to raise new AT1 capital through the issuance of CoCos.

TABLE 14.3　Actions on RBS's share capital in 2008 and 2009

Corporate Action	Capital Raised	Impact	Share Count
Original shares (1 Jan 08)			10.1 bn
Early 2008 rights issue	GBP 12 bn at 200p/share	+6 bn	16.1 bn
Dividend capitalisation		+0.4 bn	16.5 bn
Oct-08 govt. injection	GBP 15 bn at 65.5p	+22.9 bn	39.4 bn
Jan-09 pref. conversion	GBP 5 bn at 31.75p	+15.8 bn	55.2 bn
B shares issuance	GBP 25.5 bn at 50p	+51 bn	106.8 bn
Total			106.8 bn

A fifth weakness was that, in order to secure the state aid, RBS agreed to certain undertakings that limited the bank's operations. These undertakings included (i) supporting certain initiatives in relation to mortgage lending and lending to SMEs and commercial/industrial companies in the UK until 2011, (ii) regulating management remuneration and (iii) regulating the rate of growth of RBS's balance sheet.

Finally, the state aid gave the UK government the right to appoint up to three new independent non-executive directors. It meant that the UK state was able to exercise a significant degree of influence over, among other things, the election of directors and the appointment of senior management.

14.3 CASE STUDY: SAREB, THE SPANISH BAD BANK

In 2012, in the context of the Eurozone sovereign crisis, the Spanish government created Sociedad de Activos de Restructuración Bancaria ("SAREB" or "Fund for Orderly Bank Restructuring") with the sole purpose of addressing the management and orderly disinvestment of assets transferred from financial institutions that were receiving public assistance.

14.3.1 Background

At the beginning of June 2012, the Spanish Government, upon request from EU authorities, carried out two independent and private valuations of the loan portfolios of the 14 main Spanish banking groups in order to evaluate the resistance level of the Spanish financial sector in case of a significant deterioration of the Spanish economy.

On 25 June 2012, the Spanish Government presented a formal request for financial aid to the Eurogroup with a view to recapitalising Spanish credit institutions. On 29 June it was decided that the financial assistance would be provided by the European Financial Stability Facility (EFSF) until the European Stability Mechanism (ESM) was in place, and that the aid would be in the form of a line of credit for up to a maximum of EUR 100 billion, to be allocated exclusively to servicing the recapitalisation requirements of the Spanish financial sector.

This financial assistance arrangement led to the signing, on 23 July, of a "Memorandum of Understanding of Financial Sector Policy Conditions", which described the conditions related to the financial assistance granted by the EFSF or, as applicable, the ESM. Among other measures, the Memorandum required the performance of a stress test to estimate each bank's capital deficit and initiate a restructuring or dissolution process of the financial institutions with important capital shortfalls.

One of the conditions included in the agreement was that any credit institution that obtained public financial assistance was obliged to transfer some of its real estate exposure (in particular, real estate assets handed over in lieu of payment of debts and credits in the property development sector) to an asset management company that was to be created to this end before the end of November 2012. In order to meet this condition SAREB was created in November 2012 with the mission of "holding, managing and administering, both direct and indirect, and acquiring and divesting the assets transferred to it by credit institutions". SAREB was formed for a limited period of time, which was initially set at 15 years.

14.3.2 Legal Structure and Governance

A key element of the SAREB was that it was structured as a financial institution (i.e., a bank) as opposed to a government institution. Being a bank, it was supervised by the Bank of Spain. The European Commission classified the vehicle as a non-government entity based on the following conditions:

- It was a separate entity;
- It was majority privately owned. Private investors were not protected by any additional bilateral agreements with the Spanish government;
- Its main purpose was to solely address the financial crisis;
- It was established with a short, temporary duration;
- Its expected losses were small in comparison with the total size of its liabilities; and
- It had no golden share granted or any similar benefit that could increase its control by the Spanish government. The FROB (Fund for Orderly Bank Restructuring), a government entity that invested in SAREB, had the same voting rights as any other equity investors in accordance with their equity participation.

SAREB was governed on a day-to-day basis by its **board of directors**, representing its shareholders according to their participation in the vehicle's equity. The board had 15 members: six members representing the private shareholders, four members designated by the FROB and five independent members. Other two key committees were created: an **audit committee** and an **appointments and remuneration committee**. In addition to the aforementioned, the vehicle also had support committees:

- A **management committee** assisted with the company's financial and operational management and the duties of budgetary and management reporting;
- A **risk committee** oversaw and proposed contingent actions to respond to situations or activities that could lead to excessive levels of risk;
- An **investments committee** evaluated and proposed strategies or actions for investment and disinvestment; and
- An **asset-liability committee** advised on any factor that could affect the SAREB's balance sheet and, in particular, related to the equity, financing and liquidity structure.

14.3.3 Assets Composition and Pricing

As explained above, SAREB was entrusted with managing assets transferred by banks that received, or were about to receive, government assistance. The categories that were eventually included under the terms of the transfer were the following:

- Loan exposure in the real estate development sector with a net book value in excess of EUR 250,000 per borrower; and
- Foreclosed properties with a net book value of more than EUR 100,000.

The specific selection of the assets to be transferred from the institutions receiving public capital was the duty of the FROB. The vehicle acquired assets in a two-step process. In a first step (Group 1) SAREB acquired 36.7 billion of assets in December 2012 from distressed institutions in which the

FROB was the majority shareholder: BFA-Bankia, Catalunya Banc, NCG Banco-Banco Gallego and Banco de Valencia. In a second step (Group 2) SAREB acquired 14.1 billion of assets in March 2013 from a group of banks in which the FROB had not taken a holding on the reference date, but which were nevertheless going to require public assistance: BMN, Ceiss, Liberbank and Caja 3. In total, SAREB received assets with an acquisition cost of EUR 50.8 billion, of which EUR 34.4 billion related to financial assets (90,618 loans and credit lines for real estate developers) and EUR 11.3 billion related to real estate assets. The gross values of these assets were EUR 107 billion, split between EUR 74.8 billion of financial and EUR 32.2 billion of real estate assets.

Assets' Transfer Price   The transfer of assets was based on their estimated economic value (i.e., the expected loss) with an additional haircut. The valuation was provided by an independent third party and was closely monitored by the European Commission, the ECB and the IMF. The haircut took into account elements not included in the economic valuation, such as maintenance costs, financing costs, legal costs, recovery costs, etc. The haircut was fixed in a resolution adopted by the Bank of Spain and it took the form of an average cut in the gross value of each category of assets transferred.

The average haircuts (in percentage) applied to **financial assets** were the following:

- Completed housing: 32.4%;
- Projects under construction: 40.3%;
- Urban land: 53.6%;
- Other land: 56.6%;
- Other guarantee: 33.8%; and
- No guarantee: 67.6%.

The average haircuts (in percentage) applied to **real estate assets** were the following:

- New build housing: 54.2%;
- Projects under construction 63.2%; and
- Land 79.5%.

The asset transfer price could be adjusted within a 36-month deadline from the date of transfer, to incorporate inappropriate categorisation, changes in scope and errors or fluctuations in the estimated price at the date of transfer.

Simultaneously to the aforementioned transfers, SAREB signed the management and administration contracts for the transferred assets with each of the selling institutions to ensure continuity in the management of the assets over a transitional period of one year, avoiding any deterioration to the assets that could be due to a lack of attention.

14.3.4 Balance Sheet Structure

Figure 14.10 depicts the main elements of SAREB's balance sheet structure at inception:

1. The **assets** described above with an initial book value of EUR 50.8 billion, the consideration paid. Initially, the consideration was met by SAREB with the issuance of senior bonds (see next);
2. A **senior debt** tranche amounting to EUR 46 billion, representing 90.6% of the assets value. Initially the debt had maturities from one to three years and was fully subscribed by the banks selling the assets, to take into account any price transfer adjustments during their 36-month deadline. The repayment of this temporary debt, once the price adjustments were performed, was made through the issuance of new debt, fully subscribed by the FROB;
3. A **subordinated debt** tranche amounting to EUR 3.6 billion, representing 7% of the assets' book value. The subordinated debt was held by a majority of private investors (55%) and by the FROB (45%). It was designed to absorb potential losses above the expected losses. The private investors

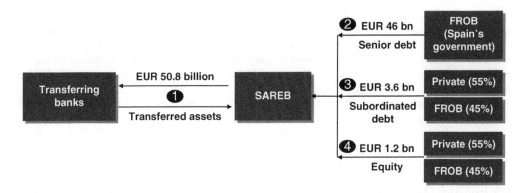

FIGURE 14.10   SAREB's balance sheet structure at inception

were 21 banks and insurance companies. The subordinated debt could be converted into share capital under certain circumstances and it entitled investors to an 8% coupon, payable in the event that sufficient profits were available for distribution; and

4. An **equity** tranche amounting to EUR 1.2 billion, representing 2.4% of the assets value. The private investors were 31 banks and insurance companies. SAREB estimated a 13% return on equity.

The duration of the vehicle was linked to the liquidation of the acquired assets. The vehicle was expected to last 15 years based on the projected timeline for divestment of the assets.

14.3.5 Further Write-downs and Balance Sheet Restructuring

Since its set-up, SAREB reported losses as the assets sold, primarily to private equity investors and banks, were executed at prices below book value. Thus, no coupons were paid to the subordinated debt holders.

In 2015 the Bank of Spain obliged financial institutions to update their provisions based on an item-by-item revaluation of their loan and foreclosed assets. The revaluation was supposed to incorporate market prices. As a consequence SAREB revalued its properties individually. After an intense valuation process, it was determined that the company should write down a further EUR 2,044 million in 2016, in addition to the EUR 968 million set aside in the previous two financial years. The write-down wiped out the vehicle's equity.

In 2016, SAREB's shareholders approved the conversion of EUR 2.17 billion of subordinated debt into equity. Through this conversion, SAREB met the capital requirements of the new accounting framework that came into effect in 2015.

The objective of the conversion of subordinated debt into capital was to absorb the losses created by this write-down using the vehicle's own shareholders' equity, without the need for additional capital injections. After this transaction, SAREB's shareholders' equity structure comprised EUR 0.95 billion capital and EUR 1.43 billion of subordinated debt.

14.4 CASE STUDY: NAMA, THE IRISH BAD BANK

Following the nationalisation of Anglo Irish Bank in January 2009 and in order to restore stability to the Irish banking system in the context of the sovereign crisis, in November 2009 the Irish government introduced an asset relief scheme for banks in Ireland through the establishment of the National Asset Management Agency ("NAMA"). NAMA acquired and managed assets from a number of participating financial institutions.

In a decision issued in July 2009, Eurostat (the statistical office of the European Union) ruled that special purpose vehicles (SPVs) which were majority-owned by private companies would be regarded as being outside the government sector if they met a number of conditions (see SAREB's case study). Among the conditions were that the SPVs were of temporary duration and were established for the sole purpose of addressing the financial crisis. As in the SAREB case study, the categorisation of NAMA as a non-government entity was key to its formation.

Another key element to a bad bank structure is the mechanism by which the assets are legally transferred to the bad bank. In the case of NAMA, a particularly complex situation was the acquisition of foreign bank assets, where an Irish statutory transfer was not be effective. The PI had to take all steps necessary to ensure that there was a binding and enforceable transfer to NAMA, as a matter of applicable foreign law, of the foreign bank asset.

Five Irish banks participated (the participating institutions or "PIs"): Allied Irish Bank (AIB), Anglo Irish Bank (Anglo), Bank of Ireland (BOI), Educational Building Society (EBS) and Irish National Building Society (INBS).

14.4.1 Loan Transfers

Bank assets (loans and derivative transactions) were acquired at an acquisition value which represented their long-term economic value. The loan portfolios acquired by NAMA from the PIs were valued on a loan-by-loan basis. The valuation process was split into the valuation of the collateral pledged (a property in most cases) and the valuation of the loan itself.

Valuation of the Collateral Pledged   The starting element in the valuation of each loan was the current market value of the property ("CMVP") or any other collateral securing the loan. The CMVP was calculated as the present value of the collateral expected cash flows, comprising the assumed disposal proceeds and any projected rental income discounted to present values using the NAMA discount rates. The CMVP was, in the first place, provided by a professional valuer commissioned by the PI but also owing a duty of care to NAMA. Each valuation was referred by NAMA to its own property valuation panel, which reviewed it and provided an opinion as to whether it considered it to be sufficiently accurate. If the NAMA panellist disagreed with the valuation, it was referred to an independent property valuer for adjudication. The aggregate value of the CMVPs was EUR 21.51 billion.

NAMA applied an uplift adjustment factor ranging from 0% to 25% to the CMVP to reflect its **long-term economic value ("LEV")**. The LEV was defined as the value that (a) a property could reasonably be expected to attain in a stable financial system when the crisis conditions prevailing at the constitution of the NAMA were ameliorated and (b) in which a future price or yield of the property was consistent with reasonable expectations having regard to its long-term historical average. The weighted average uplift factors applied by NAMA was 9.3%. The aggregate value of the LEVs was EUR 23.51 billion (=21.51 bn × 109.3%).

A discount of 5.25% was applied to the LEV to provide for due diligence (0.25%) and other costs (5%) relating to the possible enforceability of NAMA's security and title rights over loan collateral incurred or likely to be incurred by NAMA. The LEV, adjusted for the legal discount (the "**collateral available to the state**"), represented the expected proceeds that would be realised if the collateral was disposed of when the market crisis conditions had normalised. The aggregate value of the collateral available to the state was EUR 22.28 billion (= 23.51 bn × 94.75%).

TABLE 14.4 Geographical split of NAMA's collateral

Jurisdiction	CMVP (EUR)	Share
Ireland	11.5 bn	54%
United Kingdom	8.2 bn	38%
Rest of Europe	1.5 bn	7%
US/Canada	0.3 bn	1%
Totals	21.5 bn	100%

In some instances, the value of the collateral provided by the borrowers exceeded amounts owed. Where excess collateral existed, adjustments were made so that the consideration given did not exceed the borrower's debt (defined below). In some cases, the legal structure of a borrower's loans prevented cross collateralisation to other loans.

One interesting aspect of the collateral was the high percentage of non-Irish collateral pledged, as shown in Table 14.4. This aspect notably increased the complexity of the valuation process and added FX risk to the vehicle.

Valuation of the Loans   Following completion of the property and legal due diligence processes, a loan-by-loan valuation was carried out by one of five loan valuation firms employed by NAMA. The loan valuation process was independently audited by one of the Big 4 audit firms, which acted as audit co-ordinator. The audit co-ordinator provided audit certification to the EU Commission that the valuations were in line with the methodology approved by the Commission.

The starting element in each loan valuation was the "**borrower debt**". The borrower debt was calculated as the sum of (i) amounts owed by borrowers at loan valuation date and including qualifying advances made after 7 April 2009 (the date on which the Minister for Finance announced the Government's intention to establish NAMA) (the "**loan balance**") and (ii) the market value at acquisition time of the performing financial derivatives for which NAMA gave consideration (the "**derivatives**"). The aggregate borrower debt amounted to EUR 46.41 billion.

Next the market value of each loan was calculated using a valuation model, approved by the EU Commission, which discounted the expected value of future cash flows. The market value of the loans was estimated to be EUR 17.25 billion.

As in the collateral valuation, an uplift was incorporated to arrive at the long-term economic value of the loans ("**LEVL**"), which on aggregate amounted to EUR 21.39 billion. This uplift was set at 24% of the market value of the loans.

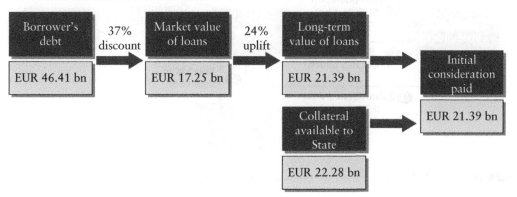

Consideration Paid   The lower of the collateral available to the state and the LEVL was the initial consideration paid by NAMA to the PIs. As a result, NAMA initially paid a EUR 21.39 billion consideration for the loan portfolio:

- The difference between (i) the borrower gross debt at loan valuation date and (ii) the initial consideration paid, was EUR 25.02 billion (= 46.41bn − 21.39bn) – a 54% (= 25.02bn / 46.41bn) discount; and
- The value-to-loan of the acquired loans was 100.6% (= 21.51bn / 21.39bn), the ratio between the CMVP and the initial consideration paid.

Subsequently, the initial consideration was adjusted (the "final consideration") to take into consideration any errors in the acquisition process or value attributed to the loan.

> One of the effects of the valuation approach approved by the EU Commission was that the initial consideration paid for the loans by NAMA was very close (a difference of EUR 120 million) to the current market value of the property (CMVP).
> The Commission treated the difference between the current market value of loans and their long-term economic value (LEVL) as a state aid.

14.4.2 Balance Sheet Structure

Figure 14.11 depicts the main elements of NAMA's balance sheet structure as at December 2010:

1. Participating banks transferred troubled loans and related derivatives to the NAMA. The sold assets comprised land, development property and associated commercial loans. The purchase price of the transferred loans and derivatives was EUR 21.4 billion. The gross debt of the loans and derivatives transferred was EUR 46.41 billion;
2. As consideration for the loans acquired, NAMA issued EUR 20.3 billion of senior debt to the PIs, pro rata to their share in the assets transferred to NAMA. The debt, which was guaranteed by the Irish Minister for Finance, accounted for 95% of the consideration paid. The debt securities paid a floating rate of interest on a semiannual basis, with the coupon based on six month Euribor. These bonds could be used by the PIs as collateral to receive financing from the European Central Bank, helping improve their liquidity position;

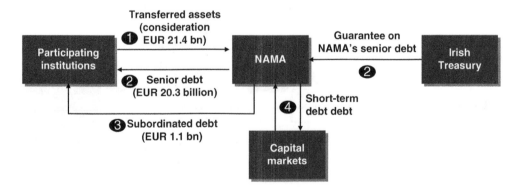

FIGURE 14.11   NAMA's balance sheet structure at 31 December 2010

3. NAMA issued EUR 1.1 billion of non state-guaranteed subordinated debt securities for 5% of the consideration paid. The issued securities were held by the PIs pro rata to their share in the assets transferred to NAMA. The subordinated dent was perpetual and its coupons were non-cumulative. It carried an interest rate linked to the yield on 10-year Irish government bonds prevailing at the time of issuance plus an interest margin of 0.75%. As a result, the interest rate was initially set at 5.26%. The payment of interest and principal on the subordinated debt was dependent on NAMA reporting sufficient profits to meet the coupon distribution;
4. NAMA managed its day-to-day liquidity and funding requirements through the issuance of short-term floating-rate notes guaranteed by the Irish government.

14.5 ASSET PROTECTION SCHEMES VERSUS BAD BANKS

Asset protection schemes (APSs) and bad banks are intended to address the issue of asset quality in the domestic banking system by allowing weakened financial institutions to protect or sell assets whose declining and uncertain value prevents the longer-term shoring-up of bank capital and the return to a normally functioning financial market. Whilst they try to accomplish a similar objective – to help a bank de-risk its balance sheet – there are substantial differences between asset protection schemes (APSs) and bad banks.

14.5.1 Advantages and Weaknesses of Asset Protection Schemes

The main **advantages** of an APS for a bank are the following:

- **De-risking:** An APS provides immediate RWAs reduction, providing capital relief. The RWA relief reduces capital needs. However, some RWAs would still be present as the assets are not fully derecognised;
- **Upside participation:** The bank retains a partial exposure to the cash flows of the assets;
- **No loss realisation:** The protected assets are typically not fully derecognised from an accounting perspective, so no loss is crystallised on the retained assets;
- **Reduction of CET1 volatility:** Notwithstanding the volatility created where the protection is recognised as a derivative (see weaknesses below), the protection reduces volatility in CET1 through a reduction of potential impairment charges in profit or loss related to the protected portfolio;
- **Cost is spread over the protection life:** The premium is paid regularly over the life of the protection, so the impact on profit or loss is spread over such life; and
- **Customer relationship is maintained:** The customer is not aware that his/her borrowing has been protected, allowing the bank to keep its relationship with the customer intact.

The main **weaknesses** of an APS for a bank are the following:

- **No funding benefit:** APSs are commonly unfunded, executed through credit default swaps or similar instruments;
- **Downside participation:** The bank retains a partial exposure to further defaults on the assets;
- **Potential profit or loss volatility:** If the protection is recognised as a derivative, the changes in its fair valuation are recognised in profit or loss, increasing its volatility and, as a result, increasing the volatility of CET1. However, this increase in CET1 volatility is likely to be offset by the reduction of CET1 volatility stemming from a reduced likelihood of impairment charges (see advantages above);
- **Complexity:** The protection agreement is complex, especially the quantification of realised losses;
- **Limited flexibility:** Decisions on the protected assets (e.g., disposals, restructurings, etc.) are constrained by the APS. The bank is less likely to sell the assets, potentially foregoing attractive offers; and
- **Scrutiny:** The protection provider monitors the actions taken on the protected assets by the bank.

14.5.2 Advantages and Weaknesses of Bad Bank Solutions

The main **advantages** of a bad bank solution for a bank are the following:

- **De-risking:** A bad bank provides immediate and full RWAs reduction, providing capital relief. However, consideration paid via government bonds may attract RWAs;
- **Derecognition:** Assets are transferred to the bad bank and, as a result, fully derecognised from the bank's balance sheet;
- **Funding benefit:** Assets are sold for cash. Whilst sometimes the consideration paid by the bad bank is via bonds guaranteed by the promoting government, these bonds can be repoed to raise financing;
- **Management focus:** Assets are transferred and management is free to focus its energy on the core businesses;
- **Reduction of CET1 volatility:** The asset transfer reduces volatility in CET1 through an elimination of further impairment charges in profit or loss related to the transferred portfolio; and
- **Greater transparency:** Investors are able to gain a clearer picture of the bank going forward, potentially regaining their trust.

The main **weaknesses** of a bad bank solution for a bank are the following:

- **Loss realisation:** Assets are normally sold at a price below their carrying amount on the balance sheet. As a consequence, a loss is crystallised;
- **Reduction in CET1:** Due to the loss realisation, CET1 capital is reduced, often requiring a simultaneous capital injection;
- **No further participation in upside:** Any recovery on the value of the transferred assets benefits the bad bank solely;
- **Customer relationship is lost:** The customer relationship is with the bad bank going forward; and
- **Sharing of risks by well capitalised banks:** Healthy banks are commonly "informally" required to invest in the equity and subordinated debt of the bad bank, having a negative impact on the capital levels of these banks.

CHAPTER 15

Approaching Capital Enhancement Initiatives

Banks have an incentive to minimise the capital they hold, because reducing capital frees up economic resources that can be directed to profitable investments. On the other hand, the less capital a bank holds, the greater is the likelihood that it will not be able to meet its obligations. Thus, banks must carefully balance the risks and rewards of holding regulatory capital.

15.1 INITIAL THOUGHTS

Previous chapters covered a good number of real-life capital enhancement initiatives. These initiatives tried to increase capital levels (in particular CET1 capital), to decrease the amount of RWAs, or both:

$$\text{Capital Ratio} \uparrow \; = \; \frac{\text{Amount of capital} \uparrow}{\text{Risk-weighted assets} \downarrow}$$

Regulatory Capital Volatility

Capital ratios provide a picture of the regulatory capital levels held by a bank as of a certain date. In theory RWAs take into account the riskiness (i.e., the uncertainty on returns) of assets and off-balance sheet items as of that date.

Assets recognised at fair value through other comprehensive income (OCI) are fair valued at each reporting date, and the difference between cost and market value is recognised in OCI, an element of CET1 capital. RWAs on these assets are calculated based on their carrying amounts in the balance sheet. In turbulent markets, asset prices may fall disproportionally relative to their credit risk. The reduction in CET1 due to changes in OCI may well exceed the offset implied by the lower RWAs (due to lower exposure values). Therefore, it is important to avoid excessively volatile capital ratios.

Some of the initiatives covered in this book had the benefit of reducing regulatory capital volatility. The European supervisor (i.e., the ECB) through asset quality reviews and stress tests periodically assesses whether banks hold sufficient capital to withstand certain adverse scenarios. These exercises provide the undertaking banks with an insight on particularly volatile items.

15.1.1 Misconceptions Regarding Capital Enhancement Initiatives

There are several misconceptions regarding capital enhancement actions:

- Misconception 1: Capital enhancement initiatives are **first order decisions**. Wrong. Capital enhancement initiatives are second order decisions. As most of us learned in Corporate Finance 101, first and foremost a bank must assess whether its businesses are providing an attractive return on capital. Therefore, a business may be attractive despite consuming a high level of capital if the business provides the bank with an adequate return. Following the 2007/08 credit crisis many banks set up the so-called "non-core" businesses, parking in those businesses capital intensive assets, frequently disregarding their return. Once results and capital were presented to investors excluding the non-core division, the bank looked like a notably enticing investment opportunity;
- Misconception 2: There is an **optimal level of regulatory capital**. Wrong. Frequently, professionals in the consulting business propose to banks "capital optimisation" projects as if, wrongly in my view, there is a level of capital which provides an optimal return. First of all, there are different types of capital (accounting, regulatory, economic, etc.). Secondly, historical returns are backward looking and forecasts of expected future returns are commonly subject to substantial uncertainty. Finally, if a bank focuses on regulatory capital, its calculation contains many "arbitrary" elements, like for instance application of prescribed risk weights that may not bear a high correlation with the riskiness of the asset portfolio;
- Misconception 3: Capital enhancement is a series of **one-off processes**. Wrong. Capital enhancement should be a continuous process. Banks frequently devote substantial energy on devising capital improvement measures when capital levels are tight and once they have achieved comfortable levels of capital they lose interest in continuing the process; and
- Misconception 4: Capital enhancement is mostly about **designing the initiatives**. Wrong. Execution is as important as design. Most of us have heard numerous times of well identified M&A transactions that have failed because of poor execution. Similarly, the implementation of sound capital initiatives may not achieve the expected benefits if those initiatives are not appropriately implemented. In addition, inculcating effective capital management as a culture is key in implementing capital enhancement initiatives.

15.1.2 The Banking Business Cycle

Observing the banking crises in the last several decades, there is a pattern of a cycle followed by the banks, as shown in Figure 15.1.

Strong Economic Growth   In a first stage banks operate in a benign environment characterised by strong growth and demand for credit. Bank capital levels are well above minimum requirements. Capital enhancement initiatives take a back seat as organic growth and DTAs utilisation generate "excessive" amounts of capital. Return on equity and earnings growth are a priority. Equity analysts and investors put pressure on the bank's management to deploy excess capital by increasing dividends or executing share buybacks. Banks embark in acquisitions generating large amounts of goodwill and other intangibles. To enhance earnings loan books expand. As competition from other banks to provide loans is notably severe, margins are narrowed and appetite for credit risk is notably raised.

Economic Recession   In a second stage the economy in which banks operate rapidly slows down. The credit riskiness of loan portfolios increase and, as a consequence, banks are required to recognise substantial provisions. DTAs are generated as recognised provisions are not yet tax deducted. Lending margins are increased as competition is low. However, wider margins are insufficient to offset the large provisions and, thus, heavy losses are reported. Dividends are withheld. As a result of these hefty losses, capital levels decrease approaching minimum capital requirements. Capital becomes a priority, taking capital enhancement initiatives and cost cutting efforts to the driver's seat.

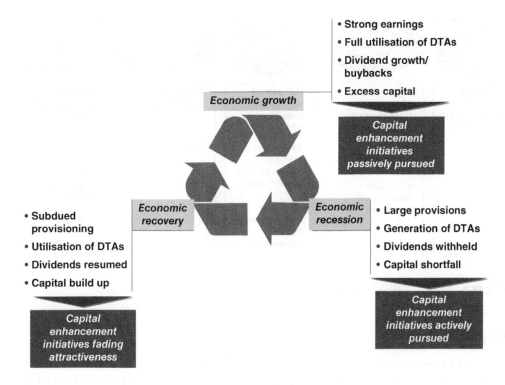

FIGURE 15.1   Common pattern of the business cycle in banking

Economic Recovery   In a third stage the underlying economy recovers and on the back of it provisioning slows down, helping earnings to grow. Capital is replenished organically through earnings retention. DTAs are starting to be consumed, accelerating capital build-up. Banks resume distributing dividends, but are cautious about providing high payout ratios and dividend growth targets. Banks are careful to assume risks but gradually, as confidence in underlying economic conditions improve, risk appetite grows. Management attention on capital enhancement initiatives fade as initiatives to boost return on equity are prioritised.

15.2 OVERVIEW OF MAIN CET1 CAPITAL RATIO ENHANCEMENT INITIATIVES

A bank may implement many types of initiatives to enhance its CET1 capital ratio. Next, the most common of these initiatives (see Figure 15.2) are briefly covered.

15.2.1 Organic Capital Generation

Organic capital generation refers to the increase in CET1 levels driven by the generation of profits and run-off of assets. The period profit or loss of a bank is reclassified to retained earnings as part of the accounting process at each reporting date. This process implies that a bank reporting a net profit will increase its retained earnings. Dividends to ordinary shares and AT1 instruments are commonly distributed out of retained earnings. Where a bank reports a profit and its dividend payout ratio (i.e., the percentage of earnings distributed as dividends) is lower than 100%, its retained earnings will grow. As a result, CET1 capital will increase if RWAs growth do not exceed retained earnings growth, assuming all other variables unchanged.

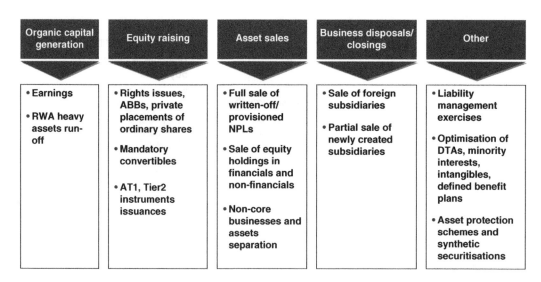

FIGURE 15.2   Main initiatives to enhance CET1 capital ratios

15.2.2 Capital Raising

Raising CET1 capital through the issuance of ordinary shares is the preferred alternative for regulatory supervisors, as it provides an additional layer of protection against losses. It is arguably the quickest way to generate a large amount of CET1 capital. Broadly speaking, there are three ways to raise capital:

- A rights issue;
- An ABB (accelerated book building) or a private placement; and
- An equity-linked instrument issuance.

I strongly recommend readers interested in gathering a deeper knowledge on these alternatives to read my *Handbook of Corporate Equity Derivatives and Equity Capital Markets* book.

Rights Issue   A rights issue, also known as a rights offering, is the most common way to increase ordinary share capital. A rights issue is a method for a listed company to raise additional capital by asking existing shareholders to invest more in the company. In a rights issue, existing shareholders are given the right to subscribe for a specific number of new shares in proportion to their existing shareholdings, at a specified price during a specified period. The case in Section 15.3 describes a rights issue implemented by Deutsche Bank.

Accelerated Book Building (ABB) or Private Placement   In an accelerated book building ("ABB") a bank issues new ordinary shares and places them with institutional investors in a quick placement transaction. The new shares are issued at a discount to the then-prevailing market price to entice investors. An ABB is quicker than a rights issue as it can be implemented in just one day.

In a private placement, a bank issues new ordinary shares to an anchor investor. During the credit crisis of 2008–09, investors were mostly sovereign funds. Sometimes, as an inducement and simultaneously to the direct investment in the shares, call options are offered to the investor giving it the right to increase its holding in the bank.

Equity-linked Instrument Issuance   The issuance of mandatory convertibles on own ordinary shares allows a bank to raise liquidity. At maturity of the bond (or upon early conversion by the bondholders) the bank delivers new (or existing) ordinary shares in exchange for the mandatory convertible bond. The main weakness of this alternative is that the positive impact on CET1 capital is not materialised until the bond's conversion, commonly several years following its issuance.

Issuance of other Capital Instruments   Where a bank's total capital comprises less than 1.5% of AT1 capital and/or less than 2% of Tier 2 capital, this implies that the bank is using CET1 capital to meet its minimum total capital requirements. As CET1 capital is, in theory, more expensive than AT1 and Tier 2 capital, a straightforward decision would be to issue AT1/Tier 2 instruments to replace existing CET1 capital.

15.2.3 Asset Sales

Asset sales are a relatively quick way to enhance capital. The challenge is to find investors that may pay a price sufficiently attractive to the selling bank and derecognise the transferred assets. A case study in Section 15.4 has been provided to cover the main elements and challenges of this type of transactions.

15.2.4 Business Disposals and Discontinuance – Barclays Non-Core

Following an assessment of the capital consumption and profitability of their various businesses, a bank may conclude that some businesses will not sufficiently attractive and, as a result, it may decide to either sell or close them.

Example: Barclays Non-Core

The British bank Barclays formed Barclays Non-Core ("BNC") in 2014 to oversee the divestment of Barclays' non-strategic assets and businesses, releasing capital to stimulate strategic growth in its Core business. BNC brought together assets and businesses that did not fit its client strategy, remained sub-scale with limited growth opportunities or were challenged by the regulatory capital environment. Non-core assets were grouped together in BNC comprising mainly business units (e.g., Barclays Spain), securities and loans (mainly commercial real estate and leveraged finance loans), and derivatives. BNC included GBP 99.1 billion of loans and GBP 31.9 billion of customer deposits. Two criteria were used to determine which businesses were placed in BNC:

- **Strategic fit**: Businesses that were either not client-driven or operated in areas where the bank did not have a competitive advantage; and
- **Returns on both a Basel III capital and leverage exposure**: Capital and/or leverage-intensive businesses, unlikely to meet the bank's target returns over the medium term.

Several of the businesses managed within BNC were profitable and were expected to be attractive to other owners. All of BNC were to be exited over time, through disposal or run-off. Reducing the capital and cost base helped improve Barclays' returns and deliver shareholder value.

Almost 80% of BNC RWAs related to assets transferred from its investment bank at the creation of BNC. It included the majority of its commodities and emerging markets businesses, elements of other trading businesses, including legacy derivative transactions, and non-strategic businesses. The key non-core portfolios outside the non-core investment bank comprised the whole of its European retail business, some European corporate exposures and a small number of Barclaycard and wealth management portfolios. BNC was run by a dedicated management team operating within a clear governance framework to optimise shareholder value and preserve maximum book value as businesses and assets were divested.

To divest BNC successfully Barclays was partly dependent on external market factors. The income from its businesses and assets, the quantum of associated RWAs and finally the market appetite for BNC components were all influenced by market environment. In addition, regulatory changes in the treatment of RWAs could significantly impact its "stock" of RWAs. These

(continued)

factors, alongside continued regulatory change, meant the market environment in which BNC operated could have positive or negative consequences for its planned run-down profile.

BNC needed a robust risk management framework to mitigate the risks inherent in its businesses and traded assets. It could take further, at its inception unforeseen, actions to achieve its run-down objectives which could include incurring additional costs of exit, or a change in direction to its planned run-down trajectory. Although the emphasis was on bringing down RWAs, reducing costs in BNC was also critical. BNC needed to be disciplined in ensuring it reduced both, although this could not always happen simultaneously.

The main benefits of the BNC strategy for Barclays were:

- It reduced both RWAs and total assets due to the run-down of legacy portfolio assets;
- It reduced the likelihood of future credit impairment charges on single name exposures and improved recoveries and delinquencies in loan portfolios; and
- It reduced operating expenses due to the savings from lower headcount.

However, the disposal strategy could bring substantial losses to Barclays' profit or loss. For example, following the inclusion of Barclays Spain in BNC and the agreement to dispose of it to the Spanish bank CaixaBank, Barclays re-examined the accounting treatment of its Spanish subsidiary concluding that it had to be fully written down to fair value less costs to sell. As a result, Barclays recognised in the third quarter of 2014 a net loss of GBP 364 million.

15.2.5 Mergers and Acquisitions – BNP Paribas Acquisition of Fortis Bank

Consolidation among banks in which weak banks are taken over by stronger banks is an alternative encouraged by governments and regulatory supervisors. The successful completion of the sale of a bank takes considerable time to execute. Moreover, frequently the acquiring bank requires a thorough clean-up of troubled assets of the acquiree before executing the transaction.

Example: BNP Paribas Acquisition of Fortis Bank

In 2008 the Belgian economy was hit by the most severe decline in economic activity since World War II. The peak of the recession came at the start of 2009 when the financial crisis was still in full force. Extensive government intervention stabilised the situation and in the second half of 2009 the Belgian economy saw growth comparable to the reviving international momentum.

In October 2008, the Belgian state, Fortis Holding ("Fortis"), and the French bank BNP Paribas signed an agreement under which BNP Paribas acquired 75% of Fortis Banque Belgium from the Belgian state and 100% of Fortis Insurance Belgium from Fortis. BNP Paribas also signed an agreement with the state of Luxembourg under which BNP Paribas acquired 16% of Fortis Banque Luxembourg (which was 51% owned by Fortis Banque Belgium):

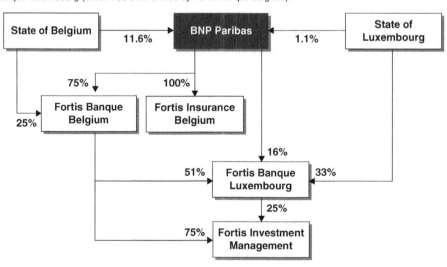

BNP Paribas paid a combination of own shares and cash for an aggregate consideration of EUR 14.7 billion: EUR 9 billion paid in BNP Paribas shares and EUR 5.7 billion in cash. As a result, the states of Belgium and Luxembourg owned 11.6% and 1.1% respectively of BNP Paribas. In addition, the Belgian state had the right to appoint two new BNP Paribas Board members. The Belgian state was required to maintain a minimum 10% stake for two years, while the state of Luxembourg was required to keep 50% of its stake for one year.

The agreement included the ring-fencing of EUR 10.4 billion of impaired structured credit assets, with a 10% interest kept by BNP Paribas.

The main advantages for BNP Paribas of the transaction were:

- The addition of two attractive retail markets: Belgium and Luxembourg, adding more than 1,100 branches and 3.3 million customers;
- Extended insurance product coverage in bancassurance and diversified alternative distribution channels;
- A reasonable price: BNP Paribas paid a price/adjusted tangible book value 0.7× for the banking business and a 1.0× life insurance embedded value for the life and non-life Belgian insurance businesses;
- A strengthened capital position: the transaction enhanced the French bank's Basel II Tier 1 ratio by 35 basis points. The newly issued shares increased its ordinary share capital by EUR 9 billion, while no goodwill was recognised. However, the transaction increased the bank's RWAs (Basel II) by 174 billion;
- A stable shareholder – the state of Belgium – for at least two years; and
- An enhanced funding position: Fortis loan/deposit ratio was close to 100%.

15.2.6 Other Capital Enhancement Initiatives

Throughout the book, a good number of cases have provided real-life examples of other initiatives implemented by banks to enhance their capital levels:

- Liability management exercises (see Co-operative Bank case study in Section 15.6);
- Reduction of excess capital attributable to minority interests;
- Optimisation of defined benefit pension plans;
- Reduction of deferred tax assets;
- Reduction of intangible assets;
- Asset protection schemes and synthetic securitisations; and
- Other capital enhancement initiatives.

15.3 CASE STUDY: DEUTSCHE BANK'S RIGHTS ISSUE

In June 2014 the German bank Deutsche Bank raised capital through a rights issue, aimed at strengthening its CET1 capital position. The public offering of new ordinary shares was via subscription rights:

- Five new share could be acquired at the subscription price for every 18 existing shares (i.e., 18:5 subscription ratio);
- Subscription price was EUR 22.5 per share;
- Subscription period was from 6 to 24 June 2014; and
- The offering was fully underwritten. Lead underwriter was UBS.

Prior to the launch of the rights offering, the German bank issued 59.9 million new shares at a price of EUR 29.20 to Paramount Services Holdings Ltd., an investment vehicle ultimately beneficially owned and controlled by Qatar, who intended to remain an anchor investor in Deutsche Bank. The gross proceeds of this offering were EUR 1.7 billion. The transaction was structured as a capital increase excluding subscription rights. This private placement was followed by a public issuance of AT1 instruments for a notional amount of EUR 3.5 billion.

Scheduled Timetable Deutsche Bank's CET1 capital raising exercise, as with any other rights issues, was not immediate. Several legal steps had to be taken before settling the new shares. The rights issue

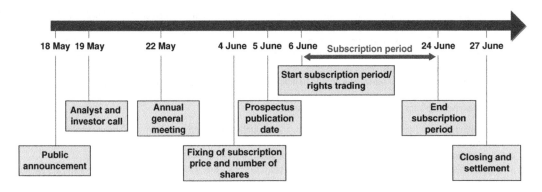

FIGURE 15.3   Deutsche Bank's rights issue timeline of key events

was completed on 27 June 2014, five weeks following its disclosure. The timeline of the rights offering is summarised in Figure 15.3.

Results of the Offering   In the public offering:

- Deutsche Bank raised 6.63 billion (EUR 6.75 billion gross proceeds less 120 million expenses);
- Deutsche Bank issued 299.8 million new ordinary shares; and
- 99.1% of the subscription rights were exercised. The remaining new shares that were not subscribed were sold on the market.

Capital Impact   As the rights issue involved the issuance of ordinary shares, Deutsche Bank's CET1 capital increased by the EUR 6.63 billion issuance's net proceeds.

Deutsche Bank agreed on a lock-up period of six months during which it could not issue new shares without the prior written consent of the lead underwriter UBS.

15.4 CASE STUDY: STRUCTURING THE DISPOSAL OF A PORTFOLIO OF NPLs

Commonly, during periods of economic slowdown the credit riskiness of loan portfolios increase and, as a consequence, banks are required to recognise substantial provisions. Simultaneously, capital levels decrease creating capital shortfalls. Asset sales are a relatively quick way to enhance capital. Often the assets sold are heavily impaired non-performing loans ("NPLs") and repossessed REOs (real estate owned). These assets consume large amounts of capital as they attract large RWAs. This case study covers some of main elements of structuring a NPLs portfolio disposal transaction.

> Sales of fully written-off portfolios are an easy win. For example, in 2014 the Spanish bank Banco de Sabadell formalised sale of fully provisioned loan portfolio, with total volume of EUR 554 million, to Aiqon Capital (Lux) Sarl. The transaction price was EUR 23.3 million, which Banco de Sabadell fully recognised as a gain.

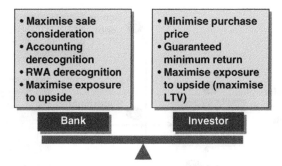

FIGURE 15.4 Conflicting interests between the bank and the investor

15.4.1 Transaction Design

This section covers the most common structure of a disposal of NPLs transaction, commenting first on the conflicting motivations by the seller bank and the investor(s).

Conflicting Objectives   The design of a NPL's disposal transaction is complicated due to the opposing objectives of the two main parties, as shown in Figure 15.4:

- The transferring bank would look to maximise the sale proceeds, to derecognise the NPLs and to avoid risk-weighting the NPLs. Normally, these two last objectives are closely related: it is highly unlikely that the banking supervisor would allow the bank not to risk weight the NPLs while they are still retained in the bank's balance sheet; and
- The objective of the investor is to maximise the return on its investment while being guaranteed an attractive minimum return. In order to achieve these objectives, the investor would try to maximise the amount of financing (i.e., to maximise the loan-to-value of the raised financing).

General Structure   Generally speaking a disposal transaction of a portfolio of NPLs to an investor (typically a private equity fund) entails the following steps, as shown in Figure 15.5:

1. A special purpose vehicle ("SPV") is set up by the bank with the sole purpose of purchasing the NPLs and issuing the instruments providing the finance of the purchase. The debt and equity instruments issued by the SPV have only recourse to the assets of the vehicle;
2. The bank sells the NPLs portfolio to the SPV in exchange for a cash consideration;
3. The private equity fund provides financing to the SPV via the issuance of senior bonds;
4. The private equity fund and the bank provide financing to the SPV via the issuance of subordinated bonds. Commonly, the investor's share of the financing is larger than that of the bank (e.g., 51% and 49% respectively);
5. The equity capital of the SPV is provided by the investor and the bank. Commonly, the investor's share of the SPV's equity capital is larger than that of the bank (e.g., 51% and 49% respectively). This equity capital assumes the first loss exposure to the NPLs;
6. The investor finances its investment in the SPV's senior debt by raising financing from the bank and other financial institutions; and
7. The collection of the cash flows associated with the NPLs and the management/sale of any related assets foreclosed are managed by the investor. The investor may delegate part of the management responsibilities to the bank. These responsibilities are formalised through a management agreement signed by the fund, the SPV and the bank.

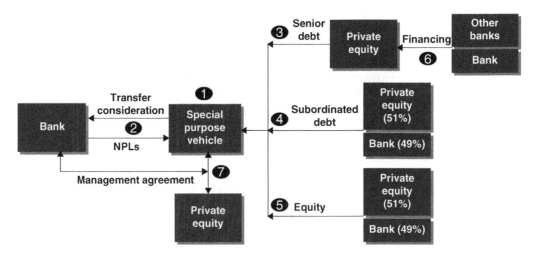

FIGURE 15.5   General structure of a disposal of a portfolio of NPLs

A good number of variations to this general structure have been implemented by banks, for example a structure in which the bank does not invest in the equity tranche. This structure notably helps the bank to derecognise the assets. Whilst this structure allows the investor to maximise its participation to the upside, it makes the investor's interest in maximising the recovery of cash flows misaligned with that of the bank. The bank has less incentive to devote resources in its recovery function that minimises first losses. This misalignment is likely to translate into a lower purchase price.

15.4.2 Accounting Considerations

This section covers the accounting treatment of the transaction depicted in the previous section.

Consolidation of the SPV   The first step in the accounting process is the assessment on whether the SPV is consolidated. The SPV is consolidated by the bank if it controls it. IFRS 10 *Consolidated Financial Statements* provides guidance on whether a bank controls an SPV: "an investor controls an investee when it is exposed, or has rights, to variable returns from its involvement with the investee and has the ability to affect those returns through its power over the investee". Therefore, the bank controls the SPV if, and only if, the bank has all the following (see Figure 15.6):

- Power over the SPV;
- Exposure or rights to variable returns from its involvement with the SPV; and
- Ability to use its power over the SPV to affect the amount of the bank's returns.

Derecognition of the Sold Assets   One of the key objectives of the transaction from the bank's perspective is to achieve derecognition of the NPLs (and any real estate assets) sold to the SPV. The assets subject to the derecognition assessment process are dependent on whether the SPV is consolidated by the bank, as shown in Figure 15.7. The derecognition assessment for each relevant asset follows the

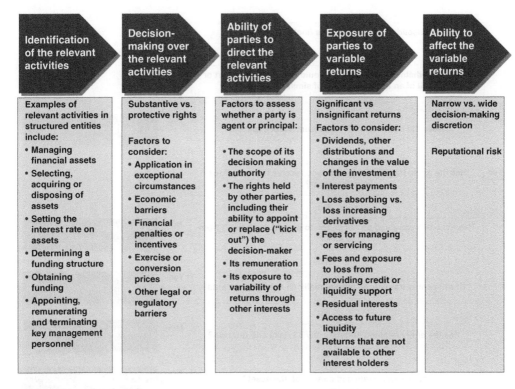

FIGURE 15.6 Accounting roadmap for the assessment of control of an entity

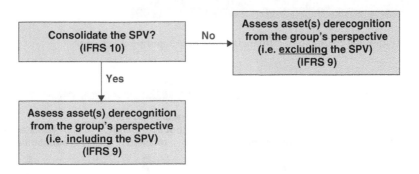

FIGURE 15.7 Assets to be included in the derecognition assessment

complex roadmap depicted in Figure 15.8. Following its derecognition assessment, an asset is categorised in one of the following situations as shown in Figure 15.9:

■ The asset continues to be recognised by the bank if it has retained substantially all the asset's risks and rewards;

■ The asset continues to be recognised by the bank to the extent of its continuing involvement if the bank has transferred some of the asset's risks and rewards but has retained control;

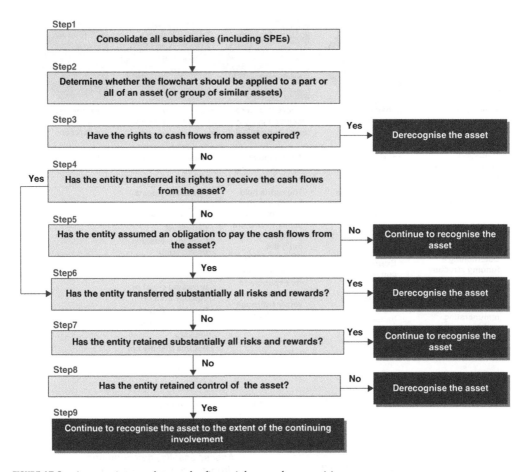

FIGURE 15.8 Accounting roadmap of a financial asset derecognition assessment

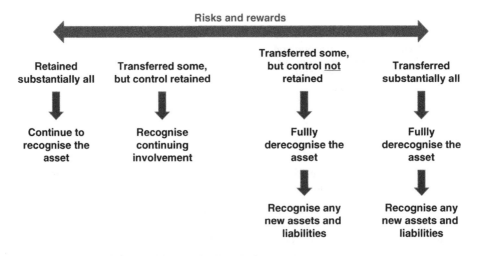

FIGURE 15.9 End result of a financial asset derecognition assessment

- The asset is derecognised by the bank and any rights and obligations created or retained in the transfer are recognised separately as assets and liabilities if the bank has transferred some of the asset's risks and rewards but control has *not* been retained; and
- The asset is fully derecognised by the bank if it has transferred substantially all the risks and rewards of ownership. The bank may also have to recognise separately as assets and liabilities any rights and obligations created or retained in the transfer.

15.4.3 Tax Considerations

A key element in the design of a robust NPLs disposal transaction is the minimisation of its tax impact. This objective is achieved by setting up entities in jurisdictions that maximise the tax deductibility of interest payments and capital losses, and that minimise the tax charges on dividends and capital gains.

An example of a structure that aims at achieving such objective is depicted in Figure 15.10, as follows:

1. The investor is commonly incorporated in a tax heaven or in jurisdictions with an advantageous tax regime. In Europe, Luxembourg is a frequent choice;
2. Similarly, the SPV (the "Parent SPV") is incorporated in an "offshore" jurisdiction (i.e., in a country other than the NPLs' jurisdiction) with an advantageous tax regime. Again, Luxembourg is a rather common country for incorporation of the SPV. The vehicle buys the NPLs portfolio and raises funding through the issuance of debt and capital instruments;
3. The default of the loans' borrowers triggers the foreclosure of the assets securing the loans (i.e., their collateral). The collateral is normally a real estate property, which is called REO ("Real Estate Owned"). Another SPV (the "REO SPV") is set up "onshore" (i.e., in the NPLs' jurisdiction) to manage and dispose of the REOs. The REO SPV is fully owned by the Parent SPV. An intercompany loan is provided by the Parent SPV to the REO SPV to acquire the REOs from the Parent SPV. Additional financing is available in the case of additional funds needed to optimise value from the property portfolio (e.g., updating or repairing the underlying properties);
4. The management of the assets (both the NPLs and REOs) is delegated to a third entity which is commonly incorporated onshore.

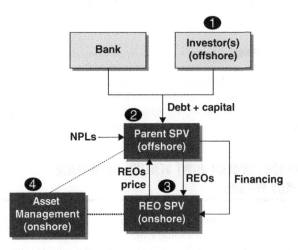

FIGURE 15.10 Example of tax efficient group structure

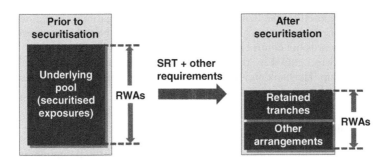

FIGURE 15.11   Significant risk transfer

15.4.4 Capital Considerations

The regulatory capital treatment of the transaction is closely related to its accounting treatment and whether the transaction is categorised as a securitisation.

Securitisation   Securitisation is defined in [CRR 4(1) 61] as a transaction or scheme, whereby the credit risk associated with an exposure or pool of exposures is tranched, having both of the following characteristics:

- Payments in the transaction or scheme are dependent upon the performance of the exposure or pool of exposures; and
- The subordination of tranches determines the distribution of losses during the ongoing life of the transaction or scheme.

In order to apply the securitisation framework for the securitised exposures the bank has to demonstrate that "significant risk transfer" ("SRT") to third parties occurs (besides other requirements). SRT tries to demonstrate that the possible reduction in RWAs, which the originator would achieve by the securitisation, is justified by a commensurate transfer of credit risk to third parties. Competent authorities decide on a transaction-by-transaction basis whether SRT has been achieved.

If SRT is achieved, the retained tranches and other arrangements between the bank and the SPV are risk-weighted based on the rating, as opposed to risk weighting the securitised pool, as shown in Figure 15.11.

My View on the Regulatory Treatment   In my view, the transaction described above was not a securitisation, although three tranches of securities were issued by the SPV (senior debt, subordinated debt and equity). The activities of the SPV included an active management of the NPLs and REOs as opposed to the passive collection of cash flows in a securitisation. Therefore, the assets were risk-weighted one by one in accordance with their accounting recognition. Therefore, the achievement of accounting derecognition was key to obtain an advantageous regulatory treatment.

15.5 CASE STUDY: BANCO POPULAR JOINT VENTURE WITH VERDE PARTNERS AND KENNEDY WILSON

This case study covers in detail an innovative solution heavily implemented by Spanish and other European banks to generate large upfront capital gains.

In December 2013 the Spanish bank Banco Popular set up a joint venture – Aliseda Sociedad de Gestión Inmobiliaria ("Aliseda") – with Värde Partners and Kennedy Wilson ("Värde & Kennedy"), as summarised in Figure 15.12. Aliseda was established to manage and sell assets, mainly NPLs and real

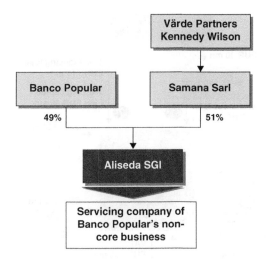

FIGURE 15.12 Aliseda SGI ownership structure

estate properties seized from non-performing customers in default of their loans. It is relevant to note that Alseda did *not* own any of such NPLs or real estate properties.

15.5.1 Transaction Structure

At its inception the main elements of the transaction are depicted in Figure 15.13, as follows:

1. Aliseda raised senior financing via a EUR 350 million syndicated loan. Banco Popular participated with a EUR 80 million take;
2. Aliseda raised subordinated financing via a EUR 222 million loan provided by Banco Popular (49% share) and Värde & Kennedy (51% share);
3. Banco Popular and Värde & Kennedy owned 49% and 51% respectively of Aliseda's equity after a EUR 150 million capital contribution;
4. Aliseda acquired Banco Popular's its NPLs and real estate management business unit. Aliseda paid EUR 715 million upfront to Banco Popular. Additionally, there was an earn-out of EUR 100 million if certain levels of return on the investment were achieved. The sale included the transfer by the Banco Popular to Aliseda of all resources required to independently carry out the NPLs and real estate management business;
5. Aliseda and Banco Popular signed a contract of services transferred. In addition, Banco Popular and Värde & Kennedy signed a shareholders' agreement;
6. Aliseda paid EUR 150 million VAT to the Spanish authorities; and
7. The tax payment and the working capital needs were financed with a EUR 115 million and a EUR 35 million loans.

15.5.2 Services Agreement

The transaction included a 10-year exclusivity contract (the "services agreement") between Banco Popular and Aliseda, with an automatic 5-year extension for managing the balance of assets remaining after the initial 10-year period had elapsed. The contract was priced at market value.

- During the first 10-year period Aliseda managed all the inventory of Banco Popular's foreclosed real estate assets, loans to property developers more than ninety days past due, loans to individuals

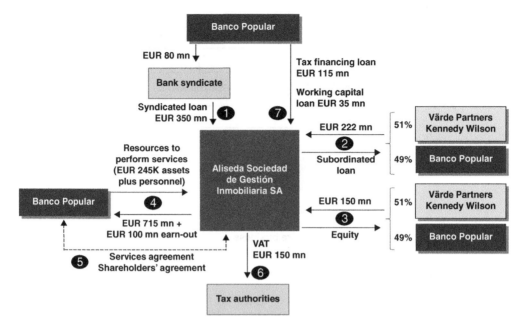

FIGURE 15.13   Aliseda initial transaction structure

secured by investment properties more than 90 days past due and 100% of the future flow stemming from these assets, and secured loans to SMEs which the Banco Popular could decide to convert to property or to sell from the balance sheet of the borrower;

- During the 5-year extension, subsequent to the initial 10-year period, no new assets were managed by Aliseda. Aliseda was, therefore, managing the disposal of the assets remaining at the end of the 10-year period; and
- Subsequent to the 5-year extension, further extensions could be implemented upon agreement of the two parties.

In addition to the services agreement, Aliseda and Banco Popular entered into another agreement with a short duration to allow the smooth transition of the material and human resources from the bank to Aliseda.

15.5.3 Aliseda: Initial Accounting Recognition

The first element that Aliseda had to assess was whether it acquired a **business** from Banco Popular. A business is defined in IFRS 3 *Business Combinations* as "an integrated set of activities and assets that is capable of being conducted and managed for the purpose of providing a return in the form of dividends, lower costs or other economic benefits directly to investors or other owners, members or participants".

The second element that Aliseda had to assess was whether the transaction constituted a **business combination**. A business combination is defined in IFRS 3 as "a transaction or other event in which an acquirer obtains control of one or more businesses". In our case the transaction met the definition of a business combination as Aliseda acquired the management business of certain NPLs and foreclosed real estate assets from Banco Popular. Consequently, and in compliance with IFRS 3, Banco Popular transferred to Aliseda a group of inputs, processes, activities, products and services that in themselves generated ordinary income and profits for Aliseda, having relinquished control over and transferred the risks and rewards of the business.

All business combinations within IFRS 3's scope are accounted for using the **acquisition method**. This method looks at the business combination from the acquirer's perspective. As a result, the third element in the business combination transaction was the identification of the **acquirer**. According to IFRS 3, the acquirer is the combining entity that obtains control of the acquiree. In our case, the acquirer was Aliseda.

A fourth element to be determined was the **acquisition date**. According to IFRS 3, this is "the date on which the acquirer obtains control of the acquiree". In our case, the acquisition date was the date on which the agreements were signed.

Recognition and Measurement of the Identifiable Assets and Liabilities   A fifth element to be determined was the classification and measurement of all assets acquired and liabilities assumed (e.g., financial instruments). According to IFRS 3, "as of the acquisition date, the acquirer shall recognise, separately from goodwill, the identifiable assets acquired, the liabilities assumed and any non-controlling interest in the acquiree". This element is one of the most complex in the application of the acquisition method.

Aliseda's balance sheet as of 31 December 2013 is shown in Figure 15.14. Aliseda's **identifiable assets** consisted mainly of deferred tax (the VAT payable that was expected to be utilised against future taxable income) and intangible assets. Excluding goodwill, the intangible assets comprised:

- The exclusivity of the service agreement with Banco Popular which was valued taking into account the exclusivity over the management of NPLs and real estate foreclosed assets;
- The Aliseda brand which was already in the market for several years under the Banco Popular patronage; and
- The general and IT services provided by Banco Popular to Aliseda.

The value of these intangible assets were estimated to be EUR 572 million by an independent third party. These assets were tested for impairment periodically.

Assets		Liabilities and Shareholders' Equity	
Current:		**Liabilities:**	
Cash	6 mn	Debt with banks	270 mn
Deferred tax	150 mn	Debt with related parties	452 mn
Non-current:		**Shareholders' Equity:**	
Goodwill	143 mn	Share capital	150 mn
Other intangibles	572 mn	Profit or loss	<0.4 mn>
Deferred tax	0.2 mn		
Other assets	0.3 mn		
Total	**872 mn**	**Total**	**872 mn**

EUR 715 mn { Goodwill, Other intangibles }

FIGURE 15.14   Aliseda's balance sheet as of 31 December 2013

Aliseda's **identifiable liabilities** comprised the senior and subordinated debt as shown in Figure 15.13. Aliseda split its liabilities into:

- Debt with banks which comprised the senior debt provided by lenders other than Banco Popular. This item amounted to EUR 270 million (= 350 mn – 80 mn); and
- Debt with related parties amounting to EUR 452 million, which comprised the EUR 80 million senior debt provided by Banco Popular, the EUR 115 million loan to finance the VAT payment, the EUR 35 million loan for working capital purposes, and the EUR 222 million subordinated debt provided by the two shareholders.

Aliseda's **shareholders' equity** included the EUR 150 million capital injection by Banco Popular and Värde & Kennedy and a small loss incurred from the acquisition date until year end.

Consideration Transferred   A sixth element to be determined was the **consideration transferred** for the acquiree. According to IFRS 3, the consideration transferred is the sum of the acquisition date fair values of the assets transferred, the liabilities incurred by the acquirer to the former owners of the acquiree and the equity interests issued by the acquirer to the former owners of the acquiree. This element took into account any previously held interest and any non-controlling interest. Aliseda had no non-controlling interests. Aliseda concluded that the consideration transferred was the EUR 715 million upfront payment.

Goodwill   According to IFRS 3, goodwill is an intangible asset representing the future economic benefits arising from other assets acquired in a business combination that are not individually identified and separately identifiable. It is calculated as the difference between (i) the aggregate of the consideration transferred, the previously held interest and the value of the non-controlling interest and (ii) the fair value of the identifiable assets and liabilities. In our case, Aliseda recognised a EUR 143 million goodwill:

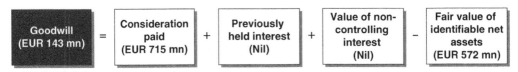

15.5.4 Banco Popular: Accounting Impact

Notwithstanding the business combination described above, in accordance with the provisions of the articles of association and shareholders' agreements, control was defined as joint. Thus, in accordance with IFRS and considering that there was a loss of control over Aliseda, the investment was classified as a "jointly-controlled entity", included in Banco Popular's consolidation scope using the **equity consolidation method**.

Initial Recognition   The initial carrying amount of its investment in Aliseda was EUR 73.5 million (49% of the EUR 150 million capital injection in the joint venture). This item comprised EUR 70 million (= 49% × 143 mn) of goodwill, based on Aliseda's EUR 143 million goodwill.

Banco Popular received a EUR 715 million consideration for the sale of Aliseda. As Aliseda was valued at nil prior to its disposal, the transaction generated a capital gain for Banco Popular of EUR 710 million, taking into account the EUR 5 million transaction costs and the EUR 0.249 million transferred assets to Aliseda. The gain was recognised under "gains on disposals of assets not classified as non-current assets held for sale" in the bank's profit or loss account. In addition, Banco Popular had to recognise the obligation to pay EUR 150 million VAT which it expected to recover using future taxable benefits. The initial accounting entries were:

Investment in Aliseda (Assets)	73.5 mn
Cash (Assets)	524.5 mn
Loans and receivables (Liabilities)	117 mn
Deferred tax asset (Assets)	150 mn
VAT payable (Liability)	150 mn
Fees payable (Liability)	5 mn
Derecognised assets (Assets)	0.249 mn
Gain on disposal (Profit or loss)	709.751 mn

Subsequent Recognition Subsequently, the carrying amount of Aliseda's investment was adjusted to take into account the bank's share of Aliseda's profit or loss and changes in OCI, the dividends received, the changes in the initial fair value adjustments and the goodwill impairment charges, as follows:

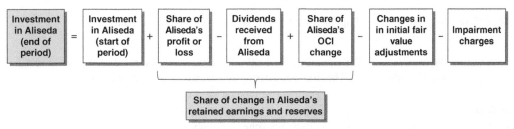

Figure 15.15, summarises the impact on its balance sheet of Banco Popular's investment in Aliseda, subsequent to initial recognition.

15.5.5 Capital Impact of the Transaction

Several items of the transaction had an impact on Banco Popular's CET1 ratio, as shown in Figure 15.16:

- The goodwill associated with the investment;
- The investment in Aliseda;
- The gain reported in profit or loss;
- The loans to Aliseda, which were risk-weighted; and
- The deferred tax asset stemming from the VAT on the transaction.

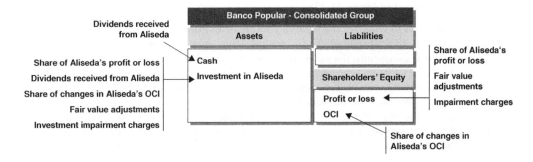

FIGURE 15.15   Impact on Banco Popular's balance sheet of its investment in Aliseda

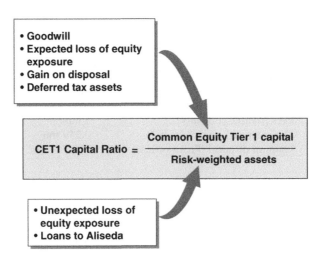

FIGURE 15.16   Impact on Banco Popular's CET1 ratio of its investment in Aliseda

Overall, the impact on CET1 capital of the EUR 710 million gain on the disposal well exceeded the impacts from the other items. The first three items are covered in more detail next.

Goodwill   The investment in Aliseda included a EUR 70 million goodwill, which was deducted from the bank's CET1 capital, in conjunction with any other intangibles.

Investment in Aliseda   The equity exposure to Aliseda was EUR 3.5 million (=73.5 mn investment – 70 mn goodwill). From a regulatory perspective, Aliseda was considered as an investment in a non-financial entity. Following the arguments covered in Chapter 12, Aliseda constituted a **qualified holding** for two reasons: (i) Aliseda was a non-financial entity and (ii) Banco Popular had a significant influence in Aliseda. Banco Popular calculated the following two thresholds:

- **The 15% threshold:** The amount representing 15% of the bank's eligible capital. The **eligible capital** was the sum of its Tier 1 and Tier 2 capital, with the Tier 2 capital been capped at 1/3 of the Tier 1 capital. Assuming that Banco Popular had EUR 9.2 billion of eligible capital, the 15% threshold was then EUR 1.38 billion (= 9.2 bn × 15%); and
- **The 60% threshold:** The amount representing 60% of the bank's eligible capital. The 60% threshold was EUR 5.52 billion (= 9.2 bn × 60%).

Following the process in Figure 15.17:

- Banco Popular had to compare the equity exposure of its equity investment in Aliseda with the EUR 1.38 billion 15% threshold. The exposure value of its investment in Aliseda was EUR 3.5 million and, consequently, the excess over the 15% threshold was nil;
- The carrying value of its investment in Aliseda was added to other qualifying holdings and compared with the 60% threshold. This aggregate was below the EUR 5.52 billion 60% threshold. Thus, the excess over the 60% threshold was nil;
- The exposure below the 15% and 60% thresholds, EUR 3.5 million, was risk-weighted using the simple risk weight approach as Banco Popular had permission to use the IRB approach. Banco Popular applied a risk weight of 370% on its investment in Aliseda. As a result, the RWAs related to Aliseda were at EUR 12.95 million (= 3.5 mn × 370%), which consumed EUR one million (= 12.95 mn × 8%))of CET1 capital;

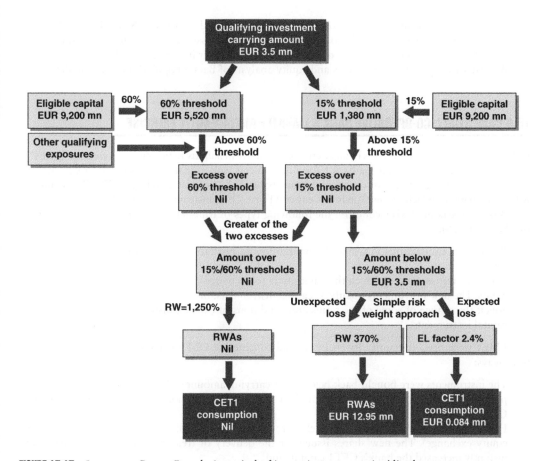

FIGURE 15.17   Impact on Banco Popular's capital of its equity exposure in Aliseda

■ Finally, and as a result of applying the IRB approach, Banco Popular had to calculate the expected loss (EL) amount. The EL factor was 2.4% of the exposure value, implying a EUR 84,000 (= 3.5 mn × 2.4%) EL amount. The EL was deducted from CET1 capital.

Gain Reported in Profit or Loss   Banco Popular reported in profit or loss a EUR 710 million pre-tax gain. Let us assume that the tax obligation of such gain utilised existing deferred tax assets, so the after-tax gain was EUR 710 million as well. As profit or loss is part of CET1 capital, the bank's CET capital was enhanced by the EUR 710 million after-tax gain.

15.5.6 Main Advantages of the Transaction

The main advantages for Banco Popular were the following:

■ An enhancement of the bank's CET1 capital levels through the EUR 710 million pre-tax capital gain;
■ A greater focus of the bank's resources on the core banking business: the supply of traditional banking products to SMEs and individuals. The transaction separated the management of the non-core NPLs and real estate assets from the management of the core banking business;

■ A greater discipline in the disposal of the foreclosed assets and recovery of NPLs. The involvement of Värde & Kennedy was likely to accelerate the pace of asset disposals due to the substantial impact of the timing of cash flows on the profitability of their investment; and

■ A greater transparency to investors and equity analysts of Banco Popular's business model.

15.6 CASE STUDY: CO-OPERATIVE BANK'S LIABILITY MANAGEMENT EXERCISE

Following the 2008–09 credit crisis banks were notably active in **liability management exercises ("LMEs")**. These exercises consisted in buying back hybrid instruments (subordinated bonds or preference shares). The instruments bought back were most of the time Basel II's Lower Tier 2 and Upper Tier 2 instruments with high coupons, which did not qualify as either AT1 or CET1 instruments under Basel III.

Broadly speaking, LMEs comprise the following types of transactions, or a combination thereof (see Figure 15.18):

■ Repurchase transactions in which the bank offers to buyback existing instruments in exchange for cash;

■ Exchange transactions in which the bank offers to exchange existing instruments for new instruments. The new instruments qualify as capital instruments; or

■ Solicit the change of some of the terms and conditions of existing instruments so they qualify as capital instruments.

LMEs were predominantly driven by a need to generate CET1 capital, which was created in three ways:

■ The instruments were bought back below their carrying amount on the bank's balance sheet. The purchase generated a capital gain recognised in profit or loss and, as a consequence, generated CET1 capital;

■ Frequently, the instruments bought back were exchanged for ordinary shares (i.e., in a debt-for-equity exchange). The new shares issued (or the delivery of treasury shares held by the bank) instantly increased the bank's CET1 capital; and

■ Often, the repurchased instruments carried high coupons. Where the instruments were exchanged for new hybrid instruments with a lower coupon, a capital benefit arouse from the coupon savings. CET1 capital was *not* generated immediately, but during the subsequent years.

The participation of investors holding the instruments underlying the LME was voluntary, and typically banks had to offer a substantial premium over the instruments' market price to entice investors to tender.

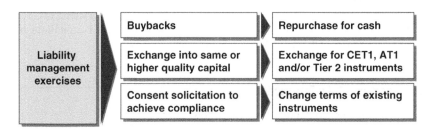

FIGURE 15.18   Types of LME transactions

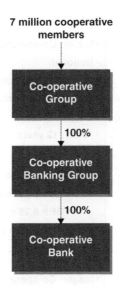

7 million cooperative members

Co-operative Group

100%

Co-operative Banking Group

100%

Co-operative Bank

FIGURE 15.19   Co-operative Bank's ownership structure

15.6.1 Background

The British bank Co-operative Bank ("Co-op") was a subsidiary of Co-operative Banking Group Limited ("Banking Group") which was itself a subsidiary of Co-operative Group, as shown in Figure 15.19. Co-operative Group was the ultimate holding entity of Banking Group and its subsidiaries. Co-operative Group was the UK's largest mutual business, owned by over 7 million consumer members. It was the UK's fifth biggest food retailer, a leading farmer and a major financial services provider. The bank's strategy was to become a retail and commercial bank focused on retail and small- and medium-sized enterprises.

During the first half of 2013, Coop reported continuing losses predominantly driven by impairment charges to the carrying value of the bank's loans, in particular corporate loans acquired as part of the merger with Britannia Building Society in 2009. The credit impairment charges were due to various factors, including the bank's strategy of targeting non-core assets for run down and exit, improvements in the bank's credit risk management approach and impairments incurred in the ordinary course of business due to changes in customer circumstances. Credit impairment charges for the six months ended 30 June 2013 were GBP 496 million, which were added to the negative effects in profit or loss of intangible IT asset impairments and customer redress provisions.

The British supervisor – the PRA – reviewed the financial position of the bank and determined that Coop needed an additional GBP 1.5 billion of CET1 capital. To meet the capital shortfall, in November 2013, Coop announced details of a recapitalisation plan to strengthen the bank's capital base by the end of 2014.

15.6.2 Recapitalisation Plan: Liability management Exercise and Direct Capital Contribution

The recapitalisation plan comprised a LME and a contribution from Banking Group (supported by Co-operative Group).

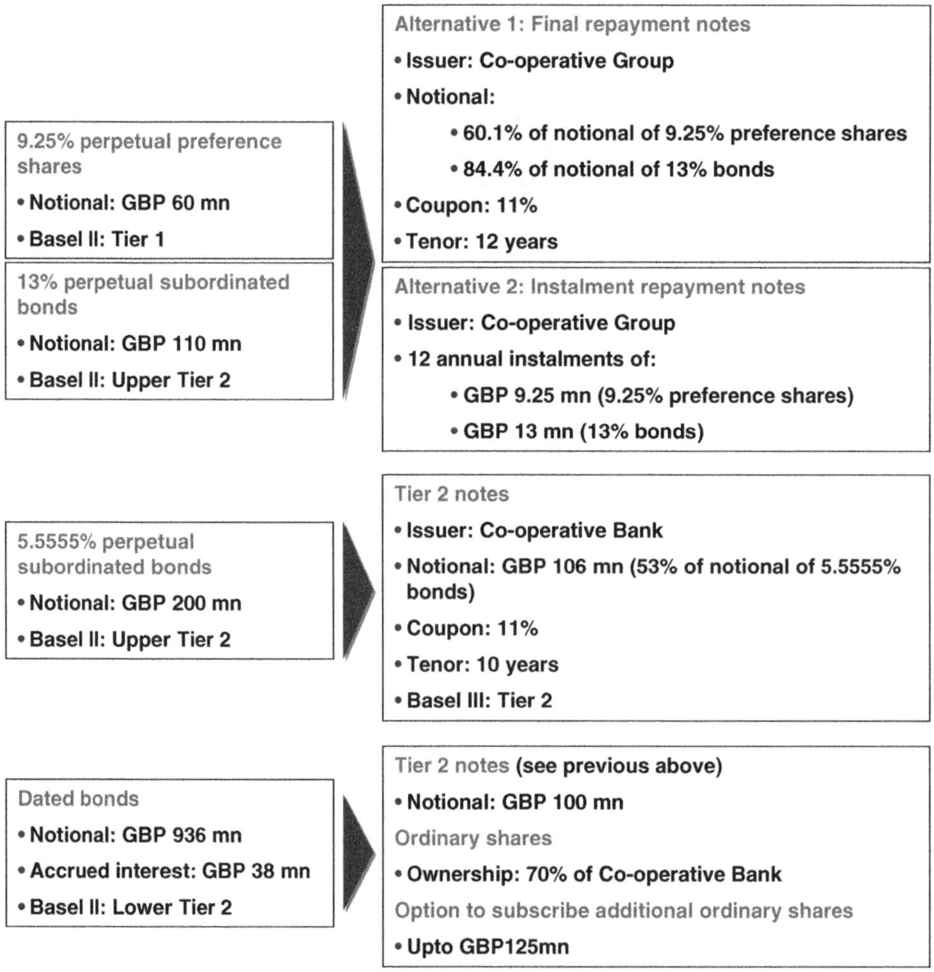

Alternative 1: Final repayment notes
- **Issuer: Co-operative Group**
- **Notional:**
  - **60.1% of notional of 9.25% preference shares**
  - **84.4% of notional of 13% bonds**
- **Coupon: 11%**
- **Tenor: 12 years**

9.25% perpetual preference shares
- **Notional: GBP 60 mn**
- **Basel II: Tier 1**

13% perpetual subordinated bonds
- **Notional: GBP 110 mn**
- **Basel II: Upper Tier 2**

Alternative 2: Instalment repayment notes
- **Issuer: Co-operative Group**
- **12 annual instalments of:**
  - **GBP 9.25 mn (9.25% preference shares)**
  - **GBP 13 mn (13% bonds)**

5.5555% perpetual subordinated bonds
- **Notional: GBP 200 mn**
- **Basel II: Upper Tier 2**

Tier 2 notes
- **Issuer: Co-operative Bank**
- **Notional: GBP 106 mn (53% of notional of 5.5555% bonds)**
- **Coupon: 11%**
- **Tenor: 10 years**
- **Basel III: Tier 2**

Dated bonds
- **Notional: GBP 936 mn**
- **Accrued interest: GBP 38 mn**
- **Basel II: Lower Tier 2**

Tier 2 notes **(see previous above)**
- **Notional: GBP 100 mn**
Ordinary shares
- **Ownership: 70% of Co-operative Bank**
Option to subscribe additional ordinary shares
- **Upto GBP125mn**

FIGURE 15.20   Main terms of Co-operative Bank's liability management exercise

Terms of the LME   The LME was broken down into three different parts, as shown in Figure 15.20:

1. The first part of the LME was directed to the holders of Coop's 9.25% non-cumulative perpetual preference shares and 13% perpetual subordinated bonds, which qualified as Basel II's Tier 1 and Upper Tier 2 instruments respectively. The LME included an invitation to exchange the 9.25% non-cumulative perpetual preference shares (with a total notional of GBP 60 million) and the 13% perpetual subordinated bonds (with a total notional of GBP 110 million) for either:

   ■ **Final repayment notes:** new 11% subordinated bonds due 2025 (i.e., a 12-year tenor) to be issued by Co-operative Group and guaranteed (on a subordinated basis) by certain subsidiaries of Co-operative Group. The notional of the new bonds would be 60.1% of the notional of the 9.25% preference shares. If for example, a holder had GBP 100 million of the 9.25% preference shares, then the investor would receive GBP 6.01 million of interest each year up to 2025 and GBP 60.1 million principal in 2025. The notional of the new bonds would be 84.4% of the notional of the 13% subordinated bonds. If for example, a holder had GBP 100 million of the 13% subordinated bonds, then the investor would receive GBP 9.284 million of interest each year up to 2025 and GBP 84.4 million principal in 2025. This alternative was aimed at holders wishing to preserve some capital but taking a reduced level of income; or

- **Instalment repayment notes**: a cash consideration payable in 12 equal instalments over 12 years up to (and including) 2025 and which would be represented by new "instalment repayment subordinated notes" to be issued by Co-operative Group and guaranteed (on a subordinated basis) by certain subsidiaries of Co-operative Group. If for example, a holder had GBP 100 million of the 9.25% preference shares, then the investor would receive GBP 9.25 million of interest each year up to 2025. If for example, a holder had GBP 100 million of the 13% subordinated bonds, then the investor would receive GBP 13 million of interest each year up to 2025. This alternative was aimed at holders wishing to preserve their level of income.

2. The second part of the LME comprised an invitation to exchange the 5.5555% perpetual subordinated bonds, which qualified as Basel II's Upper Tier 2 capital, for 11% subordinated bonds due 2023 to be issued by Coop. The total notional of the 5.5555% was GBP 200 million. The notional of the new bonds would be 53% of the notional of the 5.5555% subordinated bonds (i.e., GBP 106 million). If, for example, a holder had GBP 100 million of the 5.5555% subordinated bonds, then the investor would receive GBP 5.828 million of interest each year up to 2023 and GBP 53 million capital in 2023. Therefore, the LME gave the 5.5555% subordinated bondholders greater certainty on receiving an 11% interest but on a reduced notional amount, preserving income for 10 years. The new 11% bonds would qualify as Basel III's Tier 2 instruments.

3. The third part of the LME comprised an invitation to exchange seven series of dated subordinated bonds qualifying as Lower Tier 2 capital under Basel II. The notional of these bonds was GBP 936 million. In addition, GBP 38 million of accrued interest would not be paid if the bonds were tendered. Bondholders would receive a combination of:

- Ordinary shares representing 70% of the ordinary equity capital of Coop;
- GBP 100 million of the 11% subordinated bonds due 2023 (i.e., the bonds offered to the 5.5555% bond holders); and
- In addition, these bondholders were voluntarily entitled to subscribe for 62.5 million ordinary shares of Coop for an aggregate consideration of GBP 125 million. These shares represented 25% of the bank ordinary shares.

Direct Capital Contribution Conditional on the successful completion of the LME, Banking Group would subscribe a new issue of ordinary shares of Coop for a GBP 333 million cash consideration to be implemented during 2014. Banking Group would be funding the capital injection with the disposal proceeds of its insurance business.

Other In addition, in the period from June 2013 to September 2013, GBP 0.6 billion of non-core business loans were deleveraged, through a combination of asset sales, run-off and managed repayments, net of new drawdowns and the bank raised GBP 1.5 billion of secured wholesale funding.

15.6.3 Conditionality of the LME, Quorum and Voting Requirements

The LME was conditional to the exchange of the *entire* principal amount of all instruments pursuant to the LME.

Each of the proposals in respect of the 9.25%, 5.5555% and 13% instruments had to be approved by their holders at separate meetings convened for the purposes of voting on such proposals and the proposals had to be capable of being implemented in accordance with their terms. Table 15.1 summarises their quorum and voting requirements.

In respect of the dated subordinated bonds, which qualified as Lower Tier 2 capital under Basel II, there was no concept of quorum, first meeting or adjourned meeting. All the holders of these instruments acted as one class and approval required a combination of volume/numerosity test and the sanction by a legal court. The process started with a first court hearing, followed several weeks later by a "scheme" meeting in which the bondholders voted on the proposal. The volume/numerosity test required

TABLE 15.1   Quorum and voting requirements to obtain approval by the holders of the exchanged instruments

	Quorum First Meeting	Quorum Adjourned Meeting	Voting Threshold (%)
9.25% preference shares	2 persons holding at least 1/3 in nominal amount	Any holders who are present in person or proxy	Majority consisting of not less than 3/4 of the persons voting
5.5555% or 13% subordinated bonds	One or more persons holding or representing not less than 2/3 in nominal amount	One or more persons holding or representing not less than 1/3 in nominal amount	Majority consisting of not less than 3/4 of the persons voting

bondholders approval with a majority in number representing 75% in value of the creditors present and voting at the scheme meeting, either in person or by proxy. Once the volume/numerosity test was passed, a formal court hearing was arranged in which the legal court assessed whether to sanction the proposal.

15.6.4 Capital Impact

The LME generated CET1 capital in several ways:

- To the extent that Coop exchanged existing bonds for new ordinary shares, the new shares issued constituted CET1 capital for the bank;
- To the extent that the existing bonds were exchanged for new bonds at a discount to the carrying amount (in Coop's balance sheet) of tendered instruments, the after-tax amount of that discount was also recognisable as CET1 capital; and
- To the extent that the existing bonds were exchanged for new bonds that carried a lower coupon, interest expense savings occurred each subsequent year, which were CET1 capital enhancing.

More precisely, the combination of the LME and the direct capital contribution enhanced Co-op's CET1 capital by GBP 1,529 million (ignoring the costs related to the LME), as follows (see Figure 15.21):

- In respect of the 9.25% perpetual preference shares, as the instruments were exchanged for instruments issued by Co-operative Group, an entity external to the bank, a gain representing all their carrying amount (GBP 60 million) was recognised. As Coop did not expect to distribute a dividend on these preference shares in 2014, no additional benefits accrued to the bank's CET1 capital in 2014. As a result (assuming no tax effect), GBP 60 million of CET1 capital was generated as of the end of 2014.
- In respect of the 13% perpetual subordinated bonds, as the instruments were exchanged for instruments issued by Co-operative Group, an entity external to the bank, a gain representing all their carrying amount (GBP 110 million) and the accrued interest (GBP 12 million) was recognised. In addition, in 2014 Coop would have paid GBP 14 million (= 110 mn × 13%) interest which was foregone by the LME. As a result (assuming no tax effect), GBP 136 million (= 110 mn + 12 mn + 14 mn) of CET1 capital was generated as of the end of 2014;
- In respect of the 5.5555% perpetual subordinated bonds, as the instruments were exchanged for instruments issued by the bank, a GBP 94 million gain representing the difference between their carrying amount (GBP 200 million) and the notional amount of the new 11% Tier 2 bonds (GBP 106 million). In addition, a gain was recognised representing the saved accrued interest (GBP 6 million). Finally, Coop would have to pay GBP 1 million (= 200 mn × 5.5555% − 106 mn × 11%)

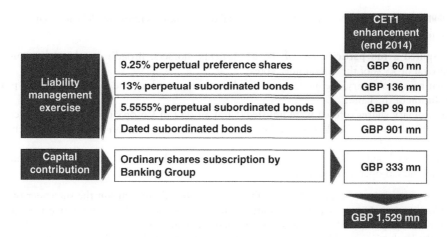

FIGURE 15.21 CET1 effects of Co-operative Bank's liability management exercise and capital contribution

higher interest in 2014 and in subsequent years. As a result (assuming no tax effect), GBP 99 million (= 94 mn + 6 mn – 1 mn) of CET1 capital was generated as of the end of 2014;

■ In respect of the dated subordinated bonds, as the instruments were exchanged for a combination of ordinary shares and GBP 100 million of Tier 2 instruments issued by the bank, it implied that the new ordinary shares were valued at GBP 874 million (= 936 mn carrying amount + 38 mn accrued interest – 100 mn Tier 2 bonds), enhancing CET1 capital by such amount. In addition, Co-op would have interest expense savings of GBP 27 million in 2014. As a result (assuming no tax effect), GBP 901 million (= 874 mn + 27 mn) of CET1 capital was generated as of the end of 2014; and

■ In respect of the capital contribution, Co-operative Group injected GBP 333 million in Co-op's capital in the form of new ordinary shares. As a result, CET1 capital increased by GBP 333 million.

In addition, the holders of the dated subordinated bonds had the right to subscribe a new issue of Co-op's ordinary shares for a maximum of GBP 125 million. If such right was exercised, Co-op's capital would be increased by the issue proceeds (i.e., GBP 125 million less related expenses).

Finally, the new Tier 2 bonds issued helped Coop meet its Total Capital requirements.

15.6.5 Additional Comments

This section briefly covers other aspects of Co-op's LME like the investors' motivations to participate in the exercise and the unusual circumstances surrounding it.

Investors' Incentive to Participate in the LME Why would investors be willing to realise a large loss in their holdings? The outcome of a successful LME was a substantially more favourable outcome to the holders of the securities pursuant to the offer than keeping their investments. If the LME was *not* successfully implemented, the bank would fail to raise sufficient CET1 capital by 31 December 2014. Co-op believed that, in such circumstances, the bank would cease to be a going concern, becoming subject to a resolution procedure. In the event that the British authorities exercised their resolution powers the bank would go into an insolvency proceedings and, as a result, it would be highly probable that the holders of the securities pursuant to the offer (if they remained outstanding in such circumstances) would receive no recovery in respect of their securities.

Other Comments   Co-op's LME was in a way unusual due to the exceptionally delicate financial position of the bank:

- It required a **full participation** of the instruments' holders. Broadly speaking, it required the approval of 75% of the bondholder votes;
- Albeit being voluntary, the instruments' holders were enticed to tender by the **threat of potential resolution** of the bank;
- The ordinary shares offered were **unlisted**. Until an IPO of Co-op's ordinary shares occurred, it was difficult for shareholders to sell their shares. The bank planned an IPO in 2014 which did not materialise; and
- Some of the bonds offered in the exchange were issued by **entities other than the bank** (Bank Group and Co-operative Group).

The combination of the LME and the direct capital contribution meant the surrender of control by the Co-operative Group. Upon successful completion of the LME, Co-operative Group owned (through Banking Group) 30% of the issued shares of the bank with the remaining 70% of the issued shares of the bank being held by holders of the bank's former dated subordinated bonds.

The LME was successfully completed in December 2013. During 2014 the bank's capital position continued to improve following an additional GBP 400 million capital raising in May, the final GBP 313 million contribution from Co-operative Group and the write back of credit impairment provisions on non-core assets and the speed and timing of the deleverage of those assets. Coop's CET1 ratio was 13.0% at the end of 2014 and whilst the bank did not yet meet the Bank of England's stress test scenario of extreme economic circumstances, a plan was in place to achieve this. This revised plan, which was accepted by the PRA, was based on the bank accelerating its strategy to significantly reduce RWAs.

The GBP 400 million capital injection in May 2014 was subscribed by US hedge funds Silver Point, Perry Capital, York Capital Management and institutional investor Invesco Asset Management through a vehicle called SP Co-op Investments Limited, which owned 12.79% of Co-op after the equity investment. The objective of these investors was to sell their shares in a subsequent IPO of Co-op. Simultaneously, Co-operative Group entered into a shareholder agreement with Silver Point and Perry Capital giving the right to these hedge funds to nominate a director for appointment to the board for so long as they continued to own 5% or more of the bank. In addition, the shareholder agreement granted the right for one director to be appointed to a sub-committee of the board, the IPO Committee, to assess the feasibility of the bank listing its ordinary shares on the London Stock Exchange.

The hedge funds' investment tried to benefit from a planned upcoming IPO. However, at the time of writing the IPO had not yet materialised.

Glossary

A-IRB Advanced IRB approach, a method of calculating credit risk capital requirements using internal PD, LGD and EAD models.

Additional Valuation Adjustment See AVA.

Advanced Measurement Approach See AMA.

AGM Annual General Meeting. AGM is an annual meeting of the shareholders of an entity in which the activities and financials of the entity during previous year are reviewed. In addition, proposals on decisions of material importance to the entity are voted, including amendments to the articles of association, the appropriation of profit, the authorisation to issue new shares and important structural changes.

AMA Advanced Measurement Approach. The AMA is used for measuring operational risk. The methodology is based upon the identification of a number of key risk scenarios that describe the major operational risks a bank faces. Each scenario is reviewed and the likelihood of occurrence and the potential severity of loss is estimated. Internal and external loss data, along with certain business environment and internal control factors, such as self-assessment results and key risk indicators, are considered as part of this process. Based on the output from these reviews and estimations, a bank enters the scenario parameters into an operational risk model that generates a loss distribution from which the level of capital required to cover operational risk is determined.

Associate An entity in which the consolidated group has a significant influence, without having control. Significant influence is deemed to exist when the group owns 20% or more of the voting rights of an investee directly or indirectly.

AVA Additional valuation adjustment, the difference between the fair value, as reported in the balance sheet including all fair value adjustments, and the prudent value. This difference shall be deducted from CET1 capital.

Baffin Bundesanstalt für Finanzdienstleistungsaufsicht, the German financial supervisory authority.

Basel III The capital adequacy framework issued by the Basel Committee on Banking Supervision in December 2010, *Basel III: A Global Regulatory Framework for More Resilient Banks* and *Banking Systems* and *International Framework for Liquidity Risk Measurement, Standards and Monitoring*. Together, these documents present the Basel Committee's reforms to strengthen global capital and liquidity rules with the goal of promoting a more resilient banking sector. In June 2011, the Basel Committee issued a revision to the former document setting out the finalised capital treatment for counterparty credit risk in bilateral trades.

Basel Committee on Banking Supervision See BCBS.

BCBS The Basel Committee on Banking Supervision, a forum for regular cooperation on banking supervisory matters. Its objective is to enhance the understanding of key supervisory issues and improve the quality of banking supervision worldwide. It seeks to do so by exchanging information on national supervisory issues, approaches and techniques, with a view to promoting common understanding. At times, the BCBS uses this common understanding to develop guidelines and supervisory standards in areas where they are considered desirable. In this regard, the BCBS is best known for its international standards on capital adequacy, the Core Principles for Effective Banking Supervision and the Concordat on cross-border banking supervision.

BIS   Bank for International Settlements, domiciled in Basel.

Capital conservation buffer   A capital buffer, prescribed by regulators under Basel III, and designed to ensure banks build up capital buffers outside periods of stress which can be drawn down as losses are incurred. Should a bank's capital levels fall within the capital conservation buffer range, capital distributions will be constrained by the regulators.

Capital requirements directive   See CRD IV.

Cash flow hedges   A type of hedge accounting in which the bank hedges the exposure to variability in cash flows attributable to a particular risk associated with a recognised asset or liability or a highly probable forecast transaction and that could affect profit or loss.

CBR   Combined buffer requirement. The aggregate of the CET1 capital requirements related to the capital conservation buffer and, as applicable, the countercyclical capital buffer, the G-SII buffer, the O-SII buffer and/or the systemic risk buffer.

CCP   Central counterparty. A CCP is a "financial market infrastructure" which interposes itself between two counterparties, becoming the seller to every buyer and the buyer to every seller, through the novation of the derivative contracts. This structure flattens out risk and uncertainty and increases efficiency and confidence in the financial operations. That is because the CCP limits exposures among counterparties (each counterparty is essentially exposed only to the CCP) and requires collateral for its open positions by all counterparties and therefore allows each counterparty to be protected against credit and liquidity risks stemming from the other counterparty. A CCP usually deals only with a limited number of trusted counterparties, the "clearing members". The CCP does not take on market risk, i.e., the exposure to a change in the market value of the trades that it enters into, because it runs a "matched book": any position taken on with one counterparty is always offset by an opposite position taken on with another counterparty.

Central counterparty   See CCP.

CET1 capital   The common equity tier 1 capital of a bank or its group, as the case may be. It is the highest quality form of regulatory capital under Basel III that comprises common shares issued and related share premium, retained earnings and other reserves excluding the cash flow hedging reserve, less specified regulatory adjustments.

CET1 ratio   With respect to a bank or its group, as the case may be, the ratio (expressed as a percentage) of the aggregate amount (in the accounting currency) of the CET1 capital at such time divided by the RWAs at such time.

CHF   Swiss franc. The official currency of Switzerland.

Combined buffer requirement   See CBR.

Covered bonds   Debt instruments issued by banks and other credit institutions and secured by a cover pool of assets which typically consist of mortgage loans or public sector debt to which investors have a preferential claim in the event of default.

Countercyclical buffer   A capital buffer which aims to ensure that capital requirements take account of the macro-financial environment in which banks operate. This will provide the banking sector with additional capital to protect it against potential future losses, when excess credit growth in the financial system as a whole is associated with an increase in system-wide risk.

CRD IV Directive   A capital adequacy legislative package issued by the European Commission and adopted by EU member states. The package implements the Basel III capital proposals together with transitional arrangements for some of its requirements. It is formalised under Directive 2013/36/EU of the European Parliament and of the Council of 26 June 2013 on access to the activity of credit institutions and the prudential supervision of credit institutions and investment firms, amending Directive 2002/87/EC and repealing Directives 2006/48/EC and 2006/49/EC or such other directive as may come into effect in place thereof.

Credit risk   Risk of financial loss if a customer or counterparty fails to meet an obligation under a contract. It arises mainly from direct lending, trade finance and leasing business, but also from products such as guarantees, derivatives and debt securities.

Credit risk mitigation   See CRM.

Credit Valuation Adjustment   See CVA.

CRM Credit risk mitigation. A technique to reduce potential credit losses associated with an exposure by application of credit risk mitigants such as collateral, guarantees and credit protection.

CRR Regulation (EU) No. 575/2013 of the European Parliament and of the Council of 26 June 2013 on the prudential requirements for credit institutions and investment firms and amending Regulation (EU) No. 648/2012 or such other regulation as may come into effect in place thereof.

CSA ISDA's Credit Support Annex, a legal agreement between the two parties to an OTC derivative transaction which contains the agreed collateral terms under an ISDA Master Agreement.

CVA Credit Valuation Adjustment, an adjustment to derivatives fair valuation – according to IFRS 13 – to take into account counterparty credit risk.

Debit Valuation Adjustment See DVA.

Deferred tax assets See DTAs.

Deferred tax liabilities See DTLs.

Defined benefit plans Post-employment obligation under which the bank, directly or indirectly via the plan, retains the contractual or implicit obligation to pay remuneration directly to employees when required or to pay additional amounts if the insurer, or other entity required to pay, does not cover all the benefits relating to the services rendered by the employees when insurance policies do not cover all of the corresponding post-employee's benefits.

Defined contribution plans Retirement benefit plans under which amounts to be paid as retirement benefits are determined by contributions to a fund together with investment earnings thereon. The employer's obligations in respect of its employees current and prior years' employment service are discharged by contributions to the fund.

DTAs Deferred tax assets. Taxes recoverable in future years, including loss carry forwards, tax credit carry forwards and tax arising from temporary differences.

DTLs Deferred tax liabilities. Income taxes payable in subsequent years.

DVA Debit valuation adjustment, an adjustment to the fair value of a financial liability – according to IFRS 13 – that reflects the possibility that the counterparty may default such that the bank would not receive the full value of the derivative.

EBA European Banking Authority. The EBA is an independent European Union Authority which works to ensure effective and consistent prudential regulation and supervision across the European banking sector. Its overall objectives are to maintain financial stability in the EU and to safeguard the integrity, efficiency and orderly functioning of the banking sector. The main task of the EBA is to contribute to the creation of the European Single Rulebook in banking whose objective is to provide a single set of harmonised prudential rules for financial institutions throughout the EU. The Authority also plays an important role in promoting convergence of supervisory practices and is mandated to assess risks and vulnerabilities in the EU banking sector.

EAD The amount expected to be outstanding after any credit risk mitigation, if and when the counterparty defaults. EAD reflects drawn balances as well as allowance for undrawn amounts of commitments and contingent exposures.

ECAIs External Credit Assessment Institutions. For the standardised approach to credit risk for sovereigns, corporates and institutions, external ratings are used to assign risk weights. These external ratings must come from ECAIs, regulator approved credit rating agencies. The table below maps the main credit rating agencies' (Standard & Poor's, Moody's and Fitch) long-term ratings to the credit quality steps:

Credit Quality Step	Standard & Poor's	Moody's	Fitch
1	AAA to AA–	Aaa to Aa3	AAA to AA–
2	A+ to A–	A1 to A3	A+ to A–
3	BBB+ to BBB–	Baa1 to Baa3	BBB+ to BBB–
4	BB+ to BB–	Ba1 to Ba3	BB+ to BB–
5	B+ to B–	B1 to B3	B+ to B–
6	CCC+ and below	Caa1 and below	CCC+ and below

The table below maps the main credit rating agencies' **short-term** ratings to the credit quality steps:

Credit Quality Step	Standard & Poor's	Moody's	Fitch
1	A–1+, A–1	P–1	F1+, F1
2	A–2	P–2	F2
3	A–3	P–3	F3
4	Below A–3	NP	Below F3

ECB   European Central Bank. The ECB is the central bank for Europe's single currency, the euro. The ECB is responsible for the prudential supervision of credit institutions located in the euro area and participating non-euro area member states, within the Single Supervisory Mechanism, which also comprises the national competent authorities. It thereby contributes to the safety and soundness of the banking system and the stability of the financial system within the EU and each participating member state.

Effective interest rate method   The method used to measure the carrying value of a financial asset or a liability recognised at amortised cost. It allocates associated interest income or expense to produce a level yield (EIR) over the relevant period.

Equity method   An accounting method for recognition of investments in companies over which significant influence can be exercised. The pro-rata share of the company's net income (loss) increases (decreases) the carrying value of the investment affecting net income. Distributions decrease the carrying value of the investment without affecting net income. An investee, other than a joint venture, recognised using the equity method is called an "associate".

EL   A regulatory calculation of the amount expected to be lost on an exposure using a 12-month time horizon and downturn loss estimates. EL is calculated by multiplying the PD (a percentage) by the EAD (an amount) and LGD (a percentage).

ESRB   European Systemic Risk Board. A European Union entity responsible for developing the principles and monitoring macroprudential risks across the Union. The ESRB was established under Regulation (EU) 1092/2010 of 24 November 2010 of the European Parliament and of the Council on European Union macro-prudential oversight of the financial system and establishing a European Systemic Risk Board. The ESRB was established in December 2010 with a mandate to oversee risk in the financial system as a whole. It can issue recommendations for remedial action in response to the risks identified and, where appropriate, make those recommendations public. The ESRB recommendations are not binding. However, if an addressee does not take appropriate action in response to a recommendation, it must provide adequate justification for inaction ("comply or explain"). In cases where national macroprudential policy has material cross-border effects, the ESRB may encourage countries to coordinate policy measures.

Expected loss   See EL.

Exposure at default   See EAD.

External Credit Assessment Institutions   See ECAIs.

EU   European Union.

EUR   The currency introduced at the start of the third stage of European economic and monetary union pursuant to the Treaty on the Functioning of the European Union.

F-IRB approach   Foundation IRB approach. A method of calculating credit risk capital requirements using internal PD models but with supervisory estimates of LGD and conversion factors for the calculation of EAD.

Fair value   Amount at which assets or liabilities would be exchanged between knowledgeable, willing and independent counterparties. Fair value is often identical to market value.

Fair value hedges   A type of hedge accounting, in which the bank hedges the exposure to changes in the fair value of assets and liabilities or firm commitments that have not be recognised, or of an identified portion of said assets, liabilities or firm commitments, attributable to a specific risk, provided it could affect the income statement.

FICOD   Financial Conglomerates Directive.

Financial Stability Board   See FSB.

Foundation IRB approach   See F-IRB.

FSB   The Financial Stability Board coordinates all of the measures to reduce moral hazard and risks to the global financial system posed by G-SIIs. It is important to note that the FSB do not establish laws, regulations or rules for any financial institution directly. It merely acts in an advisory capacity. It is up to each country's specific lawmakers and regulators to enact whatever portions of the recommendations they deem appropriate.

Fully loaded   In relation to a measure that is presented or described as being on a "fully loaded basis", that such measure is calculated without applying the transitional provisions set out in Part Ten of the CRD IV Regulation.

FVTOCI at fair value through OCI.   A category for the recognition of financial assets under IFRS 9.

FVTPL at fair value through profit or loss.   A category for the recognition of financial assets and liabilities under IFRS 9.

G-SIB   Global Systemically Important Bank. A term used when a G-SII is a bank. Each year, the FSB publishes a revised list of G-SIBs and their current assessment of the appropriate capital charge.

G-SIB buffer   A capital buffer requirement levied on G-SIBs to reduce the systemic risk that a bank poses to the larger financial system. This requirement is to be met with CET1 capital.

G-SII   Global Systemically Important Institution.

GBP   British pound. The official currency of the United Kingdom.

Goodwill   Goodwill acquired in a business combination represents a payment made by the acquirer in anticipation of future economic benefits from assets that are not able to be individually identified and separately recognised.

Higher Loss Absorbency requirement   See G-SIB buffer.

HLA requirement   Higher Loss Absorbency requirement. See G-SIB buffer.

HQLA   High-Quality Liquid Assets. Assets that are unencumbered, liquid in markets during a time of stress and, ideally, central bank eligible. These include, for example, cash and claims on central governments and central banks. Basel III requires this ratio to be at least 100%.

IAS 39   The International Accounting Standard for financial instruments that preceded IFRS 9.

IASB   International Accounting Standards Board. The independent standard-setting body of the International Financial Reporting Standards. IASB members are responsible for the development and publication of IFRS. The IASB is also responsible for approving interpretations of IFRS as developed by the IFRS Interpretations Committee.

ICAAP   Internal Capital Adequacy Assessment Process. A comprehensive assessment under Pillar 2 required to banks of their risks, to determine the appropriate amounts of capital to be held against these risks where other suitable mitigants are not available.

IFRS   International Financial Reporting Standards. Financial reporting rules as set by the International Accounting Standards Board to ensure globally transparent and comparable accounting and disclosure.

IFRS 9   The International Financial Reporting Standard for financial instruments. The IFRS 9 replaced IAS 39.

IMA   Internal model approach. An approach used to calculate market risk capital and RWAs with an internal market risk model approved by the regulatory supervisor.

Independent Price Verification   See IPV.

Internal Capital Adequacy Assessment Process   See ICAAP.

Internal Model Approach   See IMA.

Internal Ratings-Based Approach   See IRB.

International Accounting Standards Board   See IASB.

IPV   Independent Price Verification, the process by which the valuations of positions on the balance sheet are independently verified for accuracy.

IRB   A method of calculating credit risk capital requirements using internal, rather than supervisory, estimates of risk parameters.

IRB advanced approach   See A-IRB.

ISDA International Swaps and Derivatives Association, Inc. The global trade organisation that represents participants in the OTC derivatives markets, and designs and maintains the industry-standard contracts (ISDA Master Agreements) for trading OTC derivative transactions.

Joint venture A joint arrangement whereby the parties that have joint control of the arrangement have rights to the net assets of the arrangement. A joint venturer recognises its interest in a joint venture as an investment and shall account for that investment using the equity method.

LCR Liquidity cover ratio. The ratio of the stock of high-quality liquid assets (HQLAs) to expected net cash outflows over the following 30 days. High-quality liquid assets should be unencumbered, liquid in markets during a time of stress and, ideally, be central bank eligible. The Basel III rules require this ratio to be at least 100%.

Level 1 financial instruments From an IFRS accounting perspective, financial instruments with quoted prices for identical instruments in active markets.

Level 2 financial instruments From an IFRS accounting perspective, financial instruments with quoted prices for similar instruments in active markets or quoted prices for identical or similar instruments in inactive markets and financial instruments valued using models where all significant inputs are observable.

Level 3 financial instruments From an IFRS accounting perspective, financial instruments valued using valuation techniques where one or more significant inputs are unobservable.

Leverage ratio The ratio of tier 1 capital to total exposures. Total exposures include on-balance sheet items, off-balance sheet items and derivatives, and should generally follow the accounting measure of exposure. This supplementary measure to the risk-based capital requirements is intended to constrain the build-up of excess leverage in the banking sector.

Liquidity cover ratio See LCR.

LGD The estimated ratio (percentage) of the loss on an exposure to the amount outstanding at default (EAD) upon default of a counterparty. In other words, LGD is the percentage that one party expects not to recover if the other party defaults.

Loss given default See LGD.

Maximum Distributable Amount See MDA.

Market risk The risk that movements in market risk factors, including foreign exchange rates and commodity prices, interest rates, credit spreads and equity prices will reduce income or portfolio values.

Maximum Distributable Amount See MDA.

MDA Maximum Distributable Amount. Where the Combined Buffer Requirement is not met, regulatory supervisory authorities prohibit a bank from distributing more than the MDA, therefore, restricting the bank from making a distribution to shareholders, paying variable remuneration or discretionary pension benefits or making payments on AT1 instruments.

Minority interest The net amount of the shareholders' equity of a subsidiary attributable to investors outside the group (that is, the amount that is not owned, directly or indirectly, by the parent), including that amount in the corresponding part of the consolidated earnings for the period.

Net stable funding ratio See NSFR.

Non-controlling interest See minority interest.

Non-performing loans See NPLs.

Non-performance risk The risk, according to IFRS 13, that a reporting entity will not fulfil an obligation (i.e., an entity's own credit risk). The fair value measurement of a liability must reflect non-performance risk.

NPLs Non-performing loans. The balance of non-performing risks, whether for reasons of default by customers or for other reasons, for exposures on balance loans to customers. This figure is shown gross (i.e., it is not adjusted for value corrections – loan loss reserves – made).

NSFR The ratio of available stable funding to required stable funding over a one year time horizon, assuming a stressed scenario. Available stable funding would include items such as equity capital, preferred stock with a maturity of over one year and liabilities with an assessed maturity of over one year. The Basel III rules require this ratio to be over 100% with effect from 2018.

OCI   Other comprehensive income. A part of shareholders' equity that includes mostly reserves. These reserves have a temporary nature as their amounts would be reclassified at a later stage either to profit or loss or to another account within shareholders' equity.

O-SII   Other Systemically Important Institution.

Operational risk   The risk of loss resulting from inadequate or failed internal processes, people and systems, or from external events, including legal risk.

OTC   Over-the-counter securities and derivatives are not traded (and negotiated) on an exchange but via private contracts between two parties.

Over-the-counter   See OTC.

Ordinary shares   Common shares in the capital of the bank, each of which confers on the holder one vote at general meetings of the bank and is credited as fully paid up.

Other comprehensive income   See OCI.

PD   The probability that an obligor will default within one year.

Pillar 1   Minimum capital requirements. The part of Basel III setting out the calculation of regulatory capital for credit, market, and operational risk.

Pillar 2   The supervisory review process. The part of Basel III which sets out the process by which a bank should review its overall capital adequacy and the processes under which the supervisors evaluate how well financial institutions are assessing their risks and take appropriate actions in response to the assessments.

Pillar 3   Market discipline. The part of Basel III, which sets out the disclosure requirements for banks to publish certain details of their risks, capital and risk management, with the aim of strengthening market discipline.

PONV   The point of non-viability is the point at which the relevant resolution authority determines that the bank meets the conditions for resolution (but no resolution action has yet been taken) or that the bank will no longer be viable unless the relevant capital instruments are written-down or converted or the bank requires extraordinary public support, without which the relevant resolution authority determines that the relevant entity would no longer be viable.

Point of non-viability   See PONV.

PRA   Prudential Regulation Authority. The PRA is responsible for the prudential regulation and supervision of banks, building societies, credit unions, insurers and major investment firms in the United Kingdom. The PRA is a subsidiary of the Bank of England.

Probability of default   See PD.

QCCP   Qualifying central counterparty. A QCCP is an entity that is licensed to operate as a CCP (including a license granted by way of confirming an exemption), and is permitted by the appropriate regulator/overseer to operate as such with respect to the products offered.

Qualifying central counterparty   See QCCP.

Recovery Resolution Directive   See RRD.

Repo/reverse repo   Arrangements that allow counterparties to use financial securities as collateral for an interest bearing cash loan. The borrower agrees to sell a security to the lender subject to a commitment to repurchase the asset at a specified price on a given date. For the party selling the security (and agreeing to repurchase it in the future) it is a repurchase agreement or repo; for the counterparty to the transaction (buying the security and agreeing to sell in the future) it is a reverse repurchase agreement or reverse repo.

Reverse repo   See repo/reverse repo.

Risk-weighted assets   See RWAs.

RRD   Recovery Resolution Directive. A directive published by the European Commission establishing a EU-wide framework for the recovery and resolution of credit institutions and investment firms.

RWAs   Risk-weighted assets. A degree of risk expressed as a percentage (risk weight) to an exposure value. Assets are adjusted for their associated risks using weightings established in accordance with Basel III as implemented by the bank's national supervisor. Certain assets are not weighted but deducted from capital.

Sale and lease back   Transaction in which one party sells assets such as real estate to another party and at the same time enters into an agreement to lease the assets for a predetermined period of time.

SPE   Special purpose entity. An entity (also called "vehicle") set up for the solely purpose of a specific transaction.

SREP   Supervisory Review and Evaluation Process. A process carried out by the competent authorities to assess (i) the appropriate bank-specific level of regulatory capital on an individual and consolidated basis in accordance with [CRD IV Chapter 2, Title VII] and (ii) the consequent need to impose additional Pillar 2 capital requirements. The common procedures and methodologies for SREP are documented in the EBA's "Guidelines on Common Procedures and Methodologies for the Supervisory Review and Evaluation Process (SREP)" (EBA/GL/2014/13) of 19 December 2014.

Standardised approach   In relation to credit risk, a method for calculating credit risk capital requirements using ECAI ratings and supervisory risk weights. In relation to operational risk, a method of calculating the operational capital requirement by the application of a supervisory defined percentage charge to the gross income of eight specified business lines.

Supervisory Review and Evaluation Process   Ver SREP.

Tier 1 capital   With respect to a bank or its group, the Tier 1 capital of the bank or the group, respectively, as calculated by the bank in accordance with Chapters 1, 2 and 3 (Tier 1 capital, Common Equity Tier 1 capital and Additional Tier 1 capital) of Title I (Elements of own funds) of Part Two (Own Funds) of the CRR and/or applicable banking regulations at such time, including any applicable transitional, phasing in or similar provisions. Tier 1 capital is the highest-quality components of capital that fully satisfy all of the characteristics outlined under the CRR framework. It provides a permanent and unrestricted commitment of funds, is freely available to absorb losses, does not impose any unavoidable servicing charge against earnings and ranks behind the claims of depositors and other creditors in the event of winding-up.

TLAC   Total loss-absorbing capacity.

US GAAP   US accounting principles drawn up by the Financial Accounting Standards Board (FASB) and the American Institute of Certified Public Accountants (AICPA). In addition, the interpretations and explanations furnished by the Securities and Exchange Commission (SEC) are particularly relevant for entities listed on the stock exchange.

USD   US dollar. The official currency of the United States of America.

VaR   Value-at-Risk, a measure of the loss that could occur on risk positions as a result of adverse movements in market risk factors (e.g. rates, prices, volatilities) over a specified time horizon and to a given level of confidence.

Wrong-way risk   Wrong-way risk occurs when a counterparty's exposures are adversely correlated with its credit quality. There are two types of wrong-way risk: (i) general wrong-way risk occurs when the probability of counterparty default is positively correlated with general risk factors, such as, for example, where the counterparty is resident and/or incorporated in a higher-risk country and seeks to sell a non-domestic currency in exchange for its home currency; and (ii) specific wrong-way risk occurs when the exposure to a particular counterparty is positively correlated with the probability of counterparty default, such as a reverse repo on the counterparty's own bonds.

Bibliography

A good number of documents issued by Basel Committee on Banking Supervision have been consulted. The most relevant one is the document titled *Basel III: A Global Regulatory Framework for More Resilient Banks and Banking Systems*, revised version, June 2011, BCBS 189.

HM Treasury, *The Asset Protection Scheme*, Report by the Comptroller and Auditor General, 21 December 2010.

Juan Ramirez, *Accounting for Derivatives*, Wiley, 2015.

Juan Ramirez, *Handbook of Corporate Equity Derivatives and Capital Markets*, Wiley, 2012.

Regulation (EU) No. 575/2013 of the European Parliament and of the Council of 26 June 2013 on Prudential Requirements for Credit institutions and Investment Firms and Amending Regulation (EU) No 648/2012.

For the construction of the case studies, the annual reports, Pillar 3 reports and investors' presentations of the entities involved have been consulted. Frequently, the calculations use data estimated by the author.

Printed and bound by CPI Group (UK) Ltd, Croydon, CR0 4YY

23/04/2025

14660948-0003